PROFITABLE BEVERAGE MANAGEMENT

PROFITABLE BEVERAGE MANAGEMENT

John A. Drysdale
Johnson County Community College, Professor Emeritus

PEARSON

Boston Columbus Indianapolis New York San Francisco Upper Saddle River
Amsterdam Cape Town Dubai London Madrid Milan Munich Paris Montréal Toronto
Delhi Mexico City São Paulo Sydney Hong Kong Seoul Singapore Taipei Tokyo

Editorial Director: Vernon R. Anthony
Senior Acquisitions Editor: William Lawrensen
Program Manager: Alexis Duffy
Editorial Assistant: Lara Dimmick
Director of Marketing: David Gesell
Marketing Manager: Stacey Martinez
Senior Marketing Coordinator: Alicia Wozniak
Marketing Assistant: Les Roberts
Senior Managing Editor: JoEllen Gohr
Production Project Manager: Susan Hannahs
Senior Art Director: Jayne Conte
Cover Designer: Suzanne Duda
Cover Art: Getty Images, Vladan Milisavljevic
Full-Service Project Management: Anju Joshi, PreMediaGlobal
Composition: PreMediaGlobal
Printer/Binder: LSC Communications
Cover Printer: LSC Communications
Text Font: 11/13 Adobe Garamond Pro

Credits and acknowledgments borrowed from other sources and reproduced, with permission, in this textbook appear on the appropriate page within the text.

Library of Congress Cataloging-in-Publication Data
Drysdale, John A.
    Profitable beverage management / John A. Drysdale.
        pages cm
    Includes bibliographical references and index.
    ISBN-13: 978-0-13-507877-8
    ISBN-10: 0-13-507877-6
    1. Bars (Drinking establishments)—Management.   2. Bartending.   3. Alcoholic beverages.   4. Alcoholic beverage industry.   I. Title.
    TX950.7.D78 2015
    647.95068--dc23
                                                                            2013032541

2

ISBN 10: 0-13-507877-6
ISBN 13: 978-0-13-507877-8

To my wife of 50 years: Judy
Your love and support has made this possible

brief contents

contents

10
Production and Mixology 240

11
Selling to a Profit 264

12
Controlling to a Profit 286

13
Marketing 304

14
The Entrepreneur in You 327

Preface

In conversations with hospitality and culinary colleagues from around the country at various conferences and conventions, it became apparent that there was a need for a new beverage management book. It had to be complete, yet concise. It had to impart to the student the knowledge of wines, spirits, and beers; responsible beverage service; purchasing equipment; and how to make a profit. We have endeavored to write such a book. Whatever students do when they graduate and go out into the hospitality field—whether they manage a hotel, restaurant, resort, or whatever—if bar service is involved, it is hoped that this text will be a guide to their success.

The book starts out with a brief history of the business of selling beverages in the United States and goes on to give an overview of the scope of the industry. It continues with an important chapter, that of serving beverages in a responsible manner to the customer. This subject has always caused a dilemma among bar managers because the more drinks you sell, the more profit you make. However, given the nature of the product, the more drinks you sell to a patron, the more likely you are going to get yourself into an ethical dilemma of putting an inebriated person out on the highway. The effects of alcohol on the body are discussed as well as how to handle delicate situations with your customers.

The next three chapters deal with the products the bar will be selling: wine, spirits, and beer. This section delves into the ingredients used to make these goods, how they are made, and how they are packaged. Many alcoholic beverages are imported from other countries, and some are made domestically. Where they come from is important as there are subtle differences in content and taste. Each of these chapters concludes with a discussion on what to purchase for a bar.

Equipment and how to purchase it correctly and save money are covered next. How to maintain it so that it will last for a long period of time is explained. The correct way to lay out a bar is described so that employees will take minimum steps to produce drinks, thus saving on labor costs. This is an important concept because any errors made here will last the lifetime of the bar.

The final chapters cover profitable bar management. They go into the legal aspects of hiring and managing people and cover some of the more significant styles of management. Production and mixology and their importance to profitability are communicated. Controls are important to achieving profit, and methods of implementing them are discussed. A good marketing strategy is essential to any bar operation, and methods to implement one are covered. The text concludes with a discussion of entrepreneurship and how to develop a business plan, an essential instrument for anyone planning on opening his or her own business.

The alcoholic beverage industry is arguably the most regulated business in the United States. Throughout the text these regulations are discussed. It should be remembered, however, that many of the laws governing the sale of alcohol are local and vary from jurisdiction to jurisdiction. The prudent manager will be aware of the laws governing his or her particular location.

The field of serving alcoholic beverages is a challenging one. Knowing the various wines, spirits, and beers is quite intimidating as many of the names are in foreign languages. Walking a fine line between selling more beverages and ensuring the safety of your customers is a challenge indeed. Controlling your product against theft and overpouring is a challenge. Obeying all of the laws is a challenge. We have attempted to write a text that is easy to read and make sense out of all of these challenges.

Enjoy the book!

Acknowledgements

People assume that an author did all of the work that goes into the writing of a text. That could not be farther from the truth. There are many people who have had a hand in this project. First and foremost is my family, whose unwavering support and patience is most appreciated; particularly my wife Judy, who read and edited every page of the manuscript.

I would like to thank the following people for their help as well. Not in any particular order, they are:

Donald McBride, whose research assistance and tireless work on the glossary are greatly appreciated.

Theodore Revell, who contributed to the section on social media and was consulted on technology as it relates to control systems. To someone who has trouble setting the alarm clock, his help was irreplaceable.

Jeanne McBride, who created all of the line drawings that you see throughout the text.

Bill Lawrensen, the acquisitions editor at Pearson. This is the third book that Bill and I have worked on together, and his calm demeanor is deeply valued.

Lara Dimmick, the editorial assistant at Pearson who can cut through red tape and quickly answer almost any question.

Susan Hannahs, the project manager who made sense out of everything and took the manuscript and made it a finished product.

Anju Joshi, the full service project manager extraordinaire whose attention to detail is greatly appreciated.

And finally to the following people who took time out of their busy schedule to review the manuscript, offer positive criticism, and recommend suggestions to improve the text:

- Earl Arrowood, Bucks County Community College
- Timothy Barr, Syracuse University
- Mark Berkner, Delta College
- Margaret Binkley, The Ohio State University
- Janice Boyce, Texas Tech University
- Dan Crafts, Missouri State University
- Barbara Jean Bruin, Collins College of Hospitality Management
- Amy M. Green, University of Alaska–Anchorage
- Brian Hay, Austin Community College
- Frederick Ferrara, Joliet Junior College
- Paul Mach, Pennsylvania College of Technology
- Stephanie Morgan, Spartanburg Technical College
- Donald Sprinkle, Maui Community College
- Louis Woods, Anne Arundel Community College

INSTRUCTOR'S RESOURCES

Instructor's Resource materials include an Online Instructor's Manual, PowerPoints, and a MyTest.

To access supplementary materials online, instructors need to request an instructor access code. Go to www.pearsonhighered.com/irc, where you can register for an instructor access code. Within 48 hours after registering, you will receive a confirmation email, including your instructor access code. Once you have received your code, go to the site and log on for full instructions on downloading the materials you wish to use.

1
History and Scope of the Industry

OVERVIEW

The world of serving alcoholic beverages is a large one indeed. Consider that the industry covers everything from small neighborhood taverns to large entertainment complexes, from sports bars to sports stadiums and arenas, and from small meetings in hotels to large banquets serving thousands of people. Yet, despite these differences, the principles of beverage management are surprisingly similar.

In this chapter, we will look at the history of the beverage service industry in America. Keep in mind that this is only an overview as volumes have been written about the subject. Additional information regarding the history of alcoholic beverages can be found in several of the chapters. We will also study the different types of beverage outlets and discuss some of their similarities and differences. The chapter concludes with a brief overview of the field of study known as beverage management.

HISTORY

When studying history, one usually starts at the beginning. In the case of alcoholic beverages, no one knows where the beginning is. Most agree that it was probably accidental, possibly some fermented fruit lying on the ground. Perhaps, as some suggest, it was bread in a bowl left out in the rain and later heated by the sun. This makes sense as the ingredients to make a crude beer are all there. The exact beginnings of alcoholic beverages notwithstanding, we do know that they were in existence around 10,000 BC as beer jugs from that era have been discovered. It is widely believed that beer predated wine as the first evidence of wine appears in Egyptian pictographs around 4000 BC.

In the 12th century AD alcoholic beverages saw a dramatic change. The still was invented. Up until then beer and wine were the only alternatives. With the invention of the still, they were joined by distilled spirits. Distilled spirits were originally used solely for medicinal purposes but slowly caught on as a beverage. It wasn't until the 17th century that distilled spirits became accepted with the general population.

Throughout the history of alcoholic beverages, one fact holds true, and that is how closely it was aligned with religion. From ancient civilizations that had little or no contact with each other to today, alcohol has played a part in many religious rituals. In China, circa 7000 BC, a fermented drink made of rice, honey, and fruit was used to offer sacrifices to the gods. Ancient Chinese believed that this was a gift from the gods. Later the Greeks and Romans thought the same. In Central America, the Incas used a fermented liquid made from maize (corn) in their religious ceremonies. In America, even the Puritans believed that alcohol was a gift from God. Another fact that holds true for the most part among religions was the advice that alcohol should be used only in moderation. Excessive use was frowned upon and in most cases forbidden.

As the focus of this text is on beverage management, we will now turn our attention to the history of bars, taverns, and laws as they apply to managing an operation in the United States. While a knowledge of history is not an overriding factor in being a successful manager, it is important to have an appreciation of how customs and laws came into being that influence the way we do business today.

17th Century

One of the first, if not the first, operation to sell alcohol in the future United States was Cole's Ordinary. Opened in the 1630s in Plymouth Colony by James Cole, who had migrated from England, it became known as Plymouth's finest inn. As the colonies expanded, inns, which were called **ordinaries**, flourished. Inn-keeping then, much like being a hotelier today, was an important occupation, and innkeepers wielded considerable influence in their communities. As a matter of fact, most ordinaries were subsidized by the colonies as they were considered a public service. If a community did not have a suitable inn, it was not considered "civilized." Along with subsidies came regulation. Most of the regulations in those days were aimed not at the taverns, but at the customers as public drunkenness was not tolerated. From the 1600s into the 1700s, the colonies, which later became states, passed laws aimed at curtailing individuals' drinking habits.

One of the first laws that targeted taverns was passed in New York in 1697, mandating that all bars and saloons be closed on Sunday as that was the Lord's day. As far as the state was concerned, the general public should concentrate its efforts on worship rather than public carousing.

Exterior of the White Horse tavern, which was granted a liquor license in 1673.
Steven Greaves © Dorling Kindersley Limited

18th Century

At this time in history, churches wielded considerable power in the various statehouses, and in 1735 the first inkling of completely shutting down all taverns came when the colony of Georgia passed a law creating prohibition. The law was short lived, however, and was repealed several years later.

When the colonies became states and the Constitution was ratified, one of the first acts of the newly formed federal government was to figure out how to pay off the enormous debt from the Revolutionary War. The solution was to place a federal tax on liquor and spirits. This did not sit well with the citizens of the new country as they had just declared independence from heavy taxation under the British Empire. Enter **moonshine**.

The making of alcoholic beverages at that time was a cottage industry; that is, it was not dominated by large distilleries. Many of these small distillers, known as moonshiners, went on making whiskey and simply did not pay the tax. It was an economic decision rather than a defiant one as, if they paid the tax, they could not feed and clothe their families. Federal agents called revenuers would come around to collect the tax and were often fired upon by the distillers. The hatred between the revenuers and the moonshiners came to a head in 1794 in Pittsburg, Pennsylvania, when the citizens took to the streets and rioted. The Whiskey Rebellion was under way. President Washington responded by calling up the militia and sending several thousand troops into the city, who stopped the rioting and captured the leaders. While Pittsburg returned to normal, the moonshiners did not go away. They continued to flourish, most notably in the South, and are still present today although greatly diminished in numbers.

Moonshine continued to flourish underground.
sumnersgraphicsinc/Fotolia

While most ordinaries served food as well as spirits and ales, one of the most popular spirits at this time was gin. As the British Empire began its worldwide growth, wherever the British went, English-style gins went with them. In the colonies, such celebrated Americans as Paul Revere and George Washington were quite fond of gin. Even the Quakers were known for drinking gin toddies after funerals. Not only was Washington fond of gin, he also favored whiskey. In 1797, a Scot, James Anderson, who was working for Washington at the time, convinced him to use some of his crop of corn and rye to distill whiskey. In 1799 the distillery, which was one of the larger ones at the time, was opened, producing 11,000 gallons of whiskey. It is assumed that Washington paid the federal tax on his distilled spirits.

19th Century

As time went on, the ordinaries grew from a few rooms in someone's house into inns with quite a few sleeping rooms as well as a dining room and bar. Paralleling this growth were stand-alone restaurants and taverns. The Union Oyster House was opened in 1826 in Boston and is believed to be the oldest continuously operating restaurant in the United States.

In the mid-1800s a few states, not learning from Georgia's mistake in 1735 of prohibition, created their own laws enacting prohibition. Some of these laws were declared unconstitutional by the courts, and the taverns stayed open. Another problem was that Congress, not the states, regulated interstate commerce. While the states could, with some degree of success, stop the manufacture of alcoholic beverages within their own borders, they could not prevent it from being shipped in. Alcoholic

The Union Oyster House, one of the oldest continuously running restaurants in the United States.

Photograph Courtesy of the Union Oyster House, Boston Mass.

beverages could be ordered from out of state by the taverns and was often delivered via the United States Post Office.

As the 1800s drew to a close, beer was becoming more and more popular. Brought to the United States by German immigrants, it quickly became a favorite. As a matter of fact, by 1890, it had surpassed liquor as the most wanted beverage in saloons. As more and more breweries were opened, the competition became fierce. Because bottled spirits took up little space, a saloonkeeper could keep several brands of each spirit on hand. Beer, however, was another matter. Kegs took up a lot of space and had to be refrigerated. Therefore the selection of beer brands in each tavern was limited. In order to expand their market share, breweries came up with circuitous methods to encourage taverns to stock their brand.

One such method was for a brewery to set up a saloonkeeper in business. If a person had a modest amount of capital to invest, the brewery would purchase for him bar fixtures, signage, advertising, and initial inventory. The saloonkeeper would pay a little more on each keg to offset the brewery's investment. While the owner could sell distilled spirits, the only beer sold was that of the brewery that put him into business. With many breweries putting people into the bar business, taverns proliferated, and competition was fierce. Spirits and beer along with free food were not enough to withstand the onslaught of competition, so gambling and prostitution flourished. All of this brought with it social problems, and neighborhoods were concerned that there was a lack of respectability and that things were getting out of hand.

In the 1880s groups such as the Women's Christian Temperance Union and the Anti-Saloon League, among others, began to spring up. These groups along with the churches began to promote the idea of stopping the sale and use of all alcoholic beverages, whether from a package store or tavern. The idea of a national prohibition was beginning to take hold.

20th Century

The movement gathered momentum, and in 1917 an amendment to the Constitution was proposed. With the strength and energy of the faction behind it, it did not take long for the amendment to be ratified by the necessary number of states. In January 1919, the last state ratified it, and it became the 18th Amendment to the Constitution on January 29, 1920. While the amendment prohibited the manufacture, transportation, and sale of intoxicating liquor, it was unenforceable because it did not define an alcoholic beverage. Thus Congress passed the **Volstead Act**, named after a congressman from Minnesota, which defined intoxicating liquor as anything containing more than one-half of 1 percent of alcohol and gave the government

Saloons and taverns proliferated in the 1800s.

Brian Daughton © Dorling Kindersley

the power to enforce the amendment. President Wilson, not liking the provisions of the bill, vetoed it, and Congress passed it over his veto.

The idea of prohibition did not start with the Georgia law in 1735. In 1100 BC the Chinese passed a law prohibiting the making and consumption of wine (the only alcoholic beverage at that time) and eventually rescinded it. As a matter of fact, over the centuries they did this over 40 times and in 1400 AD figured out that prohibition simply would not work.

The United States was no different. Now that **Prohibition** was the law of the land, the fact remained that people who wanted to drink were going to drink and nothing was going to stop them. Thus, all sorts of illegal strategies were implemented. Many of the former taverns went "underground" and became **speakeasies**. Not wanting law enforcement to get in, customers not only had to know the speakeasy's location, but they had to know somebody to get in. In effect, they became private clubs. One major difference between the former taverns and the new speakeasies, aside from the fact that the latter were illegal, was that women were admitted. Up to this point taverns had been a bastion of males only. Not only were speakeasies illegal, but remember that Prohibition also prohibited the manufacture and distribution of alcoholic beverages. How were the speakeasies to get the product to sell to their customers? Good old American ingenuity and entrepreneurial spirit took over, and before long there were a number of ways to get alcoholic beverages.

The manufacturing process took several forms. Moonshining, which had previously been carried out to avoid taxes, flourished. Smaller distilleries moved to the hills, mountains, and backwoods of the country. They set up stills and produced grain alcohol, which was then diluted and flavored. Often this was done in large batches in bathtubs, thus spawning the term *bathtub gin*. Breweries turned to making "near beer." To do this, they merely brewed their beer and cooked off the alcohol until it fell under the one-half of 1 percent requirement. However, it was not uncommon for many of them to "accidentally" skip the last step and thus sell regular beer. While America embraced prohibition, other countries did not. Much of the product sold in the speakeasies came from foreign countries. With the manufacture of alcohol resolved, distribution became the next hurdle.

Enter organized crime. Criminals had the money, the manpower, and the organization necessary, and they were not afraid of the federal and local governments. Since the goods were illegal and therefore there were no taxes on them, the mob could make huge amounts of money. From Canada and Mexico, alcohol was "bootlegged" across the border. From Europe and the Far East, freighters would bring alcohol, distilled legally in those countries, across international waters to just outside the three-mile limit of the United States. There boats would meet them and bring the product ashore illegally.

Additionally, the people operating the stills in the mountains and hills would sell to the speakeasies, as would the local producers of bathtub gin. Often they would clash with the government. Worse yet, the mob would catch up with them, with fierce fighting and bloodshed often the result. Add to all of this the fact that organized crime fought internally, with "turf wars" becoming commonplace. With high profits at stake, these skirmishes became bloody as well. In order to keep the government out of its business, the mob infiltrated most of the city halls across the country.

While the majority of taverns and saloons went underground, a few stopped selling alcoholic beverages and concentrated on the restaurant side of their business. By serving good food and having good service, they were able to survive Prohibition. Some patrons also took the high road and went to their doctors for a prescription for what ailed them. One of the loopholes in 18th Amendment and the Volstead Act was that alcohol could be manufactured for medicinal purposes. The pharmacy business skyrocketed.

As Prohibition wore on, it became increasingly clear that it was a mistake. The federal government could not control it. Local governments had become infiltrated by organized crime. There were more speakeasies after the 18th Amendment passed than there were taverns prior to it. Crime was rampant. In short, it was a total failure. On December 5, 1933, the 21st Amendment to the Constitution of the United States was passed. It repealed the 18th Amendment, and Prohibition was over.

While Prohibition was over, the communities did not want to return to the chaos that predated it. Regulation of bars and taverns became a state and municipal issue rather than a federal one. States began regulating the distribution of alcohol, and many of them became control states. A **control state** is one in which the state either distributes alcoholic beverages itself or controls the number of distributors, often giving a distributorship a monopoly in a given area. In return for this monopoly, the distributor is heavily regulated as to which products it can sell and how much it can charge for them. In addition to control states, some states had minimal regulations while on the other side of the spectrum a few states became **dry states**, which did not allow alcoholic beverages at all. Figure 1.1 shows a map of the control states

Local governments regulated the number of bars and taverns in a given area, normally a voting precinct or neighborhood. It also regulated the hours an establishment could stay open. The states and municipalities became so zealous in not wanting to return to a pre-Prohibition situation that the bar business became one of the most regulated industries in the country. Regulation notwithstanding, the industry has flourished. In the past, almost all bars and taverns were run by individual proprietors. Today the landscape has changed. While there are still a number of one-owner businesses around, the chains have taken over a large share of the business. There are so many types of bars that are in business today that it is difficult to categorize them. We will attempt to do so, but keep in mind that many bars will fall into more than one category.

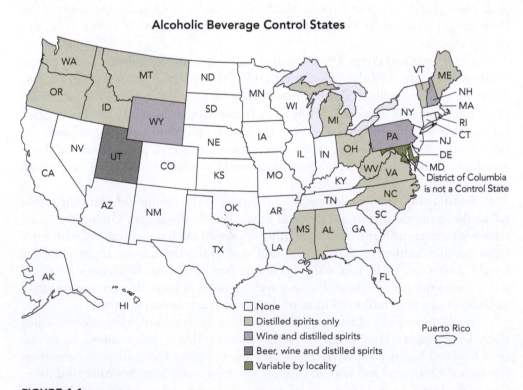

Alcoholic Beverage Control States

District of Columbia is not a Control State

☐ None
☐ Distilled spirits only
☐ Wine and distilled spirits
☐ Beer, wine and distilled spirits
☐ Variable by locality

Puerto Rico

FIGURE 1.1
Map of the control states.

TYPES OF BEVERAGE OUTLETS

First, let us define a **beverage outlet**. For the purposes of this text we will define it as a place where alcohol, namely, beer, wine, spirits, and/or liqueur, is sold to be consumed on the premises, as opposed to retail liquor stores. There are many names for such outlets, the most popular being *bars*, *pubs*, *saloons*, *taverns*, *bistros*, *nightclubs*, *honky-tonks*, and *watering holes*, among others. While the definition of a place serving alcoholic beverages is a wide one, there are several specifics that further define and categorize beverage outlets.

Neighborhood Bars

Arguably these are the most popular bars in the country today. Almost every locality, community, or small town has its neighborhood bar. It is a place where locals gather for camaraderie or to discuss local politics, sports teams, or the news of the day. Oftentimes the same people show up from day to day and everyone knows everyone. These bars are for the most part owned by one or two people, but the chains have been making inroads on these types of establishments, particularly in urban areas. Neighborhood bars may or may not sell food.

It is not at all unusual for these establishments to observe the old practice of "running a tab" for their regular customers. A **tab** is a means for the customer to charge their drinks and pay for them periodically, usually on their payday, rather than paying for each individual drink. This practice is being replaced by the use of credit and debit cards. A tab also refers to customers that pay at the end of a stay, as opposed to paying each time a drink is served.

Theme Bars

Theme bars are those outlets whose focus is on a particular theme. It could be historical like the several taverns in the Williamsburg, Virginia, Historic District. It could also be transportation related such as a train or airplane theme. It could be related to the neighborhood, town, city, or surrounding area. Whatever the theme, it is usually carried out in the décor of the establishment as well as the menu, if food is offered. Specialty cocktails relating to the theme often are featured as well.

Neighborhood bars, where locals go to have a good time.
© krsmanovic—Fotolia.com

Ethnic Bars

Ethnic bars at one time proliferated across the landscape. As different ethnic groups migrated to the United States, they tended to settle in towns and city neighborhoods where there were relatives or friends who had come before them. Bars and taverns followed. These bars would feature beverages that the immigrants were familiar with and would often feature foods from their native countries. As they assimilated into the general population and neighborhoods became more homogeneous, these taverns started to die out. They are making a comeback, however, with the new wave of immigrants from Mexico and Central America as well as Pacific Rim countries.

A derivative of the ethnic bar is one that appeals to the general population. There is hardly a city that does not have at least one Irish pub. Other examples include French, Asian, Polish, Mexican, African, German, as well as a whole list of others. More often than not these enterprises will serve food native to their respective countries. While these operations feature an ethnic group as their theme, they do not necessarily cater exclusively to that group but rather to the masses.

Sports Bars

Flat-screen televisions showing several different games at once, pennants hanging from the wall, cocktail servers and bartenders wearing the uniform or colors of a local team—there is no doubt when you walk into one of these establishments that you are in a sports bar. Sports bars are more prevalent than any other category today. They are often run by chains, but individual proprietors flourish as well. They frequently serve food, concentrating on a plethora of fried appetizers, sandwiches, and salads. They market to the younger crowd and on game day are packed with cheering fans.

Brew Pubs

Occupying a unique niche in the beverage industry, the brew pub is unusual in that it manufactures the majority of the beer and ale that is sold on the premises. While most of them serve brand-name beers as well, have a full bar, and serve food, the emphasis is on the hand crafted beers made in-house. They usually have several styles of beer and

A busy sports bar.

Alessandra Santarelli and Joeff Davis © Dorling Kindersley

ale as a core offering and several others that change on a seasonal basis. When one enters a brew pub, the vats and other production paraphernalia are usually displayed quite prominently in the establishment.

One-Product Bars

One-product bars are ones in which one type of beverage is served. They range from martini bars to beer bars. One popular variation on one-product bars is the wine bar. They will offer many varieties, brands, and vintages of wine along with tapas (small plates of appetizer-type food). One-product bars usually use premium merchandise as well as unusual and hard-to-find products. Because their market is limited, they have to be extremely good at what they do. One-product bars are usually located in large cities with a concentrated population.

Credit Bars

Credit bars are those bars where cash does not change hands with each transaction but rather a tab is run. At the end of a period, a bill is submitted to the buyer and is paid. Examples of credit bars are private clubs, such as a country club or city club. Cruise ships also run on credit with the guest paying for their bar tabs along with other expenses incurred on the ship at the end of the cruise. Neighborhood bars and others that accept tabs from some customers are not included in this category as they also accept cash from other customers. Credit bars are a total cashless operation.

The exterior of the Portland Brewing Company Brew Pub.
Bruce Forster © Dorling Kindersley

Entertainment Venues

An entertainment venue is any operation that sells alcoholic drinks but whose primary business is not selling alcohol. Alcohol is a secondary focus of the business. To put it another way, the customer goes there to be entertained rather than as a place to have a drink. This category has a wide range, running anywhere from a small intimate club featuring a jazz trio to arenas and sports stadiums.

There is usually an extra charge to get in to these establishments. In the case of a small venue, such as a club, there is a cover charge. A **cover charge** is a cost paid by the guest to enter the site. The cover charge helps absorb the cost of the entertainment to management. In the case of an arena or stadium, a ticket to the event is necessary to gain admission to the event and subsequently the bar. While the primary purpose of these venues is entertainment, make no mistake about it—alcoholic beverages make up a good portion of their income and profit.

Hotels

Hotels, particularly the larger ones, normally have several beverage outlets. In addition to these outlets, there is the banquet beverage service, which has its own set of procedures.

Outlet Bars Outlet bars are located throughout the hotel. Quite often a hotel will have a lobby bar where guests can enjoy a cocktail in a quiet, comfortable setting. Lobby bars normally are carpeted, with large comfortable chairs, sofas, and low cocktail tables. They often have a private club feel to them. Convention guests in particular like them for a place to gather and discuss issues that were raised in their sessions, as do business people who want to talk about sales figures or devise corporate strategies. The key to a successful lobby bar is that it is conducive to conversation rather than being an entertainment venue.

An elegant hotel dining room with beverage service.
Smalik/Fotolia

Other hotel beverage outlets are designed for the entertainment of guests. These could include theme, ethnic, or sport bars. Often in a large downtown hotel there are several of these venues. Frequently they will have live entertainment. These outlets normally are located on the ground floor of the hotel with an outside entrance to encourage local walk in traffic. Thus the hotel gets revenue from its guests as well as from the general public.

Large hotels will have two or more restaurants. One of these is, more often than not, a coffee shop that serves all three meals at a moderate price. Additionally, the hotel will have at least one more restaurant that has a higher price point. This could be an upscale theme or ethnic bistro or a fine dining restaurant. In almost all cases, these outlets will have beverage service.

Banquet Service   Banquets are a large part of a hotel's revenue, and beverage service, in turn, is a large part of the banquet revenue. It should be noted that while hotels are being discussed here, this dialogue also applies to catering companies and banquet halls. Breakfasts and luncheons put on by the catering department rarely have alcoholic beverage service. Occasionally, champagne, Bloody Marys, and Mimosas might be served at a breakfast or wine could be served at a luncheon. On the other hand, practically every evening banquet put on by the hotel will have some form of beverage service with it. The only exception would be for those groups that oppose alcohol for religious, ethnic, or personal beliefs.

Those banquets that do have beverage service will always have it prior to the dinner during a reception hour. This could be a full bar, beer and wine only, or wine only. Normally in banquet service the term *full bar* means that highballs, rocks, and simple mixed drinks are served along with beer, wine, and carbonated beverages. Rarely are blended or multi-ingredient drinks served. The reason for this is that the bar is portable and quite compact. It therefore has a limited amount of equipment with which to work as well as a limited amount of space. In addition to the reception hour, many banquets will keep the bar open during and after dinner. If a guest speaker is a part of the program, normally the bar will shut down for this segment.

There are several methods of handling banquet beverage service. They are a cash bar, a hosted bar, and table service. Additionally, there is in-suite or room service. While not a part of banquet service, it is covered here because it has many of the same attributes.

Cash Bars A **cash bar** is where each guest pays for his or her own drinks as opposed to having the host pay for all drinks. When cash bars are utilized, the bartender usually is allowed to receive gratuities, and often a tip jar is placed on the bar. Cash bars can be set up in one of two ways, cash or ticket.

- Cash. In this system, the guests pay for their drinks when they are purchased. They order their drinks; the bartender prepares them and then collects. The downside to this system is that it slows down service, particularly during a reception hour when there a lot of people drinking in a short span of time. It also is harder to control both cash and product with this system. For these reasons it is not used as often as the ticket system.
- Tickets. With this method, the functions of taking cash and mixing drinks are separated. A cashier sells tickets to the guest, and the guest then goes to the bar and redeems the tickets for drinks. The selling price is normally broken down into five categories: soft drinks, beer, wine, mixed drinks, and premium mixed drinks. Often beer and wine are combined, leaving four categories. The tickets are color coded to match the category. For example, a guest would purchase a ticket for a glass of Chablis from the cashier and receive a red ticket. They then give the red ticket to the bartender for their glass of wine. This method not only speeds up service but enables the house to establish a solid set of controls. Should the guests purchase more tickets than they use, they can turn them in to the cashier for a full refund. Quite often, however, the house benefits from guests who purchase tickets, do not use them, and fail to turn them in. In the case of larger banquets, only one cashier is needed for every two or three bartenders.

Hosted Bars A **hosted bar** is oftentimes referred to as an **open bar**. With this method, the host, rather than the guests, pays for the drinks. These are quite popular for wedding receptions, although with the high cost of putting on a wedding and reception, it is becoming more frequent for weddings to have cash bars. Hosted bars are also used when a company is having a sales meeting or is entertaining a group of clients. They are often used when an organization is having a fund raiser. In this case a large donation, perhaps $200, will be charged for dinner and an open bar, with part of the $200 going for the banquet and bar and the balance as a fund raiser for the organization.

There is generally no tipping at a hosted bar as the gratuity is added to the bill presented to the host at the conclusion of the event. It should be noted, however, that there are exceptions to this rule as occasionally a hosted bar will permit tipping by the guest. There are three methods that are used to figure the charges for hosted bars: by the drink, by the number of guests per hour, or by inventory.

- By the drink. In this method, each glass of wine, each bottle of beer, or each drink that is poured is tabulated by the bartender at its retail price. At the end of the event, the tab is totaled, the gratuity is added, and the tab is presented to the host. One can readily see that tabulating each drink can be cumbersome and will slow down the speed of service. For this reason, this method is used primarily at smaller events.
- Number of guests per hour. This method is used by operations that have been in business for a while as it depends on historical figures for its accuracy. The hotel knows from looking at its records how many drinks the average guest will consume

in an hour. This method takes into consideration that because drinks are free, some guests will consume an abnormally high number of drinks, some will hit the average, and some will not drink at all. This figure is then multiplied by the number of guests attending the event and then multiplied again by the number of hours the event is held. For example, if the records show that the average guest consumes $5.00 worth of alcohol per hour, there are 500 persons attending the function, and it will last for three hours, the establishment will charge the host $7500.

$$\$5.00 \times 500 \text{ persons} \times 3 \text{ hours} = \$7500$$

The hourly charge takes into consideration demographics as different groups will consume different levels of alcohol. While this may at first glance seem like a risky proposition for the hotel, as mentioned earlier, it depends heavily on an accurate historical record being kept by the property.

- Inventory. This is the most popular method of charging for hosted bars. It takes into account the actual amount of alcohol consumed during the function and adds an hourly charge for the bartender and miscellaneous overhead. It works like this: All of the product is inventoried at the start of the function. This includes all beer, wine, spirits, and mixes including soft drinks. At the conclusion of the function, the product is inventoried again. The starting inventory is subtracted from the ending inventory and is then multiplied by the retail price of each product. This is then totaled. The hourly charge is multiplied by the number of hours the function was held to get the total service charge. The total amount of product consumed plus the total service charge are added together. A gratuity is added to the bill and presented to the guest.

A banquet set up for wine service.
gmg9130/Fotolia

Table Service   Depending on the organization, table service of alcoholic beverages may or may not be offered at a banquet. When offered, it is carried out by cocktail servers in some cases or food servers in others. Table service commences after the reception when the guests have taken their seats. In addition to cocktail service, quite often wine by the bottle is offered. When this happens, wine is poured by a wine steward or a banquet server for each guest at the table. In the case of a cash bar, the server collects from the guests for their drinks. Most often, one person at the table will pay for the bottles of wine. In the case of a hosted event, there is no collection. With hosted events, it is common for several varieties of wine to be served, which correspond with each course.

In-suite Service   In-suite service is used for very small gatherings. In this case, a variety of wine, beer, spirits, and mixers is sent to the suite, often with an assortment of snacks such as pretzels, chips, or mixed nuts. In this case, the house does not provide a bartender. This duty is often performed by the person hosting the event, or it could be "everyone for themselves." With in-suite service, the host is charged for everything sent to the suite. Should there be any product left, it is the property of the host who paid for it.

Restaurants

Many restaurants sell alcoholic beverages. Some serve wine or beer solely, some serve beer and wine, and some have a full bar. To define this category, the question must be asked whether the primary purpose of the establishment is to sell food or alcoholic beverages. In other words, is it a bar that sells food or a restaurant that serve drinks? Regardless of the answer, there are a multitude of establishments that do both. As a matter of fact, each could fall into several categories. For example, an Irish pub sells both food and drink, has a banquet facility that can handle either a cash bar or a hosted bar, and brings a Celtic band in on the weekends and charges a cover charge. As we can see, there are very few establishments that qualify for one category exclusively, but rather most fall into several categories.

SCOPE OF THE BUSINESS

As we have seen, the scope of bar business is very broad. It is also very complicated. When one visits a bar and sees people having a good time, one is tempted to think "maybe I should open a bar." "After all I like to party and have a good time. All it takes is a location, buy some bottles, stick a flat screen on the wall, and let the good times roll." WRONG!!!! It is more involved than that. As you progress through this book, you will learn about the business and its intricacies. You will learn to appreciate the skill and knowledge it takes to own or manage a beverage outlet. The following is a brief description of the material that we will be discussing as we study profitable beverage management.

- Alcohol service. In marketing, we learn how to sell. We learn in accounting that sales volume is the key to profitability. From this we could deduce that the objective is to sell, sell, sell. Not so fast! Responsible alcohol service should be the primary goal of every bar manager. Knowing how a person gets inebriated and the signs to look for inebriation is important. Management, bartenders, and servers need to walk a fine line between getting optimum sales and at the same time protecting their guests and the community from an intoxicated person. In addition to moral and ethical behavior on the part of the bar, there are legal issues as well. The law comes down hard on those who serve alcohol to inebriated persons. With the large investment in both time and money on the part of ownership, it would be devastating to lose a liquor license over legal violations.

- Wine. It is crucial for you as a manager to know what you are selling; thus the study of wine, spirits, and beer. Starting with wine, many factors go into producing a wine and its ultimate color, taste, and clarity. It starts with the vineyard, goes to the harvest, then the extraction procedure, and on to aging, bottling, and ultimately tasting. In some cases, wine from different vintners or from previous harvests are blended and in other cases they stand alone on their own merits. Each step of this process is significant as any slight variation will alter the outcome of the final product. Different grapes produce different wines, and the significant varieties are examined. We will look at some of the more important wine growing regions and examine the wines they produce. We conclude with how to conduct a wine tasting. While this chapter is difficult because of the foreign terminology, it is an exciting one that only begins to explore the remarkable world of wine. Hopefully you will be inspired to learn even more.

- Spirits. All alcoholic beverages are fermented. Spirits take it a step further and are distilled as well as being fermented. Examples of spirits include bourbon, whisky, whiskey (not the same thing), vodka, rum, tequila, and gin. The distillation process increases the amount of alcohol in the beverage. To offset this, many drinks made from spirits are mixed with soda or juice, while a few are sipped "straight." While there are differences in the distillation process among spirits, the primary factor in the distinction between them is in the ingredients used, the amount of aging, and the methods used to age the product. Knowledge of each type of spirit, its ingredients, how it is distilled, and what gives it its unique character is essential for you as a future manager to know.

- Beer. There are basically two types of beer: ale and lager. Within these types are many different classifications. These classifications sometimes overlap one another, making it difficult to distinguish one from the other. That notwithstanding, knowing the key categories of ales and lagers and the attributes of each is of the essence. While the ingredients in beer (yeast, barley, hops, water, and cereal) are essentially the same, the additives, brewing process, quality of the ingredients, and their growing area are what differentiates one beer from the other.

- Bar equipment. One of the most costly purchases you will make at any given time is bar equipment. Whether purchasing one piece or outfitting an entire bar, new or used, equipment is a long-term investment expending a lot of cash. There is a right way and a wrong way to purchase equipment. If you purchase only one piece of equipment in your lifetime, by following the principles set forth, you will save enough money to pay for the course you are taking now. If you outfit an entire bar, you could well save enough to pay for your entire tuition. While knowing how to purchase equipment is important, knowing what to purchase is equally important. Purchasing something you do not need is a waste of money, as is buying something too large or too small to do the intended job. Maintaining the equipment you purchase will ensure that it will last a long time. It is imperative that you know the essentials of appropriate maintenance. With the amount of money invested in equipment, it makes good sense to keep it running as long as possible.

- Equipment layout. How and where equipment is placed is an important component to the profitability of a bar. How many times have you seen a bartender run back and forth to assemble the ingredients for one drink? Steps waste time, and time is money. In addition to proper placement of equipment, the dimensions of the work space and table placement are equally important. The consequences of an error in the layout phase of a project will last the entire life of the bar. It is essential that you get this right.

- Employment law. Managing an outgoing and cheerful group of employees is one thing, but following employment laws is another. There are a myriad of laws, going from federal to state and local, governing how employees are treated. Often these laws conflict. In some cases, federal law will supersede state law, and sometimes the reverse is true. Knowledge of these laws is important, as the penalties for failure to follow them are often severe. Not knowing the law is not an excuse. Keep in mind also that these laws change from time to time and new ones are being constantly added. It is one of your responsibilities as a manager to know these laws and to keep up with the changing landscape.

- Organization. The bar business is a people business. While bars make drinks, how they serve them goes a long way into determining how successful that business will be. How you, as a bar manager, treat your people will reflect how they, as servers and bartenders, treat their customers. There are many different management styles, and we will study some of the more prevalent ones. How you resolve conflicts between your staff members will go a long way in determining your success as a manager. Managing change is also an important component of your job. One of the keys to success as a manager is to have job descriptions that delineate the exact duties of every employee. This helps eliminate conflict between employees and lets each one know what is expected of him or her. Employee evaluations should tie into job descriptions and measure how well the person is performing what is expected.

- Production and mixology. One of the most important aspects of beverage management is the ability of the bar to produce a quality drink that is consistent time after time. To achieve this, standardized recipes are employed. This ensures consistency for the customer and also ensures that the costs are contained and therefore profit is achieved. Whether pouring wine or beer or mixing a spirit, using the appropriate glassware is important. Choosing the correct glassware for your bar will make the bartenders' job easier and will ensure correct portion control. The tools that are used in the production of drinks are also fundamental to a smooth-running bar.

A bartender serving a mixed drink.
© Kuzmick—Fotolia.com

- Selling to a profit. In order to make money in the bar business, it is essential that your product is priced correctly. Price it too high and you drive your customer straight into the arms of your competitor. Price it too low and you lose profit. In order to understand the concept of profit, it is necessary to understand the income statement and the relationship of sales and costs. Every item on the bar menu must be priced so that it can cover all costs and leave some money left over for profit. There are several formulas available for setting the correct selling price. After the selling price is determined, the psychological pricing of drinks as well as the price value perception is determined and adjustments are made. By comprehending how the selling price, sales, cost, and controls all come together to affect profit, you are well on the way to running a successful beverage operation.

- Controlling to a profit. Alcoholic beverages are expensive to purchase. While they are sitting in the storeroom, you do not get a return on your investment until that inventory is sold. The quicker it moves through the cycle of purchasing, receiving, storage, issuing, and sales, the quicker you will receive an investment return. Alcoholic beverages are also very prone to theft. Because of this, it is imperative that tight controls be exercised throughout the process from the time they are purchased to the time they are sold. This is an important concept as it outlines the steps necessary to achieve a profit.

- Marketing. Marketing starts with ascertaining who exactly your customers are and determining their wants and needs. It is also analyzing your operation for its strengths and weaknesses as well as the opportunities and threats to your business. From this data a marketing plan is developed. An important component of the plan is determining the return on investment. After all, marketing is an expense, and you want to be sure that you have spent your money wisely. One final thought on marketing is employee involvement. In order for any marketing plan to succeed, the employees must buy into it.

- Entrepreneurship. It is fitting that this chapter is the last one in the book as it also serves as a review of many of the points you have learned. The review follows a path that one must go through when starting up a new business. It begins with a discussion on demographics as it relates to location and who your potential customer is. How to put together a business plan is discussed in detail. It concludes with the regulatory laws and the agencies that you will have to deal with, not only before you open but after the business is established. If you have ever dreamed of opening your own bar, this chapter is essential to you. Even if you have no desire to own your own business, the ideas presented will tie all of the concepts together for you.

CONCLUSION

Throughout the history of the civilized world, alcoholic beverages have played a part. The same can be said of American history. While the venues have changed drastically from the early ordinaries, one thing remains constant, and that is that bars provide a place for people to congregate, to discuss the issues of the day, or to simply have a good time.

The business of running a beverage outlet, whether it is a small neighborhood tavern, a nightclub, or a large hotel, is one that takes a great deal of knowledge and discipline. While it is hard work, it is rewarding. There is nothing more satisfying than seeing people have a good time or enjoying a fine meal with a good bottle of wine or just unwinding at the end of the day.

Welcome to the world of profitable beverage management.

> **Project**
>
> Interview the beverage manager of a large hotel in your area. Ascertain how many bars are on the property, what type of bars they are, and how they are managed. How does the hotel charge the client for a hosted bar? Why does it use this method over others? Write a paper explaining the findings as a result of your interview.

QUESTIONS

True/ False

1. In the time of the colonization of America, taverns were referred to as ordinaries.
2. In 1735, the colony of Georgia passed a law creating prohibition.
3. Prohibition became enforceable with the passage of the Volstead Act.
4. During Prohibition, it was impossible for a person to obtain an alcoholic beverage.
5. There were more speakeasies during Prohibition than there were taverns before Prohibition.

6. For the purposes of this text, a beverage outlet is defined as a place where alcohol, namely, beer, wine, spirits, and/or liquor, is sold to be consumed on the premises.
7. A cover charge is a fee imposed upon a person who charges his or her drinks.
8. A cash bar and a hosted bar are one and the same.
9. In-suite service refers to a butler serving beverages in a hotel suite.
10. The business of opening a bar is, in reality, quite simple.

Multiple Choice

1. In the 17th century
   1) most ordinaries were subsidized by the colonies.
   2) regulations concerning drinking alcoholic beverages were aimed at the customer, rather than the tavern.
   A. (1) only
   B. (2) only
   C. Both (1) and (2)
   D. Neither (1) nor (2)
2. The Whiskey Rebellion
   1) refers to a riot in Pittsburg, Pennsylvania, when distillers refused to pay a federal excise tax on distilled spirits.
   2) was caused by a group of women known as the Women's Temperance Union.
   A. (1) only
   B. (2) only
   C. Both (1) and (2)
   D. Neither (1) nor (2)

3. Breweries in the late 1800s often set up individuals in the saloon business. Which of the following statements concerning this practice is not true?
   A. The saloon owner had to carry beer provided by the brewery exclusively.
   B. The saloon could carry wine and spirits.
   C. The brewery bought the fixtures and provided the initial inventory.
   D. The saloon was not to sell any food.
4. A state that does not allow the sale of alcoholic beverages by the glass is known as a
   1) dry state.
   2) control state.
   A. (1) only
   B. (2) only
   C. Both (1) and (2)
   D. Neither (1) nor (2)

5. Running a tab, in the bar business, refers to
   1) a customer charging his or her drinks and paying for them periodically, usually at the end of the week or month or on payday.
   2) a customer who pays for his or her drinks prior to leaving the establishment.
   A. (1) only
   B. (2) only
   C. Both (1) and (2)
   D. Neither (1) nor (2)
6. Outlet bars
   A. are normally quiet to encourage conversation among guests.
   B. could be an entertainment venue.
   C. are found in hotel dining facilities.
   D. all of the above.
7. A credit bar is
   A. one in which a tab is accepted as well as cash.
   B. one where credit only is accepted.
   C. most common among ethnic bars.
   D. one that is run by a credit union.

8. Tipping is acceptable at a
   A. hosted bar.
   B. cash bar.
   C. open bar.
   D. all of the above.
9. The most popular method of figuring charges for a hosted bar is
   A. the inventory method.
   B. charging a flat rate for the number of hours the event is held.
   C. by the drink
   D. by counting the glassware used and multiplying it by the cost per drink that goes into that glassware.
10. In the ticket method of charging guests attending a banquet for their alcoholic beverages,
   A. the tickets are color coded for the type of beverage paid for.
   B. a cashier sells the ticket to the guest and the guest presents the ticket to the bartender.
   C. one cashier is assigned to two or three bartenders.
   D. all of the above.

Essay

1. Make a case for the effect that Prohibition had on the saloon business in the United States. Include in your discussion how speakeasies obtained product and how they managed to flourish in an illegal business.
2. Prior to Prohibition, breweries would set proprietors up in the bar business. Discuss how this was carried out and what implications this had on the populace regarding Prohibition.
3. Discuss the difference between a control state and a dry state.
4. Write about the difference between a cash bar and a hosted bar. Include in your discussion how cash and/or charges are handled with each one.
5. Discuss the various methods of charging for alcoholic beverages on a banquet where table service is offered.

RESOURCES

Davis, Bernard and Stone, Sally, *Food and Beverage Management*, 5th ed. (Oxford, UK: Lineacre House, 2008).

Katsigris, Costas and Thomas, Chris, *The Bar & Beverage Book*, 4th ed. (Hoboken, New Jersey: John Wiley & Sons, 2007).

Kotschevar, Lendal H. and Tanke, Mary L., *Managing Bar and Beverage Operations*, (East Lansing, MI: Educational Institute of the American Hotel and Motel Association, 1996).

Plotkin, Robert, *Successful Beverage Management*, (Tucson, AZ: Bar Media, 2001).

2
Alcohol Service

Key Terms

Administrative liability
Blood alcohol content (BAC)

OVERVIEW

The material in this chapter is of extreme significance to the owner or manager of a bar. First we look at alcohol and how it affects the mind and body. It is important that your staff understand this concept so that they can recognize when a person is becoming inebriated and take action before the situation gets out of control. How to handle a condition that has gone too far is also covered.

A dilemma occurs when a business gets overzealous in its strategy to increase sales and comes in conflict with social responsibility. Additionally, the staff has this conflict because the more a customer spends and the more inebriated they become, the higher the tip. While the bar has an obligation to make a profit for the owner, it also has a social responsibility to society. It is a fine line that management must walk to maintain a balance between the two.

The last part of the chapter covers laws pertaining to the beverage industry. It is imperative that management has an understanding of these laws. Failure to do so could result in a fine, a lawsuit, or a suspension of the license to operate. Understanding alcohol's influence on the mind and body, your social responsibility to your guest and the community, and the legality of operating a bar is what this chapter is all about.

ALCOHOL'S EFFECT ON BEHAVIOR

Before we discuss how alcohol affects behavior, we need to know how it enters the body and what the body does with it after it enters. When a customer has a drink, alcohol enters the body through the mouth. When this happens a very small amount of alcohol enters the blood stream. The rest of it goes on to the stomach where approximately 20 percent of it enters the bloodstream. From here it goes on to the small intestine where rest of the alcohol (approximately 80%) enters the blood stream. As a result, the longer the alcohol remains in the stomach, the slower it will be absorbed. When alcohol gets into the bloodstream, it can reach the brain and all of the body's other organs in minutes. At the start, alcohol will relax a person and in most cases make them feel happy and outgoing; however, additional drinking may lead to blurred vision and a lack of coordination.

How Alcohol Affects the Body

As the alcohol flows through the bloodstream, it eventually reaches the liver. The liver metabolizes about 90 percent of the alcohol. **Metabolism** is the method the body uses to process those items that you ingest, such as food or alcohol. Of the remaining 10 percent that is not metabolized, about 5 percent is separated in the lungs through breathing. Alcohol separation in the lungs forms the basis for Breathalyzer testing. Another 5 percent is excreted into the urine.

There are many misconceptions and old wives' tales about eliminating alcohol from the system and advancing sobriety. Very simply put, they are not true. You have probably heard that drinking hot coffee will do the trick; not so. All this will do is create a wide-awake drunk. Other legends include breathing fresh air, taking a cold shower, or urinating. None of these fables work. Ninety percent of the alcohol is still present in the body, and only the liver will eliminate it from the system.

On average, the liver metabolizes one normal drink per hour. Heavy drinkers have more active livers and may be able to metabolize up to three drinks per hour. A normal drink is defined as 1.5 ounces of 80 proof alcohol. Proof is twice the amount of alcohol content; thus 80 proof equals 40 percent alcohol. To put it another way, one 12-ounce bottle of beer or a 5-ounce glass of wine is also equal to 1.5 ounces of 80 proof alcohol. Any consumption in addition to this cannot be processed immediately by the liver. Consequently, the alcohol backs up in the bloodstream until it can be processed. As the bloodstream becomes saturated with alcohol, the person becomes intoxicated. Note also that this takes time. Thus a person who drinks three Manhattans in a short period of time will not appear intoxicated immediately. As a matter of fact, they could become intoxicated after they leave your bar.

As previously mentioned, once alcohol is in the bloodstream it can affect every organ and tissue in the body. Excessive or prolonged use of alcohol can have the following effects:

- Blood—can increase the likelihood of infection as alcohol can weaken the function of white blood cells. Additionally, blood clotting can occur.
- Kidneys—can affect the kidneys' ability to regulate and balance the fluids circulating in the body as well as cause kidney failure.
- Liver—can cause cirrhosis, which changes the structure of the liver and its ability to regulate blood flow.
- Stomach—can cause gastritis, ulcers, and acid reflux. It can also wear away the stomach lining causing blood to ooze into the stomach.
- Brain—contracts brain tissue, which weakens the central nervous system. It also destroys brain cells. Keep in mind that while cells in the body regenerate, brain cells do not. Once they are gone, they are gone. Alcohol can also cause problems with perception and memory.
- Heart—can contribute to high blood pressure, heart disease, and heart failure. Irregular heartbeats can be caused by binge drinking.
- Bones—can cause osteoporosis and arthritis.
- Lungs—can increase vulnerability to pneumonia, infections, and lung collapse.

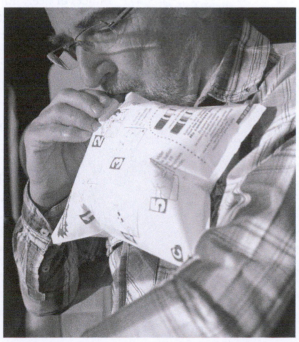

Drivers suspected of driving under the influence of alcohol (DUI) are often given a Breathalyzer test.

minicel73/Fotolia

- Reproductive system—can cause reduction in the production of sperm leading to impotence or infertility. In women, it can cause menstrual abnormalities and possible infertility.
- Muscles—can cause muscle weakness and abrupt pain.
- Esophagus—can cause cancer in the mouth, throat, and larynx as well as tearing the esophagus due to extreme vomiting.

Blood Alcohol Content

How much alcohol is in the bloodstream is measured by **blood alcohol content (BAC)**. This term should be familiar because it is used in all 50 states to determine a person's ability to drive a vehicle. It is unlawful to drive with a *BAC higher than 0.08*. Blood alcohol content is defined as the weight of alcohol per unit volume of blood, normally measured in grams and expressed as a percentage. For example, if a person had a BAC of 0.10, he or she would have one-tenth of a gram of alcohol in every 100 milliliters of blood. To put it another way, there is about one drop of pure alcohol for every 1,000 drops of blood.

Calculating BAC

Blood alcohol content is based on the fact that the liver can break down alcohol at a rate of one drink per hour. Let's review: A drink is defined as 1.5 ounces of spirits (40% alcohol or 80 proof), one 12-ounce bottle of beer (4–5% alcohol), or a 5-ounce glass of wine (12% alcohol). This is pretty simple in a perfect world, but the world of drinking is not all that simple. Consider that different brands and varieties of spirits have a different proof. Add to this the fact that quantities are different. In other words, not all bars pour 1.5 ounces of liquor, nor do they all serve 12 ounces of beer, nor do they all have 5 ounce wine glasses. Multiple-ingredient drinks complicate the matter even more. Fortunately there is a formula that can be used to make sense of this:

Ounces poured / standard = equivalent number of drinks

The standard is the same as the liver's ability to absorb alcohol and is defined as follows:

- 1 ounce of 100 proof spirits
- 1.5 ounces of 80 proof spirits
- 2.5 ounces of 40 proof spirits
- 12 ounces of beer
- 5 ounces of wine

Therefore a pint of beer would be 1.3 drinks:

Ounces poured/standard (ounces) = equivalent number of drinks
16/12 = 1.3 drinks

A pitcher of beer containing 64 ounces would be 5.3 drinks:

Ounces poured/standard = equivalent number of drinks
64/12 = 5.3 drinks

A 2 ½ ounce pour of 80 proof scotch on the rocks would be:

Ounces poured/standard = equivalent number of drinks
2.5 /1.5 = 1.6 drinks

To figure multiple-ingredient drinks, list the ingredients that contain alcohol and then proceed as above. Finally, total the number of equivalent drinks to find the total number of equivalent drinks in that recipe. For example, a multiple-ingredient drink recipe for a martini is figured as follows:

2 ounces 80 proof gin
¼ ounce 40 proof vermouth

Ounces poured/standard = equivalent number of drinks
2/1.5 = 1.33 gin

Ounces poured/standard = equivalent number of drinks
0.25/2.5 = 0.10 vermouth

1.33 gin
0.10 vermouth
1.43 total equivalent number of drinks

Factors Affecting BAC Level

Calculating BAC is not an exact science as there are several other factors that affect the body's ability to absorb alcohol. They include the following:

- Emotional condition. All things being equal, a person showing high emotion will have a higher blood alcohol content than will a tranquil person. The reason for this is that a stressed person's blood is diverted from the stomach and thus slows the dissipation of alcohol to the bloodstream. This does not reduce the amount of alcohol in the system but rather delays the assimilation of alcohol.
- Pregnancy. Fetal alcohol syndrome and fetal alcohol effects are common problems that can affect pregnant women.
- Drugs. Legal or illegal, alcohol does not care as it cannot discern the difference. Suffice it to say that the mixture of drugs and alcohol is very dangerous and in some cases can be lethal. Most often the presence of drugs in the body will increase the BAC.
- Altitude. Atmospheric pressure at high altitudes affects the body's ability to absorb alcohol. While people living in this environment adjust, vacationers are particularly susceptible to an increased BAC at higher altitudes.
- Speed of intake. This should be fairly obvious. A guest who slams down four drinks quickly will have a BAC greater than that of a guest who paces him- or herself. Consider that binge drinking, which is popular on college campuses, is quite dangerous as the alcohol backing up in the bloodstream could reach dangerous levels in short order.
- Tolerance. Persons who are experienced drinkers can build up a tolerance to the effects of alcohol. This is not to say that there is any less alcohol in their system; it's just that they can conceal it better than the occasional drinker.
- Size, body fat, and sex. Since a larger person has more blood in his or her body than does a smaller person, alcohol is diluted further and thus his or her BAC is less than that of a smaller person. Keep in mind that size is not to be confused with body fat. Alcohol is highly soluble in water and is absorbed less in fat. Therefore, alcohol is inclined to distribute itself mostly in muscles, which are plentiful in water, instead of those laden in fat. While two people could weigh the same, their bodies

Binge drinking can be dangerous as the BAC can reach dangerous levels in a short amount of time.
baronvsp/Fotolia

will be different in that they will have dissimilar proportions of tissue holding water and fat. If both people were to drink the same amount of alcohol, a short, fat person will end up with a higher BAC.

All things being equal, women's bodies have more fat and less water than men. By the same token, if a woman and a man were to drink the same amount of alcohol, the woman would reach a higher BAC than the man.

- Age. Older people, because they tend to exercise less, tend to have more body fat than younger people. Additionally, their enzymes do not absorb alcohol as quickly; thus an elderly person will have a higher BAC than a younger one.
- Dietary intake. Food will slow down alcohol's journey to the small intestine, thus keeping it in the system for a longer period of time. A person who has eaten will have a lower BAC than one who has not eaten. Note that food does not absorb alcohol, as many people believe; it merely slows down the time it takes to get to the small intestine where the majority of the alcohol enters the bloodstream. When alcohol is taken with food, alcohol absorption generally is complete in up to three hours (as opposed to one hour with no food), during which time the BAC will peak.

Result of Overconsumption

When alcohol enters the system, the effects can be felt very quickly by the average person. As it gets into the bloodstream and enters the brain, it first reduces a person's inhibition. A person with a BAC of 0.05 is very likely to be at ease and socialize more than usual. At the same time, the alcohol is beginning to obstruct their way of thinking and slowing their reaction time. All states have laws that prohibit a person with a BAC higher than 0.08 to operate a motor vehicle.

As the BAC reaches 0.10, their speech becomes affected and they begin to slur words. Additionally, their vision is impacted, and they may have trouble seeing things, particularly if it is dark out. As the BAC reaches 0.15, there is a loss of muscle control.

A BAC level of 0.3, or higher could cause a person to pass out and lose consciousness.
william casey/Shutterstock

A person may stagger, sway, or lose balance quite easily. This is why police usually have a driver walk in a straight line as one of the tests of sobriety.

When the BAC reaches 0.20–0.30, the drinking becomes quite serious. A person at this point becomes confused and could be in a daze. A BAC of 0.30–0.40 could cause a person to lose consciousness. A BAC of 0.40–0.50 affects the part of the brain that controls the heart and respiratory system and in many cases causes death.

Outward Clues of Intoxication

It is vitally important that you and your staff recognize the signs of **intoxication** that your customers may exhibit. These signs can, and usually do, predict potential problems. As a person drinks more and more, it is as if the bartender or server is watching the proverbial train wreck about to happen. There are clues that indicate a behavioral change on the part of your customer is taking place. The key word here is change. A person may be naturally clumsy or may have a physical condition that would cause them to stumble occasionally, or they may be rowdy by nature all of the time. Their behavior is not to be confused with a customer who has had too much to drink. It's when a person's behavior changes are due to alcohol, your staff needs to take notice and be ready to react.

There are four major signs that your staff should look for: decreases of a customer's inhibition, their judgment, their reaction time, and their coordination. Let's look at these signs in more detail.

Decreased Inhibitions **Inhibition** is a psychological or mental process that suppresses our actions, thoughts, or emotions. It is what keeps us from saying or doing things that we would normally find ethically or morally wrong. When alcohol gets into the bloodstream and ultimately to the brain, this suppression is relaxed, and we say and do things we normally would not say or do otherwise. Bartenders and servers should be acutely aware of a person's actions and speech when he or she enters the bar and should be careful to note any changes. One of the signs that a person's inhibitions are becoming relaxed include becoming overly friendly. A guest who all of a sudden starts putting his or her arm around another guest or starts making advances towards them needs to be observed. Other signs include swearing or becoming loud and boisterous.

The staff should also be aware that not everyone reacts in the same manner in these situations. An exact opposite could occur, in that when a customer's inhibitions are decreased, he or she could become very unfriendly, causing arguments and fights, acting depressed, or becoming unusually quiet and drinking by theirself.

Decreased Judgment **Judgment**, or a person's ability to make sound decisions, is impaired when alcohol enters the system. Customers with impaired judgment may become careless with money. They may have several dollars on the bar from the previous round and reach into their pocket to pay for the next one. They tend to buy drinks for those around them and in extreme cases will buy a round for everyone in the "house." They also tend to increase their consumption of alcohol by purchasing stronger drinks, increasing the size, or drinking faster. While doing this, they could complain about the speed of service or the strength of drinks. Some of them, as in the case of decreased inhibitions, start to become argumentative or irrational.

Decreased Reaction Time As **reaction time** becomes decreased, your customers will go into slow motion. Their speech will become slower, and they may start to slur their words. They will lose their train of thought and may even forget what they are saying in mid-sentence. Their eyes may glaze over, and they could lose their ability to focus. They become lethargic and in rare cases will take a nap right in your bar.

A customer should never be allowed to get too inebriated in your bar.
thaumatr0pe/Shutterstock

Decreased Coordination   **Coordination** is the ability of the muscles to produce complex movements. As alcohol enters the brain, it impairs the body's ability to direct the muscles to perform these movements. Guests with impaired coordination have trouble with eye–hand coordination. They have trouble lighting a cigarette or in some cases miss their mouth entirely when drinking. They drop things and cannot pick them up after they drop them. In some cases they bump into other guests and tend to stumble.

A customer in your bar should never be allowed to get in this condition as they should have been refused service long ago. Keep in mind, however, if they have been drinking at another bar, they may have entered your establishment looking and acting okay. Nevertheless, the alcohol suddenly catches up with them after only one drink in your bar, and you have inherited the problem. Do not pour this person another drink, and by all means this person should not be allowed to operate a motor vehicle.

In addition to serving alcohol to a customer who has already had too much to drink, there is the issue of serving alcohol to an underage person. While serving too much is illegal in most states, serving to a minor is illegal in all states. We will discuss the legal matters later in the chapter. Barring the legal issue, it is also unethical to take advantage of a situation in order to gain profit both for the house and for the server who is expecting a large gratuity.

TRAINING YOUR STAFF

As the owner or manager of an alcoholic beverage operation, one of your primary duties is to train your staff to handle these situations. When a bar is slammed with business, management does not have the time to look after every individual customer. Therefore the accountability falls upon the bartender and/or servers to ascertain if a customer has had too much to drink or if they are of age. Keep in mind, however, that the responsibility always rests with management. While the staff could be fined or even serve jail time in severe situations for violating the law, it is ownership that will have their license suspended or even revoked, who will suffer severe monetary damages due to a lawsuit, or who will lose their business due to adverse publicity. Since the bartenders and servers are your front line in upholding the law, it is imperative that they be trained and know what to do in any given situation.

Intoxicated Guests

One of the best ways to prevent guests from becoming intoxicated is to count drinks. This system has long been used in the beverage industry to help bartenders and servers know when they should become concerned about a customer's consumption. We have already looked at how many drinks a person can consume in a given period of time without becoming inebriated and the various exceptions due to age, weight, sex, and other factors. This is a relatively simple task as all one has to do is look at a customer's bar tab to see the amount he or she has consumed.

In spite of tracking a guest's intake, occasionally a situation will occur in which a customer becomes inebriated before you can take a proactive stand. When this happens, it becomes necessary to stop serving them alcohol, or in the industry vernacular, "shut them off." More often than not this will be a sensitive situation. As we have learned earlier, a person in this condition has decreased judgment and is often argumentative. It is a good idea to have a plan of action in place before this happens. Some of the things you can do to diffuse this situation include the following:

- Avoid being confrontational. Do not accuse the customer of being drunk. Do not in any way, shape, or form accuse them of being at fault for drinking too much. Rather, show concern for the person. Tell them you are worried about their safety. Possibly joke about avoiding the massive hangover they will get if they continue to drink. You could also empathize with them, telling them you have been in this same situation yourself.

- Privacy is best. Do not embarrass your guest in front of their friends. Take them aside and explain the situation to them. Offer them a nonalcoholic beverage. If they have been drinking gin and tonic, suggest a 7-Up with a lime wedge. In this way they will not be ill at ease in front of their cohorts. Should this approach not work, try the opposite; request the help of one of their friends. Tell them you are concerned about the person's ability to get home safely and see if they can persuade the person to leave with them. Obviously, you will want to ascertain that the person whose help you have requested is coherent enough to take care of the situation.

- Be determined. Do not back down. Often a guest will beg you for "one more and then they'll leave." Do not do it. Explain that it is the house policy and that "your hands are tied."

- Plan B. Always have a backup colleague of yours appraised of the situation. This would preferably be a member of management, but it could be anyone who would be capable of handling the situation should it get out of control and the customer would need to be subdued.

While you have stopped serving a guest who has had too much to drink, the real problem occurs when they get ready to leave. If they are not in condition to drive, it is imperative that you diffuse the situation. There are several ways to handle this.

- First and foremost, get the car keys from the intoxicated guest. If they refuse or become belligerent, call the police.

- If they are with a group, preferably someone in the group has been designated as the driver and has abstained from drinking alcohol. This makes the solution quite simple. As a matter of fact, many bars will serve complimentary nonalcoholic drinks or food to designated drivers. If there is no designated driver and someone in the group is coherent enough to drive safely, then make sure that they have the car keys of the intoxicated person.

- If the intoxicated guest has come alone, try to find out the name of a friend or relative that you can call to have them come and take the guest home. Failing that, call a cab to have that person driven home. Many municipalities have an agreement with cab companies to drive an intoxicated person home for free. These are normally funded by the municipalities, the police department, hospitals, or hospitality associations. As a last resort, have an employee drive them home. Under no circumstances allow an intoxicated customer to drive without having notified the police.

Aggressive Circumstances

If the staff is alert and paying attention, they will be aware of any impending aggression of the part of their customers. When this occurs, management should be notified immediately and the offending parties should be required to leave the premises. If there is any hint that the problem will intensify outside, the police should be notified. Occasionally, a problem will flare up unexpectedly in the bar and a fight will break out. In this case as well, the police should be notified immediately. Management and the staff should separate the other guests from the altercation to avoid having them get injured or, worse yet, get involved in the fight. Unless you or a member of your staff has been trained to restrain persons from fighting, stay out of the altercation. Many bars, particularly those with large crowds, have trained security on hand to handle these types of situations. Above all else, never try to resolve a situation with a gun or other weapon.

Illegal Behavior

While 99.94 percent of the people who frequent bars are there to have a good time, to relax and visit with friends or watch a sporting event, there are always those few who are there for illegal activities. People who sell or distribute illegal drugs or marijuana often frequent bars. Because people's inhibitions are reduced when they are drinking, prostitutes like to spend time at bars looking for prospective customers. The sale or use of date rape drugs is another possible pursuit that should be watched for. It is imperative that management and staff are constantly vigilant for these activities. It is not unreasonable to assume that if these deeds are allowed to continue, your operation could get a bad reputation.

ETHICAL ISSUES

Ethics concerns itself with distinguishing between right and wrong. Right and wrong are determined by the standards that a society, or group, deems appropriate. Thus within a society, we could have a group that believes a certain behavior is acceptable and another group that would believe it to be unacceptable. A perfect example of this is the consumption of alcohol. There are those who think that it is perfectly acceptable to enjoy a drink or two in amiable surroundings, and there are those who think that alcohol for moral or spiritual reasons should be abolished. These two groups have been at odds probably since alcohol was discovered. That certainly is true since this country was established. At various times throughout our history, one group or the other has flexed its muscle and established, or repealed, laws governing the use and consumption of alcohol.

There is, however, some agreement between the groups as to what is morally unacceptable behavior. Drinking to the point of being impaired is considered by most groups within the society as being unacceptable. Thus, for the most part, there has been an uneasy truce between the factions with occasional flare-ups between them.

While the laws of the land reflect, for the most part, society's moral and ethical beliefs in regard to alcohol, they are not all inclusive.

Ethical behavior and the goals of the bar business are constantly at odds with each other. For example, the goal of any bar is to make a profit. Bars are owned and managed anywhere from megacorporations all the way down to a single proprietor running a small neighborhood bar. Regardless, the goal is the same: make a profit. Profits are derived from sales. Thus, the higher the sales level, the more likely the bar will be profitable. Herein lies the dilemma: the owner or manager's desire to drive sales up versus the ethical consideration of persuading customers to drink more.

A decision on whether or not to serve a customer, for the most part, is left up to the bartender or server. This is made difficult by the absence of a concrete definition of what constitutes an excessive intake of alcohol. We know that all states have a BAC limit of 0.08 to operate a vehicle. But at what point is this attained? We have just learned that people have differing reactions to alcohol based on their size, age, sex, and other factors. Therefore the staff must make a judgment call on the sobriety of their guest. This is further complicated by the fact that quite often the staff is encouraged by management, using incentives, to increase their individual sales. Even if management does not encourage additional sales, bartenders and servers are paid primarily by tips, which are for the most part based on the amount the customer spends. Add to this the intoxicated customer who is spending freely, and the incentive for the staff to keep serving this person is increased.

While the laws to a large extent control the operation of bars and the serving of guests, they do not cover every situation. When a situation occurs that is not covered by law, it is up to management and the staff to decide how to handle it ethically, for the good of both the business and society as a whole. The retail liquor industry has, in the past, not handled this well; thus the plethora of laws governing the alcoholic beverage industry. Consider this: If a bar acts in the interest of society and stops serving a person who has overindulged and sees to it that they have a safe way home, they

Irrational behavior on the part of guests should alert the staff to take action.
© Blend Images / Alamy

have ethically diffused a potential crisis. While they have sacrificed short-term sales and therefore profit, they have gained a long-term result. There are many bars that have gone out of business either due to lack of sales because the public has considered them dangerous or the authorities have shut them down as a public nuisance.

LAWS

As we have previously learned, a person who is becoming inebriated is not thinking very clearly. Therefore, it would be reasonable to assume that a bartender or server is in a better position to be responsible for serving that person than it would be for the person drinking to be accountable for controlling his or her own consumption. The law clearly places the responsibility for serving alcohol on the management of bars and restaurants, as well as on the servers and bartenders. However, the law also acknowledges that a person is responsible for their own actions even if they are under the influence of alcohol. Liquor liability and server liability cases are very intricate and should only be handled by an experienced attorney.

One of the main reasons they are so complex is that the laws vary from state to state and often from county to county and even from city to city. The only thing that is consistent about liquor laws is that they are inconsistent. While the examples given in this section along with the charts and maps are up to date as of this writing, keep in mind that laws can change every time Congress, a state legislature, a county or parish commission, or a city council meets. Therefore, it is best to check with your local alcoholic beverage board or commission to keep abreast of the laws in your area.

One last thing—the intent of this section is to give you an overview of the laws and the affect they can have on your business and you personally, as manager, bartender, or server. It is *not* to give you legal advice. Legal advice should only be sought from a licensed attorney in your area.

Civil Liability

Civil liability lets a person who has been victimized bring a lawsuit against another person or company. In the case of the bar business, a person could bring a lawsuit against a bar that served alcohol to a customer that resulted in that customer becoming intoxicated. The person who served the customer can also be a party to the lawsuit. Thus a lawsuit can be filed by an innocent victim who was injured or had property that was damaged by an intoxicated person. This lawsuit can be filed against the individual, the bar where the individual was drinking, or both. In the case of death, a lawsuit can be filed by the heirs. Strange as it may seem, a lawsuit can even be filed by the intoxicated person themselves against the bar that served them.

Civil liability lawsuits are often tried before a jury. Should the plaintiff (the person who instituted the lawsuit) win, the defendant (the person being sued) will have to pay monetary damages. These damages are awarded in two stages: compensatory and punitive. Compensatory awards are for damages that the plaintiff has incurred. Punitive awards are given to punish the defendant. These awards can go anywhere from a few thousand dollars to millions of dollars. Many a bar has been put out of business as a result of a civil lawsuit.

For example, David Drinker goes into the Sir Servalot bar and is served a number of drinks by Timmy Tippme. Leaving the Sir Servalot intoxicated, David gets into his pickup truck and proceeds to drive home. He misses seeing a red light and hits a car driven by Victoria Victim. Victoria sustains a number of injuries and misses two months of work. She later sues David, Timmy, and the Sir Servalot. The trial goes to jury and they find that David, Timmy, and the Sir Servalot bar are guilty. They award

Victoria $100,000 compensatory damages for her hospital bills and to compensate her for loss of work. They also award her $1,000,000 in punitive damages to punish David, Timmy, and the Sir Servalot.

Civil lawsuits are based on three basic forms of law: common negligence, social host, and dram shop.

Common Negligence **Common negligence laws** are concerned with negligent behavior on the part of a person or persons. Negligent behavior, in this case, is defined as not doing what a reasonable person would do given a specific set of circumstances. With regard to alcohol, bartenders or cocktail servers are expected to monitor the behavior of their customers. If they feel that they are becoming intoxicated, they should stop serving them. If they are a minor, they should not be served in the first place. Should a bartender or cocktail server serve these persons, they could be considered to be acting negligently. This concept will become clearer as you study the dram shop laws.

Social Host This particular law does not apply directly to an alcoholic beverage business, but rather to a person or persons who host a party or function. It provides that hosts can be held responsible for the actions of their guests if they served them alcohol in an inappropriate manner.

Dram Shop Laws The term *dram* comes from 18th-century England where gin was served by the spoonful, called a dram. Technically, a dram is 1/16 of an ounce. Many of the pubs of that era were called dram shops as they would sell drams of liquor to a customer. The term **dram shop law** subsequently came to mean those laws that govern the liability of pubs, bars, liquor stores, or any other businesses that sell alcoholic beverages. Dram shop laws for the most part establish the liability of bars selling alcohol to visibly intoxicated persons or minors who consequently cause death, injury, or loss of property or income to another person. They were enacted to protect the general public from the perils of irresponsibly serving alcohol to minors and intoxicated patrons. When the English settled in America, dram shop laws were enacted here to protect the general public. However, their use was quite widespread, and they were not taken very seriously.

After Prohibition, the use of dram shop laws gained a stronger foothold, led primarily by organizations such as the Women's Christian Temperance Union. In 1980, the movement accelerated rapidly with the formation of Mothers Against Drunk Driving (MADD). This organization was formed by Candy Lightner, whose daughter was killed by a drunk driver who had a series of arrests for driving while intoxicated (DWI). This group has been, and still is, responsible not only for the enactment of dram shop laws in many states but also for strengthening existing laws. There are other organizations that have been formed as a result of MADD, including SADD (Students Against Drunk Driving) and RID (Remove Intoxicated Drivers). Not only are these groups responsible for enacting and strengthening dram shop laws, they are also given credit for championing other laws pertaining to drinking as well as the service of alcohol.

Dram shop laws vary widely across the country. As a matter of fact, there are eight states that have no dram shop laws at all. Figure 2.1 shows those states that have no dram shop laws. The other 42 states, plus the District of Columbia, have laws that range from minimal substance to significant subject matter with major penalties for violations. However, there is agreement in almost all of the dram shop laws that in order for there to be liability, the test of "obvious intoxication" must be met. This means that the bar owner or the staff knew, or should have known, that the customer was obviously intoxicated and a menace or danger to themselves or society. Most of

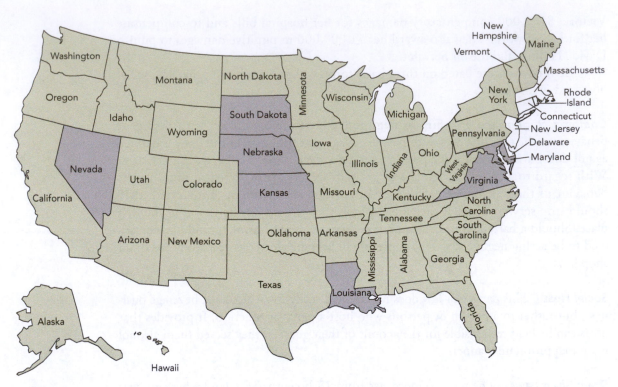

FIGURE 2.1
States shaded in gray have no dram shop laws.

the states with the stricter laws will hold retailers accountable for third-party damages. This means that if a patron in your bar has become intoxicated, you as the bar owner are liable if they leave your bar and inflict damage or harm to another person away from your premises. Additionally, some courts have ruled that if a customer becomes intoxicated in another bar, but your bar was the last place they had a drink, you are the liable party.

Dram shop laws have been enacted by some state legislatures to place the responsibility of damages to a third party squarely on the shoulders of the retailer as well as the person who is responsible for the damages, that is, the person who has been drinking. Hence, dram shop laws are also known as **third-party laws** or third-party liability. The reasoning behind this way of thinking is that the retailer is the one who profits from the sale of alcohol and therefore should be the one bearing the responsibility. It also gives an impetus to the retailers to train their staff in responsible alcohol service.

Prior to the dram shop laws, common law was applied to cases involving intoxication. In those states that have no dram shop laws, common law is still the ruling force. Under common law, there is no regulation that holds a bar responsible for selling alcohol to an intoxicated customer that results in damages caused by that customer. It goes on the premise that the cause of the injury was not the selling of alcohol but rather the act of drinking the alcohol that resulted in damages. However, many a judge has ruled in states that do not have dram shop laws and follow common law that the bar owner (or third party) is liable as well as the defendant. With the enactment of a dram shop law, in most jurisdictions, the plaintiff can sue the bar owner, be it an individual or corporation, if he or she sustains personal injury, property damage, or loss of support that was caused by an intoxicated person who was served alcohol by that bar.

Criminal Law

Dram shop laws are considered to be a part of civil law. **Criminal law** on the other hand is a different application of law that relates to the owner of a bar and the staff. Criminal liability gives the state the right to bring suit against a licensee, the owner of a bar, and/or its employees. It also applies to social hosts. These suits are different from civil suits in that they deal with the criminal aspect of irresponsible alcohol service. Many times, particularly in cases involving injury or death, a lawsuit could be brought in both civil and criminal courts and could result in both civil and criminal charges. While the cases are tried separately, the penalty in either case is not dependent on the other. Thus a party could be found innocent in the civil trial but guilty in the criminal trial or versa visa, or it could be found innocent in both or guilty in both.

As previously discussed, a civil suit typically carries a monetary judgment while a criminal suit can bring prison time. This should be a somber thought to any bar owner, manager, or staff member. The very act of not acting responsibly in the service of alcohol to their customers could result in a possible bankruptcy or prison time or both. As in the case of the previous example involving Victoria Victim who received monetary damages from a civil lawsuit, the state could have also brought a criminal lawsuit against the Sir Servalot bar and Timmy Tippme. This not only resulted in the owner of Sir Servalot and Timmy having to pay out a large sum of money, but they could also have received prison time.

Administrative Liability

Administrative liability applies to the issuing of licenses and/or permits to sell alcoholic beverages. These are normally issued to the business, and in some jurisdictions they are issued to the bartenders and servers as well. This can be either a state function or the function of a local jurisdiction such as a city or a county, or in some cases it could be all three. The issuing of licenses is normally done by a liquor control board. In addition to issuing licenses, they enforce the laws governing the service of alcoholic beverage as passed by the legislature or council. Quite often they are given the responsibility for setting the penalties for noncompliance. Establishments or servers not adhering to the law can be fined or have their license suspended. In rare cases, usually involving several violations, they could have their license revoked.

These penalties can be quiet severe to a bar considering if its license is suspended for a few days or weeks it means a loss of income, not to mention the adverse publicity that normally comes with such an action. To a server, it could mean lost income or even the loss of a job along with having one's reputation tarnished. Administrative liability is more common that the other forms of liability. Frequent causes for these penalties include allowing a person to become intoxicated, failing to properly check IDs, and serving alcohol to an underage customer.

Blood Alcohol Content (BAC) Laws

The first state to enact a BAC law was Indiana in 1939. It set the BAC level at 0.15, almost twice that of today's level of 0.08. Other states followed suit, enacting similar BAC laws with differing levels ranging from 0.15 down to 0.08. By 2000, there were 19 states, the District of Columbia, and Puerto Rico with 0.08 BAC laws. During this period, MADD and other organizations were urging state legislatures to pass BAC laws. Meeting strong resistance at the state level, they turned to Congress to pass a national law. With the states opposing a national Congressional mandate in an area that they believed they had control over, Congress relented, but only somewhat. In 2000 Congress passed the Department of Transportation Appropriations Act. In that act was a stipulation that if the states wanted federal highway construction funds, they must pass a 0.08 BAC *per se* law. (The next section discusses *per se* law.) The states, some of them begrudgingly, gave in and by 2004 all of the states, the District of Columbia, and Puerto Rico had a BAC law of 0.08.

Blood content level is determined by testing. Police officers who have a reasonable suspicion that a person has been driving under the influence of alcohol (DUI) legally have the right to do further testing. Many people are surprised to learn that they have previously consented to this testing. In every state, when you sign for your driver's license, you have consented to be tested if there is a reasonable suspicion that you have been drinking. The testing can include a blood test, urine test, or breath test. It should be noted that the term *reasonable suspicion* is a legal term that means an officer requires less evidence than *probable cause* but more evidence than a guess or a feeling.

There are several ways a police officer can ascertain if a vehicle is being driven by a person that is under the influence. Examples include the following:

- If the driver is stopped at a sobriety checkpoint or if the driver has been stopped for committing another offense and the officer notices that he or she appears to be intoxicated.
- If the driver has been in an accident and the responding officer conducting the investigation discovers intoxication.
- If the department receives a tip from a person or if an officer during a routine patrol sees a car weaving or neglecting to obey traffic laws.

Once officers have pulled a vehicle over, they will determine if they have reasonable suspicion that the driver has been drinking. Some of the telltale signs they look for include slurred speech, bloodshot eyes, alcohol odor, flushed face, or the obvious one: An open container of alcohol in the car. If they have reasonable suspicion, they will have the driver step out of the car and will continue to test them, normally with a Breathalyzer test. If the driver's BAC is greater than 0.08, he or she will be arrested.

Per se Laws

Drunken driving laws are different than other laws, in that when a person is arrested for failing a sobriety test, he or she is considered guilty in many states. This is known as a presumptive law, which is one of several ***per se* laws**. *Per se* is Latin for the term "by itself"; thus the failure of a sobriety test by itself is sufficient to consider a person guilty.

One of the most common of the *per se* laws is a license suspension law. This law is in effect in most states. The license suspension law requires the officer who conducts the arrest to suspend the driver's license of the person who did not pass the sobriety test. This is referred to as an administrative law as it is administered at the time of the violation and is not considered to be a part of any criminal procedure. When the officer takes the license, it is sent to the Department of Motor Vehicles. The driver's license is then automatically suspended unless the offending party requests a hearing. How long the license is suspended for varies from state to state. Some states also provide for a restricted license, which will allow the offending party limited driving privileges such as driving to work. Note that this administrative *per se* action is taken independently of any criminal DUI charges that could be filed later.

Another *per se* law is the ignition interlock law, which is in effect in many states. An ignition interlock is a complex system that tests a driver's breath for alcohol. It is an apparatus that involves the driver blowing into a small handheld device that is attached to a vehicle's dashboard. The vehicle will not start if the BAC is above a preset level, usually 0.02 to 0.04. In addition to needing a test to start the engine, it also requests a test every few minutes while driving. This prevents another person from starting the car and then giving the wheel to an impaired driver. While this is cumbersome for the guilty parties, it does have an advantage in that it allows them to operate a motor vehicle as opposed to having their driver's license revoked. With an ignition interlock system they can get to work and run errands without having society worrying about whether they are endangering the safety of others.

An additional *per se* law is a vehicle forfeiture law that allows the vehicle that the drunk driver is driving to be impounded. In most states, this applies only to those drivers who have had precious convictions. Note, however, that this law is applied even if the driver arrested for the DUI does not own the vehicle. Thus, you could loan your car to a friend or relative; if they get a DUI arrest and your car gets impounded, you could be left without transportation for a considerable amount of time.

Punishment for BAC Violations

There is no consistency between jurisdictions for punishment for a DUI or DWI. The penalties vary from state to state, county to county, and even city to city. Generally speaking, the severity of the penalty will depend on if it is a first violation and could include the following: fines, time in jail, impoundment of vehicle, ignition interlock device, driver's license suspension, attendance at Alcoholics Anonymous meetings, or community service. The punishment could include one of these or a combination thereof. For two or more convictions, jail time is commonly imposed. In almost all jurisdictions, mandatory attendance at an alcohol education program is required as a condition to reinstating the offending person's driver license.

The severity of the punishment can be greater if there are other circumstances surrounding the arrest. These could include excessive speeding, a BAC greater than 0.20, a child in the vehicle, refusal to take a Breathalyzer test, or an accident resulting in property damage. Additionally, if someone is injured, in many states it is considered a felony. This would include passengers in the offending driver's car. If a death occurs, the offending driver could be charged with vehicular manslaughter or murder.

Sales to Minors

Underage drinking is a huge problem today as alcohol is the drug of choice among teenagers. As a result, in 1984 Congress passed a law that required the states to set their minimum drinking age at 21 years. Failure to do so would result in that state not receiving any highway funds. Note that this method of withholding money from the states unless they passed the legislation that Congress wanted was so successful that it was used again in 2000 when the 0.08 BAC law was passed. Consequently, all states have enacted *per se* BAC laws for minors operating motor vehicles. You will recall that exceeding the BAC limit established in a *per se* statute is itself a violation. While this may seem like a universal law at first glance, it should be noted that many of the states allow exceptions to this law and that the penalties are not uniform.

Closely following this legislation was the Zero Tolerance Legislation, which was passed in 1998. The line of reasoning behind this law was that since it was illegal for minors to drink in the first place, any amount of alcohol in their system was illegal. As a result of the financial incentives established in this legislation, all states and the District of Columbia have enacted very low legal BAC limits of 0.02 or less for drivers under the legal drinking age of 21.

Several states beginning in the 1980s began passing Use/Lose laws as a penalty for minors purchasing, possessing, or consuming alcohol. As the name implies, if you use alcohol, you lose your driver's license. Not only does the law include alcohol, it also includes other drugs as well. The states enacting this law did so because the previous method of fining the violators was not discouraging minors from purchasing or consuming alcohol. To a teenager, losing their license is more of a major deterrent than paying a fine, as their parents more often than not paid the fine for them.

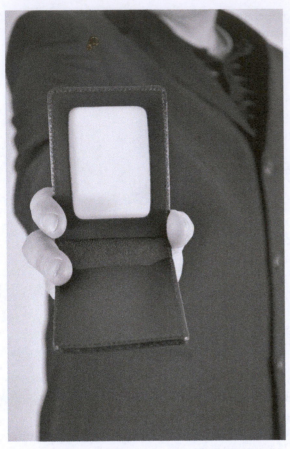

It is the bar's responsibility to check customer IDs for date of birth and authenticity.
kilukilu/Fotolia

Bar owners and their staff are responsible for ascertaining that alcoholic beverage sales are made only to customers who are officially allowed to buy alcohol. If there is any doubt that a customer is not of legal age, a government-issued identification document should be requested. This could include a driver's license, non-driver identification card, passport, or military identification. Teenagers are a resourceful lot. They can, and will, find a means to obtain and use what would appear to pass as valid identification. Additionally, they may alter the birth date on a valid identification or use someone else's identification.

Persons working in a bar should become familiar with current valid driver's licenses and IDs. Evaluate the customer's identification with a standard. If it looks like it was altered or changed, do not accept it. Alterations can include discoloration, changed lettering, or logos. A photo of the person presenting the card could be placed over the photo of a person that the card was issued to.

Given the proliferation of false IDs and their artificial authenticity, there is some protection for the bar owner and their staff. Note that all states prohibit minors from using false identification to acquire alcohol. Additionally, some states have adopted specific legal provisions that are intended for minors who use false identification to obtain alcohol. Still other states have provided what is called an affirmative defense to retailers who sell alcohol mistakenly to an underage customer.

CONCLUSION

Responsible alcohol service is one of the more important tasks of a bar manager. While social responsibility to your guests, your staff, and the community at large is important, there are other serious implications for not acting conscientiously. Laws enacted to protect the general public have been passed. Failure to comply with these laws could result in a fine, a suspension of business for several days, or a worst-case scenario of a loss of one's liquor license. Another thing to consider is that a loosely run operation will soon develop a reputation and could drive away desirable business while attracting unwelcome business.

Knowledge of alcohol's effect on the mind and body, social responsibility, and the law are an integral part of responsible bar management.

QUESTIONS

True/ False

1. On average the liver metabolizes one normal drink per hour.
2. Breathing fresh air will help eliminate alcohol from the system.
3. Intoxication incurs as the bloodstream becomes saturated with alcohol.
4. A person who has eaten before drinking will not get drunk as readily, as the food will absorb alcohol.
5. Having the bartender or server count the number of drinks a guest has had in order to avoid intoxication is rarely used as it is cumbersome and difficult to execute.

6. Under no circumstance should a person be allowed to leave your establishment intoxicated with his or her car keys.

7. For the most part, liquor liability laws vary from state to state, county to county, and city to city.

8. Civil lawsuits are based on three basic forms of law: common negligence, social host, and dram shop.

9. Dram shop laws exist in all 50 states and the District of Columbia.

10. An example of a *per se* law is that when a person fails a sobriety test, he or she is considered guilty without a court appearance.

Multiple Choice

1. Alcohol enters the bloodstream via the
   A. mouth.
   B. stomach.
   C. small intestine.
   D. all of the above.

2. It is unlawful to drive with a blood alcohol level in excess of
   A. 0.06.
   B. 0.08.
   C. 0.10.
   D. 0.12.

3. In calculating "one drink per hour" for BAC purposes, a 2-ounce pour of an 80 proof Scotch on the rocks with a standard of 1.5 ounces will have a BAC equivalent of
   A. 1.3 drinks.
   B. 1.5 drinks.
   C. 2.0 drinks.
   D. 3.0 drinks.

4. A person with a BAC of 2.0
   A. could become dazed and confused.
   B. could lose consciousness.
   C. could die.
   D. would be normal.

5. When having to tell a customer that you can no longer serve them alcohol as they are showing signs of intoxication you should
   A. confront them in private.
   B. not be confrontational.
   C. be empathetic.
   D. do all of the above.

6. The responsibility for the consequences of service to an intoxicated guest lies with the
   A. bartender.
   B. server.
   C. management
   D. doorman or bouncer.

7. Dram shop laws were enacted to protect the general public from the perils of
   1) serving alcohol to minors.
   2) serving alcohol to intoxicated patrons.
   A. (1) only
   B. (2) only
   C. Both (1) and (2)
   D. Neither (1) nor (2)

8. In a lawsuit against a bar brought in both a civil court and criminal court,
   A. a verdict or penalty in one case is not dependent on the other case.
   B. the penalty in a criminal court is usually monetary.
   C. a civil court penalty is usually time in prison.
   D. none of the above apply.

9. The law creating the 0.08 BAC threshold is a
   1) federal law
   2) state law
   A. (1) only
   B. (2) only
   C. Both (1) and (2)
   D. Neither (1) nor (2)

10. The issuance of a license to sell alcoholic beverages is a function of
    A. the state.
    B. the county.
    C. the city.
    D. one or more of the above.

Essay

1. Weigh a bar owner's desire to make a profit and the fact that the higher a bar's sales, the higher the probability of making a profit against the ethical considerations of encouraging people to drink. In other words, where do you draw the line of increased sales and social responsibility?

2. Discuss the pros and cons of having the bartender or server determine if a customer has had too much

to drink. Give examples of both sides of the issue.

3. Discuss the pros and cons of organizations such as MADD as they relate to the ability of bars to maintain a level of sales.

4. Compare the application of civil law and criminal law as they pertain to the bar business. Where are they similar and different? Is one dependent on the other?

5. Discuss dram shop laws. Are they fair to the alcoholic beverage industry? Defend your answer.

RESOURCES

Davis, Bernard and Stone, Sally, *Food and Beverage Management*, 5th ed., (Oxford, UK, Lineacre House, 2008).

Katsigris, Costas and Thomas, Chris, *The Bar & Beverage Book*, 4th ed., (Hoboken, New Jersey, John Wiley & Sons, 2007).

Kotschevar, Lendal H. and Tanke, Mary L., *Managing Bar and Beverage Operations*, (East Lansing, Michigan: Educational Institute of the American Hotel & Motel Association, 1996).

National Restaurant Association Educational Foundation, *ServSafe Alcohol*, (Chicago, IL, National Restaurant Association Educational Foundation).

Plotkin, Robert, *Successful Beverage Management*, 1 ed., (Tucson AZ, Bar Media, 2000).

3
Wine

OVERVIEW

When you are relaxing and enjoying a glass of wine, you rarely, if ever, think about what went into producing it. Why does one bottle taste different than another, even though it is the same type of wine, has the same label, and is from the same vintner? In this section, we will answer those and many other questions as we explore the fascinating world of wine making, from the vineyard, to production, to aging, to blending, to bottling, and finally to tasting. In this chapter there are a number of terms that will be unfamiliar. Do not try to memorize them as you will become quite confused, but rather familiarize yourself with them.

PRODUCTION

The Vineyard

Let's begin by clearing up a misconception held by many. Farmers grow grapes, and **vintners** process the grapes into wine. In a few instances, these tasks are done at the same location and the distinction becomes blurred. But for the most part, these tasks are completed separately. Is farming a science or an art? It is both, and never is this more true than when growing grapes for wine. The soil, moisture, temperature, weather conditions, fertilizer, and climate along with the skill of the farmer all determine the outcome and the quality of the grape harvest. The French refer to this as **terroir**. All of the variables coming together to produce a good, or bad, harvest.

Grapes are not all the same even though they come from the same family. The majority of wine comes from the *Vitis vinifera* family of grapes, although some others are used. In addition to the family, grapes are also classified by color. Green grapes are referred to as white grapes by the vintner while purple ones are referred to as red grapes. We will get into the specifics of grapes when we study the various classifications of wine.

The farmer who grows grapes is more interested in the quality of the grape than the quantity of grapes grown. After all, if the grapes do not meet the vintner's specifications, he or she will not buy them and the farmer is left with an unsalable crop. To get the maximum quality, in cooler climates, the farmer carefully prunes the vines to allow the grapes to get the greatest exposure to sunlight. Conversely, in warmer climates the vines are trained to grow tall to shelter the grapes and keep them from ripening too quickly. In addition to this, the vines are cut back so that

Objectives

Upon completion of this chapter, the reader should be able to:

- Comprehend the production of wine, including the growing of grapes, extraction, aging, blending, bottling, and corking.
- Compare the various classifications of wine.
- Identify the varietals of red and white grapes and describe which grapes make which wines.
- Identify the major wine-producing countries, what wines they produce, their growing regions, and their governmental requirements.
- Explain the unique methods of producing Champagne and other sparkling wines.
- Plan the procedure for executing a proper wine tasting experience.

Key Terms

Aperitif wine
Bouquet
Brix
Carbonation method
Chaptalization
Charmat method
Château
Classic Champagne
Cru
Cuvee
Dessert wine
Dosage
Estate bottled
Fining
Flor
Fortified wine

An Austrian vineyard.
Elena Schweitzer/Fotolia

fewer bunches of grapes are grown. With fewer grapes competing for nutrients, the remaining ones will be healthier. The pruning is quite drastic, with over 90 percent of the previous year's growth removed, and is usually done in the winter when the vines are dormant.

The soil has a large impact on the quality of the grape grown. Nutrients and minerals from the soil are absorbed into the grape as it grows, which will influence the flavor and taste of the grape and ultimately the wine produced from it. A paradoxical fact about grapes is that they grow well where nothing else will grow and do not grow well where other crops thrive. Grapes are best grown in poor, grainy soil on a hillside facing the sun. Mulching is important as the farmer will take the vine cuttings along with the pressings from the grapes and return them to the soil. If this is not sufficient to suitably enrich the soil, additional fertilizer must be added. A grape vine, properly cared for, will last for over fifty years.

Another factor is the water, both the quality and quantity of it. Too much water will produce large, juicy grapes, but they will lack flavor as they will be watered down. Too little water and the grapes will be small with a poor yield. While most water for a vineyard comes from rain, sometimes it needs to be augmented. This can be done either by irrigation or by tapping into an aquifer (an underground river) if one is available.

Last but not least is the climate. This is very important, as the grapes need sufficient time at the right climate to develop their sugars, which create alcohol to produce a fine wine. The sugar content is measured in **Brix**. Knowing the sugar content, the vintner can predict the alcoholic content of the wine by using the formula

$$\text{Brix} \times 0.55 = \text{percent alcohol}$$

A grape picked at 22 Brix will yield a wine with approximately 12 percent of alcohol and no residual sugar. Since most countries outlaw additional sugar during the wine-making process to increase the alcohol content, it is imperative that the grapes provide the optimum amount of sugar. It takes 100–120 days of warm, sunny conditions for the grapes to develop; however, each grape variety is different. Some grapes grow well in one climate while other varieties grow well in a different climate.

All of this—the soil, water, and climate—come together to determine which grape should be grown in which location. For years, scientists and agronomists have studied the conditions that produce the best grapes. The French have even taken it so far as to pass laws as to what grapes can be grown in what region.

Harvesting

When the grapes are at 20–25 Brix, they are ready for harvest. In addition to Brix, the acidity of the grape is also measured. As the grape ripens, the sugar content becomes greater than the acidity. Different wines have different ratios of sugar to acid. Timing is of the utmost importance as additional rain will quickly go from the root of the plant to the grape and thus dilute the flavor of the grape as well as the acid-to-sugar ratio. During harvest time, the grower watches the weather forecast as well as tasting the grapes and testing Brix on a daily basis. When the flavor, the sugar content, and the acidity are at their optimum and the weather is cooperating, the grapes are harvested.

The grapes are harvested either by hand or mechanically. In Europe and South America, on many farms the harvest is done by hand. This is due to the smaller size of the farms and also the terrain. In Germany, for example, the topography is so hilly that a mechanical harvest is impossible. Many of the European vineyards have been handed down from generation to generation, resulting in many people now owning one vineyard. With so many people involved, it makes sense to harvest by hand. When harvesting by hand, bunches of grapes are cut using a knife or shears. Bunches, rather than individual grapes, are cut as picking grapes one by one would be too time consuming, making the process too expensive. Only in rare cases are they picked individually and only for very expensive wines.

On the other hand a very large vineyard owned by one farmer or conglomerate will use mechanical harvesting. Many of the large vineyards in the United States use mechanical harvesters. While it takes many hours to pick grapes by hand, one mechanical harvester can collect an acre in less than an hour. While the mechanical method is economically more efficient, the preferred method is still hand picking as the pickers can use their judgment to select only those grapes that meet the criteria for picking.

As previously mentioned, the quality of the grape and ultimately the quality of the wine is dependent on limiting the number of bunches of grapes per vine. Because of this, the yield per acre is substantially reduced. That being said, what is the yield that a farmer could expect? The answer is "it depends." A very high quality wine would have a grape yield of less than 2 tons per acre while a low quality wine would have a yield of over 14 tons per acre. As you can see, there is quite a variance between high

Harvesting grapes by hand.
linomax/Fotolia

The grape harvest arrives at an Italian winery.

Judy Edelhoff © Dorling Kindersley

quality–low yield and low quality–high yield. While the United States does not regulate the yield, some countries do. France, for example, limits its highest quality wine to 2 tons per acre. Keep in mind also that soil condition, climate, and rainfall all play a part as well in regard to quality.

The Vintner

As soon as the grapes are picked, they are rushed to the vintner, who extracts the juice, which then goes through the fermentation process, is aged, may be blended, and is then bottled. Throughout this process, keep in mind that the color of the wine is determined by the color of the grape's skin; thus white grape skins produce white wine while red grape skins produce red wine. Having said that, as always, there are exceptions.

Extraction Within twelve hours after being picked, the juice of the grapes is extracted. For centuries, the grapes were placed in a large vat and crushed by people walking over them and crushing them with their feet. While this method is rarely used today, it can often be seen in local ceremonies celebrating the first harvest of the grapes.

Nowadays, the grapes are washed and go into a crusher-stemmer. This must be done very carefully as too much pressure will result in the stem being crushed as well as the grapes, resulting in a bitter-tasting wine. When the grapes are crushed, the resulting liquid is called a **must**. If a white wine is being produced, the must is immediately separated from the skins, cleaned to remove any impurities, and then put into a fermentation tank. If a rose or red wine is being produced, the must and skins are both cleaned and put into a fermentation tank. For a rose, they are left in the tank for 12–24 hours, and then the skins are removed from the must and the must is placed in a separate tank. Red wines are left in a while longer until the correct color is attained before the must is sent to an alternate tank. The distinctive color and taste of rose or red wine comes from the skins of the grapes.

Ceremonial crushing of the grapes.

alexandco/Fotolia

Prior to fermentation, a small amount of sulfur dioxide is added to the must to kill any wild yeast that could be present on the grape skins. Wild yeasts can cause unwanted consequences such as premature oxidation or not being able to control the oxidation process once it has begun. In most countries, the amount of sulfur dioxide that can be added is controlled by law. Some vintners are now using a sterile filtration process rather than sulfur dioxide.

Fermentation   As the grape juice goes into the fermentation stage, some decisions have to be made by the vintner. When the grapes are picked they may lack sweetness or acidity. This is usually due to weather conditions not allowing them to be picked at an optimal time. Grapes lacking sweetness will not produce adequate alcohol. When the vintner adds sugar to the must, it is called **chaptalization**. This process will affect the taste of the wine very slightly. As a matter of fact, chaptalization can only be detected by the most discerning palate. For grapes lacking acidity, some unripened grapes can be added to the must to increase the acid content, or acid can simply be added to the must.

Originally, all wine was fermented in wooden vats. These were replaced by cement vats, and today practically all wine is fermented in stainless steel vats. While different wines ferment at different temperatures, there is wide disagreement among vintners over what exactly is the correct temperature for various wines. Generally speaking, white wines are fermented at a lower temperature of 45–65°F, while red wines are fermented at 70–90°F.

As the wine ferments, the yeast feeds on the sugar until the alcohol content reaches about 14 percent, at which time the sugar is either used up or the high alcohol content kills the yeast. If there is sugar left in the must, the wine will be sweet. If the sugar is all used up, the wine will be dry. This process usually takes two weeks or in some cases longer. Occasionally the vintner will stop the process earlier than that to get the desired product.

Wine fermenting in stainless steel vats.
ArenaCreative/Fotolia

Aging   After fermentation, the wine goes on to the aging process where it will undergo some changes.

- Most of the red wines (and a few whites) are aged in oak containers. These can be small oak casks, oak barrels, or large vats which have been lined with oak. The wood imparts tannins that affect the flavor and texture of the wine, with the result being a smoother, more delicate wine.
- Most whites and roses are aged in vats made of stainless steel or vats that have been lined with plastic or glass.
- During the aging process, the sediment in the wine, which is called **lees**, settles to the bottom of the storage container. This happens as the wine stabilizes. Every so often, the wine is bled off and put into a new cask where it will settle some more. This process is referred to as **racking**.
- After racking, some very small microscopic solids may still remain. These are removed by a process called **fining**. The vintner uses one of several methods to achieve this. The predominant method is to use filters. Care must be exercised when using this method as too many solids may be removed, thus affecting the wine's taste and body. Another popular method is to use electrical charges that attract the floating elements. Other methods include gels, gelatin, silica, and animal blood. One last method, with which many of you may be familiar, is using egg whites. This process is very similar to the one used to clarify a stock.
- As the wine ages, some of it evaporates. Since the vintner wants the casks full to prevent further oxidation, which could ruin the batch, more wine is added to keep the casks full. This process is referred to as **topping off**.
- The amount of time a wine is kept in the aging process depends on the type of wine. For the most part, white wines and roses are aged for a few months. Normally, a fall harvest will be aged over the winter and the wine bottled in the spring. Red wines and a few whites are aged for six months to over two years. In some areas, the amount of time a wine is aged is controlled by law. It should be mentioned that that the aging process has a "point of no return" in that the wine will deteriorate, rather than improve, after a certain point in time.

Red wine being aged in oak vats.
PANORAMO/Fotolia

Only after a wine has been aged is its value determined. While the farmer and the vintner may have proclaimed a certain year to be a great harvest, the final determination is made after the wine has been fermented and aged. At this point the wine is classified as exceptional, good, medium, or ordinary. Also at this point the wine can either be bottled as is or be blended with other wines.

Blending   *Blending* is a term that could be used any time during the process of producing wine. For example,

- Different varieties of grapes could be blended prior to the destemming and crushing process.
- Grapes from different vineyards or even from different parts of a country could be blended.
- Different varieties of grapes from the same vineyard could be blended.
- Wines made from different varieties of grapes could be blended.
- Wines from different wineries could be blended.
- Wines from different years could be blended.

And so on and so forth. Keep in mind that while all of the above are true, when the term *blending* is used, it most often refers to the blending of wines already produced and aged.

Many of today's wines are blends. Do not assume that a wine is inferior if it is blended. While in a few cases this could be true, for the most part it is not. There are many reasons for blending. For example, one wine may be lacking in a certain characteristic, and by blending it with another wine lacking a different characteristic will result in an improvement of both wines. Others are blended to maintain a certain flavor profile for a particular variety or brand year after year. Wine from a poor harvest could be combined with wine from a good harvest. Still, a few others are blended to simply make more profit.

Most countries regulate the blending process. In the United States, for example, if a wine is labeled as coming from a particular varietal, it must contain 75 percent of that varietal. In France, a far stricter regulation exists in that a varietal labeled as such must contain 100 percent of that varietal.

Bottling   Bottling the wine can be done in one of two ways, either at the winery or at a bottling plant. Wine bottled at the winery is known as **estate bottled**. There are those who consider estate-bottled wine to be the very finest. After all, a vintner would not put their name on a bottle if it were not of the highest quality. In the past, very few wineries could afford to maintain their own bottling operation, and estate-bottled wine was quite rare. Today, however, more and more wine is bottled by the vintner. This is made possible by companies that have trucks equipped with bottling equipment that go from vineyard to vineyard bottling wine.

If a vintner does not bottle their own wine, they sell it to a general bottler. The bottler goes to the vineyard, samples the wine, and negotiates with the vintner. When a deal is struck, the wholesaler loads the casks of wine onto a truck and ships it to the bottling plant where it is bottled as is or blended and then bottled.

While a few of the low-priced wines are packaged in plastic bags and then boxed, the vast majority of wine is bottled in glass. The glass is tinted or colored to protect the wine from harmful rays. Many of the bottles are made of heavy glass, particularly sparkling wines, in order to hold in the intense pressure caused by the carbon dioxide in the wine. After bottling, the wine is allowed to rest for a short period of time before being shipped to a wholesaler.

Bottling French wine by machine.
Albo/Fotolia

Corking   To paraphrase Shakespeare, "to cork or not to cork, that is the question." There is a great deal of debate regarding wine corks today. For years, cork was seen as the only way to properly seal a bottle of wine. Its malleability allows it to be inserted into the neck of a bottle and completely seal it, thus effectively keeping air out and not allowing any evaporation. The primary drawback of cork is that the bottle must be placed on its side in order to keep the cork moist so that it does not shrink and allow air to enter the bottle.

Cork is harvested from suberin oak trees, which grow primarily in Portugal and Spain. The cork is actually the outer part of the tree and is carefully stripped from the tree. It takes over forty years before the tree will produce cork. It does not harm the tree to have the bark removed; however, it will take the tree several years to regrow its outer bark. A good cork will last up to fifty years. Environmentalists are obviously opposed to the desecration of these trees and have weighed in on the controversy. It should be known, though, that the harvesting of cork is strictly regulated by the Portuguese government.

Modern science has come to the rescue with screw tops and plastic stoppers to replace the cork. One advantage of these stoppers is that the bottles no longer have to be stored on their side, allowing for more efficient shipping and taking up less display space in bars and retail stores. A downside is that they are not biodegradable like cork.

While one would think that technology would be embraced, it is not that simple. Some people cling to the tradition of the cork; some say that corked wine tastes better, while others say screw tops connote cheap wine. Some vintners and bottlers like the convenience of the new tops. Environmentalists do not like the harvesting of cork and the fact that the new tops are not biodegradable.

To cork or not to cork, that is the question.

Wine corks.
babimu/Fotolia

CLASSIFICATIONS

Wine can be divided into six classifications: table, natural, fortified, aperitif, dessert, and sparkling. The first five are also known as **still wines** as they have no bubbles. It should be noted that a wine can be put into more than one classification. For example, a table wine can also be classified as a natural wine.

- **Table wines** belong to the largest classification of wines and are so called because they are often served at the table with food. They can be further classified as to their color: red, white, and rose. We will discuss these wines in further detail later in the chapter.
- **Natural wines** are those wines that are made without additional alcohol or sugar. As we learned earlier, fermentation stops when all of the sugar is used up or when the alcohol level reaches 14 percent. In some natural wines, the fermentation process is stopped before this stage, and they will therefore have a lower alcohol content. For the most part, natural wines are between 7 and 14 percent alcohol by volume.
- **Fortified wines** are much higher in alcohol content than natural wines, ranging anywhere from 14 to 24 percent. This is due to the fact that, in many cases, additional alcohol (normally brandy) is added to the wine during the fermentation stage. Because of this not all of the sugar that was originally in the grapes is fermented, resulting in a sweeter wine. Those fortified wines that are not made in this manner have a complete fermentation of the sugar and add a sweetener after the fermentation process.
- **Aperitif wine** is precisely what the name implies—a wine served prior to a meal. The term *aperitif* is probably familiar to you, as it is the French word for appetizer. Aperitifs are normally fortified wine, and some are flavored with herbs and spices.
- **Dessert wines** are exactly the opposite of aperitif wines as they are served at the end of the meal. They are almost always a sweet wine. While most are fortified, some are not. Those that are not fortified are made from over-ripened grapes that have an extremely high sugar content.
- **Sparkling wines** are those wines with bubbles. The most widely known wine in this classification is Champagne. International law decrees that to be called Champagne, the wine should come from Champagne, France; however, this is generally ignored. In the United States, for example, the term *sparkling wine* should be used, although the point of origin can be used, such as California champagne.

  These wines are made by double fermentation; that is, the fermented wine goes through another fermentation process by adding yeast and sugar to the wine. It is then bottled in one of three ways. The most expensive method, which is reserved only for very high priced sparkling wines, is one in which the fermentation takes place in the bottle in which it is sold. It is a very tedious and delicate process. In the second method, the wine is filtered and transferred to another bottle. The third method involves double fermenting the wine in a large vat, filtering it, and then transferring it to the bottles.

There is still another method in which wine is identified, and that is by the variety of grape that is used to produce it. This is called a **varietal**. A great deal of wine comes from one variety of grape only. Other wine is made from a blend of grape varieties. When this happens, depending on the laws of the country involved, if there is a predominant grape variety in the blend, the wine takes the name of the predominant variety. Where a large blend of grape varieties is used, it is called a **generic wine**. When a wine is a varietal, the name of the grape will be on the label. When it is a generic wine, it will have a "house" name on the label. Countries have differing laws governing the branding of varietals and generics, and these will be discussed in detail later in the chapter.

GRAPE VARIETIES

There are many varieties of grapes grown to produce wine. We have listed some of the more popular ones; however, keep in mind that this is not a complete list. Be that as it may, there are still quite a few of them. You will probably recognize some of them because a wine sold as a varietal is called by the name of the grape from which it was produced. Some of the more popular *red* grape varietals are as follows:

- Barbera. Grown primarily in Italy, this grape produces a low-tannin, high-acid wine.
- Cabernet Sauvignon. This is arguably the most popular grape grown. It is a small grape that produces a strong flavored wine, which gets mellower with age. Known as Cabernet for short.
- Gamay. A grape that produces a light red wine. It does not age well and is best ingested when young. Beaujolais Nouveau made from the Gamey grape is one of the first wines of the year to be produced.
- Grenache Noir. Known as Grenache for short, it turns out a light red wine that is high in alcohol. It is also used in the making of some roses and ports. Its counterpart is a white grape known as Grenache Blanc.
- Lambrusco. A grape that is predominantly grown in northern Italy and produces a semisweet wine. Popular with those who prefer a less intense wine.
- Merlot. This grape produces a mild red wine similar to a Cabernet. As a matter of fact, it is often blended with Cabernet. Merlot is a very popular wine in the United States.
- Mourvedre. A robust red grape that is used primarily for blending with other grapes to produce generic red and rose wines.
- Pinot Noir. This grape produces some of the most celebrated wine in the world, including some of the best Champagne. It is difficult to grow and requires constant care on the part of the farmer.
- Nebbiolo. A small, thick-skinned grape that produces a very dark red wine that is bold in taste and aroma.
- Tempranillo. A grape grown primarily in Spain that is used both for blending with other wines and also as a standalone wine. It has a thick skin and produces a wine that is colorful and low in alcohol.
- Sangiovese. A grape grown in Italy in the Tuscany area and best known for making Chianti. It is one of the oldest grapes known with some historians dating it back over 3,000 years.
- Syrah. Depending on the country it is grown in, it is also known as the Shiraz grape. Regardless of the country, it produces an outstanding wine heavy with taste and aroma.
- Zinfandel. A California grape popularly known as Zin. It is used both as a blend in other wines as well as bottled on its own.

Some of the more popular *white* grape varietals are as follows:

- Chardonnay. This grape produces a bold dry wine. It can be grown almost anywhere and is therefore the most popular of all the grapes grown for producing

Red and white varieties of grapes.
Nenov Brothers/Fotolia

wine. It develops the characteristics of the area that it is grown in and therefore has a wide range of flavor and aroma.

- Chenin Blanc. A popular grape used as a blend to make white wine as well as sparkling wines. This grape usually has a high acidity.
- Gewurztraminer. A pink grape that falls under the white grape classification. The name is taken from the German word *gewurz*, which means spicy, and that is the flavor that this wine embraces. When harvested early it produces a dry wine, and when harvested late it produces a sweet wine.
- Muller-Thurgau. A hybrid grape that has been crossed with the Riesling and Silvaner grapes. It can be grown in colder climates and therefore has a wider growing area than most grapes. It produces a wine that is low in alcohol and acid.
- Muscat. This grape has both a red and white variety. The white Muscat produces the popular Italian wine Asti Spumante.
- Pinot Blanc. A white grape used primarily for making sparkling wine.
- Riesling. This grape grows best in cooler climates. It produces a wine that has a heavy fruit flavor, but some areas produce a wine that is very dry. Late harvest Riesling grapes produce some fine dessert wines.
- Semillon. A grape grown for both a varietal and blended wine. As a varietal, it mellows with age and has a full fruit flavor. It is often blended with the Sauvignon Blanc grape and the Chardonnay grape.
- Sauvignon Blanc. A very popular white grape, it is used to make many other dry wines with a heavy fruit flavor. The name of the wine often denotes the area in which it was grown.
- Viognier. Because it is an extremely difficult grape to grow, it is quite uncommon and consequently very expensive. It is produced both as a varietal and as a blend. It should be consumed when it is young as it does not have lasting characteristics.

A TOUR OF THE WORLD

It is no secret that a great wine starts in the vineyard, and vineyards can be found the world over. As a matter of fact, grapes are the largest fruit crop grown, with over 18 trillion acres planted.

Grapevines for the most part like a temperate climate, with warm, dry summers and mild winters. Approximately four months of temperatures above freezing are required. While grapevines need a dormant winter period, extremely harsh winters will kill the vines. On the other hand, hot tropical temperatures will disrupt the cycle of winter dormancy. High humidity is also bad, as it promotes vine disease. Generally speaking, grapevines can be grown between 20° and 50° latitude north or south of the equator. They are not very fussy about the type of soil they are grown in as they will grow in soils ranging from light sand to packed clay.

While a complete discussion of grapes, vineyards, and their locations is beyond the scope of this text, we discuss the top eight countries, which include France, Italy, Spain, the United States, Argentina, Australia, Chile, and Germany. These countries account for over 75 percent of the world's production of wine, which is estimated at over 26 trillion liters. They are presented in the order of their production.

France

When one thinks of the most important wine-producing country, one automatically thinks of France. While it may arguably be the most important, surprisingly it was not the most prolific. Italy was. It was not until 2009 that France barely overtook Italy as the most productive wine country in the world, producing over 4 trillion liters of wine. Whether or not that claim to fame holds up remains to be seen. Production notwithstanding, France has always considered itself to be the most significant. This is attributable to the fact that it exports wine to more countries and produces more varieties of wine than any other country in the world.

There are six major wine-producing regions in France. They include Alsace, Bordeaux, Burgundy, Champagne, Cotes du Rhone, and Loire. We will examine each of these regions, their vineyards, and the wines they produce. While these are the significant regions, keep in mind that almost all of France is covered with vineyards.

Alsace

As the Rhine River meanders along its course, it separates the countries of France and Germany. On the French side lies the region of Alsace. Figure 3.1 shows the Alsace region. This area's cool climate makes it ideal for growing white grapes. While most of the wines produced in France carry the name of the vineyard, the majority of wine from the Alsace region is varietal. These wines are dry and very flavorful, with a full body. The majority of grapes grown here consist of four varieties:

- Gewurztraminer, which produces a fruity wine with spice overtones.
- Muscat, which makes a brisk, delicate wine with a definite Muscat flavor.
- Pinot Blanc, which makes a delicate white wine and is also used in blends.
- Pinot Gris, also known as the Tokay d'Alsace grape, which produces a substantial, dry, and full-bodied wine.

Alsace Region

Paris

Strasbourg

France

Germany

FIGURE 3.1
Map of the wine-producing areas of Alsace.

- Riesling, perhaps the most widely used grape from the Alsace area, which produces a dry, traditional white wine with a light, subtle bouquet.

Bordeaux As the Garonne and Drodogne Rivers amble through France, they join forces to form the Gironde River. On the banks of these rivers lies the Bordeaux region of France where many of the premium wines of the world are produced. Refer to the map of Bordeaux at Figure 3.2. To the north is the right bank and to the south is the left bank. Within this region are over 50 districts. Among the more significant are the Medoc, Graves, Barsac, Margaux, St. Julien, and Pauillac districts on the left bank and the Pomerol and St. Emilion districts on the right bank. While these are important districts, do not discount the others as many of them produce outstanding wines as well.

Bordeaux's mild winters and high humidity coming in from the Atlantic Ocean promote sturdy vine growth. It is here that the Cabernet Sauvignon and Cabernet Franc grapes are grown to produce some of the finest red wines of the world. The area also produces Merlot grapes as well as Malbec and Petit Verdot, which are blended into the bold reds to temper the wine.

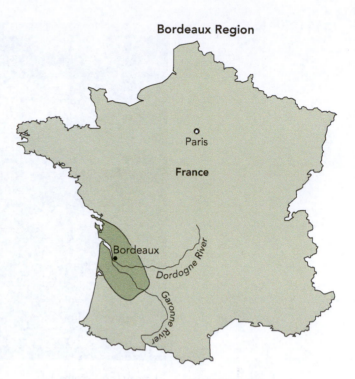

Bordeaux Region

FIGURE 3.2
Map of the wine-producing areas of Bordeaux.

While the area is known for its red grapes, some outstanding whites are also grown, including Sauvignon Blanc, Muscadelle, and Semillon. They produce some outstanding dessert wine. The sweetness is caused by **noble rot**, which is a mold that grows on the grapes. The mold causes the moisture in the grapes to evaporate, causing them to shrivel, thus concentrating the sugars. The Semillon grape is particularly susceptible to noble rot and is used in the making of fine Sauterne and Barsac wines. Approximately 80 percent of the makeup of these wines comes from this grape while the other 20 percent is made up of the Sauvignon Blanc grape, which is also susceptible to noble rot. These wines have an alcohol content of 12.5 percent.

It is in the Bordeaux region that some of the finest wines of the world are produced. The left bank houses some of the most famous vintners that set the standard for the rest of the world, among them Château Haut-Brion, Château Margaux, Château Latour, Château Lafite-Rothschild, and Château Mouton-Rothschild. You will notice that the name of the wine carries the name of the **château**. These châteaux not only house the vineyard, the wine is also produced and bottled there. Thus, they control virtually the entire process.

The French government, in 1855, issued a classification rating for Bordeaux wines. It classifies each château's wines according to a standard of excellence, and is divided into five tiers called growths. The top tier, first growth, is the finest wine and therefore obtains the highest price. The list has gone unchanged since 1855 with one exception. In 1973, the government added Château Mouton-Rothschild to the first growth.

Not all of the wine from this area is bottled under the name of the château that grew the grapes. Bottlers will purchase grapes from different growers and put their own labels on them. These labels could denote the Bordeaux region, a district such as Graves or Barsac, or a varietal. When using a varietal label, the wine must be 100 percent of that varietal.

Burgundy Just north of Dijon lies the Chablis section of France. From here, travel south to Lyon, a journey of about 300 miles. It is in this area that the Burgundy region of France is located. The Burgundy region consist of four areas: Chablis, Cote d'Or, Southern Burgundy, and Beaujolais. Figure 3.3 shows the Burgundy region.

Château Lafite-Rothschild.
Philippe Giraud © Dorling Kindersley

Many of the vineyards in the Burgundy region are in the possession of multiple owners. The reason for this is that, prior to the French Revolution, the land was owned by the Catholic Church. After the revolution, the land was divided into little parcels and sold to the general populace. Over time, many of these owners joined their parcels together to form a large vineyard while others retained their independence but joined together in selling their grapes or must to a bottler. Still others kept their small parcels and produced a limited number of bottles per season. Thus, if a wine is bottled at the vineyard, either a small independent or large conglomerate, it will carry the name of that vineyard. If sold to a bottler, it will carry either the name of the bottler, the location, or both.

Chablis Seventy-five miles north of Dijon lies the Chablis area of Burgundy. It is here that Chardonnay grapes are grown to produce the finest white wine in the world. French law dictates that only the Chardonnay grape may be used to produce Chablis. In France, the highest ranking for wine is called a **cru**, and while there are other considerations regarding grade, alcohol content is one of the most important. The rankings are as follows:

- Chablis Grand Cru   11 percent alcohol
- Chablis Premier Cru   10.5 percent alcohol
- Chablis   10 percent alcohol
- Petit Chablis   9.5 percent alcohol

Burgundy Region

France

Paris

Dijon

Lyon

Rhone River

FIGURE 3.3
Map of Burgundy showing the four wine-producing areas.

Cote d'Or The Cote d'Or district of Burgundy consists two areas, north (Cote de Nuits) and south (Cote de Beaune). Some of the most famous red wines come from the north, while the southern part produces some very fine white wines in addition to the reds. Literally translated, *Cote d'Or* means "slope of gold." It is here that some of the finest burgundies in the world are produced. French law stipulates that all red wines produced in this region come from the Pinot Noir grape. While most of the wine produced in this region is red, a small percentage of the vineyards also produce a very fine white wine. White Burgundy is referred to as Chardonnay. It is aged in oak barrels that have been used several times, thus allowing the distinctive flavor and taste of the grape to come through.

Like the Chablis region, the wines produced in Cote d'Or are classified by the government as follows:

- Grand Cru. Includes the name of the vineyard. This classification is given sparingly and therefore is quite expensive
- Premier Cru. Contains the name of the vineyard and is a very good wine.
- Appellation Communale, also known as Village. Has the name of the village only. The grapes must come from the village listed on the label. This is higher in quality and more expensive than the Bourgogne classification.
- Bourgogne, also known as generic. A classification given to wine from vineyards that do not meet the above standards. The grapes can come from anywhere in the Cote d'Or region.

Even though the Cote d'Or wines are government classified, they present a case of "buyer beware." For example, a Grand Cru wine could bear the name of a famous vineyard but be from an inferior year. The buyer cannot rely on information from the label only but must be knowledgeable about the region and the practices of certain bottlers.

Southern Burgundy   The Southern Burgundy region is made up of the Cote Chalonnaise and the Maconnais areas. It produces a respectable red wine but not of the quality of the widely acclaimed reds of the Cote d'Or region. For the most part, the reds come from the Gamay grape.

While the region produces a respectable amount of red wine, it is widely acclaimed for its whites. As a matter of fact, white wine from Southern Burgundy that has an alcohol content of 11.5 percent or higher can carry the Premier Cru label. This region also produces the famous Pouilly-Fuisse, a light golden wine with a full flavor.

Beaujolais   In the extreme southern part of Burgundy lies Beaujolais. Almost all of its production is in red wine from the Gamay grape. Its wine does not age well, and most of it is sold within three years of harvest. The Beaujolais Nouveau (new) has a shorter life span and is usually consumed within nine months of harvest. Not being aged in oak allows the delicate flavors to come through. Beaujolais reds must have an alcohol content of 9 percent, with Cru being an exception. There are four levels of quality for wine from the Beaujolais area. They are as follows:

- Cru Beaujolais, which is the highest ranking and must have an alcohol content of 10 percent. The label will denote the town that the wine came from. Cru Beaujolais is not normally served chilled but rather at a cool room temperature.
- Beaujolais Village is normally a blend of grapes from different vineyards from a particular village. Even though it is classified as Village, the name of the village does not appear on the label.
- Beaujolais, while one of the lesser ranked classifications, oddly enough accounts for the majority of wine sold from this area. It does not age well and should be consumed with in a year.
- Beaujolais Nouveau, while ranked low, enjoys great popularity as it is the first wine released each year (*nouveau* being French for "new"). It gives a first indication as to the quality of the French harvest for that year.

Champagne Region

Reims

Paris

France

FIGURE 3.4
Map of the wine-producing area of Champagne.

Champagne   From the north-central part of France comes one of the most widely recognized wines in the world, Champagne. The location of Champagne can be found in Figure 3.4. While the French made it famous, its origins are mostly unknown. Some say it was developed in a Catholic monastery in Spain. Whatever its origins, a monk by the name of Dom Perignon is widely credited with perfecting the process of making and bottling Champagne. While other areas of the world make sparkling wines, only wine made in the Champagne region of France can be called Champagne. This is enforced with trade agreements made by France with most other countries of the world. The most notable exceptions to this rule are Russia and the United States. Here the word *champagne* (lower case) can be so labeled on a bottle of sparkling wine. Let the buyer beware! Since the making of Champagne or a sparkling wine is different than other wines, we will go into detail here.

Champagne is not the product of one vineyard but rather is a blend of many different wines. Thus, the majority of Champagne is made by companies that purchase wine from many different growers or grower cooperatives. The blending of these wines is a complex operation and is a well-guarded secret as the process defines a brand's essence and flavor.

While many different growers are used, Champagne, by law, can only come from three different grapes: the red Pinot Noir, the red Pinot Meunier, and the white Chardonnay, with the Pinot Noir normally being the predominant grape. When red grapes are used exclusively, the wine is known as Blanc de Noir (literally translated, white from red). When the white Chardonnay grapes are used 100 percent, it is called Blanc de Blanc (white from white). To get a clear or golden-colored Champagne out of red grapes requires a process by which the skins are removed quickly after squeezing them. The red color is not in the grape itself but rather in the skin only. If the skins are removed quickly, the wine will be clear. If they are left in for a short time it will be a rose wine, and if for a longer period the wine will be red.

After harvest, the wine is fermented until spring. At this time it is blended. This is a very important process as this will determine the final outcome of the Champagne. While Champagne must come from the three grapes, as many as thirty different wines coming from those varieties may be used to get to the final blend. The bottlers keep their formulas secret to protect their brand. In addition to different wines, different years of production may be used. When this is done it is called **Classic Champagne**. When one year is used exclusively, and the harvest is of high quality, it is called **Vintage Champagne**. Do not be misled that Vintage is better than Classic. It probably is not. Vintage years are few and far between. By blending the good years with the not so good, the bottler can come up with a superior product that adheres to their profile year after year. French law stipulates that each producer has to set aside 20 percent of that year's wine for future use. However, most producers set aside more than that to protect themselves for upcoming use.

The process of blending is called **cuvee**. The cuvee is put into bottles with the addition of sugar and yeast and capped. The bottles are then stored in caves where they undergo a second fermentation. In this process the cuvee produces more alcohol, but more importantly creates a carbon dioxide gas that cannot escape and therefore is forced into the wine. This process creates extreme pressure on the bottle and the cap, reaching as high as 110 pounds per square inch. This second fermentation results in the tiny bubbles that make Champagne famous.

The second fermentation takes quite a while, up to three years. During this time the wine is not sitting idly in some cave. It is stored on its side, neck down, on an A-frame rack. This allows the sediment to settle in the neck of the bottle. The bottle is occasionally shaken slightly and turned to advance the process. While this is still done manually in some wineries, much of it is done by machines that can handle over 4,000 bottles at a time. After the sediment has settled, the bottles are then placed neck down in an ice-cold brine, which freezes the sediment to the cork. The cork along with the sediment is then quickly removed, leaving behind clear, clean Champagne.

In the process of removing the sediment, some of the Champagne is lost and is replaced by the **dosage**, which is addition of wine and/or brandy and sugar. The amount of sugar added will greatly affect the dryness or the sweetness of the Champagne. The additional sugar can range from zero to over 50 grams of sugar per liter. The label on the bottle will indicate the degree of sweetness:

- Extra Brut   Driest, no sweetness
- Brut   Not as dry
- Extra dry/Extra Sec A little dryness
- Sec   Some sweetness
- Demi sec   Sweet
- Doux   Especially sweet

Champagne bottle with cap, wire cage, and foil.
Gary Ombler © Dorling Kindersley

After the wine and sugar are added, the bottle is recorked, a wire cage is put over the cork to secure it (as it is under extreme pressure), and the cork and cage are covered with foil. The bottles are then returned to the caves, where they are aged from one to five years. This method of bottling and infusing bubbles is called **Methode Champenoise**.

There are other methods used for bottling sparkling wine or "champagne." These are used primarily in other parts of the world and are considered by some to be inferior to the method just described. Some wine makers in the United States, Germany, and other countries use the **transfer method**, which follows the procedure just outlined except for the clarification process after the second fermentation. Here the wine is placed in a pressurized vat where it settles and is then clarified by filtering and rebottled. Additional wine and sugar (dosage) is added and the bottle is corked, wired, and foiled.

The **Charmat method**, which the Italians use for Spumante, is where the wine is put into a pressurized tank; sugar and yeast are added, and the fermentation begins. After several weeks, it is then pumped into a second tank and clarified, with additional wine and sugar added, and is then bottled. While this procedure costs less, its bubbles are not of the quality of Champagne and do not last as long. On the plus side, critics contend that it has a clean grape flavor.

One last method, the **carbonation method**, which is used solely by those makers who want to produce a very low cost sparkling wine, is to force carbon dioxide into the wine under pressure. But drink it fast because the bubbles are large and do not last long.

Flute of champagne.
seen/Fotolia

Cotes du Rhone   Travel directly south from Champagne, past the Burgundy region, and you will come to the Cotes du Rhone region of France. This region follows the Rhone River from Lyon as it flows southward. Refer to Figure 3.5 for the Cotes du Rhone region. Being in the south of France, the summers are long and give the grapes the opportunity to ripen to their fullest. This produces a grape that is deep red, almost black, in color and in time a wine that is bold and rich in taste with a high alcohol content.

Approximately 90 percent of the wine produced in the Cotes du Rhone area is red. In the northern part of the region, the primary grapes grown are the Cinsault and Syrah. The southern part grows these grapes as well as the Grenache and Clairette varieties. The reds are aged in casks for several years as they are quite stark when young.

Cote du Rhone Region

FIGURE 3.5
Map of the wine-producing
areas of Cotes du Rhone.

After bottling they are aged more until the wine has matured. As a matter of fact, they can age for over twenty years. The wines produced in this region are usually dependable year after year.

Like the reds, the white wine produced in the Cotes du Rhone region is also high in alcohol content. For the most part, they are dry with a subtle flavor and aroma. Roses are also made in this region, mostly from the Grenache grape. They have a medium body and a definite fruit-like flavor.

Loire The Loire River flows through central France on its way to the Atlantic Ocean. Figure 3.6 show the Loire region of France. As it meanders along, it passes many famous castles as well as fertile farms and vineyards. The wine-growing region consists of the lower Loire (Bas-Loire) and the upper Loire (Haute-Loire). It is here that mostly white wine is produced along with some roses.

The lower Loire is most noted for the whites and roses from the Anjou area, the dry whites of Muscadet, and the still whites and sparkling whites of Vouvray. While the Chenin Blanc grape is the predominant one grown in this area, a substantial number of vineyards grow the Gamey grape. The area produces a highly acidic wine ranging from dry to very sweet.

The upper Loire is most noted for the white wine of Pouilly-Fume as well as the lesser known Sancerre. Both are made from the Sauvignon Blanc grape. The Pouilly-Fume is higher in alcohol content and tends to have a more creamy body and flavor.

The majority of wines coming from the Loire region should be experienced when young, less than five years, as they do not age well. Only the very sweet whites may be kept for a longer period. For the most part, the wines from this region are fruity, clean, light, and quite subtle.

Italy

Somewhere around 900 BC, grapes were discovered in Italy around the Tuscan region, and shortly thereafter wine was produced. As far as we know it is the oldest wine-producing area in the world. However, it wasn't until the Greeks planted grapes on the island of Sicily that the wine industry took off, and it has been an integral part of Italian society ever since. As a matter of fact, Italy consumed and produced more wine than any other country in the world until 2009, when France edged it out. The production output of both countries is so close that by the time you read this, Italy could well be back in first place. The reason for this see-saw could be attributed to the favorable climate of both countries.

The Denomisazione di Origine Controllata (DOC) controls the certification of wine. The DOC controls, among other things, the types and amount of grapes that can be used in different wines, the production per acre, the alcohol content of the wine, and the length of aging. A wine must adhere to these standards to be certified DOC. Another classification that is more stringent is DOCG (DOC Guaranteed). In it the producer must adhere to the DOC standard, plus the number of grapes grown per acre is restricted and the wine must achieve a higher minimum alcohol level.

Loire Region

FIGURE 3.6
Map of the wine-producing
areas of Loire.

FIGURE 3.7
Map of Italy showing the wine-producing regions.

There is hardly an area in Italy where wine is not produced. The DOC has divided the country into twenty wine-producing regions. A map of these regions is shown in Figure 3.7. We will examine some of the more important ones.

Emilia-Romagna In the north-central part of Italy lies the Emilia-Romagna region. It is here that the Lambrusco grape is grown. The vast majority of the best wine produced in this region is made from this grape. Most are Frizzantes, which are a slightly sparkling wine, and a few are Spumantes. which are a full sparkling wine. Several have the DOC rating, but only one has the rare DOCG rating, the Albana di Romagna, which is a white wine.

Also grown in the Emilia-Romagna region is the Trebbiano grape. While it is grown in almost every region in Italy, it is here, as well as in the Abruzzio region, where it is most prolific. The Trebbiano grape is the foremost grape in wine production the world over, but it is not well known as it is used

Picture of Denomisazione di Origine Controllata (DOCG) label.

Neil Mersh © Dorling Kindersley

primarily as a blending and distilling grape. A few wineries make a wine exclusively from the Trebbiano grape, but it is a bland, flavorless wine with a high acid content. The grape is also used in the making of brandy.

Latium-Lazio   Surrounding Rome is the Latium-Lazio region. Here is where several DOC white wines are produced. There are other fine wines produced in this area, although they are not recognized by the DOC. Among them are the wines of Castelli Romani, whose wine makers believe that the DOC regulations restrict them from making an outstanding product.

Lombardy   Directly north of the Emilia-Romagna region lies the Lombardy region, which surrounds the city of Milan and borders on Switzerland. The Nebbiolo grape grows well here. This area produces some very fine wines, several of which are recognized as DOC. These wines have a relatively short life span and should be enjoyed early on.

Piedmont   Descending from the Alps, west of the Lombardy region of Italy is the Piedmont region. It is the home of the famous Asti Spumante, Italy's version of Champagne. In addition to this outstanding sparkling white, the Piedmont region also produces some exceptional reds. Barolo is one of them. It is made from the Nebbiolo grape, a small, thick-skinned grape, and carries the prestigious DOCG designation. It is a rich, full-bodied wine that ages well and is best consumed when aged up to fifteen or even twenty years. It is one of the few wines that has to be decanted as, more often than not, it contains a substantial amount of sediment.

Sicily   From Piedmont, travel south down the west coast of Italy, to where the "toe" of the "boot" is kicking an odd-shaped football. The odd-shaped football is Sicily. This is where it all began in terms of modern Italian wine making. The warm climate and abundant sunshine make it an ideal climate for growing grapes. The island is best known for producing an outstanding dessert wine called Marsala. There are three characteristic that identify Marsala, and they are referred to as the **Triple Trinity**.

- Sweetness: Secco, dry; Semisecco, semi dry; and Dolce, sweet.
- Color: Oro, golden; Ambra, amber; Rubino, ruby.
- Quality:
  - Marsala Fine. Minimum alcohol content of 17 percent, aged a minimum of one year in wood
  - Marsala Superiore. Minimum alcohol content of 18 percent, aged a minimum of two years in wood.
  - Marsala Vergine. The finest Marsala made, minimum alcoholic content of 18 percent, aged for five years

On the slopes of volcanic Mount Etna, white grapes are grown to produce Corvino, a dry white wine.

Tuscany   In the north-central part of Italy on the west coast lies the region of Tuscany. It surrounds the city of Florence and produces the famous Chianti. DOC-approved Chianti is made with 90 percent red grapes, normally Sangiovese, and 10 percent white. It is a robust, dry, well-balanced wine that is ruby red in color. Some vintners in the area produce a similar wine that is outstanding and is made from all red grapes; however, by law it cannot be called Chianti. Chianti has three classifications:

- Chianti Classico Riserva. The highest quality and most expensive
- Chianti Classico. An excellent quality wine from choice districts
- Chianti. A basic category for all Chianti-type wines

A bottle of Marsala wine.
Clive Streeter © Dorling Kindersley

The Sangiovese grape is being replaced with other red grapes such as Merlot and Cabernet Sauvignon, with these wines being called Super Tuscans. Other DOC wines produced in the Tuscany region include Brunello, Vin Santo, Galestro, and Bianco Toscano.

Spain

Like many other countries, Spain regulates its wine industry. But it did so only recently in 1972 when it established the Instituto de Denominaciones de Origen (INDO). Its regulations emulate France's system and, as such, grant the Denominacion de Origen (DO) to those wines that meet its directives. While the wine industry in France is dominated by the growers (châteaux), wine in Spain is dominated by the wine producers (bodegas) who buy the grapes from many vineyards and process them into wine.

INDO has recognized 28 regions of Spain that produce wine, and of these, three stand out as being the most important: Jerez de la Frontera, Rioja, and Catalonia. See Figure 3.8 for a map depicting these three regions.

Jerez de la Frontera   On the southern coast of Spain lies the region of Jerez de la Frontera that is home to Spain's most famous wine—sherry. The making of sherry is curtailed to this region by INDO, and only wine produced in this region can be labeled sherry. All others must have their point of origin on the label behind the word *sherry*.

The making of sherry is interesting. The majority of sherry is made with the Palomino grape, and the rest made up of the Pedro Ximenez grape. Only the first pressing of these grapes is used in the process of fermentation. The second pressing is used to produce brandy, which is added to the sherry after fermentation to increase the alcohol content and add flavor.

The aging of the first pressing is done using the **solera system**. With this system, the first pressings are blended by the producers according to their own formulas, which are a carefully guarded secret. The casks used are made from American white oak. Casks are tiered by row, with a minimum of three casks high and as many as ten casks high. As the tiers go up, there are fewer casks in each row. The casks are placed outside to get the full effect of the sun warming the summer air. When the aging process is complete, by law a maximum of 33 percent of the sherry is removed from the bottom cask. The bottom cask is then filled with some of the sherry from the cask above it. That cask is then filled from the cask above it, and so on until the top row is reached. The new sherry, blended from the first pressing, is then placed into the uppermost row of casks.

Some sherry, as it goes through the aging process, develops a film called a **flor**, which slows the oxidation process and gives the sherry flavor. The longer it is in contact with this film, the finer the sherry. It should be noted that some sherry is discouraged from developing this film, resulting in a heavier product.

As the sherry is fermenting, all of the sugar from the grapes is turned into alcohol, thus leaving the product considerably dry. To offset this, after the sherry goes through the solera process, it is sweetened by the addition of a sweet wine made from Muscat grapes. Further sweetening and additional flavor is created by supplementing the wine with coloring, sweeteners, and unaged fresh wine. Sherry is classified as follows:

- Manzanilla. A pale, light-bodied, very dry sherry with a hint of saltiness. It has a heavy growth of flor and should be served chilled.

Wine Growing Regions of Spain

FIGURE 3.8
Map of Spain showing the three of the important wine-producing regions.

An example of the solera aging system.
John Woodcock © Dorling Kindersley

Glass of sherry.
Steve Gorton © Dorling Kindersley

- Fino. Pale, but with more body and sweetness. It is not aged. It also has a flor growth and should be served chilled.
- Amontillada. A dry golden sherry that is aged for a short period. It has a thin coat of flor and should be served at room temperature, although some prefer it over ice.
- Amoroso. A medium dry, light amber sherry. Its flavor profile varies significantly from maker to maker.
- Oloroso. Light brown to tan in color; sweet and rich. Many are aged for years. Dry oloroso should be served over ice and sweet oloroso at room temperature.
- Cream. Very sweet and rich; brown color.

Remember the brandy that was made from the second pressing of the Palomino grape? That is added at the end to increase the alcohol content of the sherry from 13 to 15–20 percent.

Rioja   Southwest of Bordeaux in France is the Rioja region of Spain. The wine that is produced here is often compared to the wine produced in Burgundy and Bordeaux. The primary grape of this area is the Tempranillo, which is sometimes blended with other grape varieties. The reds fall under two classifications: tinto and rioja. The tinto is a heavy, full-bodied, deep red wine often compared to a French Burgundy. The rioja has a more subtle flavor, is lighter in body, and is compared to a French Beaujolais.

Because this region has a great deal of sun during the summer months, the grapes develop a large amount of sugar, resulting in a high alcohol content. The whites produced here are also high in alcohol but are not as brusque as the reds.

Catalonia   East of Rioja, near Barcelona, is the Catalonia region. The prominent wine maker here is Bodega Torres. While it has been in the same family for over 300 years, it is quite up to date, with modern techniques being employed. Stainless steel vats are used, replacing the traditional clay *tinajas*. Grapes are being planted that are not indigenous to the region. In addition to other wines, Bodega Torres produces a Cabernet with a blackberry-tinged bouquet.

The United States

While California leads America in wine production, over forty states have wineries that produce wine. Indeed, the United States, as a whole, has the climate and soil to produce good vineyards. As a matter of fact, of the sixty countries that produce wine, over 10 percent of it comes from the United States. While it has been producing wine commercially for almost 200 years (a relative newcomer to the wine industry), its wines are recognized as being among the finest produced worldwide. In this section we will examine three of the more important areas in terms of total production: California, the Pacific Northwest, and New York. Keep in mind, however, that there are many other fine wineries scattered across the country that produce excellent wines, just not in the volume of these three regions.

California   California, with its diverse climate ranging from the desert in the south to the mild climate of its north coast, produces a wide variety of grapes. Such production yields a wide variety of wines including red, white, rose, and sparkling. The production areas are divided into four regions: the North Coast, the North Central Coast, the South Central Coast, and the Central Valley. Refer to Figure 3.9 for a map of the California regions.

In the northern part of California, just off the coast of the Pacific Ocean, lies the North Coast region. It consists of the counties of Sonoma, Mendocino, and Lake, as

California Wine-Growing Regions

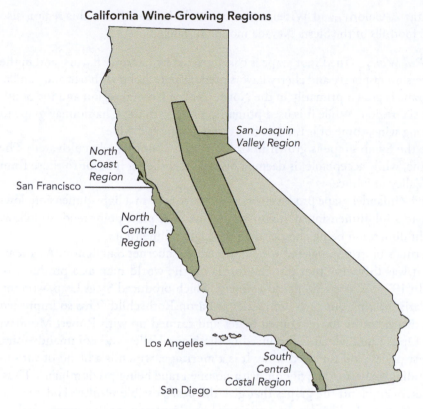

FIGURE 3.9
Map of California showing the wine-producing areas.

well as the Napa Valley. It is here that some of the most famous wineries in the United States, indeed the world, are located. To name a few: Fetzer, Parducci, Gudnoc, Sebastiani, Stony Hill, Robert Mondavi, Inglenook, Domaine Chandon, Beringer, and Freemark Abbey. This is just a small sampling of the many outstanding wineries that dot the region.

Traveling south into the San Francisco area lies the North Central region, consisting of the counties of Livermore, Santa Clara, and Monterey. East of San Francisco Bay is the Livermore area that produces some outstanding white wine, both dry and sweet. South of San Francisco are Santa Clara, Santa Cruz, San Mateo, and Monterey counties. Some of the major wineries of this area are Wendt Brothers, Concannon, Almenden, Taylor, Paul Masson, Jeckel, and Martin Rey.

Traveling down the coast even farther, you will come to San Luis Obispo, and further south Santa Barbara. Within this area is the South Central Coastal region.

Go east from the North Central Coastal and the South Central Coastal regions and you will come to the Central Valley, or more notably the San Joaquin Valley. This enormous valley transverses the central part of California, stretching over 400 miles. It is here that most of the state's wine is produced. As a matter of fact, it harvests so many grapes that it supplies not only its own wineries but others outside its region as well. Here are housed many wineries, some small and some as a part of large corporations. Names include Gallo, Almaden, Italian Swiss

Beringer Winery, Napa, California.

© John Elk III / Alamy

Colony, Franzia, Colony, and Winemaster. It should be noted that this region also includes the foothills of the Sierra Nevada mountain range.

California Red Wines   The Pinot grape is characterized by its fruity flavors, and in the California version raspberry and cherry flavors predominate along with oak and vanilla. The pinot grape is grown primarily in the North Central Coastal region and the South Central Coastal region. While it is used primarily along with the Chardonnay grape to make sparkling wine, some of it is made into a standalone still wine.

While the Syrah grape is grown in California, it is not widely cultivated. The resulting wine, while acceptable, is deemed by experts as being inferior to those from the Rhone Valley in France.

The red Zinfandel grape produces a range of flavors from a light-dimension, low-tannin wine to a full-dimensioned, high-tannin wine. The price point tends to follow, with the light dimension being cheaper than the higher dimension.

California's most popular red wine is arguably Cabernet Sauvignon. As a matter of fact, it was this wine that put California on the world map as a producer of fine wines. In 1976, Warren Winiarski's winery, which produced Stags Leap, won top honors in Paris, beating out such luminaries as Baron Rothschild. This so impressed Rothschild that he came to the United States and teamed up with Robert Mondavi to produce Opus One, which is produced in the Napa Valley and commands some of the highest prices paid for a red wine. It is a **meritage**, which is a blend of various grapes, including Cabernet Sauvignon, with no one grape being predominant. Thus, the winemaker can blend the grapes that give the best possible results. To be called Cabernet Sauvignon, the blend must contain at least 75 percent of that grape.

Another popular red wine from California is Merlot. Along with the imports from France and other countries, Merlot is one of the most popular wines sold in the United States. The reason for this could be attributed to the fact that it is lighter than a Cabernet Sauvignon and easier to drink.

A bottle of wine from Stags Leap Winery. © ZUMA Press, Inc. / Alamy

California White Wines   The Chardonnay grape is the most widely grown grape in California. As a matter of fact, over 20 percent of the state's grape production is Chardonnay, and it is grown in all four regions, with the Central Valley being the largest producer. Having said that, it is definitely a quantity issue rather than a quality issue, as the Chardonnay wineries considered outstanding are few and far between. Nonetheless, there is a strong demand for California Chardonnay. It has an oak flavor along with several type of fruit overtones and is higher in alcohol content than its French counterpart.

In California's North Central Coast, the vast majority of the Riesling, Gewurztraminer, and Pinot Blanc grapes are grown. As Riesling and Gewurztraminer are thought of as primarily German wines, they are often compared to them as the standard. California being warmer with more sunshine than Germany, the grapes tend to be sweeter, with less acid and a higher alcohol content than their German counterparts. This results in a drier wine than the German equivalent.

The Sauvignon Blanc grape is one of the more popular white grapes grown in California. As the growing season is longer here than in other parts of the world that grow this grape, the wine tends to favor the taste of stewed or cooked fruit. Often it is blended with the Semillon grape to produce a more intricate wine. By law, wineries are limited to a 25 percent addition of other grapes for the wine still to be called Sauvignon Blanc.

Other California Wines   Sparkling wines from California have a sweeter taste than their French counterparts from Champagne. This is due to the fact that the climate is warmer and the grapes ripen more quickly, thus giving them more sugar and less acid. The primary grapes used are the Pinot Noir, Chardonnay, and Pinot Blanc. California

Cave at Spring Mountain Winery, St. Helena, California.
© Hemis / Alamy

sparkling wines use all of the traditional methods for making Champagne: the traditional Champagne method, the Charmet process, the transfer process, and the forced carbonation method.

Coming primarily from the southern part of the state are the California dessert wines. Here the hot sun ripens the grapes quickly, which gives them a sweet taste. The brandy coming from this area is considered by many to be more of a caliber for mixed drinks rather than a standalone brandy. The sherries from this region are made by the traditional solera method as well as being heated by mechanical means to give them a sherry-like flavor.

The Pacific Northwest States Comprising the states of Oregon and Washington, the Pacific Northwest is second only to California in wine production. Well over 800 wineries, some of them quite small, thrive in this area. The reason for this could be that the state of Washington lies on the same latitude as Bordeaux and Burgundy in France, and Oregon's climate and soil is almost identical with the soil and climate of the Rhone, Bordeaux, and Alsace regions of France. Because of its northern location, the growing area is cooler and shorter than California, while at the same time it receives more sun per day. Figure 3.10 depicts the Pacific Northwest regions.

Pacific Northwest Red Wines The Willamette Valley is Oregon's home to the Pinot Noir grape as it is the most extensively grown grape in the area. It is here that award-winning wines have helped put Oregon on the world wine map. The Pinot Noir grape is also grown in other areas of Oregon and Washington with great success. Not as successful is the Cabernet Sauvignon grape as this area is too far north to produce bumper crops. However, it has met with some degree of success in Washington and in the Rogue River Valley in Oregon.

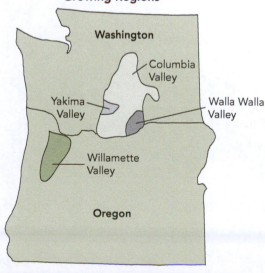

Pacific Northwest Wine-Growing Regions

FIGURE 3.10
Map of the Pacific Northwest wine areas.

Red Hill Vineyard, Dundee, Oregon.
Bruce Forster © Dorling Kindersley, Courtesy of Red Hills Vineyard, Dundee Oregon

Pacific Northwest White Wines   The Riesling grape does well in the Pacific Northwest and produces a wine that ranges from dry to sweet, depending on the time of harvest. The Gewurztraminer grape, while grown there, is declining in popularity. The Semillon grape is used primarily as a blend with other grapes. However, in Washington it is often used as the only grape. When it is blended, it is the predominant grape.

The Pinot Gris grape is becoming quite popular in Oregon, as vintners can make a quick profit on it. The wine is ready to market within six months of bottling. The Chardonnay grape thrives in Washington and Oregon and compares favorably with those grown in Burgundy, France. The reason, as given above, is that they share the same latitude. The Chardonnay from the Pacific Northwest has a medium body with a fruity flavor.

New York   The state of New York can be divided into three grape-growing regions: west of Buffalo along Lake Erie, the Finger Lakes region south of Syracuse, and Long Island. Go to Figure 3.11 for a map of the New York wine regions. The largest of these is the area west of Buffalo; however, most of the grapes grown there are made into grape juice. The Finger Lakes area is the largest wine-producing area in the state. The winters are harsh here as far as the grape vines are concerned, and the roots have to be covered by a foot of soil in order to survive.

Most of the wines coming from New York are white. The Riesling produced here measures up favorably with that produced in Germany and can vary from dry to sweet. It comes primarily from the Finger Lakes region but is also produced in Long Island. The Gewurztraminer grape is also grown in these regions but does not compare to its European counterparts. The Chardonnay grape is grown in all three regions and produces a full-bodied wine.

New York Wine-Growing Areas

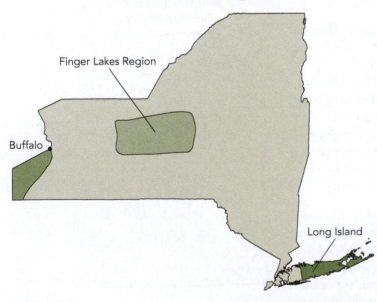

Finger Lakes Region

Buffalo

Long Island

FIGURE 3.11
Map of New York wine areas.

Inniskillin Winery vineyards, Niagara on the Lake, New York.
© Buddy Mays / Alamy

Argentina

Argentina is the fourth largest producer of wine, turning out almost 5 percent of the world's output. As a matter of fact, Argentina has been producing wine for over 400 years. As most of it is consumed in South America, it is not widely known in the United States and Canada, although this is changing as more Argentine imports are finding their way into the United States. San Juan is an important wine-growing region; however, most of the production takes place in Mendoza. Refer to Figure 3.12 for a map showing the wine-producing areas of Argentina.

Sangiovese, a grape that is usually blended with other grapes because of its high acidity, is a recent newcomer to Argentina. Tempranillo, a grape usually associated with Spain, also thrives here. The Cabernet Sauvignon wine produced in Argentina was considered for years to be inferior to other Cabernet Sauvignons, but that is rapidly changing. The quality is surprisingly good while the price is relatively low. Another good bargain is Merlot, which along with Cabernet Sauvignon makes up a good portion of Argentina's output. Other grapes grown here include Malbec, which produces a very good red wine, and Torrontes, which produces a sweet white wine.

Australia and New Zealand

Australia along with New Zealand makes over 5 percent of the world's production of wine. The major wine-producing region is in the southwestern part of Australia with an exception being Hunter Valley, which is north of Sydney. Hunter Valley is one of the oldest producers of wine in Australia. Much of the wine produced is exported, with Great Britain being the recipient. However, the United States is becoming a major player as the wines sell for a reasonable price and are of good quality. In New Zealand the major growing areas are Hawke's Bay, Gisborne, and Wairarapa. Refer to Figure 3.13 for a map showing the wine growing regions of Australia and New Zealand.

Australia has a unique blending law. Unlike most jurisdictions where 75 percent of the grape listed on the label must be of that grape, Australian wine makers are not thus restricted. Therefore, the Shiraz blends coming from Australia have a unique flavor that cannot be duplicated anywhere in the world. As a result, these wines are enjoying an immense popularity. One of the more predominant grapes that the Australians use to blend with the Shiraz is the Cabernet Sauvignon grape.

Wine-Growing Region

Argentina

San Juan
Mendoza

Buenos Aires

FIGURE 3.12
Map of Argentina wine-producing areas.

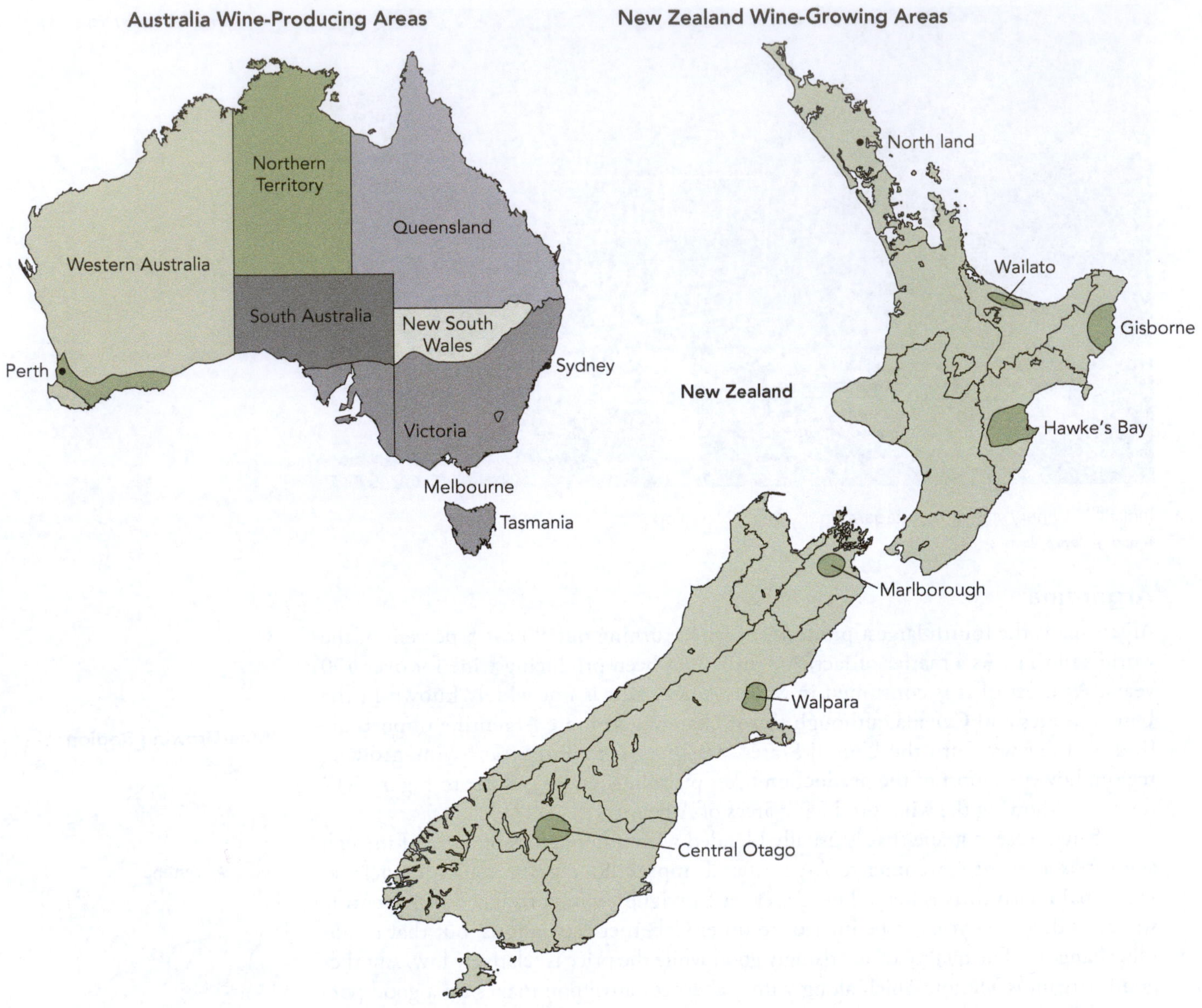

Australia Wine-Producing Areas

New Zealand Wine-Growing Areas

Northern
Territory

Queensland

Western Australia

South Australia

New South
Wales

Perth

Sydney

Victoria

Melbourne

Tasmania

North land

Wailato

Gisborne

Hawke's Bay

New Zealand

Marlborough

Walpara

Central Otago

FIGURE 3.13
Map of Australia and New Zealand wine-producing areas.

Rieslings from Australia have a distinct flavor of strong lime overtones, which is attributable only to Australian Rieslings. New Zealand Rieslings, on the other hand, have more of a grapefruit overtone. The Sauvignon Blanc grapes grown in New Zealand produce an outstanding wine that is different from that produced anywhere else. It is aged in stainless steel vats rather than oak barrels, thus allowing the natural flavors to predominate. Chardonnay wines that are produced in Australia and New Zealand are two entirely different products. The Australian Chardonnays are aged in stainless steel, giving them a full fruit flavor, while the New Zealand Chardonnays are aged in oak, which affects the flavor profile. Both are high in acid and alcohol content. The Semillon grape is grown primarily to blend with the Chardonnay grape; however, some vintners use the Semillon as the primary grape.

Chile

Over half of Chile's wine is exported, which is a good deal for the United States as it is usually low priced and of decent quality. It should be mentioned that the quality

Votager Estate Winery, Margaret River Region, Australia.
Terry Carte © Dorling Kindersley

Chile Wine-Producing Areas

• Santiago

FIGURE 3.14
Map of Chile wine-producing areas.

has improved over the last decade and continues to improve. The main production region starts near Santiago and covers a narrow band of land for almost 500 miles. Figure 3.14 show this narrow band. As the region is quite arid, the majority of vineyards are irrigated.

The Sauvignon Blanc grape is the most widely grown white grape in Chile followed by the Chardonnay. The Chardonnays from here have a fruity flavor but are not of the same quality as those from France or the United States. White grapes account for only about a third of Chile's output of wine. The king of the reds is Cabernet Sauvignon, accounting for almost half of Chile's wine output, with Merlot right behind it. Carmenere, a blending grape, is also grown here.

Vina La Posada Winery, Colchagua Province, Chile.
Nigel Hicks © Dorling Kindersley

Germany Wine-Growing Region

FIGURE 3.15
Map of Germany wine areas.

Vineyards in Edenkoben, Germany.
Pawel Wojcik © Dorling Kindersley

Germany

One of the attributes of German wine is that most of it is hand picked. The steep and hilly terrain does not allow for mechanized picking; thus only the grapes that are ripe are hand picked. This could explain the fact that German wines are usually high in sugar content as well as acid and low in alcohol content. Figure 3.15 shows the growing areas of Germany.

The Riesling grape is widely grown in Germany and produces a white wine, which is light with a good deal of fruity overtones. Another white, while not grown as much, is associated with Germany because of its name: Gewurztraminer. *Gewurz* translated from German means "spice," and that word best describes this wine—spicy and sweet. The wines made from the Muller-Thurgau grape are uncomplicated and basic. Germany's cooler climate is ideally suited for this grape.

The Pinot Noir grape in Germany is known as Spatburgunder. It is grown in southern Germany and is not very widely planted. A rare and expensive wine that is produced in Germany is Eiswein. The grapes are harvested very late in the year, usually in late November after a hard freeze. While the grapes are still frozen, they are harvested and pressed while frozen. The ice particles are removed and the fermentation process begins. As most of the water (ice) has been removed the wine has a rich heavy flavor that is both sweet and tart. The conditions to produce this wine (heavy frost when the grapes have ripened) occur on the average of every four years. Thus the production is very limited, not to mention the yield with the water removed is low, causing Eiswein to be very expensive.

WINE TASTING

Now that you have a very basic—and I emphasize basic—understanding of what goes into the making of wine, you can see that it a very complex procedure from the growing of the grapes to the uncorking of the bottle. You can read volumes about wine, but not until you actually taste it, evaluate it, and compare it with other wines and vintages can you get a true appreciation for the art of wine making.

Wine tasting for the beverage manager can take on different formats. It could be very informal with several friends getting together for an evening of trying out several different wines. It could be a business meeting with one of your suppliers trying to sell you some different brands or varietals of wine. It could be you, as the beverage manager, conducting a formal wine-tasting seminar with your customers. Whatever the occasion, it is tasting, evaluating, and discussing the virtues and the differences of the wine. There will be differences of opinion as people will not always agree on the aromas and flavors they are tasting. This is okay as personal likes and dislikes come into the picture.

To conduct a proper wine tasting, you will need certain materials. Glassware is very important. It should be a stemmed glass, thin in body, with the bowl of the glass bowed out so that the top is narrower than the base of the bowl. The reason for using this style of glass is so that the taster can swirl the wine by holding the stem and not warm the wine by the hand holding the bowl. The design of the glass keeps the wine in the glass while swirling. You will need a clean glass for each wine tasted. Therefore the number of glasses needed will be the number of people in attendance times the number of wines being tasted.

In addition to glassware, you will need a white background such as a tablecloth, placemat, or white cardboard. This is needed so that the taster can see the clarity and evaluate the color of the wine. Additionally you will need some water so that the tasters can rinse their mouths as well as some crackers or french bread and cheese to clear their palates.

Tasting and evaluating wine is not simply drinking a glass of it and going "wow" or "yuk"! It is rather a set procedure that involves six steps. The procedure is see, swirl, smell, sip, swallow (spit), and savor.

An example of a wine glass for tasting.
Photo courtesy of Libbey Glass Inc.

- See. Pour a small amount of wine into a glass. Hold the glass at a slight angle up to a light or above a white tablecloth or towel. What is its color? Reds should be light pink in a young wine to a reddish brown in a mature wine. A rust or amber color is a sign of oxidation, which signifies spoilage. Whites should be green yellow, signifying a young wine probably from a cooler climate, to a tan-like color, signifying an older wine from a warmer climate. Again beware of an amber color, signifying that a wine is beyond its time. Roses should be pale orange to pink. Too much color means trouble. Red wines tend to become lighter in color as they age, turning their reddish purple color into a brown. Whites tend to become darker as they age, also turning brown. Color is not only an indication of age; it can also indicate the grape skin contact with the wine, the aging vessel (stainless steel, barrel, degree of char on the barrel), and exposure to air. Check the clarity. Tilt the glass so that when there is a thin line of wine, it should be nearly transparent. If it is full of sediment, then it is probably past its prime. A word of caution here: Some wines, as we have already learned, are aged with some sediment in them and are decanted before being served. These should be evaluated after the decanting process.

Seeing the color and clarity of the wine.
shock/Fotolia

- Swirl. Take the wine glass, holding it by the stem, and slowly rotate it, letting the wine swirl against the side of the glass. The true character of the wine will evaporate to create a better bouquet. The complex components will be released, giving the taster a true sense of the wine's traits. To prove this point, pour two glasses of wine. Without swirling, smell one. All you will sense is alcohol and probably grape. Swirl the other glass and you will smell a much more complex bouquet.

- Smell. After swirling, smell the wine. Put your nose in the glass. Breathe deep and then hold it in. What do you initially detect in the first phase of the sniff? Now what additional aromas begin to reveal themselves over time? Is it flowers, fruit, spice, vegetables, wood, or nuts? Try and pinpoint the exact kind, for instance apples, berries, cinnamon, green beans, or oak, etc. If the wine is complex, you may not be able to pick out a specific smell but rather a combination of smells. This is referred to as a wine's **bouquet**. If on the other hand you detect vinegar, chemicals, or sulfur, the wine should be rejected and not sold to your customers.

- Sip. Take a small sip. Pull some air into your mouth through a small hole in your lips and allow the wine to bubble. This will aerate the wine some more and allow more of the flavors to come through. As the wine passes over your tongue, which contain taste buds, it detects flavors: sweet, salt, sour,

Smelling the wine.
S Chantal/Fotolia

Tasting the wine.
Knut Wiarda/Fotolia

bitter, umami, and spicy. The first flavor detected is sweetness, as these flavor buds are located at the tip of the tongue. Since saltiness is normally not part of a wine's component, the taste buds that detect saltiness do not apply here. Farther back on the tongue are the taste buds that detect sourness. Sour is present in many of wine's components such as apples and citrus fruits. Sour is also present in vinegar. If you detect this flavor when tasting wine, it is a clear indication that the wine has turned bad. Still farther back on the tongue are the taste buds that detect bitterness. Bitter flavor can come from tannins that occur naturally on grapes or from the tannin in oak barrels. Umami refers to a wine's savoriness or flavor intensity. It was discovered by Japanese scientists and refers to the level of glutamate in a food or beverage. Glutamate intensifies the flavor. Finally, the heat or spiciness of the wine is caused by the amount of alcohol in the wine. The higher the alcohol content, the more prevalent this flavor becomes.

- Swallow (spit). After you have evaluated the wine, should you swallow it or spit it out? It depends. If you're sitting down with a wine representative and evaluating a few different wines to add to your wine list, it's probably okay to swallow it. If you're conducting a wine tasting with a group of customers, you'll probably want to keep your wits about you and should spit it out. Remember also to drink some water and eat a cracker or french bread with some cheese between each tasting to cleanse your palate so that you can properly evaluate the next wine.
- Savor. Enjoy the experience. Talk about the wine you have just tasted with others. Describe it. Do you agree on what you tasted or do some others have a different flavor profile? Discuss it. One thing is for sure, and that is that several people can taste the same wine from the same bottle and come up with diverse opinions.

CONCLUSION

Unless you're familiar with the European languages, by now your head is probably spinning. If so, answer the questions at the end of the chapter, and if you don't know the answer go back and look it up. It will eventually become clearer to you. With wine it seems the more you know, the more you need to learn. Remember that your customers feel the same way. On the one hand, there are those who know relatively little about the subject and are confused about what wine to order with their dinner. They may even be embarrassed. As a

beverage manager you will need to lead them through the maze either verbally or though menu listings. Your servers will need to be well trained on the subject as well. On the other hand are wine aficionados who will either try to impress you with their knowledge or will call on you to increase your knowledge. Either way, this is a large part of your business. We have scratched the surface here. It is up to you to delve deeper into the fascinating world of wine.

QUESTIONS

True/ False

1. Farmers who grow grapes are more interested in the quality of the grape than the quantity of grapes grown.
2. Sugar content is measured in Brix.
3. Given that one of the factors affecting the quality of wine is the yield per acre, the United States limits the yield per acre that a grape farmer can produce.
4. Red wine comes from red grapes, while white wine comes from white grapes.
5. Of the many varieties of grapes grown, some are quite familiar as the name of the wine is identical to the grape.
6. Grapes are the largest fruit crop grown worldwide.

7. Until the early part of this century, Italy was the largest producer of wine grapes in the world.

8. By French law, any wine labeled as Champagne must come from Champagne, France. While most countries observe this law, the United States does not.

Multiple Choice

1. Grapes grown for wine
   1) grow well where nothing else will grow.
   2) do not grow well where other crops thrive.
   A. (1) only
   B. (2) only
   C. Both (1) and (2)
   D. Neither (1) nor (2)

2. Grapes are harvested when
   A. the flavor of the grape is at its optimum.
   B. the sugar content of the grape is at its optimum.
   C. the acidity of the grape is at its optimum.
   D. all of the above.

3. Practically all white and rose wine produced today is fermented in
   A. stainless steel vats.
   B. wooden vats
   C. copper vats.
   D. cement vats.

4. Wines are blended
   A. to maintain a certain brand profile.
   B. for profit.
   C. to improve the wine produced from a bad harvest.
   D. all of the above.

5. Environmentalists
   1) do not like cork because it is stripped from trees and leaves the tree susceptible to disease.
   2) do not like plastics stoppers in wine bottles as they are not biodegradable.
   A. (1) only
   B. (2) only
   C. Both (1) and (2)
   D. Neither (1) nor (2)

6. France
   1) produces more wine than any other country in the world.
   2) does not produce as many significant wines as does Italy.
   A. (1) only
   B. (2) only
   C. Both (1) and (2)
   D. Neither (1) nor (2)

7. For a wine tasting, in addition to the proper glassware, you will need
   1) a white background such as white cardboard or tablecloth.
   2) water.
   A. (1) only
   B. (2) only
   C. Both (1) and (2)
   D. Neither (1) nor (2)

8. Which of the following is not one of the six "s" of a wine tasting?
   A. Seeing
   B. Salability
   C. Swallow
   D. Savor

9. When evaluating a wine some of the factors would include the wine's
   1) bouquet.
   2) umami.
   A. (1) only
   B. (2) only
   C. Both (1) and (2)
   D. Neither (1) nor (2)

10. The reason for having crackers or french bread and cheese at a wine tasting is
   A. to cleanse the palate.
   B. to make the occasion more sociable.
   C. to slow the alcohol's absorption into the blood stream.
   D. to sell the cheeses as well as the wine.

9. For a wine tasting, the glass should have a stem and the top of the glass should be wider than the bowl of the glass.

10. In a formal wine tasting, personal likes and dislikes should not enter into the evaluation of the wine.

Essay

1. Explain in your own words the process used to ferment and age wine.

2. Discuss the six categories of wine. Tell the attributes of each. Which are still and which are sparkling? Give some examples of wines which fit into more than one category.

3. Pick a grape, any grape, and tell where it is grown, what wine(s) it produces, what other grapes or wines it is blended with, and any other interesting facts associated with that grape.

4. There are over forty other countries, other than those covered in this chapter, that produce wine.

Pick one of those countries not covered and do some research in your library or on the web (using reliable sources). Tell what wines are produced there; whether they are exported to other countries, and if so, where; and any other interesting facts you can uncover.

5. Assume that you are a beverage manager of a fine dining restaurant and you are going to conduct a wine tasting with some of your customers. Tell what materials you would have to assemble prior to the tasting.

RESOURCES

Henderson, J. Patrick and Rex, Dellie, *About Wine*, 7th ed. (Albany, NY: Delmar Publishing, 2006).

Johnson, Hugh and Robinson, Jancis, *World Atlas of Wine*, 7th ed. (London: Mitchell Beazley Publishers Limited, 2007).

Robinson, Jancis, *The Oxford Companion to Wine*, 3rd ed. (Oxford, UK: Oxford University Press, 2006).

Schmid, Albert, *The Hospitality Manager's Guide to Wines, Beers, and Spirits*, 2nd ed. (Upper Saddle River, NJ: Pearson Education, 2008).

4
Spirits

OVERVIEW

Spirits are alcoholic beverages that are distilled. Keep in mind that all alcoholic beverages are fermented, but the distillation process takes it one step further in that the alcohol is separated from the fermented liquid. Yeast and fermentation can produce only so much alcohol. After this, distillation must occur to increase the alcohol content of a beverage. We will study the distillation process in detail in this chapter. Spirits are sometimes referred to as liquor, and these terms are often used in place of each other. Spirits include, but are not limited to, all whiskey, gin, vodka, rum, tequila, and brandyies.

Speaking of whiskey, let's set the record straight on its spelling. You have probably seen it spelled *whisky* as well as *whiskey*. Which one is correct? They both are. *Whisky* refers to Scotch and Canadian whisky, while *whiskey* refers to bourbon, Irish, rye, and Tennessee whiskey. There are a few exceptions, but for the most part these spellings hold true.

ALCOHOL CONTENT OF SPIRITS

Distilled spirits are the strongest of all alcoholic beverages in terms of alcohol content. Consider that beer and ale for the most part have 2.5–5 percent alcohol content by weight, while wine is 7–14 percent by volume, and distilled spirits are 35–75 percent by volume. One could question why you would not get inebriated quicker with distilled spirits than with beer or wine, and the answer is in the portions served. A bottle of beer is typically 12 ounces, a glass of wine is normally 5 ounces, while a mixed cocktail using a distilled spirit is typically around 1.5 ounces. A glass of wine would, therefore, be equal to a typical mixed drink using 80 proof liquor.

Speaking of **proof**, this is the term that is used to measure the alcohol content in distilled spirits. How the term *proof* became the standard for the alcohol content in distilled spirits is quite interesting. It seems that many distillers would water down their product and the consumer would have no way of knowing exactly what they were purchasing. An Englishman mixed gunpowder with a spirit and lit it. If there was enough alcohol to keep the fire lit, it was proof that it was considered a legal spirit.

Objectives

Upon completion of this chapter, the reader should be able to:

- Calculate the proof of distilled spirits.
- Discuss the methods of distillation and identify the types of stills.
- Differentiate between white and brown goods.
- Compare the various types of spirits, identify their major attributes, and describe how they are distilled and, if applicable, how they are aged.
- Determine what type of spirits to stock.

Key Terms

Bottled in Bond
Brown goods
Clear goods
Condenser
Congener
Distillation
Fermentation
Genever
Gin-head
Grist
Mash
Mash tun
Patent still
Pot still
Proof
Still
Wort

Gay Lussac	American	British/Canadian
100%	200 proof	175 proof
50%	100 proof	87.5 proof
45%	90 proof	79 proof
40%	80 proof	70 proof
35%	70 proof	61 proof

FIGURE 4.1
Comparison of the different methods of establishing proof.

If the flame burned a steady blue, it was considered to have 50 percent alcohol or 100 percent proof that it was legitimate. Thus the formula that "proof" is double the alcohol content of the spirit. Therefore if a spirit is labeled 80 proof, it is 40 percent alcohol. Most spirits are between 80 and 100 proof. An exception, which is quite popular, is 151 proof rum, which is often used in flambéing or tableside cooking. Because its alcoholic content is greater than 50 percent (which gives off a blue flame), it flares up in a dramatic fashion. Another exception is cordials, which are distilled spirits that are lower at 35–60 proof. Still another exception, which is not used in bars today for obvious reasons, is white lightening, which can be as high as 190 proof. It should be noted that 200 proof can only be achieved in laboratory conditions and would evaporate almost instantaneously.

The system just described is the American system, which is doubling the alcoholic volume to establish proof. There are two other methods used in other countries to measure the alcoholic content of spirits. The first is the Gay-Lussac method, which is the actual percentage of alcohol by volume. It is used in several European countries. The second is the British system, which is also used in Canada. It takes the Gay-Lussac figure, multiplies it by 7, and then divides it by 4. Figure 4.1 compares these different methods.

LABELING DISTILLED SPIRITS

All distilled spirits sold in interstate commerce in the United States must adhere to the regulations of the Alcohol and Tobacco Tax and Trade Bureau (TTB). This bureau oversees the manufacturing, distribution, and sales of alcoholic beverages in the United States. One of the areas regulated is the labeling of distilled spirits. The label of each bottle of spirits sold in interstate commerce must contain the following information:

- Brand name. This is used by the distiller or bottler to identify its company. The name cannot be misleading as to the age, identity, origin, or other characteristic of the distilled spirit.
- The name and address (normally just city and state) of the bottler.
- Alcohol content. This must be expressed in terms of alcohol content in percent by volume. The bottler can in addition, at its discretion, express this in proof.
- Health warning statement. Required on all alcoholic beverages containing 0.5 percent or more of alcohol by volume.
- Country of origin. Required on all imported distilled spirits.
- Net contents. Should be stated in metric units of measure. Distilled spirits must be bottled in sizes of 1.75 l, 1 l, 750 ml, 375 ml, 200 ml, 100 ml, or 50 ml.

- Classification. The label must contain a designation that accurately describes the product. The regulation includes the ingredients and method of production inherent in that classification. For example, gin must derive its flavor from juniper berries. (The characteristics of all classifications will be studied later in this chapter.)

Please refer to Figure 4.2 for an example of a distilled spirit label.

DISTILLATION PROCESS

We all know (or should know) that water boils at 212°F. In the process of boiling, the water turns into a vapor. Alcohol boils at 176°F and at that point, like water, it turns into a vapor. Because alcohol boils at a lower temperature than water, a fermented mixture can be heated to 176°F or higher (but lower than 212°F), and the alcohol in that mixture will vaporize, thus setting itself apart from the fermented liquid. This process is called **distillation**. It is how a fermented liquid can be made stronger with a higher alcohol content than other fermented liquids like beer or wine.

To distill a liquid, a piece of equipment called a **still** is used. Very basically, it is a vessel in which a fermented mixture is heated to between 176°F and 190°F. At this point, the alcohol in the mixture boils and the alcohol's vapor goes into a **condenser** where it is cooled, and as it cools it is condensed into a liquid state. Depending on the spirit, the vapor could pass through a **gin-head** during which the vapors pick up an infused flavor.

Types of Stills

There are two types of stills in use today, each of which will produce a different end product. The first is a **pot still** which, as its name implies, is a pot which is covered with a funnel device at the top. The vapors are captured at the top of the funnel and go into a pipe that carries them to the condenser, where they are condensed and become distilled spirits. Most distillers will use only the middle portion of the distillate. The first and last portions are returned to be redistilled.

The second type of still is called a **patent still** and is also known as a Coffey still, a column still, or a continuous still. This is the most common type of still used to produce commercial spirits. It is basically a very tall cylinder. The heat source for the patent still is normally steam, which is piped into the bottom of the cylinder with the pipes going to the top. Preheated wort or fermented liquid goes into the top of the cylinder and drops down. As it drops, it hits baffles and is heated until the alcohol vaporizes. As it continues through the process, it is redistilled. The baffles have different temperatures as various components are vaporized at different temperatures. This method of distillation can result in a product that is close to 190 proof and is a much purer product than that achieved in a pot still. The alcohol is drawn off and put into storage.

The other components that have been vaporized are drawn off. Some of them are sold as by-products. These include, but are not limited to, cattle feed, paint solvent, mulch, and others. The advantage of a patent still is that it is a continuously run operation. As product is drawn off, new fermented liquid is added and the process continues. Another advantage is that patent stills can produce more alcohol in a given period of time than a pot still.

Regardless of the type of still used, some spirits are distilled once, while others are distilled several times. Scotch, for example, is normally distilled twice and Irish whiskey three times.

FIGURE 4.2
An example of a distilled spirit label.
Clive Streeter © Dorling Kindersley

An example of a pot still.
mweber67/Fotolia

Congeners

Congeners are the substances that give a particular spirit its unique taste as well as its aroma. They are inherent in the ingredients that are used in the fermented liquid. As a rule, the more expensive a spirit, the fewer the congeners, as the distillation process will filter out a higher percentage of them. Another rule of thumb states that the darker the spirit the greater the number of congeners. Therefore, whiskey, brandy, and red wine have more congeners than do vodka, gin, and white wine. Some research has suggested that congeners are directly responsible for hangovers. It has also been suggested that the higher the level of congeners the greater likelihood of a hangover and the more severe the hangover.

Aging

Spirits can be broken down into two categories: **clear goods**, also known as white goods, and brown goods. All spirits when distilled are clear. As a general rule, white or clear goods are not aged and are stored in stainless steel or glass barrels prior to bottling. Examples of clear goods are vodka, gin, tequila, and some rums.

Brown goods on the other hand are stored and aged in oak barrels. The aging of brown goods does two things. One, it gives the spirit color, and two, it develops its flavor and aroma. Two types of oak are generally used, French and American, with French oak being subtler, while American oak gives stronger aromas.

Those spirits that go through the aging process undergo quite a change. First, because the wooden barrels are porous, there is a small amount of evaporation of water and alcohol. The amount of alcohol that evaporates from the barrel is known as "the angel's share." As the product evaporates, a small amount of oxygen enters the barrel. The oxygen interacts with the congeners in the spirit as well as additional congeners being picked up from the wood. The result being that these additional flavors are merged with the spirit, giving it its final taste and aroma. Generally speaking, aged spirits cost more than nonaged, and the longer a spirit is aged the higher the price. This is because of the cost of keeping the spirit in inventory as it ages. Examples of brown goods include Scotch whisky, Irish whiskey, Canadian whisky, some rums, and bourbon.

Bonding

When whiskey was first commercially produced in the United States, many distillers advertised and labeled their product as straight whiskey. As a matter of fact, very few of them were straight whiskey, and some of them were not even close to being considered whiskey at all. Rather, they were artificially flavored water, which was colored with tobacco or iodine. At this point, the federal government stepped in and passed the Bottled in Bond Act of 1897. There were two purposes to this law, with one being the assurance that the customer was purchasing "real" whiskey and the second ensuring that the government collected the excise tax due on the sale of the whiskey. To entice the distillers to go along with the law, the excise tax was not collected until the whiskey had aged.

Aging barrels.
wiangya/Fotolia

To be labeled **Bottled in Bond**, the whiskey must come from one distiller, must be distilled in one distillery, and must be the product of one distillation season. It must be aged for a minimum of four years in a bonded warehouse and be bottled at 100 proof.

The term *bottled in bond* does not guarantee the quality of product, only that it has met the criteria set out in the above statement. There are a few bottled in bond products on the market that are quite inferior to other products. However, the general public has come to believe that whiskey labeled as such is of better quality.

TYPES OF DISTILLED SPIRITS

As was previously mentioned, distilled spirits can be classified as clear or white goods and brown goods. Another method of differentiating spirits is by their ingredients or method of distillation. When grouped this way there are five types:

- Grain liquors. Examples include whisky, whiskey, and vodka.
- Plant liquors. Examples are rum and tequila.
- Fruit liquors. Brandies.
- Liqueurs. Cordials.
- Bitters. Aromatic or fruit.

Classification notwithstanding, the following is a description of the major spirits, in alphabetic order, in use in today's bars.

Aquavit

Aquavit is a product of Scandinavia and is primarily distilled from potatoes, similar to some vodkas. It is normally flavored with herbs, spices, and fruits. Some of the more common flavors are derived from caraway, anise, dill, cumin, or fennel. A more common name for aquavit is schnapps, particularly in the United States, with the most popular flavor being peppermint. Schnapps are discussed in further detail in the liqueur section. The name *aquavit* comes from the Latin *aqua vitae*, which means "water of life."

An interesting aquavit is Linie, which is shipped in wooden barrels over the equator twice before it is bottled and sold. Some claim that the motions of the vessel, the sea air, and the warm temperature improve its characteristics, while others dismiss it as an advertising ploy.

Bitters

Bitters is a spirit that is not consumed by itself but rather is used as an ingredient in cocktails such as an Old Fashioned. The ingredients used in making bitters are a highly protected secret among the few distillers that produce them. They can contain over 30 different components including bark, herbs, spices, roots, fruit, and berries, among others. One thing that is known is that their bitter taste comes from the fact that no sugar or sweetener is added.

One of the more popular brands of bitters is Angostura, made in Trinidad. Peychaud's is another popular brand that is from New Orleans. Vermouth and bitters are used in the same way, that is, as an ingredient in cocktails. Some people think that vermouth is a spirit, but it is actually a wine and is covered in the wine chapter.

Brandy

Brandy is basically a wine that has gone through a distillation process. The name *brandy* is a translation of the Dutch word *brandewijn*, which is burnt or boiled wine. It is believed to have originated in the Muslim countries around the Mediterranean Sea in the 7th century. It soon spread to other countries and in the 8th century into Europe and the British Isles by traveling missionary monks. While it is predominately made from grapes, it can be made from almost any fruit. There are three classifications of brandy:

- Grape brandy, which is distilled from fermented grape juice or crushed grape pulp and skin. It is aged in oak casks, which give it a mellow flavor and aroma as well as color.
- Fruit brandy is all of the brandies that are made from fermented fruit other than grapes.
- Fruit flavored brandy is a grape brandy that has been flavored with the extract of another fruit. In European countries, the word *flavored* is left off of the label. Fruit flavored brandies sold in the United States require that the word *flavored* be included on the label of grape flavored brandies.

Distillation   The distillation mechanism depends on the country. For example, almost all brandy distilled in the United States is distilled in column stills, while in Europe both the pot stills and column stills are used. While some brandies are distilled once, others are distilled twice. All cognac, for example, is distilled twice. Brandy is distilled to produce a lower alcohol content in order to preserve its unique flavor. As a result, it has a larger number of congeners.

Aging   Most brandies are aged in a wooden cask, usually oak, which gives them a rich amber color and smooth taste. Aging also adds additional flavor and aroma. The oak barrels of aging brandy are stored in warehouses or caves for temperature control. As they age, they pick up the characteristics of the oak, giving the brandy

A picture of a Linie aquavit bottle and label.

Frits Solvang © Dorling Kindersley

A picture of an Angostura bitters bottle.

David Murray © Dorling Kindersley

Three bottles of Russian brandy.
Jon Spaull © Dorling Kindersley

a musky flavor and at the same time giving it smoothness. While it is aging, some of the product evaporates through the pores in the wood, up to 2.5 percent a year. This is known as the angels' share. Some brandies that are aged over a long period can lose up to 25 percent of their original volume, which results in increasing the selling price.

A few brandies, pomace for one, are not aged in oak and are aged only for a very short time. Pomace has a fresh, grape aroma and flavor, which would be lost if it were aged in oak for a long period.

Types of Brandy   Unlike other spirits, brandy is dependent on the season. Since its main ingredient is grapes or fruit that cannot be dried and distilled later like grain, its production occurs soon after it is harvested. For the most part the types of brandy produced tend to be named after the area in which they were grown and distilled. Some of the more popular types of brandy and their characteristics are as follows.

Applejack   Applejack is an American brandy. It is produced from fermented apple cider. For the most part, it is distilled in a continuous still. Straight applejack that is bottled in bond is aged for four years and is bottled at 100 proof. Some applejack is a blended product and does not have the intense flavor of straight applejack. These products are aged for a minimum of two years and are bottled at 80 proof.

Armagnac   Armagnac is a grape brandy and is produced in the southwest corner of France in the province of Gascony. It dates back to the 15th century and is believed to be the oldest brandy produced in France. It is distilled in a column still called an alambic armagnacais. The finest Armagnac is aged in Monlezun oak casks; however, some of the lesser brands use other oak. While single vintage and single vineyard output can be found, the vast majority of Armagnac is blended. It is not unusual to have older vintages blended with younger vintages to achieve the desired flavor and aroma. Armagnac has a rustic and assertive character and aroma.

Calvados   Calvados is a fruit brandy made from apples. It comes from the Normandy region of France in the northern part of the country. There are three classifications of calvados:

- Calvados du Pays d'Auge is the finest of the three. It is distilled in a pot still two times and aged for a minimum of one year and many times much longer.
- Calvados is the middle classification and while not as exceptional as Calvados du Pays d'Auge, it is considered by most to be a highly regarded product. It is distilled in a continuous still at a lower temperature and is aged for two to three years.
- Eau-de-vie de cidre is the least of the three in terms of quality.

Cognac   Cognac is another grape brandy and comes from the central part of the west coast of France. It is the most widely known brandy in the world and is the standard by which all other brandies are compared. The grapes used to produce brandy are poor in quality and low in alcohol, which make them a poor choice for producing wine, but conversely they produce an excellent brandy. For the most part, cognac is produced in pot stills and is double distilled. After distillation, it is stored in casks made of new oak. Some cognacs are aged for a short term and some for a longer term. Those that are stored for a longer term are removed from the new barrels and stored in older seasoned casks.

Practically all cognacs are a blend. Local vineyards sell their harvest to cognac distillers who in turn sell their product to cognac blenders. Often these blends are from different vintages and different growing zones. Even cognacs from one vineyard or one distiller will be a blend from different casks. The reason behind blending is to give a consistent taste and flavor to a particular brand. The blending is more of an art than science, and blenders pass their knowledge and secrets down from generation to generation.

There are no age or quality requirements or laws regarding cognac. As a result, the industry has developed standards; however, no one is required to follow them. Figure 4.3 illustrates the industry standards.

Framboise   Framboise is a fruit brandy produced from raspberries. While it is produced in Germany and Switzerland, the finest framboise come from the Alsace region of France. It has a very dominant raspberry flavor but at the same time is quite delicate. The Swiss and German versions do not have the full flavor and presence of the French framboise.

Kirschwasser   Kirschwasser is also known as Kirsch in the United States. It is a fruit brandy that is made from cherries. It is distilled in France, Germany, and Switzerland,

E	Extra or Especial	S	Superior or Special
O	Old	V	Very
P	Pale	X	Extra or Extremely

Letters	Label	Rating	Minimum Age
VS	Very Superior	3 Star	5 years
XO	Extra Old	5 Star	6 years
VSOP	Very Superior Old Pale	4 Star	5 years

FIGURE 4.3
Cognac Lettering Standards

with the French variety being more subtle and lighter. It has a well-defined and strong flavor of cherry.

Marc   Marc is a grape brandy made in France and is distilled from the leftovers of winemaking. It is aged for a very short time and has a stark bite to it along with a full grape flavor. Italy produces a similar brandy called Grappa.

Ouzo   Ouzo is a famous Greek brandy. It contains anise and therefore has a licorice flavor to it.

Poire Williams   Aptly named, it is made from William pears (*poire*), which grow in Switzerland. William pears are very similar to Bartlett pears grown in the United States. While its aroma is definitely pear, its taste lacks a pear flavor. An interesting note is that often a young pear is placed in the empty bottle and continues to grow. When it reaches maturity, the bottle is filled with pear brandy.

Slivovitz   Slivovitz is a Balkan brandy. It is a fruit brandy made from yellow plums. France, Germany, and Switzerland make a plum brandy as well; however, the product from the Balkans is considered to be superior. It is aged for a long period of time, sometimes up to 12 years, and has an abundant plum flavor and aroma.

Bottles of Greek ouzo.
Rob Reichenfeld © Dorling Kindersley

Gin

Gin is a juniper berry–flavored distilled grain spirit. The word *gin* is taken from *genever*, the Dutch word for juniper. While gin had its originations in Holland, it was the English that made it famous. When the Dutch Protestant William of Orange and his English wife Mary became co-rulers of England, he imposed a tax on brandy, which was imported. At the same time, he encouraged the local production of spirits, such as gin, by abolishing the taxes and fees imposed on them. It did not take long for many households to become involved in the production of gin. Public drunkenness became a serious problem. Government controls were reimposed, and commercial distillers took over the production of gin, reducing the problem. By this time, however, gin was firmly entrenched as an English drink of preference.

The foundation of gin is primarily grain, normally wheat or rye, which results in a light-bodied spirit. Its primary flavor comes from the addition of the berries of a juniper bush, which is in the evergreen family. Most distillers add an assortment of other fruits, herbs, and spices such as anise, orange or lemon peel, caraway, coriander seeds, fennel, and almonds, among others. Gin makers add from four to fifteen of these ingredients to develop their own distinctive flavor.

It should be noted here that sloe gin is not gin but rather a liqueur made from wild plums called sloe berries. As such, it will be covered in the section on liqueur.

Distillation   Most gin is distilled in patent stills which produce a high-proof spirit that is light-bodied and clean with very few congeners. At this point in the distillation process, the procedure varies. Low-quality gin is made by mixing the base spirit with juniper extract as well as the extract of the additional ingredients. A higher quality gin, but one that is still mass produced, is made by soaking juniper berries and the additional ingredients in the base spirit and then redistilling the mixture. Top quality gin is flavored by hanging dried juniper berries with the other ingredients, which have

A martini with an olive garnish.

Clive Streeter © Dorling Kindersley

also been dried, in a chamber. As the gin goes through its last distillation, it passes through this chamber and picks up the flavors on its way to the condenser.

Classifications   There are basically two styles of gin, English and Dutch. While a Dutchman by the name of Dr. Franciscus de le Boe Sylvius is credited with inventing gin, it is the English version that is most popular today. While there are a few lesser selling gins, London Dry gin is the dominant English style. English gin is made in patent stills at 180 proof and diluted with distilled water to 90 proof.

Gin made in the United States is of the English variety with two methods being employed. One is using the distillation process much like the English and the other is by compounding, which is made by adding compound of juniper berries and other ingredients. Only the gin that is made by distillation is allowed to have *distilled* on the label. American Dry gins, often termed soft gins, for the most part are 80 proof which is lower than English gins and are considered to be not as flavorful as English gins. English gins are usually combined into mixed drinks.

The Dutch style of gin is often referred to as Holland or **Genever**. It is generally distilled in a pot still, as opposed to a patent still, from a malted grain mash similar to what is used for whisky. A few are aged in oak casks for one to three years giving them a straw color as well as a moderate sweetness. As a result, they have a fuller body than their English counterparts. Genevers tend to be lower proof than English gins in the 72–80 proof range. They are usually served chilled and neat (no ice). A small number are distilled directly from fermented juniper berries, creating a gin that is quite strong in flavor. Figure 4.4 shows some of the more popular brands of gin.

While there are a multitude of gin-based cocktails, probably the best known is the martini, a combination of 2 parts gin and 1 part dry vermouth. While the creation of the martini is disputed, it is generally believed to have been created at the Knickerbocker Hotel in New York City in the early 20th century. While the ratio of gin to vermouth started out at 2 to 1, it has been getting drier (less vermouth) ever since. Today many people prefer just a splash of vermouth.

Liqueurs and Cordials

Liqueur and *cordial* are synonymous; that is, they both mean the same thing. As *liqueur* is the more accepted name in the United States, we will use it in this section. However, keep in mind that if someone refers to it as a cordial, they are not incorrect.

A liqueur has its start as a distilled spirit. It could be Irish or Scotch whisky, rum, a neutral spirit, or any one of countless others. To this is added one or more of a myriad of other ingredients: spices, herbs, fruits, or flowers, to name a few. Some add

Some Popular Gin Brands

Barton London Extra Dry

Beefeater

Bengal

Bombay

Booth's London Dry

Broker's London Dry

Burnett's London Dry

Fleischmann's

Gordon's

House of Lords

McCormick

Old Mr. Boston

Seagram's Extra Dry

Tanqueray London Dry

FIGURE 4.4
Some popular gin brands.

AN INTERESTING ASIDE

Old Tom Gin has a fascinating story connected to the origination of its name. In what was a precursor to our present-day vending machines, English pubs in the 18th century would have a wooden replica of a black cat mounted on the outside wall in front of their pub, hence the name Old Tom. Customers on the outside would put a penny in the cat's mouth and the bartender on the inside of the pub would pour a shot of gin down a tube that went between the cat's paws and into the customer's mouth.

one flavor, some a few, and some add many flavors. There are several ways that these flavors are incorporated into the spirit, but three methods are predominant:

- Maceration. A method in which the flavorings are soaked in the spirit itself.
- Percolation. In this method, the spirit is poured over the flavorings, then pumped back up over the flavorings, and the process is repeated several times. If you think about the percolation method of brewing coffee, you have a good idea as to how this process works.
- Distillation. When the spirit is redistilled, the flavoring is added during the redistillation process.

Sugar—a lot of it—is then added in the form of corn syrup, maple syrup, or honey. Liqueur can be made up of anywhere from 2 to 35 percent sugar. It is what characterizes liqueur and differentiates it from the other spirits. Some liqueurs add color to improve their appearance and to merchandise them better. When this is done the additional coloring must be a natural vegetable coloring or a USDA-approved food dye.

Originally, liqueurs were used to start and end a meal. *Aperitifs* were developed to whet the appetite and were served prior to the start of the meal. *Digestifs* were developed to aide in the digestion of the meal and were served at the end. While some liqueurs are served this way in the United States, the vast majority of liqueurs are used, along with other ingredients, to make cocktails.

Before we go over some of the more popular types of liqueur, we must mention absinthe. It has a nerve-damaging ingredient and prior to its being regulated could cause convulsions and hallucinations. It has a very high alcohol content with most brands at over 60 percent. As a matter of fact, one shot of some brands of absinthe equal two shots of Scotch. Its flavor comes from wormwood, sweet fennel, and anise, and its color is green. It is referred to as *la fee verte*, French for the green fairy. Today it is highly regulated and was only made legal in the United States in 2007. Some experts claim absinthe is a spirit, while others claim it is a liqueur. Absinthe notwithstanding, here are some of the more common liqueurs on the market today. While the list may seem long, keep in mind that these are only a few of what is available. There are literally hundreds of liqueurs to be had. The listings are the common name for the liqueur, and when brand names are listed, they are so indicated.

- Amaretto. An almond flavored liqueur. 50–56 proof
- Anisette. A sweet liqueur made with anise as its primary herb along with several other herbs and fruit. 40–96 proof
- Aurum. An orange flavored Italian liqueur made from brandy. 80 proof
- Bailey's Irish Cream. A brand name for a liqueur with Irish whiskey as its base. 34 proof
- Benedictine. A brand name for a French herb-based liqueur made by the Benedictine monks. It is one of the most recognized names in liqueur. 86 proof
- B&B. A brand name for a cognac-based liqueur that is dark gold in color. 86 proof
- Blackberry. Can be sold as either a liqueur or cordial and made primarily from brandy. It has a blackberry (purplish red) color to it. 60 proof
- Chambord. A brand name for a cognac-based black raspberry liqueur. 33 proof
- Chartreuse. A brand name for a brandy-based liqueur made by monks since the 17th century. It has a flowery, fruit-and-honey flavor to it and is gold in color. 86 proof
- Cointreau. A brand name for a citrus flavored liqueur made from cognac. It is clear in color. 80 proof
- Crème de bananes. Made from a neutral spirit and has the flavor of ripe bananas. 50–60 proof

A bottle of Amaretto.
Joff Lee/Getty Images, Inc.

A bottle of Benedictine.
Steve Gorton © Dorling Kindersley

A glass of Kirsch.
© Christian Jung—Fotolia.com

- Crème de cacao. Has the flavor of chocolate with a vanilla twinge. It is made from a neutral spirit and is either clear or brown in color. 50–60 proof
- Crème de menthe. Made from a neutral spirit and is either clear or green in color. It is flavored heavily with mint. 60 proof
- Curacao. Made in Curacao and other Caribbean Islands, it is made from the peel of bitter oranges. Cointreau is a brand name for Curacao. 50–80 proof
- Drambuie. The brand name of a liqueur made from Scotch with the addition of honey. 70 proof
- Frangelico. A brand name of an Italian liqueur flavored with hazelnut. 40–80 proof
- Galliano. The brand name of an herb-based liqueur made in Italy. Its popularity increased with the introduction of the Harvey Wallbanger cocktail. 80 proof
- Glayva. A Scotch-based liqueur with the additional flavor of orange. 80 proof
- Goldwasser. Has an orange flavor with anise overtones. It is a clear liqueur with gold flecks, thus the name gold water (*wasser* being German for water). 60–80 proof
- Grand Marnier. A brand name for a cognac-based liqueur blended with Curacao and aged in oak barrels. 80 proof
- Kahlua. The brand name of a liqueur flavored with coffee and vanilla. It is made in Mexico and is often mixed with cream. 53 proof
- Kirsch liqueur. Made from kirschwasser brandy and is a cherry flavored liqueur. 90–100 proof
- Malibu. A coconut flavored liqueur. 56 proof
- Maraschino. Distilled from neutral spirits and has a cheery almond flavor. 50–100 proof
- Midori. A brand name liqueur from Japan with a melon flavor. 46 proof.
- Ouzo liqueur. Made from ouzo brandy, it is Greek in origin. It is a clear, thick liqueur. 90–100 proof

A bottle of sloe gin and a cocktail of sloe gin and sparkling water.

Peter Anderson © 'Dorling Kindersley

- Pastis. An absinthe. See the discussion on absinthe on the previous page. 90 proof
- Peach cordial. Also known as a liqueur, has a peach flavor (obviously), and is clear. 60-80 proof
- Pernod. A brand name for a liqueur that has an anise or licorice flavor to it. 90 proof
- Pimms. Made from London gin, it is an orange flavored liqueur. 50 proof
- Poire William liqueur. A clear liqueur made from Poire William brandy. It has a pear flavor. 60 proof
- Schnapps. A fruit or mint flavored liqueur in the United States. Among the more popular flavors are peach or peppermint. In Europe it has a dry herb flavor. (See the previous discussion on aquavits.) 40–60 proof
- Sloe gin. A plum flavored liqueur distilled from neutral spirits. Note that sloe gin is not a form of gin but a liqueur. 42–60 proof
- Southern Comfort. A brand name liqueur made from bourbon and flavored with peach. Many customers will order it in place of bourbon. 70 or 100 proof
- Tia Maria. A brand name for a coffee flavored liqueur made in Jamaica and often substituted for Kahlua. 53 proof
- Triple sec. Made from neutral spirits and flavored with orange peel. 60–80 proof
- Yukon Jack. A brand name liqueur made from Canadian whisky. 80 or 100 proof

Rum

The primary ingredient in rum is sugar or a sugar derivative. Like many of the other spirits, rum can be classified in several different ways: by the ingredients used, the method of distillation, the type and length of aging, blending, color, and point of origin.

Ingredients   Some rum producers use sugar or sugar cane syrup to produce their rum. These producers will use several different types of sugar to obtain the desired flavor, taste, and aroma. These rums contain a high level of floral and herbal aromas. Still other producers will use molasses. The molasses is extracted from the sugar cane juice by boiling the juice until crystals start to form and produce a thick liquid. The grade of molasses is dependent on how long they boil the juice and how much sugar they take out. Grade A is the best with the highest amount of fermentable sugar left, followed by grades B, C, D, and lastly black strap, which is the lowest quality. There is a direct relation in that the best rums are made with the highest grade of molasses, while lower quality and cheaper rums are made with lower quality molasses. A few distillers will use beet sugar to make their rum; however, it is illegal to use anything other than cane sugar in most countries. For the most part, if it says rum, it is made from cane sugar.

Distillation   Like several of the other spirits, rum is commercially distilled in either a pot still or a column still. The pot still produces a single distillate since it is processed through the still only once. Most distillers will process the rum a second time to give it a cleaner taste and to increase the alcohol content. Some of the better brands will distill a third and even a fourth time. As with other spirits, the amount of rum that can be produced is limited by the size of the pot. Remember that the pot must be cleaned after each batch, making this a very labor-intensive procedure.

Many of the rum producers have gone to the column still, which injects steam at the bottom of the still and the fermented liquid at the top. As the liquid drops down the column, the alcohol is vaporized and then condensed. Depending on the strength of alcohol desired, several columns can be employed with each one going into the next.

Most rum is distilled at 160 to 190 proof, then diluted and bottled at 80, 86, or 151 proof. The high alcohol content of 151 proof rum allows it to be ignited, thus its popularity with flambéing dishes such as beef tournedos, cherries jubilee, and bananas foster.

Aging   Rum can be aged in either stainless steel barrels, bottles, or oak barrels. Rum aged in stainless steel barrels or bottles is normally aged for a minimum of one year. There are those that would argue that rum aged in this method is not aged at all, as there is no flavor or aroma that is imparted into the product from stainless steel or glass. The age of a rum that is aged in an oak barrel refers to the amount of time the rum spends inside that barrel prior to bottling. If the rum is blended, the age printed on the label depends on the country in which it is bottled and sold. In the United States, the stated age has to be the age of youngest rum in the blend. On the other hand, in Europe, the label can display the age of the oldest rum in the blend.

Rum being distilled in Barbados in a pot still.
Nigel Hicks © Dorling Kindersley

Some warehouses will refill their barrels as evaporation reduces the amount of rum in the barrel. Others do not, which results in a stronger, more pungent rum. Some countries have outlawed refilling. Keep in mind that age is not a gauge of quality.

Rum being aged in oak barrels.

Nigel Hicks © Dorling Kindersley

Blending   Most rums are blended after aging to attain a particular taste, aroma, color, or body. This usually takes place in a large vat. Individual barrels are selected based on their characteristics and are mixed together to ensure a consistent product. Rum from both pot stills and column stills is often used to achieve the desired result.

Another method, used by a few distillers, is the solera method. In this method, barrels are placed in a row and stacked four or five high. Each row contains rum of a different age with the youngest rum on the top row and the oldest on the bottom row. When the rum on the bottom row is ready to be bottled, approximately one third of it is drawn off. The barrels in the bottom row are then filled up with rum from the row above it and so on. The top row is then replenished with "young" rum. As it progresses down, it picks up the flavor of the older rums with the end result being a consistent product. Chapter 3 (page 57) shows a picture of the solera method.

Not all rum is blended. When it comes from one barrel, it is known as single barrel rum. In this case, the label on the bottle will identify from which barrel that particular rum came. Because barrels vary due to many circumstances, these brands will not be consistent from bottle to bottle.

Color   One of the methods used to classify rum is by color. There are three classifications: white, amber, and dark.

- White. The white classification has several other names associated with it: silver, clear, crystal, blanco, and plata. While these rums are the lightest in color, they have the highest alcohol content. They are the cheapest to produce as they are aged for only a year or so, which probably accounts for the fact that they are the best sellers. They are aged for the most part in stainless steel barrels which account for their light color.
  - Amber. Also known as gold or oro. The color of this rum comes from being aged at least three years in oak barrels. These rums have more flavor than white rums and tend to be mellower as well. Some ambers are colored with caramel or molasses. When properly aged, the aroma and taste of the rum should have a hint of oak.
  - Dark. If made properly, this is aged for six or more years. Like amber, some distillers add adjuncts and coloring to short circuit the process. When properly done, the dark rum will have a rich golden color with a full-bodied flavor. The alcohol content is normally lower than an amber or white rum.

Origin   Rum is made worldwide wherever sugar cane is grown. Rums distilled in different areas have different properties. We will explore some of the more popular rum-producing countries and the characteristics of their product.

- Cuba. A clear, light rum whose flavor comes from blending various batches and also from proper aging.
- French. Rum made in French-speaking countries is spelled _ruhm_. For the most part, they are distilled in pot stills and use only sugar cane juice as opposed to molasses. They contain a sizeable amount of congeners.

The main factory of the Bacardi rum distillery, San Juan, Puerto Rico.

Tim Draper © Rough Guides / Dorling Kindersley

AN INTERESTING ASIDE

In 1731 an admiral in the British Royal Navy authorized each of his sailors to be provided with a half a pint of rum a day. This was done to keep up the morale of the sailors and to quell any ideas of a mutiny. After all, the work of a sailor was quite hard and the pay was quite low. Later that year, the British Navy picked up on the idea, and it was authorized for the entire navy.

The navy developed a recipe which was based on Jamaican rum but included rum from Barbados and Guyana as well. As a result, it was a heavy, full-flavored, dark, pungent rum. This tradition lasted for well over 200 years into the 20th century when on July 31, 1970, the British Navy discontinued the practice and the day became known to the sailors as Black Tot Day. Many of them were so upset with this action that they chose to retire on that day rather than continue their service without this great tradition.

Some Popular Brands of Rum

10 Cane Rum
Admiral Nelson's Premium Spiced Rum
Angostura Old Oak White
Bacardi
Barton
Bundaberg
Captain Morgan
Castillo White
Fernandes White
Gosling Brothers
Mount Gay
Myers
New Orleans Rum
Old Mr. Boston
Ron Rico
Tommy Bahama White Sand

FIGURE 4.5
Some popular brands of rum.

- Jamaica. A heavy-bodied rum with a pungent taste, loaded with congeners giving it a rich flavor.
- Puerto Rico. A light rum very similar to a Cuban rum.
- Spain. Spanish-style rums have a fruity flavor and are considered to be almost brandy-like. Most are produced in pot stills.
- United States. There are two types of rum distilled in the United States. One is a heavy-bodied rum similar to the ones produced in Jamaica and the second is a lighter medium-bodied rum.

In addition to these countries, rum is also produced in the Dominican Republic, Haiti, Venezuela, Mexico, the Philippines, and British Guiana. Refer to Figure 4.5 for some of the more popular brands of rum.

Tequila

An early form of tequila was used in religious rituals by the Aztecs some 2000 years ago.

It evolved over the years, and in 1656, the town of Tequila was formed and soon thereafter tequila, as we know it today, was distilled. After the Mexican-American-War, tequila found its way into the United States, and after World War II it became a staple spirit.

Ingredients Tequila is a spirit that is distilled from the blue agave plant. The agave plant is grown in the desert, and while there are many varieties of the plant only the blue agave is used in making tequila. The center part of the plant, called a *pina*, contains sugar, which is what is used in the distillation process. The blue agave is a slow-growing plant, taking almost 10 years to reach maturity. It is quite large, weighing anywhere from 50 to 200 pounds, and is harvested by hand.

Distillation The pina is quartered and baked at a very low temperature in a steam oven until the starch is converted to a sugar, when it is then crushed into a juice and fermented.

It is then distilled in a pot still until it reaches 110 proof. After distillation, tequila is a clear liquid that contains a large amount of congeners, which gives it a strong flavor with an intense kick. Most often the distillers will distill the tequila a second time, which results in a cleaner liquid that is significantly blander than the single distillate. Most tequila is bottled at 38–40 proof, but it can get as high as 50 proof.

An agave plant.
James Young © Dorling Kindersley

Tequila distillation process.
Francesca Yorke © Dorling
Kindersley

Blending   Expensive tequila is 100 percent agave. Mexican law requires these tequilas, known as *tequila puros* (pure tequila), to be produced in Mexico under strict regulations. Because of these regulations, very few distillers produce 100 percent agave tequila, driving the price even higher.

Most tequila is blended with sugar and water during the distillation process. This tequila is called *mixtos* (mixed) and must be at least 51 percent agave. Mixtos can be distilled in countries other than Mexico.

Aging   Most tequila is not aged. When it is aged, it is from two to four years, sometimes in oak barrels, which give it a rich gold color. The buyer should beware, however, as some distillers add caramel coloring to unaged tequila giving it an aged appearance.

Types of Tequila   There are four types of tequila. They are as follows:

A bottle of Cuervo Gold
Especial Tequila.
Neil Mersh © Dorling Kindersley

- Silver. Also known as clear, white, or *blanco* (Spanish for white). Silver tequila can be either puro (100 percent agave) or mixto. Some of them are aged for less than sixty days, but most are not aged at all. Some prefer this type of tequila as it does not pick up the flavor of barrel aging and gives a true agave taste. However, most of it is used in mixed drinks.
- Gold. Unaged tequila, also known as *joven* (young). It has caramel added to it for flavor and color and is a mixto. It is used in mixed drinks and is popular in margaritas. It is a top seller in the United States.
- *Resposado* (rested). Must be aged for 2–11 months by law with the higher quality brands being aged for 3–9 months. It can be either puro or mixto and has a robust flavor. It is the most popular type of tequila in Mexico and is excellent for sipping.
- *Anejo* (aged). This tequila is aged in white oak barrels and often uses old bourbon barrels for additional flavor. It must be aged for a minimum of one year; however, most mixtos are aged for eighteen months to three years, while puros are aged up to four years. Most aficionados will argue that aging over four years destroys the flavor. It is also a sipping tequila and should be served in a brandy snifter to allow the aroma to escape.

Figure 4.6 shows some of the popular brands of tequila.

Tequila Blanco (Silver)	Tequila Añejo
• El Jimador Blanco	• 1800 Añejo
• Jose Cuervo Clasico Silver	• Amate Añejo
• Juarez Silver	• Don Agustin Añejo
• Margaritaville White	• Jose Cuervo Black Medallion
• Puerto Vallarta Blanco	• Puerto Vallarta Añejo
• Sauza Silver	• Sauza Conmemorativo Añejo
• Tarantula Plata	• Sauza Tres Generaciones Añejo
• Cazadores Blanco	• Cabo Wabo Añejo
• Corazon Blanco	• Chinaco Añejo
• Corralejo Blanco	• Don Eduardo Añejo
• Dos Manos Blanco	• Mi Tierra Añejo
• Herradura Blanco	• Patron Añejo
• Milagro Silver	• Cuervo La Reserva
• Sauza Tres Generaciones Plata	

Tequila Reposado	Tequila Joven (Gold)
• 1800 Reposado	• Antano Gold
• Calende Reposado	• Jose Cuervo Especial Gold
• Dos Manos Reposado	• Margaritaville Gold
• El Ultimo Agave Reposado	• Montezuma Gold
• Real Hacienda Reposado	• Olmeca Gold
• Sauza Hacienda Reposado	• Pepe Lopez Gold
• Sauza 100 Anos Reposado	• Sauza Extra Gold
• Tarantula Reposado	• Two Fingers Gold
• Tevado Reposado	• Herradura Gold Reposado
• Tequila 30-30 Especial Reposado	• Zafarrancho Gold
• Cuervo Tradicional Reposado	• Chinaco Reposado Artisan Gold
• El Tesoro Reposado	• Los Azulejos Gold
• Herradura Reposado	
• Oro Azul Reposado	
• Mapilli Reposado	

FIGURE 4.6
Some Popular Brands of Tequila

Mescal   Mescal is very similar to tequila in that is made from the agave plant. While tequila uses only the blue agave, mescal can be made from one of several agave plants, with the green agave being the most popular. Another difference is that mescal is usually distilled once, while tequila is distilled twice. Probably the most distinguishing characteristic is the worm in the bottle. Tequila does not have a worm, while many mescals do. The worm is the larva of a moth that lives on the agave plant and is completely safe to consume and quite tasty (so they say). Figure 4.7 shows some of the popular brands of mescal.

Vodka

Although vodka became popular in the United States in the 1950s, it has been around for much longer than that. It was known to be prevalent in the 1400s in Poland, and

A bottle of mescal.
Andrew McRobb © Dorling Kindersley

- Gusano Rojo
- Hacienda de Chihuahua Plata
- Monte Alban
- Zacatecano Reposado
- Embajador Silver
- Hacienda de Chihuahua Añejo
- Scorpion Añejo
- Talapa Reposado
- Embajador 5 year
- Del Maguey
- Del Maguey Pechuga
- Scorpion Añejo 7 year

FIGURE 4.7
Some popular brands of mescal.

A bottle of Passover plum vodka.
© maglara—Fotolia.com

Some Popular Brands of Vodka

Luksusowa
Olifant
Seagrams
Smirnoff
Svedka
101 Vodka
Absolut
Blue Ice
Finlandia
Reyka
Skyy
Stolichnaya
Tanqueray
360 Vodka
Charbay
Christiania
Emperor Vodka
Grey Goose
Stoli

FIGURE 4.8
Some popular brands of vodka.

there is speculation that it was here long before that. It is believed to have originated in an area consisting of Poland, Belarus, Ukraine, and western Russia.

Ingredients   Vodka has a neutral taste, that is to say, it has no taste at all. Therefore it can be made from any plant that is rich in starch or sugar. Some of the more popular plants used today are sorghum, corn, rye, or wheat. Additionally some vodka is made from potatoes, molasses, soybeans, or grapes. While pure vodka has a neutral taste, some vodkas are flavored with fruit, herbs, or other flavorings.

Distillation   Vodka today is produced virtually everywhere in the world. Even so, there are some common attributes to its production. In order to get it to a neutral taste, it is filtered several times. The filtering begins in the distillation process. Most vodka is produced in column stills, and as it goes through the distillation process it is filtered. Some are distilled once, while some are distilled three or four times.

After distillation, it is filtered again, most often through a charcoal filter until all congeners, taste, and impurities are eliminated. Other methods of filtering include using sand or ground seashells. One distiller is said to use diamond dust. A more modern method is to spin the distilled spirit in a centrifuge, separating the spirit and its impurities. The method notwithstanding, the only thing left in the vodka should be pure water and pure alcohol.

Vodka is distilled at 190 proof and bottled at 80–110 proof. Vodka is not aged.

Types of Vodka   There are two types of vodka; unflavored and flavored. The unflavored adheres to the United States Government's Standards of Identity as "a neutral spirit … without a distinctive character, aroma, taste, or color." One of the reasons for the great success of vodka is the fact that because it is neutral, it can be combined with practically any mix to produce a cocktail. The popularity of Bloody Marys and screwdrivers, among others, attest to its mixability. Figure 4.8 shows some of the more popular brands of vodka. While the majority of vodka sales are unflavored, the flavored vodkas are coming on strong.

Since the attraction of vodka is its neutral taste, why would one want to flavor it? The answer is probably to cover the intense harshness of the spirit. Flavored vodka can come in a multitude of fruit flavors: citrus, strawberry, raspberry, and peach. Other flavors include pepper, vanilla, coffee, and cinnamon, among others.

Whiskey

Whiskey, whisky, and brandy are collectively known as brown goods due to their color. This is as opposed to white or clear goods such as vodka, gin, tequila, and others. As we discuss whiskey in general, we will use the *whiskey* spelling. Keep in mind however, that the discussion also applies to whisky.

A misconception of whiskey is that it is more potent than other spirits because of its rich color and hearty taste. This is not true as its proof is consistent with the clear goods.

Each category of whiskey has its own distinct flavor and taste. A person who likes one whiskey will not necessarily like another. For example a Scotch drinker may not like bourbon and versa visa. The differences between whiskeys notwithstanding, including the spelling, there are some commonalities among all of them. While it may be an oversimplification, whiskey is not much more than distilled and aged beer.

Whiskey starts with a grain. While barley and corn are most often used, wheat and rye are used as well, and often these grains are combined. Next, the grain must be converted into a sugar. To accomplish this, malt is added to the grain. As in the beer brewing process, barley is used to create the malt via an enzyme know as diastase. The malt and grains are combined with hot water to create a mixture called **mash**. The mash liquid is then combined with yeast that causes **fermentation**. After fermentation, the product is distilled.

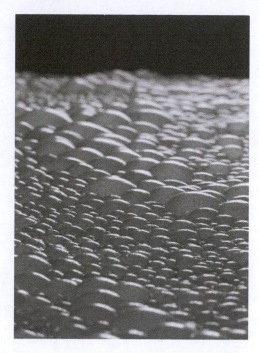

Mash fermenting after the addition of yeast.

Ian O'Leary © Dorling Kindersley

Two types of stills are used to distill whiskey, the smaller pot still and the larger continuous or column still. The type of still has an impact on the flavor and aroma of the final product in that the pot stills produce a more concentrated flavor and the column stills a more subtle product.

After distillation, the product is aged for a minimum of two years and often much longer. The aging takes place in wooden barrels most often made of oak. Frequently the barrels have been previously used to age other products such as wine, sherry, or bourbon. The type of oak tree, the origin of the tree, and its previous use (if any) all have a direct bearing on the flavor, taste, and aroma of the final product. Distillers are very particular about the barrels that age their product. As a matter of fact, they may use one type of barrel for the initial aging and another type to finish the aging process.

Whiskey can be categorized as either straight or blended. If it is straight, it must contain a minimum of 51 percent of a single grain distillate. Straight whiskeys are bottled immediately after aging. Blended whiskeys go through one more step in that two or more batches, ages, or still outputs are combined. This is a very exacting science and art and is carried out by master blenders known as noses. They blend by smell rather than taste and combine various outputs until the exact flavor and aroma are achieved. Many of the straight whiskeys have the distiller's name on the bottle while blends always are a brand name. Since many of your customers will order a particular brand based on its taste, it is easy to appreciate the value of a good blender who will ensure that it tastes the same time after time.

There are several different types of whiskey: bourbon, Canadian, Irish, rye, Scotch, and Tennessee whiskey. We will now examine their individual characteristics.

Bourbon While many religions around the world have an aversion to liquor, it may seem odd that the creation of bourbon is credited to a Baptist minister by the name of Elijah Craig in Bourbon County, Kentucky, circa 1789. By federal law,

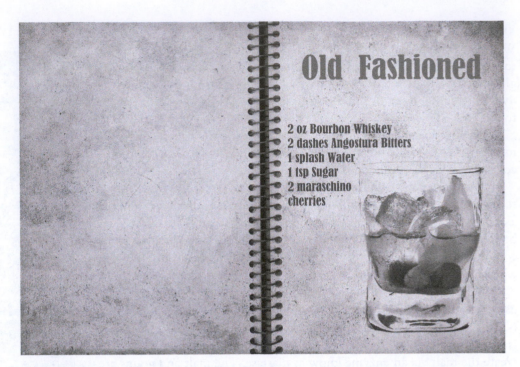

A recipe for an Old Fashioned.
Boyan Dimitrov/Fotolia

- Bourbon must be made in the United States and can be made in any state. Currently bourbon is distilled in Kentucky, Illinois, Indiana, Missouri, Ohio, Pennsylvania, and Tennessee.
- The only state that can be listed on the bottle label is that made in Kentucky.
- Bourbon must be a made from a mash that contains a minimum of 51 percent corn. Most distillers exceed this amount, some as high as 80 percent. In addition to corn, rice, rye, and wheat are also used.
- The distillation of bourbon should not exceed 160 proof.
- The only thing that can be added is water.
- Bourbon must be put into charred white oak barrels at 125 proof and aged for a minimum of two years. It should be noted that most bourbons are aged from four to six years.

Barley malt is added to the grains, and it is ground into a mash, fermented, and distilled. Most distillers use a continuous or column still. The aging of bourbon in the charred barrels add to its corn favor and also colors it, although some distillers add additional color. Bourbon can be bottled in one of three ways: straight, in which the bourbon is from one distillation; blended straight bourbon; or blended straight bourbon with grain neutral spirits added. Bourbon is bottled at anywhere from 80 to 110 proof. For some of the more popular brands of bourbon refer to Figure 4.9.

Canadian   No one grain can compose more than 49 percent of a mash according to Canadian law. However, the predominant grain in most Canadian whisky is corn, with rye, wheat, and barley malt, or some variation thereof, making up the difference. It is distilled in a Coffey still, which allows it to have a lighter taste and body. It is distilled at 140–185 proof. Canadian is aged for a minimum of three years in oak barrels; however, most distillers age it for six or more years. It is a mild and delicate whisky. See Figure 4.10 for some of the brands of Canadian.

Corn   Corn whiskey, as its name implies, must be made from a minimum of 80 percent corn. It is light in color as its oak casks are not charred. It is distilled using a

---

Some Popular Brands of Bourbon

Ancient Age
Bakers
Benchmark
Blanton's Single Barrel
Buffalo Trace
Eagle Rare
Early Times
Four Rose's Single
    Barrel
Jefferson's Reserve
Jim Beam
Knob Creek
Makers Mark
Ten High
Wild Turkey 101
Willet 28 Year

FIGURE 4.9
Some popular brands of bourbon.

***Some Popular Brands
of Canadian***

Canadian Club

Canadian Mist

Crown Royal

Black Velvet

Forty Creek Barrel

J.P. Wiser's Red Letter

Mountain Rock

Pendelton

Seagrams VO

Windsor Canadian

Wisers Deluxe

FIGURE 4.10
Some popular brands of
Canadian.

***Some Popular Brands
of Corn Whiskey***

Buffalo Trace White
Dog Mash #1

Copper Run Distillery

George Moon Corn
Whiskey

Roughstock Seet Corn
Whiskey

Ole Smoky Distillery

FIGURE 4.11
Some popular brands of
corn whiskey.

Bottles of Irish whiskey.
Steve Gorton © Dorling Kindersley

continuous or column still and goes into the cask at a minimum of 125 proof. As would be expected from a whiskey containing 80 percent corn, it has a definite corn flavor to it. Refer to Figure 4.11 for some of the popular brands of corn whiskey.

Irish   Irish whiskey and Scotch whisky are distilled in much the same manner with similar outcomes. As Scotch is the more predominant of the two beverages in the United States, we will discuss the distillation process in more detail in the section on Scotch later in the chapter. That said, however, there are some differences. Unlike Scotch, Irish whiskey is hardly ever made from a single malt, but rather from several grains. These include corn, oats, rye, and wheat.

Another major difference is that the barley, which is smoked for Scotch, is rarely smoked for Irish, giving it less of a harsh, peaty flavor. It is triple distilled and aged in barrels that have previously been used for bourbon or sherry. It must be aged for a minimum of three years but is normally aged much longer, for five to eight years.

For the most part Irish is a blended whiskey, which makes it lighter. Such whiskey must be labeled *Blended Irish Whiskey* or *Irish Whiskey—a Blend*. There are two separate governments in Ireland; Northern Ireland and the Republic of Ireland. Irish whiskey is produced in both of these jurisdictions, and the laws governing distillation are very similar in each. Figure 4.12 shows some of the brands of Irish whiskey.

Rye   During the Revolutionary War, and for quite a while after, rye was the predominant whiskey. As our agrarian society progressed and other grains became plentiful, it was replaced in popularity by other spirits. Rye whiskey contains a minimum of 51 percent rye, although most distillers use more. Corn is the preferred grain that makes up the balance. In a few rare instances, distillers will use 100 percent rye. United States law requires it to be aged for a minimum of two years, but most distillers age it for four or more years in new, charred, white oak barrels. It has the taste of a full bourbon, with a caraway seed overtone. It is normally bottled at 80–110 proof. For a list of some of the more popular brands of rye whiskey refer to Figure 4.13.

Scotch   While the history of Scotch is unknown, it is believed that it was first distilled in pot stills built by Christian monks. They used barley grown on the local farms, peat from the ground, and the pure sparkling water from the local streams and rivers. As time progressed, the local farmers took up the trade and the practice spread throughout the

***Some Popular Brands
of Irish Whiskey***

Bushmill

Black Bush

Clontarf Single Malt

Feckin

Finian's

Greenore

The Irishman The
Original Clan

Jameson

Kilbeggan

Merry's

Michael Collins

Middleton

Power and Son

Tullamore Dew

Tryconnell

FIGURE 4.12
Some popular brands of
Irish whiskey.

FIGURE 4.13
Some popular brands of rye whiskey.

Slabs of peat air drying at the Bruichladdich Distillery, Scotland.
Ian O'Leary © Dorling Kindersley

A bottle of Glenlivit, a single malt Scotch.
Steve Gorton © Dorling Kindersley

country. In Scotland, peat is collected from the ground, and in years past, Scots used it for fuel to heat their cottages. It is made up of decayed vegetable matter which has hardened and could be compared to a very soft coal that gives off a great deal of very pungent smoke.

Scotch is a whisky that is made from malted barley that has been smoked and dried over peat. It is this smoke that give Scotch its distinctive flavor and aroma. There are two types of Scotch: single malt and blended. Single malt consists of 100 percent smoked barley and water and comes from a single distillery. Blended Scotch on the other hand has several subcategories;

- Blended Scotch. A blend of one or more single malts with one or more single grain Scotch whiskys.
- Blended malt Scotch. A blend of single malts that come from different distilleries.
- Blended grain Scotch. A blend of single grain whiskies that have come from more than one distillery.

The only components in a blended Scotch are single malts and grain Scotch. No other distillates can be used. The more malt used in a blended Scotch, the heavier its flavor. Even with additional malt, blended Scotch is lighter than single malt and because of this has a higher degree of sales in the United States.

Because blended Scotch is sold by a brand name, it must be consistent each and every time a customer buys it. This is not easy to achieve as each batch of whisky is different, due to grains not being consistent, climates being different year after year, and water conditions changing. As a matter of fact, blenders will use as many as forty to fifty different Scotches to achieve a consistent product. Some Scotches are bottled at 80 proof while most are bottled at 86 proof.

Single malts on the other hand, coming from a single distiller, will not have this degree of consistency. This does not bother the single malt drinker. Real aficionados will discuss different batches (as well as different distillers) much like wine connoisseurs will discuss different vintage years.

For the most part, grain Scotch is distilled in the Scottish lowlands. Single malts are distilled in different areas of Scotland, primarily in the Highlands. While each area

The Glenfiddich distillery, Scotland.
Alex Havret © Dorling Kindersley

has its own distinct differences, each distiller, due to different distillation methods, has its differences as well. The areas are as follows:

- Orkney Isles. A robust and balanced Scotch that is full of smoke flavor.
- Campbelltown. Similar to Highland, but with a distinct peat flavor.
- Isle of Islay, Being by the ocean, it has a somewhat salty flavor and has a high degree of peat in a full-bodied Scotch.
- Speyside. Scotch from the Spey River valley has sherry overtones and is milder, more like a lowland Scotch than the others.

Scotland's harsh, cool, and wet climate makes it ideal for growing barley. Because barley is so important to the flavor of Scotch, its selection is essential to producing a good product. After harvesting, the barley is put in warm water where it sprouts. It is in the process of sprouting that the malt flavor is developed. The sprouts are then placed over burning peat until they are dried. This smoky, malty essence is the basis for Scotch's taste and aroma.

After the sprouts have been dried, they are then ground. The ground barley sprouts are called **grist**. You may be familiar with this term, as it is used when wheat is ground into flour. The ground barley is then mixed with warm water in a tank called a **mash tun**. After the starch turns into maltose, the liquid, which is referred to as **wort**, is drawn off and is fermented. The solids remaining behind are sold to farmers for cattle feed. (Is it any wonder that Scotland raises such excellent Black Angus beef?) After fermentation, the wort is distilled. Malt Scotch is distilled twice in pot stills while grain Scotch is distilled once in a patent or column still.

Whether a Scotch is straight single malt or blended, by law it must be aged in a used white oak bourbon barrel or a used sherry barrel for a minimum of three years. That said, most distillers and blenders choose to age it longer. Most blends are aged for five or six years while many single malts are aged for eight years or longer. For a list of some of the brands of single malt and blended Scotch whisky, refer to Figure 4.14.

Tennessee Whiskey Tennessee whiskey is very similar to bourbon. This stands to reason as bourbon was first distilled in Kentucky and the two states adjoin each other. As a matter of fact, the same principles that apply to bourbon apply to Tennessee whiskey. (See the discussion on bourbon above.) The most notable exception is the fact that the distillate is filtered through a maple charcoal prior to being placed in barrels. This

Some Popular Single Malt Scotch Brands	Some Popular Scotch Blends
Balvenie	Ballantine'
Corryvreckan	Bell's Special Reserve
Cragganmore	Black & White
Dalmore	Black Bottle
Glenfiddich	Chivas Regal
Glengoyne	Cutty Sark
Glenlivet	Dewar's
Glenmorangie	Famous Grouse
Laphroaig	Grant's
Macallan	J & B
Oban	Johnnie Walker
Talisker	Teacher's

FIGURE 4.14
Popular brands of single malt Scotch and blended Scotch.

Some Popular Brands of Tennessee Whiskey
Jack Daniels
George Dickel
Collier and McKee
Benjamin Prichard's Tennessee Whiskey

FIGURE 4.15
Some popular brands of Tennessee whiskey.

process adds a slight maple flavor and removes some of the abrasiveness found in bourbon. Figure 4.15 shows some of the brands of Tennessee whiskey

WHAT TO BUY?

That is a good question, and the answer is, it depends. Certainly with spirits costing a great deal of money, you do not want a lot of cash tied up in inventory, particularly if the inventory is not turning over at a fairly good rate. One guideline would be your business model and who you are trying to attract as a customer. If you are trying to attract an upper level clientele, you would want to stock premium brands. If on the other hand you are managing a neighborhood bar, well spirits and a few call spirits would suffice. Let your customer dictate what to stock. By all means, do not try to be all things to all people and stock brands that will never sell and will sit on the shelf gathering dust. Most point-of-sale programs will give usage figures on the inventory. If it is not selling, get rid of it.

AN INTERESTING ASIDE

One of the more popular Tennessee whiskeys is Jack Daniels. which is distilled in Lynchburg, Tennessee. Lynchburg is a small town of less than 400 souls and is completely dry and has been since Prohibition. It is one of the few producers of alcoholic beverages that does not (or cannot) sample its product. In the mid-1990s, the city fathers loosened the law just a little bit and allowed Jack Daniels to sell commemorative bottles in its store, but with no tasting it on site.

CONCLUSION

You now have a glimpse into the fascinating world of spirits: their history, how they are made, and some of the particular distinctions of each. Spirit aficionados are much like wine enthusiasts; they will debate the merits and nuances of their favorite spirit ad infinitum. In a later chapter, we will go into some detail on how spirits are used in the making of some of the more popular cocktails. As a beverage manager, it behooves you to look more deeply into this subject as it is a major segment of your business.

QUESTIONS

True/False

1. Using the American system of establishing the proof of alcoholic beverages, the stated proof is double the alcohol content of the beverage.
2. Spirits for the most part are distilled once.
3. As a general rule white and clear spirits are aged for a minimum of three years.
4. As a rule of thumb, the longer a spirit is aged, the higher its price.
5. Bitters are oftentimes consumed alone, either as a straight shot or on the rocks.
6. Tequila is named after the town of Tequila, Mexico.
7. Contrary to popular opinion vodka is not, for the most part, made from potatoes.
8. By law, in order to be called bourbon, it must be distilled in Kentucky.
9. Corn is the predominant grain in most Canadian whisky.
10. During the Revolutionary War, rye was the predominate whiskey in the United States.

Multiple Choice

1. All alcoholic beverages are
   1) fermented.
   2) distilled.
   A. (1) only
   B. (2) only
   C. Both (1) and (2)
   D. Neither (1) nor (2)
2. A patent still goes by several different names. Which of the following names is *not* a synonym for a patent still?
   A. Continuous still
   B. Pot still
   C. Column still
   D. Coffey still
3. Which of the following statements is *not* true of congeners?
   A. The darker the spirit, the more congeners it contains.
   B. The more congeners in a spirit, the greater the hangover.
   C. The more expensive the spirit, the more congeners it contains.
   D. Congeners give a spirit its unique flavor and aroma.
4. The Bottled in Bond Act of 1897 states that whiskey that is labeled "Bottled in Bond"
   A. must come from one distiller, be distilled in one distillery, and be the product of one distillation season.
   B. must be aged for a minimum of four years in a bonded warehouse.
   C. be bottled at 100 proof.
   D. is the consumer's guarantee of product quality.
5. The primary flavor of gin comes from
   A. the agave plant.
   B. peat.
   C. the juniper berry.
   D. fermented apples.
6. In most countries it is illegal to produce rum from
   A. cane sugar.
   B. grade D molasses.
   C. dark molasses.
   D. beet sugar.
7. The difference between tequila and mescal is that
   1) mescal is made from one of several agave plants rather than solely from the green agave.
   2) mescal has a worm in the bottle.
   A. (1) only
   B. (2) only
   C. Both (1) and (2)
   D. Neither (1) nor (2)
8. Which is (are) the correct spelling(s)?
   1) *Whiskey* for Scotch and bourbon
   2) *Whisky* for Canadian
   A. (1) only
   B. (2) only
   C. Both (1) and (2)
   D. Neither (1) nor (2)

9. Which of the following is not true of Irish whiskey?
    A. The barley for Irish is smoked over peat.
    B. Irish is rarely made from a single malt.

C. Irish is triple distilled.
D. Irish is normally aged for five to eight years.

Essay

1. Discuss the labeling requirements for spirits as established by the Alcohol and Tobacco Tax and Trade Bureau.
2. Discuss how brandy is different from other spirits. Include in your discussion its distillation process and aging. Pick four different brandies, research them on the web or in your library, and write a paragraph on each.

3. Pick five liqueurs and research them. Tell what cocktails they are ingredients in.
4. Discuss in detail the difference between single malt Scotch whiskey and blended. Explain the various methods of blending.
5. Where are the predominant distilling areas in Scotland located? What type of Scotch is distilled in these areas?

RESOURCES

Davis, Bernard and Stone, Sally, *Food and Beverage Management*, 5th ed. (Oxford, UK: Lineacre House, 2008).

Kotschevar, Lendal H. and Tanke, Mary L., *Managing Bar and Beverage Operations*, (East Lansing, MI: Educational Institute of the American Hotel & Motel Association, 1996).

Lerner, Daniel, *Single Malt and Scotch Whisky*, (New York:, NY, Black Dog and Leventhal Publishers, 1997).

Plotkin, Robert, *Successful Beverage Management*, (Tucson, AZ: Bar Media, 2001).

5
Beer

OVERVIEW

As a professional in the hospitality industry, it is important that you have a knowledge and understanding about the products you sell, namely, food, wine, spirits, and beer. In this chapter, we will look at beer: how it is made, its ingredients, and the various types of beer. Unless you are a real connoisseur of beer, it will surprise you how many types there are. Until recently, most bars served only a pilsner beer, which is a type of lager. However, with the proliferation of microbreweries and brew pubs, the selection that is offered has grown dramatically. Not only that, the customer's knowledge of beer has grown as well. It should be noted that most of these brews are not new but are steeped in the history and traditions of brewing.

A HISTORY OF BEER

Water notwithstanding, beer is one of the oldest beverages known to man. An interesting theory is that the process of brewing beer was discovered by several different civilizations almost simultaneously and unknown to each other. It dates back to the 6th millennium and is recorded in the histories of Mesopotamia and Egypt. Archeologists have discovered ancient pictograms that show bread being baked and ground up, mixed with water, and allowed to ferment. As we shall learn later in this chapter, these are the basic ingredients in making beer.

By 3000 BC, beer was known to be brewed in Iran, China, Peru, and also in Europe and Great Britain by the Germanic and Celtic tribes. From the beginning, beer was brewed in small batches at home for personal consumption. This began to change when monks began brewing it in large batches in the monasteries in the 7th century AD. They would sell it to individuals and as such controlled the brewing of beer for the next several hundred years. By the 11th century, individuals were brewing in large quantities, and in Belgium the first known guild of brewers was formed. It was the Germans, however, who were the first to regulate the brewing of beer. One of the stipulations of these regulations was that malt, hops, yeast, and water were the only ingredients to be used in the production of beer. For the most part, these regulations are still followed today.

As the early settlers left England and Europe to come to America to establish a new country, beer played an important role. Water was a risky commodity on sailing vessels in those days, as it would easily become contaminated over a period of time. Beer, however, with its high alcoholic content was deemed safe for the entire voyage. As the settlers arrived, taverns (called ordinaries back then) were opened and breweries established. Due to the high popularity of beer and spirits, these taverns and breweries were heavily regulated and taxed. An interesting fact was that many of the Founding Fathers as well as other leaders in the United States were either tavern or brewery owners.

As history evolved into the Industrial Revolution, more and more beer was commercially produced by larger and larger breweries. Competition became fierce and the breweries would find "front" men to open taverns which would sell their beer exclusively. Then Prohibition hit and the breweries either went out of business or went underground. Prohibition was short lived, and after it was lifted, many of these breweries came back into business, but more regulated than before. Today, practically all beer is brewed commercially by several international conglomerates as well as by thousands of regional breweries and brewpubs.

TYPES OF BEER

There are primarily two types of beer: lager and ale. These types are further subcategorized into many variations. Some beers have the characteristics of both lagers and ales and are therefore difficult to categorize. The primary difference between lagers and ales is in the type of yeast used in the brewing process.

The alcohol content of beer normally runs at around 5 percent, but can be as low as almost 0 percent (near beer) and as high as 15 percent and in a few cases even higher. The alcohol content, color, and flavor of lagers and ales are similar and in some cases are the same. Generally speaking, it can be said that ales are sweeter and have a fuller body than lagers.

Monks began brewing beer in large batches in the 7th century AD.
Denys/Shutterstock

The name *lager* comes from the German word *lagern*, which means "to store." Originally, breweries in Bavaria stored their beer in caves or cellars. In this environment, the air was quite cool and encouraged the beer to ferment. While the beer was fermenting, the sediment settled and the beer became quite clear. Additionally, the cooler temperatures inhibited the development of by-products, resulting in the beer having a clean taste. The beer we drink today is based on a lager that was brewed in the 1800s in Pilsen, in the Czech Republic. As it was then, today's pale lager is light gold in color, has an alcohol content of around 5 percent, and has a definite carbonation. Pale lagers are by far the most popular selling beers in the world. Some of the more popular brands of pale lager sold in the United States are Heineken, Budweiser, Coors, and Miller.

Ales are further categorized into other varieties such as pale ale, stout, and brown ale.

INGREDIENTS

For any food product, the quantity, quality, and type of ingredients that go into it will determine its outcome. Beer is no different. While the ingredients of all beers are essentially the same, the amount and type used, as well as their growing areas, are different. Slight differences in the production process affect the final outcome as well. The common ingredients found in beer are yeast, barley, hops, water, cereal, and other additives.

Yeast

Yeast is the microorganism that is responsible for fermentation in beer. Yeast metabolizes the sugars extracted from grains, which produces alcohol and carbon dioxide and thereby turns wort into beer (more on this later). In addition to fermenting the beer, yeast influences the character and flavor. Yeast is a living organism and like any living life form requires food, water, and the proper temperature to live and reproduce. Yeast is nourished by sugar and needs a temperature of between 68°F and 113°F to live. Since yeast is such an important part of the brewing process, many brewers grow their yeast in their own laboratories.

As previously mentioned, the primary difference between lagers and ales is in the type of yeast used in the brewing process. Lagers are brewed with bottom fermenting yeast while ales are brewed with top fermenting yeast. As their name implies, bottom fermenting yeast used in lagers ferments in the bottom of the fermenting tank while ale, using top fermenting yeast, ferments in the top of the fermenting tank. The bottom fermenting yeast used for lagers is a slower-acting yeast, and ferments at lower temperature. The effect of this is that most of the sugars are removed, which results in a clean, dry beer. Ale on the other hand uses fast-acting yeast, which leaves behind residual sugars. It is interesting to note that the yeast used in ale is the same yeast used in making bread.

Barley

The majority of beers produced use a malted barley. It is produced from the seeds of the barley plant. There are several varieties of barley that are used, with the type having two rows of seeds in its head being considered the best. Four- and six-row barley is used in the less expensive brands.

Water is added to the barley seeds, and their starch is converted to sugar. This process is facilitated as barley contains a rich source of amylase, a digestive enzyme that

Hop cones with barley.
Václav Mach/Fotolia

facilitates conversion of starch into sugars. This sugar is used by the yeast to produce alcohol during the fermentation process. When the seeds begin to sprout, they are roasted to produce **malt**. The longer they are roasted, the darker they become. Since the roasted malt will give the beer its color and some of its flavor, the brewer will stop the process when the proper degree of color has been obtained.

Cereal

Most breweries in the United States add cereal grains to the malt. These cereals include wheat, rice, and corn and are referred to as **adjuncts**. Less widely used starch sources include millet and sorghum. In addition to cereals, adjuncts could include sugar or potato starch. Other countries use different starch sources such as cassava root in Africa, potato in Brazil, and agave in Mexico. These adjuncts influence the beer's color and flavor as well as its body. A rule of thumb is that when a greater amount of barley is used in relation to cereal additives, it will result in a more flavorful beer with a better body and head. It is interesting to note that adjuncts cost less than barley; thus the lower cost beers will have more adjuncts and less barley than the premium or super premium beers. Some of the so-called light beers produced in the United States have reduced the amount of barley and cereals, thus producing a beer that is not only lower in calories but also has a reduced alcohol content. While the addition of adjuncts is popular in the United States, many imported beers do not have them. As a matter of fact, the use of adjuncts is prohibited in many European countries.

Hops

Hops are important as they help give beer its flavor and aroma. They come from a vine-like plant, and the flowers look like tiny little pine cones. These flowers of the hop vine are used as a flavoring and preservative agent in nearly all beer made today. While they are not essential in the process itself of brewing beer, they are important in that in addition to giving beer flavor, they give it a longer shelf life as they act as a preservative. Most brewers will blend a variety of hops to achieve a desired degree of bitterness that balances the sweetness of the malt. Additionally, hops contribute floral, citrus, and herbal aromas and flavors to beer.

Hops are a vine plant and are trained to grow up poles.
Pawel Wojcik © Dorling Kindersley

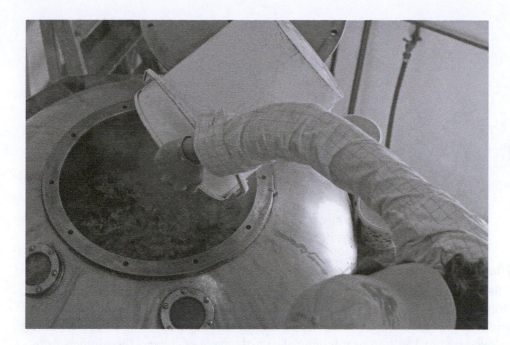

There are two main categories of hops: boiling and finishing. Boiling hops are taken from the female hop vine. They are put in during the first boil and give the beer its bitter flavor. Finishing hops are put in at the end of the boil and give the beer aroma.

Water

From a stream high in the Rocky Mountains to the Coors brewery, from "it's the water" in Olympia beer, to Hamm's "the beer from the land of sky blue waters," brewers have often touted the water in their beer, and for good reason: beer is mostly water. Different regions have water with dissimilar mineral components, and as a result, some regions are better suited to making certain types of beer. Different waters react differently with the ingredients that go into the beer. Yeast, for example, is affected by the type of water used. A low level of calcium sulfate will produce a good pilsner beer while a high level would be good for ale. Chloride will bring out a malt flavor in the beer.

Water is often boiled or filtered to remove undesirable characteristics and then modified by adding certain minerals. By doing this, the brewer can have water that is consistent and ultimately produce a consistent tasting beer. Keep in mind also that water that is acceptable in one brand of beer may not be acceptable in another brand.

Additives

While some brewers use **additives** to enhance the beer, many do not. Those that do not use additives use superior ingredients and carefully tested production techniques to produce their beer. Those that do use additives use them to stabilize the beer, produce better foam, and/or to extend the shelf life of their product. Additives are also used to shorten the production process in the fermentation stage.

THE BREWING PROCESS

The function of the brewing process is to change a starch into a sweet liquid, called wort, and to convert the wort into an alcoholic beverage known as beer. This is accomplished by a fermentation process affected by yeast. There are seven steps to this process: malting, mashing, brewing, fermentation, pasteurization, carbonation, and packaging.

Roasted barley.
alb470/Fotolia

Malting

This first step in the brewing process does not always take place in the brewery. Many brewers purchase malt already roasted and dried, while others prefer to carry out this process themselves. Aside from where it is done, the malting process involves cleaning barley and then steeping it in warm water. This induces the barley to sprout and create malt enzymes, which convert the starch into a sugar called **maltose**. As soon as this occurs, the barley is dried in a hot kiln, which stops the barley from sprouting. The barley is then roasted. How long it is roasted and at what temperature will determine the color and sweetness of the final product. It should be noted that not all brewers use barley as some of them will use wheat. Also those brewers that brew a less expensive product will use a malt extract.

Mashing

The malted barley is then ground and placed into a mash **tun**, which is a large vessel. Water is added along with precooked adjuncts, usually rice or corn, and cooked for one to six hours. The temperature at which it is cooked varies from brewer to brewer, anywhere from 154°F to near boiling. The malt enzymes convert the adjuncts from a starch to a sugar. This mash is then strained through a filter to make it clear, and the resulting liquid is called **wort**.

Brewing

The wort goes into large kettles made of copper or stainless steel. Hops are added, and the combination is then boiled. Some breweries add hops at more than one point in the process. This procedure pulls out the flavor of the hops as well as sterilizes the wort. It is the flavoring of the hops that give beer its unique flavor. It should be noted that the longer hops are boiled, the more bitterness is extracted. When this procedure is complete, the hops are strained off and the wort is allowed to cool. It is at this point that the differentiation between lager and ale begins. Wort for lager is cooled to 37–50°F, while the wort for ales is cooled to 50–70°F.

Copper mash tun.
Nataliya Hora/Shutterstock

Fermentation

Yeast is then added to the wort, and the fermentation process begins to take place. This step ripens the beer and is what gives it its smooth full flavor. This occurs as the yeast converts the sugar into alcohol and also creates carbon dioxide. There are two different strains of yeast used, one for lager and a different strain for ales.

The yeast used for **lagers** settles to the bottom of the fermenting tank and is referred to as bottom fermented. It is a slow process and works at a relatively low temperature. Brewers refer to this as lagering, hence the term *lager* to delineate this type of beer. It produces a smoother and mellower product than ale. It produces no foam, and only a few bubbles of carbon dioxide come to the top of the tank.

Ale on the other hand is top fermented. This takes place quickly, fermenting in several days, and produces a heavy foam. Often, the carbon dioxide is siphoned off, stored, and added back later in the brewing process. In addition to ale, top fermented beers include porters and stouts.

Fermentation vats.
ewwwgenich1/Fotolia

Pasteurization

Not all beer is pasteurized. Draft beer is not and is therefore a perishable product with a relatively short shelf life. Additionally, it should be stored at 36–42°F. Most canned and bottled beers on the other hand are pasteurized. This is a process that heats the beer to 140–150°F. which kill the bacteria that cause the beer to spoil. However, it is important to note that even though the beer is pasteurized, it will not last forever in its bottle or can. Most pasteurized beers have an expiration date of four months.

While most canned and bottled beers go through the pasteurization process, a few do not, resulting in can or bottle draft beer. When this is done, the beer goes through a process called **sterile filtration** in which the beer goes through a series of filters to eliminate the bacteria that cause spoilage. Like draft beer, it must be refrigerated and has a shorter shelf life. As most bars serve both draft and bottle (or canned) beer, it is important that management recognize that whether pasteurized or not, the shelf life is limited and proper stock rotation is a must. All bars should use the first in first out (FIFO) method of stock rotation.

Carbonation

The last step prior to packaging is the addition of carbon dioxide to beer. There are several methods that are used to achieve this process. One is called **krausening**. It is achieved by a second fermentation process whereby wort is added to the brew and it ferments under pressure, causing the gas to be entwined in the beer. Because it is a natural process of fermentation, it is often called natural carbonation. Another method, which is not natural, is to pump gas directly into the beer, and still a third method is to add the carbon dioxide, which was saved during the first fermentation, to the beer during the packaging process. Carbonation does nothing for the flavor of beer, but it is important in that it gives beer its bubbly effervescence. It is also responsible for the foam, or head, on a glass of beer.

Packaging

The next and final step in the brewing process is to package the beer. See Figure 5.1. It goes into either a keg, bottle, or can. As previously mentioned, if it goes into a bottle or

FIGURE 5.1
A model showing the
beer-making process.

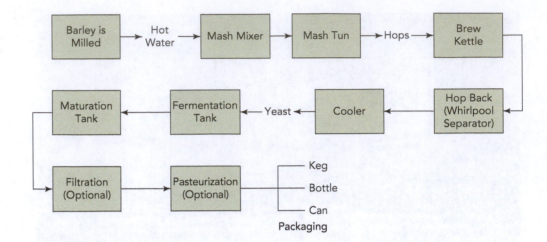

can it is probably pasteurized. Federal law states that if a beer has been pasteurized, it cannot be labeled as draft beer. Keg beer is not pasteurized.

Most keg beer is 15.5 gallons and is referred to as a half barrel. Smaller kegs are available measuring one-eighth of a barrel. These are handy for bars that want to sell a large variety of draft beers. They take up less space in the walk-in and their smaller size helps keep the product fresh. While their cost is higher than a normal keg, the advantages can offset the higher cost. Also, keep in mind that draft beer regardless of keg size commands a higher gross profit than canned or bottled beer.

The most popular size of domestic bottled or canned beer for bar use is 12 ounces. Many breweries also package in 16, 29, 25, and 40 ounces, although these are more popular with the retail trade than the bar trade. It should also be noted that many imports will come in sizes other than 12 ounces. While canned beer is most popular with the retail trade, bottles are preferred by far in bars. Figure 5.2 illustrates some of the more popular bottle sizes.

ALCOHOL CONTENT

The quantity of sugar in the wort and the variety of yeast used to ferment the wort are the primary factors that determine the amount of alcohol in beer. Additional fermentable sugars are sometimes added to increase alcohol content, and enzymes are often added to, for light beers to convert more starch to fermentable sugar.

The pale lagers that most of us are familiar with fall in the range of 4–6 percent alcohol by weight, with a typical alcoholic content of around 5 percent. A lower

Name	U.S. Oz	
U.S. Can/Bottle	12.0	
Canadian Bottle	11.5	
Euro Can/Bottle	14.9	Odd size used in Guinness and others
Euro Can/Bottle	16.9	Common size for imported cans and bottles
Imperial Pint	19.2	Canadian imperial pint
Australian Bottle	12.7	

FIGURE 5.2   Some common beer bottle sizes.

content of 3.2 percent or less is brewed for those states that outlaw a higher alcoholic content. Malt liquor, which is not liquor, but is a beer, is in the 6–7 percent range. A nonalcoholic beer is also produced for those who prefer the taste of beer but for one reason or another do not want the alcoholic effects of regular beer.

ALES AND LAGERS

As previously mentioned, beer is categorized as ale or lager with ale primarily being a top fermented beer and lager a bottom fermented beer. Within these two categories are a number of classifications, some of which become blurred with each other, and sometimes blurred between ales and lagers. Classification and categories notwithstanding, listed below are some of the more popular types of beer. Be advised that this is not a complete list but rather an overview of the vast variety that can be purchased.

Ales

- Altbier. A beer native to northern Germany, it is crisp and clean with a bitter taste. It has a copper-like color with a thick head. A balance of both malt and hops is quite common in a classic altbier.
- Amber ale. A miscellaneous classification of ale that has a wide variety of characteristics. They have moderate to high malt and hop content with citrus aromas and flavors being common. They have more color than an American pale ale but less than a brown ale.
- Barley wine. Its name notwithstanding, barley wine is actually beer, as it is made from grain rather than grapes or other fruit. It is among the highest strength beers available, 10–14 percent alcohol, which is probably why it is called a wine. Barley wine is normally amber to light brown in color and is sometimes cloudy, with a thick body. American barley wine is different from its English counterpart in that it uses American hops, which give it a more intense hop flavor.
- Belgium ales. In addition to the category of Belgium ales, there is a subcategory known as abbey beers; these beers originated in Belgian monasteries in the Middle Ages. While a few monasteries still brew this ale, most of it is brewed commercially under license by various religious communities. There are several types of Abbey beer, including the following:
  Abbey dubbel, which is a double fermented ale (hence *dubbel*) that is dark amber in color with a long-lasting head. Dubbels have a hint of flavors such as fruit, chocolate, nuts, and caramel.
  Abbey tripels are triple fermented Belgian ales. Tripels are light amber in color with an abundant head. Their flavors can be yeasty, spicy, fruity, or floral.
  Abbey quadrupels are quadruple fermented ales that present the richest and most multifaceted flavors in the abbey ales. They are dark red-brown with a creamy taste. The flavors are malty with yeasty overtones. They are stronger, with alcohol levels in the 10 percent and higher range.
  Belgian ale is very similar to the pale, amber, and brown ales of the United States. The pale varieties are fruity with a light malt aroma, while the dark types have a more pronounced malt flavor. The color of pale ale varies from gold to amber while the darker ales are amber to a brownish red. Belgium ales have a low alcohol content of less than 6 percent.
  Belgium strong ale is similar to the regular Belgian ales in both color and flavor. They are, however, significantly stronger, with an alcoholic content of 7 percent and higher.

A bottle of Adnams Suffolk strong ale.
Steve Gorton © Dorling Kindersley

A bottle of Newcastle brown ale.
Kellie Walsh © Dorling Kindersley

A glass of pale ale.
Kellie Walsh © /Dorling Kindersley

- Bitter ale. This ale was established in the early 1900s in England and is still popular today in English pubs. It has three subcategories: ordinary bitter, special bitter, and extra special bitter, which are dependent on the bitterness of the hops as well as the alcohol content.
- Blond ale. A brew that is named after its color and is sometimes referred to as golden ale. It has a fruity and sometimes sweet flavor.
- Brown ale. As its name implies, this ale is light to dark brown in color and unlike other beers has a tan head. It has a degree of popularity in Belgium, England, and the United States. Its flavor varies depending on where it was brewed, but generally speaking it has a bittersweet taste with a hint of malt.
- Cream ale. While this beer is very similar to a lager, it is definitely ale. It has a high level of carbonation with a light, crisp flavor. It has a light golden color.
- Fruit beer. A classification that includes just about any beer that has fruit or fruit flavoring added to it during the brewing process. It does not include beer that derives a fruit flavor from hops, yeast, or malt.
- India pale ale. Also known as IPA, there are several versions of this ale:
  English IPA. The original India pale ale was developed to make the long voyage from England to the British troops stationed in India. As hops act as a preservative, pale ale was brewed with a large quantity of them. Today's version contains fewer hops.
  American IPA is a bolder version with more hops and malt than the English version. The alcohol content of both the American and English versions is from 5 to 7.5 percent.
  Imperial IPA is often referred to as a double IPA as it is a stronger brew. It is similar in flavor to a regular IPA, albeit with more intensity. The alcohol content of double IPA is in the 7.5–10 percent range.
- Irish red ale. This beer originated in Ireland and is a very drinkable ale. It is also made as a lager. It has a sweet flavor with a low hop presence. Its alcohol content is in the 4.5 percent range.
- Kölsch. An ale with lager tendencies as it is fermented at cooler temperatures and lagered for a month. It is protected by law to be brewed in only twenty breweries in Cologne, Germany. It is a clean and crisp beer with fruity overtones. Its alcohol content is around 5 percent.
- Lambic. A Belgian ale that spontaneously ferments. It comes in several varieties:
  Faro. Rarely produced today, it has a sweet flavor with added sugars, fruit, and spices.
  Fruit lambic. Tart ale with the addition of raspberries, peaches, cherries, or currants.
  Gueuze. A blend of one- to three-year-old lambics that should be sour in taste, but today are normally sweetened.
  Unblended. Just as the name implies, it is a straight lambic that is tart and acidic.
- Mild ale. An ale that is low in alcohol content, usually less that 4 percent, and is mildly flavored. It can be either pale or dark in color.
- Old ale. Just as its name implies, old ale has been aged longer than ordinary ales and has a stronger alcohol content than most ales.
- Porter. Originating in England, it is an ale that is enjoyed by blue-collar workers (hence the name *porter*). It is very similar to stout. In addition to English porters, there are Baltic porters, which originated in those countries around the Baltic Sea, and American porters, also known as Imperial porters.
- Rye beer. An ale that is brewed with a minimum of 20 percent rye, it is light to dark amber in color and is comparable in flavor to a wheat beer.
- Scotch ale. As can be expected, this ale has a smoky, peaty taste. The alcohol content ranges from a low of 2 percent to a high of 10 percent. Hops are not grown

in Scotland and are an expensive import. The Scots, being Scots, use very few hops in brewing this ale.

- Stout. A generic category in which the malt is roasted until it is very dark, almost black, which gives stout a dark color. There are several subcategories of stout.

  Imperial stout. As the term imperial implies, this stout is the strongest of the stouts both in alcohol content and intense malt flavor. It was originally brewed in England and exported to the Baltic States.

  Extra stout. These stouts are not as strong as the imperial stouts either in flavor or alcohol content. They were originally brewed for export to tropical islands.

  Dry stout. While a smooth beer, it has a bitter dryness to it. Also known as Irish stout.

  Sweet stout. Also known as milk stout, cream stout, or oatmeal stout, these stouts are brewed with either lactose or oatmeal. They are sweeter than other stouts with a full, silky body.

- Wheat beers. These are for the most part ales, but they can be produced as lagers as well. They are primarily German beers but are produced in America as well. American wheats are varied in flavor and usually contain 50 percent or more wheat in the malt component. There are several German-style wheat ales, as follows:

  Weisse. Also known as Berliner weisse, it is an unusual ale that is hard to get as only two breweries brew it. These ales are quite sour and are normally served with a shot of fruit syrup. They have a low wheat content.

  Dunkel weizen. Dunkel, meaning dark in German, is what its name implies: a dark, cloudy ale. It contains over 50 percent wheat malt and has a strong, full-bodied flavor.

  Hafeweizen is one of the lightest German wheat beers. It has a golden color and is cloudy as it is an unfiltered ale.

  Krystal weizen is a clear version of the hafeweizen as it is filtered.

  Weizenbock is a dark, murky ale with a fruit-like flavor. Its alcohol content is higher than other wheat beers, ranging from 7 to 9 percent.

- Witbier. Belgium's answer to wheat beer, being brewed with around 50 percent wheat malt. It often has spices and/or citrus added. Its alcohol content is between 5 and 7 percent.

A glass of stout ale.
Steve Gorton © Dorling Kindersley

Lagers

As previously mentioned, practically all beers are classified as lagers or ales. Larger was first brewed by the Germans in the 7th century. The word *lager* comes from the German word *lagern*, which means "to store." These beers are brewed at lower temperatures and require a longer fermentation period as well as a longer maturation period. Lagers are normally served cold at around 40°F. The classification of lagers is as follows:

- Bock. Originated in the 13th or 14th century in the town of Einbeck, Germany. It has a golden to brown color and is higher in alcohol content than other beers. It has a full-bodied, sweet malt flavor. The word *bock* translated from German means "billy goat." There are two subcategories of bock beer:

  Doppelbock, translated from German, means "double bock," and while its alcohol content is higher than a bock (7.5–9 percent), it is not double as the name would imply. Its label customarily ends in "ator," for instance, Celebrator and Salvator.

  Eisbock, translated from German, means "ice bock." Its name comes from the fact that the beer is frozen and some of the ice particles are removed. When the

A glass of pilsner lager beer.

Jules Selmes and Debi Treloar ©
Dorling Kindersley

ice (water) is removed, the alcohol remains, and, consequently, the beer has a higher alcohol content, up to 10 percent.

- California Common. Created during the California gold rush where ice was not easily accessible and is therefore fermented at a higher temperature. It is also known as steam beer, which is trademarked and brewed by the Anchor Brewing Company.
- Dortmunder. A full-bodied beer that originated in Dortmond, Germany. It is golden in color with a white head. Its alcohol content is around 5.5 percent.
- Dunkel. A German beer that translated means "dark." It is a brown-colored beer with a balanced taste of malt and hops.
- Marzen. Marzenbier, which literally means "March beer," originated in Bavaria, Germany. It was brewed in the spring, matured in cool caves, and finished in time for the German fall festivals. It is also known as Oktoberfest beer and has an alcohol content of around 6 percent.
- Kellerbier. Literally means "cellar beer" when translated from German. It is a cloudy beer that is matured in underground vaults. It is sweeter and has less carbonation than typical lagers.
- Light beer. Also spelled "lite" beer, it is, as the name implies, a beer that is lighter in taste as well as carbohydrates and calories. Most brands are below 100 calories per 12 ounce container. Some brands have a lower alcohol content as well.
- Malt liquor. Not liquor, but is rather a strong lager with an alcohol content of 6–8 percent. It has a heavy malt flavor, hence its name. The American version has a high adjunct (rice and corn) ratio.
- Pilsner. Originated in 1842 in Czechoslovakia and has become the best-selling beer style of beer in the world. It is a very clear beer with a considerable amount of carbonation and a white head. Most pilsners have an alcohol content of around 5 percent. An exception to this is the imperial pilsner, which has a greater alcohol content and is usually more bitter than a regular pilsner.
- Rauchbier. Different from most other beers in that the malt is beachwood smoked. The level of smoky flavor varies depending on the degree of smoking that the malt receives. The alcohol content is around 5 percent.
- Vienna. First brewed in Vienna, Austria, it is an amber or copper-colored brew with a slight sweet and malty taste to it.

OTHER BEVERAGES

There are other beverages that are in a sort of no-man's land in that they have characteristics of both wine and beer. Controversy surrounding their classification notwithstanding, we will place them here under a miscellaneous beer category.

A pint of Guinness Black lager.

© Steve Stock / Alamy

Cider

Cider is made from fermented apple juice and is not considered a beer as there is no grain malt used in its production. Often adjuncts are added to increase the alcohol level. Ciders have achieved a level of acceptance in the United States, and many bars serve them. Similar to cider is Perrie, which is made from pears rather than apples.

Mead

Mead is one of the earliest forms of fermented beverages, dating back to the Greek and Egyptian periods as well as the Inca and Aztec cultures of Central America. It is a fermented product made from honey, water, and yeast. Because it lacks malt, it is not considered a beer. The alcohol content of mead varies from 8 to 12 percent. Often other ingredients are added that affect its taste such as fruit or tea.

Sake

Sake is a Japanese beverage that is fermented from rice. As a matter of fact, the translation of the word *sake* is "the essence of the spirit of rice." Because of its ingredients and its brewing procedure, many classify it as beer. Others, however, classify it as a wine. One of the reasons is that sake has a very high alcohol content ranging from 12 to 17 percent. While it is most often served warm, sake can be served chilled, "on the rocks," or at room temperature.

A jug of Sheppy's Cider.
Kim Sayer © Dorling Kindersley

WHAT TO SELL

As you can see, the list of beers can be quite intimidating, and the above is not a complete list. Add to the numerous styles the number of brewers for each style, and it becomes readily apparent that one bar cannot sell all of them. While there are some bars that specialize in beer exclusively and have extensive beer lists, the average bar will carry only some of those listed. How many is enough? That depends on the demographics of your customers, storage space, inventory turnover, and product mix.

Middle to upper income, college educated, white-collar types tend to be more daring when it comes to trying new things. This demographic sector will probably welcome new brews that are either imported or a limited edition from a local microbrewery. Often with this group, being seen with the "in" beer is as important as the taste of the beer itself. On the other hand, middle income, blue-collar types will opt for the more traditional American lagers. Enjoying the taste is more important than perception to this group.

Storage space will go a long way in determining the number of beers to offer. In the United States, most beers are enjoyed cold as opposed to Europe and Great Britain, where many of them are served at room temperature. Therefore, adequate refrigeration must be available. The more styles of beer and the greater the selection of breweries offered, the more refrigerated storage space is needed. Closely aligned with storage space is inventory turnover. Remember that draft beer is a perishable product and must be turned over every fourteen days. Bottled beer, while having a longer shelf life, will also go stale and therefore must be sold in a timely manner. Last is your product mix: how much of your sales will be in beer? More often than not, the customer will make this decision for you, but it is wise to have a budget as to how much will be spent on beer inventory.

While all of the above will go into determining how many varieties to sell, most experts recommend that a bar should offer a *minimum* of ten to twelve different beers. These can be divided between draft and bottled beers as well as major domestic breweries, microbreweries, and imports. Figure 5.3 shows the top ranking brands of beer by sales and Figure 5.4 shows the top craft breweries in the United States, ranked by sales.

FIGURE 5.3

Beer rankings by brand.

Beer	Brewery
Bud Light	Anheuser-Busch InBev
Budweiser	Anheuser-Busch InBev
Coors Light	Millercoors Brewing
Miller Lite	Millercoors Brewing
Natural Light	Anheuser-Busch InBev
Corona Extra	Crown Imports
Busch Light	Anheuser-Busch InBev
Busch	Anheuser Busch InBev
Heineken	Heineken
Michelob Ultra	Anheuser Busch InBev
Miller High Life	Millercoors Brewing
Keystone Light	Millercoors Brewing
Natural Ice	Anheuser Busch InBev
Modelo Especial	Crown Imports
Bud Light Lime	Anheuser Busch InBev
Icehouse	Millercoors Brewing
Bud Ice	Anheuser Busch InBev
PBR	Pabst Brewing Co.
Yuengling Lager	D G Yuengling & Sons
Corona Light	Crown Imports

FIGURE 5.4

Top craft brewing companies.

	Brewery	City
1	Boston Beer Co.	Boston, MA
2	Sierra Nevada Brewing Co.	Chico, CA
3	New Belgium Brewing Co.	Fort Collins, CO
4	The Gambrinus Company	San Antonio, TX
5	Deschutes Brewery	Bend, OR
6	Matt Brewing Co.	Utica, NY
7	Bell's Brewery, Inc.	Galesburg, MI
8	Harpoon Brewery	Boston, MA
9	Lagunitas Brewing Co.	Petaluma, CA
10	Boulevard Brewing Co.	Kansas City, MO
11	Stone Brewing Co.	Escondido, CA
12	Dogfish Head Craft Brewery	Milton, DE
13	Brooklyn Brewery	Brooklyn, NY
14	Alaskan Brewing & Bottling Co.	Juneau, AK
15	Long Trail Brewing Co.	Burlington, VT
16	Shipyard Brewing Co.	Portland, ME
17	Abita Brewing Co.	Abita Springs, LA
18	Great Lakes Brewing Co.	Cleveland, OH
19	New Glarus Brewing Co.	New Glarus, WI
20	Full Sail Brewing Co.	Hood River, OR

CONCLUSION

With the proliferation of beers available today, it is important that you, as a hospitality professional, are aware of the different types and styles of beer. It is also important that you know and understand your customers who enjoy trying new and different beers. Knowledge of the history and origin of the styles of beer should be essential knowledge to you, so that you can be conversant with your guests. Knowing which beers to carry in inventory will bring additional sales to your bar. On the other hand, not knowing and understanding beer will drive customers to your competition.

> ### Case Study/Project
>
> Take a tour of a brewery in your area. Explain what, if any, deviations they make in the brewing process that is different than the norm. In terms of ingredients, what do they do that makes their beer stand out from the rest of the beers on the market?

QUESTIONS

True/False

1. Outside of water, beer is one of the oldest beverages known to man.
2. Some beers are difficult to classify as they have the characteristics of both lagers and ciders.
3. The amount of and type of ingredients used in the brewing of beer are the same from brewery to brewery.
4. The same type of yeast is used in brewing lagers and ales.
5. Fermentation ripens the beer and gives it its smooth flavor.
6. The longer hops are boiled, the more bitterness is extracted.
7. Lager produces a heavier foam or head than ale.
8. One of the several methods that are used to achieve carbonation in beer is referred to as krausening.
9. Stout beer is in the ale category.
10. The best-selling beer style of beer in the world is a pilsner.

Multiple Choice

1. One of the first countries to regulate the brewing of beer was
   A. the United States.
   B. Germany.
   C. Japan.
   D. Mesopotamia.
2. Beer is normally classified as either
   1) lager.
   2) ale.
   A. (1) only
   B. (2) only
   C. Both (1) and (2)
   D. Neither (1) nor (2)
3. The alcohol content of beer
   1) is normally around 5 percent.
   2) can run as high as 15 percent and higher, or as low as almost 0 percent.
   A. (1) only
   B. (2) only
   C. Both (1) and (2)
   D. Neither (1) nor (2)
4. Malt for beer is made from
   A. hops.
   B. cereal.
   C. yeast.
   D. barley.
5. Cereal when used in the brewing of beer is
   A. referred to as an adjunct.
   B. referred to as an additive.
   C. made exclusively from corn.
   D. not used in the brewing of beer as it is strictly a breakfast item.
6. Hops are used in brewing beer as
   A. a flavoring agent.
   B. a preservative.
   C. a means of giving beer its aroma.
   D. all of the above.

7. The malting process
   1) takes place in the brewery.
   2) creates malt enzymes that convert the starch into a sugar called maltose.
   A. (1) only
   B. (2) only
   C. Both (1) and (2)
   D. Neither (1) nor (2)

8. The result of the mashing process is a clear liquid called a
   A. tun.
   B. wort.
   C. lager.
   D. maltose.

9. Bottom fermentation is a slow process and works at a relatively low temperature and produces a product known as
   A. ale.
   B. tun.
   C. lager.
   D. mead.

10. The most popular beer sold in the United States is a(n)
    A. lager.
    B. cider.
    C. ale.
    D. mead.

Essay

1. In your own words, describe the difference between lagers and ales.
2. Give the basic ingredients used in the brewing of beer, explain the importance of each, and discuss how brewers differentiate their product using these ingredients.
3. Explain in detail each step of the brewing process in chronological order.
4. Give a brief description of the type of bar you would like to run and then review the list of ales given in the chapter. Tell which of the ales you would sell in your establishment, why you chose those particular types, and whether they would be bottled or draft.
5. Give a brief description of the type of bar you would like to run and then review the list of lagers given in the chapter. Tell which of the lagers you would sell in your establishment, why you chose those particular types, and whether they would be bottled or draft.

RESOURCES

Davis, Bernard and Stone, Sally, *Food and Beverage Management*, 5th ed. (Oxford, UK: Lineacre House, 2008).

Katsigris, Costas and Thomas, Chris, *The Bar & Beverage Book*, 4th ed. (Hoboken, NJ: John Wiley & Sons, 2007).

Kotschevar, Lendal H. and Tanke, Mary L., *Managing Bar and Beverage Operations*, (East Lansing, MI: Educational Institute of the American Hotel and Motel Association, 1996).

Plotkin, Robert, *Successful Beverage Management*, (Tucson, AZ: Bar Media, 2001).

6

Purchasing Bar Equipment

OVERVIEW

Before any discussion of equipment purchasing can begin, there are some terms regarding the equipment's power source that you should be familiar with.

- **Ampere**. Commonly called an amp, it measures the amount of electricity. There is a limited amount of amps going into any building. You need to know this number to avoid purchasing more electrical equipment than the system will allow.
- **Volt**. Volts measure the force or push of electricity. Some equipment operates on 110, 115, or 120 volts, some operates on 208, 210, 220, 230, or 240 volts; and some on 440 or 480 volts. Each piece of electrical equipment is designed to operate on a specific voltage. You need to know the voltage coming into your building to specify the correct piece of equipment. Too much voltage will burn the equipment out; too little will not allow it to run at its full potential. Additionally, some equipment will not even run on the incorrect voltage. All buildings with electricity will have the 100 series of volts. They may or may not have the 200 or 400 series.
- **Watt**. This is the amount and force of electricity or amps times volts.

$$\text{(amps} \times \text{volts} = \text{watts})$$

- **Kilowatt**. 1,000 watts. This is the number seen on an electric bill showing the electrical usage for a period.
- **British thermal unit**. Abbreviated BTU; the amount of heat needed to raise one pound of water 1° F. It is used to measure gas.
- **Pounds per square inch**. PSI for short; used to measure water pressure and steam. Water pressure is what cleans glasses and dishes.
- **Cubic feet per minute**. CFM for short; used to measure air movement in heating and cooling the building. It is also used in the kitchen for air movement in the exhaust hood and makeup air systems.

Purchasing bar equipment is an expensive undertaking. Knowing what to purchase and how to purchase it is the thrust of this chapter. Purchasing for a new operation has a different set of criteria than buying a single piece or replacing an obsolete piece. The menu, the number of seats, the bar's personnel, and the clientele all have a bearing on which piece of equipment to purchase. Having an understanding of how equipment works, what it can and can't do, and its limitations can be of great value when it comes to selecting specific pieces of equipment.

One of the most complicated types of equipment to understand is refrigeration. How a compressor, condenser, evaporator, and thermostat all work together to cool product will be explained. The various pieces of refrigeration equipment such as bottle and keg coolers, ice machines, reach-ins, and walk-ins are discussed. Beverage machines such as cappuccino and carbonated beverage machines are explained. Methods of glass washing are also covered. The makeup of the front bar, commonly called the bar die, and the back bar are conveyed. What to look for in a point of sale (POS) is explained.

There is a right way and a wrong way to purchase equipment. First, an understanding of the distribution system is essential. After this, choosing the manufacturer and the exact piece of equipment you want is important. To do this, you need to know specifically what you want the equipment to do, what options (if any) you want, and the quality level of construction and the price you are willing to pay. There are several ways to select equipment, which include the Internet and going to trade shows and seeing the actual pieces on display. Once it is determined what you want, writing a specification for that piece of equipment is necessary. By writing a specification, various dealers can then bid on the equipment. When there are several dealers bidding, the price goes down and you save money. Another consideration is purchasing used equipment. Knowing when to purchase new and when to purchase used is important as sometimes the "good deal" isn't as good as it looks.

While purchasing bar equipment seems confusing at first, compare it to buying a car. Do you want a sedan or an SUV? Two doors or four doors? Automatic or stick? Radio or full sound system? Is color important? New or used? When you go to purchase a car, in your mind, you have in effect written a specification for that car. Bar equipment is no different.

The chapter concludes with a section on bar equipment maintenance. This is a very important section as large sums of money have been invested, and by properly maintaining the equipment that investment will be protected.

WHAT TO PURCHASE

Knowing what to purchase can be approached in three ways. First, and the most complicated, is purchasing equipment for the new operation. Second is purchasing a piece of equipment that is new to an existing operation. While this is not overly complicated, there are several points to consider. Third, and relatively easy, is replacing an existing piece which has worn out or become obsolete.

The New Operation

Before the decision is made as to what equipment to purchase for a new bar, it must be decided what the operation is going to sell. As we will learn later, when laying out a menu for a particular operation, the customers, and their wants and needs, must be taken into consideration. This is important because the menu will determine the *type* of equipment needed. The size of the operation or the number of seats will determine the *amount* of equipment needed. Whether or not the equipment is designed to be labor saving should also be considered. Cost, of course, is always a prime issue. Taking all of these facts into consideration, what equipment to purchase can be categorized in three ways:

- Essential. This is the equipment that is absolutely necessary to operate the bar. Business cannot be conducted without it.
- Desirable. This is equipment that would enhance the operation and should be purchased if funds are available.
- Extraordinary. This is equipment that would be really, really neat to have if there is still money left over.

For example, every bar needs to have a cash control system and a place to store cash. The least expensive way to go would be to purchase a simple cash register. This would be an essential piece of equipment. However, a POS (point of sale) system, while more expensive, would be better as it would give a greater control over the operations and would also speed up service. It therefore would be desirable. Suppose we added an automated liquor dispensing system to the POS. While this would be very expensive it would give us even greater cost control as well as product control and would speed up service even more. Note that these factors could mean different things to different operations. A POS system could be considered desirable in one bar while in another it would be considered essential.

The menu for a country and western bar and the menu for a bar in a sophisticated white-table-cloth restaurant are different. The former would require a large amount of refrigeration for bottled and draft beer while the later would require less refrigeration but more mechanical equipment for blended drinks as well as an extensive wine display. Bear in mind also that due to local regulatory restraints or customer reference, some bars will sell beer only, while others might sell beer and wine only.

While there are considerable differences among beverage outlets, there remains some basic equipment that the average bar must have. These pieces include, but are not limited to, the following:

Front Bar   This is where the customer sits on one side while the bartender works on the other side and is normally referred to as the bar die. It will be covered in more detail in the next chapter. The following are located underneath the bar die on the bartender's side.

- Ice bin. Built with a drain that empties into a floor drain. There should be an air space between the ice bin drain and the floor drain to avoid sewage backup into the ice bin.
- Speed rail. Houses the spirits normally called the "house" or "well" liquors.
- Blender stand. A work area for the bartender, normally constructed of stainless steel.
- Blender. Used for blended drinks.
- Server pick-up area. Contains the carbonated beverage gun and condiment trays. Normally blocked off from the customer area with bar rails on each side.
- Four-compartment bar sink. Used to wash glasses and bar utensils.
- Storage area. For backup liquor, unrefrigerated mixes, napkins, straws, and stir sticks, and other supplies.

Back Bar   The following are normally located on the back bar:

- Shelving or steps for "call" and premium liquor, glassware, and/or display of wine and bottled beers offered by the establishment.
- Cash register or POS system.

The following equipment can be located either under the front bar, as a part of the back bar, or located directly adjacent to the bar area:

- Refrigerated bottle box.
- Draft box or draft dispensing heads coming from the walk-in cooler.
- Refrigeration for wine fruit and mixes.
- Glass storage. *Note*: Some bars hang their stemmed glassware inverted over the front bar. Many health departments will not allow this as customers seated at the bar cough, sneeze, and do other despicable things, thus contaminating the glassware. Also, in any of those rare areas that still allow smoking, the tar and nicotine adhere to the glassware.
- Hand-washing sink, soap, and disposable paper towels.

An illustration of an underbar, which is located directly under the bar die where the customer sits.
Courtesy of the Gaf

While this is a bare-bones list for an average bar, keep in mind that as a bar menu expands the equipment list also expands. Also, as a bar becomes more specialized, the equipment list changes accordingly.

Replacing Existing Equipment

This normally is not difficult if a few points are followed.

- Match the electrical requirements (if applicable) of the equipment being replaced, because if the wrong voltage is specified, the equipment will not work. Also, if the amps (amperes) are greater on the new piece of equipment than the old piece, check with the electric company to make sure there is sufficient power coming into the building to handle the additional amperage. If the voltage and amperage are the same on the new piece as the old, there will be no electrical problems.

- Check the dimensions of the new piece of equipment. If they are the same as the old, no problem. If they are greater, ascertain if the new piece will fit in the designated space. Also check to see if it will fit in the door. Most equipment will fit through the doorway of a newer building; however, it is always wise to check. For example, a new side-by-side refrigeration unit is approximately 6 feet high by 5 feet wide by 3 feet deep. Most doors are 5½ feet high by 3 feet wide. By placing the refrigerator on its side, it would be 5 feet high by 3 feet wide and would go through. Keep in mind that it is a tight fit and the door may have to be removed from its hinges in order for it to go through.

- If the replacement piece of equipment is to go in the same space as the old one, there is no problem. If it is going elsewhere, not only should it be checked for fit, but the electrical and/or plumbing (if applicable) need to be checked. For example, if a new ice machine is being ordered and will go in a new location, a water line, floor drain, and electrical line need to be in place. This can be very costly, particularly if the floor is concrete and has to be jack hammered for the floor drain to be connected to an existing drain line.

Adding New Equipment

When adding a new piece of equipment to the bar or lounge area, basically the same questions must be answered as were answered when replacing equipment. The most important consideration is where to put it. As will be observed in the next chapter, one of the important considerations in bar design is to have little or no wasted space. Thus if the bar was laid out properly in the first place, there is little or no room to add new equipment. Water and electrical lines need to be considered as well.

TYPES OF EQUIPMENT

When selecting equipment, it is important to know its characteristics. In other words, what should you look for? It is also important to know how the piece that is being bought actually works. Knowing this will help make a more informed decision and will probably save money in the long run.

Refrigeration Overview

As some of the most costly equipment in the bar is refrigeration, it is important to have a basic understanding of how refrigeration works. To begin with, we ask the question, is heat the absence of cold or is cold the absence of heat? In the case of refrigeration, clearly, cold is the absence of heat; that is, for something to become refrigerated or frozen, heat must be removed. To do this, refrigeration systems rely on latent heat, which is the amount of heat necessary to change a liquid into a gas. This is also known as vaporization. For example, if a pan of water is put on a stove and the stove is turned on, eventually the water boils or, to put it another way, the liquid (water) turns into a gas (vapor). The water pulls heat from the heat source and keeps on pulling until it changes from a liquid into a gas.

How does all of this discussion about heat relate to keeping something cold? Simple. Refrigeration systems use a **refrigerant** called R-22, which boils at –32°F (–36°C). The R-22 refrigerant goes throughout the refrigeration system as a liquid. As it goes, it pulls out heat from the products in the refrigerator or freezer. It keeps on pulling until it boils and turns into a gas at –32°F (–36°C).

It should be noted that R-22 is being phased out by the Environmental Protection Agency (EPA). Replacing it is R-410A, as well as several others, which are undergoing tests at this time. R-22 can still be used in existing units. When a unit is repaired, R-22 can be used until 2020, after which the newer type of refrigerant must be used. This can get quite costly as the new refrigerant will necessitate modifications to the existing refrigeration system. Therefore, when buying refrigerated equipment, make sure that it uses the new approved refrigerant or at least is convertible in the future at a minimal cost.

Refrigerant, both R-22 and R-410A, is very expensive. Because of this, we do not want it to evaporate when it turns into a gas. We also do not want our refrigerators and the products in them to be at –32°F (–36°C) all of the time; therefore, we need additional parts to operate a refrigeration system. To look at it in its most basic format, we need a compressor, condenser, evaporator, and thermostat. There are other components, but comprehending these and how they work gives you a basic understanding of how a refrigeration system operates. Refer to Figure 6.1 as we discuss the various components.

- The **compressor**. The refrigerant, which is in a gaseous state, is compressed until it gets very hot.
- The **condenser** takes the hot gas and condenses it into a liquid form.
- The **evaporator** takes the refrigerant, now in a liquid state, and circulates it. As it circulates throughout the refrigerator or freezer, it picks up heat from the air

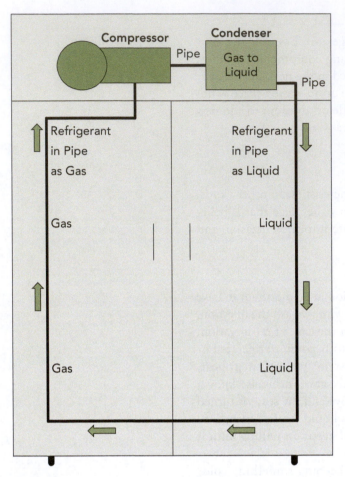

FIGURE 6.1
Diagram of a refrigeration system.

in the box as well as from the products. As it picks up this heat, it heats up until it comes to the boiling point and turns to a gas. It returns to the compressor, where the process starts over and repeats itself.

- The **thermostat** controls the temperature in the box. There are normally <u>two temperatures on the thermostat</u>, a low setting and a high setting. When the temperature in the box reaches the high setting, the refrigeration system is turned on. The liquid refrigerant

  1. Circulates throughout the evaporator (the box) picking up heat.
  2. Comes to a boil and turns into a gas.
  3. Returns to the compressor and gets compressed.
  4. Goes to the condenser and gets condensed into a liquid.
  5. Goes on to the evaporator as a liquid.

  This continues until the temperature in the box reaches the low setting on the thermostat. When this happens, the thermostat shuts the system down. For example, if you wanted the temperature in your refrigerator to be 35°F (2°C), you could set the parameters on your thermostat at 37°F (3°C) and 33°F (1°C), when the temperature in the box reaches 37°F (3°C), the system goes on. When it reaches 33°F (1°C), the system goes off.

- The **thermometer**. Most commercial units contain exterior thermometers on their refrigerators and freezers. These work by use of a probe that is in the interior cabinet of the refrigerator or freezer. The probe relays the interior temperature to the exterior thermometer.

Freezers work in the same way as refrigeration systems except that they use a different refrigerant.

It should be noted that the condenser gives off considerable heat. This heat has to go somewhere, and it can go either into water or into the air surrounding the refrigeration system. Thus, we have two types of refrigeration systems: water cooled or air cooled.

Water-cooled systems have a series of pipes containing water. The water picks up the heat given off by the condenser and becomes quite hot. In state-of-the-art facilities, where having a green restaurant is important, this water is circulated into the hot water system. By doing this the water heater does not have to work as hard to get the water up to the desired temperature and therefore uses less energy. In operations that do not do this, the hot water is simply wasted and emptied into a floor drain.

Air-cooled systems are the most popular and are therefore found in most commercial refrigerators and freezers. In this system, a fan blows the hot air off the condenser into the surrounding air in the room. It is critical that, for this system to operate most efficiently, the fins on the condenser be cleaned on a regular basis, preferably monthly.

Another thing to consider is that the Built-in refrigeration system or a remote refrigeration system can be built into the unit or can have a remote location. Thus you have a **built-in system** or a **remote system**. Built-in systems are the more popular as they are less costly. However, with a remote system the heat generated by the compression system will be away from the bar area, making it more comfortable for your customers. When repairs are necessary, a remote system can be worked on without having the repair person working behind the bar and getting in everyone's way.

This applies to all refrigeration units. Therefore when the decision is made as to which model to choose, water cooled or air cooled will have to be decided on as well as whether the refrigeration system should be built in or remote. It should be noted that the systems will normally have different model numbers. In other words, when a unit is selected, the model number will be different for a water-cooled unit than an air-cooled unit even though everything else in the unit is identical. The same scheme holds true for a built-in or a remote system.

Reach-in Refrigerators, Bottle Boxes, and Keg Boxes

Reach-in refrigerators can be either upright or under counter reach-in boxes. Using the same technology are bottle and keg boxes. All of these are used to store bottled beer, wine, cocktail mixes, and fruit. When selecting a refrigerator, take into consideration the following:

- Hardware. The hinges, catches, and door handles should all be strong and durable. Commercial refrigeration takes a lot of abuse particularly in a high-volume bar. The author remembers one particular brand of refrigerator where the door handles kept falling off. Often, the cheapest is not necessarily the best.
- Gaskets. This is the rubber tube-like piece that fits around the door to give it a complete seal, keeping the cold air in and the hot air out. Make sure that the unit selected has replaceable gaskets as some manufacturers provide these and some do not. Gaskets all wear out over time and are necessary to keep a tight seal so that the unit will not work overtime and wear out the refrigeration system.
- Insulation. This should be a minimum of 3 inches of rigid urethane, which is a material that looks a lot like Styrofoam.
- Interior lighting. This applies to reach-in boxes only. Some units have it and other do not. If this is important, make sure that the model selected has it.
- Locking devices. Not all units have locks. This is a very important feature to have especially in a bar where expensive and sought-after merchandise is stored. Make sure the unit selected can be secured.
- Shelving. Make sure the shelving is adjustable in reach-ins. In beer boxes the same applies for the bottle dividers. This is important as inventories change and occasionally bottle or container sizes change and you need the ability to adjust. Not all manufacturers or models come with adjustable shelving.
- Thermometers. Some models have exterior thermometers, some do not. Make sure that the unit selected has an exterior (preferably digital) thermometer.

While the above applies to most reach-ins, bottle, and keg boxes, there are some attributes that apply specifically to each of them.

When selecting a reach-in, both upright and under counter, there is a choice of doors. They can be left open, right open, or sliding. When selecting one over the other, consider the traffic pattern where the unit will be located. For example, if the bartender's work station is on the left side of a reach-in and the door is a left open door, it will open in his or her face, and employees will have to walk around the door to retrieve product. Doors can be solid or glass, allowing the bartender to see inside for a particular product without opening the door and causing the refrigeration unit work overtime. On upright reach-ins, the doors can also be full or half doors.

Bottle and keg boxes are both under-counter units and are constructed the same except for the door location. On most bottle boxes, the doors are sliding and are located on the top of the unit. While some models have the doors on the front of

An alternative to a bottle box is an ice bin with bottles of beer iced down. This saves time in that the bartender does not have to open the box each time a beer is ordered.

Conroy's Public House

the unit, these are cumbersome for the bartender to retrieve beer bottles and are not recommended. On keg boxes, they are located in the front and are either left or right open. Bottle boxes have dividers to separate the brands of beer. While called bottle boxes, they can also be used to store cans of beer.

To dispense draft beer, you can have either a keg box or it can be dispensed directly from a walk-in cooler. The decision as to which system to use is predicated on the volume of draft beer sold. If it is a minimal amount, a draft box will suffice. If it is a large amount it is best to go with a walk-in system.

Keg boxes can be sized to accommodate one, two, or three kegs of beer. A one-keg unit can be placed on wheels to accommodate a portable bar set up for a banquet. Keg boxes are self-contained in that the draw spigot is located on the top of the unit and the unit is equipped with a drain. In the portable one-keg unit, the drain goes into a bucket located inside of the unit, while on the permanent two-, three-, and four-keg units the drain is hooked into the floor drain system.

In both the keg box and the walk-in system, the beer is "pushed" from the keg to the dispensing head by either an air compressor or a CO_2 tank. To accomplish this, several components are needed. For example using a CO_2 tank the following are necessary:

- A keg box or a walk-in cooler to store the keg(s).
- A keg, or kegs, of beer and/or ale.
- A CO_2 tank.
- A pressure regulator with a gauge indicating the pressure (pressure gauge).
- Vinyl or nylon hoses running from the CO_2 tank to the keg and from the keg to the tap.
- Couplings that connect the lines in the keg to the hoses.
- A tap, which is essentially a faucet to dispense the beer or ale.

There are two methods to drawing beer out of the keg. One is on the top of the keg and the other is on the bottom of the keg. There are two lines. First, the CO_2 line hooks up to a coupling on the keg. The second line is "tapped" into the keg and is hooked up to a coupling as well. The CO_2 line pushes the beer or ale out of the keg into the second line and on to the tap. Figure 6.2 illustrates a tapping device.

The CO_2 cylinder has carbon dioxide gas in it at a pressure of 1,000 PSI (pounds per square inch). The gas goes through the pressure regulator and is reduced to 12 to 15 PSI at room temperature. The key words in that sentence are room temperature. Therefore the CO_2 tank must be stored in the room outside of the refrigerated keg box or walk in. If it is stored in the box it will not work accurately. The tank should be stored upright and chained to a wall to prevent it from tipping over. When changing tanks, they should be handled very carefully. A mishap on a full tank could cause the tank to act like a torpedo causing severe injury and/or damage.

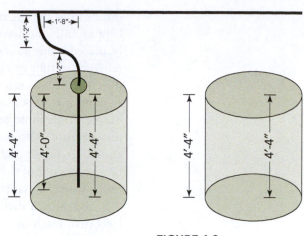

FIGURE 6.2

Diagram of a tapping device.

Draft beer is not pasteurized and must be kept cool at all times. When drawing draft beer, one of the more common problems is improper temperature. Draft beer should be stored at a temperature between 32 and 38° F. At warmer temperatures, beer will foam. At temperatures lower than 30° F., the beer will freeze, causing the alcohol to separate, bringing about a beer that will be cloudy with an "off" taste. Figure 6.3 illustrates a draft beer system.

Walk-in Refrigeration Units

Walk-in coolers for bars are designed for long-term storage, while reach-in coolers and bottle boxes are intended for short-term storage. Hence, bottle boxes will be used primarily for the beer that will be sold during a shift, while the back-up cases will be stored in the walk-in. Also many bars, particularly those that sell a large amount of draft beer, do not use keg boxes but rather dispense the beer directly from the walk-in. When using this system, the beer is basically dispensed the same as it is in keg boxes, using a CO_2 system. Recent innovations have included adding nitrogen to the CO_2 to help maintain the integrity of the product.

In an ideal world, the walk-in should be located directly adjacent to or in the basement directly under the bar. There are several reasons for this, one being that as the beer

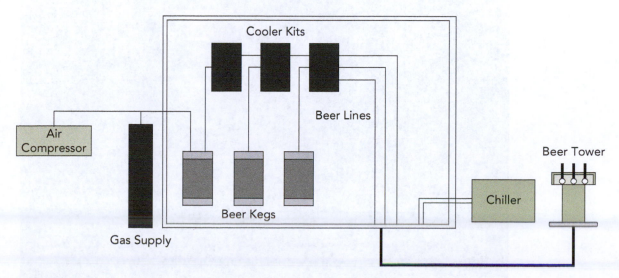

FIGURE 6.3

Diagram of a draft beer system.

travels from the keg to the dispensing head, the temperature, for most beers, should be kept at 38°F. To accomplish this, if the distance is short, the beer dispensing tube can be placed inside an insulated tube. For longer distances, it will need to travel thorough a refrigerated tube at a greater expense. While traversing this distance, it is important that the correct temperature be maintained the entire distance. When purchasing dispensing systems, it is important that the temperature can be adjusted to accommodate different brews. While most beers are served at 38°F, some beers are ideally served at a different temperature. Also, when traveling long distances the proper pressure must be maintained. To accomplish this, pumps should be installed to maintain this pressure. When beer comes out of the tap, if the temperature and/or pressure is not at its proper setting, excess foaming, flat beer, or an inferior-tasting product will result.

Because of their size, walk-ins take longer to recover to their proper temperature level than reach-ins when the door is opened. Hence, the less a walk-in is entered, the better. The products stay at their intended temperature, and less energy is expended. Plastic strips or air curtains can be used to reduce the cold air escaping when the walk-in door is opened.

There are three different methods of construction for walk-in coolers and freezers. The first type is a walk-in that is actually built as part of the building, similar to a room. This method is normally reserved for extremely large walk-ins that are found in a large food distribution warehouse, a central commissary, or a large institutional kitchen.

The second type, used for small walk-ins, is completely built in the factory as an integral unit. It is transported from the factory on a flatbed truck to the foodservice operation. Normally, this type is used as an outdoor unit as opposed to a unit in the kitchen, as it is too large to fit through a standard door frame.

The third type, which is the most popular for restaurants and bars, is a modularly constructed unit. For most manufacturers, the wall modules are 8 feet high, 4 inches thick, and 1 to 3 feet in width. These modules are hooked together on site. The floor and ceiling of the walk-in are assembled in a similar manner. The door module contains

Kegs in a walk-in cooler hooked up to the draft beer system.
Conroy's Public House

Pressure valves regulating the various amounts of pressure of the beer or ale being delivered to the draft heads.
Conroy's Public House

the interior light, light switch, and thermometer; thus all of the electrical components are located on this section. Consequently, any size walk-in can be constructed without having to worry about getting it through a door or ripping out an exterior wall to get the walk-in into the kitchen.

When choosing a walk-in, consideration should be given to the following:

- Door. Can be left opening, right opening, or sliding. The same considerations that were used to determine a left or right opening door on a reach-in would be taken into account here. *Note*: All walk-in doors must be fitted with an inside release on the door latch to prevent a person from being trapped inside. This release must function whether or not the door is padlocked.
- Door gasket. The rubber strip that goes around the door to ensure a tight fit when the door is closed. Make sure that it is replaceable.
- Door-heating strip. A wire that goes around the perimeter interior of the door to slightly heat the door edge, thus preventing excessive condensation from forming. This strip is particularly important in freezers since the condensation could freeze the door shut. In most walk-ins, the strip is located in the door gasket.
- Door panel. On most small to medium-sized walk-ins, several additional components are located on the door panel, including the following:

  ○ The interior light switch.
  ○ Interior light enclosed in a vapor-proof glass.
  ○ Thermometer.
  ○ Pressure relief vent, needed to avoid a vacuum from being created by different temperatures and air pressures when the door is closed.

In operations where there is a restaurant in conjunction with a bar, the bar should have its own walk-in due to the high propensity for theft for bottled beer. The walk-in should be kept locked at all times.

Ice Machines

When purchasing ice machines, a general understanding as to how they work is helpful when deciding which model to purchase. While there are minor differences in the method of making ice, the majority of manufacturers use the same process:

- A prechilled evaporator contains cube cells. An even level of water flows across the evaporator and into each cube cell, where it freezes.
- The water continues to flow until a complete cube of ice has formed in the cube cell. Having water flow continuously across the evaporator results in a clear cube of ice as opposed to simply filling the cube cell once, which would result in a cloudy cube of ice. With a continuous flow, the impurities in the water do not settle in the cube cell. An ice thickness probe determines when the cube cell is filled and an ice cube has formed. The water flow is then shut off.
- At this point, a hot gas is sent into the evaporator, warming it and causing the ice cubes to slide off the evaporator sheet.
- The cubes slide into a curtain that opens the bin, and the cubes slide into the ice storage bin.
- After the cubes pass the curtain, the curtain closes and the process repeats itself. These last three steps are known as the ice harvest.
- After a number of harvests, the ice-storage bin gets full. The ice being harvested has nowhere to go and consequently it holds the curtain open. When this happens, the ice machine stops functioning.
- At some point, when ice is removed from the bin, the ice that is "hung up" and is holding the curtain open slides down into the storage bin, thus closing the curtain. The ice machine starts up again and the process is repeated.
  Note: Instead of a curtain, some machines have a probe in the ice-storage bin. When the bin fills, ice touches the probe, which in turn shuts the ice production down until some of the ice is removed from the bin.

Some ice machines, rather than having cube cells, form the ice on a sheet. When the proper thickness of ice forms on this sheet, a hot wire grid comes down on the sheet, cutting the ice into cubes. Flaked ice is made in this fashion with the thickness of the sheet being much less than for cubes. Rather than having a hot wire grid, the thin sheet is broken into flakes.

In addition to cubes, ice can also be formed into half cubes, mini-cubes, moons, half-moons, circles, and several other sizes and shapes. It can also be manufactured as flaked or crushed. When purchasing an ice machine, keep in mind that most bar drinks, that is high balls and rocks, are made with cubes or some form of a cube. While blended drinks can be made with cubes as well, flaked ices works better. In high-volume bars, consideration should be given to purchasing separate machines. In moderate-size bars, cubes work best as an all-purpose ice shape.

The ice is transported from the ice bin to the area of use, such as a wait station or bar, where it is put into an ice-service bin. Never store wine, soda, or mixer bottles or fruit in the ice-service bin.

The capacity for an ice machine is predicated on a 24-hour day, 60°F (16°C) water temperature, and 70°F (21°C) room temperature. For every 10° difference in either the water or room temperature, there is a 10 percent variance in the ice production. Thus, if a 750-pound ice machine were placed in the middle of a kitchen with an average temperature of 90°F (32°C), it would produce only 600 pounds of ice in a 24-hour period.

750 pounds less 150 pounds {20 percent of capacity} = 600 pounds

An oft asked question is "what capacity of ice machine should I purchase?" While the average ice consumption per customer varies with the type of service and product offered in a bar, as well as the climatic conditions, a rule of thumb is 3 pounds of ice per customer per day. Keep in mind that this is a rule of thumb only and should be used with some common sense. If you are running a country and western bar in West Texas that sells primarily beer, you will need less ice than an upscale New York City nightclub that sells an abundance of blended drinks.

While ice machines and ice-storage bins look like one piece of equipment, for the most part, they are separate elements—often purchased and shipped separately. For example, you could purchase an ice machine with a 750-pound production capacity and place it on a bin. If you needed more capacity, another 750-pound machine could be stacked on top of your present machine, doubling the ice output. Most manufacturers can stack up to three machines. The only caveat is that the storage bin should be large enough to handle the output of the two or three machines. This system works in your favor because if the 750-pound capacity is insufficient for your operation, another machine can be added without purchasing a whole new setup and having to run another water line and install a floor drain at considerable expense. Figure 6.4 shows an ice machine on top of an ice bin.

FIGURE 6.4
An example of a single ice machine unit on top of an ice bin.
Scotsman Ice Machines

Frozen Beverage Dispensers

While frozen beverage dispensers are not an essential piece of equipment for a bar, they are invaluable where great volumes of high-profit-margin frozen drinks are produced. Whereas frozen cappuccinos, margaritas, daiquiris, and many other exotic cocktails can be offered in any bar that has an ice machine and a blender, they are labor intensive. With a frozen beverage dispenser, they can be produced quickly and efficiently.

There are basically two types of frozen beverage dispensers, one that produces slushes only and one that can produce frozen dairy products such as ice cream, custard, or soft serve as well as slushes. The refrigeration unit can be either built in or remote, air cooled or water cooled. The product can be poured directly into the machine and frozen, or it can be pumped in from a walk-in cooler. Several models have smart technology, which monitors product usage. They can also notify the operator when the machine needs maintenance or cleaning.

Blenders

The real workhorse of many bars is the blender. The blender containers vary in size from 32 ounces to 64 ounces. The container can be made from glass, stainless steel, or polycarbonate, a plastic-like substance. As glass can break, the stainless steel or polycarbonate is recommended. The power of a blender is rated by the horsepower rating of its motor with a ½ horsepower being the smallest to a very powerful 3½ horsepower blender. On most models, the blades will rotate from 27,000 to 40,000 rotations per minute (RPM). Most blenders have two speeds while the more expensive models have four or more speeds.

Espresso Machines

Many bar and beverage outlets have introduced a variety of European-style coffees such as cappuccino, espresso, and lattes. The machines that produce these coffees vary from the simple to complex.

There are three different types of espresso machines: steam driven, piston driven, and pump driven. While all of these machines are different, some of them carry common traits. In most machines whole coffee beans are stored in the appliance and ground to order, and the coffee is brewed to order. The taste of espresso is determined by how fine the bean is ground and the amount of pressure used to tamp the grinds. An espresso machine may also be equipped with a refrigerated compartment to store fresh milk as well as a steam wand, which is used to steam and froth milk for cappuccinos and lattes.

- Steam driven. The earliest espresso machines were all steam driven. They work by having a steam-driven unit force water through the coffee using steam pressure. They are still in use today; however, they are more prevalent in home machines rather than commercial ones.
- Piston-driven. This machine pressurizes the hot water by use of a pump, which is operated by the barista using a lever to drive the pump, sending the hot water through the coffee grounds. The coffee is then dispensed by pulling a long handle to dispense the espresso, hence the term "pulling a shot." There are two types of piston machines; one is a manual piston in which the operator directly pushes the water through the grounds and the other is a spring piston which provides the pressure.
- Pump driven. With a pump-driven machine, a motorized pump rather than manual force pushes the hot water through the grounds. Commercial machines are normally pump driven.

There is one other type of machine on the market to produce espresso, and that is one that uses all powdered products. Several hoppers inside the machine contain all of the ingredients necessary to produce European coffees. With the push of a button, anyone can be an "expert."

Carbonated Beverage Dispensers

There are two types of carbonated beverage dispensers: premix and postmix. Additionally, there are two methods of dispensing carbonated beverages. One is a hand-held device with buttons, commonly known as a bar gun. Each button corresponds to a particular flavor of beverage. When the button is pushed, the product is dispensed. The second is a tower-style box with a lever for each dispensing head, which represents each flavor of beverage. When the lever is pushed, product is dispensed. Bar guns are typically used in bars while the towers are used in restaurants and quick-service operations.

An espresso machine.
Nuova Simonelli S.P.A.

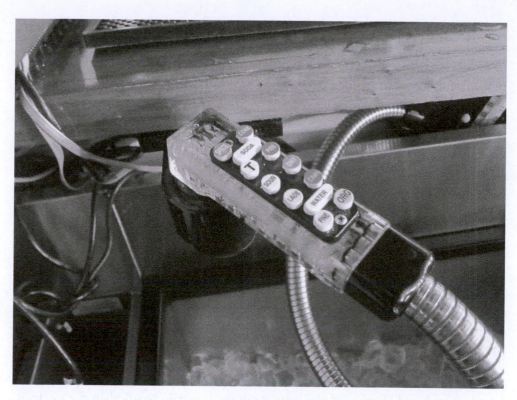

An example of a bar gun.
Photograph courtesy of Easybar
Beverage Management Systems Inc.

In a premix system, the carbonated beverage is delivered to the bar operation completely mixed in 5-gallon containers. The product in boxes, ready to use, is identical to the soda you would purchase in a grocery store in a 1-liter bottle. The only difference is the method of dispensing the product. While it is fairly easy to pick up a chilled 1-liter bottle and pour it into a glass of ice, 5 gallons is a different matter. That fact, along with the need to maintain product integrity and pour it at the proper temperature, means that some additional equipment is needed.

To commercially dispense carbonated beverages, a CO_2 tank is hooked up to a series of boxes of carbonated beverages. When a button is pushed on the dispensing head, the CO_2 pushes the product from the box, through a chilling device, and on to the dispensing valve, where it goes into a glass.

The chiller that it passes through can be either an electrical mechanical chiller or a cooling plate located in the bottom of the ice bin. If a cooling plate is used, no electricity is needed. Since the product is already mixed, no water is needed. Therefore, with the use of a cooling plate, the entire operation can be portable. Hence, premix setups are very popular with portable bars used at banquets.

On the other hand, the dispensing of postmix carbonated beverages is a little more complicated. It also uses 5-gallon boxes, but they contain syrup only.

1. The syrup is pushed from the box by the CO_2 gas and goes through the chiller and then on to the dispensing valve.
2. Incoming tap water goes through a filter process, then to the chiller and on to the carbonator, where it picks up its effervescence (carbonation).
3. The carbonated water then goes on to the dispensing valve. When the button is pushed on the bar gun, it is mixed with the chilled syrup, usually at a ratio of 5 parts of carbonated water to 1 part of syrup.

While postmix has a higher initial investment cost because of additional equipment, the product is much less expensive to purchase than premix. As a result, postmix gives a higher gross profit than premix and is thus the more popular of the two systems. Premix, however, has its advantage when a portable bar is necessary.

Caution: A problem arises in that the beverage or syrup line can be hooked up to the wrong box, resulting in the wrong flavor being dispensed from the dispensing head. To overcome this, each beverage or syrup line should be tagged, naming the flavor of the box to which it should be attached.

Glass Washing

There are several methods that can be employed to clean the glassware behind the bar. If the bar is being operated as a part of a restaurant, the glassware can be sent to the kitchen to be washed with the china. This has its advantage in that valuable bar space is not used for ware-washing equipment, nor is there a capital expense to purchase it. The downside is that additional labor is required to move the soiled glassware from the bar to the kitchen and the clean from the kitchen to the bar. Another problem could occur if the restaurant is busy and the dishwashers are getting "slammed," the bar could run out of glassware. Additionally, fragile stemware tends to get broken more easily when sent to the kitchen to be washed. Perhaps the biggest argument against this method is that the glassware does not get "bar clean." Detergent and rinse additives cling to the glassware resulting in difficulty getting a perfect head on a draft beer. While some restaurant and bar operations use this method, the majority opt to keep the bar glassware in the bar area and wash them there.

Cleaning glassware behind the bar can be done either manually or mechanically. If done manually, it will be necessary to have a four-compartment bar sink with a drain board on each end. The soiled glassware is put on one drain board, then the ice, fruit, and/or leftover beverage is dumped into the first sink. The second sink is for washing and will require upright brushes to aid in the cleaning process. These brushes can be either stationary or mechanically rotated. The third sink is for rinsing, and the fourth sink is for sanitizing. The clean glassware is then put on the other drain board to be air dried. Never hand-dry glassware as this is liable to contaminate it. This operation can be done either left to right or right to left depending on the bartender or bar back's preference.

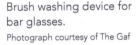

Brush washing device for bar glasses.
Photograph courtesy of The Gaf

Mechanical washing of glassware will require purchasing a glass washer. There are several styles from which to choose. All glass washers have several things in common. First and foremost, their primary purpose is to clean and sanitize. The key words here are *clean* and *sanitize*. Glasses are cleaned primarily by water pressure. While detergents are used to loosen any soil on the glasses, the water pressure ultimately cleans them. Most commercial glass washers have water coming out of the wash arms at 15 to 20 PSI, and this pressure removes the soil.

The glasses are then sanitized by either high water temperature or chemicals. Thus there are two types of glass washers: high temperature and low temperature. While their operating characteristics are essentially the same, the means of sanitizing are vastly different. High-temperature glass washers sanitize by killing bacteria with heat. They do this in the final rinse cycle when the glasses are rinsed with clear water that is at a minimum of 180°F (83°C). Low-temperature glass washers, on the other hand, sanitize by using chemicals and have a temperature of 135°F (58°C) maximum. Notice that the temperature on the high-temperature machine is a minimum and the temperature on the low-temperature machine is a maximum. On the low-temperature machine, this is to avoid having the chemicals being dissipated by evaporation.

An under-counter bar glass washing machine.
Photograph Courtesy of Moyer Diebel

Bar Die

What people normally refer to as "the bar" is technically called the **bar die**. It is often custom built to fit the room both in terms of size and aesthetics. Behind and underneath the bar die, in many cases, is the four-compartment sink or glass washing machine, ice bin, blender stand, and liquor well.

Since the bar die is custom built, the specification for it must be very detailed. The dimensions must be accurate and the materials carefully detailed. While all bar dies look different to the casual observer, their dimensions, except for the length are, in most cases, the same. They are 42 inches high. The top of the bar is 2 feet in depth, which includes a 4-inch water drain and an arm rest. On the front of the bar at the base is a foot rest. While many bars do not have them, it is a good idea to provide a hook under the bar overhang for ladies to hang their purses. Chapter 7 goes into detail about the dimensions of bar dies.

Back Bar

Like the bar die, the back bar is also custom built. It normally houses the premium and call spirits, glass storage, and sometimes a display of the various bottled beers, ales, and lagers served by the operation. The cash register or POS monitor is usually located there as well. In bars that have a high volume of draft beer, the back of the back bar is up against the walk-in keg cooler. Where a lower volume of draft beer is sold, a keg cabinet could be located on the back bar or under the front bar die. As will be explained in the next chapter on design, there are many variations as to what is located where.

Cash Registers and Point-of-Sale Systems

The handling of cash and recording of sales are very important. In small bars where the owner is on the premises most of the time, a simple cash register will suffice.

The front section of a bar die.
photograph courtesy of The Gaf

A section of a back bar
showing call and premium
spirits.
Photograph courtesy of The Gaf

In beverage outlets with high or even moderate volume, the POS system is the best option. Consider what this system can do:

- It records the customer's order, which goes directly to the bar and is printed out, thus reducing verbal mistakes.
- Reduces the time it takes between the customer's order and the delivery of his or her product.
- Simultaneously, it integrates that order with all of the other orders for the shift and gives management a total of the sales with a breakdown of what has been sold by server, by bartender, by drink and category.
- It can accept debit cards, credit cards, and gift cards and process them for payment.
- If the servers have handheld devices, as soon as the customer orders, the request is transmitted to the bartender, saving more time between order and delivery.
- It can clock all of the employees in and out, reducing labor costs for unworked time.
- It can be integrated with other software that gives a perpetual inventory, thus allowing for management to purchase goods and run checks and balances on its controls.
- The next generation of POS systems will have the customer order food and drinks on a handheld device or one built in to the table or bar. The server will deliver the order to the customer. When the customer is ready to leave, they insert their credit or debit card into the device and complete the transaction. The advantage of this system is that the server never handles the debit or credit card, thus giving a sense of security to the customer. The downside is that the server cannot up sell, and it also curtails interaction with the customer, thus establishing an impersonal relationship with the guest.

When writing specifications for a POS system, make sure that it can do all of the things that you want it to do or can at least be modified in the future to accommodate additional functions.

A Point of Sale (POS) system.
Photograph courtesy of The Gaf

Portable Bars

Portable bars are very expedient for receptions, often in conjunction with a large banquet. They are used in ballrooms or large meeting rooms where the room arrangement is different with each event. They give management the ability to configure the room to any layout because of their ability to be moved anywhere. Portable bars can also be moved outdoors for receptions.

A portable bar must be totally self-contained. Rarely is there an accessible water line or drain and often there is no electricity available either. While these are obstacles, they can be overcome. Keep in mind that a portable bar mixes and serves drinks only and does not wash glasses. These are taken to the kitchen and run through the dishwasher, or disposable glassware is used. Water for mixing drinks is put in pitchers.

When setting up a portable bar, it is important that it be totally self-sufficient. What is stocked on the bar is dependent on the menu. A portable bar can be as simple as a 6-foot skirted banquet table in front and another 6-foot skirted banquet table to serve as the back bar. Plastic bins are used to store ice for drinks. They can also be used to ice down bottled beer, wine, and soft drinks (*note*: Do not use this ice for mixed drinks).

A more professional look can be had by using a manufactured portable bar on wheels. These usually contain an ice bin that drains into a bucket, a work area, and a liquor well. They can have a self-contained premix set up for mixes and soft drinks. The back bar is also on wheels and has an ice bin and drain bucket for cooling beer and wine. Glassware is stored on the back bar. A single-keg beer dispenser on wheels can also be added if the client wants draft beer. Note that it will be necessary to have electricity available if this is used.

Another consideration is how cash is to be handled. If the event is a host bar, there is no issue. If the guests are paying for their drinks, a cash register must be added to the equipment list. This also will require an electrical outlet. Often a cashier is employed to take cash and dispense tickets, which are then turned in to the bartender, and other times the bartender collects the cash. As you will recall, these issues were discussed in Chapter 1.

GREEN EQUIPMENT

There is a major emphasis today on making bars and other establishments more environmentally friendly. One of the most important aspects of this movement involves purchasing equipment, as the majority of the bar's utility usage comes from equipment operation. Along with all of the other considerations in selecting the make and model that are right for your operation, comes the conundrum of choosing the one that uses the least amount of energy or water. Fortunately, the government has done the homework on this issue with the Energy Star rating system. Purchasing Energy Star equipment for new bar construction or as a replacement for aging equipment can save significant amounts of money and energy on an operator's electric, gas, water, and sewer bills. The Energy Star rating system is available on the following categories of commercial restaurant and bar equipment: fryers, hot-food holding cabinets, refrigerators and freezers, steam cookers, dishwashers, ice makers, griddles, and ovens. Qualified products can save up to 50 percent over their conventional counterparts.

For example, an average commercial refrigeration unit that carries the Energy Star designation is more energy efficient because it is designed with improved evaporator and condenser fan motors and high-efficiency compressors, which results in reducing energy consumption and ultimately your electric bill. Keep in mind that these improvements cost money and that an Energy Star piece of equipment will normally cost more than a standard piece of equipment. However, compared to standard models, Energy Star commercial refrigerators can achieve energy savings of as much as 30 percent with a 2.9 year payback. In other words, the additional cost to the purchaser will be recouped by saving in energy costs in 2.9 years on the average. This means that purchasers can expect to save $200, more or less, depending on the utility rates in their area, annually per refrigerator. Figure 6.5 gives an example of the cost effectiveness of an Energy Star refrigerator.

HOW TO PURCHASE EQUIPMENT

There is a right way and a wrong way to purchase equipment. All too often bar owners or managers simply call up their local equipment distributor or their full-line foodservice wholesaler and tell them they need a new piece of equipment. They get a price quote of one or more manufacturers and models, make a decision, and then purchase the equipment. WRONG!!! Consider this: Purchasing equipment is like buying a car; you never, never, never, pay the list price. Before a discussion on the correct method to purchase equipment can begin, it is necessary to examine how equipment moves through the distribution system and how the owner or manager needs to work within that system to obtain the best price possible.

Equipment Distribution System

To fully understand the correct method of purchasing equipment, it is necessary to understand the **distribution system**. First there is the **manufacturer**. They design and build the equipment. Very few of them sell directly to a restaurant or lounge. Instead, they hire **manufacturer representatives** or reps that represent their products to dealers. Most manufacturer reps will speak for several manufacturers. They work with consultants, architects, and builders to specify their client's equipment when new operations are being built. They also work with large corporations and chains to induce them to purchase their manufacturer's brand. Their primary job, however, is to get the dealers, who sell to the end user, to carry the brands they represent and to market and sell those brands. Often times this is done by offering incentives to the dealers

Products that earn the ENERGY STAR prevent greenhouse gas emissions by meeting strict energy efficiency guidelines set by the U.S. Environmental Protection Agency and the U.S. Department of Energy.
www.energystar.gov

CHANGE FOR THE BETTER WITH ENERGY STAR

Life Cycle Cost Estimate for 1 ENERGY STAR Qualified Commercial Refrigerators

This energy savings calculator was developed by the U.S. EPA and U.S. DOE and is provided for estimating purposes only. Actual energy savings may vary based on use and other factors.

Enter your own values in the gray boxes or use our default values.

Number of units	1	
Electricity Rate ($/kWh)	$0.095	

	ENERGY STAR Qualified Unit	Conventional Unit
Initial cost per unit (estimated retail price)	$2,450	$2,122
Volume (ft^3)	44	44
Unit energy consumption (kWh/year)	2,351	3,548

Annual and Life Cycle Costs and Savings for 1 Commercial Refrigerators

	1 ENERGY STAR Qualified Units	1 Conventional Units	Savings with ENERGY STAR
Annual Operating Costs*			
Energy cost	$224	$338	$114
Maintenance cost	$0	$0	$0
Total	**$224**	**$338**	**$114**
Life Cycle Costs*			
Operating cost (energy and maintenance)	$2,100	$3,170	$1,070
Purchase price for 1 unit(s)	$2,450	$2,122	−$328
Total	**$4,550**	**$5,292**	**$742**
Simple payback of initial additional cost (years)†			**2.9**

Annual costs exclude the initial purchase price. All costs, except initial cost, are discounted over the products' lifetime using a real discount rate of 4%. See "Assumptions" to change factors including the discount rate.

†*A simple payback period of zero years means that the payback is immediate.*

Summary of Benefits for 1 Commercial Refrigerators

Initial cost difference	$328
Life cycle savings	$1,070
Net life cycle savings (life cycle savings - additional cost)	$742
Simple payback of additional cost (years)	2.9
Life cycle energy saved (kWh)	14,369
Life cycle air pollution reduction (lbs of CO_2)	22,128
Air pollution reduction equivalence (number of cars removed from the road for a year	1.84
Air pollution reduction equivalence (acres of forest)	2.28
Savings as a percent of retail price	30%

FIGURE 6.5

An example of an energy savings chart using an Energy Star refrigerator.

Chart courtesy of the United States Department of Energy.

Assumptions for Commercial Refrigerators

Category	Value	Data Source
Power		
ENERGY STAR Qualified Unit		
Initial cost per unit (estimated retail price)	$2,450	Industry Data 2007
Volume	44 ft^3	FSTC 2007
Unit Energy Consumption	2,351 kWh/year	ENERGY STAR Specification
Lifetime	12 years	FSTC 2007
Conventional Unit		
Initial cost per unit (estimated retail price)	$2,122	Industry Data 2007
Volume	44 ft^3	FSTC 2007
Unit Energy Consumption	3,548 kWh/year	FSTC 2007
Lifetime	12 years	FSTC 2007
Maintenance		
Labor cost (per hour)	$20	EPA 2004
Labor time (hours)	0	EPA 2004
Usage		
Number of operating days per year	365 days/year	EPA 2004
Discount Rate		
Commercial and Residential Discount Rate (real)	4%	A real discount rate of 4 percent is assumed, which is roughly equivalent to the nominal discount rate of 7 percent (4 percent real discount rate + 3 percent inflation rate).
Energy Prices		
Commercial Electricity Price	$0.0952 $/kWh	EIA 2008
Residential Electricity Price	$0.1059 $/kWh	EIA 2008
Carbon Dioxide Emissions Factors		
Electricity Carbon Dioxide Emission Factor	1.54 lbs CO_2/kWh	EPA 2008
CO_2 Equivalents		
Annual CO_2 sequestration per forested acre	9,700 lbs CO_2/yr	EPA 2007
Annual CO_2 emissions for "average" passenger car	12,037 lbs CO_2/yr	EPA 2007
For questions or comments, please send your email to: Escalcs@cadmusgroup.com		
Constants updated 08/08		

FIGURE 6.5   *(Continued)*

to sell a particular brand or model number. The dealers then sell, deliver, and in some cases install the equipment to the restaurants, bars, and lounges.

The Bid Process

Once again, manufacturers sell to dealers via the manufacturer rep. Manufacturers do not generally sell directly to the end user. The markup on equipment from the manufacturer to the dealer is quite high, leaving ample room for the dealer to negotiate price. For this reason, the best and only way for the buyer to obtain the lowest price for equipment is to have several dealers **bid** on the equipment. In order for the bidding to be accurate, a specification for the equipment must be written. A **specification** lists all of the important data pertaining to the equipment so that each dealer is bidding on the exact same piece. Specifications will be covered in more detail later in the chapter. Suffice it to say for now that bidding is the only way to properly purchase equipment at the lowest possible price.

For example, if the owner of a bar wanted to replace an ice machine and went to an equipment dealer, the dealer would quote a price and maybe to close the deal would offer a discount of 10 percent. If on the other hand the bar owner wrote a specification for the ice machine and sent it to several dealers to bid, the discount would likely be in the 40–45 percent range. The savings by using the bid process is considerable. Imagine if it were a new business that planned on investing $100,000 in equipment and furnishings.

Another factor to consider is the relationship between the manufacturer, the rep, and the dealer. If the manufacturer had a particular model number they were having trouble selling, they would have their rep push that particular model. Remember that the manufacturer's rep called on the dealer and offered them monetary incentives to sell the brand. If the bar manager went to a dealer and said "I need a new ice machine," guess which one they would get. The point is that the owner or manager, by researching exactly what they wanted in terms of a piece of equipment, writing a specification, and bidding it out, would get what was best for their bar, not what is best for the manufacturer or dealer.

This is not to say that manufacturers, their reps, or dealers are unscrupulous or dishonest. To the contrary, most are very ethical businesses. Like any other business, they need to maximize profits. They want to sell their products at the highest possible price. If they need to offer incentives to move a slow-moving item, they will. This is not unlike a bar, which wants to charge the highest price that the traffic will bear and will offer incentives like happy hours to induce customers to come into their place of business.

Selection

As previously discussed, when purchasing equipment for a new operation, the menu in terms of what beverages are to be sold, the extent of the wine selection, and the types of beers, ales, and lagers to be offered is consulted (or, in the case of an existing operation, what is to be replaced or what new equipment is desired). From this, the decision can be made as to the specific piece of equipment to purchase. Included in this decision should be the capacity of that equipment. The next step is to select the manufacturer and the model number. Keep in mind that often the model number, among other things, determines the capacity.

There are two ways to select equipment. The first is by going through the manufacturers' catalogs. Each piece of equipment is listed on a **cut sheet**, which explains the equipment, its design, its capacity, how it is constructed, its dimensions, and any electrical, gas, or water data. See Figure 6.6 for an example of a cut sheet. While you can go to a dealer and peruse their catalogs, for reasons mentioned earlier, it is probably best to avoid the dealer at this stage of the process and go to the manufacturer rep's office. This process is time consuming, and often the catalogs are not kept up to date. Should you opt to do this it will be necessary to photocopy the cut sheet of the equipment you select. The easiest and best way to shop for equipment is on the Internet. By utilizing the various manufacturers' Web sites, information can be obtained quickly and accurately. All of the manufacturers can be located by using one of the Internet search engines.

Another excellent method is to visit the various shows like the National Restaurant Association (NRA) Show in Chicago, the American Hotel and Lodging Association (AHLA) in New York, or the National Association of Food Equipment Manufacturers (NAFEM) show, which is held in various cities. Many state associations also have state or regional shows that display equipment.

Scotsman®

PRODIGY®
smart thinking

C0522 – 500 lb Cube Ice Machine

Prodigy® Modular Cube Ice Maker

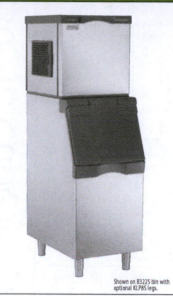

Shown on B322S bin with optional KLP8S legs.

Features

Prodigy® cubers use significantly less energy and water than other cube ice machines, exceeding California and Federal energy efficiency regulations.

AutoAlert™ indicator lights constantly communicate about operating status and actually signal your staff when it's time to descale, sanitize, and more— making upkeep practically foolproof.

The patented WaterSense adaptive purge control delivers maximum reliability by reducing scale buildup for a longer time between cleanings.

Preventative maintenance is simpler than ever with easily-removed panels allowing clear access to internal components and a diagnostic code display insuring the right fix the first time. Reusable air filter is easily removable from the outside.

All external panel components are crafted for optimal aesthetic appeal through superior fit and finish.

An optional advanced feature Smart-Board™ provides NAFEM data protocol and additional operational data that can be displayed on-screen or transmitted remotely, resulting in early alert and fast diagnosis of operating issues.

An optional Vari-Smart™ ultrasonic ice level control sensor allows you flexibility to program ice levels, for up to 7 days, keeping just the right amount of freshly made ice in the bin.

24 Hour Volume Production

Air Cooled			Remote			Water Cooled		
70°F/21°C 50°F/10°C lb/kg	Air Water	ARI 90°F/32°C 70°F/21°C lb/kg	70°F/21°C 50°F/10°C lb/kg	Air Water	ARI 90°F/32°C 70°F/21°C lb/kg	70°F/21°C 50°F/10°C lb/kg	Air Water	ARI 90°F/32°C 70°F/21°C lb/kg
475/216		380/160	517/235		460/209	549/250		480/218

  c(UL)us NSF

  CE CERTIFIED ISO 9001:2000

Modular Bin Options

Model Number	Dimensions W″ x D″ x H″	ARI Certified Bin Capacity lb/kg	Application Capacity lb/kg	Finish	Ship Weight lb/kg
B222S	22 x 34 x 32	190/86	242/110	SS	120/55
B322S	22 x 34 x 44	290/132	370/168	SS	140/64

 ARI PERFORMANCE CERTIFIED agion Nature's antimicrobial

NAFEM DATA PROTOCOL COMPLIANT

Bin: B222S

Cube Ice

Small Cube
⅞″ x ⅞″ x ⅜″
(2.22 x 2.22 x .95 cm)

Medium Cube
⅞″ x ⅞″ x ⅞″
(2.22 x 2.22 x 2.22 cm)

Common ice form, ideal for mixed drinks.

Warranty

• 3 years parts and labor on all components.
• 5 years parts and labor on the evaporator.
• 5 years parts on the compressor and condenser.

Warranty valid in North, South & Central America. Contact factory for warranty in other regions.

FIGURE 6.6 An example of a cut sheet for an ice machine and bin.
Scotsman Ice Machines

Scotsman®
The smart choice in ice.™

C0522 – 500 lb Cube Ice Machine

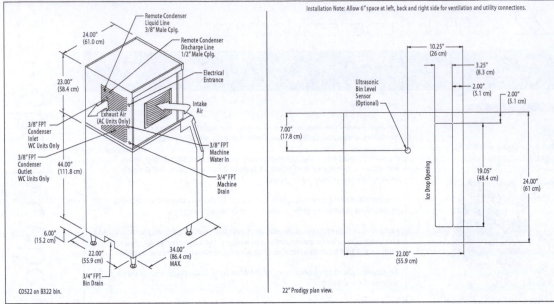

C0522 on B322 bin.

22" Prodigy plan view.

Specifications

Model Number* Cube Size: medium or small	Condenser Unit	Basic Electrical Volts/Hz/Phase	Max. Fuse Size or HACR Circuit Breaker (amps)	Circuit Wires	Min. Circuit Ampacity	Energy Consumption kWh/100 lb (45.4 kg) 90°F(32°C)/70°F(21°C)	Water Usage Gallons/100 lb (liters/45.4 kg) Potable 90°F(32°C)/ 70°F(21°C)	Condenser 90°F(32°C)/ 70°F(21°C)
med. C0522MA-1A	Air	115/60/1	15	2	13.8	6.7	18.5/70.2	-
C0522MR-1A	Remote	115/60/1	15	2	14.9	6.5	18.2/69.0	-
C0522MW-1A	Water	115/60/1	15	2	12.2	4.7	18.4/69.7	160.0/605.7
sm. C0522SA-1A	Air	115/60/1	15	2	13.8	6.7	18.5/70.2	-
C0522SR-1A	Remote	115/60/1	15	2	14.9	6.5	18.2/69.0	-
C0522SW-1A	Water	115/60/1	15	2	12.2	4.7	18.4/69.7	160.0/605.7

* 208-230/60/1 Voltage - Substitute "-32" in place of "-1", i.e. C0522SA-32A.

All Models

Dimensions (W x D x H):
Unit:
    22" x 24" x 23"
    (55.9 x 61.0 x 58.4 cm)
Shipping Carton:
    25.5" x 27.5" x 28"
    (64.8 x 69.9 x 71.1 cm)
Shipping Weight:
    160 lb / 73 kg
BTUs per hour:
    7,900

Accessories

Model Number	Description
KVS	Vari-Smart™ Ice Level Control - Program ice bin levels to match ice needs.
KSB	Smart-Board™ Advanced Control - Use additional operational data for fast diagnosis.
KSB-N	Smart-Board™ Advanced Control with Network - Network capable.
ERC111-1A	Remote Condenser for C0522xR, 115/60/1 - Consult Remote Condenser Spec Sheet for details.
RTE10	Line set, Precharged, R-404A, 10ft.
RTE25	Line set, Precharged, R-404A, 25ft.
RTE40	Line set, Precharged, R-404A, 40ft.
RTE75	Line set, Precharged, R-404A, 75ft.

* Scotsman recommends all ice machines have water filtration. See Scotsman Sanitation Matrix for details.

Operating Requirements

	Minimum	Maximum
Air Temperatures	50°F (10°C)	100°F (38°C)
Water Temperatures	40°F (4.4°C)	100°F (38°C)
Remote Cond. Temps	-20°F (-29°C)	120°F (49°C)
Water Pressures	20 PSIG (1.4 bar)	80 PSIG (5.5 bar)
Electrical Voltage	-10%	+10%

Specifications and design are subject to change without notice.

FIGURE 6.6   *(Continued)*

Should you opt out of spending the necessary time to select the proper equipment, a consultant could be the answer. More often than not the fee they charge will be offset by the savings to be had by bidding the equipment rather than going to one dealer. Plus you get their expertise on which piece of equipment and which model would be best for your operation. When hiring a consultant, always check references. Many of the top consultants belong to the Foodservice Consultants Society International and have the FCSI initials behind their name.

New versus Used

There is a common misperception among restaurant and bar owners that by purchasing used equipment, they can save large sums of money. This may or may not be true depending on several factors.

First and foremost, the person doing the buying must be knowledgeable about equipment, know what to look for, and be familiar with its price. All too often, people get caught up in a buying frenzy at an auction or with an overzealous used equipment salesperson's spiel and pay almost as much for the item as it would have cost new. Consider that most new equipment comes with either a guarantee or warranty, and the difference could well merit buying new and being protected. Consider also the working condition of the equipment. How long will it last? When purchasing used, the economic theory of *caveat emptor*, "let the buyer beware," applies. When you leave the auction or the person selling the used equipment, it is yours and there is no recourse.

A good rule of thumb to follow is that the more moving parts there are to the equipment, the greater propensity to purchase new. For example, if purchasing a stainless steel worktable, used would be fine. Other than a drawer slide there are no moving parts. If a four-compartment bar sink, were being considered, the only part that could wear out would be the faucet. If the price to be paid for a used sink plus the price of a new faucet were less than a new sink, then it would be a good value. On the other hand, when purchasing a keg cooler, there are many parts that could need replacing: the compressor, condenser, evaporator, refrigerant, door hinges and handles, and shelving, not to mention that most new coolers come with a five-year warrantee on parts and labor. When purchasing any refrigeration unit, strongly contemplate buying new.

As with buying new, make sure the piece that is being purchased will fit into the space allotted and that the power source matches up. Also remember that when buying new, the equipment is delivered. When purchasing used at an auction or from another bar owner, you do the hauling.

Bid Conditions

When purchasing new bar equipment, the first part of the bid process concerns itself with the **bid conditions**, sometimes referred to as conditions to bid or invitation to bid. Either way they are the same thing and outline the rules that the bidders, in this case the dealers, need to follow. This is an important document as it eliminates any confusion between the buyer and the seller. It also makes it a level playing field for all bidders. In other words, everyone is bidding on the same item under the same conditions. An invitation to bid is often a lengthy text, or it can be as short as one or two pages. Regardless, it is a legal document and should be constructed carefully and contain the following information:

- Construction schedule. If one piece of equipment is being purchased, this is quite simple. When will it be delivered? If it is a new operation being constructed, this becomes a major scheduling process, often with a bonus if work is completed ahead of schedule and a penalty if it is completed behind schedule.

- Payment schedule. When and how will the buyer pay? The standard payment schedule in this industry is 30/60/10. This means that the winning bidder will receive 30 percent of the bid price when the bid is awarded, 60 percent on delivery of the equipment or completion of the work performed, and 10 percent thirty days later. It is important that the last 10 percent be held back in case the equipment malfunctions or there are other problems.
- Insurance held by bidder. The primary insurance that the bar owner should be concerned with is liability and workman's compensation is case there is an accident during delivery or installation. Evidence of insurance should be presented to the bar owner prior to awarding the bid.
- Delivery conditions. Is the equipment to be delivered and left on the loading dock, is it to be set in place, or is it to be installed and hooked up to the utilities?
- Installation. This criterion can get quite problematic. Some dealers will hook equipment up to the utilities and others will not. It should be clearly stated who is to perform this work. If it is a new operation and the dealer is to install the equipment and connect to the utilities, will there be any union issues? Experience has shown that the best possible scenario is to have the dealer install and hook all of the equipment up. Problems arise when everything is installed and turned on and the ice machine does not work or the dish machine will not get hot enough, and so forth. If the contractor hooks it up and it does not work, they will blame it on the fact that the equipment does not work. The dealer will say it was hooked up wrong, and the owner is left resolving the issue. If the dealer hooks it up and it does not work properly, there is only one person to deal with to have the situation rectified.
- General construction criteria. This pertains to how the equipment is to be constructed. It is particularly important when purchasing several pieces of equipment. Generally, the certification or approval of regulatory agencies is sufficient to ensure that the equipment is constructed properly. While most equipment constructed in the United States meets these criteria, many imports do not. With the advent of the global economy, it is wise to make sure that the equipment is approved. Some of the agencies that approve commercial restaurant and bar equipment include the following:

  ○ Underwriter's Lab (UL)
  ○ National Sanitation Foundation (NSF)
  ○ American Gas Association (AGA)
  ○ National Electric Manufacturers Association (NEMA)
  ○ National Fire Protection Association (NFPA)

Specifications

Once the invitation to bid has been written, it will be necessary to write out the specification or, in the case of a new operation, specifications. The information on a specification is found on the cut sheet or from the manufacturer's Web site. An equipment specification has seven parts:

1. Equipment name
2. Manufacturer's name
3. Model number
4. Dimensions
5. Material
6. Power source
7. Miscellaneous information

FIGURE 6.7

A written specification that is based on an ice machine and bin based in Figure 6.6.

Specification
Equipment name: Cube ice machine with bin
Manufacturer's name: Scotsman
Model number: CO522 Ice maker with B322S bin
Dimensions: Ice maker 22"/24"/23" Bin 22"/34"/44"
Material: Stainless steel
Power source: 115 volts/60 cycles (HZ)/Single phase
Miscellaneous information:
- Ice bin shall sit on four KLP8S legs
- Shall produce a medium sized cube 7/8" × 7/8" × 7/8"
- Shall include a KVS ice level controls system
- Warranty to include three years parts and labor on all components, five years parts and labor on the evaporator, five year parts on the compressor and condenser.

The first four parts of the specification are self-explanatory. Number five, material, will often necessitate a decision. What do you want the equipment made of? For example, a refrigerator could have an exterior made of stainless steel or aluminum. Number six, power source, is very important. Some equipment can be powered by either electricity or gas. A good example would be the booster heater on the glass washing machine in which the water can be heated by either gas or electricity. With equipment running on electricity, the exact voltage must be specified or the equipment will not work. Number seven, miscellaneous information, is data that is not covered in sections one through six. Most equipment comes with options that can be purchased at an additional cost. Should any of these options be desired, they would be listed here. Figure 6.7 gives an example of a specification.

In order for the dealer to bid properly, they must know exactly what you want. If there is any question in their mind or if the specification is not accurately written, rest assured they will bid on the cheaper of the alternatives in order to come in with the lowest price. The result is that you will not get what you thought you were getting.

CLEANING AND MAINTENANCE

Refrigeration Units

Maintenance duties on bar equipment concern themselves primarily with refrigeration equipment. If a glass washer is used, there are some maintenance duties to be performed on it as well. Regarding refrigeration, the following maintenance duties should be performed on a monthly basis on all units. Stage the duties so that one duty is performed each week. For example,

- Deep cleaning. Remove all items from the refrigeration unit and place in another unit. On walk-ins, move the items to another shelf. Wipe down the interior and exterior walls, ceiling, floor, and shelving with a clean cloth that has been saturated and wrung dry in a solution of water and mild detergent. For heavy stains, a mild nonabrasive cleanser can be used. If the exterior is stainless steel, a thin coat of stainless steel polish can be applied according to the manufacturer's directions.
- Door gaskets. Clean the door gaskets using a solution of baking soda and warm water to wash them. Wipe the gaskets dry with a clean cloth. If the gaskets are

cracked or worn, they should be replaced. The purpose of the gaskets is to ensure a complete seal around the door, trapping the cold air in and keeping the warm out. A cracked or worn gasket also allows moisture into the unit and forces the unit to work overtime, drastically shortening the life of the refrigeration component.

- Condenser coils. Prior to performing this procedure, disconnect the unit from the power source. Clean the condenser coils with a vacuum cleaner or stiff brush, being careful not to bend the fins. If the fins are completely blocked when the unit is cleaned, this procedure should be increased to every other week.
- Defrost cycle. Should there be a frequent frost buildup on the evaporator, increase the number of defrost cycles per day on the defrost time clock.
- Door hinges. Lubricate the door hinges with petroleum jelly. Check the hinge screws and tighten them if necessary.

There are a few additional duties to be performed monthly on walk-ins. First, check the heater wire around the door opening. It is normally located inside the door gasket. It should be warm to the touch. Also check for frost or sweating around the wire. If this occurs, call a qualified service contractor to replace the heater wire. If the unit is a modularly constructed unit, check the interior of the walk-in for missing plug buttons and replace them if they are missing. This prevents moisture from getting into the insulation inside the wall panel.

Ice Machine

The exterior of the ice machine and storage bin should be cleaned on a regular basis as needed. Use a damp clean towel for routine cleaning. For heavier soil, use a nonabrasive cleaner according to the manufacturer's directions. The machine and bin should be cleaned at least every six months and more often than that if the water conditions require it. When cleaning the interior of the ice machine, there are two functions to complete. One is the cleaning procedure that removes lime and other mineral deposits. The other is the sanitizing procedure, which removes algae and slime. Both should be done separately.

Note: Do not mix cleaner solutions and sanitizing solutions in order to do both procedures at the same time.

- When the machine has completed a harvest cycle, turn it off. If more than one machine feeds a bin, turn all machines off.
- Empty all ice from the ice storage bin.
- Turn the switch to the Wash or Clean position.
- Use rubber gloves, an apron, and eye protection when working with the cleaning and sanitizing solutions.
- Adding the cleaning solution to the machine requires that you read the manufacturer's directions. Some manufacturers specify that it be added to the water trough, while others specify that it be added to water level control tube or the control stream box. Use only the cleaning solution that came with the machine. Replacement cleaning solution can be ordered directly from the manufacturer. Failure to correctly use the recommended solution in the proper amount could void the warranty.
- After the cleaning solution has been added, the machine goes through a self-cleaning process. This lasts approximately half an hour.
- Rinse the machine according to the manufacturer's directions.
- Repeat this procedure using the sanitizing solution recommended by the manufacturer.

- When the sanitizing cycle is complete (in approximately 15 minutes), turn the switch from the Wash or Clean position to the Ice or On position.

While the ice machine is self-cleaning and sanitizing itself, clean the ice-storage bin, which has already been emptied. Use a solution of a half cup of baking soda per gallon of warm water. Rinse the bin and sanitize it with a solution of 1 teaspoon of household bleach per quart of warm water. Do not use strong detergents, appliance polishes, or finish preservatives in cleaning the interior portion of the bin.

In addition to cleaning and sanitizing the ice-machine and ice-storage bin, it is also necessary to clean the condenser (assuming it is an air-cooled machine) on a monthly basis. A dirty condenser reduces the capacity of ice production in the machine and also shortens the life of the condenser. *Note*: Prior to cleaning the condenser, disconnect the electric power to the machine.

Clean the condenser fins either with a soft brush or with a vacuum and brush attachment. Be careful not to bend the condenser fins. Should they become bent, they should be straightened with a fin comb. If the brush or vacuum does not adequately clean the fins, either blow compressed air from the inside through the fins or clean the fins with a commercial condenser coil cleaner.

The fan blades should also be cleaned at this time. Use a damp cloth to wipe the blades and the exterior of the motor. Do not allow water to get into the motor.

Check waterlines and fittings for leaks. Make sure that the tubing is not rubbing or vibrating against other tubing or panels.

Carbonated Beverage Dispenser

Daily, take the temperature of the beverage by pouring out the first one and taking the temperature of the second drink. The temperature should be 40°F (4°C) or less.

Weekly, clean the syrup box storage area. Check the syrup connector valves for leaks and clean around the connectors with soap and warm water. Rinse off all soap. When hooking up a fresh box or tank of syrup, clean the inside of the syrup connector with soap and warm water. Thoroughly rinse off all soap.

On a quarterly basis, check for proper carbonated water flow by using a Brix cup and syrup separator. The flow should be 5 ounces in four seconds. Also check for proper syrup-to-water ratios, normally 1:5. If either of these rates is not at their proper level, call a qualified person to adjust the system. In addition to a Brix cup and syrup separator, a refractometer can be used to measure the syrup-to-water ratio. If the refrigeration unit is equipped with an air-cooled condenser, clean it with a vacuum cleaner.

The entire carbonated beverage system should be thoroughly inspected by a competent carbonated beverage specialist every three months. Leading syrup manufacturers (e.g., Coca Cola, Pepsi Cola, and others) normally provide this service at no charge to their customers.

Beer Taps

The entire beer system, including the faucet, beer line, and tapping devices should be cleaned chemically once a month. Additionally, the entire system should be flushed with clean water each and every time a keg is changed. This is important if you want to serve a good-tasting glass of beer. Failure to do so will result in the following:

- Bacteria growth. Bacteria, like humans, love beer. While these bacteria are not harmful, they will affect the quality of the beer. By regular cleaning, this bacterial buildup is prevented and the quality level is maintained. Green- or yellow-colored material on a faucet may indicate bacterial growth.

- Yeast fermentation. Remember that all domestic draft beers contain yeast from the fermentation process. A small amount of this yeast remains in the beer. When the temperature of draft beer exceeds 50°F, a process of secondary fermentation may take place. The beer faucet may display a yeast buildup, which looks like a white-colored material if not cleaned on a regular basis.
- Beer Stone. All beer contains calcium, which is present from the grains used in the brewing process. It is important to the draft system in that as it oxidizes, it coats the internal parts of the beer lines and equipment. This coating prevents the beer from picking up strong metallic or plastic flavors as it flows through the system. While it is helpful, it will continue to build if the system is not cleaned regularly and will cause drawing problems if it begins to flake off. Beer stone is present if flakes that are brownish in color appear in the beer or if there is a brownish color on the faucet or inner wall of the beer line.

To clean the lines, a sterilizer attachment should be purchased when purchasing the dispensing system. This unit attaches to the dispensing head, and the sanitizer is pumped throughout the system. To clean the interior and exterior of the cabinet, use a mild detergent and water. Monthly, clean the condenser using a stiff brush.

As previously mentioned, temperature is very important in the proper dispensing of beer. The temperature of most keg storage units is set at the factory. However, if they need to be changed, there is a control by the refrigeration mechanical unit. Using a screwdriver, turn the adjusting screw to the right to increase the temperature and to the left to decrease the temperature.

Glass Washers

Automated glass washers should be cleaned daily at the end of the day. While there are some differences among manufacturers and model numbers, they all basically adhere to the following procedure:

- At the end of each day, drain the machine.
- After the unit has drained, turn the power switch to the off position.
- Open the door and remove the lower spray arm.
- Inspect the spray nozzles to make sure that they are free of any debris that could affect their spray patterns.
- Remove the end caps from the spray manifold and clean with a brush.
- Flush the manifold with water.
- Remove and clean the scrap and pump intake screens carefully to avoid any waste particles from falling into the tank.
- Clean the inside of the wash tank with clean water.
- Remove the scrap tray carefully from the drain sump to avoid any waste particles falling into the drain sump.
- Thoroughly clean the interior of the drain sump.
- Check the levels of the chemical containers and fill if necessary.
- Replace all of the parts.
- Leave the door(s) open overnight to allow drying.

Espresso Machines

As with all equipment, cleaning the espresso machine and its parts is an essential function to ensure its proper operation. Since the majority of espresso machines are manufactured overseas, their makeup and therefore their maintenance and cleaning are vastly different. It is best to consult the manufacturer's instructions for these functions. Be that as it may, there are a few commonalities among the machines:

- The grounds drawer should be emptied daily and washed with mild soapy water.
- The bean hopper should be removed daily, the beans emptied, and the hopper wiped clean with a clean, dry towel.
- Vacuum any grounds or beans that may have collected around the grinder.
- Remove the drip tray and clean with mild soapy water.
- The exterior of the machine should be wiped with a damp towel using mild soapy water.
- Steam wands should be cleaned after every use with a damp towel and a small amount of steam dispensed after the pitcher has been removed to clear steam wand.
- Daily remove, empty, and clean the milk tank.
- If the machine has any electronic functions, care must be taken to avoid these areas getting wet. Use only a barely damp towel to clean this area.

CONCLUSION

There is a lot of information to be absorbed in this chapter, and much of it will save you a great deal of money if followed properly. Purchasing bar equipment is an expensive undertaking. Knowing what to purchase and how to purchase is important. Having an understanding of how bar equipment works can be of great value when it comes to selecting specific pieces of equipment.

While there are different types of equipment used in bar layouts, refrigerated equipment is the most prevalent. The predominant parts of a refrigeration system are the compressor, condenser, evaporator, and thermostat. The refrigerant that is used to cool the system is R-22. The various types of refrigerated equipment include bottle boxes to store bottled and canned beer and keg boxes used to store kegs of beer. Operations that sell a large amount of draft beer dispense it from a walk-in cooler. Ideally, the walk-in cooler should be located near the bar. The longer the line, the more beer that is wasted. In a well-designed bar, the back wall of the walk-in cooler will abut the wall of the back bar.

Another type of refrigeration equipment is the ice machine, which manufactures ice in cube form as well as many other shapes and sizes including flaked and crushed. The capacity for an ice machine is predicated on a 24 hour period, 60°F (16C) water temperature, and 70°F (21C) room temperature. For every 10° difference in either the water or room temperature, there is a 10 percent variance in the ice production.

Other types of equipment include frozen beverage dispensers, espresso machines, juice dispensers, and carbonated beverage dispensers. There are two types of carbonated beverage dispensers: premix and postmix. Premix is used predominately in portable beverage service such as that used in banquets while postmix is used mainly in permanent bar layouts. In both types of bars, carbonated beverages are normally dispensed from a bar gun.

Glass washing is still another type of equipment needed to operate a bar. It can be as simple as a four-compartment underbar sink with brushes, either mechanical or manual, in the wash compartment or as sophisticated as an automatic dish machine also located under the bar.

Most of the bar equipment is located either under the bar die, which is the front part of the bar, or under or as part of the back bar. There are many different ways to design a bar, which will be covered in the next chapter.

When purchasing bar equipment, it is important to remember to purchase green equipment when all possible. While the cost is greater initially, the energy savings will more than make up for the initial excess investment. The government has developed the Energy Star rating system with qualified products saving up to 50 percent over their conventional counterparts.

The correct method to purchase equipment was discussed. Whether you are purchasing a single piece of equipment or equipping an entire bar, consider this: If you buy one piece of equipment, you will probably pay for this course that you are presently taking. If you are opening a new bar, you will probably pay for one or two years of your education, and if you open a large bar, you will probably pay for your entire tuition. It is that important to get it right.

The distribution system starts with the manufacturer. They design and build the equipment. They hire manufacturer representatives that represent their products to dealers. The dealers then sell, deliver, and in some cases install the equipment to the restaurants, bars, and lounges.

The correct way to purchase equipment is to have several dealers bid on the equipment. In order for the bidding to be accurate, a specification for the equipment must be written. A specification lists all of the important data pertaining to the equipment so that each dealer is bidding on the exact same piece. By purchasing equipment by bidding, you are assured of getting the lowest possible price for that equipment. There is a common misperception among restaurant and bar owners that by purchasing used equipment, they can save large sums of money. This may or may not be true.

After the equipment is purchased and installed, it is important to properly maintain it. Refrigeration interiors should be deep cleaned and the condenser coils cleaned on a monthly basis on all units. When cleaning

the interior of the ice machine, there are two functions to complete. One is the cleaning procedure that removes lime and other mineral deposits. The other is the sanitizing procedure, which removes algae and slime. The entire beer system, including the faucet, beer line, and tapping devices, should be cleaned chemically once a month. Additionally, the entire system should be flushed with clean water each and every time a keg is changed. This is important if you want to serve a good-tasting glass of beer. Automated glass washers should be cleaned daily at the end of the day. By properly maintaining equipment, it will last longer and give you a greater return on your investment.

Case Study/Project

You have just purchased a bar in your neighborhood. It has been there for several years and does a steady, if not robust, business. The beverage menu is typical of a neighborhood bar; however, the bottled beer is limited to several brands. Several of your friends have told you that while they like the bar, they would go there more often if it had a larger selection of beer. The under part of the back bar is a storage area. You have determined that the items stored there could be stored elsewhere and that it would be an excellent

place to locate an under-counter refrigeration unit. There are 70 inches (length) to work with and electricity is available. You need to write a specification in order to put the refrigerator out to bid. Using the Web, write a specification for an under-counter box. You may use any manufacturer you wish; however, the one listed here is an easy site to follow: Go to www.beverage-air.com. Then click Products, then Bar Equipment, then Deep well bottle coolers (select which cooler you want), then Spec Sheet.

Write the specification from the information given.

QUESTIONS

True/ False

1. The speed rail on a front bar is that area where the server picks up the drinks that have been prepared by the bartender.
2. Refrigeration works by having cold air infused into the refrigeration cabinet.
3. There are two temperatures on a refrigeration setting, a high setting and a low setting.
4. A clear cube of ice is made when water runs continuously over the evaporator.
5. The proper and only method of sanitizing glassware is by using hot (180°F) water.
6. The bar die and back bar are normally custom built.

7. When an equipment dealer sells you a piece of equipment, they are responsible for the delivery and hook up of that equipment.
8. If the opportunity comes up to purchase a used ice machine at a low price, it is best to purchase it over a new piece as the savings will probably offset any repairs necessary to get the used piece working.
9. Most equipment manufactured in the United States conforms to the regulatory and certification agency's requirements.
10. Because it is so expensive to perform maintenance on bar equipment, it should only be performed when it is absolutely necessary.

Multiple Choice

1. The formula for figuring wattage is
   A. Volts + amps = watts
   B. Volts/amps = watts
   C. Volts − amps = watts
   D. Volts × amps = watts

2. In a new bar operation, the menu will determine
   1) the type of equipment to be purchased.
   2) the amount or capacity of equipment to be purchased.
   A. (1) only
   B. (2) only
   C. Both (1) and (2)
   D. Neither (1) nor (2)

3. Management in its infinite wisdom has decided to add a freezer in the bar for the purpose of frosting beer mugs. It is important that they check the building's electrical capacity for
   A. volts.
   B. amps.
   C. watts.
   D. ohms.

4. The component of a refrigeration system that picks up heat particles from the refrigeration cabinet is called a (an)
   A. compressor.
   B. condenser.
   C. evaporator.
   D. thermostat.

5. The capacity of an ice machine is predicated on
   A. 70°F room temperature.
   B. 60°F water temperature.
   C. 24-hour day.
   D. All of the above.

6. A refrigeration unit can be either
   1) air cooled or water cooled.
   2) built in or remotely located.
   A. (1) only
   B. (2) only
   C. Both (1) and (2)
   D. Neither (1) nor (2)

7. Which of the following is *not* true of the top of a bar die?
   A. It is 2 feet in length.
   B. It has an arm rest.
   C. It has a 4-inch water drain.
   D. It is normally custom built.

8. Which of the following is *not* included on an equipment specification?
   A. Material
   B. Cost
   C. Power source
   D. Dimensions

9. Maintenance on refrigeration units should be performed
   A. as needed.
   B. daily.
   C. weekly.
   D. monthly.

10. When cleaning an ice machine it is necessary to
    1) perform a cleaning process, which removes lime and mineral deposits.
    2) perform a sanitizing procedure, which removes algae and slime.
    A. (1) only
    B. (2) only
    C. Both (1) and (2)
    D. Neither (1) nor (2)

Essay

1. Define BTU, CFM, and PSI by giving their full names, a definition of each, and in what context they are used.
2. Differentiate among the criteria that are used to select equipment for a new operation, to select a piece of additional equipment for an existing bar, and to select replacement equipment.
3. Discuss the differences between premix and postmix carbonated beverages, including equipment needed, cost, and profitability.
4. What are the advantages of a POS system over a cash register? Give an example of an application where each would be used and tell why it would be used in that particular application.
5. Discuss the proper method of purchasing bar equipment.

RESOURCES

Birchfield, John C., *Design and Layout of Foodservice Facilities* (New York, NY: John Wiley & Sons, 2008).

Drysdale, John A., *Restaurant Foodservice Equipment* (Upper Saddle River, NJ: Pearson Prentice Hall, 2010).

Kazarian, Edward A., *Foodservice Facilities Planning*, 3rd ed. (New York, NY: John Wiley & Sons, 1997).

Scriven, C. & Stevens, J., *Food Equipment Facts* (New York, NY: John Wiley & Sons, 1982).

7

Bar Layout and Design

Objectives

Upon completion of this chapter, the reader should be able to:

- Explain the components of planning for the layout of a bar.
- Assess the importance of space utilization as well as traffic and product flow.
- Design a bartender's workstation for maximum utilization of space with minimum travel and worker effort.
- Execute a conceptual bar layout.
- Draw a bar layout showing where each piece of equipment is to go.
- Communicate with the architect, consultant, interior designer, and building codes people regarding bar construction.
- Select the various elements of design for the interior of the bar.

Key Terms

Bar die

Circular bar

Cold storage

Computer Assisted Design (CAD)

Conceptual layout

Decibel

Dry storage

Elevation drawing

Foot candles

"L" shaped bar

Material flow

Plan drawing

Rectangular bar

Scale

Service bar

Speed rail

Straight line bar

OVERVIEW

In Chapter 6, the various pieces of equipment that are necessary to operate a bar were examined. In this chapter, we will learn where to put this equipment so that the operation can function in an efficient and cost-effective manner. This is an important chapter, as any mistakes made during the planning phase will last the lifetime of the business. After the plan is drawn, go over it several times. Walk through the process of receiving goods, storing them, and producing drinks and serving them. Ask yourself: Is this the best place to locate this equipment, or would it work better in another location? Show your plan to others in the industry, people you can trust for solid advice. No one knows better than a bartender how to lay out a bartender's work center or a server how to layout the cocktail service area.

There are others that you will have to work with in the planning process that will also have a say in how the final plan will evolve. These are the government individuals such as zoning, building codes, fire codes, liquor control, and the health department personnel. The laws and codes are on the books for a reason: to protect you as well as your customers. While these people may seem adversarial at times, keep in mind that, overall, they are there for everyone's benefit. Others that you will work with include the architect, the builder, and possibly a layout consultant or interior designer. By relying on your own expertise and taking into account the advice of others, you will end up with a good plan that will last the lifetime of the business.

PLANNING

The food and beverage business is quite unique among retail stores in that it is one of the few types of ventures that manufactures what it sells. In a typical retail operation, you have a small storeroom and a large sales area and that is all. In a food and beverage setting, you have a storeroom, manufacturing space (kitchen and bar), and a sales floor (seating area). Because of this, careful planning for a new operation is a must if the business is to meet its maximum potential. In developing a floor plan, several broad concepts must be looked at and decided on before the plan can move forward.

The layout of the operation is an integral part of this plan. As the layout plan develops, management must keep in mind that the object of any business is to make a profit. Investors, be they an individual, a partnership, a corporation, or lenders, want to see a return on investment. The planning stage is critical to obtaining this return on investment as well as to the future success of any beverage outlet. Each decision made at this juncture will have a lasting effect. For example, if an electrical outlet is placed in the wrong location for a blender, it is either a permanent problem or an expensive proposition to have it moved to its proper location. When putting together a layout, there are many things to consider. This process should not be rushed but rather thought through carefully.

Demographics and the Menu

As we learned in the previous chapters, demographics and therefore the menu dictate the type and amount of equipment you are going to buy. It is important to reiterate here the question, who are the customers? What are they going to buy? A bar located in a blue-collar, middle-income demographic area will want a large selection of beer as well as simple drinks such as "on the rocks" or highballs. Contrast this with a high-end, upscale wine bar and you can readily see that there is going to be a vast difference in the menu offerings, décor, equipment purchases, and ultimately the layout.

All too often prospective owners buy unnecessary equipment. They rush off to an auction and buy things, half of which does not work and the other half they do not need, or they are persuaded by an overzealous salesman that "they must have this." If you are not going to sell a lot of margaritas, you do not need a margarita machine; a blender will suffice. Once the menu is formulated, an equipment list can be drawn up and a layout of where that equipment will go can be planned.

Placement of the equipment is very important and must be done in a logical sequence. There are several areas that need to be considered when placing equipment, and they include the utilization of the available space, the shape of the bar, traffic and material flow, and future planning.

Space Utilization

The end result of any layout should be the maximum utilization of space. To maximize profit and return on investment, you must maximize sales. Sales come from seats. Therefore the space devoted to seats should be maximized and the space devoted to everything else minimized. Unless you are designing your own building, the allocated space is either a leased storefront or is part of another complex such as a hotel, conference center, or stadium. Therefore the space is unique to that operation, and this is where careful planning comes in. Because there is no common shape or size to the space that a bar will occupy, there is no "cookie cutter" layout scheme for beverage outlets. That being said there are certain concepts that need to be followed, and how they fit into the assigned space is the challenge.

In order to discuss space utilization, we must first discuss how much area will be taken up by equipment, how much area is necessary for the employees to do their work, and how much is needed for customer seating. Some general rules of thumb are as follows:

- Bar die. This is the area where the customer sits and is referred to as the bar die. Bar dies are typically 2 feet wide front to back plus 1 foot for under bar equipment.
- Back bar. This is the area behind the bar, and it is usually 3 feet wide as well. This are is used for storage and often displays the call and premium brand spirits.
- Work aisle. This is the area between the bar die and the back bar and is where the bartender works. It should be a minimum of 3 feet wide and could be as much as 5 feet. The amount of space allocated here is determined by traffic. If the bar is going to be busy and warrants more than one bartender, the space allocated

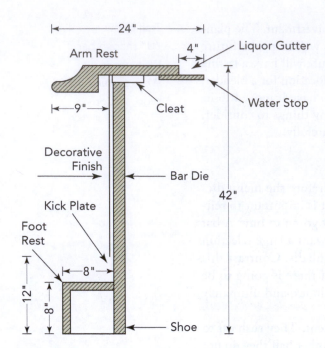

FIGURE 7.1
Side view of a typical bar die.

should be closer to 5 feet. If only one bartender is expected to work, then 3 feet is adequate. The reason for this is that a person can stand in one spot and simply turn around to get something from behind him- or herself. Anything over 3 feet means they must take steps to retrieve items.

- Bar stools. Bar stools are placed on the customer side of the bar die. Allow 2 feet from the edge of the bar die to the back of the stool.
- Customer aisle. Behind the bar stools and to the back of customers is an aisle, and the space allocated for it should be a minimum of 3 feet, with 4 feet being more comfortable. Figure 7.1 shows a side view drawing of a bar die.

Bar Shape

When deciding on the shape of the bar, keep in mind that corners encourage conversation between bar patrons, as they can see each other. While corners are not always feasible, they should certainly be considered if there is space available. Consider that there is nothing that will affect the usage of overall space more than the shape of the bar itself. That being said, there are several shapes that could be utilized; they are the straight line, "L" shaped or corner bar, rectangle, "U" shaped, and circle.

- Straight line bar. This is best utilized in a building that is long and narrow. As a matter of fact, it may be the only option. Keep in mind that the minimum width for a bar is approximately 14–17 feet. (See Figure 7.2.) This allows 3 feet for the back bar, 3 feet for work space (which is a minimum; it ideally should be 3–5 feet), 3 feet for the bar die, 2 feet for the stools, and 3–4 feet for an aisle. One of the drawbacks of a straight line bar is that quite often people patronize a bar to socialize with one another, and a straight line is not very conducive to this type of social interaction.
- "L" shaped bar. While this shape could be utilized in any shape room, it is often found in buildings that are "L" shaped. The minimum width requirements are the same as for a straight line bar. An advantage of an "L" shape is that with the corner, your guests can be facing one another when carrying on a conversation. Figure 7.3 shows a plan view of an "L" shaped bar.

FIGURE 7.2

A layout of a straight line bar.

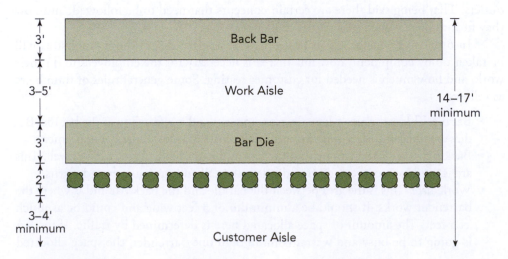

An example of an "L" shaped bar.
Lars Christensen/Fotolia

- Rectangular bar. This shape takes up a lot of space. Look at Figure 7.4 and you can readily see that a minimum of 25–28 feet is needed. Essentially what is happening is that you have two straight line bars back to back. There are some drawbacks to this type of configuration. Many rectangular bars utilize the back bar space for call liquor, which blocks the view of the other side of the bar. Not only does this cut back on social interaction among the guests, it makes it difficult for the bartender to see if anyone needs to be served on the other side.

This problem can be eliminated by storing call and premium liquor elsewhere so that the view is unobstructed from one side to the other. This configuration allows for the bartender to see the whole bar as well as allowing customers to talk

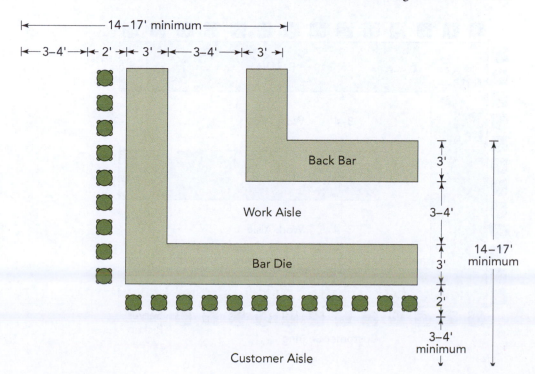

Customer Aisle

FIGURE 7.3

A layout of an "L" shaped bar.

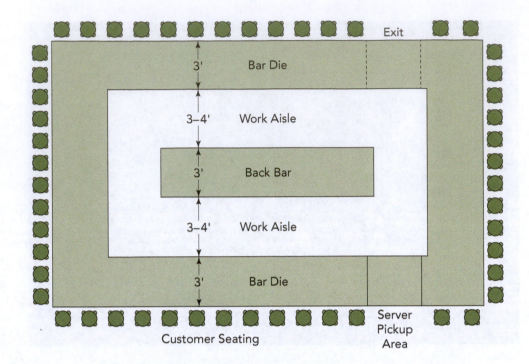

across the bar. Additionally, a rectangular bar has more corners for the customers to interact with each other. A drawback is the distance the bartender has to travel to keep all sides of the bar serviced.

- "U" shaped bar. This is essentially a rectangular bar with a wall at one end. Quite often, the wall is directly adjacent to the walk-in cooler where the kegs are stored for draft beer. Refer to Figure 7.5 for the layout of a "U" shaped bar.
- Circular bar. This is another variation of a rectangular bar; however, it is not very popular because it tends to have wasted space associated with it. It is most prevalent where the building has been designed in a circle to house a circular bar and

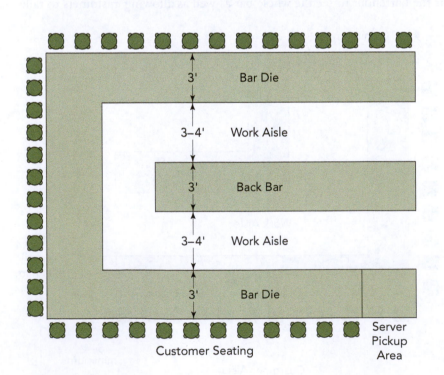

A picture of a circular bar.
© National Geographic Image Collection/Alamy

the tables are arranged in a circular manner around the bar. A plus for this design is that it looks good and is a conversation piece. Figure 7.6 shows a plan view of a circular bar. Note the wasted space in this layout.

• **Service bar.** This bar normally does not impact space to any degree as it is quite compact and is used only by the wait staff. While it is a fully stocked bar capable of producing any drink on the menu, there are no accommodations for customers. Additionally, it can be located almost anywhere as long as it is accessible to the service staff.

FIGURE 7.6

A plan view of a circular bar.

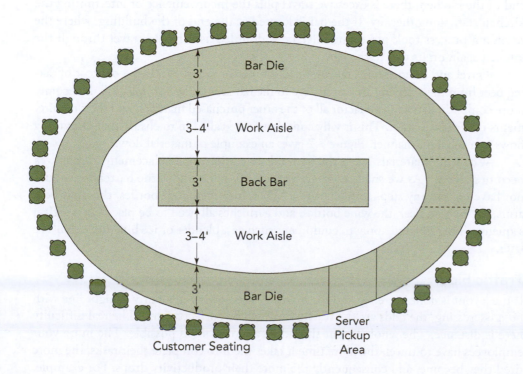

Material Flow

A critical component of the layout process comes in determining the **material flow** in the operation. After goods are purchased, they are shipped to the business and received. The receiving function is the first step in the flow of goods throughout the bar. From receiving, they travel to storage and then on to production and finally service. As they go from function to function, they should travel in a straight line as much as possible with no cross traffic or crisscrossing. A minimum of travel distance is preferred.

To illustrate, consider a shipment of bottled beer. It is received at the back door and goes into storage in the walk-in cooler. If the walk-in cooler is located at the far end of the kitchen, there is excessive travel plus the inconvenience of interrupting the kitchen staff along the way. If the bar is located at the end of the building, where the receiving process took place, the mistake is doubled as it has to travel through the kitchen again on its way to the bar.

Travel and interruptions take time, and time is money. While the concept of taking beer from the receiving area to storage to the bar seems like a simple task, it becomes more complicated when you factor all of the other purchased materials and their requirements into the equation. This is why consultants are called in to ensure that everything flows in a coherent manner. Figure 7.7 gives an example of material flow.

When the materials reach the bartender's station, their placement in that area becomes critical. As we shall see later, in the ideal bar station, the bartender should not have to take any steps to fill an order. Therefore the liquor bottles, the draft beer arms, the bottled beer, the wine bottles, and garnishes all need to be placed in a logical sequence. This will also apply to equipment such as a blender or ice bin, as we shall see later.

Traffic Flow

If the layout is done correctly and the materials are flowing in a fairly straight line with no crisscrossing, the odds are the **traffic flow** will be correct as well. The real difficulty here is distance. The whole layout should be as compact as possible. The more your employees have to travel, the more time it takes them to complete their tasks, the more tired they become, and consequently the more their productivity drops. For example,

```
                           ┌───────────┐
                           │ Receiving │
                           └───────────┘
                 ┌───────────────┴───────────────┐
          ┌─────────────┐                  ┌─────────────┐
          │ Cold Storage│                  │ Dry Storage │
          └─────────────┘                  └─────────────┘
      ┌──────┬──────┬──────┐          ┌──────┬──────┬──────┬──────┐
  ┌──────┐┌──────┐┌──────┐┌──────┐┌──────┐┌──────┐┌──────┐┌──────┐
  │ Wine ││Bottle││Draft ││Mixes ││ Wine ││Liquor││ Soda ││Supplies│
  │      ││ Beer ││ Beer ││      ││      ││      ││      ││      │
  └──────┘└──────┘└──────┘└──────┘└──────┘└──────┘└──────┘└──────┘
                           ┌────────────┐
                           │ Production │
                           └────────────┘
                           ┌────────────┐
                           │  Service   │
                           └────────────┘
```

FIGURE 7.7 An illustration of proper material flow.

we said that in the ideal bar station, the bartenders would not have to take any steps. In reality, this ideal is rarely achieved, and they will have to take some steps. The objective is to have them take as few steps as possible. While this may not seem like a big deal, consider that a few steps to fill each order over an eight hour shift will wear an employee down.

Future Planning

The final concept that needs to be investigated is planning for the future. All too often a bar opens, becomes successful, and wants to expand but discovers that the entire operation has to be discarded because the original layout did not take into consideration that the management may one day want to enlarge the business. When looking at the big picture of what shape the bar is going to be, where it is going to be located, how the equipment is going to be situated, and what the traffic and material flow is going to look like, think about the "what if" of expansion.

For example, if the storefront next door were to become available and the sales warranted it, how would the operation merge into that space with the least amount of disruption and cost? Is the bar die adequate for handling the additional business? If not, can it be expanded? Would the addition of a service bar for the additional seats be the answer? Is the walk-in adequate to accommodate the additional kegs and bottles of beer? Are the restrooms located in such a manner that they are convenient to the entire room? If a restaurant is involved, can the kitchen handle the additional production load? Proper planning at this juncture could go a long way in saving money down the road.

EXECUTING THE PLAN

Now that we have looked at the broad picture and we know what the shape of the room is and how much space we have to work with, we can start to get more detailed. Restaurant layouts involve two parts: work centers and work sections. A **work center** is where one task or a group of similar tasks are completed by one employee. A **work section** is where a group of similar functions takes place. For example, in a kitchen one person may work on prepping and plating salads. This is a work center. Another person nearby may be preparing cold platters for a buffet and another preparing cold canapés for a reception. These functions all take place at work centers, and they are joined together to make up work sections, in this case a *garde mange* kitchen.

Kitchen layout is quite complex, and while many beverage outlets have full service restaurants, we will limit our discussion here to bars. Bar layout is much simpler. For starters, there are no work sections, only work centers. The work centers are receiving, storage, bartender, glass washing, service, customer area, and auxiliary.

Receiving

This is a small area that should be located directly adjacent to the loading dock. It should contain a small desk or table, an area for the delivery person to place the merchandise to be inspected and counted, and if a kitchen is involved, a scale for weighing meat and produce. This is an important area and is overlooked in many layouts. Considering the high cost of liquor, wine, and beer, it is imperative that it be received correctly, that everything is in good condition, and that everything that is paid for is actually received.

Storage

There are two parts to this work center, **dry storage** and **cold storage**. Dry storage should be a locked storeroom. Liquor and room temperature wines would go directly into this room immediately after they are inspected and signed for. If the operation has a restaurant, garnishes such as maraschino cherries and olives as well as paper supplies would normally go into the general storeroom. Keg and bottled beer go into cold storage which, depending on the bar's volume, is normally a walk-in cooler and is also kept locked at all times. Wine can go here as well; however, many bars that have a large wine selection will have a separate locked storage area.

Bartender

The bartender's work center is the nerve center of the entire bar production activity. It is where all of the drinks are produced as well as the pouring of beer and house wines. It is imperative that the workstation be laid out properly. The majority of drinks served should be produced with the minimum amount of movement by the bartender. Each step taken is lost time and energy, and while it may be minimal on a per-drink basis, it adds up during a busy shift.

Exactly how the work center, sometimes called a pour station or workstation, is laid out depends on the demographics of the business and what is being predominantly served. In most bars the majority of sales are in mixed drinks, followed by beer, wine, and finally nonalcoholic beverages. Everything the bartender needs to mix the majority of drinks should be at his or her fingertips, and few, if any, steps should be taken. A good rule of thumb to follow is that the average person has a reach of 3 feet. Therefore everything the bartender needs should be within this range. Keep in mind that there can be materials in front of them as well as behind them, so by simply turning around you can double the workstation capacity. The parts of the workstation are as follows:

- **Ice bin**. This is for short-term ice storage only. Ice is produced in the ice machine, usually located in the kitchen or the back of the house, and transported to the ice bin. The capacity of the ice bin in a normal bar is usually sufficient for a shift; however, in high-volume bars it may need refilling several times during a shift.
- **Speed rail**. This is also called a speed rack or liquor well. The **speed rail** contains all of the well brands or house brands. These are used to mix drinks when the customer does not specify (call for) a particular brand. They normally, but not always, cost less than call brands and consequently sell for a lower price.

Tradition calls for bourbon to be placed in the well first, followed by (left to right) scotch, gin, vodka, rum, tequila, whiskey, and triple sec. However, many bartenders prefer to line their distilled spirits up in the order in which they are most ordered or in some cases in another order that they prefer (for whatever reason). The important thing here is that the bottles are in a specific order and

A double rack speed rail.
Courtesy, Conroy's Public House

that they are replaced in the same order after use. When a drink order is placed, the bartender can grab the bottle without looking at the label as he or she knows exactly where everything is located. This is extremely important in a busy bar during a rush, as seconds are important in expediting orders. In bars where there is a high demand for call liquor, a second rail is added below the speed rail, which is used to house the most popular call brands.

- **Mix bin**. These are usually stored to the right or left (or both) of the ice bin. While they are separated from the ice bin itself, they should be kept iced down to prevent spoilage. Mixes stored here would include, but are not limited to, orange juice, Bloody Mary mix, pina colada mix, and margarita mix. Carbonated beverages are usually dispensed from a device called a bar gun, which is located above the ice bin where the bartender as well as the cocktail servers have access to it.
- **Blender stand**. Normally located immediately adjacent to the workstation either to the left or right. Either way, it should be handy for the bartender to fill the blender with ingredients from the speed rail and the mix bin and blend the drink without taking any steps. Some bars use a malt mixer rather than a blender for blended drinks.
- **Glass rail**. This is located on top of the bar die directly above the ice bin. It is a 4-inch-wide trough that is usually lined with a webbed rubber or plastic matting. The bartender fills the glasses with ice, places them on the glass rail, and proceeds to mix the drinks.

Glass Washing

Washing glasses at the bar can be done either manually or by machine. The sink or machine is usually located under the front bar behind the bar die. When washing glassware manually, a four-compartment sink is recommended.

- The first compartment is for any ice or unfinished product in the glass.
- The second compartment is for washing. It is filled with warm water and a detergent. A series of three brushes is placed in the sink. The bartender holds the glass

A four-compartment sink, left to right: drainboard for soiled glasses, dump sink, wash sink with brushes, rinse sink, sanitizing sink, drainboard for clean glasses.
Courtesy Conroy's Public House

and using an up-and-down motion cleans both the inside and outside of the glass simultaneously. The brushes can be either stationary or mechanically rotated.

- The third compartment is for rinsing. A rinse agent is added to the water.
- The fourth compartment is for sanitizing. A sanitizing agent is added to the water. After sanitizing, the glass is placed on the drainboard to air dry. Do not towel dry glassware as it could contaminate the glass.

There are a number of glass washing machines on the market. While these are expensive, they will affect cost savings in a bar that does a large volume of business by freeing up the bartenders to do what they are paid to do: mix drinks. See Chapter 6 for a complete discussion on glass washing machines.

Service Area

This is the area of the bar where the bartender places the filled orders for the service personnel to pick up. Therefore it is also known as the pickup station. This area contains a garnish tray, napkins, straws, stir sticks, and the bar gun for carbonated beverages. Again, everything should be in reach of the server. Depending on house policy, the server may or may not finish each drink by filling the glass with the appropriate carbonated beverage and garnishing it. There should be a guard rail on each side of the server station to designate the area for service personnel and to keep the guests from congregating there.

Seating Area

It is important to lay this area out properly so as to seat the maximum number of customers. What the maximum is depends on two things: the fire code and the ambiance the operation wishes to project. In most jurisdictions, the fire code will determine the maximum number of people that can be in the building at one time. The ambiance is determined upon what type of atmosphere the bar wants to project. Some bars want a

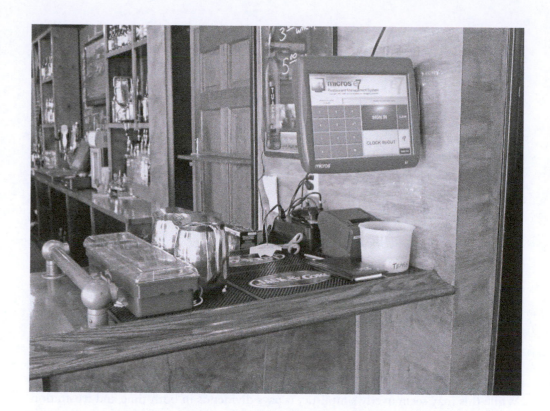

Service area with garnish tray on left and touch-screen POS on right.
Conroy's Public House

quiet setting with comfortable furniture and plenty of space, while other bars want it crowded and noisy.

Tables come in all sizes and shapes. If the operation serves cocktails only, a smaller table will suffice, thus giving additional seating capacity. However, if meals are served in the bar area, the table should be of sufficient size to accommodate the various plates and flatware. Booths and banquettes give a sense of privacy but take up a lot of space. Square and rectangular tables can be put together to accommodate larger parties, while with rounds everyone seated can see each other. As you can see, there are pros and cons. What you decide on should reflect the atmosphere that you are trying to project.

Auxiliary Areas

This is the miscellaneous area of work centers and includes the waiting area, host stand, wait stands, and restrooms. With the exception of restrooms, not every bar will have all of these options. Operations with a very heavy volume will have a host stand and possibly a waiting area for their patrons. The purpose of the host stand is twofold; one is to make sure that the bar does not exceed its seating capacity, and the other is to check the guests' IDs. Both of these are extremely important as the fire department conducts spot checks on popular bars to make sure that they are within code and the beverage control board or the police department makes sure that those imbibing are of age.

Wait stands are limited to those operations that serve food in the bar. For those that sell drinks only, the service area at the bar is sufficient for all of the necessary supplies to serve the guests.

Restrooms should be of sufficient size and capacity to handle the volume of guests in the establishment. As a matter of fact, many jurisdictions will dictate how many toilets, urinals, and hand washing sinks are required. This is normally based on either the square footage of the operation or the number of seats. The location of the restrooms is important as well, as they should be conveniently located. If the operation has a restaurant, they should be located between the restaurant dining room and the bar. Restaurant customers should not have to walk through the bar to get to the restrooms.

THE CONCEPTUAL LAYOUT

Bar layouts are done in two stages: the conceptual layout and the actual layout. The **conceptual layout** is made up of deciding where each work center is going to go and how they will be joined together. In reality, it is nothing more than doodling on paper with words defining each work center. When done in this manner with no detail, the conceptual layout can be changed quickly with a minimum of wasted time. Refer to Figure 7.8 for an example of a conceptual layout.

When joining work centers, there are a few rules of thumb that should be followed. They include the following:

- Tasks should proceed in proper progression with a minimum of crisscrossing and backtracking.
- Effortless and rapid production and service should be planned with a minimum waste of worker time and energy.
- Workers and materials should travel minimum distances.
- Maximum utilization of space and equipment should be achieved.

While this may seem overly simplistic, it pays dividends in both time and frustration when the actual layout is being drawn. As we shall see, layouts are very time consuming and detailed drawings. Changes, while common, take time and slow the project down. A well-conceived conceptual drawing will eliminate many of these changes and will speed up the process.

When doing the conceptual drawing, keep in mind plumbing and drain connections. Try and locate these in a straight line, if possible, as well as having equipment and fixtures that require plumbing grouped together. This will save considerable expense during construction. A word of caution: Traffic patterns and work flow take precedence here. For example, if moving an ice machine to get it closer to other plumbing violates the rules given above, the money saved in construction could well be outweighed by the cost of an employee traveling further and crisscrossing existing traffic lines. Remember that the cost of an employee taking extra time to complete a task costs money day after day, year after year.

FIGURE 7.8

An example of a conceptual layout.

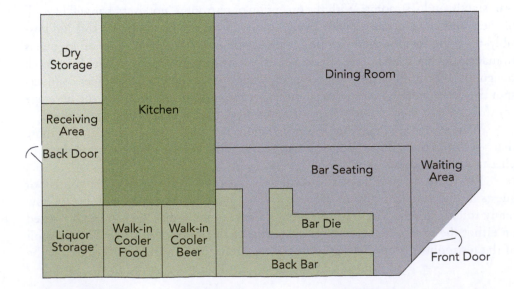

THE ACTUAL DRAWING

Unless you are opening a small neighborhood bar and are well versed in construction, you are probably going to need an architect to execute the actual drawings. As a matter of fact, many jurisdictions will not issue a building permit without drawings submitted by an American Institute of Architects (A.I.A.) architect. Keep in mind that you will need a building permit even if you are remodeling an existing space. While there are a few architects that specialize in bars and restaurants, most have little or no experience in this area. It is therefore important that you furnish the architect with a detailed drawing as to how you want the bar laid out.

The drawing should show the entire area of the building that the business will occupy and where each piece of equipment is to go. This is what is known as a **plan drawing**. It is as if you were situated on the ceiling and looking down at the operation. As the main concern here is to ascertain how much space everything is to take, there are only two dimensions used for the equipment: length and width (depth). Aisle spaces are in width only. A plan drawing is very similar to the layout drawings you have seen in this chapter.

Another type of drawing the architect will use is an **elevation drawing**. This type of drawing is as if you were standing in the room and looking straight ahead at a wall with equipment lined up against it. Elevation drawings use two dimensions as well: length and height. They are important for locating items that go over equipment such as a shelf over a worktable or equipment located under the bar die. They are also useful for items that need to be custom built such as the back bar, showing detail as to how the keg box will fit into the back bar and how the call and premium liquor storage shelving is to look. Another advantage of an elevation plan is that it helps the owner to envision how the operation will look when completed. Elevations are very difficult to draw and are best left to the architect.

All drawings should be drawn to **scale**. There are two scales used by architects: ¼ inch and ⅛ inch scale. The scale refers to the number of feet represented by 1 inch on the drawing. Thus a ¼ inch scale will represent 4 feet of actual space for every inch

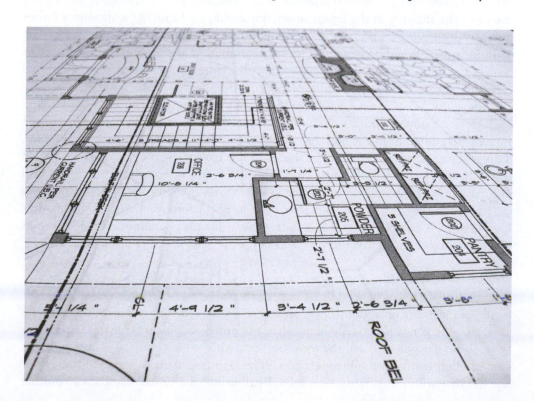

An architect's drawing is a blueprint for the layout of the operation.
charles taylor/Fotolia

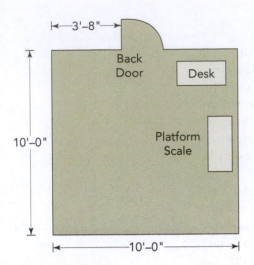

FIGURE 7.9
Drawing of a receiving area.

used on the drawing and a ⅛ inch scale will represent 8 feet for every inch on the drawing. For example a two-door reach-in refrigerator measures on the average 5 feet in length by 3 feet deep. On a ¼ inch scale drawing, you would draw a rectangle 1¼ inches by ¾ inch.

There are two options for doing your drawing. It can either be hand drawn or it can be done on a computer using a **computer assisted design (CAD)** software program. CAD programs are usually quite expensive, and it will take some time to learn them. As an architect is going to do the final drawing anyway, if you are not proficient at CAD drawings, it is probably best to draw it by hand. As ¼ inch scale is easier to work with than ⅛ inch scale, purchase some ¼ scale graph paper from a local office supply store or an artist's supply store.

We are now going to go step by step through the drawing that you will present to the architect. We will be designing a bar that has a restaurant but will not detail the kitchen or restaurant dining room. We will be assuming that the operation sells wine but does not have a sommelier or a particularly extensive wine list.

Receiving Area

Start by drawing the outline of the building or storefront on the graph paper using one square (¼ inch) for each foot that the building measures. Once this is done, it is easiest to start at the back of the building and draw in the receiving area first. As stated earlier, this is a fairly easy work center as it contains only a desk and a receiving scale (if a restaurant is involved). You will need some space for the delivery personnel to set the items down so they can be inspected and counted or weighed. Figure 7.9 show an example of a drawing of a receiving area.

Storage Area

Next is the storage area: a locked liquor and wine storage room, a walk-in cooler for the bottled and keg beer and chilled wine, and the general storage room for the kitchen. The shelving in the liquor storeroom should be 12 inches wide with a 3-foot aisle. With shelving on both sides, this should be a minimum of 5 feet in width. The walk-in cooler should be large enough to accommodate the anticipated inventory of bottles and kegs. The inventory figures will come from your business plan, which has estimated the percentage of customers drinking beer as well as the number of seats in the operation. We will draw an 8 foot by 10 foot walk-in. Refer to Figure 7.10 for a representative storage area. As mentioned earlier, the walk-in ideally should be located immediately adjacent to the back bar so that the draft beer does not have to travel far. This will pay dividends later as the lines will not have to be bled as much to get rid of flat beer as well as cleaning the lines. This will result in both labor savings as well as liquor cost. If the walk-in cannot be located there, it should be located as close as possible to the bar area. This is a perfect example of the importance of laying out your bar properly. A good layout will save money every day the operations is open. A layout error could cost money day after day after day.

Bartender Station

As mentioned earlier, it is essential to get this work center right as this is the nerve center of the entire operation. There are several layout schematics that will accomplish this, and one is not necessarily better than the other. A critical piece to the puzzle is what is the bar going to sell the most of: beer, wine, or cocktails. This information can be obtained from the business plan. The layout illustrated here is for an average bar that will have a fairly even sales distribution of all three categories. Another

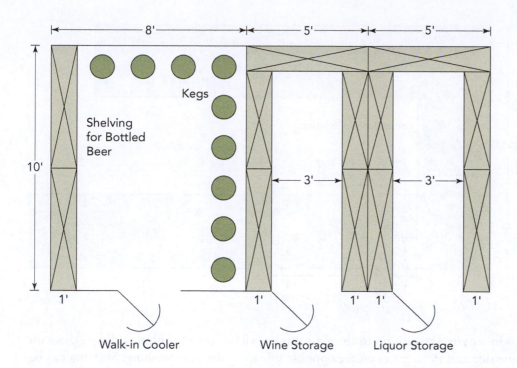

FIGURE 7.10
Drawing showing the storage area with a liquor and wine storeroom, as well as the beer walk-in cooler.

consideration is who is going to garnish the drinks. In this illustration, the service personnel will be doing the garnishing. The bartender station is located under and protruding from the back of the front bar die. Note that practically everything the bartender needs to produce a cocktail is within arms' reach. The glasses are stored to the left, the ice bin is directly in front, the mixes are on either side of the ice bin, the carbonated beverage gun is located to the bartender's right by the service station, and the house liquor is in the speed rail in front of the ice bin. A blender shelf is located to the right of the ice bin.

See Figure 7.11 for a bartender station. The approximate dimensions for these items are as follows:

- Glass storage. 18 inch minimum length, 30 inches deep
- Ice bin. 24–36 inches length, 30 inches deep
- Refrigerated or iced-down mix storage. 6 inches length, 30 inches deep
- Speed rail. 36 inches length, 6 inches deep
- Blender shelf. 12 inches length, 30 inches deep

If the bar is expected to have a high volume, a second identical work center can be planned on the far side on the bar die. A hand sink should be located near the bartender station. Wine, draft beer, bottled beer, and call liquor will be dealt with when the back bar is designed.

Glass Washing

As previously mentioned, this can be done either manually or mechanically. Either way, the glass washing equipment is located under the front bar die and, like the bartender's station, protrudes out. If the glasses are washed manually, a four-compartment bar sink is recommended. This takes quite a bit of linear footage. Depending on the size of the sink bowl and the size of the drainboard, it can go from 6 feet to 10 feet in length and 2 feet in depth. If space is at a premium, consider using a smaller bowl with a three-compartment sink. In this case, you will need to provide a receptacle to empty the glasses of unused ice, garnishes, straws, and other debris. Mechanical glass washers vary in size based on the style and manufacturer selected but are typically 24 inches or

FIGURE 7.11
An example of a bartender's
workstation.

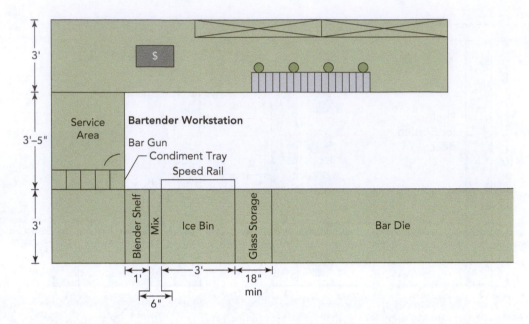

so in length. In addition to the glass washer, allow space for placing dirty glasses on
one side and clean gasses on the opposite side to air dry after washing. Shelving can be
placed underneath to accommodate additional glasses. Figure 7.12 shows a schematic
of a four-compartment underbar sink with a 36-inch drainboard on each side.

Back Bar

After the front bar has been laid out, the length of the bar die will be known. The back
bar will have an identical length. The width (depth) is from 24 to 36 inches depending on whether a keg or bottle cooler is located within it. The height of the back bar
varies depending on the type of bar being designed. For a straight or "L" shaped bar,
the height typically goes to the ceiling. For a rectangular or circle bar, the height is less,
typically 3 to 5 feet.

Back bars for the most part contain shelving for all of the call and premium
liquor, an underbar cooler for bottled beer, space for the draft beer heads including a
drainboard, a refrigerated unit for chilled wine, shelving for room temperature wine,
and a cash register or POS unit. Any leftover space should be used for cabinetry to
store supplies and "stuff." In most bars, there is never enough storage space. When
locating these items, keep in mind that the bartender should take minimal steps to
complete an order. Figure 7.13 shows a back bar layout.

Having said all of this, keep in mind that this is not the only way to do a bar
layout. There are many variations that are caused by numerous circumstances. First
and foremost is the menu. For example, if the operation is going to sell primarily beer,
you may want the bottle box and the draft heads located on the front bar and put
the refrigerated mix storage on the back bar. The shape of the room, the space available, and other architectural considerations will also determine its layout. For example,

FIGURE 7.12
Schematic of a four-
compartment glass washing
sink with drainboard.

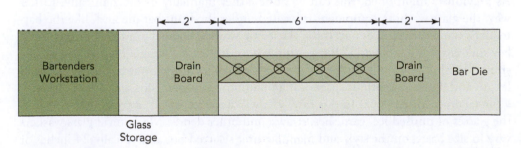

Back Bar Shelving for Premium/Call Liquor or Beer or Wine Bottle Display

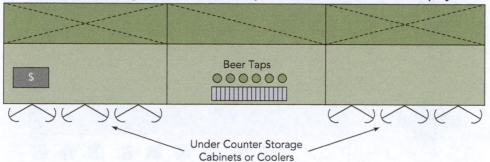

Under Counter Storage
Cabinets or Coolers

FIGURE 7.13
Schematic of a back bar.

there may be a column located in the middle of the bar's work aisle. (Columns hold up the roof, which makes them rather important. Back bars can be moved on a plan, columns cannot.)

Again, and this cannot be stressed enough, the bartenders work center should be laid out so that the bartender takes minimal, if any, steps to complete an order. The next time you are in a bar, notice how much traveling the bartender does. If he or she takes only a few steps to fill each order, then this is a good layout. Check it out. How is it laid out? What is located where? If on the other hand the bartender is going up and down the bar to finish an order, this is a poor layout. While you are nursing your drink and ignoring your friends, try to mentally rearrange the bar so that the bartender does not have to work as hard.

Service Area

The service area is where the cocktail servers pick up their drinks. It is a relatively small area, measuring approximately 36 inches long by 30 inches deep, but an important one. As we mentioned earlier about our hypothetical operation, the servers will be garnishing the drinks. Therefore it contains a garnishment tray, which measures 4–6 inches in width and is 12–18 inches in length. If the servers are going to get their own carbonated beverages, a carbonated bar gun should be located there as well. A backup supply of napkins, straws, swizzle sticks, and coasters (if used) should be nearby. It is a good idea to separate this area from the rest of the bar die with a curved railing to indicate that this is the server's area and to keep the patrons from congregating there. Figure 7.14 gives a drawing of a service area.

Seating

More than anything the number of seats will determine the level of sales. Therefore, it is important that this area be laid out correctly. How many seats will go into the space is determined by local fire codes and the ambiance the operation wants to convey—a crowded, noisy bar or a quiet, laid-back club with a relaxing atmosphere. The environment notwithstanding, there are some rules to follow when placing tables and chairs in the layout. The *minimum* aisle space with a customer seated at the table should be as follows: 18 inches for a customer aisle, 30 inches for a service aisle, and 48 inches for main aisles throughout the room. Allow a *minimum* of 18 inches from the edge of the table to the back of the chair with a customer seated. Thus when laying out the seating area, you need to allow 66 inches (5 feet 6 inches) from table edge to table edge. (18 inches from table edge to back of chair + 30 inches aisle space + 18 inches from chair

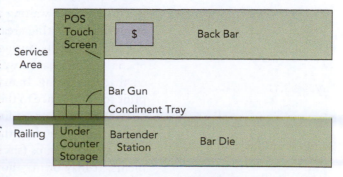

FIGURE 7.14
Service area.

FIGURE 7.15

An example of a seating area.

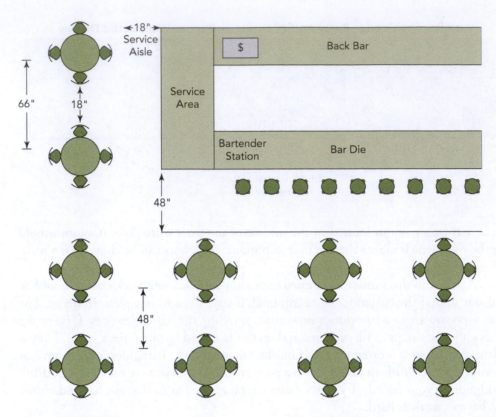

back to table edge.) Refer to Figure 7.15 for an example of the space relationships between table and chairs.

In addition to seating, this area, in many cases, will house other functions such as a stage for a band or DJ, a dance floor, pool tables, or video arcade games. As such, they must be accounted for in the planning stage. Keep in mind that they will take away from the space available for seating; however, if they are important for sales, they must be accounted for.

If part of the seating area is raised or terraced, it must be accessible according to the Americans with Disabilities Act (ADA). A ramp leading up to the raised area will satisfy this rule.

Auxiliary Areas

The auxiliary areas include a waiting area, host stand, wait stations, and restrooms. Most bars will not have a waiting area. These are limited to those operations that have a large following such as a nightclub that would have a waiting line to get in. If the operation has a restaurant, it would also have a waiting area, but this would primarily be for the restaurant as opposed to the bar. As a matter of fact, the bar is usually an extension of the waiting area as guests will often go there to enjoy a cocktail prior to dinner. The waiting area is important as the guests should not be expected to stand outside, especially during extreme weather such as rain, sleet, heat, and cold. Those operations that have a waiting area will also have a host stand to keep track of customers that are waiting. In many operations, the customer's ID is checked at the host stand prior to admittance to the bar area; therefore the stand should be well lighted.

Wait stations are limited to those operations that sell food. The size of the wait station will depend on the menu being served; however, it should be of sufficient size to store extra setups (silverware and napkins), water glasses, cups, saucers, and condiments. It may or may not have, depending on customer needs, a coffee warmer, iced tea dispenser, ice bin, and water. The area should be blocked from the customers' view with a half wall allowing the service personnel to see the seating area.

Restrooms should be conveniently located, not at the rear of the building so that the guest will have to walk through the storage area to get to them. If a restaurant is involved, they should be located between the dining room and the bar. Some restaurant patrons for religious, ethnic, or other reasons abhor alcohol. If they have to walk through the bar area to get to the restrooms, they probably will not return to your establishment. Restrooms should be of sufficient size to accommodate all guests. Many jurisdictions have codes that will determine the number of sinks, toilets, and urinals that the business must provide. Restrooms should be spotlessly clean at all times with sufficient soap and towels or hand dryers provided.

DÉCOR

There are countless ways to decorate a bar. As a matter of fact, the only limit is your imagination. When deciding on a décor, consider your customer demographics and the ambiance you want to project. Do you want crowded, loud, and noisy, or do you want quiet and comfortable, or something in between? There are many decisions to be made concerning what will go on the walls and floors as well as what type of ceiling material to choose. If you are not familiar with such terms as *thread count*, warp and woof, *breaking strength*, *weaves*, *gloss*, *semi-gloss*, and *veneer*, it would behoove you to hire an interior decorator to guide you through this process. In addition to knowing all of the technical terms and how they apply to the finished product, an interior decorator will take your ideas and incorporate them into an overall design that will be pleasing to your patrons.

Walls

Walls are the focal point of the bar and as such deserve careful attention. The wall surface can be plaster, in older buildings, or plaster board in newer buildings. This surface can be covered with paint, wall paper, vinyl, or another synthetic material. In addition to plaster or plaster board, other surfaces include wood paneling or exposed brick. Mirrors can also be used to reflect light and to make the operation seem larger.

The walls can be covered with paintings, photographs, or artifacts that carry out the theme of your bar. Millers Pub in Chicago covers its walls with photographs

An example of bar décor.
krsmanovic/Fotolia

of sports figures and stars that have been and are customers. On a national scale, Applebee's features photos, posters, and artifacts of local high school and college students and athletes to give it a neighborhood feel. If you want to decorate your bar "on the cheap," contact your beer, wine, or liquor distributors. They have a plethora of pictures, mirrors, posters, and advertisements that can be hung on the walls.

a

d

b

e

c
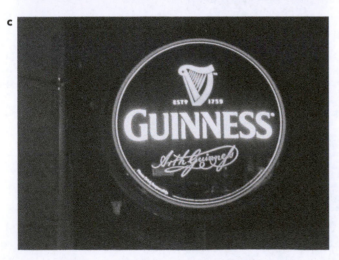

f
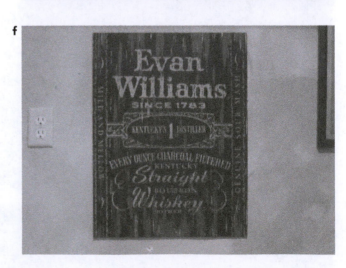

Examples of décor supplied by suppliers.
Courtesy of The Gaf

Windows

Windows can either be an asset to a bar or a major nuisance. If they are the latter, consider removing them altogether in the construction process or, barring that, covering them with heavy draperies. Replacing windows with a wall will give you more space to display artifacts, while covering them with drapes will give you substantial sound absorption. Draperies should always be treated with a flame-resistant chemical.

Many bars use windows as a focal point. The cocktail lounge in the Banff Springs Hotel in Banff, Alberta, Canada, has floor-to-ceiling windows overlooking a gorgeous view of a valley in the Canadian Rocky Mountains. Many other bars have views of gardens, courtyards, busy streets, or other sights. Keep in mind that blinds, curtains, or window tinting will be needed for that period when the sun will shine into the room. Some operations use window etchings or stained glass to display their logo or other scenes depicting the atmosphere of the operation. One last consideration regarding windows is that they are not energy efficient. However, if they are important to the overall ambience, by all means use them to your advantage.

Floors

In most operations, different types of flooring will be used depending on the area. In the area in front of the bar and the work area behind the bar, the flooring should be hard, nonporous, and slip resistant. If carpeting is used in the seating area it should end 4–5 feet in front of the bar and a heavy-duty tile or slate should be used, as the bar stools being constantly moved back and forth will quickly wear the carpeting thin. Many back bars are sealed concrete or, if the flooring is wooden, are covered with a heavy-duty tile. Most often a rubber mat will cover the concrete or tile to make walking back and forth easier and more comfortable on the bartender's feet. While some operations will use portable wooden slats behind the bar, these are not approved in many jurisdictions for sanitary reasons.

There is a wide choice of floor coverings that can be used in the seating area including carpeting, tile, sealed concrete, and wood. They all have their advantages and disadvantages. Carpeting is expensive and must be vacuumed nightly. It also must be shampooed regularly as drinks get spilled and absorbed into the carpet. On the plus side, if it is properly maintained, it looks good and helps in sound absorption. Tile and sealed concrete should be swept and mopped on a nightly basis and polished regularly. While cheaper than carpeting to install, they reflect sound more readily than carpeting. A wood floor is arguably the most expensive flooring particularly, if a hardwood or parquet is used. When properly maintained it looks good and adds style to a room. If the operation has a dance floor, it is normally made of wood, although there are a

 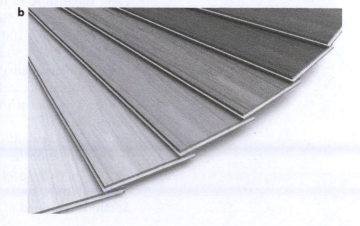

Examples of carpet and wood flooring selections.
(a) Steschum/Fotolia, (b) Scanrail/Fotolia

number of synthetic materials on the market. Regardless of the material used, a dance floor should have a degree of slipperiness to it.

Ceilings

As with the walls, windows, and floors, there are several different treatments for the ceiling. It can be completely open, exposing all of the ductwork and pipes. These can be painted various colors to highlight them or painted with a dark color to deemphasize them. All of the pipes and ducts can be enclosed with a plaster board ceiling or a tinplate ceiling, which is popular in operations with an old-time theme to them. An open ceiling notwithstanding, the most popular type of ceiling is a hung ceiling using acoustical tiles. An advantage of this type of ceiling is that it absorbs a great deal of sound. A disadvantage of a hung ceiling is that between the "false" hung ceiling and the actual ceiling is space, and this space tends to become a wind tunnel. Should a fire break out, this tunnel will quickly sweep the fire up and across the ceiling, spreading it faster than would be normal. Consequently, all ceiling tile should flame resistant to slow this process down and give the fire department a chance to extinguish the fire.

Guest Surroundings

One of the most important aspects of the planning process is the comfort of the guest. The temperature, a smoke- and odor-free atmosphere, the sound level, and the lighting in the room all contribute to a pleasant environment. If a customer does not notice any of these things, management has been successful in controlling them. If on the other hand the guest is too cold, perceives the music as too loud, can smell kitchen grease, or cannot read the menu because it is too dark, then management has failed. Some of the characteristics that make up a good quality environment include the following:

- Air. The air in a bar should have a proper temperature and humidity and be clear of smoke and odors. A good temperature is between 65°F and 80°F with a higher number, around 76–78°F in the summer and a lower temperature of around 70–72°F in the winter. The air handling system should be designed so that air is circulated around a room and should avoid having a direct discharge on a table or confined area. The relative humidity should be between 40 and 60 percent, with 50 percent considered best. In those areas where smoking is still allowed in bars, an air purifier should be installed. If the bar has a kitchen, the exhaust from the kitchen should be adjusted with the amount of air going into the bar. Normally there should be more air going in than is being exhausted out. In most jurisdictions, this is governed by code.

- Lighting. One of the main factors in creating ambiance in the bar is lighting. Light is measured in **foot candles**, which is defined as the amount of light provided by a candle 1 foot from an object. In work areas such as behind the bar or in the kitchen, 100 foot candles is recommended while in the seating area it could go as low as 30 foot candles. Lighting that is too low can make it difficult to read a menu and also makes it hard for people to feel comfortable moving around. Lighting can be either direct or indirect. Direct lighting is used to enhance an object such as a picture or artifact, while indirect lighting is used for atmosphere.

- Sound. The amount or level of sound that you want in your bar is governed by the ambiance that you want to project. Keep in mind, however, that there are limits, even if you desire to have a noisy, fun-filled operation. A good rule of thumb to follow is that if you cannot carry on a conversation, it is too loud. Sound is measured in frequency and loudness. Frequency is measured in **hertz**

Example of direct and indirect lighting.
krsmanovic/Fotolia

and is the number of sound waves per second. A more important number is **decibels**, which measures the loudness of sound. A person speaking in a normal tone is around 50 decibels. Occupational Safety and Health Administration (OSHA) requirements state that workplace sound should not be higher than 90 decibels. Background noise should be reduced to as low a point as is possible. To a person who is hard of hearing, background noise will drown out a conversation. Background noise comes from air ducts, motors, and fans. This is one of the reasons why, as noted in the previous chapter, refrigeration condensers and compressors should be located remotely away from the public areas. Soft materials such as draperies, carpeting, acoustical ceiling tile, and upholstery will absorb sound while hard surfaces such as tables, the bar die, wood floor, and tin or plaster ceilings will reflect sound.

CONCLUSION

This all may seem a little overwhelming, but it is not as bad as it seems. Take it one step at a time. Look at your space. How will the components fit in the most efficient manner? How will the traffic and product flow throughout the operation? Where will the bar go? What will it look like? When these questions are answered, draw up several conceptual drawings. When a conceptual is selected, place each piece of equipment on an actual drawing using grid paper. Walk though each function. Mentally mix some cocktails or draw some beer based on where you have placed things. Mentally wash some glasses and serve some customers. When you are satisfied, show the plan to others. Remember that a plan keeps evolving and hopefully gets better with each change. Take your plans to your architect, who will probably make more changes and who will take it to the codes people, who will make even more changes. When you and everyone else is satisfied, it is time to begin construction.

Case Study/Project

You have taken a job at a local restaurant and lounge to help defray some of your expenses while attending college. The owner-manager wants to put a service bar in the dining room to take the pressure off of the lounge, which is quite busy. She knows that you are taking a course in beverage management and has asked you to help her in designing it. The area she has in mind is an old storeroom located immediately adjacent to the dining room. It measures 10 feet by 10 feet. Draw a floor plan as to how you would lay out the service bar.

QUESTIONS

True/ False

1. Demographics and the menu are instrumental in determining what type of equipment to purchase for a bar.
2. The space devoted to seats should be maximized, and the space devoted to everything else minimized.
3. If the service bar for the dining room augments the regular bar, it does not need to have the equipment or inventory to make every drink on the menu.
4. As materials travel through an operation from the receiving area and ultimately into the customer's drink, they should travel in a straight line with no crisscrossing or backtracking.
5. When hand washing glasses, after sanitizing they should be hand dried with a clean towel.
6. When laying out a bar, it is best to locate the beer walk-in cooler directly adjacent to the back bar.
7. Wait stations in a bar are limited to those operations that sell food.
8. While windows could be an important design element, they are not necessary in all bars.
9. The amount of light intensity is measured in hertz.
10. Once a flooring material has been decided on, it can be used throughout the bar area.

Multiple Choice

1. Referring to a straight line bar, the minimum amount of space from the front edge of the bar die to the back side of the back bar is
   A. 3 feet.
   B. 5 feet.
   C. 6 feet.
   D. 9 feet.
2. In a long, narrow building the most ideal shape for a bar would be a
   A. straight line bar.
   B. "U" shaped bar.
   C. service bar.
   D. circle bar.
3. An area where one task or similar tasks are performed by one person is known as
   A. a workstation.
   B. a pour station.
   C. a pickup center.
   D. a work center.
4. The average person has a reach of
   A. 2 feet.
   B. 3 feet.
   C. 4 feet.
   D. 5 feet.
5. Auxiliary areas are made up of
   A. the pour station, the pickup stations, and the service area.
   B. restrooms, wait stations, and the host stand.
   C. host stand, waiting area, and seating area.
   D. dining room, bartender station, and service station.
6. A plan that is drawn showing work centers only is known as a(n)
   A. conceptual plan.
   B. floor plan.
   C. elevation plan.
   D. actual plan.

7. In a drawing using ¼ inch scale, a four-compartment bar sink measuring 10 feet by 2 feet would be shown on the drawing measuring
   A. 5 inches by 1 inch.
   B. 1¼ inches by ¼ inch.
   C. 2½ inches by ½ inch.
   D. 10 inches by 2 inches.

8. In a restaurant–bar operation, the restrooms should be located
   1) between the dining room and the bar.
   2) in such a way that the guest does not have to go through the bar to get to the restroom.
   A. (1) only
   B. (2) only
   C. Both (1) and (2)
   D. Neither (1) nor (2)

9. The best floor covering for a bar that wants an elegant, quiet, laid-back, relaxing atmosphere would be
   A. expensive wood parquet.
   B. Italian marble tile.
   C. imported slate.
   D. plush carpeting.

10. A temperature of 76–78°F is ideal
   A. for summer.
   B. for winter.
   C. year round.
   D. never.

Essay

1. Discuss the various shapes of bars, including their advantages and disadvantages. Tell which one you prefer if space is not an issue and why you prefer it.
2. Describe the parts of a bartenders work center. Tell, or draw, where you would locate these parts.
3. You have leased a space that measures 35 feet wide by 125 feet deep. The entrance is on the front side on the right. The receiving door is on the back side center. Sketch a conceptual drawing showing where you would locate the various work centers.
4. Go to a bar in your area. Observe the bartender and how many steps they must take to fill an order. Sketch the bartender's station as it exists and do another sketch showing how you would improve the layout.
5. You are going to open a sports bar in a vacant building in your area. Give a brief description of how you would treat the décor including the walls, floor, and ceiling. What would the noise level be? How would you control air and lighting?

RESOURCES

Birchfield, John C., *Design and Layout of Foodservice Facilities* (New York, NY: John Wiley & Sons, Inc., 2008).

Drysdale, John A., *Restaurant Foodservice Equipment* (Upper Saddle River, NJ: Pearson Prentice Hall, 2010).

Kazarian, Edward A., *Foodservice Facilities Planning*, 3rd ed. (New York, NY: John Wiley & Sons, Inc., 1997).

Scriven, C. & Stevens, J., *Food Equipment Facts* (New York, NY: John Wiley & Sons, Inc., 1982).

8
Employment Law

OVERVIEW

If you are a manager, or aspire to become one in the hospitality industry, this chapter is essential to your success. There are a number of laws that dictate what you can and cannot do in regards to the management and leadership of your employees. These laws are summarized in this chapter. Please note that the purpose of this chapter is to familiarize you with these laws and is not intended to give legal advice. This should only be done by a licensed attorney in your area. While most of the laws cited here are federal, there are many state and local laws that pertain to the management of your staff. In some cases, federal law supersedes local laws, and in some cases the reverses is true. Another thing to keep in mind is that every time Congress, your state legislature, or the local council meets, the laws will probably change and new ones will be added. This is an additional reason to consult an attorney regarding these issues. This is an area of hospitality management that you need to keep on top of, as many times the penalties for noncompliance are severe, both monetarily and in terms of serving prison sentences for violations.

FAIR LABOR STANDARDS ACT OF 1938

The **Fair Labor Standards Act (FLSA)** was passed into law in 1938 primarily to level the playing field between management and labor. It also sought to end child labor among other things. It has been amended several times since then including the addition of the minimum wage provision. This arguably was one of the most sweeping additions to this law and affected much of the hospitality industry. In addition to the minimum wage, there are a few other provisions to the law regarding wages and hours worked that affect bars, clubs, and restaurants.

The act establishes standards for minimum wages, overtime pay, recordkeeping, and child labor. These standards affect more than 130 million workers, both full time and part time, in the private and public sectors. In order to be covered, an establishment must have in excess of $500,000 in annual dollar volume of business or be engaged in interstate commerce, the production of goods for interstate commerce, or an activity that is closely related and directly essential to the production of such goods.

Minimum Wage

The federal **minimum wage** for covered, nonexempt employees is $7.25 per hour effective July 24, 2009. The federal minimum wage provisions are contained in the Fair Labor Standards Act and are administered and enforced by the U.S. Department of Labor (DOL) Employment Standards Administration's Wage and Hour Division. Many states also have minimum wage laws. In cases where an employee is subject to both the state and federal minimum wage laws, the employee is entitled to the higher of the two minimum wages.

Wages required by FLSA are due on the regular payday for the pay period covered. Deductions made from wages for such items as cash or merchandise shortages, employer-required uniforms, and tools of the trade are legal, but they cannot reduce the wages of an employee below the minimum rate or reduce the amount of overtime pay due.

The FLSA contains some exceptions (or exemptions) from the minimum wage requirement. For example, youths under 20 years of age may be paid a minimum wage of not less than $4.25 an hour during the first 90 consecutive calendar days of employment with an employer. Employers may not displace any employee to hire someone at the youth minimum wage. The act also permits the employment of certain individuals at wage rates below the statutory minimum wage under certificates issued by the Department of Labor. This includes vocational education students, full-time students in retail or service establishments, and individuals whose earning or productive capacities for the work to be performed are impaired by physical or mental disabilities, including those related to age or injury. Executive, administrative, and professional employees are also exempt from the act.

Tipped Employees

An employer of a tipped staff member is only required to pay $2.13 an hour in direct wages if that amount plus the tips received equals at least the federal minimum wage and the employee customarily receives more than $30 a month in tips. This is known as the **tip credit provision**. If an employee's tips combined with the employer's direct wages of at least $2.13 an hour do not equal the federal minimum hourly wage, the employer must make up the difference. Some states have minimum wage laws specific to tipped employees. When an employee is subject to both the federal and state wage laws, they are entitled to the provision that provides the greater benefits.

If management elects to use the tip credit provision and pay tipped employees $2.13 per hour, they must do the following:

- Inform each tipped employee about the tip credit allowance before the credit is utilized.
- Be able to show that the employee receives at least the minimum wage when direct wages and the tip credit allowance are combined.
- Allow the tipped employee to retain all tips, whether or not the employer elects to take a tip credit for tips received, except to the extent the employee participates in a valid tip pooling arrangement.

The requirement that an employee must retain all tips does not preclude a valid tip pooling or sharing arrangement among employees who customarily and regularly receive tips, such as waiters, waitresses, bellhops, counter personnel who serve customers, busboys/girls, and service bartenders. Tipped employees may not be required (although they can at their own discretion) to share their tips with employees who have not customarily and regularly participated in tip pooling arrangements, such as dishwashers, cooks, chefs, and janitors. Only those tips that are in excess of tips used for the tip credit may be taken for a pool. Tipped employees cannot be required to contribute a greater percentage of their tips than is customary and reasonable.

Equal Employment Opportunity Commission (EEOC)

Equal Pay Act

Fair Labor Standards Act (FSLA)

Family Medical Leave Act (FMLA)

Federal and State Unemployment Compensation Program

Form I-9

Minimum wage

National Labor Relations Act

Overtime pay

Taft-Hartley Act

Tip credit provision

Title VII of the Civil Rights Act of 1964

Wage garnishment

There are several other provisions that apply to management using the tip credit; they are as follows:

- Dual jobs. When an employee is assigned to both a tipped and a nontipped job, such as a host or hostess and a cocktail server, the tip credit is available only for the hours spent in the tipped occupation (cocktail server). The different rates of pay when combined are known as blended pay.
- Retention of tips. The law forbids any arrangement between management and the tipped employee where any part of the tip received becomes the property of the employer. A tip is the sole property of the tipped employee. If an employer violates any part of the tip credit provisions of the Act, no tip credit may be claimed and the employees are entitled to receive the full minimum wage ($7.25 in 2009), in addition to retaining tips they should have received.
- Credit cards. Where tips are charged on a credit card and the employer must pay the credit card company a percentage on each sale, the employer may deduct the service charge from the tip. The charge on the tip may not reduce the employee's wage below the required minimum wage. The amount due the employee must be paid on the regular pay day and may not be held while the employer is awaiting reimbursement from the credit card company.
- Service charges. A compulsory charge for service, for example 15 percent of the bill, is not a tip. Such charges are part of the employer's gross receipts. Where service charges are imposed and the employee receives no tips, the employer must pay the entire minimum wage ($7.25 in 2009) and overtime required by the act. There's a fine line here. If the policy is that a gratuity will be added to the bill, then it is a tip and is given to the server. If it is stated that a service charge will be added, then management keeps the money received from the service charge and pays the server $7.25 (2009) or more.

Overtime Pay

Management that requires or permits an employee to work overtime is generally required to pay the employee premium pay for such overtime work. Employees covered by the Fair Labor Standards Act must receive **overtime pay** for over 40 hours worked in a workweek. The rate for overtime is at least one and one-half times the regular rate of pay. Management is not required to pay overtime for work on Saturdays, Sundays, holidays, or regular days of rest, unless overtime hours are worked on such days, nor is it required to pay double time. Extra pay for working weekends or nights is a matter of agreement between management and the employee. The FLSA, with some exceptions, requires bonus payments to be included as part of an employee's regular rate of pay in computing overtime.

When an employee works two jobs at different rates of pay, for instance host/hostess and cocktail server, the overtime is calculated on what is known as a blended rate of pay. When this occurs, the employee's overtime rate is determined by calculating time and a half of the employee's blended rate of the two positions. This is figured by dividing all compensation received by all hours worked, not simply time and a half of the lower rate of pay or the rate of pay for the position in which the overtime hours were worked. For example, if Sally worked 30 hours as a cocktail server and 20 hours as a hostess in a one week period and the rate of pay was $2.13 for cocktail servers and $7.50 for the hostess position, the blended rate of pay would be $4.278, or $4.28:

30 hours cocktail server @ $2.13: 30 × $2.13 = $63.90

20 hours hostess @ $7.50: 20 × $7.50 = $150.00

$63.90 + $150.00 = $213.90/50 hours worked = $4.278 or $4.28

Her gross pay would be as follows:

20 regular hours @ $2.13 = $42.60

20 regular hours @ $7.50 = $150.00

10 overtime hours @ $4.28 × $1.5 = $64.20

$42.60 + $150.00 + $64.20 = $256.80

Garnishment

Wage garnishment occurs when an employer is required to withhold the earnings of an individual for the payment of a debt in accordance with a court order or other legal procedure. Management is prohibited from terminating employees because their earnings have been subject to garnishment. However, the employee is not protected from termination if they have been garnished a second time.

Employees are protected by limiting the amount of earnings that may be garnished in any workweek; however, a greater amount may be garnished for child support, bankruptcy, or federal or state tax payments. Up to 50 percent of an employee's disposable earnings can be garnished for child support if the employee is currently supporting a spouse or child who is not the subject of the support order, and up to 60 percent if the employee is not supporting a current spouse or child. An additional 5 percent may be garnished for support payments over twelve weeks in arrears.

Termination and Severance Pay

Employers are not required by federal law to give former employees their final paycheck immediately. However, they must give the terminated employee their final check on or before their regular payday. Some states, however, may require immediate payment upon termination.

Severance pay is an amount of money that is given to employees when they are terminated. It is over and above the amount that they earned during their last pay period. Look at it as a bonus for being terminated. Severance pay is usually based on the length of employment and is normally given only to management. Hourly workers as a rule do not get severance pay, but there are exceptions. There is no requirement in the FLSA for severance pay, as it is a matter of agreement between an employer and an employee.

Other Provisions

There are some things the Fair Labor Standards Act does not do. For instance,

- The FLSA does not provide collection procedures for an employee's wages or commissions in excess of those required by the FLSA. However, some states do have laws under which such claims may be filed.
- The FLSA does *not* require vacation, holiday, severance, or sick pay; meal or rest periods, holidays off, or vacations; premium pay for weekend or holiday work; pay raises or fringe benefits; or a discharge notice, reason for discharge, or immediate payment of final wages to terminated employees.
- The act does not limit either the number of hours in a day or the number of days in a week that an employer may require an employee to work, as long as the employee is at least 16 years old.

Notices and Posters

Every business subject to the minimum wage provisions must post a notice or poster explaining the act in a conspicuous place in all of its establishments. Although there is no size requirement for the poster, employees must be able to readily read it. There is no requirement to post the notice in languages other than English. The Department of Labor will furnish such posters. Figure 8.1 dipicts the minimum wage poster.

FIGURE 8.1
A minimum wage poster must be displayed prominently in all places of employment that are required to pay minimum wage.

Poster courtesy of the Department of Labor

EMPLOYEE RIGHTS
UNDER THE FAIR LABOR STANDARDS ACT
THE UNITED STATES DEPARTMENT OF LABOR WAGE AND HOUR DIVISION

FEDERAL MINIMUM WAGE
$7.25 PER HOUR
BEGINNING JULY 24, 2009

OVERTIME PAY At least 1½ times your regular rate of pay for all hours worked over 40 in a workweek.

CHILD LABOR An employee must be at least **16** years old to work in most non-farm jobs and at least **18** to work in non-farm jobs declared hazardous by the Secretary of Labor.

Youths **14** and **15** years old may work outside school hours in various non-manufacturing, non-mining, non-hazardous jobs under the following conditions:

No more than
- **3** hours on a school day or **18** hours in a school week;
- **8** hours on a non-school day or **40** hours in a non-school week.

Also, work may not begin before **7 a.m.** or end after **7 p.m.**, except from June 1 through Labor Day, when evening hours are extended to **9 p.m.** Different rules apply in agricultural employment.

TIP CREDIT Employers of "tipped employees" must pay a cash wage of at least $2.13 per hour if they claim a tip credit against their minimum wage obligation. If an employee's tips combined with the employer's cash wage of at least $2.13 per hour do not equal the minimum hourly wage, the employer must make up the difference. Certain other conditions must also be met.

ENFORCEMENT The Department of Labor may recover back wages either administratively or through court action, for the employees that have been underpaid in violation of the law. Violations may result in civil or criminal action.

Employers may be assessed civil money penalties of up to $1,100 for each willful or repeated violation of the minimum wage or overtime pay provisions of the law and up to $11,000 for each employee who is the subject of a violation of the Act's child labor provisions. In addition, a civil money penalty of up to $50,000 may be assessed for each child labor violation that causes the death or serious injury of any minor employee, and such assessments may be doubled, up to $100,000, when the violations are determined to be willful or repeated. The law also prohibits discriminating against or discharging workers who file a complaint or participate in any proceeding under the Act.

ADDITIONAL INFORMATION
- Certain occupations and establishments are exempt from the minimum wage and/or overtime pay provisions.
- Special provisions apply to workers in American Samoa and the Commonwealth of the Northern Mariana Islands.
- Some state laws provide greater employee protections; employers must comply with both.
- The law requires employers to display this poster where employees can readily see it.
- Employees under 20 years of age may be paid $4.25 per hour during their first 90 consecutive calendar days of employment with an employer.
- Certain full-time students, student learners, apprentices, and workers with disabilities may be paid less than the minimum wage under special certificates issued by the Department of Labor.

For additional information:
1-866-4-USWAGE
(1-866-487-9243)   TTY: 1-877-889-5627
WWW.WAGEHOUR.DOL.GOV

U.S. Wage and Hour Division

U.S. Department of Labor | Wage and Hour Division

WHD Publication 1088 (Revised July 2009)

Recordkeeping

Every business covered by the FLSA must keep certain records for each covered employee. Most of this data is the type that employers generally maintain in ordinary business practice. There is no required form for the records. However, they must include accurate information about the employee and data about the hours worked and the wages earned. The following is a listing of the basic payroll records that an employer must maintain:

- Employee's full name, as used for Social Security purposes, and on the same record the employee's identifying symbol or number if such is used in place of name on any time, work, or payroll records
- Address, including zip code
- Birth date, if younger than 19

- Sex and occupation
- Time and day of week when employee's workweek begins
- Hours worked each day and total hours worked each workweek
- Basis on which employee's wages are paid (e.g., "$9 per hour," "$440 a week," "piecework")
- Regular hourly pay rate
- Total daily or weekly straight-time earnings
- Total overtime earnings for the workweek
- Documented tips for the workweek
- All additions to or deductions from the employee's wages
- Total wages paid each pay period
- Date of payment and the pay period covered by the payment

Employers are required to preserve for at least three years payroll records, collective bargaining agreements, and sales and purchase records. Records on which wage computations are based should be retained for two years. These include time cards and piecework tickets, wage rate tables, work and time schedules, and records of additions to or deductions from wages.

Penalties and Sanctions

The Department of Labor (DOL) uses a variety of remedies to enforce compliance with the act's requirements. When Wage and Hour Division investigators encounter violations, they recommend changes in employment practices to bring the employer into compliance, and they request the payment of any back wages due to employees.

Willful violators may be prosecuted criminally and fined up to $10,000. A second conviction may result in imprisonment. Employers who willfully or repeatedly violate the minimum wage or overtime pay requirements are subject to civil money penalties of up to $1,100 per violation. For child labor violations, employers are subject to a civil money penalty of up to $11,000 per worker for each violation of the child labor provisions. In addition, employers are subject to a civil money penalty of $50,000 for each violation that causes the death or serious injury of any minor employee. This penalty may be doubled, up to $100,000, when the violations are determined to be willful or repeated.

When the DOL assesses a civil money penalty, the employer has the right to file an exception to the determination within 15 days of receipt of the notice. If an exception is filed, it is referred to an administrative law judge for a hearing and determination as to whether the penalty is appropriate. If an exception is not filed, the penalty becomes final.

The DOL may also bring suit for back pay and an equal amount in liquidated damages, and it may obtain injunctions to restrain persons from violating the act.

EQUAL PAY ACT

Employers who are required to comply with the Fair Labor Standards Act (FLSA) are also required to comply with the **Equal Pay Act**. This act reads in part that no employer shall discriminate between employees on the basis of sex by paying wages to employees at a rate less than the rate at which it pays wages to employees of the opposite sex for equal work on jobs the performance of which requires equal skill, effort, and responsibility, and which are performed under similar working conditions. In other words, the act mandates equal pay for equal work. An exception comes in where such payment is made pursuant to a seniority system, a merit system, a system which measures earnings by quantity or quality of production, or a differential based on any factor other than sex. Figure 8.2 Shows an equal employment opportunity poster.

Equal Employment Opportunity is

THE LAW

Private Employers, State and Local Governments, Educational Institutions, Employment Agencies and Labor Organizations

Applicants to and employees of most private employers, state and local governments, educational institutions, employment agencies and labor organizations are protected under Federal law from discrimination on the following bases:

RACE, COLOR, RELIGION, SEX, NATIONAL ORIGIN

Title VII of the Civil Rights Act of 1964, as amended, protects applicants and employees from discrimination in hiring, promotion, discharge, pay, fringe benefits, job training, classification, referral, and other aspects of employment, on the basis of race, color, religion, sex (including pregnancy), or national origin. Religious discrimination includes failing to reasonably accommodate an employee's religious practices where the accommodation does not impose undue hardship.

DISABILITY

Title I and Title V of the Americans with Disabilities Act of 1990, as amended, protect qualified individuals from discrimination on the basis of disability in hiring, promotion, discharge, pay, fringe benefits, job training, classification, referral, and other aspects of employment. Disability discrimination includes not making reasonable accommodation to the known physical or mental limitations of an otherwise qualified individual with a disability who is an applicant or employee, barring undue hardship.

AGE

The Age Discrimination in Employment Act of 1967, as amended, protects applicants and employees 40 years of age or older from discrimination based on age in hiring, promotion, discharge, pay, fringe benefits, job training, classification, referral, and other aspects of employment.

SEX (WAGES)

In addition to sex discrimination prohibited by Title VII of the Civil Rights Act, as amended, the Equal Pay Act of 1963, as amended, prohibits sex discrimination in the payment of wages to women and men performing substantially equal work, in jobs that require equal skill, effort, and responsibility, under similar working conditions, in the same establishment.

GENETICS

Title II of the Genetic Information Nondiscrimination Act of 2008 protects applicants and employees from discrimination based on genetic information in hiring, promotion, discharge, pay, fringe benefits, job training, classification, referral, and other aspects of employment. GINA also restricts employers' acquisition of genetic information and strictly limits disclosure of genetic information. Genetic information includes information about genetic tests of applicants, employees, or their family members; the manifestation of diseases or disorders in family members (family medical history); and requests for or receipt of genetic services by applicants, employees, or their family members.

RETALIATION

All of these Federal laws prohibit covered entities from retaliating against a person who files a charge of discrimination, participates in a discrimination proceeding, or otherwise opposes an unlawful employment practice.

WHAT TO DO IF YOU BELIEVE DISCRIMINATION HAS OCCURRED

There are strict time limits for filing charges of employment discrimination. To preserve the ability of EEOC to act on your behalf and to protect your right to file a private lawsuit, should you ultimately need to, you should contact EEOC promptly when discrimination is suspected:

The U.S. Equal Employment Opportunity Commission (EEOC), 1-800-669-4000 (toll-free) or 1-800-669-6820 (toll-free TTY number for individuals with hearing impairments). EEOC field office information is available at www.eeoc.gov or in most telephone directories in the U.S. Government or Federal Government section. Additional information about EEOC, including information about charge filing, is available at www.eeoc.gov.

Employers Holding Federal Contracts or Subcontracts

Applicants to and employees of companies with a Federal government contract or subcontract are protected under Federal law from discrimination on the following bases:

RACE, COLOR, RELIGION, SEX, NATIONAL ORIGIN

Executive Order 11246, as amended, prohibits job discrimination on the basis of race, color, religion, sex or national origin, and requires affirmative action to ensure equality of opportunity in all aspects of employment.

INDIVIDUALS WITH DISABILITIES

Section 503 of the Rehabilitation Act of 1973, as amended, protects qualified individuals from discrimination on the basis of disability in hiring, promotion, discharge, pay, fringe benefits, job training, classification, referral, and other aspects of employment. Disability discrimination includes not making reasonable accommodation to the known physical or mental limitations of an otherwise qualified individual with a disability who is an applicant or employee, barring undue hardship. Section 503 also requires that Federal contractors take affirmative action to employ and advance in employment qualified individuals with disabilities at all levels of employment, including the executive level.

DISABLED, RECENTLY SEPARATED, OTHER PROTECTED, AND ARMED FORCES SERVICE MEDAL VETERANS

The Vietnam Era Veterans' Readjustment Assistance Act of 1974, as amended, 38 U.S.C. 4212, prohibits job discrimination and requires affirmative action to employ and advance in employment disabled veterans, recently separated veterans (within three years of discharge or release from active duty), other protected veterans (veterans who served during a war or in a campaign or expedition for which a campaign badge has been authorized), and Armed Forces service medal veterans (veterans who, while on active duty, participated in a U.S. military operation for which an Armed Forces service medal was awarded).

RETALIATION

Retaliation is prohibited against a person who files a complaint of discrimination, participates in an OFCCP proceeding, or otherwise opposes discrimination under these Federal laws.

Any person who believes a contractor has violated its nondiscrimination or affirmative action obligations under the authorities above should contact immediately:

The Office of Federal Contract Compliance Programs (OFCCP), U.S. Department of Labor, 200 Constitution Avenue, N.W., Washington, D.C. 20210, 1-800-397-6251 (toll-free) or (202) 693-1337 (TTY). OFCCP may also be contacted by e-mail at OFCCP-Public@dol.gov, or by calling an OFCCP regional or district office, listed in most telephone directories under U.S. Government, Department of Labor.

Programs or Activities Receiving Federal Financial Assistance

RACE, COLOR, NATIONAL ORIGIN, SEX

In addition to the protections of Title VII of the Civil Rights Act of 1964, as amended, Title VI of the Civil Rights Act of 1964, as amended, prohibits discrimination on the basis of race, color or national origin in programs or activities receiving Federal financial assistance. Employment discrimination is covered by Title VI if the primary objective of the financial assistance is provision of employment, or where employment discrimination causes or may cause discrimination in providing services under such programs. Title IX of the Education Amendments of 1972 prohibits employment discrimination on the basis of sex in educational programs or activities which receive Federal financial assistance.

INDIVIDUALS WITH DISABILITIES

Section 504 of the Rehabilitation Act of 1973, as amended, prohibits employment discrimination on the basis of disability in any program or activity which receives Federal financial assistance. Discrimination is prohibited in all aspects of employment against persons with disabilities who, with or without reasonable accommodation, can perform the essential functions of the job.

If you believe you have been discriminated against in a program of any institution which receives Federal financial assistance, you should immediately contact the Federal agency providing such assistance.

EEOC 9/02 and OFCCP 8/08 Versions Useable With 11/09 Supplement

EEOC-P/E-1 (Revised 11/09)

FIGURE 8.2 An equal employment opportunity poster must be displayed in all businesses that are covered by the law.

FEDERAL LAWS REGARDING AGE

The federal government does not have any laws regarding age limits for working in bars per se, but they do have several that pertain to restaurants. Since many bars serve food, some of these regulations are covered here. The following are taken from a part of the Fair Labor Standards Act (FLSA), which is administered by the U.S. Department of Labor's Wage and Hour Division.

- Minors under age 18 may not set up, operate, or assist to operate power-driven slicers or mixers, including countertop models.
- Minors under 16 years of age are prohibited from using conventional ovens and convection ovens.
- Minors 14 and 15 years old are prohibited from working in walk-in freezers and coolers. This includes duties such as taking inventory or performing cleanup work, which would require them to enter and remain in coolers or freezers for prolonged durations. These minors may enter such refrigeration equipment momentarily as when retrieving an item for use outside the equipment if the equipment is designed to prevent the worker from being locked inside.
- Minors 14 and 15 years old may perform cooking that (1) involves the use of electric and gas grills that do not entail cooking over an open flame and (2) involves the use of deep fat fryers that are equipped with and utilize devices that automatically raise and lower the "baskets," but not pressurized fryers. They may operate office machinery, vacuum cleaners, floor waxers, and machines and devices used in connection with preparing and serving food and beverages, such as dishwashers, toasters, popcorn poppers, milk shake blenders, and coffee grinders.
- Minors 14 and 15 years old may not work during school hours. The term *outside school hours* means such periods as before and after school hours, holidays, summer vacations, Sundays, or any other day or part of a day when the school normally attended by the minor is not in session.
- Minors 14 and 15 years old may not be employed before 7:00 A.M. on any day.
- Minors 14 and 15 years old may not be employed past 7:00 P.M. from the day after Labor Day through May 31. This applies even if there is no school the next day, such as a Friday or Saturday night, as well as in weeks when school is not in session such as during spring break. These same minors may not work past 9:00 P.M. between June 1 and Labor Day.
- Minors 14 and 15 years old may work up to 8 hours a day on Saturdays and Sundays and on other days when school is not in session, as long as they do not exceed the maximum permissible hours in any workweek. They may work up to 18 hours in any week school is in session and up to 40 hours in any week school does not meet.
- Minors 13 years of age and younger are generally not allowed to work under the federal youth employment provisions. Permissible employment for such minors is limited to exempt work and working for a parent who is the sole owner of a business.
- Employers are required to maintain and preserve certain records, including the date of birth for all employees who are less than 19 years of age.

STATE LAWS REGARDING AGE

One would think that if you had to be 21 to drink alcohol, you would have to be 21 to serve it. If one were to think that, one would be wrong. As a matter of fact, as of this writing, thirty-seven states and the District of Columbia permit persons age 18 or older to serve alcoholic beverages in on-premises establishments, which include bars, clubs, and restaurants. Figure 8.3 shows the minimum age by state to serve alcohol. Twenty-four states in the United States permit adults age 18 or older to tend bar. Figure 8.4 shows the minimum age by state to bartend. Generally, the term *server* refers to a person who delivers alcohol to a customer, whereas *bartender* refers to a person who mixes drinks or generally dispenses alcoholic beverages. In some of these states, persons under 21 may be allowed to serve alcohol only in restaurants, not bars or clubs. In still other instances, employees may be allowed to stock coolers with alcohol or clear alcoholic beverages from tables but not be allowed to serve it. Some states require that a manager or supervisor who is over 21 be on the premises when an underage person is serving alcoholic beverages. Additionally, in some cases the underage server must take additional beverage server training.

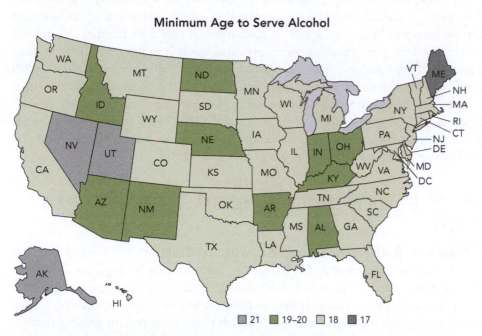

Minimum Age to Serve Alcohol

Legend: ■ 21 ■ 19–20 □ 18 ■ 17

FIGURE 8.3
Minimum age by state to serve alcohol.

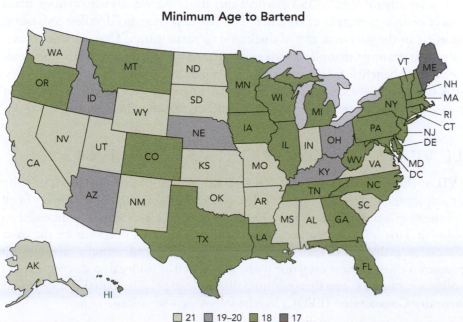

Minimum Age to Bartend

Legend: □ 21 ■ 19–20 ■ 18 ■ 17

FIGURE 8.4
Minimum age by state to bartend.

While all of this may seem confusing, it is. Keep in mind also that minimum age laws are passed by the legislatures in each state, but in several states local jurisdictions may override the state law if the local law is stricter. To be on the safe side, consult with your local beverage control commission to ascertain the law in your area and avoid hiring someone who is legally not of age to serve or dispense alcoholic beverages in your operation.

CONSOLIDATED OMNIBUS RECONCILIATION ACT OF 1985 (COBRA)

The **Consolidated Omnibus Reconciliation Act of 1985 (COBRA)** generally requires that group health plans sponsored by businesses with twenty or more employees offer employees and their families the opportunity for a temporary extension of health coverage (called continuation coverage) in certain instances where coverage under the plan would otherwise end. It gives workers and their families the right to choose to continue group health benefits provided by their group health plan for limited periods of time under certain circumstances such as voluntary or involuntary job loss, reduction in the hours worked, transition between jobs, death, divorce, and other life events. Qualified individuals may be required to pay the entire premium for coverage up to 102 percent of the cost to the plan. COBRA beneficiaries generally are eligible for group coverage during a maximum of 18 months for qualifying events due to employment termination or reduction of hours of work.

EMPLOYEE RETIREMENT INCOME SECURITY ACT (ERISA)

The **Employee Retirement Income Security Act (ERISA)** is a federal law that contains detailed requirements for businesses who offer their employees a welfare benefit plan or retirement plan. It sets minimum standards for retirement and health benefit plans in private industry. It does not require any employer to establish a plan; however, it requires that those who do establish plans meet certain minimum standards. Among other things, ERISA provides that those individuals who manage plans must meet certain standards of conduct. The law also contains detailed provisions for reporting to the government and disclosure to participants. There also are provisions aimed at ensuring that plan funds are protected and that participants who qualify receive their benefits. ERISA has also been expanded to include new health laws. COBRA (see previous section) amended ERISA to provide for the continuation of health care coverage for employees and their beneficiaries for a limited period of time.

TITLE VII OF THE CIVIL RIGHTS ACT OF 1964

Title VII of the Civil Rights Act of 1964 prohibits employers from discriminating against employees on the basis of race, color, national origin, religion, or gender in all parts of the employment process from recruitment through termination. In order to comply with Title VII, an employer must make employment decisions on the basis of business necessity rather than based upon a particular individual's membership in a protected class. Almost everyone understands that it is illegal to discriminate in the workplace, but what exactly constitutes discrimination? The **Equal Employment Opportunity Commission (EEOC)** has the following suggestions:

- Race. In general, it is assumed that pre-employment requests for information will form the basis for hiring decisions. Therefore, employers should not request information that discloses or tends to disclose an applicant's race unless it has a legitimate business need for such information.

- Height and weight. Height and weight requirements tend to disproportionately limit the employment opportunities of some protected groups. Unless the employer can demonstrate how the need is related to the job, it may be viewed as illegal under federal law.

- Credit rating or economic status. Inquiry into an applicant's current or past assets, liabilities, or credit rating, including bankruptcy or garnishment, refusal or cancellation of bonding, car ownership, rental or ownership of a house, length of residence at an address, charge accounts, furniture ownership, or bank accounts generally should be avoided because they tend to impact more adversely on minorities and females. Exceptions exist if the employer can show that such information is essential to the particular job in question.

- Religious affiliation or beliefs. Questions about an applicant's religious affiliation or beliefs (unless the religion is a bona fide occupational qualification, such as working for a religious organization) are generally viewed as non-job-related and problematic under federal law. Employers should avoid questions about an applicant's religious affiliation, such as place of worship, days of worship, and religious holidays and should not ask for references from religious leaders, for instance a minister, rabbi, priest, imam, or pastor.

- Citizenship. Employers should not ask whether or not a job applicant is a United States citizen before making an offer of employment. The Immigration Reform and Control Act makes it illegal for employers to discriminate with respect to hiring, firing, or recruitment based on an individual's citizenship or immigration status. For example, the law prohibits employers from hiring only U.S. citizens or lawful permanent residents unless required to do so by law, regulation, or government contract; it also prohibits employers from preferring to hire temporary visa holders or undocumented workers overqualified U.S. citizens or other protected individuals, such as refugees or individuals granted asylum.

- Marital status or number of children. Questions about marital status and number and ages of children are frequently used to discriminate against women and may violate Title VII if used to deny or limit employment opportunities. Such inquiries may be asked after an employment offer has been made and accepted if needed for insurance or other legitimate business purposes. The following pre-employment inquiries may be regarded as evidence of intent to discriminate when asked in the pre-employment context:
  ○ Whether applicant is pregnant
  ○ Marital status of applicant or whether applicant plans to marry
  ○ Number and age of children or future child bearing plans
  ○ Child care arrangements
  ○ Employment status of spouse
  ○ Name of spouse

- Gender. Questions about an applicant's sex (unless it is a bona fide occupational qualification and is essential to a particular position or occupation), marital status, pregnancy, medical history of pregnancy, future child bearing plans, number or ages of children or dependents, provisions for child care, abortions, birth control, ability to reproduce, and name or address of spouse or children are generally viewed as non-job-related and problematic under Title VII.

- Arrest and conviction. There is no federal law that clearly prohibits an employer from asking about arrest and conviction records. However, using such records as an absolute measure to prevent an individual from being hired could limit the employment opportunities of some protected groups and thus cannot be used in this way. Since an arrest alone does not necessarily mean that an applicant has committed a crime, the employer should not assume that the applicant committed the offense. Instead, the employer should allow him or her the opportunity to explain the circumstances of the arrest(s) and should make a reasonable effort to determine whether the explanation is reliable. Even if the employer believes that the applicant did engage in the conduct for which he or she was arrested, that information should prevent him or her from employment only to the extent that it is evident that the applicant cannot be trusted to perform the duties of the position when considering the nature of the job, the nature and seriousness of the offense, and the length of time since it occurred. This is also true for a conviction. Several state laws limit the use of arrest and conviction records by prospective employers. These range from laws and rules prohibiting the employer from asking the applicant any questions about arrest records to those restricting the employer's use of conviction data in making an employment decision.

- Security or background checks for certain religious or ethnic groups. If the employer requires all other applicants to undergo background checks before being offered a position, the employer may require members of religious or ethnic groups to undergo the same pre-employment investigations.
- Disability. Under the law, employers generally cannot ask disability-related questions or require medical examinations until after an applicant has been given a conditional job offer. This is because, in the past, this information was frequently used to exclude applicants with disabilities before their ability to perform a job was evaluated.
- Medical questions and examinations. The ADA places restrictions on employers when it comes to asking job applicants to answer medical questions, take a medical exam, or identify a disability. An employer also may not ask a job applicant to answer medical questions or take a medical exam before making a job offer. An employer may ask a job applicant whether they can perform the job and how they would perform the job. The law allows an employer to condition a job offer on the applicant answering certain medical questions or successfully passing a medical exam, but only if all new employees in the same job have to answer the questions or take the exam. The law also requires that the employers keep all medical records and information confidential and in separate medical files.

Sexual Harassment

Sexual harassment is a form of sex discrimination that violates Title VII of the Civil Rights Act of 1964 and applies to employers with fifteen or more employees. Unwelcome sexual advances, requests for sexual favors, and other verbal or physical conduct of a sexual nature constitute sexual harassment. It applies when this conduct affects an individual's employment, unreasonably interferes with an individual's work performance, or creates an intimidating, hostile, or offensive work environment. Sexual harassment can occur in a variety of circumstances, including but not limited to the following:

- The victim as well as the harasser may be a woman or a man. The victim does not have to be of the opposite sex.
- The harasser can be the victim's supervisor, an agent of the employer, a supervisor in another area, a coworker, or a nonemployee.
- The victim does not have to be the person harassed but could be anyone affected by the offensive conduct.
- Unlawful sexual harassment may occur without economic injury to or discharge of the victim.
- The harasser's conduct must be unwelcome.

The victim should inform the harasser directly that the conduct is unwelcome and must stop. Barring this, the victim should use any employer complaint mechanism or grievance system available.

When investigating allegations of sexual harassment, the EEOC looks at the whole record: the circumstances, such as the nature of the sexual advances, and the context in which the alleged incidents occurred. A determination on the allegations is made from the facts on a case-by-case basis. Prevention is the best tool to eliminate sexual harassment in the workplace. Employers are encouraged to take steps necessary to prevent sexual harassment from occurring. They should clearly communicate to employees that sexual harassment will not be tolerated. They can do so by providing sexual harassment training to their employees and by establishing an effective complaint or grievance process and taking immediate and appropriate action when an employee complains.

As you can see, most areas of EEOC law are fairly cut and dried, but there are a few areas that are gray. If you are managing a themed bar which calls for young female servers or young male servers, you could be in trouble, the key words being *young* and specifying a specific sex. If you are running a Japanese restaurant and lounge you could be in trouble by hiring all Japanese workers. When in doubt, check with the EEOC or your attorney.

IMMIGRATION AND THE I-9

Closely aligned with discrimination is immigration and who exactly is eligible to work in the United States. The U.S. Citizenship and Immigration Services administers and enforces the **employment eligibility verification** process, commonly known as **Form I-9**. The instructions they give are as follows.

All employers must complete and retain a Form I-9 for each individual they hire for employment in the United States. This includes citizens and noncitizens. On the form, the employer must examine the employment eligibility and identity document(s) an employee presents to determine whether the document(s) reasonably appear to be genuine and relate to the individual and record the document information on the Form I-9. The list of acceptable documents can be found on the last page of the form. Refer to Figure 8.5 for a list of acceptable documents.

Form I-9 must be kept by the employer in a file separate from the employee's personnel file, either for three years after the date of hire or for one year after employment is terminated, whichever is later. The form must be available for inspection by authorized U.S. government officials (e.g., Department of Homeland Security, Department of Labor, and Department of Justice).

AGE DISCRIMINATION IN EMPLOYMENT ACT (ADEA)

The **Age Discrimination in Employment Act (ADEA)** is a law that was passed by Congress in 1967 to protect individuals over the age of 40 from discrimination based upon their age. It prohibits businesses from discriminatory treatment in hiring, promotion, and firing based on an employee's age. It applies to businesses with twenty or more employees. It does allow age to play a factor in an extraordinary situation where age is an occupational qualification. Many bars hire only young, good-looking, and energetic persons. Prior to doing this, however, it would be wise to consult with an attorney to make sure that you are complying with the law. Forcing early retirement or refusing to train or promote older employees is a violation of the law.

Instructions for Employment Eligibility Verification

Department of Homeland Security
U.S. Citizenship and Immigration Services

USCIS
Form I-9
OMB No. 1615-0047
Expires 03/31/2016

Read all instructions carefully before completing this form.

Anti-Discrimination Notice. It is illegal to discriminate against any work-authorized individual in hiring, discharge, recruitment or referral for a fee, or in the employment eligibility verification (Form I-9 and E-Verify) process based on that individual's citizenship status, immigration status or national origin. Employers **CANNOT** specify which document(s) they will accept from an employee. The refusal to hire an individual because the documentation presented has a future expiration date may also constitute illegal discrimination. For more information, call the Office of Special Counsel for Immigration-Related Unfair Employment Practices (OSC) at 1-800-255-7688 (employees), 1-800-255-8155 (employers), or 1-800-237-2515 (TDD), or visit **www.justice.gov/crt/about/osc**.

What Is the Purpose of This Form?

Employers must complete Form I-9 to document verification of the identity and employment authorization of each new employee (both citizen and noncitizen) hired after November 6, 1986, to work in the United States. In the Commonwealth of the Northern Mariana Islands (CNMI), employers must complete Form I-9 to document verification of the identity and employment authorization of each new employee (both citizen and noncitizen) hired after November 27, 2011. Employers should have used Form I-9 CNMI between November 28, 2009 and November 27, 2011.

General Instructions

Employers are responsible for completing and retaining Form I-9. For the purpose of completing this form, the term "employer" means all employers, including those recruiters and referrers for a fee who are agricultural associations, agricultural employers, or farm labor contractors.

Form I-9 is made up of three sections. Employers may be fined if the form is not complete. Employers are responsible for retaining completed forms. Do not mail completed forms to U.S. Citizenship and Immigration Services (USCIS) or Immigration and Customs Enforcement (ICE).

Section 1. Employee Information and Attestation

Newly hired employees must complete and sign Section 1 of Form I-9 **no later than the first day of employment**. Section 1 should never be completed before the employee has accepted a job offer.

Provide the following information to complete Section 1:

Name: Provide your full legal last name, first name, and middle initial. Your last name is your family name or surname. If you have two last names or a hyphenated last name, include both names in the last name field. Your first name is your given name. Your middle initial is the first letter of your second given name, or the first letter of your middle name, if any.

Other names used: Provide all other names used, if any (including maiden name). If you have had no other legal names, write "N/A."

Address: Provide the address where you currently live, including Street Number and Name, Apartment Number (if applicable), City, State, and Zip Code. Do not provide a post office box address (P.O. Box). Only border commuters from Canada or Mexico may use an international address in this field.

Date of Birth: Provide your date of birth in the mm/dd/yyyy format. For example, January 23, 1950, should be written as 01/23/1950.

U.S. Social Security Number: Provide your 9-digit Social Security number. Providing your Social Security number is voluntary. However, if your employer participates in E-Verify, you must provide your Social Security number.

E-mail Address and Telephone Number (Optional): You may provide your e-mail address and telephone number. Department of Homeland Security (DHS) may contact you if DHS learns of a potential mismatch between the information provided and the information in DHS or Social Security Administration (SSA) records. You may write "N/A" if you choose not to provide this information.

FIGURE 8.5 The I-9 form, which must be filled out by all employees.

Form illustration courtesy of the United States Citizen and Immigration Services.

All employees must attest in Section 1, under penalty of perjury, to their citizenship or immigration status by checking one of the following four boxes provided on the form:

1. **A citizen of the United States**

2. **A noncitizen national of the United States:** Noncitizen nationals of the United States are persons born in American Samoa, certain former citizens of the former Trust Territory of the Pacific Islands, and certain children of noncitizen nationals born abroad.

3. **A lawful permanent resident:** A lawful permanent resident is any person who is not a U.S. citizen and who resides in the United States under legally recognized and lawfully recorded permanent residence as an immigrant. The term "lawful permanent resident" includes conditional residents. If you check this box, write either your Alien Registration Number (A-Number) or USCIS Number in the field next to your selection. At this time, the USCIS Number is the same as the A-Number without the "A" prefix.

4. **An alien authorized to work:** If you are not a citizen or national of the United States or a lawful permanent resident, but are authorized to work in the United States, check this box.

   If you check this box:

   a. Record the date that your employment authorization expires, if any. Aliens whose employment authorization does not expire, such as refugees, asylees, and certain citizens of the Federated States of Micronesia, the Republic of the Marshall Islands, or Palau, may write "N/A" on this line.

   b. Next, enter your Alien Registration Number (A-Number)/USCIS Number. At this time, the USCIS Number is the same as your A-Number without the "A" prefix. If you have not received an A-Number/USCIS Number, record your Admission Number. You can find your Admission Number on Form I-94, "Arrival-Departure Record," or as directed by USCIS or U.S. Customs and Border Protection (CBP).

      (1) If you obtained your admission number from CBP in connection with your arrival in the United States, then also record information about the foreign passport you used to enter the United States (number and country of issuance).

      (2) If you obtained your admission number from USCIS *within the United States*, or you entered the United States without a foreign passport, you must write "N/A" in the Foreign Passport Number and Country of Issuance fields.

Sign your name in the "Signature of Employee" block and record the date you completed and signed Section 1. By signing and dating this form, you attest that the citizenship or immigration status you selected is correct and that you are aware that you may be imprisoned and/or fined for making false statements or using false documentation when completing this form. To fully complete this form, you must present to your employer documentation that establishes your identity and employment authorization. Choose which documents to present from the Lists of Acceptable Documents, found on the last page of this form. You must present this documentation no later than the third day after beginning employment, although you may present the required documentation before this date.

Preparer and/or Translator Certification

The Preparer and/or Translator Certification must be completed if the employee requires assistance to complete Section 1 (e.g., the employee needs the instructions or responses translated, someone other than the employee fills out the information blocks, or someone with disabilities needs additional assistance). The employee must still sign Section 1.

Minors and Certain Employees with Disabilities (Special Placement)

Parents or legal guardians assisting minors (individuals under 18) and certain employees with disabilities should review the guidelines in the *Handbook for Employers: Instructions for Completing Form I-9 (M-274)* on **www.uscis.gov/ I-9Central** before completing Section 1. These individuals have special procedures for establishing identity if they cannot present an identity document for Form I-9. The special procedures include **(1)** the parent or legal guardian filling out Section 1 and writing "minor under age 18" or "special placement," whichever applies, in the employee signature block; and **(2)** the employer writing "minor under age 18" or "special placement" under List B in Section 2.

FIGURE 8.5 *(Continued)*

Section 2. Employer or Authorized Representative Review and Verification

Before completing Section 2, employers must ensure that Section 1 is completed properly and on time. Employers may not ask an individual to complete Section 1 before he or she has accepted a job offer.

Employers or their authorized representative must complete Section 2 by examining evidence of identity and employment authorization within 3 business days of the employee's first day of employment. For example, if an employee begins employment on Monday, the employer must complete Section 2 by Thursday of that week. However, if an employer hires an individual for less than 3 business days, Section 2 must be completed no later than the first day of employment. An employer may complete Form I-9 before the first day of employment if the employer has offered the individual a job and the individual has accepted.

Employers cannot specify which document(s) employees may present from the Lists of Acceptable Documents, found on the last page of Form I-9, to establish identity and employment authorization. Employees must present one selection from List A **OR** a combination of one selection from List B and one selection from List C. List A contains documents that show both identity and employment authorization. Some List A documents are combination documents. The employee must present combination documents together to be considered a List A document. For example, a foreign passport and a Form I-94 containing an endorsement of the alien's nonimmigrant status must be presented together to be considered a List A document. List B contains documents that show identity only, and List C contains documents that show employment authorization only. If an employee presents a List A document, he or she should **not** present a List B and List C document, and vice versa. If an employer participates in E-Verify, the List B document must include a photograph.

In the field below the Section 2 introduction, employers must enter the last name, first name and middle initial, if any, that the employee entered in Section 1. This will help to identify the pages of the form should they get separated.

Employers or their authorized representative must:

1. Physically examine each original document the employee presents to determine if it reasonably appears to be genuine and to relate to the person presenting it. The person who examines the documents must be the same person who signs Section 2. The examiner of the documents and the employee must both be physically present during the examination of the employee's documents.

2. Record the document title shown on the Lists of Acceptable Documents, issuing authority, document number and expiration date (if any) from the original document(s) the employee presents. You may write "N/A" in any unused fields.

    If the employee is a student or exchange visitor who presented a foreign passport with a Form I-94, the employer should also enter in Section 2:

    a. The student's Form I-20 or DS-2019 number (Student and Exchange Visitor Information System-SEVIS Number); **and** the program end date from Form I-20 or DS-2019.

3. Under Certification, enter the employee's first day of employment. Temporary staffing agencies may enter the first day the employee was placed in a job pool. Recruiters and recruiters for a fee do not enter the employee's first day of employment.

4. Provide the name and title of the person completing Section 2 in the Signature of Employer or Authorized Representative field.

5. Sign and date the attestation on the date Section 2 is completed.

6. Record the employer's business name and address.

7. Return the employee's documentation.

Employers may, but are not required to, photocopy the document(s) presented. If photocopies are made, they should be made for **ALL** new hires or reverifications. Photocopies must be retained and presented with Form I-9 in case of an inspection by DHS or other federal government agency. Employers must always complete Section 2 even if they photocopy an employee's document(s). Making photocopies of an employee's document(s) cannot take the place of completing Form I-9. Employers are still responsible for completing and retaining Form I-9.

FIGURE 8.5 (Continued)

Unexpired Documents

Generally, only unexpired, original documentation is acceptable. The only exception is that an employee may present a certified copy of a birth certificate. Additionally, in some instances, a document that appears to be expired may be acceptable if the expiration date shown on the face of the document has been extended, such as for individuals with temporary protected status. Refer to the *Handbook for Employers: Instructions for Completing Form I-9 (M-274)* or I-9 Central (www.uscis.gov/I-9Central) for examples.

Receipts

If an employee is unable to present a required document (or documents), the employee can present an acceptable receipt in lieu of a document from the Lists of Acceptable Documents on the last page of this form. Receipts showing that a person has applied for an initial grant of employment authorization, or for renewal of employment authorization, are not acceptable. Employers cannot accept receipts if employment will last less than 3 days. Receipts are acceptable when completing Form I-9 for a new hire or when reverification is required.

Employees must present receipts within 3 business days of their first day of employment, or in the case of reverification, by the date that reverification is required, and must present valid replacement documents within the time frames described below.

There are three types of acceptable receipts:

1. A receipt showing that the employee has applied to replace a document that was lost, stolen or damaged. The employee must present the actual document within 90 days from the date of hire.

2. The arrival portion of Form I-94/I-94A with a temporary I-551 stamp and a photograph of the individual. The employee must present the actual Permanent Resident Card (Form I-551) by the expiration date of the temporary I-551 stamp, or, if there is no expiration date, within 1 year from the date of issue.

3. The departure portion of Form I-94/I-94A with a refugee admission stamp. The employee must present an unexpired Employment Authorization Document (Form I-766) or a combination of a List B document and an unrestricted Social Security card within 90 days.

When the employee provides an acceptable receipt, the employer should:

1. Record the document title in Section 2 under the sections titled List A, List B, or List C, as applicable.

2. Write the word "receipt" and its document number in the "Document Number" field. Record the last day that the receipt is valid in the "Expiration Date" field.

By the end of the receipt validity period, the employer should:

1. Cross out the word "receipt" and any accompanying document number and expiration date.

2. Record the number and other required document information from the actual document presented.

3. Initial and date the change.

See the *Handbook for Employers: Instructions for Completing Form I-9 (M-274)* at www.uscis.gov/I-9Central for more information on receipts.

Section 3. Reverification and Rehires

Employers or their authorized representatives should complete Section 3 when reverifying that an employee is authorized to work. When rehiring an employee within 3 years of the date Form I-9 was originally completed, employers have the option to complete a new Form I-9 or complete Section 3. When completing Section 3 in either a reverification or rehire situation, if the employee's name has changed, record the name change in Block A.

For employees who provide an employment authorization expiration date in Section 1, employers must reverify employment authorization on or before the date provided.

FIGURE 8.5 (*Continued*)

Some employees may write "N/A" in the space provided for the expiration date in Section 1 if they are aliens whose employment authorization does not expire (e.g., asylees, refugees, certain citizens of the Federated States of Micronesia, the Republic of the Marshall Islands, or Palau). Reverification does not apply for such employees unless they chose to present evidence of employment authorization in Section 2 that contains an expiration date and requires reverification, such as Form I-766, Employment Authorization Document.

Reverification applies if evidence of employment authorization (List A or List C document) presented in Section 2 expires. However, employers should not reverify:

1. U.S. citizens and noncitizen nationals; or

2. Lawful permanent residents who presented a Permanent Resident Card (Form I-551) for Section 2.

Reverification does not apply to List B documents.

If both Section 1 and Section 2 indicate expiration dates triggering the reverification requirement, the employer should reverify by the earlier date.

For reverification, an employee must present unexpired documentation from either List A or List C showing he or she is still authorized to work. Employers CANNOT require the employee to present a particular document from List A or List C. The employee may choose which document to present.

To complete Section 3, employers should follow these instructions:

1. Complete Block A if an employee's name has changed at the time you complete Section 3.

2. Complete Block B with the date of rehire if you rehire an employee within 3 years of the date this form was originally completed, and the employee is still authorized to be employed on the same basis as previously indicated on this form. Also complete the "Signature of Employer or Authorized Representative" block.

3. Complete Block C if:

    a. The employment authorization or employment authorization document of a current employee is about to expire and requires reverification; or

    b. You rehire an employee within 3 years of the date this form was originally completed and his or her employment authorization or employment authorization document has expired. (Complete Block B for this employee as well.)

    To complete Block C:

    a. Examine either a List A or List C document the employee presents that shows that the employee is currently authorized to work in the United States; and

    b. Record the document title, document number, and expiration date (if any).

4. After completing block A, B or C, complete the "Signature of Employer or Authorized Representative" block, including the date.

    For reverification purposes, employers may either complete Section 3 of a new Form I-9 or Section 3 of the previously completed Form I-9. Any new pages of Form I-9 completed during reverification must be attached to the employee's original Form I-9. If you choose to complete Section 3 of a new Form I-9, you may attach just the page containing Section 3, with the employee's name entered at the top of the page, to the employee's original Form I-9. If there is a more current version of Form I-9 at the time of reverification, you must complete Section 3 of that version of the form.

What Is the Filing Fee?

There is no fee for completing Form I-9. This form is not filed with USCIS or any government agency. Form I-9 must be retained by the employer and made available for inspection by U.S. Government officials as specified in the **"USCIS Privacy Act Statement"** below.

USCIS Forms and Information

For more detailed information about completing Form I-9, employers and employees should refer to the *Handbook for Employers: Instructions for Completing Form I-9 (M-274)*.

FIGURE 8.5 *(Continued)*

You can also obtain information about Form I-9 from the USCIS Web site at www.uscis.gov/I-9Central, by e-mailing USCIS at **I-9Central@dhs.gov**, or by calling **1-888-464-4218**. For TDD (hearing impaired), call **1-877-875-6028**.

To obtain USCIS forms or the *Handbook for Employers*, you can download them from the USCIS Web site at www.uscis.gov/forms. You may order USCIS forms by calling our toll-free number at **1-800-870-3676**. You may also obtain forms and information by contacting the USCIS National Customer Service Center at **1-800-375-5283**. For TDD (hearing impaired), call **1-800-767-1833**.

Information about E-Verify, a free and voluntary program that allows participating employers to electronically verify the employment eligibility of their newly hired employees, can be obtained from the USCIS Web site at www.dhs.gov/E-Verify, by e-mailing USCIS at **E-Verify@dhs.gov** or by calling **1-888-464-4218**. For TDD (hearing impaired), call **1-877-875-6028.**

Employees with questions about Form I-9 and/or E-Verify can reach the USCIS employee hotline by calling **1-888-897-7781**. For TDD (hearing impaired), call **1-877-875-6028.**

Photocopying and Retaining Form I-9

A blank Form I-9 may be reproduced, provided all sides are copied. The instructions and Lists of Acceptable Documents must be available to all employees completing this form. Employers must retain each employee's completed Form I-9 for as long as the individual works for the employer. Employers are required to retain the pages of the form on which the employee and employer enter data. If copies of documentation presented by the employee are made, those copies must also be kept with the form. Once the individual's employment ends, the employer must retain this form for either 3 years after the date of hire or 1 year after the date employment ended, whichever is later.

Form I-9 may be signed and retained electronically, in compliance with Department of Homeland Security regulations at 8 CFR 274a.2.

USCIS Privacy Act Statement

AUTHORITIES: The authority for collecting this information is the Immigration Reform and Control Act of 1986, Public Law 99-603 (8 USC 1324a).

PURPOSE: This information is collected by employers to comply with the requirements of the Immigration Reform and Control Act of 1986. This law requires that employers verify the identity and employment authorization of individuals they hire for employment to preclude the unlawful hiring, or recruiting or referring for a fee, of aliens who are not authorized to work in the United States.

DISCLOSURE: Submission of the information required in this form is voluntary. However, failure of the employer to ensure proper completion of this form for each employee may result in the imposition of civil or criminal penalties. In addition, employing individuals knowing that they are unauthorized to work in the United States may subject the employer to civil and/or criminal penalties.

ROUTINE USES: This information will be used by employers as a record of their basis for determining eligibility of an employee to work in the United States. The employer will keep this form and make it available for inspection by authorized officials of the Department of Homeland Security, Department of Labor, and Office of Special Counsel for Immigration-Related Unfair Employment Practices.

Paperwork Reduction Act

An agency may not conduct or sponsor an information collection and a person is not required to respond to a collection of information unless it displays a currently valid OMB control number. The public reporting burden for this collection of information is estimated at 35 minutes per response, including the time for reviewing instructions and completing and retaining the form. Send comments regarding this burden estimate or any other aspect of this collection of information, including suggestions for reducing this burden, to: U.S. Citizenship and Immigration Services, Regulatory Coordination Division, Office of Policy and Strategy, 20 Massachusetts Avenue NW, Washington, DC 20529-2140; OMB No. 1615-0047. **Do not mail your completed Form I-9 to this address.**

FIGURE 8.5 *(Continued)*

Employment Eligibility Verification

Department of Homeland Security
U.S. Citizenship and Immigration Services

USCIS
Form I-9
OMB No. 1615-0047
Expires 03/31/2016

▶**START HERE.** Read instructions carefully before completing this form. The instructions must be available during completion of this form.
ANTI-DISCRIMINATION NOTICE: It is illegal to discriminate against work-authorized individuals. Employers **CANNOT** specify which document(s) they will accept from an employee. The refusal to hire an individual because the documentation presented has a future expiration date may also constitute illegal discrimination.

Section 1. Employee Information and Attestation (Employees must complete and sign Section 1 of Form I-9 no later than the **first day of employment**, but not before accepting a job offer.)

Last Name (Family Name)	First Name (Given Name)	Middle Initial	Other Names Used (if any)

Address (Street Number and Name)	Apt. Number	City or Town	State	Zip Code

Date of Birth (mm/dd/yyyy)	U.S. Social Security Number	E-mail Address	Telephone Number

I am aware that federal law provides for imprisonment and/or fines for false statements or use of false documents in connection with the completion of this form.

I attest, under penalty of perjury, that I am (check one of the following):

☐ A citizen of the United States

☐ A noncitizen national of the United States (See instructions)

☐ A lawful permanent resident (Alien Registration Number/USCIS Number): _____

☐ An alien authorized to work until (expiration date, if applicable, mm/dd/yyyy) _____ . Some aliens may write "N/A" in this field.
(See instructions)

For aliens authorized to work, provide your Alien Registration Number/USCIS Number **OR** Form I-94 Admission Number:

1. Alien Registration Number/USCIS Number:_____

OR

2. Form I-94 Admission Number: _____

   If you obtained your admission number from CBP in connection with your arrival in the United States, include the following:

   Foreign Passport Number: _____

   Country of Issuance: _____

Some aliens may write "N/A" on the Foreign Passport Number and Country of Issuance fields. (See instructions)

3-D Barcode
Do Not Write in This Space

Signature of Employee:	Date (mm/dd/yyyy):

Preparer and/or Translator Certification (To be completed and signed if Section 1 is prepared by a person other than the employee.)

I attest, under penalty of perjury, that I have assisted in the completion of this form and that to the best of my knowledge the information is true and correct.

Signature of Preparer or Translator:	Date (mm/dd/yyyy):

Last Name (Family Name)	First Name (Given Name)

Address (Street Number and Name)	City or Town	State	Zip Code

STOP *Employer Completes Next Page* **STOP**

Form I-9 03/08/13 N

FIGURE 8.5 (Continued)

Section 2. Employer or Authorized Representative Review and Verification

(Employers or their authorized representative must complete and sign Section 2 within 3 business days of the employee's first day of employment. You must physically examine one document from List A OR examine a combination of one document from List B and one document from List C as listed on the "Lists of Acceptable Documents" on the next page of this form. For each document you review, record the following information: document title, issuing authority, document number, and expiration date, if any.)

Employee Last Name, First Name and Middle Initial from Section 1:

List A	OR	List B	AND	List C
Identity and Employment Authorization		**Identity**		**Employment Authorization**
Document Title:		Document Title:		Document Title:
Issuing Authority:		Issuing Authority:		Issuing Authority:
Document Number:		Document Number:		Document Number:
Expiration Date *(if any)(mm/dd/yyyy)*:		Expiration Date *(if any)(mm/dd/yyyy)*:		Expiration Date *(if any)(mm/dd/yyyy)*:
Document Title:				
Issuing Authority:				
Document Number:				
Expiration Date *(if any)(mm/dd/yyyy)*:				
Document Title:				**3-D Barcode**
Issuing Authority:				**Do Not Write in This Space**
Document Number:				
Expiration Date *(if any)(mm/dd/yyyy)*:				

Certification

I attest, under penalty of perjury, that (1) I have examined the document(s) presented by the above-named employee, (2) the above-listed document(s) appear to be genuine and to relate to the employee named, and (3) to the best of my knowledge the employee is authorized to work in the United States.

The employee's first day of employment *(mm/dd/yyyy)*: _____ *(See instructions for exemptions.)*

Signature of Employer or Authorized Representative	Date *(mm/dd/yyyy)*	Title of Employer or Authorized Representative	
Last Name *(Family Name)*	First Name *(Given Name)*	Employer's Business or Organization Name	
Employer's Business or Organization Address *(Street Number and Name)*	City or Town	State ▼	Zip Code

Section 3. Reverification and Rehires *(To be completed and signed by employer or authorized representative.)*

A. New Name *(if applicable)* Last Name *(Family Name)* First Name *(Given Name)*	Middle Initial	B. Date of Rehire *(if applicable) (mm/dd/yyyy)*:

C. If employee's previous grant of employment authorization has expired, provide the information for the document from List A or List C the employee presented that establishes current employment authorization in the space provided below.		
Document Title:	Document Number:	Expiration Date *(if any)(mm/dd/yyyy)*:

I attest, under penalty of perjury, that to the best of my knowledge, this employee is authorized to work in the United States, and if the employee presented document(s), the document(s) I have examined appear to be genuine and to relate to the individual.

Signature of Employer or Authorized Representative:	Date *(mm/dd/yyyy)*:	Print Name of Employer or Authorized Representative:

FIGURE 8.5 *(Continued)*

LISTS OF ACCEPTABLE DOCUMENTS
All documents must be UNEXPIRED

Employees may present one selection from List A
or a combination of one selection from List B and one selection from List C.

LIST A Documents that Establish Both Identity and Employment Authorization		LIST B Documents that Establish Identity	LIST C Documents that Establish Employment Authorization
	OR		AND
1. U.S. Passport or U.S. Passport Card		1. Driver's license or ID card issued by a State or outlying possession of the United States provided it contains a photograph or information such as name, date of birth, gender, height, eye color, and address	1. A Social Security Account Number card, unless the card includes one of the following restrictions: (1) NOT VALID FOR EMPLOYMENT (2) VALID FOR WORK ONLY WITH INS AUTHORIZATION (3) VALID FOR WORK ONLY WITH DHS AUTHORIZATION
2. Permanent Resident Card or Alien Registration Receipt Card (Form I-551)			
3. Foreign passport that contains a temporary I-551 stamp or temporary I-551 printed notation on a machine-readable immigrant visa		2. ID card issued by federal, state or local government agencies or entities, provided it contains a photograph or information such as name, date of birth, gender, height, eye color, and address	2. Certification of Birth Abroad issued by the Department of State (Form FS-545)
4. Employment Authorization Document that contains a photograph (Form I-766)			3. Certification of Report of Birth issued by the Department of State (Form DS-1350)
		3. School ID card with a photograph	
5. For a nonimmigrant alien authorized to work for a specific employer because of his or her status: a. Foreign passport; and b. Form I-94 or Form I-94A that has the following: (1) The same name as the passport; and (2) An endorsement of the alien's nonimmigrant status as long as that period of endorsement has not yet expired and the proposed employment is not in conflict with any restrictions or limitations identified on the form.		4. Voter's registration card	4. Original or certified copy of birth certificate issued by a State, county, municipal authority, or territory of the United States bearing an official seal
		5. U.S. Military card or draft record	
		6. Military dependent's ID card	
		7. U.S. Coast Guard Merchant Mariner Card	
		8. Native American tribal document	5. Native American tribal document
		9. Driver's license issued by a Canadian government authority	6. U.S. Citizen ID Card (Form I-197)
		For persons under age 18 who are unable to present a document listed above:	7. Identification Card for Use of Resident Citizen in the United States (Form I-179)
6. Passport from the Federated States of Micronesia (FSM) or the Republic of the Marshall Islands (RMI) with Form I-94 or Form I-94A indicating nonimmigrant admission under the Compact of Free Association Between the United States and the FSM or RMI		10. School record or report card	8. Employment authorization document issued by the Department of Homeland Security
		11. Clinic, doctor, or hospital record	
		12. Day-care or nursery school record	

Illustrations of many of these documents appear in Part 8 of the Handbook for Employers (M-274).

Refer to Section 2 of the instructions, titled "Employer or Authorized Representative Review and Verification," for more information about acceptable receipts.

FAMILY MEDICAL LEAVE ACT (FMLA)

Under the **Family Medical Leave Act (FMLA)**, employers must allow employees to take the equivalent of 12 weeks of unpaid leave each year

- Due to the birth or adoption of a child.
- To attend to a serious health condition of an immediate family member.
- To attend to their own serious health condition.

A serious health condition is defined as an illness, injury, impairment, or physical or mental condition which involves an overnight stay in a hospital, hospice, or residential medical-care facility. It includes a period of incapacity of more than three consecutive days or a period of incapacity that is permanent or long-term due to a condition for which treatment may be ineffective. It also includes absence to receive multiple treatments from a health care provider. The right to take a leave applies to both male and female employees alike. The FMLA also states that an employee should be given the same job back or an equivalent job if the original position is no longer available when they return.

The FMLA applies only to businesses with fifty or more employees.

UNIONS AND THE LAW

Unions in hospitality organizations are sporadic in the United States. They are primarily limited to large organizations such as hotels, convention centers, arenas, restaurant chains, and large clubs. In addition, they are usually confined to large cities. Nonetheless, there are a great many bars that fall under laws that pertain to unionized work agreements. Even if your bar is not unionized there is always the threat that it could be, and there are laws governing what you can and cannot do regarding a union organization of your business.

Unions can be traced back to the late 1700s and at that time were called societies. When the members would band together to demand certain rights from their employers, the employers would go to court and get an injunction against the workers, thus restricting their right to strike. In the early 1900s, there were often riots between the workers who wanted to strike and management who did not want them to strike. Often the police were called in to uphold the law. Some of the bloodiest riots were between railway workers and management. Congress became alarmed that the economy, which was dependent at that time on the railways getting goods to the consumers, and the national security were at risk. Consequent they passed the Railway Labor Act in 1926. This act gave the workers the right to join unions. Additionally, the railroads had to bargain with the union representatives, and they could not discriminate against union workers.

In 1935, Congress passed the **National Labor Relations Act**, also known as the Wagner Act, which extended the Railway Labor Act to give all workers in private business who were not a part of management the right to form unions. This bill also gave the right to workers to strike. As a result, management complained that the unions held an advantage, and in 1935, Congress passed legislation known as the **Taft-Hartley Act**, which leveled the playing field.

If a union decides to attempt to organize an operation that you are managing, there are some things that you can do to try to prevent the union from becoming recognized. They include the following:

- Informing employees that they do not have to vote for the union even if they have signed an election authorization card.
- Telling employees that they will lose wages if there is a strike and the bar will lose customers.

- Relate positive aspects of the company's relationships with the employees.
- Indicate to employees those statements made by the union that management feels are false.
- Inform them of the disadvantages of union membership.

Some of the things you should *not* do include the following:

- Asking employees how they intend to vote.
- Secure benefits to those employees who vote against the union.
- Attend union organizing meetings to see which employees have shown up to those meetings.
- Give unscheduled wage increases or improved benefits during the pre-election period.
- Meet with employees within 24 hours of the election.
- Prevent employees from wearing union buttons.

The above "cans" and "cannots" are representative of the law and are not a complete list. Since the union will be watching every move made by management, it is best to consult a labor attorney to advise you as to exactly what you can and cannot do.

When a business becomes unionized, management loses many of the prerogatives that it had prior to unionization. It is imperative that management hold on to as many of these prerogatives as possible when the contract is being negotiated. These rights include, but are not limited to, the right to set performance standards, policies, procedures, and schedules; modify job descriptions; require tests for employment; and determine eligibility for promotions.

One of the most difficult aspects of dealing with a unionized operation is the fact that you will lose some authority and in some cases cannot deal directly with your employees on certain issues. These will be handled by the union steward who will act as an intermediary between you and your employee. Additionally, you cannot discriminate against any employee because they favor the union or are involved in union activities. This pertains to transferring or demoting employees, refusing to rehire them after a strike, or terminating them. In other words, you need a tight case with documentation to discipline an employee who does not meet company standards or has violated a company work rule. This will be necessary to offset the claim that will inevitably be made by the employee that you are discriminating against them because they are a union member.

UNEMPLOYMENT COMPENSATION

One of the provisions of the Social Security Act of 1935 was to create the **Federal and State Unemployment Compensation Program**. One of the objectives of the program is to provide an unemployed worker time to find a new job, which is the same or similar to the one they lost without undue financial burden. Another objective is to help stabilize the economy during recessions. The U.S. Department of Labor oversees the system, but each state administers its own program. It is based on a dual program of federal and state statutes.

Each state administers its own unemployment insurance program. This program must be approved by the Secretary of Labor based on federal standards. All state laws provide that a person claiming unemployment compensation be able to work and be available for work. In addition to registering for work at a local employment office, most states require that a person look for work on his or her own or at least makes a reasonable effort to obtain work.

Much of the federal program is financed through the Federal Unemployment Tax Act (FUTA). The tax is paid by businesses at the rate of 0.8 percent on the first

$7,000 of annual pay to each employee. In addition, many states impose an additional tax on employers to cover administration costs. The amount a business pays to the state is normally based on the amount of wages they have paid, the amount they have contributed to the unemployment fund, and the amount that their discharged employees have been compensated from the fund.

One of the caveats of the law is that a person may be disqualified from collecting unemployment compensation if they have been terminated for misconduct, quit without cause, or resigned because of illness.

It is important that management is fully aware of this law. Remember that the amount of tax that you pay is partially predicated on the amount the system pays out to former employees of your business. For example, if an employee is terminated for misconduct and files for compensation, you are notified by the state. If you do not file an appeal, the former employee will collect and your tax could go up. This is one of the reasons it is imperative that you keep excellent records of disciplinary actions taken so that you can defend yourself in the case of an appeal.

CONCLUSION

As you can see, the laws are many and in some cases quite complex. There are sure to be more to follow as legislatures pass additional laws regulating the gap between management and labor. It is imperative that management always keeps abreast of the law as ignorance is no excuse for noncompliance. Careful record keeping is also imperative. You never know when you will have to defend yourself before a commission or court of law. Areas of particular concern to hospitality managers are in the area of wages and sexual harassment as most often these appear to be the areas of noncompliance. The bar business is particularly vulnerable to these issues.

This chapter has given you an overview of the major employment laws affecting the industry. It is, however, just that: an overview. As stated earlier, do not attempt to interpret law by yourself. It is too complex a subject. Always engage the services of an attorney to advise you in this area. You pour the drinks; let them handle the law.

QUESTIONS

Note: All questions assume that the operation in question is eligible for and comes under the jurisdiction of all of the laws covered in this chapter.

True/ False

1. The current minimum wage for nontipped employees is $7.25 per hour.
2. The minimum wage law applies to all bars in the United States and its territories.
3. In the United States, all bartenders must be a minimum of 21 years old.
4. COBRA offers employees the chance to continue their health coverage at their own cost should they be laid off from work.
5. Title VII of the Civil Rights Act of 1964 is administered by the Equal Employment Opportunity Commission (EEOC).
6. You may require an applicant to undergo a physical examination prior to making a job offer to him or her.
7. Under the Family Medical Leave Act, you must allow an employee to take a paid leave for up to twelve weeks for a medical cause.
8. If a union is attempting to organize your bar, you, as management, can attend the organization meeting to see what is going on.
9. As a manager you may tell your employees the disadvantages of forming a union.
10. As the labor laws are readily available to management, it is not necessary to go to the expense of hiring an attorney unless you are sued by a disgruntled employee.

Multiple Choice

1. You decide to add to your dishwashing staff and hire a 19-year-old for the position. The lowest wage you can give is
   A. $7.25.
   B. $4.25.
   C. $3.15.
   D. $2.13.

2. One of your employees works three nights as a cocktail server and two nights as a hostess for a total of 40 hours per week. Tips are quite good, and there is no problem meeting the minimum wage requirement for tip credit for the 40 hours, even though she makes no tips as a hostess. Legally you can pay $2.13 per hour
   1. while she is a cocktail server.
   2. while she is a hostess.
   A. (1) only
   B. (2) only
   C. Both (1) and (2)
   D. Neither (1) nor (2)

3. According to the FLSA, garnishment
   A. refers to the withholding of wages to satisfy a debt.
   B. applies only to child support.
   C. does not have to be executed by the employer.
   D. refers to the little umbrella and fruit on a cocktail.

4. Title VII of the Civil Rights Act of 1964 prohibits you from not hiring a person based on their
   A. height and weight.
   B. credit rating.
   C. race.
   D. all of the above.

5. Which of the following is *not* considered to be sexual harassment according to the Civil Rights Act?
   A. The victim is of the same sex.
   B. The harasser is a customer.
   C. There is no economic injury.
   D. All of the above could be sexual harassment.

6. Under the Family Medical Leave Act, you are required to allow an employee up to twelve weeks of unpaid leave

1. to attend the needs of an immediate family member who is ill.
2. and to give them the same or equivalent job back at the same rate of pay when they return.
   A. (1) only
   B. (2) only
   C. Both (1) and (2)
   D. Neither (1) nor (2)

7. The Unemployment Compensation Program created under the Social Security Act of 1935
   1. is overseen by the Department of Labor.
   2. is administered by the individual states.
   A. (1) only
   B. (2) only
   C. Both (1) and (2)
   D. Neither (1) nor (2)

8. The amount of tax a business pays for unemployment compensation is predicated on
   1. a flat rate determined by each state.
   2. the amount that former employees have been compensated from the fund.
   A. (1) only
   B. (2) only
   C. Both (1) and (2)
   D. Neither (1) nor (2)

9. Which of the following can you *not* do if a union is attempting to organize your business?
   A. Give a wage or benefit increase to those employees who vote against the union.
   B. Tell employees they will lose wages if there is a strike.
   C. Tell employees the disadvantages of belonging to a union.
   D. You cannot do any of the above.

10. Regarding employees who go on strike,
    1. you can refuse to rehire them after the strike.
    2. you can put them in a lower-paying job.
    A. (1) only
    B. (2) only
    C. Both (1) and (2)
    D. Neither (1) nor (2)

Essay

1. You are the manager of a large bar and pay your bar backs $5.00 per hour. They also receive tips from the bartenders. These tips over a period of time average about $2.00 per hour. Three of your bar backs have sued you for back wages, claiming that you have not paid them the prevailing minimum wage. Discuss the merits of this case including what evidence you could bring forth to win the case and what would be the potential penalties should you lose.

2. If an employee works 20 hours as host or hostess at $7.25 per hour and 20 hours as a cocktail server

at $2.13 per hour, how much would you pay them per hour for overtime during a week in which they had to work 10 hours of overtime?

3. Title VII of the Civil Rights Act of 1964 is quite explicit regarding what questions you can and cannot ask in interviewing a prospective employee for a job. Discuss how those parameters affect your ability, both positively and negatively, to choose the best applicant for the job opening.

4. A cocktail waitress comes to you and states that a table of hers is making her very uncomfortable with suggestive comments and wanting to meet her after work. Explain how you would handle this situation.

5. A distinguished-looking gentleman applies for the bartender opening in your establishment. During the interview, you decide that he has all of the qualifications you are looking for. You guess his age to be around the mid-fifties. Your bar caters to the young, hip crowd, and all of your other employees are in their mid-twenties. Do you hire this applicant? Defend your answer.

RESOURCES

The following Acts and Commissions can be found on the Department of Labor website at www.dol.gov (then type in the agency in the search box.)

Age Discrimination in Employment Act (ADEA)

Consolidated Omnibus Reconciliation Act of 1985 (COBRA)

Employee Retirement Income Security Act (ERISA)

Equal Employment Opportunity Commission (EEOC)

Equal Pay Act

Fair Labor Standards Act (FSLA)

Family Medical Leave Act (FMLA)

Federal and State Unemployment Compensation Program

National Labor Relations Act

Taft-Hartley Act

Title VII of the Civil Rights Act of 1964

9
Organization

OVERVIEW

From small neighborhood taverns to large multi-unit corporations, all bars have employees. Regardless of size, how management treats their people will go a long way in determining the success of that business. This is an important chapter as it will delve into the organizational structure of bars, job descriptions, and how these tie into hiring and management practices. How to manage people and the different management styles are also covered. Conflict resolution is an essential part of management, as is managing change. The savvy manager will do these things well and will have the luxury of managing a well-run staff of people who enjoy their work.

ORGANIZATIONAL STRUCTURE

The organizational structures of beverage outlets are as varied as the industry itself. That said, let's look at some representative organizational configurations starting with a small operation and working up. As we go through these, we will simply be listing the titles of the personnel; job descriptions will follow later in the chapter. Also keep in mind that the titles are per shift. If the operation is open more than one shift, the positions will be duplicated.

Neighborhood Bars

There are thousands of small bars scattered across the country in almost every city, town, and neighborhood. Unless you live in a "dry area," there is probably a bar in your neighborhood. They are normally owned by one person or possibly a limited partnership. Their organizational structure is very simple: a bartender, who is quite often the owner, and a server. As sales increase, more servers are added. As servers are added, another bartender is added, one to tend to the customers at the bar and one to mix drinks for the servers. These operations serve little if any food, and when they do it is limited to packaged snack foods, premade microwave products, or limited grill items. Figure 9.1 shows a small bar organization chart.

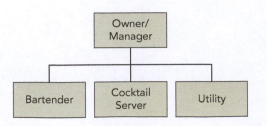

FIGURE 9.1
Small bar organization chart.

Restaurant Bars

There are many restaurants that offer alcoholic beverage service just as there are many bars that serve food. The basic difference between the two is a philosophical thought by management on what the operation stands for and how they want to be branded in the business community. In other words, is it a restaurant that sells drinks or a bar that sells food? In addition to the job positions in small neighborhood bars, there is usually a general manager who oversees both the food and beverage sides of the business. In larger operations, these duties are split with a restaurant manager overseeing the food production and restaurant service side of the business and a beverage manager overseeing the bar and its service. In independent operations, the manager(s) report to the owner or, in the case of a partnership, the owner's representative. Many of these types of operations are owned by regional and national chains, in which case the unit management reports to a district or regional manager. Refer to Figure 9.2 for a restaurant bar organization chart.

Hotel Bars

In most hotels, particularly the larger ones, there are several beverage outlets. These are usually under the direction of the hotel's beverage manager, who oversees the individual bar managers. In addition to the standard bars, there are the banquet bars, which are normally portable operations and are only used in the event of a banquet. They are also under the direction of the beverage manager, although in some instances they could be under the direction of the banquet manager. Figure 9.3 depicts a hotel beverage department organization chart.

Showrooms and Nightclubs

While Broadway theaters and many movie theaters have bars, the discussion here is limited to large showrooms, such as one would find in Las Vegas, and large nightclubs. In addition to the aforementioned job positions, large showrooms also have a maitre d'hotel who seats the guests. These positions can be quite lucrative as many guests are willing to tip the maitre d' large sums to sit close to the stage. These operations as a rule are limited to service bars with the servers delivering drinks to the clientele. Large nightclubs also have additional positions usually in the area of security. Highly popular nightclubs will have a doorperson who will check identification to ascertain that the customer is old enough to consume alcoholic beverages and will also control the number of people admitted to the club so as to not violate the fire code regarding maximum occupancy. Refer to Figure 9.4 for a showroom organization chart.

Key Terms

Bar back
Bartender
Beverage manager
Closed question
Cocktail server
Employee evaluation
Employee training
Employment application
Exit interview
Labor cost
Leadership style
Mixologist
Open-ended question
Performance review
Professional development
Semi-variable cost
Sommelier
Standard
Termination

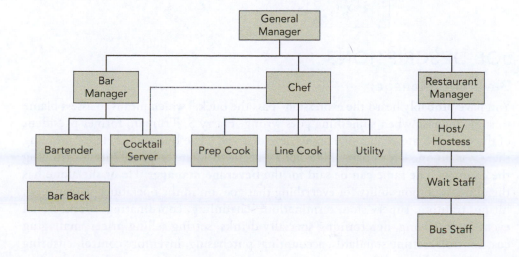

FIGURE 9.2
Restaurant bar organization chart.

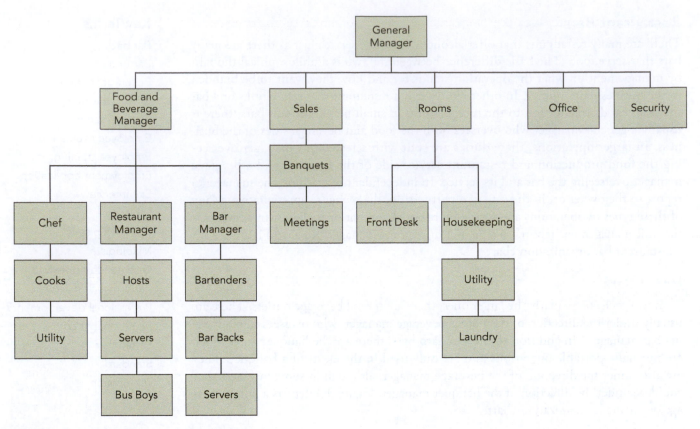

FIGURE 9.3   Hotel beverage organization chart.

FIGURE 9.4
Showroom organization
chart.

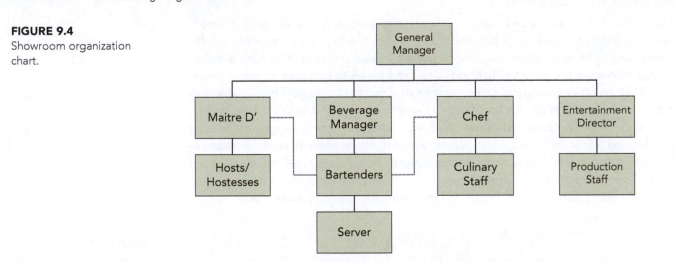

JOB DESCRIPTIONS

Beverage Manager

You have probably heard the expression "pass the buck," which means to assess blame to someone else when something goes wrong. Harry S. Truman, former president of the United States, had a sign on his desk that said "The Buck Stops Here," meaning there was no one left to blame. He alone had the ultimate responsibility for running the country. The same can be said for the **beverage manager**: He or she alone has the ultimate responsibility for everything that goes on in the operation—organizing, hiring, training, supervision, termination, scheduling, coordinating, promotional events, advertising, determining specialty drinks, setting selling prices, managing cost controls, setting standards, accounting, purchasing, inventory control, ensuring adherence to laws and codes, licensing, and the overall profitability of the operations, among many other things.

In a small operation, it is the owner/manager who does most of these things. In larger operations, some of these duties are delegated to others, but it is the beverage manager who has the responsibility to see to it that they are carried out in an acceptable manner. In chain operations, some of these duties, such as the marketing plan, menu, accounting, legal, and the operational plan, are created in the corporate office and executed by the beverage manager at the local level.

Regardless of whether the business is large or small, corporate or independent, someone must manage the operation. The entire scope of management is too broad to fit in this section; after all, this entire text is about bar management. Suffice it to say that management reduced to its basic level is about leadership. It is about achieving objectives through individuals. One person cannot carry out all of the functions necessary in running a bar by themselves; they must have help. Figure 9.5 gives an example of a beverage managers job description.

Job Description

TITLE: Beverage Manager

REPORTS TO: General Manager

JOB SUMMARY: The bar manager is responsible for the overall operation of the bar/lounge area including but not limited to hiring, training, evaluation, discipline, and terminating employees. Additional responsibilities include purchasing, maintaining company standards on production and service, establishing controls, meeting sales budget, and producing a profit.

DUTIES:
- Using the daily sales forecast, create a work schedule and assign duties, responsibilities, and work stations to bar employees.
- Train workers in drink production, wine and beer service, sanitation and safety procedures, ABC laws, health department regulations, and responsible customer service.
- Diffuse potential altercations between guests and/or staff and ensure that responsible drinking practices are being upheld.
- Supervise employees to ensure that quality standards and service are being met.
- Carry out personnel functions such as hiring and firing staff, evaluation of employee's job performance, and complete disciplinary write-ups as necessary.
- Enact measures for improving worker performance to increase service quality.
- Interact with customers to ensure that they are having a good experience and that their expectations are being met or exceeded.
- Inspect equipment and work areas to ascertain that they conform to standards.
- Develop equipment maintenance schedules and repair as necessary.
- Purchase alcoholic and nonalcoholic beverages and supplies necessary to run the operation.
- Control inventories of liquor, beer, wine, and supplies.
- Establish procedures to alleviate theft and waste.
- Ensure that cash is handled properly and deposited in a timely manner.
- Evaluate new products to ensure that they are saleable and compatible with the operation.

QUALIFICATIONS:
- College degree or five years' experience in hospitality management.
- Ability to solve problems, select and train staff, and be a team leader.
- Must be up to date on all health department and ABC regulations.
- Must possess an outgoing personality and enjoy interacting with people.

FIGURE 9.5 Beverage manager job description.

In addition to all of bartenders' other duties, one of the most important is to have friendly conversation with their guests.
© CandyBox Images—Fotolia.com

Bartender

Bartenders are essentially responsible for the functional operation of the bar itself. At the start of their shift, they see to it that the bar is adequately stocked for business. They fill out a requisition for spirits, beer, and wine and give it to the general manager, who retrieves it from the locked liquor storeroom. They stock the bottled beer cooler, check the mixer inventory, restock the supplies (napkins, straws, stirrers, etc.), fill the ice bin, and prepare the garnishes (limes, oranges, lemon peels, etc.). They count their change bank to ascertain that it is accurate.

During their shift, they prepare drinks according to the house standards, pour beer, and decant wine for the guests at the bar and for the cocktail servers. They handle cash and debit or credit cards for the bar customers. They wash glassware as necessary and keep the bar area clean and sanitary. They restock the bar as necessary for the next shift.

At the end of their shift, they balance the cash register and turn in the shift's receipts to the general manager. Figure 9.6 shows an example of a bartenders job description.

Mixologist

Mixology is a term that is becoming more and more popular in the beverage industry. It is generally defined as an advanced study of the art of mixing cocktails. Quite often the terms *bartender* and *mixologist* are used interchangeably, but there is a distinct difference. While a **mixologist** often tends bar, he or she practices mixology as well.

Mixologists are often referred to as alcohol chefs as they use innovative techniques to create new drinks. This includes using different vegetables, fruits, herbs, and spices heretofore not used in creating cocktails. It also includes using molecular mixology, which is mixing drinks using foams, liquid nitrogen, gels, mists, heat, and solidifying liquids. A mixologist not only creates ground-breaking cocktails but revives nostalgic drinks of the past. Thus they are not only innovators but also guardians of bartending traditions.

Many people have the misconception that a mixologist is better or more important than a bartender. Nothing could be farther from the truth. They incorporate, quite simply, two different skill sets. A bartender needs to be able to produce any number of popular cocktails, serve all of the people at the bar and mix drinks for the cocktail servers, think quickly, and be an entertaining, friendly, and outgoing person. While mixologists may practice all of these skill, they tend to concentrate on the art, skill, and technique of mixing drinks, creating

---

Job Description

TITLE: Bartender

REPORTS TO: Beverage Manager

JOB SUMMARY: Responsible for meeting and exceeding the expectations of all customers. Provide friendly, attentive, and timely service to create an exceptional experience. This position requires constant customer interaction as well as an understanding of the food and beverage menu. The ability to prepare a wide range of drinks according to the company's standards is a must. The bartender should have a basic understanding of the ABC laws, proper sanitation practices, and responsible beverage service.

DUTIES:
- Present drink menus, make recommendations, and answer questions regarding beverages.
- Take orders from guests seated at the bar and from the cocktail servers.
- Check the identification of customers seated at the bar to verify age.
- Prepare and serve drinks consistent according to the standard drink recipes.
- Record drink orders immediately into the POS system.
- Keep track of tabs and collect money or process credit cards for drinks served.
- Serve food items to customers seated at the bar.
- Limit problems and liability related to excessive drinking by persuading customers to refrain from ordering and arrange transportation for intoxicated guests.
- Prepare garnishes for drinks.
- Clean and sanitize glasses, utensils, bar, equipment, work areas, and tables.
- Maintain bottles, equipment, and supplies in a practical manner to provide for efficient drink preparation.
- Order or requisition liquors and supplies.
- Balance cash receipts at end of shift.
- Report all maintenance and equipment problems to the beverage manager.
- Assist in planning bar menus, drink specials, and promotions.
- Attend all employee meetings.

QUALIFICATIONS:
- High school diploma or equivalent.
- Three years' experience or graduate of bartending school.
- Ability to mix a wide selection of drinks.
- Must be familiar with health department and ABC regulations.
- Must possess an outgoing personality and enjoy interacting with people.

FIGURE 9.6 Bartender job description.

new and unusual cocktails, experimenting with uncommon spirits and mixes, studying the classics from yesteryear, and, overall, taking bartending to the next level. Refer to Figure 9.7 for an example of a mixologist's job description.

Bar Back

In many bars, particularly those with high sales volumes, **bar backs** are employed. This position is essentially an assistant to the bartender. Quite often bar backs are actually bartenders in training. Their primary role is to take over some of the bartender's more mundane duties so that the bartender can concentrate solely on mixing drinks and keeping up with the volume.

They do such things as restock ice, beer, and wine as well as wash glassware and may bring food from the kitchen for the customers seated at the bar. Since most of their duties are performed at the bar itself, they will have limited interaction with the bar customers. Depending on company policy and their level of training, they may

Job Description

TITLE: Mixologist

REPORTS TO: General Manager

JOB SUMMARY: Tend bar in an upscale restaurant and club.
Working with the general manager and chef, create new and unusual cocktails to complement the menu. Be able to interact with the customers and discuss the various nuances of different spirits, liqueurs, beers, and wines.

DUTIES:
- Perform the general duties of bartender.
- Have a general knowledge of all spirits including their makeup, history, and local producers.
- Have a general knowledge of lagers and ales, their makeup, history, and local breweries and brewpubs.
- Have a general knowledge of all wines served by the establishment, suggest pairings with food to the customer, and be familiar with local wineries and their products.
- Using spirits and liqueurs along with fruits, vegetables, and spices, create new and unusual cocktails.
- In conjunction with the culinary staff, create beverages to pair with the menu.
- With the general manager, develop the alcoholic and nonalcoholic beverage menu.
- Have an appreciation of the history of cocktails and impart this knowledge in the implementation of mixing drinks at the bar.

QUALIFICATIONS:
- Five years' experience as a bartender.
- Demonstrate knowledge of wines, beers, and spirits.
- Have an ability and knowledge to create new and unusual cocktails using different and unique ingredients.

FIGURE 9.7 Mixologist job description.

in some instances pour beer or wine and possibly mix some basic drinks. Figure 9.8 shows an example of a bar back job description.

Cocktail Server

Cocktail servers are an integral part of any bar business. They, like the bartender, are the face of the operation. Cocktail servers should be friendly, outgoing, and have a type A personality. They should be able to "up sell" from a well drink to a call drink. For the undecided customer, they should have the ability to ascertain the guest's likes and dislikes and suggest appropriate drinks. They also need to be well organized. Consider that they must keep the guest's order straight, handle cash or debit/credit cards from customers, and balance the transactions at the end of their shift, all the while maintaining a pleasant personality. Cocktail servers should also be team players. Their personalities should mesh, and they should look out for one another. Nothing can destroy camaraderie quicker than a team member complaining or tearing down a coworker. When customers walk into a bar, they can sense the atmosphere immediately. If the environment is positive and everyone is having a good time, they will return again and again and become regular customers and a part of the "family."
A good cocktail server when serving drinks will do the following:

- Come up to the guests, smile, introduce him or herself, and if necessary check IDs.
- Ask guests what they would like to drink. Try to up sell if possible. If the guest orders a draft beer, suggest the larger size. If they order a cocktail, suggest one or two call brands. Write the order down if necessary.
- Input the order into the POS terminal or call it out to the bartender.

Job Description

TITLE: Bar Back

REPORTS TO: Beverage Manager and Bartender

JOB SUMMARY: The bar back serves as an assistant to the bartender. He or she will interact with customers seated at the bar and will keep the bar area well stocked, clean, and organized.

DUTIES:
- Properly stock the bar at the start of the shift and ensure that the stock is maintained at an adequate level during the shift.
- Interact with the customers seated at the bar.
- Notify the bartender if a customer wants to order a drink or food.
- Retrieve food from the kitchen and serve it to customers seated at the bar.
- Wash and sanitize glasses and tools as needed.
- Keep the bar area clean and organized.

QUALIFICATIONS:
- High school diploma or equivalent.
- Capable of lifting heavy loads including kegs and cases of supplies.
- Must be of age to serve alcoholic beverages.
- Ability to prioritize duties.
- Friendly and outgoing personality.

FIGURE 9.8 Bar back job description.

- Pick the order up from the bar and deliver the drinks to the guest.
- Ask guests if they want to pay now or start a tab. If they want to pay as they go, give them the amount, accept the money, and place their change on a change tray and leave it on the table. If they want to run a tab, many operations require that they present a credit or debit card for security. *Note*: Some bars require that all drinks are paid for when delivered and do not allow tabs.
- Keep an eye on all of their tables at all times. When the drinks are getting low, ask if guests would like another round. Nothing irritates bar customers quicker than being ignored. When their drink runs out and they want another one, they want it now! At the same time, however, the cocktail server needs to ascertain if they have had enough.
- When all is under control at your station, help out other servers who may be "swamped." If servers are allowed behind the bar, help the bartender by washing glasses or restocking. By doing this, servers demonstrate that they are team workers, and the others will appreciate their efforts. They will also reciprocate when you are "in the weeds."
- If the customer has been running a tab and is ready to leave, present them with their total. Run their debit or credit card through the system and present them with the receipt to sign. Keep the receipt, as this is confirmation to management for your tip. If they are paying their tab with cash, promptly give them their change on a change tray.

At the end of the servers' shift, they will have to cash out. There are several ways this is done depending on the house policy for cash controls. If they were given a bank at the start of their shift and paid for drinks as they received them, then add cash plus charge receipts and subtract the amount of the bank. The amount left over is the server's tips. If the house dispenses drinks by a POS system or guest check, each server's sales are totaled. Cash and credit/debit cards are totaled and subtracted from sales. The amount left over is the server's tips. Figure 9.9 shows an example of a cocktail server's job description.

Job Description

TITLE: Cocktail Server

REPORTS TO: Beverage Manager

JOB SUMMARY: Cocktail servers are responsible for taking food and beverage orders from the guests. You should have a basic understanding of product ingredients and their preparation. You should be familiar with proper service techniques and customer relations as well as the ABC laws. This is a fast paced position and requires carrying heavy trays and being on your feet for long hours. You should provide a professional image at all times.

DUTIES:
- Greets guests in a friendly and courteous manner.
- Present guests with a drink and/or food menu, explain promotions and daily specials, and answer the guest's questions.
- If necessary, check guest's IDs to verify age.
- Serve beverage and food orders.
- Respond quickly to any requests from the guest.
- Follow up to ensure that the guest's expectations are being met.
- Present guest with their bill at the conclusion and collect money or process charge card.

QUALIFICATIONS:
- High school diploma or equivalent.
- Must be familiar with health department and ABC regulations as they pertain to service.
- Must be of age to serve alcoholic beverages.
- Must possess an outgoing personality and enjoy interacting with people.

FIGURE 9.9   Cocktail server job description.

Sommelier or Wine Steward

This position is normally reserved for fine dining restaurants, that is, white tablecloth, exquisitely prepared food, and elegant service. The terms *wine steward*, *cellar master*, *wine master*, *wine captain*, or *wine waiter* are, for the most part, interchangeable. The term **sommelier** is reserved for a person who has been certified. There are three levels of certification: Introductory, Advanced Sommelier, and Master Sommelier. A sommelier's role is much more than working with wines; as a matter of fact, it includes all aspects of the restaurant's beverage service, with an enhanced focus on wines.

The wine steward or sommelier works with management to create the restaurant's wine list or in some cases creates it him- or herself. Often purchasing wine, maintaining inventory, and storage security are delegated to them. They coordinate with the culinary team in pairing wines with the menu listings. They also work with the wait staff, training them on service techniques and conducting tastings with them so that the wait staff is knowledgeable about the restaurant's offerings.

Their primary duty, however, is to interact with the guests to help them make an appropriate wine selection. In doing so, they should do the following:

- Converse with the guest to ascertain their desires, likes and dislikes, and their budget and only then make a recommendation. Oftentimes, guests are panicky over the number of selections offered on the wine list. Other guests, who are more experienced with wine, may simply want a second opinion. Sommeliers are people who have a love of wine and are excited to pass on their knowledge to the customer. They can describe the grapes, the vineyards they were grown in, the winery, and the vintages of an assortment of wines.

- Present the bottle to the customer after a selection has been made. They should describe the wine's components and bring it to life before the guest even tastes it.
- Uncork the wine. The sommelier should pour a small amount of wine into the proper wine glass and encourage the patron to smell the wine first and then let the customer taste the wine.
- Pour the wine for the customer and their guests.

With the recent proliferation of brew pubs, a new title has emerged, which is beer sommelier. This position is carried out in much the same way as a traditional sommelier only with the emphasis on beer. Figure 9.10 shows an example of a sommelier's job description.

Security

Security personnel in bars are usually limited to those operations that either do a large volume of business or attract people that customers want to see and be seen with—luminaries such as entertainers, sports figures, and media types. They are also used in those establishments that are located in a less desirable location such as a high crime area or that attract a type of clientele that would tend to get rowdy from time to time. There are three types of security personnel that could be utilized by a bar:

- Door person. This position is used by those operations that have a high volume of business or have a cover charge. The duties of a door person start with maintaining decorum in the line outside of the bar. Consider that the people standing in line have probably had a few drinks prior to arriving and the fact that they

---

Job Description

TITLE: Sommelier

REPORTS TO: Beverage Manager

JOB SUMMARY: The sommelier works with the culinary and service staff to ensure outstanding wine service to the guest. He or she is responsible for all wine products including the development of a wine list and maintaining and controlling an inventory of same. The sommelier will from time to time conduct wine tastings and pairings and work with local wineries to promote their product.

DUTIES:
- Develop, maintain, and update wine list.
- Select, purchase, and store wine properly.
- Ensure that the wine cellar is properly maintained within a clean and temperature controlled environment.
- Manage the wine inventory.
- Interact with guests and assist them in selecting wine.
- Decant and serve wine to guests.
- Train the serving staff on the nuances of different wines and give instruction in proper wine service.
- Conduct wine tastings.
- Work with the culinary staff to pair wines with the various menu offerings.
- Attend trade shows.
- Work with regional wineries and help promote their products.

QUALIFICATIONS:
- A minimum of three years' experience as a wine steward or sommelier.
- Certified or willing and qualified to seek certification.
- Must possess a friendly and outgoing personality and have the ability to interact with guests.

FIGURE 9.10 Sommelier job description.

Some security members are quite visible, while others work undercover.

Thibault Renard/Fotolia

have to wait to get another drink is getting on their nerves, or seeing a VIP get preferential treatment while they stand in line can cause some uneasiness. In addition to maintaining good line behavior, the door person admits customers to the bar as other customers leave. This is an important function as the establishment does not want to violate the fire code or allow a dangerous situation to erupt because there were too many guests in the bar. As they let the guests in, they check IDs and ascertain that the guests adhere to the company's dress code.

• Internal security. These are often referred to in the industry as bouncers. The image of a bouncer is a large, mean-looking individual who in their past life was a football lineman or a professional wrestler. While this could be true in some instances, in most cases the bouncers look like a regular bar customers. They dress in the same manner as the clientele and circulate throughout the room looking for potential trouble, such as a guest who has had too much to drink or an argument that looks like it could escalate into something more serious. Their job is to diffuse incidents before they become a problem. They will attempt to cope with a problem by quietly asking the person(s) to leave the premises and will only resort to physical confrontation if it is absolutely necessary. They work closely with the cocktail servers and bartenders who can point out any potential difficulties.

• External security. Normally external security is used only if the bar is located in a particularly unsafe area. They could be used to patrol the parking area, escort patrons to their cars if the parking area is not located directly adjacent to the bar, or to patrol the line waiting to get into the club.

All security personnel regardless of their job description need to be proactive in their area of responsibility. They need to anticipate a conflict before it escalates into a problem and do everything they can to try resolve the issue. They need to be able to sense, on one hand, when a conflict will resolve itself or, on the other hand, when to call the police in for assistance. Simply separating the parties or removing them from the premises will normally not solve anything. The conflict will continue to fester and will probably intensify later, either in the bar or outside.

For example, if a fight breaks out and security simply escorts the parties outside to the parking lot, calm will return to the bar. However, it will be anything but calm in the parking lot as the fight will escalate, with weapons possibly being used. When the police arrive at a situation such as this, you can be assured that the media are right behind them. The net result of all of this is that people are being unnecessarily injured, the reputation of the neighborhood is being damaged, and it is a public relations nightmare for the business.

Because security is outside the normal business of providing food and drink and the fact that it takes a different skill set than is normally found in the hospitality business, the security function is quite often contracted out to a private security company that has the expertise to handle this function. When this occurs, a contract should be drawn up between the bar and the security company outlining the exact functions the security company is to perform and the relationship between the bar employees and the employees of the security company. The security company should be checked to ascertain that it has adequate liability insurance, that its personnel are bonded, and that it has the proper licenses from the law enforcement community to do business as a security company.

Any incidents, whether minor in nature or serious, should be put in writing. This applies not only to security personnel but to the entire bar staff as well. Any and all details should be noted, including "he said, she said," the location of the conflict, the parties involved, witnesses, and any injuries that might have occurred. Often, these conflicts end up as an insurance claim or in court as a result of an arrest or lawsuit. By having written documentation, the business can protect itself in these situations.

Personnel Standards

Regardless of their size, all bars have **standards**. In the case of small, locally owned taverns, they may be informal and unwritten, whereas large corporate bars would have formal written standards. Standards are very important. They are determined by management and convey the level of service or product that the business wants to give its customers. They ensure that the customers get the same product and the same level of service each and every time they go to that bar. In the case of a chain operation, every time a guest visits that brand name, regardless of what city it is in, the product and service should be identical. Once standards have been implemented, it is up to management to see to it that they are carried out. This is achieved by properly training the employees in those standards and then following through to see to it that they are executed. Businesses have many standards. Those that apply to personnel include the following:

- Product. These standards refer to the drinks poured and are usually controlled by recipe cards. The ingredients used in drinks and the amount should be consistent each and every time that drink is made. The garnishment should be the same. The shots should be the same quantity in highballs and rocks drinks. This is important not only for customer consistency but also for cost control. This will be discussed in greater detail in Chapter 10 on production and Chapter 12 on cost control There are many standards that apply to service, and they are too numerous to mention all of them here. They apply to such things as the house policy of checking IDs, how to explain to a guest that he or she has had too much to drink, paying with personal checks, handling credit cards, placing a cocktail napkin or coaster before each guest prior to taking their order, up selling procedures, calling out drinks in

A server, in uniform serving guests.
© auremar—Fotolia.com

the proper order to the bartender, and so on. If all of the service standards are followed correctly, the operation runs smoothly with minimal disruptions.

- Appearance. There should be written standards on appearance, and they should be enforced fairly and equally. Many a bar has gotten into trouble with the Equal Employment Opportunity Commission (EEOC) and the Department of Labor (DOL) because its policy on appearance was neither written nor uniformly enforced. Are visible tattoos or body piercing allowed? Facial hair? Are closed toe shoes required? Clothes pressed with no wrinkles? Put it in writing, have all employees sign off on it, and enforce it fairly.

- Uniforms. Many bars have uniforms that they require their employees to wear. Often they are compatible with carrying out the establishment's theme. If this is the standard, it should be strictly enforced by management. Care should be exercised when choosing uniforms so that the EEOC law is followed. It does not allow for discrimination against religious beliefs, ethnicity, or race. If in doubt about your uniform, consult with your attorney to make sure you are not violating the law.

HIRING PRACTICES

Staffing a beverage operation is not simply hiring someone off of the street to fill a vacancy; it is much more than that. Many a manager has hired a friend or relative solely on their relationship with that person, only to have disastrous results in the business and often losing that relationship. The first step in hiring is to know what position you are hiring for. We have just discussed job descriptions, which will give us some insight into what attributes to look for in an applicant and what level of expertise they need to bring with them to fulfill that job. When applicants with the proper traits have been identified, it will be necessary to interview them, primarily to judge their personality to ascertain if they will fit in with the team and be a team player. References also need to be checked. There are several laws that govern the selection process, and it is important that these are followed in order to avoid government fines or lawsuits.

Recruitment

Recruiting new employees, depending on the economy at the time, can be either an easy or difficult task. In the hospitality business, the pendulum swings back and forth. If the jobless rate is high, there is a plethora of applicants. If the jobless rate is low, management has to go out and find prospective employees. Regardless of how easy or hard it is, it is imperative to recruit and hire competent employees who will carry out the company standards and be an asset to the business.

Recruiting is undergoing a rapid change. Gone are the old ways of placing a want ad in the local newspaper or placing a card in the window stating "Help Wanted." All this does is tell the public that you are desperate for help and that since you are looking for employees, the service will probably be poor. Job fairs and the Internet are more ideally suited for recruiting employees. There are several Internet sites that job applicants can refer to for job openings. Most local newspapers also have an Internet site for available openings. Social networking sites, such as Facebook and Twitter, are also good recruiting tools. Speaking of Facebook, Twitter, and other such Web sites, be careful what you post on them, as it could come back to haunt you when seeking employment yourself.

In addition to external sources, internal recruiting is another good resource for finding potential employees. Your current staff probably knows people they have previously worked with who would be an asset to your business. After all, they know your culture and your expectations and would most likely recommend someone who would fit in. Additionally, look at your own staff to see if anyone is ready for a promotion into the job you are trying to fill. One of the key factors of employee loyalty is promotion from within.

When recruiting prospective employees, it is necessary to keep in mind what attributes are being looked for in the applicant and how much experience, if any, they need to have. In addition to this, it is also essential that you remember the laws that govern recruitment and hiring that we studied in the previous chapter. They are many, and one mistake could land you in serious trouble.

The Application

Having prospective employees fill out an **employment application** is an important part of the hiring process. It allows management to look over several applicants quickly and ascertain which ones have the qualifications and background necessary to become a longtime employee. If you have twenty applicants, you do not have time to interview them all. By reviewing the applications, the field can be narrowed to three or four to be called for an interview.

When reviewing applications, there are several questions that should be answered:

- Is the application filled out completely? This will give you some insight into whether the applicant is thorough in his or her ability to complete tasks correctly and according to instructions.
- Has it been signed by the applicant? The signature on most applications acknowledges that the statements on the application are true. If it is not signed, is the applicant hiding something, or are they inattentive to detail? Both are bad.
- What is the applicant's type and level of education? This will give you valuable information about the candidate. Is the level of education commensurate with the position? If the applicant has an advanced degree and is applying for a server's position, this should be a red flag. If, on the other hand, he or she just graduated from a trade school for mixology and is applying for a bartender's job, this could be a good fit.
- What is an applicants' work experience? What is their salary history? Is it compatible with what you are paying for the job opening? If the applicant is working for another bar and, for whatever reason, the tips are substantially higher at that bar, this person, if hired, probably will not stay too long. If the applicant is a highly paid programmer analyst, they probably will not stay long either as they are looking for a temporary job while they are looking for an available position in their own industry. Look for someone who has experience and is making about the same money or less than what they would make in your establishment.

Remember that the application form should not have any reference to race, credit rating, religious affiliation, citizenship, marital status, number of children, gender, or disability or ask any questions that would infer any of these traits such as what clubs, fraternal organizations, or church they belong to.

Many firms keep applications on hand for thirty days in case another opening comes up or if none of the interviewees are hired. For the person that is hired, the application becomes a part of their personnel record. If the applicant give you a resume in addition to the application, that should be kept as well. Figure 9.11 gives an example of an employment application.

The Interview

From the available pool of applicants, three or four should be selected and called in for an interview. The interview process is a two-way procedure. You will want to find out as much information as you can about the applicant, and the applicant will want to find out as much information as he or she can about your business.

Questions In the interview, there are two types of questions to ask: open-ended and closed. An open-ended question leads the applicants into an answer that requires them

Overland Bar & Grill
Employment Application Page 1 of 2

APPLICANT INFORMATION			
Last Name	First	M.I.	Date
Street Address		Apartment/Unit #	
City	State	ZIP	
Date Available	Social Security Number	Desired Salary	
Position Applied for			
Are you a citizen of the United States? Yes ☐ No ☐ if no, are you authorized to work in the U.S? Yes ☐ No ☐			
Have you ever worked for this company? Yes ☐ No ☐ if so, when?			
Have you ever been convicted of a felony? Yes ☐ No ☐ if yes, explain?			

EDUCATION			
High School		Address	
From To	Did you graduate? Yes ☐ No ☐	Degree	
College		Address	
From To	Did you graduate? Yes ☐ No ☐	Degree	
Other		Address	
From To	Did you graduate? Yes ☐ No ☐	Degree	

REFERENCES	
Please List three professional references.	
Full Name	Relationship
Company	Phone ( )
Address	
Full Name	Relationship
Company	Phone ( )
Address	
Full Name	Relationship
Company	Phone ( )
Address	

FIGURE 9.11   Employment application.

respond with a considerable degree of information, for example, "What caused you to leave your previous job?" or "Tell me about your favorite sport." On the other hand, a closed question is one that requires a short, sometimes one-word response, for example, "What was the name of the last bar you worked at?" or "Including tips, how much do you expect to make here?" There are advantages and disadvantages to each type of question, and a good interviewer will use a mix of each and also be able to switch a specific question from open to closed or vice versa as the situation dictates.

Open-ended questions require the candidates to think about their answer, organize their thoughts, and do it quickly. This gives the interviewer insight into how quickly they can think on their feet. This is an important trait for a cocktail server or bartender to have, as situations constantly come up that require quick assessment and action. Another advantage is that with an open-ended question, the applicants have the opportunity to express themselves and to demonstrate their depth of knowledge

Employment Application Page 2 of 2

PREVIOUS EMPLOYMENT		
Company		Phone ( )
Address		Supervisor
Job Title	Starting Salary $	Ending Salary $
Responsibilities		
From To	Reason for Leaving	
May we contact your previous supervisor for a reference? Yes ☐ No ☐		
Company		Phone ( )
Address		Supervisor
Job Title	Starting Salary $	Ending Salary $
Responsibilities		
From To	Reason for Leaving	
May we contact your previous supervisor for a reference? Yes ☐ No ☐		
Company		Phone ( )
Address		Supervisor
Job Title	Starting Salary $	Ending Salary $
Responsibilities		
From To	Reason for Leaving	
May we contact your previous supervisor for a reference? Yes ☐ No ☐		

MILITARY SERVICE	
Branch	From To
Rank at Discharge	Type of Discharge
If other than honoreble, explain	

DISCLAIMER AND SIGNATURE
I Certify that my answers are true and complete to the best of my knowledge.
If this application leads to employment, I understand that false or misleading information in my application or interview may result in my release.
Signature   Date

FIGURE 9.11 *(Continued)*

on a given subject. A disadvantage is that the respondent may take forever to answer a question. With a given amount of time for each interview, management may not have enough time to get a good image of the applicant. It is important that open questions be constructed carefully. If the question is too general in nature, the candidate may not know how to answer it.

Closed questions on the other hand solicit short answers and may provide the interviewer with little information. A disadvantage to the candidates is that they may not be able to expound on their knowledge of the subject. On the other hand it could play into the applicants' hand if they know nothing about the subject. For example; "How do you make a Bloody Mary?" requires a response of the ingredients and mixology used. "Do you know how to make a Bloody Mary" requires a simple yes-or-no answer. The applicant may not have a clue as to how to make one, but the interviewer does not know that. Closed questions are often used if the respondent has taken too much time answering an open question and the interviewer has to move on to

complete the interview within the time frame allotted. Generally speaking, however, the interviewer will want to ask more open questions than closed.

There are some other things to remember when asking questions in the interview. KISS: Keep it simple, stupid. Do not try to get too much information from one question by asking a complicated multiple-subject question. Rather use several simple one-subject questions. If the applicant does not give you sufficient information in his or her answer, be ready with a follow-up question. Another technique to elicit further information is to use a "nudging" question such as "And then what happened?" or "Anything else?" At the end of the interview, use a "clearinghouse" question such as "Is there anything else you want me to know about you?" or "Is there anything else that you want to know about our club?"

The Second Interview and Testing   If the applicant pool was narrowed to three or four candidates from the applications and the job is hourly, one interview is usually enough to make a decision. However, if there are many applicants to interview or if there are several openings, two or more interviews may be necessary. This is quite common when a new operation is being opened and a multitude of people must be hired. If this is the case, the first interview is brief, with the purpose of weeding out those applicants who clearly do not meet the standards of the business. The second interview is usually conducted by a different person and is more in depth. If the job is for a management position, two or three interviews are common.

While testing is not common in small, single-proprietor bars, it is common in some of the large corporations that operate restaurant bars or clubs. There are a number of tests that are given to prospective employees; however, the two common ones in use in the beverage industry are achievement tests and personality tests.

Achievement tests measure a prospective employee's skills that are pertinent to the job. For example, when hiring a bartender, an achievement test would measure the ability to prepare a number of types of drinks from memory. While this test could be written, a practical test would show manual dexterity as well as the ability to organize and prioritize.

Personality tests measure an applicant's emotional and mental state as well as their ability to get along with others. This type of test would be most important with an applicant who has no experience in the bar business to ascertain if they were suited to it. As with all testing, it is not 100 percent absolute and should be used only as a part of the procedure. No decision should be based solely on the testing portion on the interview process.

Checking References Checking references is a time-consuming process but very important to the hiring procedure. Because of this, they should not be checked until the very end. After the applications have been reviewed, the interviews given, and the testing completed, the field is narrowed once again to one or two candidates. It is at this point that the references should be verified. There are two sets to be checked: past employers and the references that were furnished by the applicant.

Past employers, due to federal and state laws as well as lawsuits, are reluctant to give out much information. The EEOC, while allowing essential information to be given as to a person being qualified to perform a given job, prohibits them from giving any information that would discriminate against an applicant regarding their race, gender, national origin, age, religion, or any disability that the candidate may have. Some state laws are stricter than the EEOC. Many companies have a policy of only giving information regarding the dates the employee worked for them, their job title, and their job description. Others have a more open policy and will give out additional information.

Some savvy managers will read the applicant's work history from the application or resume to the past employer and ask them to verify it. Since the prospective employee signed the form that all statements are true, this potentially relieves the past employer from a potential lawsuit. Some companies opt to get a credit report on potential employees. These will give an immense amount of information regarding the candidate. They are very expensive, however, and most operations use them only for management positions or for employees who will be handling large amounts of money. Another drawback to using credit reports is that there are a lot of "gotchas" in the law. Therefore it is best to consult an attorney prior to utilizing this method of pre-employment screening.

With applicant references, it is generally easier to get the information you are looking for. These individuals are not as fearful of a lawsuit and are not as burdened by governmental regulations as are employment references. By talking with these people, you can find out a great deal about the applicant's personality, how they react under stress, their work habits, and their overall sense of ethics. Keep in mind, however, that the applicants have probably chosen these references very carefully and will only list those who will heap praise on them.

References, like testing, should only be a part of the decision-making process. Do not hire or reject an applicant based solely on what others have to say about them. Some businesses do not check references because former employers are afraid to say too much and applicant references often give glowing reports. They feel the time spent on this task is not worth the value received from it.

The Hiring Process

After the interviews have been completed and a decision has been made as to which candidate to hire, there are several factors that need to be considered. An offer has to be made, possible negotiations conducted, wages agreed on, and a personnel file started with the necessary forms.

Making the Offer When making an offer to a prospective employee, there is normally some negotiation that takes place. If the position is at a management level, then as a rule there is more negotiation than there would be for an hourly level. The big negotiating point is usually salary, but fringe benefits come into play as well. The employer must decide how far they want to go with the total dollar outlay and also how much they can afford without putting the business in financial jeopardy. If the candidate holds out for too high of a figure, then negotiations end and the business goes with their second choice.

With hourly applicants, such as servers and bartenders, there is less negotiating taking place. Normally this is limited to such things as schedule and days off. Many people in the beverage industry are students with class schedules or are persons who are working a second job. To them, the schedule is extremely important. Rarely is pay negotiated as most of this group of employees' pay comes from tips. The bar's ability to produce high tips far outweighs the hourly wage. As a matter of fact, many operations will only pay minimum wage. The rare exception would be if a bar did not generate much business and in order to find and retain competent people, they would pay a higher hourly rate than normal to offset low tips. Another example would be private clubs, many of which do not allow tipping. Here the hourly rate would be quite high.

Permits   Many states, counties, and municipalities require that persons working in a bar be licensed. Some require this only of those persons working behind the bar, while others require it of all bar employees. Most often it is nothing more than the governing jurisdiction making sure that the person has no arrests and is of good moral character. There is often a fee involved. Check with your governing body to ascertain if such a permit is required for your employees.

Getting All of the Forms   After an offer has been given to a prospective employee and accepted, it will be necessary to establish a personnel file for that employee. It should contain the following:

- The application, completely filled out and signed.
- The employee's federal income tax withholding form, completed and signed.
- If the employee is tipped, a signed acknowledgement that the employer is taking the tip credit.
- Evaluations forms as they are completed should be added to the file.
- Any disciplinary action should be kept in the file.
- The I-9 form should be kept in a separate I-9 file according to government regulations.

New Employee Orientation

After the new employee is hired, he or she needs to be trained. The amount of training depends on the complexity of the operation and the experience level of the new employee. In a small neighborhood bar, where the majority of customers drink beer and highballs, the training period would be simple and short. Contrast this with an upscale operation that serves food and whose customers order exotic drinks and drink expensive wines. Here the training would be quite extensive, both in terms of time and rigor. The amount of experience a new employee has will also define the training period. An experienced person will have to learn the house policies, how to operate the POS if they are unfamiliar with your system, and little else. A person with no experience will have to learn how to call drinks out to the bartender, in what order; the garnishment for each; wines and their components; the differences among stouts, ales, and lagers; and so on.

The first step in training new employees is to provide them with an orientation session. This should be conducted by management. Keep in mind that everything is new to this person and he or she could be quite bewildered and probably a

Part of the orientation process is introducing new employees to the staff.
Steve Gorton © Dorling Kindersley

little nervous. Things that are taken for granted by experienced employees are totally unknown to new ones. Take them on a tour of the facility showing them trivial things, like the employee entrance (if applicable), how to time in using the time clock or the POS system, and the location of the employee restrooms.

After the tour, sit down with them in a quiet place and give them a history of the operation. Go over such things as uniforms, personal appearance, and employee conduct. Explain the wage policies and pay periods, fringe benefits, and the employee evaluation procedures. Cover things the business will not tolerate such as sexual harassment, drinking on the job, fraternization with employees or customers, and drug use. At this point, they have been given more than they can handle. To overcome this, many companies have an employee orientation manual that is given to the new hire during this meeting. It is a good idea to have the employees sign off that they have read the manual and understand the company policies. This form should be included with their personnel files. Should they violate a company policy in the future, this precludes them from saying "I didn't know about that policy."

Overall, the hospitality industry does a poor job of training its new employees. All too often, management delegates this job to experienced employees who proceed to pass on to the trainee all of their bad habits, the ways to short cut the system, the reasons they do not like working there, and the other employees they do not like and why. However, it does not have to be this way. With a little bit of planning on the part of management, a new employee's orientation can be a very positive experience. First, there is nothing wrong with having a new employee follow an experienced employee if, and this is a big "if," the experienced employee has been carefully selected and trained to train new employees. In other words, management has to train the trainer.

Orientation training is very important to the employees. It gives them the self-confidence to do their job properly according to the company standards. They understand what is expected of them and the value of their position to the overall success of the business. By the same token, it is very important to the business. The same message is going to all new employees regarding what is expected of them, the company's policies, and its care values. Turnover is reduced when the employees feel comfortable doing their job. A well-conceived and properly executed orientation period for new employees is a win–win for all concerned.

Continuing the Training Process

Employee training does not stop with the orientation process. There should be an ongoing training program that addresses changes in company policies or procedures, new laws, or just simply continuing education for the employees. The training can be formal or informal but should always be conducted by a member of management. This is not to say that you cannot have guest speakers, but they should be introduced by a manager and the session overseen by a manager.

Managers should be familiar with the tasks each job classification is supposed to perform. They also should have a good knowledge of the company procedures and standards for each job. Remember that the objective of training is getting each employee to perform his or her duties according to the standard. When the standards change, employees need to be aware of them and be trained to carry out the new standards. When employees perform to the level of the standard, they are more confident in themselves, the customer receives better service and product, and the business does well.

Good trainers have the following traits:

- They are self-confident. They have a positive attitude and are respected by their employees.
- They understand the overall business as well as the individual job. They train to the company standards. They know what attributes a model employee has and train others to help them achieve those attributes.
- They encourage the employees and applaud their achievements. They support them whenever and wherever possible.
- Most of all they enjoy teaching. They are patient and get along with a diverse group of people. They have good communication skills and are enthusiastic, flexible, and have a good sense of humor. They encourage questions and group discussion.

Training sessions should be informative, lightweight, and have employee involvement.
© Alexander Raths—Fotolia.com

Training Styles

There are several different methods of training that can take place. They are as follows:

- Lecture. This is an effective method to get a message across to all of your employees quickly and efficiently. It can be used when introducing new drinks or menu items. It would be a good idea to let the employees taste the new items so they can effectively sell them. Lectures can also be used to explain a change in company policy, introduce a new ordinance in your area regarding alcohol service, or reiterate an existing policy that you see a number of employees disregarding. It should be noted that employees do not like to be lectured too constantly, so this method should only be used when it is the most effective way to get your message across.

- Discussion. This is a practical method to use when there is a problem that needs to be solved. For example, if there is an issue with food being delivered to the bar area in a timely manner, a group discussion with the bartenders and servers could be held. While you as a manager may have a solution to the problem, if the group comes up with a viable solution, they have already bought into it, as it was their idea. If they decide that a runner could bring the food to the guest rather than have the bartender or server go back to the kitchen, thus slowing the production and serving of drinks, agree with the plan and give it a trial run.

- Guest speaker. This is a great tool to use to educate your staff. Have sales representatives, who are very knowledgeable about their product, speak to your staff and conduct a tasting. This will give your team confidence to talk to their customers about that product. This could be used to expand their knowledge about various single malt scotches, beers, wines, or other products that you sell. In addition to outside speakers, your bartender could explain a new drink or your chef tell about some new menu offerings, again with a tasting.

- Role play. This method is employed when you want to train your employees in engaging with the customer. It is used primarily for teaching them to suggestive sell or up sell. It can also be used to teach them how to sell a drink or menu item that is being introduced or how to engage a customer who has had enough to drink. In role play, one person is the server or bartender and the other person is the guest. After their dialog, they switch roles. When both employees have had their turn, they critique each other and do it again.

- Line up. This method is used by larger operations where the servers and bartenders line up prior to a shift. Often a uniform and appearance inspection takes place. Additionally, the day's special is explained as well as any announcements that need to be made, and a pep talk is given. Line ups are generally brief, five minutes or so, and the participants are normally standing throughout the meeting.

- One on one. This method is used when one or a few employees need further training in some facet of their work or conduct. Rather than have the whole group go through a training session, the one (or few) are given instruction in a private meeting.

Organizing the Training Session

Since employees must be paid for training sessions and, in some cases, material and supplies purchased, training sessions can get to be quite expensive. As a result, the trainer must be organized and ready to go. The session should also have a benefit not only to the employee but to the business. All too often training sessions are held once a month for no other reason than someone decided training sessions should be held once a month.

The key to a successful training session is organization. What is the objective? Is it a new company policy that needs to be explained or demonstrated? Is it a new product, a changed menu, new pricing, or an upcoming promotion? Whatever the objective, the trainer must decide which method of training will best get the message across to the employees. After the style, or method, is selected, the trainer must then organize the session. He or she needs to write an outline so that the session will be concise and the material presented in a logical order. The employees must understand what is being presented and not be confused by the presentation.

The trainer should also select the best venue for the session. Should it be held in the bar itself, during a period when the bar is closed, or should it be held in a separate meeting room? Whatever the venue, it should be set up prior to the meeting with all handouts printed and ready to go. If audiovisual equipment or a computer web link is being used, it should be checked out prior to the meeting to make sure that everything is in working order. A time frame should be developed with the amount of time needed to get the message across and allow for questions and answers. The session should start on time and end on time. With proper planning and organization, the training session will be beneficial to the employees, making them more proficient at their jobs, and ultimately benefit the organization.

Professional Development

While all training is in essence professionally developing the worker, the term here refers to education outside of the normal work environment. For the most part it is conducted off premises. It can be as simple as a meeting of the local restaurant or hotel association, the chamber of commerce, or the visitors and convention bureau. Often these organizations bring in guest speakers whose talks expand the knowledge of the attendees.

Professional development also includes attending industry seminars, which often charge a fee. It can involve going to a national convention like the Wine and Spirit Exposition at the National Restaurant Association Show in Chicago, the American Hotel and Lodging Association Show in New York, or any other of the

Making sure the meeting room is set up and the equipment is working properly will help ensure a smooth training session.
sixninepixels/Fotolia

numerous conventions and conferences held throughout the year. These almost always include a fee and, if travel is involved, can become quite costly, not to mention time away from the business. As a result, professional development is almost always used solely for management employees.

Another professional development activity is the webinar. These are often put on by various trade associations or companies. While some charge for the webinar, often they are free. This, along with no travel and limited time away from the operation, make them a very cost effective tool for professional development. Most times webinars are hooked up with a conference call allowing for dialog to take place with the presenter and the participants. Occasionally a web cam will be used, and if your computer has a camera, face-to-face meetings can be held. Skype is a popular offering of this method.

SUPERVISING EMPLOYEES

While managing a bar has many duties associated with it, very few are as important as supervising the staff. While at first glance this may seem like a nice job to have, namely being the boss, there are many obstacles and constraints to supervising people. These come from many sources.

First and foremost are the company policies and standards. You cannot always have the number of staff that you would like, as you must meet the payroll standards the company has established. You must follow corporate protocol regarding disciplining staff. Managing conflict between employees is often a difficult task. Your own supervisor or owner may make demands of you that you think are unreasonable or attempt to control your actions regarding employee supervision. When the owner or corporation changes policy, this can often be unsettling to employees. It is your job to effect change without unnerving the staff.

Then there is the customer. They are sometimes demanding and unreasonable. You must balance valuing their business against protecting the employees. How far is too far in deciding if customers have had enough to drink or if they are harassing your bartender or server? Who is responsible if they "walk" on their tab?

Last but not least are the governmental agencies that put many constraints on your supervisory ability: the age that a person can work, overtime pay, the hours the bar can be open, health department concerns, liquor laws, OSHA, FLSA, and immigration laws, just to name a few. Between company policies, your supervisor, the employees themselves, the customers, and the government, supervising is not an easy or enviable task. In this section we will look at the various styles of management, how to lead your staff, motivation, managing conflict and change, and some other management topics.

Leadership Styles

We will examine four **leadership styles**: autocratic, bureaucratic, participative, and laissez-faire. The purpose here is not to choose the best one but rather to determine which style fits which situation for each employee at a given time. Employees are people with differing wants and needs. They come from different backgrounds and therefore will respond differently to each of the styles. Some employees want everything spelled out for them and work best in a controlled environment, while others thrive on complete freedom.

- Autocratic. This style is used by supervisors when the situation requires strict adherence to a set of rules or job procedures. There is no discussion with the autocratic style of leadership. The supervisor sets forth the rules, and they should be

Letting people be involved in the decision making process will help them buy in to the solution.
aletia2011/Fotolia

followed verbatim Chapter 10 on production. with no exceptions. The autocratic style is used best when training a new employee. The expectations and procedures are laid out in precise terms for the employee. This style also works well with those employees who do not want to make decisions but want everything laid out for them by the numbers.

- Bureaucratic. This is a leadership style in which the manager enforces rules and policies which have been set by upper management. Persons using this style of management would rarely make a decision regarding the interpretation of policy but rather would rely on someone above them to interpret it. This style fits the role of an enforcer of policy more than the role of a leader. It works well with a manager who supervises jobs that require repetitive tasks, such as dishwashers.

- Participative. Also known as democratic leadership, this style is the opposite of the autocratic method. Here the manager is a true leader. The decision making process is a joint venture with the employees, as is solving any problems that happen to come along. It is particularly effective where there is a group problem. For example, during an employee meeting the servers note that the drinks are slow coming from the bar. It is not that the bartenders are slow; they have too much to do. The servers decide that if they garnish the drinks rather than the bartender doing so, service will improve. Managers embracing the participative style encourage their employees to expand their horizons and get promoted. They help them establish goals and achieve them.

- Laissez faire. From the French for "let people do as they please." This method is also called free reign, and in it the manager does very little. He or she provides minimal leadership and direction, letting the employees establish goals and solve problems. This method only works with highly educated and skilled employees and as such is not used much in the hospitality business managing hourly employees. It could be used in a situation where a group of investors open a bar, hire a manager, let him or her run the business, and as long as it makes a profit, leave him or her alone.

Combining the Methods

Few managers utilize only one of these tactics, but rather most use a combination. In bar management, the combination of autocratic and participative management is the most common. Managers may use the autocratic style as certain procedures must be followed at all times in order for the lounge to operate smoothly and profitably. For example, drinks must be made according to standardized recipes for customer consistency and cost control. Requests must be given from the server to the bartender according to the POS procedures or be called out and picked up in a certain order.

On the other hand the atmosphere that is created in a bar should be friendly and have a party flair to it. Here the manager will act as a leader. He or she will let the employees collectively make certain decisions regarding operations and promotions. This allows the employees to "buy in" to the management of the bar and make them feel like they are a part of the team. In this environment, they work together, help each other, and collectively create a fun atmosphere. The effective bar manager will strike a balance between the two methods in order to create an operation that runs smoothly yet has a cohesive team attitude.

The Manager as a Leader

Simply put, leadership is the ability to influence the activities of others. In the case of a bar manager, the big goal is to make a profit. This is made up of many smaller goals such as how to increase sales or how to control costs. The successful leader influences the activities of others to achieve these goals. In the autocratic approach to management, the leadership role is relatively easy. In this approach, the manager has the power to insist that tasks be performed in a certain way. Thus the influence managers have over employees comes from the power of their position.

The participative style of management, however, is harder to achieve because the manager has to earn the respect of the employees in order to influence their activities. Here the manager is acting more as a coach than an authority figure. In the participative approach to management, the manager as leader will see to it that the team exudes the following traits:

- They are committed to giving excellent service and product to their customers. They take pride is working together to achieve this goal. They are loyal to each other and support each other.
- They meet regularly with management to discuss common problems. These meetings are amiable. Disagreement and diversity of opinion is encouraged, but trust and respect for others' opinions is displayed. They come to consensus easily and support the decision of the group.
- They are flexible and are open to change.
- They display a positive attitude, do not complain, and do not criticize or put others down.
- They are open to learning new systems and procedures. They are always eager to improve their skills. They help each other with ideas and encourage each other to advance their abilities.

Regardless of which method, or combination of methods, a manager uses, as a leader he or she must motivate the employees. In order for motivation to succeed there must be an open environment that is predicated on trust between the manager and employees. There should be a two-way communication with the employees, who should be able to be involved in the decision making process in matters which affect them. While this may not always be possible, it should be used as often as is feasible. The manager should be willing to give credit to the employees when things go well and accept part of the blame when things go awry.

Managing Change

To employees, change can be either good or bad. It could mean an improvement to their working environment, or it could be a threat, perceived or real, to their job security. In a well-managed bar, change is inevitable. Change can be driven by the market, a desire to improve service or product, a need to improve profitability, or a plethora of other reasons. You have probably heard the saying "a business that is not constantly changing is falling behind." Change can be business driven and detrimental to the employee, such as downsizing the staff during an economic downturn. It can be employee driven, such as introducing a 401K retirement benefit program. It can also be beneficial to both the business and employee, such as introducing a new POS system that will benefit the bar by giving tighter controls and benefit the servers by allowing them to handle more customers. How management handles change with their employees is crucial to the change being seen as an improvement or threat. The staff could well be afraid of the new POS system at the onset, but after an excellent training program see the benefits that the system provides them.

To make change a positive experience for employees, managers first need to know their employees. How will they react to this? Another perspective is how you would react if you were an employee. Anticipating the reaction can lead to an effective method to introduce and explain the change to the staff. By anticipating opposition, the manager can identify strategies that will overcome resistance prior to introducing the change. It is critical that the manager is well prepared. For example, a salesperson who is doing his or her job properly anticipates a customer's objection to the product, then overcomes these by pointing out the product's attributes: "Yes, our mimosas are higher priced than our competitors', but we use fresh squeezed orange juice rather than canned." The same principle applies to managing change and overcoming employee resistance.

SERVER: *I don't like this new POS system.*
MANAGER: *I know it may take some getting used to, but you'll be able to serve more customers quicker and therefore make more tips by using it.*

Managing Conflict

In your role as a manager, you are going to face conflict. Bet on it. How you handle it will either strengthen your department or weaken it. Conflict can come in many forms. Among the most common in bar management are the following:

- Personal conflict. This could be as simple as "he said, she said," or it could be more complicated. It could be a diversity or cultural conflict, age related, or related to division of duties. Personal conflict can also become quite serious such as a sexual harassment allegation.

     Personal conflict is difficult to handle as it is usually between two persons and sometimes can fester unbeknownst to the manager. Open communication at all times with employees is a strong deterrent to this type of conflict. Knowing their personalities and mood swings can also help. Having an open door policy where employees can bring their problems to you helps as well. Understanding the cultural differences and beliefs among your employees is also important. When personal conflict is of a discriminatory nature or there is a sexual harassment case, it should be dealt with quickly and effectively according to company policy and the law.

- Communication conflict. This is a very common conflict within departments or entire organizations. It comes about mostly from someone saying one thing and meaning another or when one person interprets a statement differently than what was intended, with the result being a conflict between two persons. Another form of communication conflict is the rumor mill, which is rarely accurate but can cause a great deal of stress among the employees.

To counteract communication conflicts, managers should always be up front with their employees, telling them in advance what is happening within the company that affects them. This can be accomplished with memos, bulletin board notices, or staff meetings. When a rumor gets started and management becomes aware of it, they should suppress it immediately, telling the employees what is in reality going on.

- Internal conflict. This occurs where there is a dispute between departments. It could occur in a smaller operation where there is a conflict between the bar and the kitchen over such things as the dishwasher's priority in getting clean glassware to the bar or clean dishes to the cook's line. It is most common, however, in larger operations, such as hotels, where a person's job is dependent on the actions of many other people. For example, a bartender is dependent on the purchasing agent procuring product to sell, the storeroom for filling out the supply requisition, the laundry department for supplying a clean uniform and bar towels, the human resources department for hiring a new bar back, and so on. If any of these departments fail to produce, the bartender is in real trouble.

Internal conflict is more difficult for managers to solve because they cannot do it alone. In conflicts between employees that report to one manager, the outcome is based on that manager's ability to solve it. Internal conflict normally takes two or more managers to solve as they are interdepartmental in nature. These are best solved by the managers involved sitting down and discussing the difficulty. It helps if the managers have empathy for each other's problems and are willing to compromise to achieve a win–win situation for all parties. However, this is not always the case. One manager could be power hungry or dominant to the point of taking care of his or her department and not being concerned with the overall good of the operation. Or managers could be stubborn, with a "it's not my problem, it's yours" attitude. This being the case, the conflict must go to a higher authority that will make a decision to resolve the dilemma. Rarely is this a win–win for all concerned but rather a win–lose (one side takes precedent over the other) or, worse yet, a lose–lose situation.

Managing Grievances

Managing grievances is much the same as managing conflict, the major difference being that conflict is usually between individuals or departments, whereas grievances are between an employee, or group of employees, and the company itself. For example, the employee parking lot is a block away from the nightclub. A group of employees have approached management claiming that they do not feel safe walking that block to get to their cars at 3:00 A.M. after the club has closed. Management agrees that they have a legitimate concern and has arranged to have security walk them to their cars and make sure that they are safely on their way.

In smaller operations grievances are usually handled informally and are resolved quickly. In bigger operations there is more bureaucracy and they take longer to resolve. Many large operations, particularly hotels, are unionized, and this brings with it a different set of rules to handle grievances, as unionized operations have rigid rules for handling grievances. Managers no longer have authority over matters contained in the union contract. They meet with a union steward rather than the employee who has filed the grievance. This means that a simple grievance which normally could be handled with a meeting between an employee and management is no longer a simple procedure.

While all union contracts are different, there is a commonality among them regarding grievances. First the department manager and the union steward meet. If they cannot resolve the problem satisfactorily, then it goes to the next level of management, who meets with the grievance committee and attempts to reach a solution. If this fails, top management meets with the committee and in extreme cases with the union's top representatives. If no agreement is reached, the dispute goes to mediation in which a disinterested third party, a mediator, attempts to bring both sides together and advises them on how to reach a resolution. Either party or both parties can reject the mediator's solution or advice. If one or both reject the mediation, it then goes to arbitration in which the arbitrator meets with both sides and makes a decision resolving the issue. Both parties must then abide by the arbitrator's decision.

Managing to Standards

All chain operations and most independent bar owners have standards or goals that they want to achieve. A standard, in this case, is defined as the level at which an outcome should be. In regards to labor, there are standards for performance, productivity, production, and labor costs among other things. For example, if the standard station for a cocktail server is thirty seats, then a server who cannot handle that many is not performing up to standard. Additional training may be needed to bring that server up to the standard.

All employees should understand the standards that pertain to their job. As mentioned earlier, they should be a part of their job description. Good managers will have knowledge of the job performance standards set forth by the company. As they supervise the employees, they should ascertain that these standards are being met. Additionally, managers are also responsible for standards that apply to solely to their job. One of the most important of these is controlling **labor cost**. As we switch our discussion from supervising the staff, we will be concentrating on those devices a manager can use to perform this significant task.

As we will learn in Chapter 12, standard costs are carefully calculated to ensure that the operation achieves profitability. Standard costs are measured against the actual cost. For example, a bar that has a standard labor cost of 28 percent will compare this with the actual labor cost on the income statement at the end of the month. If the actual labor cost is 30 percent, then adjustments to the schedule must be made to bring that cost back into line with the standard. If there is no variance, then the procedures and controls that are in place are working and no further action is taken at this time.

Labor: A Semi-variable Cost

Prior to a discussion on scheduling, it is necessary to review how labor costs react to sales. We have three types of costs: variable, fixed, and semi-variable. Variable costs are those costs that go up and down as sales go up and down and do so in direct proportion. Fixed costs are those costs that remain the same regardless of sales volume. They go on 24/7, whether or not the restaurant is open. **Semi-variable costs** go up and down as sales go up and down, but not in direct proportion. Semi-variable costs are made up of both fixed costs and variable costs. An example of a semi variable cost is labor.

Management is normally paid a salary. The salary remains the same regardless of the bar's sales volume. If the bar manager and assistant bar manager were collectively paid $100,000 per year, they would receive that amount regardless of whether the bar brought in $1,000,000 or $1,300,000 per year. Thus, management's salary is a fixed cost. That is, it remains the same regardless of volume. Granted, management is often paid a bonus for increasing sales and maintaining costs, but that is not taken into consideration here, only management's salary.

On the other hand, staff members such as the cocktail servers, bartenders, and bar backs are paid an hourly wage and are scheduled according to anticipated sales. As a result, the cost of hourly employees goes up as sales go up and goes down as sales go down. If proper scheduling is used, the cost will go up and down in direct proportion to sales as they go up and down. Putting this all together, there is a fixed cost (management's salary) and a variable cost (hourly staff wages) that result in a semi-variable cost (one that goes up and down as sales go up and down, but not in direct proportion).

Scheduling Employees

Creating a good work schedule for a bar is difficult. The reason for this is that there are many variables. Schedule too many people and profit is sacrificed. Don't schedule enough people and service and ultimately sales are sacrificed. Then there is the mix of bartenders, bar backs, and servers. How many are needed in each area to get the job done? Additionally, the right number of reliable people with the right experience and the right productivity must be available to work that shift.

While the art of putting a schedule together may be difficult, figuring the amount of payroll dollars that can be spent on that schedule is not. It is tied to a standard. Remember that a standard is what a cost should be. It is determined by management and is designed so that the operation can achieve a profit. Labor being a semi-variable cost, is a standard that is expressed as a percent. The standard labor cost percent is multiplied by the anticipated sales for the payroll period to get the amount of dollars that may be spent on labor for that period. The anticipated sales are determined by forecasting. To obtain an accurate forecast, the manager takes the sales from a prior period, usually the same time last year, and uses this as a base. This base number is adjusted for such factors as the following:

- Inflation. If selling prices are going up, the forecast is adjusted upwards. In the case of deflation, the opposite would be true.
- Sales trends. If sale overall are increasing, the forecast is adjusted upwards, or if they are decreasing, it is adjusted downward.
- Special events. If there is an event going on in town, the forecast needs to be increased.
- Extenuating circumstances. This would include such things as bad weather a year ago which would have lowered sales last year thereby increasing the forecast this year, road construction, or any other circumstances which would have affected sales a year ago or are presently affecting sales this year.

labor cost standard % × projected sales = $ available for labor

For example, if the standard was 28 percent and the anticipated sales for next week were $17,000, the amount of money available for labor would be $4760.00.

28% labor standard × projected sales of $17,000 = $4760.00 available for labor

Labor is an inclusive cost. That is, it includes payroll (the amount of money paid each week to the employees), FICA/Medicare, and fringe benefits. To get an accurate number that can be spent on payroll, FICA/Medicare and fringe benefits must be backed out of the total projected labor cost.

total $ available for labor
− FICA/Medicare
− Fringe benefit expense
= $ available for payroll

FICA stands for Federal Insurance Contribution Act. It provides for setting aside money for social security payments. Both the employer and employee contribute to this fund. The contribution rate is currently set at 6.2 percent. This means that every employee contributes 6.2 percent of his or her paycheck to the FICA and each employer contributes the same amount for each of its employees. Likewise, a contribution to Medicare is set at 1.5 percent. Combined, the two taxes total 7.7 percent. When figuring FICA/Medicare contributions for payroll expenses, only the employer's share is figured, as that is the only expense for the employer. The employee share is borne by the employee. Fringe benefits vary widely from bar to bar and company to company. They could include all, some, or none of the following: paid holidays, paid vacation, paid sick days, health insurance, life insurance, dental insurance, and company paid retirement plans. The total annual cost of the fringe benefit package is divided by the number of periods in a year for which the labor forecast is being prepared, in this case, 52 weeks. The dollar amount available for payroll now looks like this:

$4760 available for labor
−232 FICA/Medicare (0.062 FICA + 0.015 MC = .077 × 3012)
−1516 fringe benefits
= $3012 available for payroll

Now that the dollar amount that is available for scheduling employees has been figured, the next step is to figure how much of payroll is a fixed cost (management salaries) and how much is variable (hourly employees). This is important because, for the most part, when creating a work schedule, only the variable cost employees are listed. As stated earlier, management is responsible for the overall operation and does not work a specific group of tasks, nor do they work a specific rigid schedule. To figure how many dollars are available for scheduling hourly employees, subtract the total of management salaries from the total dollars available for payroll.

Total $ available for payroll − fixed cost salaries = variable $ available for schedule

In the example above, assume that management salaries were $1550 a week. The amount of payroll dollars available for hourly employees would be $1462.

$3012 (total payroll dollars) − $1550 (fixed cost) = $1462 (variable cost)

Once the amount of money that can be spent on hourly personnel is known, it must be broken down by position. The reason for this is the difference in hourly wages paid to the employees. Servers, for the most part, receive tips from their customers and are therefore paid less than other job classifications. While bartenders receive tips, the skill level that is necessary to do their job is such that they can command a higher rate of pay. If it is a large operation, employing a host or hostess and security, these would be included on the schedule as well.

To illustrate, let's assume, for simplicity's sake, that the bar is open from 4:00 P.M. until midnight and is closed on Sunday. Let's further assume that it is in a nice area and there is no need for security. Seating is open and therefore a host or hostess is also unnecessary. The employees are paid as follows:

- Cocktail servers: $2.13 per hour
- Bartenders: $12.00 per hour
- Bar backs: $8.00 per hour

There are 25 seats at the bar and 120 seats in the lounge area. A cocktail server can handle 30 seats (customers). One bartender can deal with a slow night. As business increases, a bar back is brought in to help the bartender, and on very busy nights two bartenders and a bar back are necessary. Forecasted sales for a typical week are as follows:

- Monday: $1000
- Tuesday: $1000

	Monday	Tuesday	Wednesday	Thursday	Friday	Saturday	Hours	Rate	Total
Sales	1,000	1,000	2,000	3,000	5,000	5,000			17,000.00
Bartender A	3:00–1:00	3:00–1:00			3:00–10:00	3:00–10:00	34	12.00	408.00
Bartender B			3:00–1:00	3:00–1:00	6:00–1:00	6:00–1:00	34	12.00	408.00
Bar Back				6:00–1:00	6:00–1:00	6:00–1:00	21	8.00	168.00
Server A	3:00–11:00			6:00–12:00	3:00–11:00	3:00–11:00	30	2.13	63.90
Server B	5:00–1:00			6:00 –1:00	3:00–11:00	3:00–11:00	31	2.13	66.03
Server C			3:00–10:00		5:00–1:00	5:00–1:00	23	2.13	48.99
Server D			6:00–1:00		5:00–1:00	5:00–1:00	23	2.13	48.99
Server E		3:00–11:00		4:00–10:00	6:00 –1:00	6:00 – 1:00	28	2.13	59.64
Server F		5:00–1:00	5:00–11:00	5:00–12:00			23	2.13	48.99
									1,320.54

- Wednesday: $2000
- Thursday: $3000
- Friday: $5000
- Saturday: $5000
- Sunday: Closed

Given this data, a master schedule is then drawn up. A master schedule contains no names but includes the positions necessary to run the operation for the forecasted sales, the average hourly wage paid for each position, and the projected payroll cost.

As you can see, the projected variable payroll cost for the week is $1321 (rounded off) and is well below the budget of $1462. In putting together the master schedule some assumptions were made, and they may not always hold true:

- The sales forecast could change. In a bar that has a relatively steady business, the forecast will probably not change much from week to week. However, such things as a holiday weekend could cut into sales or a local festival could increase sales. A bar that has live entertainment could see a drastic change in its forecast depending on the band that is booked. Also, keep in mind that a forecast is an estimate and anything that would affect that estimate must be reacted to immediately in order to keep the payroll on course to meet the standard as well as to give outstanding customer service.
- Not all servers can handle thirty seats. Some can do more, some less. The experience level of the servers, how organized they are, the distance from the bar to the server's station, and the speed of the bartender filling the orders all come into play. Additionally, if the server has to retrieve and deliver food from the kitchen, service will be slower.
- The bar menu also has a lot to do with the schedule. An upscale lounge specializing in mixology with hand-crafted drinks will require more people on the schedule than will a bar that serves primarily draft and bottled beer.
- The wage per hour on the master schedule is an average. A person making more than the average will drive the payroll cost up, while a person making less will drive it down. However, if management is doing its job properly, the person making more than the average should be more efficient and be able to handle more business.

Name	Position	Monday	Tuesday	Wednesday	Thursday	Friday	Saturday
Jennifer	Server	10–3	10–3	10–3	10–3	10–3	10–3
Sung Lee	Server	11–3	11–3	11–3	11–3	11–3	11–3
Bill	Server	11–2	11–2	11–2	11–2	11–2	11–2
Tony	Server	11–2	11–2	11–2	11–2	11–2	11–2
Wendy	Host/Cashier	10–3	10–3	10–3	10–3	10–3	10–3
Mike	Bus person	11–3	11–3	11–3	11–3	11–3	11–3
Rubin	Dishwasher	11–3	11–3	11–3	11–3	11–3	11–3
Carlos	Line Cook 1	8–2	8–2	8–2	8–2	8–2	8–2
Judy	Line Cook 2	9–3	9–3	9–3	9–3	8–2	8–2
Tonya	Pantry	8–2	8–2	8–2	8–2	8–2	8–2

- Remember that all businesses, including bars, which fall under the Fair Labor Standards Act have to pay all of their employees a minimum wage of $7.25 per hour. An exception to this is servers, who can be paid a minimum of $2.13 per hour provided that their tips on an hourly basis bring them to or above the $7.25 figure. Some states also have a minimum wage law. In that case, the higher minimum wage prevails.

Now that the master schedule has been written and meets the company payroll standard, the actual schedule with the employee names can be written. While at first glance this would seem like an easy task, there are some important factors to be contemplated. Each employee's knowledge of his or her job, experience, and productivity rates need to be considered. For the most part, experienced, highly productive employees need to be interspersed with newer, inexperienced employees. By doing this, the newer employees will benefit from the training and mentoring of the older employees and eventually be brought up to the company performance standard. Another factor is the anticipated volume. During high sales periods, a higher concentration of experienced employees should be scheduled in order to maximize table turnover and consequently achieve higher sales. The following table illustrates how a schedule that is to be posted for the employees will look.

Protocol regarding posted schedules should be established. It does no good to go through the entire exercise only to have an employee want to change the schedule after it is posted. Almost all restaurants and bars have policies regarding schedules. Most of these allow for no changes to be made after a schedule is posted. Some allow for employees to request a certain day or shift off with management approval prior to the schedule being written. Whatever the policy, strong discipline is needed, because if a schedule is changed, the domino theory takes effect and the whole schedule unravels quickly.

Calculating Actual Labor Costs

Up to this point, everything has been a forecast. That is, if all goes well, what labor cost is likely to occur? Because of careful planning, the future should not hold any surprises. Therefore when the forecast is compared to the actual, the numbers should be identical or at least very close to each other. The actual labor cost for the operation is taken from the income statement. The income statement reflects what has really happened. For comparison purposes, the actual labor cost is converted into a percentage by dividing the actual labor cost by sales.

$$\text{labor cost (from income statement)}/\text{sales (from income statement)} =$$
$$\text{actual labor cost percentage}$$

If the forecast and actual labor cost percentages match, management has done a good job of planning. If they are different, then they must be analyzed to see what went wrong and take corrective action so that in the future the numbers will match.

Employee Evaluations

In addition to standards being an important component for controlling labor cost, standards also play a significant role in **employee evaluations**. The employees' job description becomes the standard against which their performance is measured. Periodic **performance reviews** are valuable to both the employee and the operation. Figure 9.12 gives an example of an employee evaluation form.

Employees who know exactly where they stand, what they are doing well, and what areas need improvement will be more secure in their job and consequently will perform better. A performance review should also focus on an employee's career goals.

Overland Bar & Grill
Employee Performance Review

EMPLOYEE INFORMATION	
Name	Employee ID
Job Title	Date
Department	Manager
Review Period	to

Ratings					
	1 = Poor	2 = Fair	3 = Satisfactory	4 = Good	5 = Excellent
Job Knowledge	☐	☐	☐	☐	☐
Comments					
Work Quality	☐	☐	☐	☐	☐
Comments					
Attendance/Punctuality	☐	☐	☐	☐	☐
Comments					
Initiative	☐	☐	☐	☐	☐
Comments					
Communication/Listening Skills	☐	☐	☐	☐	☐
Comments					
Dependability	☐	☐	☐	☐	☐
Comments					
Overall Rating					

EVALUATION
ADDITIONAL COMMENTS
GOALS (As agreed upon by employee and manager

VERIFICATION OF REVIEW	
By signing this form, you confirm that you have discussed this review in detail with your supervisor. Signing this form does not necessarily that you agree with this evaluation.	
Employee Signature	Date
Manager Signature	Date

FIGURE 9.12 An example of an employee evaluation form.

For example, if a cocktail server's goal is to become a bartender, the supervisor can suggest some courses that he or she could take at a local school to achieve that goal. When an opening for a bar back comes up, the employee could be moved into that post to receive on the job training leading to a bartender position.

The operation benefits because there is a closer understanding between the supervisor and the employee. The supervisor develops an awareness of potential problems the employee may be facing that has inhibited him or her from performing up to standard. These barriers can then be knocked down, thus enabling the employee to improve his or her performance. If several employees are having the same or similar problems, the supervisor can develop some training programs to assist the staff. A properly conducted performance review will also assist management in deciding who will receive bonuses or who will receive merit increases.

An effective performance review does not just happen. It takes preparation from both the employee and the supervisor. Prior to the review, the employee should be given an evaluation form to fill out. This serves several purposes. First, it puts the employees at ease because they understand what the meeting is about and what will be discussed. It also gives them an opportunity to evaluate their own performance and make comments on it. For example, if they know that they are not performing to standard on a particular task, there may be a reason. If they put this on the evaluation form, it can then be discussed with the supervisor and a solution arrived at to the help the employee improve. Often employees will grade themselves lower than their supervisor will. Where there is a discrepancy, the differences can be discussed and a rating agreed upon. By filling out their own form, employees can also list any accomplishments they may have achieved and be given an opportunity to rate themselves high where they think they deserve it.

The supervisor fills out an evaluation form as well. A word of caution here: People often do not like to be critical of others. If an employee is not performing up to standard, many supervisors will gloss over this and rate the employee as satisfactory, thus avoiding a potential confrontation. This action effectively destroys the value of the performance review. Remember the purpose of the review is to communicate to the employees those aspects of the job that they are performing well and those aspects that need improvement. Only by giving an honest evaluation of the employee will improvement be accomplished. The meeting should not be confrontational but rather should be conducted in a friendly manner with the sole purpose of job performance development. The meeting should be conducted privately in a comfortable environment. The supervisor should have a plan that includes going over the performance review, discussing it with the employee, praising the employee where applicable, and setting up a plan for improvement where necessary. This plan should be measurable, with a timetable for completion and a date set for a progress report.

Voluntary Terminations

There are two types of **terminations**: voluntary and involuntary. A voluntary termination is when an employee decides to leave the organization of his or her own free will. Exactly why the employee is leaving is something that you as a manager need to know. Therefore, with all voluntary terminations it is important to have an **exit interview**. It could be something as simple as they were working at your bar to help defray some of their college expenses and now that they are graduating they are going to pursue a career in their chosen field. It could be that their spouse has been transferred to another city. Even if they are leaving on good terms you can learn something from the exit interview. On the other hand, they could be leaving because they do not like working there.

To conduct a good exit interview you will want to do the following:

- Hold the meeting in a private room with comfortable surroundings. Do not allow interruptions or distractions.
- Listen to the employee. In a good exit interview the manager will ask a few questions and let the employee do most of the talking.
- Do not act defensive. If the employee is critical of the company or other people, do not rationalize or argue. The purpose here is to learn, not justify.
- If the employee is leaving due to circumstance beyond your control, for instance a graduation or a spousal transfer, you can still learn. Ask what they would change about the operation of the bar if they could change anything they wanted.
- Go over any "housekeeping" details, such as when they can expect their last check, any vacation or personal days they have coming, when their insurance (if applicable) will end, how to apply for COBRA benefits, and how they can retrieve any retirement or 401K benefits.

Immediately after the exit interview, analyze the findings. What did you learn? Do any policies or procedures need to be changed? Are there flaws in the selection process? Are there troublemakers on the team? Is training adequate? Decide what, if anything, needs to be changed and set up a plan to implement the change.

Involuntary Terminations

Even if you, as a manager, have done an outstanding job of employee selection and training, it will occasionally be necessary to terminate an employee. Before this decision is made, however, ask yourself if everything possible has been done to save this employee. The most important thing to do when conducting an involuntary termination is to document everything: the events leading up to the termination should be documented, warnings to the employee should be saved, and the employee's performance reviews should be available. In many cases when employees are terminated, they will file for unemployment, and you will need documentation to plead your case before the unemployment commission. In the termination meeting, do not forget to cover the housekeeping details mentioned earlier.

CONCLUSION

The success of your bar will ride on many factors, not the least of which is how well you manage your staff. While bars range in size from small neighborhood ventures to large mega operations in hotels, casinos, and arenas, the management principles remain largely the same. An exception would be where Federal Law requires a minimum sales volume for that operation to come under its jurisdiction.

The basic tool for management is the job description. It sets forth the responsibilities and performance expectations for the employee. It also sets the standards for that job and becomes the basis for hiring new employees. The selection process is important as it sets the tone for the interaction between the staff

members. Customers enjoy going into a bar where the tone is teamwork and camaraderie. The hiring process when done correctly takes time for such things as recruitment, interviewing, reference checks, and selection. When the right candidate is selected, the training process begins.

Training begins with the orientation of the new employee. It does not end there, however. It is an ongoing process using a variety of training methods. In addition to training, leadership is also expected of the successful bar manager. The savvy manager will use a combination of leadership styles to guide the team. By using both participatory and autocratic methods, the staff will feel a part of the decision-making process yet will be expected to follow the proper procedures in carrying out their duties.

One of the key functions of management is controlling costs. As payroll is one of the major costs in any bar, it behooves management to see to it that this cost meets the company standard. Careful planning is the key to success, using a budgeted sales forecast and having the correct number of staff on hand to handle those sales levels.

Project

Interview a bar manager in your area. What type of management style(s) do they use, and why do they use it? Observe the employees. How do they respond to the style used by their manager? Why is it successful, or, conversely, why is it not successful?

QUESTIONS

True/False

1. The organizational structure of most bars is identical.
2. The general manager is ultimately responsible for everything that happens in an operation.
3. There is little or no difference in the job descriptions of a bartender and a mixologist.
4. When hiring, you should hire the person who has had the best job and the highest educational degree.
5. Checking references is a waste of time as the previous employer will probably give a poor reference because the employee left them or, if it is a friend of the prospective employee, they will give an excellent reference.

6. After the new employee orientation and initial job training has been completed, employee training is essential over.
7. Professional development most often refers to training done off premises or away from the business.
8. In resolving conflicts in a unionized operation, mediation and arbitration are essentially the same.
9. In a well-run bar, actual labor costs are measured against the standard labor cost for that operation.
10. Where states have a higher minimum wage than the federal minimum wage, it is irrelevant as federal law supersedes state law.

Multiple Choice

1. Hotel bars are normally under the direction of the
   A. rooms manager.
   B. restaurant manager.
   C. general manager.
   D. beverage manager.
2. Goods are retrieved from the liquor storeroom by the
   A. bartender.
   B. general manager.
   C. bar back.
   D. cocktail server.
3. Bar backs
   1) are often bartenders in training.
   2) have as their primary function assisting the bartender by washing glasses, getting ice, restocking beer, and so on.
   A. (1) only
   B. (2) only
   C. Both (1) and (2)
   D. Neither (1) nor (2)
4. In fine dining establishments, the person most knowledgeable about wine is the
   A. sommelier.
   B. bartender.
   C. general manager.
   D. mixologist.

5. Regarding employee orientation, when a new cocktail server has been hired who has a great deal of experience, the orientation and training
   1) is unnecessary.
   2) can be handled by another cocktail server.
   A. (1) only
   B. (2) only
   C. Both (1) and (2)
   D. Neither (1) nor (2)
6. For budgeting payroll costs, hourly employees are considered a
   A. variable cost.
   B. semi-variable cost.
   C. fixed cost.
   D. none of the above.
7. After the total payroll dollars has been budgeted, which of the following, if any, must be subtracted to get the dollar amount available for scheduling the variable cost personnel?
   A. FICA
   B. Medicare contribution
   C. Fixed cost personnel
   D. All of the above

8. Employee evaluations should be tied to
   1) company standards.
   2) job descriptions.
   A. (1) only
   B. (2) only
   C. Both (1) and (2)
   D. Neither (1) nor (2)
9. When conducting a performance review,
   A. the action plan for the employee should be measurable.
   B. it should be confrontational only if the employee is underperforming.
   C. it should be held in a corner of the bar so that the customers cannot overhear.
   D. it should be one-sided with the manager in control at all times.
10. An exit interview should be conducted
    A. in the case of an involuntary termination.
    B. in private.
    C. in the case of a voluntary termination.
    D. all of the above.

Essay

1. What is the difference between an open-ended question and a closed question? Which type of question should you use in an interview and why? When would you use the other type of question?
2. Explain the various styles of training; tell when each would be used and why you would use them in those circumstances.
3. Discuss the four basic styles of leadership. Which style, or combination of styles, do you prefer? Defend your selection.
4. The payroll cost in the bar you are managing is not meeting standard because sales are not meeting budget. This is because of construction in the area, which makes it difficult for customers to get to your establishment. The construction is expected to last for three months. How do you handle this situation: lay people off, cut their hours, or ride it out? Defend your answer.
5. You have a relatively new bartender who is not performing to the company's standard in terms of productivity and is not following the standardized recipes for cocktails. Tell how you would handle this situation. How long will you give him or her to meet the standard? What steps will you take if he or she does not meet the standards in a reasonable time?

RESOURCES

Davis, Bernard and Stone, Sally, *Food and Beverage Management*, 5th ed. (Oxford, UK: Lineacre House, 2008).

Katsigris, Costas and Thomas, Chris, *The Bar & Beverage Book*, 4th ed. (Hoboken, NJ: John Wiley & Sons, 2007).

Kotschevar, Lendal H. and Tanke, Mary L., *Managing Bar and Beverage Operations*, (East Lansing, MI: Educational Institute of the American Hotel & Motel Association, 1996).

National Restaurant Association Educational Foundation, *ServSafe Alcohol*, (Chicago, IL: National Restaurant Association Educational Foundation).

Plotkin, Robert, *Successful Beverage Management*, (Tucson, AZ: Bar Media, 2001).

10
Production and Mixology

OVERVIEW

The production aspect of any bar is critical to its success. Consider all of the things that must happen. The drinks must be prepared according to a standardized recipe time after time after time, regardless of who is tending bar. Consistency is one attribute that will bring customers back. They know what to expect. If the drinks are different each time, they do not know what to expect and will go somewhere else. Therefore, it is imperative that the bar has a standardized recipe for every drink on the menu.

In addition to consistency being important from the customer standpoint, it is also important for cost control. The selling price and therefore the profitability of the bar are predicated on the standardized recipe. If it is not followed, the cost of beverage sold goes awry and profit is not achieved.

In order for the efficient production of cocktails and the delivery of beverages to the customer, the bar must be laid out correctly. Although this was discussed in detail in Chapter 7, it is mentioned again here because an inefficient layout will hamper the ability of the bartender and the server to perform their job in a competent manner. Speed and efficiency are paramount, especially in a high volume operation.

The art of bartending is known as mixology, and it is an involved field of study. To become a bartender or mixologist takes hours of study and practice, not to mention years of experience. This chapter will give you an overview of the study of mixology.

Also discussed are how glassware is constructed, what styles to select for your bar, and what glass to use for what drink. The tools a bartender uses to produce drinks are covered as well as some basic mixing techniques. How to properly draw a beer and the correct method to serve wine are included, and finally the marketing of nonalcoholic drinks including coffee and tea is covered.

GLASSWARE

There is a wide array of glassware available on the market today as there are many styles, shapes, and sizes from which to choose. The style of the glass refers to how it is constructed. There are three parts to a glass: the bowl, the stem, and the base (sometimes referred to as the foot). Figure 10.1 illustrates these parts.

Glassware Styles

Not all glasses contain all of these parts. For example, stemware will contain all three. Refer to Figure 10.2 for some examples. **Stemware** can be used for cocktails such as margaritas or daiquiris or straight-up drinks. It is very popular in wine service. Because of its construction with a tall, thin stem, it is easily broken. Excessive breakage will result in higher operating costs for your business. This should be kept in mind when deciding whether or not to use this style for your cocktails. On the other hand, it gives a very elegant presentation, and if style is important to the ambiance of your operation, it would be an excellent choice.

Footed ware refers to glasses with either a very short, stubby stem or no stem at all. These glasses also have an elegance about them but incur less breakage as there is no stem involved. They can be used for most drinks served by the bar and come in various sizes. The bowl can have either straight sides or be rounded, such as a brandy snifter. In addition to serving brandy, the brandy snifter is very popular for single malt Scotch tastings as the Scotch can be swirled and sniffed prior to tasting. A variation of a footed ware glass is the pilsner, which is used to serve beer. Its sides taper down to the footed base. Figure 10.3 shows some examples of footed glassware.

A **tumbler** is a glass with neither a base nor a stem. It comes in a variety of shapes either straight, flared, or bowled. It is the most popular of bar glassware as it is the most durable. It can be used, depending on size, for almost every cocktail served by the bar. The size and style of tumbler is sometimes referred to by the drink that is served in it. Some of the more popular nicknames given to the tumbler include rocks, highball, collins, old fashioned, and shot glasses. A variation of the tumbler is the mug, which is a tumbler with a handle. Oftentimes mugs will have a false bottom to them, giving the illusion of a larger serving. Mugs are most often used for beer service but can be used for hot beverages such as coffee, tea, hot cider, or cocoa. Figure 10.4 shows some examples of tumbler glassware.

Choosing a Style and Size

What styles and size a particular bar should carry depends on several factors: the bar menu, ambiance of the bar, and portion size. First and foremost is the bar's menu. What you are going to sell will dictate which glassware to purchase. For example, a bar specializing in wine will need several styles and sizes of wine glasses, while a typical bar would need only one style of glassware for wine.

The ambiance of the bar and its price point will help decide the style of glassware. A neighborhood bar will most likely use tumblers for its cocktails, while an upscale operation would use stemware. Granted, stemware is more expensive and breaks easier, but its elegance far outweighs the cost in terms of the image it provides. Some operations eschew the bar glassware altogether, choosing to go a different route. For example, a restaurant or lounge with a farm theme or western theme will opt to use Mason jars for their cocktails to fit in with the theme and décor of their operation.

Portion control is another factor to consider when deciding what size to purchase. The amount of spirits that you are going to pour in a highball, for example, will dictate the size of the highball glass to purchase. A 1½ ounce pour will need a slightly larger glass than a 1 ounce pour. Consider also that a glass is, in some cases, a portion control device. The price that you are going to charge for wine or beer for example is predicated on the cost of that product and the amount served. Therefore, the glass size should be in agreement with your cost structure. Remember also that the size of the glassware does not denote the portion size. For example, a 12 ounce pilsner will not pour out at 12 ounces of product.

Key Terms

Arabica
Beer stein
Black tea
Blended drink
Decant
Flaming drink
Floated drink
Footed ware
Garnish
Goblet
Green tea
Jigger
Mocktail
Nonalcoholic beverage
Oolong tea
Pilsner
Pourer
Robusta
Shaken drink
Shot glass
Stemware
Stirred drink
Straight pour
Tumbler
Virgin drink
White tea

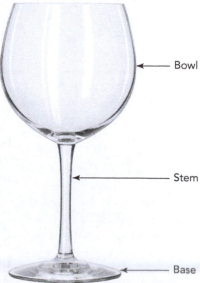

Bowl

Stem

Base

FIGURE 10.1
The three parts of a glass.
Libbey Glass

FIGURE 10.2
Some examples of stemware.
Libbey Glass

FIGURE 10.3
Some examples of footed glassware.
Libbey Glass

FIGURE 10.4
Some examples of tumbler glassware.
Libbey Glass

Handling Glassware

Glassware is extremely fragile and as such is vulnerable to excessive breakage. How a glass is manufactured can help control breakage to a degree. Stemware is the most susceptible to damage, while footed ware is sturdier, with tumblers being the sturdiest of all. When purchasing glassware, check the stress points, which is where the stem meets the base of the bowl. Some manufacturers make glassware sturdier at these stress points by using additional material.

Manufacturing notwithstanding, how glassware is handed can go a long way in reducing breakage. Proper training of the staff and vigilant supervision are essential. One of the most common causes of glass breakage is using the glass as an ice scoop when mixing a drink. Yes, it eliminates a step when you are busy, but when (not if, but when) that glass breaks, the operation is virtually shut down. The ice must be emptied from the bin, the bin washed down to ensure that all glass shards are removed, and the ice bin refilled before service can be resumed. Other causes of breakage include stacking glasses inside of each other, overloading bus tubs, or trying to carry too many glasses on a tray. Abrupt temperature change can also cause glassware to break. During busy periods, a bartender will take a glass straight out of a glass washer and place ice in it to cool it down so it can be used immediately. If there is a flaw in the glass, it will crack or shatter due to the quick temperature change.

In a business that has both a restaurant and a bar, it is highly recommended that the glassware for the bar not be washed in the dish room with the restaurant dishes. The handling of the heavier duty dishes and silverware does not mix well with the more fragile bar glassware. If they are cleaned together, there should be separate bus tubs for glassware as excessive breakage will occur if they are mixed with the dishes and silverware. Another reason that they should be washed separately is that some rinse agents used in kitchen dish machines put a film on the glassware which causes draft beer to not foam properly. In other words, it is not "beer clean." By washing the glasses in the bar area, the proper rinse agent can be used.

PORTION CONTROL DEVICES

Of all of the equipment and smallware that a bartender uses, portion control devices are probably the most important. They not only ensure that a consistent drink is poured each and every time but also ensure the profitability of the operation. Of course they must be used properly by the bartenders for this to happen, and it is management's responsibility to see to it that it does. As previously mentioned, glassware can be a portion control device. After all, if the portion size of a draft beer is 12 ounces, then the maximum amount of beer that can be poured into a 12 ounce pilsner glass is 10–11 ounces. In addition to glassware, there are other portion control devices.

The most popular control device when mixing cocktails is the **jigger**. The most often used jigger is a two-sided (top and bottom) stainless steel container with one side being larger than the other. The size of jigger that you use is dependent on the amount of distilled spirits that you want in your drinks. This is turn is predicated on your standardized recipes and ultimately your selling price. The most common size jiggers are as follows:

- ½ ounce small side, 1 ounce large side
- ¾ ounce small side, 1 ounce large side
- ¾ ounce small side, 1½ ounce large side
- 1 ounce small side, 1½ ounce large side

A two-sided jigger.
Courtesy of the GAF

A shot glass with one etched line. Some shot glasses have more than one etched line. The lines make it easier for the bartender to pour the correct amount of liquor.
Libbey Glass

Another jigger that is used is one made of glass. This is often referred to as a **shot glass**. It can have a plain bottom or an elevated false bottom to give the customers the illusion of receiving more that they really are. Glass jiggers come in a variety of sizes from ⅞ of an ounce to 3 ounces. Some glass jiggers have an etched line to mark different measures while others do not. When lined, the pour is to the line that the formula calls for. For example, if a 1½ ounce glass jigger was lined at ½, ¾, and 1 ounce and the formula called for ¾ ounce, the bartender would pour to the ¾ line. Some bars will use a glass jigger with a deceptive line etched into it. If the house formulas call for 1½ ounces of spirits to be poured, the glass jigger will be 1½ ounces but will have a deceptive line at 1 ounce. When the bartender pours to the rim, the customers think that they are getting extra but in reality they are getting what the house intended.

One more control device is the **pourer**. It fits into the top of the bottle and has a channel through which the liquor is poured. Pourers can be made of either stainless steel or plastic. While the stainless steel models last longer than plastic ones, they are considerably more expensive. Plastic models have an advantage in that they can be color coded to match the different types of spirits. Pourers give the bartender a steady stream of product, therefore making it easy to pour and at the same time makes measuring more accurate, especially if the bar is free pouring. There is a variation of the pourer that is available, which measures an amount of liquor as it is being poured. These are preset to meet the bar's portion control requirements. They are an excellent control device; however, they are somewhat hard to handle and slow down service.

The final control device is the automated beverage control system, which is a fully computerized beverage dispensing system that is designed to control beverage pour sizes. It can be controlled to pour any size shot, depending on your portion control standards. It can prevent liquor loss by eliminating overpouring, breakage, spillage, and theft. Most systems can interface with your POS system to ensure that every drink that is poured is also recorded and (hopefully) paid for.

An example of a pourer.
Courtesy of Conroy's Public House

Some of the more advanced systems can make multi-ingredient cocktails, thus increasing the bartender's speed as well as accuracy. Depending on which system you purchase, it can handle anywhere from fifteen brands of liquor to over a hundred brands. The liquor is stored in a locked storeroom and can be pumped to each bartender work station on the bar or, in the case of large operations, such as hotels, can be dispensed to multiple bars.

There are two systems for dispensing liquor. One is a hand-held bar gun, which can dispense up to sixteen brands of liquor. The second is a tower, which can dispense over a hundred brands and in some cases mix cocktails.

While at first glance an automated system is seen as a panacea for all of a bar's control problems, it does have its drawbacks, and the most obvious is that it is very expensive. Therefore its use is limited to high volume operations and those operations where control is of paramount importance. There is also no guarantee that it will stop theft, although it is a very difficult system to beat. Another drawback is that customers for the most part do not like it. They are more comfortable with watching a bartender pour their drink from a bottle whose label they recognize. There is also the taste factor, particularly with straight shots or "on the rocks" drinkers. Since the line bringing the liquor from the storeroom to the bar is plastic, if the product has been in the line too long it will pick up a plastic taste.

THE BARTENDER'S TOOLBOX

In addition to the aforementioned portion control devices that the bartender uses to produce drinks, there are many other tools that are used. They are as follows:

- Paring knife. A small knife that is used for cutting small items. The blades of all knives should be made of cutlery-grade stainless steel. Handles can be made from either wood or plastic, with plastic being preferred for sanitation reasons.

An example of an automated beverage dispensing system. Bottles are stored in a locked storage room and pumped to the dispensing mechanism.
Courtesy of ProBar

An example of a liquor
dispensing gun.
Courtesy of ProBar

Fruit squeezer.
Courtesy of Conroy's Public House

Examples of various
corkscrews.
Giuseppe Porzani/Fotolia

- Utility knife. Slightly larger than a paring knife and used for cutting small fruit such as limes, lemon, and oranges. Its blade can be either solid or serrated. Serrated is preferred as it works better when cutting fruit.
- French knife. A large knife used for cutting larger items such as watermelon or pineapple garnishes.
- Cutting board. Can be made of either wood or plastic, with plastic being preferred. Many health departments will not approve wood-cutting boards. Plastic cutting boards can be cleaned and sanitized in the dish machine. They should always be placed on a level surface with a damp bar towel underneath to prevent the board from slipping.
- Zester. Also known as a router or stripper. This implement is used to peel the outer skin of a lemon for drinks that call for a twist of lemon. The oils from the lemon are contained in the peel and flavor the drink. It is important to not get any of the white part of the lemon flesh as it is quite bitter.
- Fruit squeezer. A hand-held device that squeezes a lemon or lime wedge to extract juice.
- Corkscrew. There are a number of corkscrews available on the market. The one referred to here is the one that is most popular with bartenders. Some of the other corkscrews used by servers and sommeliers will be covered under wine service later in the chapter. A corkscrew should be long enough and have enough spirals to take it completely through the cork, approximately 2½ inches. It should be made of stainless steel.
- Bottle opener. Should also be made of stainless steel. A bottle opener is a necessary tool even with the proliferation of easy-open bottles. It will save the bartender from getting blisters and calluses, particularly if the bar does a high volume of bottled beer.
- Ice scoops. Two sizes of ice scoops are necessary: a large one for retrieving ice from the ice machine that will be transported to the ice bin at the bar and a smaller one (6–8 ounces) for placing ice from the ice bin into the glass. *Never, Never, Never,* scoop ice out of the ice bin using a glass.
- Tongs. Used in rare instances for placing ice in glasses, particularly if the ice cubes are large. They are more often used for fruit and garnishes. It should be noted that many bartenders and servers use their hands for garnishes. Proper service dictates that hands should never be used for ice or garnishes. Yes, the use of tongs slows down service, but the safety of your guests should take precedence over speed.
- Fork. Also known as a long stem fork or a relish fork; used for extracting olives or cocktail onions from a jar or condiment tray.
- Mixing glass. As the name implies, a heavy glass for mixing cocktails such as martinis or Manhattans. Ice is placed into the glass with the cocktail ingredients and is mixed with a barspoon. Some mixing glasses are not glass at all but rather stainless steel.
- Bar spoon. Also called a mixing spoon, a bar spoon is a long-handled, stainless steel spoon approximately 10 inches long, often with a bead on the top. Barspoons are used to stir cocktails in either a mixing glass or cocktail glass.

A bar spoon or mixing spoon.
Courtesy of Conroy's Public House

- Muddler. Also known as a muddling stick; a wooden staff with a rounded end. It is used for crushing ingredients such as mint for a mint julep or mojito.
- Cocktail shaker. Also known as a hand shaker, mixing cup, or mix can. It is used for mixing cocktails by shaking rather than by stirring as in a mixing glass. It is made of stainless steel and has a strainer that fits over the top of the can for straining ice and /or fruit pulp and seeds from entering the serving glass. In cases where the ice is part of the drink the strainer is not used, or in some cases a mixing glass is placed over the cocktail shaker, the drink is shaken, and then it is poured into the serving glass.
- Blender. A mechanical device with blades in the bottom that rotate at a high speed. It is used primarily to mix frozen and ice cream drinks. The canister can be made of heavy duty glass or stainless steel. A rubber cap fits over the top of the canister to keep product from splashing out of the top. A similar device is the spindle mixer, also known as a shake or malt mixer. It has a spindle with blades at the end which are used for mixing. Most bars will have either a blender or spindle mixer, although some bars have both.
- Glass rimmer. A plastic device that is used to rim a glass with either salt or sugar. It contains three compartments. One compartment has a sponge that contains either lemon or lime juice, another compartment has salt, and the third compartment has sugar. The bartender pushes the rim of the glass on the sponge and then in either the salt or sugar, resulting in the rim of the glass being covered.
- Condiment tray. Holds garnishes for drinks such as orange, lemon, and lime wedges or slice, lemon twists, olives, and

A muddler.
Courtesy of Conroy's Public House

Cocktail shaker (left) and strainer (right).
Courtesy of Conroy's Public House

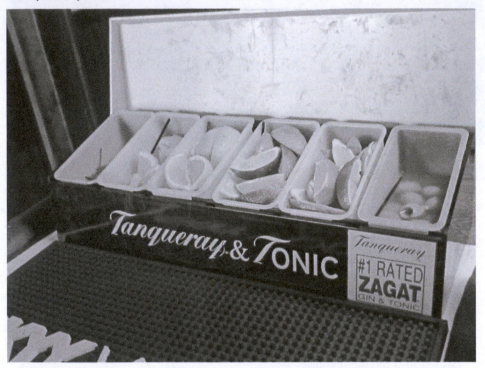

A condiment tray.
Courtesy of Conroy's Public House

cocktail onions, among other items. It can be built into the bar die or be a portable plastic tray that sits on the top of the bar die.

- Juice containers. Normally ½ gallon plastic containers to hold juices and mixes such as orange juice, cranberry juice, Bloody Mary mix, pina colada mix, and margarita mix among others.
- Funnels. Used to fill the juice containers.
- Serving trays. Usually round trays that are lined with cork to prevent the glasses from sliding. Normally come in 14 or 16 inch diameters.
- Cocktail napkins. Small (4–5 inches square) paper napkins. Either a napkin or coaster should be placed under every drink. Cocktail napkins are very important to your customers as many business plans, architectural drawings, governmental regulations, and even songs have been written on them.
- Accoutrements. These include but are not limited to such merchandising items as cocktail picks, straws, swizzle sticks, and small paper umbrellas.
- Bar towels. Made of cloth, they are indispensable for wiping up spills and keeping the bar neat and clean.

MIXOLOGY

There are several methods that a bartender uses to mix and/or serve drinks: a straight pour, stirred, shaken, blended, floated, and flamed. The simplest is the **straight pour**. It can be poured as a shot or in a rocks glass. Bourbon, whiskey, Scotch, and Irish are examples of straight pours. They can be served with ice cubes (on the rocks), crushed ice (mist), or no ice (straight or neat).

Stirred Drinks

A **stirred drink** is where one or more ingredients are added to a spirit or spirits. The ingredients are normally poured together in a glass and stirred by the bartender; however, they are sometimes stirred in a mixing glass and then poured into the serving glass. Cocktails that contain carbonated beverages are always stirred, as shaking would affect the carbonation. Perhaps the most common cocktail that is stirred is the highball. Other stirred drinks include Manhattans, gin and tonic, mojitos, and martinis (although there is great controversy over whether a martini should be stirred or shaken). Shaking gin gives it a cloudy texture. When gin is mixed with other clear ingredients and a clear drink is desired, it should be stirred rather than shaken.

Shaken Drinks

A **shaken drink** is also a multiple-ingredient drink. Ice is placed in the shaker along with the rest of the ingredients. The bartender then places a lid on the shaker and proceeds to shake the drink until it is well chilled, normally about 10 seconds. The lid is removed, a strainer is placed over the top of the shaker, and the drink is poured into the serving glass. The neat thing about a shaken drink is that it provides somewhat of an entertainment value to the customer as the bartender shakes the drink. Some examples of shaken drinks are daiquiris, margaritas, and martinis (though these are sometimes stirred; see "Stirred Drinks").

Blended Drinks

The blending method is normally used for frozen drinks. Ice is placed in a blender canister or metal can along with the drink ingredients, and the canister is placed either on a blender or spindle mixer. It is mixed until it becomes slushy and is then poured into the serving glass. Examples of **blended drinks** include frozen pina coladas, margaritas, and daiquiris.

Floated Drinks

A **floated drink**, also known as a layered drink, should only be attempted by a mixologist or a highly experienced bartender. It is a very colorful drink where various alcohols are layered on top of each other. The alcohol with the highest specific gravity or density is poured in the bottom of the glass while another alcohol of lesser specific gravity is poured on top of that and another alcohol of even lesser density is poured on top of that one. The process is repeated until the desired number of layers is achieved. When layering, the liquor is poured over the back of a bar spoon so as to not penetrate the layer below it. A very good bartender can layer about ten or so layers while an outstanding one can achieve even more. Folklore has it that over thirty layers have been poured at a given time.

Flaming Drinks

Flambéing or tableside cooking is quite popular in exclusive white-tablecloth restaurants. Not as popular, however, are **flaming drinks**. These should only be done by a mixologist or highly experienced bartender. When flaming a drink, the glass and alcohol are both heated and the alcohol is ignited with a lighter. Obviously, great care should be exercised when attempting this.

Garnishes

Garnishes should always be prepped during slow periods with a sufficient amount being prepared to get through the next rush period. There is nothing worse than having a bartender running around cutting fruit when he or she should be pouring drinks. There is a right way and a wrong way to prep garnishes. A sharp knife is a must. It will give a cleaner cut and will reduce accidents. Lemons and lime are almost always cut in wedges, although some bars will cut them in circles. Oranges on the other hand are most often cut in circles; however, they can be cut in wedges. Fruit should always be washed and dried to prevent contaminating the knife and cutting board and ultimately contaminating the cut fruit. If the cutting board does not have suction cups on the bottom, place a damp towel underneath it to prevent sliding.

To cut citrus fruit in wedges, follow these steps:

1. Using a utility knife, grasp the fruit firmly and cut off the ends.
2. Place the fruit on one of the flat sides and cut it lengthwise in half.
3. Place it on the lengthwise cut side and cut into wedges. Depending on the size of the fruit, it can be cut into two, three, or four wedges.
4. Take each wedge and cut a slit in the middle of the wedge so that it can be slipped easily onto the side of a glass.

To cut citrus fruit in circles, follow these steps:

1. Using a utility knife, grasp the fruit firmly and cut off the ends.
2. To get a half circle, place the fruit on one of the flat sides and cut it lengthwise in half. Place it on the lengthwise cut side and cut into slices.
3. To get a full circle, grasp it firmly and cut into slices.
4. Take each slice, full or half, and cut a slit in the middle of the slice so that it can be slipped easily onto the side of a glass.

Pineapple and watermelon are normally cut in wedges and then into slices as follows:

1. Using a French knife, hold the fruit firmly and cut off the ends.
2. Place the fruit on one of the flat sides and cut it lengthwise in half.
3. Place it on the lengthwise cut side and cut into wedges. Depending on the size of the fruit, it can be cut into several wedges. You will want a piece of fruit that is 2–2½ inches across the top. With pineapple, remove the inner core, which is tough.
4. Take each wedge and cut it into slices
5. Take each slice and cut a slit in the middle of the slice so that it can be slipped easily onto the side of a glass.

Lemon twists should be cut using a zester, being careful not to get any of the white part of the lemon rind as it is bitter and will affect the quality of the drink.

Another garnish that may need to be prepped is celery, if it is used in your Bloody Marys. The best part of the celery to use is the inner ribs with the leaves on top as this makes for a very striking garnish. Carefully remove the ribs of celery from the stalk and wash thoroughly. Send the outer ribs to the kitchen for other uses and cut the inner ribs with the leaves attached to a length that will allow the top part to stick out of the glass.

Prepped garnishes should be stocked in the garnish tray. A backup supply should be stored separately in covered containers in the refrigerator. Other garnishes that will not need any prepping but will need to be stocked include maraschino cherries with stems, olives, and cocktail onions.

FORMULAS

Depending on the source you consult, there are over 9,000 or 10,000 cocktail formulas. I do not know who counts such things, but such numbers seem plausible as mixologists and bartenders everywhere are dreaming up new combinations every day. Whatever the number is, it keeps growing. While we are not going to list all of the cocktail formulas, the following is a list of some of the more popular ones. You should be familiar with them and their basic ingredients. Notice that the ingredients are listed in parts as opposed to ounces as each bar differs in its standard portion sizes.

Rum Drinks

Daiquiri

Ice cubes 4 parts rum
1 part lime juice
1 teaspoon sugar or simple syrup
Martini glass
Garnish: Lime wedge

Mojito

Crushed ice
10 mint leaves
0.25 parts simple syrup
1 part lime juice
2 parts light rum
Soda water
Highball glass
Garnish: Lime wedge

Cuba Libre

Crushed ice
2 parts rum
1 part lime juice
Coca Cola (or other cola)
Highball glass
Garnish: None

Zombie

Ice cubes
2 parts light rum
1 part dark rum
1 part apricot brandy
0.5 part pineapple juice
Splash of simple syrup
Splash of 151 proof rum
Highball or hurricane glass

Gin Drinks

Singapore Sling

Ice cubes
4 parts gin
1 part cherry brandy
1 part freshly squeezed lemon juice

0.25 parts simple syrup or a teaspoon of sugar
Soda water to taste
Highball glass
Garnish: In-season fruit. Serve with a straw.

Gin Fizz

Ice cubes
2 parts gin
1 part lemon or lime juice
Sugar or simple syrup
Soda water to taste
Highball glass
Garnish: Lemon wheel

Gimlet

Ice cubes
2 parts gin
1 part lime cordial
soda water
Martini glass
Garnish: Twist of lime

John Collins

Ice cubes
2 parts gin
Freshly squeezed lemon juice
Simple syrup
Soda water
Highball glass
Garnish: Lemon wheel
Note: If you use Old Tom gin, this becomes a Tom Collins

Dry Martini

Ice cubes
1 part gin
1 part dry vermouth
Martini glass, chilled
Garnish: Green olive on a cocktail stick

Perfect Martini

Ice cubes
2 parts gin
1 part sweet vermouth
1 part red vermouth
Martini glass, chilled
Garnish: Maraschino cherry or lemon twist

Vodka Cocktails

Black Russian

Ice cubes
1 part vodka

1 part Kahlua or coffee liqueur
Martini glass
Garnish: None

Bloody Mary

Ice cubes
2 parts vodka
6 parts tomato juice
Dash of Worcestershire sauce
Dash of Tabasco sauce
Salt and black pepper
Highball or hurricane glass
Garnish: Celery stick

Harvey Wallbanger

Ice cubes
2 parts vodka
5 parts orange juice
1 part Galliano
Highball glass
Garnish: Slice of orange, cherry

Screwdriver

Ice cubes
2 parts vodka
4 parts orange juice
Highball glass
Garnish: Slice of orange

Vodka Gimlet

Ice cubes
2 parts vodka
1 part lime cordial
1 teaspoon of simple syrup
Martini glass
Garnish: Slice of orange

Vodka Martini

Ice cubes
1 part vodka
1 part dry vermouth
Martini glass, chilled
Garnish: Green olive on a cocktail stick

White Russian

Ice cubes
1 part vodka
1 part Kahlua
Splash half and half
Martini glass
Garnish: None

Whisky(ey) Cocktails

Manhattan

> Ice cubes
> 2 parts whiskey (Canadian or bourbon preferred)
> 1 part dry vermouth
> 4 dashes Angostura bitters
> *Martini glass*
> *Garnish: Maraschino cherry*

New York

> Ice cubes ice
> 2 parts whiskey (Canadian preferred)
> 1 part lime juice
> 0.5 parts simple syrup or a teaspoon of fine sugar
> *Low ball glass*
> *Garnish: None*

Old Fashioned

> Ice cubes
> 2 parts bourbon
> Cube of sugar or 0.25 parts simple syrup
> 2 dashes Angostura bitters
> Soda water
> *Lowball glass*
> *Garnish: Orange slice or lemon twist and maraschino cherry*

Hair of the Dog

> Ice cubes
> 2 parts whisky (Scotch preferred)
> 2 parts cream
> 3 teaspoons honey
> *Martini glass*
> *Garnish: None*

Whiskey Sour

> Ice cubes
> 4 parts whiskey (bourbon preferred)
> 3 parts lemon juice
> 1.5 parts sugar syrup
> *Lowball glass*
> *Garnish: Orange slice and maraschino cherry*

Rob Roy

> Ice cubes
> 2 parts Scotch whisky
> 2 parts sweet vermouth
> 2 dashes Angostura bitters
> *Lowball glass*
> *Garnish: Twist of orange*

Leprechaun

> Ice cubes
> 2 or 3 parts whisky (Irish preferred)

Tonic water
Highball glass
Garnish: Lemon peel

Godfather

Ice cubes
1 part whisky
1 part Amaretto
Teaspoon of sugar or simple syrup
Lowball glass
Garnish: None

Irish Coffee

Ice cubes
2 shots Irish whiskey
Hot coffee
1 shot cream, lightly whipped
Serve in a mug.
Garnish: None

Tequila Cocktails

Margarita

Crushed ice
3 parts tequila
1 part lime juice
1 part triple sec
Cocktail glass
Garnish: Salted rim, lemon or lime wedge

Tequila Sunrise

Ice cubes
2 parts tequila
5 parts orange juice
0.5 part grenadine syrup
Highball glass
Garnish: Maraschino cherry

Brandy Cocktails

Stinger

Ice cubes
2 parts brandy
1 part white peppermint liqueur
Martini glass, chilled
Garnish: None

Brandy Alexander

Ice cubes
2 parts brandy
1 part coffee liquor
1 part half and half
Martini glass, chilled
Garnish: Nutmeg sprinkled on top

Sidecar

> Ice cubes
> 3 parts brandy or Cognac
> 3 parts triple sec
> 1 part lemon or lime juice
> *Martini glass, chilled*
> *Garnish: None*

Miscellaneous

Spritzer

> 3 parts wine
> Soda water
> *Champagne flute*
> *Garnish: Lemon zest or twist*

Grasshopper

> Ice cubes
> 1 part green crème de menthe
> 1 part white crème de menthe
> Splash cream
> *Martini glass*
> *Garnish: Mint leaves*

Mimosa

> 1 part champagne
> 1 part orange juice
> *Champagne flute*
> *Garnish: Orange twist*

Sangria

> 3 parts red wine
> 2 parts orange juice
> 1 part tequila
> 0.5 parts triple sec
> Soda water
> Chopped fruit
> *Usually presented in a punch bowl and served in cups*
> *Garnish: Chopped fruit*

Long Island Iced Tea

> Ice cubes
> 1 part vodka
> 1 part tequila
> 1 part rum
> 1 part triple sec
> 1 part gin
> 2 parts lemon juice
> 3 parts sugar syrup
> Dash of cola
> *Highball glass*
> *Garnish: Lemon wheel or twist*

BEER AND ALE SERVICE

Unless beer or ale is an ingredient in a cocktail, there is no mixing involved. As a matter of fact, it is simple, straight-forward service. That being said, there are a few rules that should be followed to ensure that the customer receives a good tasting brew.

- Glassware. Before we start a discussion on glassware, keep in mind that many of your customers will prefer to drink their beer from a bottle. While this tends to damage the beer as it sloshes from side to side while drinking, bottle drinkers claim that the beer hold its effervescence longer in the bottle. If your customers prefer glass, there are three styles from which to choose:

  1. **Pilsner**. A tall glass shaped like a funnel with a base. Some styles of pilsners are fluted towards the bottom to form a base.
  2. **Beer stein**. Often referred to as a beer mug. Beer steins are usually heavy and have a handle on the side. Sometimes they come with a lid. They are normally made of glass; however, porcelain or china can be used.
  3. **Goblet**. Usually made of heavy glass, a goblet is a bowl shape sitting on a stem.

- Cleanliness. Speaking of glassware, it should be clean. As a matter of fact, it should be "beer clean." When washing beer glasses, use a detergent that has been designed for beer glasses. Many detergents that are used to clean dishes and restaurant glassware contain petroleum, which leaves a film on the glass. This causes the beer to over foam and break down quickly, which results in a flat-tasting beer with no head. This in turn results in a beer that does not look good to the customer and also causes an increased beverage cost. Beer served in a clean glass will not have any bubbles adhering to the inside of the glass and will also have a firm head with small bubbles.

- Pouring. There is some controversy over the correct method to pour beer. The method preferred most by experts in the art of pouring beer is to open the tap all the way. Hold the glass at a slight angle 1 inch below the faucet. Do not let the glass touch the faucet. Let the beer hit the bottom of the glass until the amount of head that you want is obtained, usually ¾ inch to 1 inch. When this occurs, tilt the glass so that the remainder of the beer hits the side of the glass. Keep in mind that beer that hits the bottom of the glass produces a head while beer that touches the side of the glass produces virtually no head. Another consideration in producing a proper head is the regulation of the keg's pressure, which should be at 12–14 pounds per square inch (PSI). Too much pressure will produce excess foam, while too little pressure will produce a flat beer.

- Temperature. This is very important when pouring beer. Lager should be poured at 38–45°F, while ale should be poured at 45–55°F. Most brewers have specific temperatures at which to serve their beer, so consult them for their recommended temperature. Serving beer at the improper temperature will reduce its flavor. Another consideration regarding temperature is that beer glasses should never be frozen. Even though the glass was totally dry when it was put into the freezer, condensation will form on the inside of the glass when it is taken out. This will water down the beer as well as create a layer of ice inside of the glass that will cause excess foaming and increase your beverage cost.

The correct method of pouring a beer.
pabijan/Fotolia

WINE SERVICE

When a glass of house wine is ordered by a guest, the server turns the order in to the bartender, who pours it into a wine glass. In operations where there is a high volume of house wine served, it may be poured from a tap, similar to a draft beer setup. After

Wine presentation to the guest.
auremar/Shutterstock

the wine is poured, the server delivers it to the guest—a fairly simple procedure. When a bottle of wine is ordered by the guest, the procedure becomes a little more complicated. As previously noted, most fine dining establishments have a wine steward or sommelier handle this duty. In establishments that do not have these personnel, the wait staff serves the bottled wine. All too often, when the wait staff performs this task, it is done improperly. There is no excuse for this, as with appropriate training, proper wine service is expected by the customer and is a credit to your business. Correct wine service by the bottle is as follows:

- Temperature. Red wines should be served in the 60–65°F range, while white and rose wines should be served in the 45–55°F range. Sparkling wines should be served a little cooler at 45°F.
- Presentation I. The bottle of wine is brought to the table and is presented to the guest in such a way as to allow the guest to read the label and verify that it is the correct wine.
- Opening the bottle. First cut and remove the foil that is covering the cork. Then insert the corkscrew into the cork very gently. Turn the corkscrew until the last ring enters the cork and pull the prongs on the top of the corkscrew up. Gently push the prongs down. As you do this the cork will rise up out of the bottle. When it is almost out, gently tug and remove the cork.
- Presentation II. Remove the corkscrew from the cork and present the cork to the host or hostess. This is tradition more than anything. Some guests will sniff the cork, for no apparent reason other than they think are expected to sniff the cork. This ritual will tell them absolutely nothing about the quality of the wine. However, it is part of the ritual.
- Presentation III. Wipe the top lip of the bottle with a clean napkin and pour a small portion of wine (1–1½ ounces) into a wine glass and present it to the host or hostess. He or she will probably swirl it to allow the wine to "breath," hold it up to the light to check for sediment, sniff it for aroma, and taste it to check for flavor. If the wine passes muster on all of these counts, then it is approved.
- Pouring. The server then pours wine for all of the guests seated at the table, serving the ladies first, then the men, and serving the host last. When pouring the wine, the bottle is tilted down. When the glass is half full (about 4 ounces), the server lifts the bottle and twists it slightly to remove any drips.

Serving Champagne and Sparkling Wines

Like wine service, the bottle is presented to the host first for his or her approval. Here the service similarities end. At the top of the bottle is some foil covering a wire mechanism called a cage. Remove the foil and place your thumb on the top of the cork. Remove the cage by twisting the wire fastener, which will loosen the cage. Place a napkin over the top of the bottle to prevent the cork from flying out and possibly injuring someone or damaging any glassware or wall artifacts. With the napkin over the cork, firmly grasp the cork with one hand, and with the other hand twist the bottle. which is at a 45° angle, to equalize the pressure in the bottle. Keep twisting the bottle in the same direction until the cork loosens and begins to come out. It should come out with a soft "kathunk." It should not come out with a loud bang, spraying champagne all over the dining room.

The cork is set next to the host or hostess and a small amount is poured for him or her to taste. It is then served to the rest of the guests in the same manner as serving wine. One notable exception is that champagne is served in two steps. The first pour will be mostly foamy effervescence. Allow that to settle for a second and then pour some more, which will be more wine than foam.

Decanting

Occasionally the wine steward or sommelier will have to **decant** some of the aged red wines. There are two reasons to decant wine: to remove the sediment that has been formed while the wine has aged and to aerate the wine to release its aroma. By exposing the wine to air, it allows it to breathe, which increases the complexity of the aroma. Aeration is important because most of the impressions people have from wine come through the nose. Older red wines benefit the most from decanting, because they tend to have the most sediment. To decant wine, allow the bottle to stand up for several hours to allow the sediment to settle to the bottom. Remove the cork and place a candle, or other light source, behind the bottle. Pour the wine gently and slowly into the decanter in front of the light source. When the sediment begins to travel up the neck of the wine bottle, stop pouring. Let the wine aerate in the decanter for a while before serving.

NONALCOHOLIC BEVERAGE SERVICE

While the emphasis has been and will continue to be on alcoholic beverages, do not forget that there is a market out there that does not drink alcohol. There are many reasons for this: religious and moral beliefs, ethnic values, people on prescription drugs, the advent of the designated driver, and the fact that some people just plain do not like alcohol. While some bars choose to ignore this market, this is a big mistake. This is a group that should be catered to with heavy marketing. After all, it is additional sales with no investment.

Nonalcoholic beverages, often referred to as **virgin drinks** or **mocktails**, are quite plentiful. Most blended drinks on the menu can be made without alcohol. The key to making a successful virgin drink is to treat it like any other drink on the menu, using the same base ingredients and garnishes but omitting the alcohol. In addition to mixing drinks, nonalcoholic beer and wine are also available on the market. Add to the list coffee, tea, and carbonated beverages and you have a large menu catering to those patrons who choose not to have alcohol. The nice thing about this is that you can do this without having to add substantially to your inventory.

Coffee

Most bars, at the very least, will have a cup of coffee available for their customers. Many bars, however, have taken coffee to the next level and serve espresso and many of its variations as well as other coffee drinks. To go to this level you will need additional equipment and also additional training for your bartenders. Even if you only sell regular coffee, you will need to select a blend that your customers enjoy.

The two main species of coffee plants are Arabica and Robusta. From these two species there are an abundance of subvarieties. Given the fact that most coffee that is purchased today is a blend of these varieties, the selection is endless. The most traditional coffee plant is **Arabica**, which is deemed superior in flavor. The other variety, **Robusta**, is higher in caffeine and is more acidic. It also has a bitter taste to it. Since it can be cultivated in more areas than arabica it sells for a lot less. Because of this, many coffee roasters will add robusta to their blends to bring down the price and thus make more profit. Because of its acidity and bitter taste, some of the higher quality robusta beans are often used in espresso blends.

Should you opt to sell coffee drinks and/ or espresso, here are some of the terms that you will need to be familiar with.

- Black coffee. Coffee that has been brewed or French press–style coffee served straight, without milk.
- Cafe au lait. Similar to caffe latte, except that it is made with brewed coffee instead of espresso.
- Cafe breva. A cappuccino made with half and half instead of milk.

Roasted coffee beans.

Ikunl/Fotolia

- Cappuccino. 1/3 part espresso, 1/3 part steamed milk, and 1/3 part frothed milk, often with cinnamon or flaked chocolate sprinkled on top.
- Cappuccino, dry. A regular cappuccino with a smaller amount of foam and no steamed milk.
- Double. Two shots of espresso mixed with the regular amount of other ingredients.
- Espresso. Prepared by pushing hot water through finely ground coffee. It is thicker than regular drip coffee and served in small cups.
- Espresso con panna. Espresso with a shot of whipped cream on top.
- Frappe. A cold espresso with sugar, water, milk, and ice.
- Iced coffee. A regular coffee served with ice and sometimes milk and sugar.
- Irish coffee. Coffee spiked with Irish whiskey and cream on top.
- Latte. Also known as a caffe latte; a single shot of espresso in steamed milk in a 3:1 ratio of milk to coffee. Often flavored with coffee syrup.
- Lungo. A long pull that lets twice as much water pass through the coffee grounds.
- Mocha. Cappuccino or latte with chocolate syrup.
- Turkish coffee (also known as Greek coffee). Made by boiling finely ground coffee and water together in an ibrik to form a muddy, thick coffee. Sugar is optional and is added during brewing. Cream or milk is not added. It is served in demitasse cups with the fine grounds included. Spices are often added to the cup.
- Vietnamese style coffee. An intense brew made by dripping hot water through a metal mesh filled with ground coffee and poured over ice and sweetened condensed milk.
- White coffee. Black coffee with milk added.

Tea

Tea is the second most consumed beverage in the world after water and dates back over 5000 years. Tea comes from the *Camellia sinensis* plant, and there are approximately 3000 varieties of these plants. They are grown in mountain ranges worldwide. The different varieties of tea are dependent on the harvesting and processing procedures made on the tea leaves and buds. Most of the world's tea is grown in large plantations. The major varieties of tea are black tea, oolong tea, green tea, and white tea.

- **Black tea** is the most popular among the varieties of teas and is easily available all over the world. It has a deep red color and comes in a variety of flavors and tastes ranging from flowery and fruity to spicy and nutty.
- **Oolong tea** is believed to be the most difficult to process. It is a medium-bodied brew and has the freshness of green tea and the aroma of black tea.
- **Green tea** is a variety of tea that is lower in caffeine than other teas and high in antioxidant properties. This is because when green tea is processed, oxidation in the leaves is prevented from taking place.
- **White tea** is minimally processed and tastes like fresh leaves or grass. White tea is obtained from the little buds and the tiny white hair grown on them.

There are countless blends of tea, which are made by combining different varieties from different plantations and locales. In addition to these blends, these are also herbal teas that are made from different herb combinations. Some of these herbal blends contain tea leaves as well. Black tea, green tea, and white tea are all common ingredients in commercial herbal tea blends. Also there are flavor infused teas, where the tea leaves are imparted with a different flavor.

To brew tea, start with cold water instead of hot water, as hot water will reduce the amount of oxygen. Bring the water to a rolling boil. Do not boil the water for a long time as it also will reduce the oxygen. Pour the hot water over the tea bag or loose tea as follows:

Green Tea	160°F	1–3 minutes
White Tea	180°F	4–8 minutes
Oolong Tea	190°F	1–8 minutes
Black Tea	Rolling boil	3–5 minutes
Herbal	Rolling boil	5–8 minutes

A good way to guess at the water temperature without a thermometer is to bring the water to a boil, remove it from the heat, and wait about 30 seconds for 180–190°F or 60 seconds for 160°F.

Harvesting tea leaves.
© eycool—Fotolia.com

CONCLUSION

As a future manager, production is an important aspect of bar management. It is, after all, the nerve center of the entire operation. It is here where the customers are either satisfied with their purchase or dissatisfied. It is here that profit is made or lost. Standardization is the key: standardized recipes and standard procedures. Consistency is important as well: consistency in using the proper glassware, a consistent pour of beer with a foamy head, consistent tasting cocktails, and consistently serving wine in the proper manner. Consistency will keep customers coming back and help ensure profitability.

Project

Interview a beverage manager of a large hotel in your neighborhood and interview an owner or manager of a small neighborhood bar. Compare the philosophies of the two operations in regards to standardized recipes and portion control devices. Are the operations similar or different? How do they relate the importance of controls to the profitability of their respective beverage operations?

QUESTIONS

True/False

1. One of the keys to a properly laid out workstation is that the bartender should have to take a minimal number of steps to fill an order.
2. The style of the glass most often refers to how it is constructed.
3. In order to control labor costs, glassware from the bar should be washed in the dish room with the other dishes.
4. The three steps in washing bar glasses are wash, rinse, and dry.
5. A shot glass is considered to be a form of a jigger.
6. All pourers measure the amount of product going into a drink.
7. A glass rimmer contains two compartments, one for sugar and one for salt.
8. A stirred drink is one in which only one ingredient is being used.
9. The two main species of coffee plants are arabica and robusta.
10. The major varieties of tea are black tea, oolong tea, green tea, and white tea.

Multiple Choice

1. A tumbler is often refered to as a
   A. rocks glass.
   B. shot glass.
   C. highball glass.
   D. all of the above.
2. Due to its construction, the glassware most likely to break is
   A. tumblers.
   B. footed ware.
   C. oblets.
   D. stemware.
3. In an operation with a restaurant, the best place for washing the bar glassware is
   1) at the bar.
   2) in the dish room.
   A. (1) only
   B. (2) only
   C. Both (1) and (2)
   D. Neither (1) nor (2)
4. Which of the following statements is not true?
   A. A jigger is a stainless steel pouring device.
   B. A shot glass is a form of a jigger.
   C. Most jiggers have two sides consisting of two different portions.
   D. Some shot glasses have deceptive lines etched into them.
5. A wooden stick used to crush mint leaves among other things is known as a
   A. crusher.
   B. muddler.
   C. zester.
   D. minter.
6. A margarita served on the rocks is an example of
   A. a straight pour.
   B. a frozen drink.
   C. a shaken drink.
   D. a layered drink.

7. A layered drink is made by
   1) pouring the alcohol with the highest specific gravity in the bottom of the glass.
   2) pouring the alcohol over the back of a spoon as it goes into the glass.
   A. (1) only
   B. (2) only
   C. Both (1) and (2)
   D. Neither (1) nor (2)

8. A gimlet contains
   A. gin.
   B. Scotch.
   C. tequila.
   D. bourbon.

9. "Beer clean" most nearly means
   A. clean beer lines.
   B. clean dispensing heads.
   C. clean beer coolers.
   D. clean glasses.

10. Decanting wine
    1) involves pouring the wine so as not to allow sediment to get into the guest's glass.
    2) generally applies to very young wines.
    A. (1) only
    B. (2) only
    C. Both (1) and (2)
    D. Neither (1) nor (2)

Essay

1. You have been hired to manage an upscale restaurant in an upper-class suburb of a large city. The restaurant is owned by a well-known chef in the area and will feature an extensive wine list as well as cocktails and a few imported beers. The restaurant is due to open in a month, and the owner has asked you to pick out the glassware for the bar. Tell what type of glassware you would purchase and why you would select that particular style.

2. Give the advantages and disadvantages of purchasing an automated beverage control system. Include in your answer when it would be feasible to use and when it would not.

3. You are training a new bar back how to pour a draft beer. Give the correct procedure, as well as any other pertinent information he or she would need to pour a perfect beer.

4. Explain in detail how to serve a bottle of wine to a table of guests.

5. You are part of the management team of a popular club in a college town. In a meeting, the team is brainstorming ideas to improve sales. You suggest marketing nonalcoholic drinks as a method to get new customers into the bar. Your idea is met with skepticism. Sell it to the rest of the team.

RESOURCES

Drysdale, John A. and Galapeu, Jennifer, *Profitable Menu Planning*, 4th ed. (Upper Saddle River, NJ: Pearson Prentice Hall, 2008).

Dopson, Lea R. and Hayes, David, *Food and Beverage Cost Control*, 5th ed. (New York, NY: John Wiley & Sons, 2010).

Keister, Douglas C., *Food and Beverage Control*, 2nd ed. (Upper Saddle River, NJ: Prentice Hall, 1990).

Pavesic, David V. and Magnant, Paul F., *Fundamental Principles of Restaurant Cost Control*, 2nd ed. (Upper Saddle River, NJ: Pearson Prentice Hall, 2005).

Plotkin, Robert, *Successful Beverage Management*, (Tucson, AZ: Bar Media, 2001).

11
Selling to a Profit

OVERVIEW

In this chapter, we will discuss setting a selling price. This is a very important element of bar management. However, prior to the discussion on selling price, one point should be made clear: the object of any business is to make a profit. There should be no argument over this point. It is fact. Far too many bar managers lose sight of this and, consequently, do not develop a profit mentality. To be sure, many factors go into achieving profit. Certainly sales are important because sales must exceed costs before a profit can be realized. Controls are important, for without them waste and theft eliminate any profit potential. The selling price, however, is the starting point on which profit is built. It is the key ingredient in making a profit. Without the proper selling price, all the promotions and all the controls will not assist in producing earnings. If the selling price is too high, sales will be lost. If the selling price is too low, profit will be lost.

We begin our discussion by studying the various categories of costs. We continue with a discussion of the income statement. By comprehending this document, an appreciation of how selling price, sales, cost, and controls all come together to affect profit. Next we will learn how to figure the cost of drinks. The reason for this is that the selling price is predicated upon what the drink costs to produce. We will then delve into the formulas for setting the price. We will also discuss the psychological pricing of drinks as well as price–value perception.

COSTS

Costs can be classified in several different ways. In the hospitality industry, the most common classifications are controllable and noncontrollable costs as well as fixed, variable, and semi-variable costs. The reason for classifying costs is to differentiate between those costs that management can control and those costs that management has little or no control over. Cost categorization is also important when preparing budgets and forecasts and when figuring break-even points.

Controllable and Noncontrollable Costs

One method of classifying costs is to categorize them as either controllable or non-controllable costs. These are not mysterious terms, as they are basically self-explanatory. **Controllable costs** are those costs that management can control and **noncontrollable costs** are those costs that management cannot control.

Controllable Costs   An example of a controllable cost is beverage cost. This cost can be controlled by using standardized recipes, standard mixing procedures, portion control, and pricing along with other constraints. For example, if the price of vodka were to increase and no action was taken, the bar's beverage cost would increase. At this point, management can raise the selling price of all drinks that use vodka as an ingredient or reduce the amount of vodka in each drink. By taking action, the increased cost of vodka has been controlled, which means the bar's beverage cost percent will not increase. It should be pointed out, however, that in exercising these options, management must always be careful not to alienate customers. If the selling price of vodka drinks were increased too much or the amount of alcohol were decreased too much, customers would quickly find a new place to patronize.

Noncontrollable Costs   Again, a noncontrollable cost is one which management has no control over. An example of a noncontrollable cost would be insurance. Once an insurance policy has been negotiated, management has no control over the cost of that policy. It is what it is. Another example would be the restaurant's lease. Once signed, management has virtually no control over its cost.

In addition to controllable and noncontrollable, costs can also be expressed as variable, fixed, or semi-variable.

Variable Costs

Variable costs are those costs that go up and down as sales go up and down and do so in direct proportion. An example of a variable cost is beverage cost. As sales go up, more spirits, wine, and beer are purchased to replenish inventory, and as sales go down, less beverages are purchased. If adequate controls are in place and there is no waste or theft, the amount of beverages used is in direct proportion to sales.

Fixed Costs

Fixed costs are those costs that remain the same regardless of sales volume. They are always there; they do not go away. If the bar is open, they are there. If the bar is closed, they are there. Insurance is an example of a fixed cost. As previously mentioned, once the policies have been negotiated, the cost remains the same. For example, if the cost of insuring the business were $1000 per month, it would remain at $1000 every month. If the bar's sales were $10,000 in March and $20,000 in April, the cost of insurance would remain the same at $1000 per month. Unlike a variable cost, it would not change because sales changed.

Semi-Variable Costs

Semi-variable costs go up and down as sales go up and down, but not in direct proportion. Semi-variable costs are made up of both fixed costs and variable costs. An example of a semi-variable cost is labor. Management is normally paid a salary. The salary remains the same regardless of an operation's sales volume. If the bar manager is paid a salary of $65,000, it remains the same if the bar does $500,000 or $600,000 a year. Thus, management's salary is a fixed cost. In other words, it remains the same regardless of volume. (*Note*: Do not confuse salary and bonuses here. Salaries stay the same regardless of volume, while bonuses are normally predicated on cost containment, sales, and/or profit and are paid in addition to salaries.)

On the other hand, staff members such as the cocktail servers, bartenders, and bar backs are paid an hourly wage and are scheduled by management according to sales predictions. As a result, the cost of these employees goes up as sales go up and goes down as sales go down. If proper scheduling is used, the labor cost will go up and down in direct proportion to sales as they go up and down. Putting this all together, there is a fixed cost (management's salary) and a variable cost (hourly staff wages) that result in a semi-variable cost (one that goes up and down as sales go up and down, but not in direct proportion).

Classifying Costs

As can be seen, there are some interchangeable terms here. Variable and semi-variable costs are normally controllable costs. That is, management can control costs that go up and down as sales go up and down. They can adjust schedules, inventories, or purchases. Fixed costs are normally noncontrollable costs, and management has little or no control over them. While management's ability to control or not control costs does not always hold true, for the most part it does.

Another thing to consider is that a particular cost could be classified in a different way depending on how it is structured. A good example of this is in negotiating a lease. For example, if a bar's lease were negotiated at $5000 per month, the monthly rental fee would be a fixed cost. It would not vary. It would not go up as sales went up or down as sales went down. It would always be $5000. If, on the other hand, the lease were negotiated at 6 percent of sales, rent would be a variable cost. The dollar amount would go up as sales went up and down as sales went down and would do so in direct proportion. Let's examine a third scenario: If the lease called for a monthly payment of $1000 plus 3 percent of sales, then rent would be a semi-variable cost. The $1000 would be paid regardless of the sale volume and would be a fixed cost. The 3 percent of sales would be a variable cost, which would go up or down as sales went up or down in direct proportion. Thus we have a fixed cost of $1000 and a variable cost of 3 percent, which when we put them together gives us a semi-variable cost.

From this example, it can be seen that some of the costs on the income statement, depending upon how they are structured, can be classified as either fixed, variable, or semi-variable. This is also a good example of the exception to the rule stated previously that variable and semi-variable costs are normally controllable. In this case, they are noncontrollable as the lease cannot be changed until it expires; thus management has no control over the lease payment.

Let's look at another example of how costs could be classified differently. If management were to budget 2 percent of sales on advertising, it would be a variable cost. The amount of money spent on advertising would be in direct proportion to sales. Conversely, if advertising were budgeted at $3000 a month, it would then be a fixed cost. It would not go up or down as sales went up or down.

UNDERSTANDING THE INCOME STATEMENT

To understand fully the relationship between the menu selling price and profit, it is necessary to examine an income statement. While it is not the purpose of this chapter to explain accounting, it is necessary to have some basic knowledge of the subject to determine how much to charge for an item as well as to analyze how successful the operation was financially. An **income statement** is nothing more than a report on how much money a business brings in (normally sales) and what its expenses are. If the sales exceed expenses, there is a profit. If the expenses exceed sales, there is a loss.

Sales

Referring to the income statement in Figure 11.1, the first line on the income statement is sales. The composition of sales on the income statement is determined by multiplying the selling price of each item by the number of units of that item sold and then totaling the sales for all the items sold in the bar. Thus, if a bar sold 100 gin and tonics at $7.00 each, its sales for gin and tonic would be $700. If it sold 100 draft beers at $4.00, its sales

Beverage sales		$135,600	
Cost of sales			
Opening inventory	$ 8,190		
Plus: Purchases	$40,240		
Equals: Total available	$48,430		
Less: Closing inventory	$10,980		
Cost of beverage sold		$ 37,450	27.6%
Less: Adjustments		$ 763	0.6%
Net cost of beverage sold		$ 36,687	27.1%
Gross profit		$ 98,913	72.9%
Labor		$ 40,750	30.1%
Music and entertainment		$ 10,640	7.8%
Supplies		$ 2,850	2.1%
Advertising		$ 2,900	2.1%
Rent		$ 10,000	7.4%
Utilities		$ 3,440	2.5%
Repairs and maintenance		$ 1,110	3.0%
Legal and accounting		$ 750	0.6%
Miscellaneous		$ 940	2.3%
Total Expenses		$ 73,380	54.1%
Profit before depreciation and taxes		$ 25,533	18.8%

FIGURE 11.1 Example of a bar income statement.

for draft beer would be $400. Let's assume for simplicity's sake that it only sold those two items. Its sales for the period would be $1100 ($700 + $400 = $1100). While the composition of sales is the selling price times the number of units sold, sales can also be looked at another way, and that is as the total of all of the bar tabs for the period. One is actually the result of the other; that is, a bar tab is the result of the number of items a customer purchased times the selling price, which is then totaled. Thus, the sales figure of $500,000 is all of the bar tabs totaled *or* all of the items sold times their selling price.

Figuring Percentages

Notice on the income statement that the figures are expressed in both dollars and percentages. Both of these are important in the analysis of the income statement. Dollars are what is brought in (in terms of sales) and expended (in terms of costs) and what is left over (in terms of profit). Percentages put the dollar numbers on an even scale for comparative purposes from period to period. For example, if an expense line such as labor went up, it could be acceptable if sales went up also in a corresponding manner. It would not be acceptable if the expense went up and sales did not or if sales dropped. Analysis of percentages makes it possible to relate cost directly to what happened to sales. Therefore, on an income statement, sales are always 100 percent and cost percentages are compared with sales. Referring to Figure 11.2 look at sales as a whole and at expenses and profit as parts of the whole.

Income Statement Pie Chart

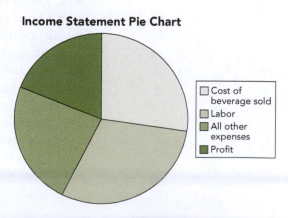

Legend:
- Cost of beverage sold
- Labor
- All other expenses
- Profit

FIGURE 11.2
Pie chart illustrating the income statement in Figure 11.1.

To obtain a percentage for a cost line, divide the cost in dollars by sales in dollars. The result is that line's cost percentage. For example, if rent was $500 and sales for that period were $5000, the percentage of rent paid to sales would be 10 percent.

$$\text{cost/sales} = \text{cost percentage}$$
$$\$500/\$5000 = 0.05 \text{ or } 5 \text{ percent}$$

The same holds true for profit. Simply divide profit in dollars by sales in dollars to obtain a profit percentage.

Cost of Beverage Sold

The second line on the income statement is **cost of beverage sold**. It is figured by taking opening inventory plus purchases minus closing inventory, which equals cost of beverage sold:

	Opening inventory
+	Beverage purchases
=	Beverage available for sale
−	Closing inventory
=	Cost of beverage sold

To simplify matters, let's assume that we are running a beer concession at the ballpark and sell only Budweiser draft beer. At the beginning of the week, we have two kegs of beer in inventory. During the week, we purchased 10 more kegs. At the end of the week, we had 3 kegs left. Assuming the kegs cost $100 each, the formula would look like this:

	Opening inventory	$200 (2 kegs @ $100 each)
+	Beverage purchases	$1000 (10 kegs @ $100 each)
=	Beverage available for sale	$1200 (12 kegs @ $100 each)
−	Closing inventory	$300 (3 kegs @ $100 each)
=	Cost of beverage sold	$900 (9 kegs @ $100 each)

Note: "Cost of beverage sold" could be a misnomer. We assume all of the beer was sold, but it may not have been. If some beer was spilled or if someone walked away without paying, the beer would be gone, but there would be no sales.

Adjustments to the Cost of Beverage Sold

Another factor to consider is the adjustments that are often made to cost of beverage sold. This is particularly true where there is a restaurant in conjunction with the bar or in a hotel setting. In these cases, quite often food is transferred from the kitchen to the bar, such things as limes, lemons, oranges, maraschino cherries, olives, to be used for drink garnishes. By the same token, liquor, beer, or wine is transferred from the bar to the kitchen for cooking purposes. When items are transferred to the bar, they are added to the cost of beverage sold. When they are transferred from the bar, they are subtracted. Another adjustment that is made is comps. A comp is when management buys a round of drinks or a bottle of wine for a customer. This is often done for a very good customer, as a means of apologizing to a customer for an incorrect order, or to pacify them for an unusually long wait for a table. Comps are subtracted from the cost of beverage sold. Given these changes, our formula now looks like this:

	Opening inventory
+	Beverage purchases
=	Beverage available for sale

−		Closing inventory
=		Cost of beverage sold
+		Transfers to bar
−		Transfers from bar
−		Comps
=		Net cost of beverage sold

Referring to the income statement in Figure 11.1, the cost of beverage sold is a compilation of all of the beverage usage of a typical bar. In other words, all of the beer, wine, spirits, mixers, and garnishes as well as every ingredient that goes in to the selling of those beverages is included in the cost of beverage sold.

To figure the percentage, take the net cost of beverage sold and divide it by sales:

$$\text{net cost of beverage sold} / \text{sales} = \text{beverage cost percent}$$
$$\$36,687 / \$135,600 = 27.1 \text{ percent}$$

Gross Profit

The next line, gross profit, is the amount of money that a business makes on its raw product. In the case of the beverage industry, it is the amount of money made on beverage ingredients, namely beer, wine, spirits, mixes, and garnishes. **Gross profit** is determined by subtracting the cost of beverage sold from sales.

		Sales
−		Cost of beverage sold
=		Gross profit

To figure the gross profit percentage, take gross profit in dollars and divide by sales in dollars. Referring to Figure 11.1, the gross profit percentage looks like this:

$$\text{gross profit} / \text{sales} = \text{gross profit percentage}$$
$$\$98,913 / \$135,600 = 72.9 \text{ percent}$$

Note: If you subtract the beverage cost percent from the sales percentage, the result will be the gross profit percentage, which will be the same percentage as when you divided gross profit by sales:

$$\text{beverage cost percent} - \text{sales percent} = \text{gross profit percent}$$
$$27.1\% - 100\% = 72.9\%$$

Labor Expense

The next line, labor expense, is the total labor cost for the operation. This includes fixed (management's salaries) and variable (hourly workers' pay) cost. This also includes payroll taxes, FICA, and fringe benefit expenses. FICA and payroll taxes were discussed in Chapter 9. Fringe benefits include (where applicable) employees' hospitalization insurance, life insurance, vacation and holiday pay, company-paid retirement benefits, and so on.

Prime Cost

Labor expense and beverage cost added together are known as **prime cost** because, together, these two expenses are the largest operating costs that are controlled by management. Note that in a restaurant operation, prime cost refers to food and labor cost. In an operation that has both a restaurant and a bar, prime cost would be food, beverage, and labor costs combined.

Other Expenses

The next line, supplies, includes such items as paper napkins, stir sticks, little paper umbrellas, dish machine detergent, and cleaning supplies. These are expenses that can be controlled by management. The following line, music and entertainment, is also one that can be controlled by management and includes expenses allocated to entertainment in the bar.

The following lines are, for the most part, noncontrollable expenses; however, there could be some exceptions depending on how the expenses are allocated. All of the expenses, controllable and noncontrollable, except beverage are then totaled on the line "Total Expenses." Total expenses are subtracted from gross profit to get the bar's income. Note that the income is prior to any depreciation and before income taxes are paid.

To put all this into perspective, let's review. In order for a bar to make a profit, sales must exceed costs. As we saw earlier, sales are nothing more than the selling price times the number of items sold. Therefore, one of the major keys to producing a profit is to determine the correct selling price. In other words, we need to charge a price that not only will cover the cost of goods (beverage cost) but also will cover all of our other expenses *and* produce a profit. Of course, we must market our business to get people in the door to buy our product. We must also control our costs so they do not get out of line and become greater than sales. If we set the right selling price, market properly, and control costs, we will make money.

SETTING THE SELLING PRICE

When we look at the percentage column on the income statement in Figure 11.1, we see that sales are 100 percent. If we add up all of the costs and profit before depreciation and taxes, we see that they add up to 100 percent. (*Note*: When you add these up, do not include gross profit.) Look at it as if sales are the whole pie and expenses and profit are parts of the pie. See Figure 11.2.

Since costs and profit add up to 100 percent, if one were to increase, another would have to decrease since we cannot go over 100 percent; or to put it another way, we cannot spend more than we bring in. Normally what happens is if an expense goes up, profit goes down. But it does not have to be this way. For example, if labor were to increase 1 percent, we could cut advertising 1 percent and profit would stay the same. This is the most common practice in the beverage industry. When one expense goes up, cut another one. When the business can cut no more, then profit will suffer. When profit drops to a point where there is an inferior return on investment, business has no other choice than to increase the selling prices. When the selling price increases, sales increase, and the 100 percent (sales) has a larger dollar pool for which to pay expenses and make a profit. A word of caution here: If management raises prices too high, it will drive customers away and sales will not increase.

In addition to increasing selling prices, there are other methods available to increase sales. These include marketing campaigns to increase the bar's traffic count and introducing new drinks, which have a higher selling price and a more favorable cost structure. However, there comes a point when the only alternative is to increase selling prices. One would hope that this does not occur too often, but when it does, it should be done very carefully.

Product Mix

In the income statement (Figure 11.1), a beverage cost of 27 percent with a gross profit of 73 percent covers all of the expenses and gives the bar owner a nice profit. Just because a bar desires, for example, a 27 percent beverage cost, not every item is marked up to give that specific cost. The 27 percent beverage cost comes from an aggregate of all items sold at their various costs. This is known as **product mix**. It is the product mix, the actual number of items sold at their various markups, that makes up the cost of beverage sold on the income statement.

Product Classifications

For the purpose of developing a selling price, bar inventories are broken down into various categories according to their cost. This greatly simplifies things when it comes to determining selling price. By bundling various brands and labels according to cost, one selling price can be determined for all of the brands and labels in that group. For example, while Passport and House of Stuart Scotches have different costs, they are at least close to each other. Rather than have a separate selling price for each, they are categorized together, and the drinks made from them will sell at the same price. The inventory classifications are as follows:

Liquor

- Well stock. Also known as house brand; made up of the low-cost liquor. This is used when a customer orders a drink without expressing a preference. For example: Scotch and soda.
- Call stock. A higher cost liquor that a customer will order by brand. For example: Bacardi and Coke.
- Premium stock. A liquor that costs more than call, normally single malt Scotch or Irish whisky and high-end domestic whiskey. Also called for by the customer.
- Super premium. The very highest priced liquor, again called for by the customer.

Beer

- Bottled. Domestic, imported, and microbrewed. Some bars charge the same for all bottled beers while others break it out into these classifications, while still others break it out according to cost categories much like the liquor categories.
- Draft. Domestic, imported, and microbrewed. Again, the same strategy is used for draft beer as for bottled beer.

Wine

- Glass. House wine by the glass is usually priced the same regardless of its type, while wines that are called for are priced according to their costs much like the liquor calls. The selection of wines by the glass is normally limited as many wines are sold by the bottle only.
- Bottle. Bottle wines are normally marked up according to their individual cost. Unlike other products in the bar, they are not categorized and grouped together to have one selling price.

Nonalcoholic Drinks

- This group includes coffee, tea, and carbonated beverages, which, for the most part, will have the same selling price. It also includes virgin drinks, which are drinks made without alcohol. They will all have the same selling price unless there are extensive labor or ingredient costs associated with a particular drink. For example, a virgin tumbleweed made with premium ice cream will normally command a higher price than a virgin Bloody Mary. Also in this group are specialty coffee drinks such as lattes and cappuccinos. Each of these will be priced individually. Having determined the categories of the bar stock, we can now determine a range of costs associated with those categories. Most experts agree on the following cost percentages and gross profit as an industry average.

Category	Cost (%)	Gross Profit (%)
Well stock	12	88
Call stock	16	84
Premium stock	19	81
Super premium	18	82
Bottled beer	25	75
Draft beer	30	70
Wine—glass	20	80
Wine—bottle	50	50
Nonalcoholic	30	70

Keep in mind that these percentages are nothing more than a rule of thumb. The exact cost percentages will vary bar to bar depending on the mix of items sold within each category. For example, if a bar were to sell a higher number of imported bottles of beer at a higher cost than domestic, their cost percentage would be higher.

Total Sales/Cost Mix

By combining the above categories into sales of liquor, beer, wine, and nonalcoholic beverages, we can get a clearer picture of the bar's product mix. Assume that the bar in Figure 11.1 had a mix that looked like this:

Category	Sales	Cost	Cost (%)	Product mix
Liquor	$50,240	$8541	17	37%
Beer	$38,680	$10,830	28	29%
Wine	$33,120	$13,248	40	24%
Nonalcoholic	$13,560	$4068	30	10%
Total	$135,600	$36,687	27	100%

As we can see, liquor must maintain a cost of 17 percent, beer 28 percent, wine 40 percent, and nonalcoholic drinks 30 percent in order to achieve an overall cost of 27 percent. Keep in mind that this is an example of a representative bar. Not all bars will have this breakdown of beverage costs. As a matter of fact, not all bars will have a 27 percent beverage cost. There are many factors that influence the cost of beverage sold. Some states mandate that bars purchase their alcoholic beverages from retailers, others must purchase from the state, and if they can buy from a wholesaler, all are taxed at different rates by their state.

Standard Beverage Cost

A **standard beverage cost** is that cost percentage that management has determined is necessary for that operation to make a profit. The actual cost on the income statement is measured against the standard. Any deviation from the standard must be corrected if the bar is to remain profitable. Each bar has to determine its own standard beverage cost based on the markup necessary to maintain an overall profit for that business. Each bar is different. They all pay different rents, have different overhead costs, and charge different prices depending on their demographic situation. While there is not a specific industry standard for beverage costs, experts agree that it should be in the 18–28 percent range. Take for example two extremes. Why does beer at a major league sports stadium cost more than the same beer at a neighborhood tavern? Captive audience aside, concessionaires at most sports stadiums pay an extremely high rent. This high rent pays for a substantial part of the upkeep of that stadium, therefore their overhead (fixed) costs are higher than those the neighborhood bar. The neighborhood bar with a lower fixed cost can charge less for beer and still make a profit. Once again, the selling price must be high enough to cover all costs and make a profit.

Once a standard beverage cost has been determined and the breakdown figured for each category to obtain that cost, we can move ahead to figuring the selling prices. The first step in doing so is to figure the cost of each item we are going to sell. As you recall, the selling price is predicated on an item cost and must be high enough to cover all of the bar's costs and profit.

FIGURING COST

How the cost of items sold is figured depends on the category. Liquor and some nonalcoholic drinks are figured using recipe cost cards as they normally have multiple ingredients. Beer, wine, and the other nonalcoholic drinks are figured on an individual basis as they normally are single-ingredient items. As usual, however, there are exceptions. Some liquor is straight shots while wine and beer are occasionally used in mixed drinks.

Multi-Ingredient Items

Multi-ingredient drinks should have a standardized recipe. While standardized recipes were discussed in detail in Chapter 10, it is important to note here that they are an integral part of determining the correct selling price. As a matter of fact, **standardized recipes** are an important component of the overall cost control system in any bar. They control the quantity and quality of ingredients used to prepare a particular drink as well as control the portions that are to be served. They are also essential tools when it comes to figuring costs. Simply having standardized recipes in an operation is not enough; it is imperative that everyone follow them. Any deviation from the standardized recipe not only results in poor quality but also in inaccurate costs being figured for that item and, consequently, an incorrect selling price. Figure 11.3 shows an example of a standardized recipe.

To figure costs based on a standardized recipe, it is advisable to use a cost card. To make the entire cost-control system effective, there should be a cost card for every

Amount	Unit	Name: Pina colada	Glassware: Collins glass
		Ingredient	Methodology
1.5	Oz	Light Rum	
2	Oz	Coco Lopez	
2	Oz	Pineapple Juice	
		Crushed Ice	Blend all until smooth
1	Ea	Pineapple Slice	
1	Ea	Maraschino Cherry	Garnish

FIGURE 11.3 A standardized recipe for a pina coloda.

multiple-ingredient drink regularly served at the bar. The object of cost cards is to get an accurate cost per portion so that the proper selling price can be determined. To properly fill out a cost card and determine the standardized costs, follow these steps:

- Copy all the ingredients for a particular drink from the standardized recipe to the cost card. The ingredients listed on the cost card should match the ingredients listed on the standardized recipe card exactly.
- List the amount and unit used for each ingredient in the appropriate column.
- From an invoice, list the cost of each ingredient as well as the unit listed on the invoice. Notice that the unit called for in the recipe is quite often different from the unit listed on the invoice. For example, a recipe unit could be in ounces while that particular item was purchased in metric. Figure 11.4 lists some of the more common unit conversions.
- Break the invoice unit down to the same unit for the recipe in the recipe column and figure the cost per recipe unit.
- In the last column, figure the extended cost by multiplying the number of units needed for the recipe times the recipe cost per unit.
- Add the cost of all ingredients in the extension column.
- If the recipe is for a large batch, for instance margarita mix, divide the total cost by the number of portions the recipe produces to get the cost per portion.

Distilled Spirits

Bottle size	Equivalent fluid ounces	Bottles per case	Liters per case	U.S. gallons per case	Corresponds to
1.75 liters	59.2 fl. oz.	6	10.50	2.773806	½ gallon
1.00 liters	33.8 fl. oz.	12	12.00	3.170064	1 quart
750 milliliters	25.4 fl. oz.	12	9.00	2.377548	4/5 quart
375 milliliters	12.7 fl. oz.	24	9.00	2.377548	4/5 pint
200 milliliters	6.8 fl. oz.	48	9.60	2.536051	1/2 pint
100 milliliters	3.4 fl. oz.	60	6.00	1.585032	1/4 pint
50 milliliters	1.7 fl. oz.	120	6.00	1.585032	1, 1.6, and 2 oz.

Official conversion factor: 1 liter = 0.264172 U.S. gallon

Wine

Bottle size	Equivalent fluid ounces	Bottles per case	Liters per case	U.S. gallons per case	Corresponds to
3 liters	101 fl. oz.	4	12.00	3.17004	4/5 gallon
1.5 liters	50.7 fl. oz.	6	9.00	2.37753	2/5 gallon
1.00 liters	33.8 fl. oz.	12	12.00	3.17004	1 quart
750 milliliters	25.4 fl. oz.	12	9.00	2.37753	4/5 quart
500 milliliters	16.9 fl. oz.	24	12.00	3.17004	1 pint
375 milliliters	12.7 fl. oz.	24	9.00	2.37753	4/5 pint
187 milliliters	6.3 fl. oz.	48	8.976	2.37119	2/5 pint
100 milliliters	3.4 fl. oz.	60	6.00	1.58502	2, 3, and 4 oz.
50 milliliters	1.7 fl. oz.	120	6.00	1.58502	1, 1.6, & 2 oz.

Official conversion factor: 1 liter = 0.26417 U.S. gallon

FIGURE 11.4   Some common bar recipe conversions.
Courtesy of the United States Department of the Treasury.

While this may seem complicated and confusing at first glance, in reality it is quite simple. For example, refer to Figure 11.5 to compose a cost card for a pina colada.

- Step 1. The recipe calls for 1.5 ounces of light rum, but rum is purchased by 1.75 liter bottles. Refer to the conversion chart in Figure 11.4 to find that a 1.75 liter bottle will yield 59.2 ounces of product. Take the cost of the bottle, in this case $20.00, and divide by 59.2 to get $0.34 (rounded off) cost per ounce. The recipe calls for 1.5 ounces, so multiply $0.34 by 1.5 to get a total cost of $0.51.
- Step 2. Coco Lopez costs $6.00 for a 1.75 liter bottle. The methodology is the same as for the rum, that is, divide the cost of the Coco Lopez ($6.00) by 59.2 to get $0.10 per ounce. The recipe calls for 2 ounces, so multiply $0.10 by 2 to get a total cost of $0.20.
- Step 3. Pineapple juice cost $3.50 for a #5 can, which contains 46 ounces of juice. Divide the cost of the can ($3.50) by 46 to get a total cost of $0.08 per ounce. Multiply the $0.08 per ounce by 2 ounces to get $0.16 total cost for the pineapple juice.
- Step 4. Fresh pineapples costs $4.60 each. We cut the pineapple into 48 slices. Therefore the cost of the pineapple is determined by dividing $4.60 by 48 to get a total cost of $0.09 per slice. *Note*: We cut the pineapple into four quarters, then slice it. If you cut it into six sections or cut it thicker or thinner, you will get a different yield. It is important when costing fresh fruit to do a yield test to determine the exact cost for your particular operation.

Date		Name: Pina colada	Portions: 1		Portion size: 5.5 Oz		
Recipe Amount	Recipe Unit	Ingredients	Invoice Cost	Invoice Unit	Recipe Cost	Recipe Unit	Total Cost
1.5	Oz	Light Rum	$20.00	1.75 Ml	$0.34	Oz	$0.51
2	Oz	Coco Lopez	$6.00	1.75 Ml	$0.10	Oz	$0.20
2	Oz	Pineapple Juice	$3.50	46 Oz	$0.08	Oz	$0.16
		Crushed Ice	NA				$0.00
1	Ea	Pineapple Slice	$4.60	Ea	$0.09	Slice	$0.09
1	Ea	Maraschino Cherry	$13.75	1/2 gallon	$0.09	Cherry	$0.08
						Total	$1.04
						# Portions	1
						Cost/Portion	$1.04

Amount	Unit	Ingredient	Methodology
1.5	Oz	Light Rum	
2	Oz	Coco Lopez	
2	Oz	Pineapple Juice	
		Crushed Ice	Blend together
			Pour into collins glass
1	Ea	Pineapple Slice	Garnish
1	Ea	Maraschino Cherry	

FIGURE 11.5 Pina colada cost card.

- Step 5. Maraschino cherries cost $13.75 per half gallon. The yield is 173 cherries per jar. Divide $13.75 by 173 to obtain a cost of $0.09 per cherry. *Note*: Cherries come in different sizes, with and without stems. Consult the label for the correct yield.
- Step 6. Add up the total cost column to get a total cost of $1.04 for the recipe.
- Step 7. Divide the number of portions for the recipe by the total cost to get the cost per portion. Since this recipe was for one portion, the total cost and the cost per portion are the same.

Many hospitality accounting software programs on the market will do everything discussed in this section. The user enters the data concerning the recipe and the invoice costs. The program does the rest by completing the math and figuring the cost per drink on the cost cards. Some of the more sophisticated programs that have a complete accounting package change cost cards as invoices are posted to the accounts payable ledger. Thus, as costs increase or decrease, the cost cards are automatically adjusted. As a result, cost per portion is monitored and management is alerted when costs increase above predetermined level.

Single-Ingredient Items

Many of the items sold in a bar have only one ingredient but are concentrated and must be mixed with water to make a sellable product. Examples of these are carbonated beverages, some mixes, and coffee. Their costs are figured as follows:

Carbonated Beverages   In costing carbonated beverages, there are two types to consider: premix and postmix. Premix is where the syrup and carbonated water are mixed at the factory and filled into 5 gallon cartons. Postmix, on the other hand, is where the syrup and carbonated water are mixed on location. The syrup is delivered in 5 gallon cartons, mixed with water that has passed through the carbonator to give it its effervescence, and then combined in the mixing chamber at the point of service.

There are some major differences between the two. Postmix is less expensive than premix and therefore has a lower cost per drink and a higher gross profit. However, to install a postmix system requires a water line, electricity, and a drain all running to the unit and requires a larger investment in equipment. Because of this, some operations opt for the premix, which requires minimal investment, even though the profit margin is lower. Additionally, the costs of premix and postmix are figured differently. Premix is relatively simple because the product is ready to serve as purchased.

When costing cold beverages, if the bar has an ice machine, the cost of ice is not figured in, as it is negligible. However, ice displaces product going into the glass, and ice displacement is figured into the formula. For example, if a 12 ounce glass of cola is served with 6 ounces of ice, the net serving of cola would be 6 ounces. *Note*: In the rare instance where an operation purchases ice from a vendor, the cost of ice would be great enough to be added as an ingredient cost of any drink that uses ice.

Costing Premix Carbonated Beverages   To figure the cost of premix, refer to Figure 11.6 and use the following steps:

1. Multiply 128 (the number of ounces in a gallon) times 5 (the number of gallons in a premix box) to get 640 ounces (ounces in a 5 gallon box).
2. Divide the cost of the box by 640 to get the cost per ounce.
3. Subtract the amount of ice displacement from the total ounces of the serving container to get net ounces of product served.
4. Multiply net ounces of product served by the cost per ounce to get net cost.

FIGURE 11.6
Premix cost example.

Premix Carbonated Beverages

Cost per 5 gallon tank: $30.00
Serving size: 16 ounces
Ice displacement: 8 ounces
Ice cost: N/A

Step 1 Ounces in a gallon $\times$ gallons in box $=$ ounces in box

$128 \times 5 = 640$

Step 2 $\dfrac{\text{Cost per box}}{\text{ounces in box}} = \text{cost per ounce}$

$\$30.00/640 = \$0.046$

Step 3 Ounces per serving $-$ ounces displaced by ice $=$ ounces of product served

$16 - 8 = 8$

Step 4 Cost per ounce $\times$ ounces of product served $=$ net cost per serving

$\$0.046 \times 8 = \$0.368$

Costing Postmix Carbonated Beverages and Other Water-Added Bases To figure the cost of postmix, use the following formula and assume mixing the water and syrup at a 5:1 ratio (i.e., 5 parts water to 1 part syrup). If a different ratio is used, the formula should be changed accordingly. Refer to Figure 11.7.

1. Multiply 5 gallons of water (for every gallon of syrup) by 5 gallons of syrup to get 25 gallons of water (5:1 ratio).
2. Add the 5 gallons of syrup to the 25 gallons of water to get a 30 gallon yield per 5 gallon box of syrup.
3. Multiply 30 gallons of product by 128 (number of ounces per gallon) to get total ounces of product per syrup box (3840 ounces). (*Note*: If the ratio does not change, then the number of ounces does not change and you can start the formula with step 4.)
4. Divide the cost per box of syrup by 3840 to get the cost per ounce of product.
5. Subtract the amount of ice displacement from the size of the serving container to get the amount of product served.
6. Multiply the amount of product served by the cost per ounce of product to get the total cost.

To figure the cost of other beverages that require the addition of water, such as frozen juice concentrates or powdered concentrates, for example pina colada or margarita mixes, simply follow the formula for postmix carbonated beverages. Be careful in step 1 as these products all have varying water-to-base ratios.

Coffee

Coffee sales are substantial enough in many bars to warrant getting an accurate cost per cup. Following are the steps to be taken to obtain a coffee cost (refer to Figure 11.8):

1. Multiply the number of gallons of water (usually 2.5 gallons per pound of coffee) times 128 (number of ounces per gallon) to get 320 total ounces.
2. Multiply total ounces by 10 percent (water absorbed by the coffee grounds).
3. Subtract the loss from total ounces to get the net yield per urn of coffee.

Postmix Carbonated Beverages

Cost per 5 gallon box of syrup: $25.00
Serving size: 16 ounces
Ice displacement: 8 ounces
Ice cost: N/A
Water cost: N/A
Water-to-syrup ratio: 5:1

Step 1   Gallons of water needed per gallon of syrup $\times$ gallons of syrup = total gallons of water needed
5 gallons of water $\times$ 5 gallons of syrup = 25 gallons of water needed

Step 2   Total gallons of water + gallons of syrup = total gallons of product
25 gallons of water + 5 gallons of syrup = 30 gallons of product

Step 3   Total gallons of product $\times$ ounces per gallon = total ounces of product
30 gallons of product $\times$ 128 = 3840 ounces of product

Step 4   Cost of syrup / number of ounces of product = cost per ounce
$25.00/3840 = $0.007

Step 5   Ounces per serving container − ounces displaced by ice = ounces of product per serving
16 ounces − 8 ounces = 8 ounces of product per serving

Step 6   Cost per ounce of product $\times$ ounces per serving = net cost per serving
$0.007 $\times$ 8 ounces = $0.056

FIGURE 11.7   Postmix cost example.

4. Divide the net yield by the number of ounces served per cup to get the number of cups per pound. (*Note*: If the brewing ratio and cup size do not change, then this number stays the same and you can start the formula with step 5.)
5. Divide the cost per pound by the number of cups per pound. The result is the cost of coffee per cup.
6. Take the cost of cream and sugar per serving and divide by 2 (assuming 50 percent of the customers use cream and sugar).
7. Add the cream and sugar cost to the cost of the coffee per cup. The result is the net cost per cup to serve.
8. Multiply the net cost per cup times the average number of refills per customer plus the original cup. (If you charge per cup with no refill, then ignore this step.)

Different sections of the country brew coffee in varying strengths, so the brew ratio (step 1) may change. If the brewing ratio is different in your area, then substitute the correct ratio. If the coffee is being used as an ingredient in a mixed drink, use the figure in step 5.

Ready-to-Serve Items

Draft Beer   There are 15.5 gallons of beer in a keg, which translates to 1984 ounces. If a bar were to pour a 14 ounce glass, common logic would dictate that there would be about 141 draws to a keg. In this case, common logic would be wrong. With draft beer, there is waste. As a matter of fact, the industry average is about a 20 percent loss. This includes such things as overpouring, excess foam, and giveaways. While this number can be substantially reduced by having clean lines and proper pressure in the lines along with a tight control system, there still will be some loss. As a matter of fact,

Coffee

Brew ratio: 3:1
Coffee cost: $4.00 per pound
Cream cost: $1.80 per quart (1 ounce serving)
Sugar cost: 0.35 pounds (½ ounce serving)
Customers using cream and sugar 50 percent
Serving size: 6 ounces
Refills: 1

Step 1 Ounces in a gallon × brew ratio = total ounces

128 × 3 = 384 ounces

Step 2 Total ounces × absorption loss = total loss

384 × 0.10 = 38.4 ounces lost

Step 3 Step 1 − step 2 = net volume

384.0 ounces − 38.4 ounces. = 345.6 ounces net volume

Step 4 Net volume/ounces per serving = cups per pound

345.6 ounces/6 ounces per cup = 57.6 cups per pound

Step 5 Cost per pound/cups per pound = Cost per cup

$4.00/57.6 = $0.069

Step 6 Cost per quart of cream/ounces per quart = cost per cup of cream

$1.80/32. = $0.056 cost of cream

Cost per pound of sugar/servings per ounce = cost per cup of sugar

$0.35/32 (1/2 ounce servings per pound) = $0.011 cost of sugar

$0.056 cost of cream + 0.011 cost of sugar = $0.067 total

Total cream and sugar × percentage (50%) of customers using cream and sugar = cost per customer

$0.067 × 50 percent (0.50) = $0.034

Step 7 Cost of coffee + cost of cream and sugar = total cost per cup to serve

$0.069 + 0.034 = $0.103

Step 8 Total cost per cup × cups per customer = net cost

$0.103 × 2 = $0.206

FIGURE 11.8   Coffee cost example.

the distance of the line from the keg to the dispensing arm will increase the amount of waste, with the longer the line, the greater the waste. The reason for this is the cost to clean and bleed the line increases with distance. Using the industry average to figure a cost, the formula will look like this:

1984 ounce in a keg × 20 percent loss = 397 ounces lost − 1984 = 1587 net ounces

OR

1984 × 0.80 = 1587 net ounces (100% full keg − 20% loss = 80%)

1587 net ounce in a keg/14 ounce draws = 113 draws per keg

$100 cost of keg/113 draws = $0.88 per draw

Wine   Ready-to-serve beverages, such as wine or bottled beer, are relatively easy to figure. (We saved the easiest until last.) If you are pouring a drink from a larger container, wine for example, simply divide the cost per container by the number of ounces per container and multiply this figure (cost per ounce) by the number of ounces served.

Cost of 750 ml bottle/25.4 ounces = cost per ounce × number ounces = cost per serving
$10/25.4 = $0.39 per ounce × 5 ounce serving = $1.95 cost per serving

Bottled Beer

Cost of case/24 bottles per case = cost per bottle
$16.00/24 = $0.67 cost per bottle

FIGURING THE SELLING PRICE

With an understanding of where profit comes from, the interrelationship of expenses to sales, and the fact that the selling price is predicated on the cost of the item to be sold, the various methods determining a selling price can be explored. There are many formulas available to assist the bar manager in determining what should be charged for an item. Some are simple, some are complicated, and some make absolutely no sense at all. There are, however, a few that have passed the test of time and are most often used in the industry today. Two of these are the factor method and the markup on cost method. We will use these methods to illustrate how to determine selling prices for cocktails and beer. Bottled wine has its own separate pricing system, and this will be covered as well. Keep in mind that you may encounter other methods used in the industry; however, they should come up with approximately the same selling price as it is the selling price that determines if the operation is to be profitable.

Factor Method

Perhaps the simplest formula to use is the **factor method**. In this method, it is necessary to have already determined what the beverage cost should be. Remember that when we grouped the items being sold in the bar into categories, they had different beverage cost percentages. In referring to the product mix chart on page 270, for example, the beverage cost for bottled beer would be 28 percent. When using the factor method to price bottled beer, 28 percent is the percentage to be used.

To obtain the selling price, take the desired beverage cost percentage and divide it into 100 percent; the result is the factor. Next, take the factor and multiply it by the cost of the item. The result is the selling price of that item. Once the factor has been determined, it is unnecessary to repeat step 1 each time a selling price is needed. Simply multiply the item cost by the factor to determine what to charge for that item. If all controls are effective and the costs remain constant, the desired beverage cost percentage will be accurate. If the cost of that item increases or decreases, multiply the new cost by the factor to determine a new selling price that reflects the change in cost.

1. Determine desired beverage cost percentage.
2. Divide 100 percent by the desired beverage cost percent. The result is the factor.
3. Multiply the factor times the cost of the item to find the correct selling price.

For example, a bottle of beer costing $0.90 a bottle would have the following selling price:

desired beverage cost percentage = 28 percent
1.00 (100%)/0.28 (28%) = 3.571 or 3.6 (factor)
$0.90 × 3.6 = $3.24

Let's take another example, this time for a pina colada. Using the cost in Figure 11.5 and a product mix value of 17 percent, the formula would be:

$$\text{desired beverage cost percentage} = 17 \text{ percent}$$
$$1.00 \ (100\%)/0.17 \ (17\%) = 5.882 \text{ or } 5.8 \text{ (factor)}$$
$$\$1.04 \times 5.8 = \$6.03$$

Markup on Cost Method

Another simple method, very similar in nature, is the **markup on cost** method. Take the beverage cost of the item and divide it by the desired beverage cost percentage; the result is the selling price to be charged for that item. As in the factor method, management must know that the desired beverage cost is adequate to obtain a satisfactory gross profit to cover all other expenses and achieve a net profit.

1. Determine the desired beverage cost percent.
2. Divide the cost of the item by the desired beverage cost percent.
3. The result is the selling price of that item.

Using the prior example of a bottle of beer, which costs $0.90, the formula would look like this:

$$\$0.90/0.28 = \$3.21$$

The cost for the pina colada would be as follows:

$$\$1.04/0.17 = \$6.12$$

Notice that the selling prices are very similar from the two formulas.

Wine Markups

To determine the selling price of wine by the bottle, there are two methods widely used in the industry today. One is the factor method, where the factor for a lower priced bottle is 4 (25% beverage cost), a mid-range bottle is factored at 2.5 (40% beverage cost), and high priced wines are multiplied by a factor of 2 (50% beverage cost).

The second method, which is normally used in white-tablecloth operations where a sommelier is on the staff, is to double the cost of the bottle of wine and add a constant to that figure. The constant is established on such factors as the cost of extra labor (the sommelier) and the overhead of having an extensive wine selection. Therefore, the selling price of a $20.00 bottle of wine with a constant of $7.00 served in an establishment such as this would be $47.00.

$$\$20.00 \text{ cost} \times 2 \text{ (double the cost)} = \$40 + \$7.00 \text{ constant} = \$47.00 \text{ selling price}$$

SETTING THE FINAL SELLING PRICE

Now that we have figured what the selling price *should be* to achieve the desired beverage cost on the income statement, it is time to *set* the final selling price. Several things need to be considered here: the product mix, bundling, the price–value relationship, psychological pricing, the business, the market, and the competition.

- Product mix. Recall that this was discussed earlier. The bar inventory was broken down into four categories—liquor, beer, wine, and nonalcoholic beverages—and a percentage was assigned for each category in order for the aggregate to give us the desired beverage cost percent. Remember that this was an example only and that each bar will have to determine for itself what its beverage cost percent should be in order to meet all costs and achieve a profit. It is therefore important that when the selling price is set that it does not stray too far from the category percentage. For example, mixed drinks should be very close to the operations standard beverage cost for liquor (17% in the example given).

- Bundling. The term **bundling** refers to grouping together the selling prices of various drinks or beverages within a category. For example, all drinks made with well liquor would have the same selling price, even though the cost for each would be different; that is, Scotch would have a different cost than vodka. All drinks made with call liquor would have the same selling price albeit a higher one than well drinks. All domestic 12 ounce bottled beer would have the same selling price, and so on. There are three different methods to figure bundle prices: worst case scenario, average, and weighted average.

  1. Worst case scenario is to take the highest cost item and figure all drinks in that group accordingly. For example, if Scotch is the highest cost item in the well drink group, then all drinks would be marked up according to the cost of Scotch. The highest cost domestic bottled beer would be used for all domestic bottled beers.

  2. Average cost is where the cost of all components in the group is averaged. Thus the costs of Scotch, bourbon, vodka, and gin are averaged, and that average is used for the cost in all well drinks.

  3. Weighted average is where the cost for the group is figured based on the individual sales of each item. For example, if vodka is used more that gin in well drinks then the cost of vodka would weigh heavier in figuring the cost of well drinks. This method, while the most accurate, is also the most time consuming. However, with the advent of the POS systems, it has become much more prevalent as this system gives you the weighted averages.

- **Price—value relationship**. Before a customer purchases anything, he or she must recognize it as a value. A cocktail or a beer, in the customer's eyes, must have a value associated with it that is as great as or greater than the stated selling price. In the hospitality industry, this is sometimes referred to as the **price point**, or the dollar point beyond which a customer will no longer purchase that item. In other words, it is the point of resistance. Keep in mind that it is not the same price that a customer will pay everywhere. Consider that customers will pay a premium price for a beer at the airport because they want that beer and there is no other place to get it. They will not pay that price at their neighborhood tavern, however, as they could go elsewhere and get it at a more favorable price.

  Another example, and one which customers complain about constantly, is the selling price of a bottle of wine. Most people who are wine connoisseurs are well aware of what their favorite wine costs at a retail shop. While they are willing to pay more at a fine restaurant where the sommelier will decant the wine and serve it to them, they will only pay so much before they recognize that the price–value relationship is not worth the additional price.

  Bar managers must be constantly aware of what their customers' price point is and what they consider to be a price–value relationship when determining their selling price in order to not drive customers away from their establishment. Keep in mind that customers could just as easily buy a six pack and take it home for less money that they could purchase it in your bar. They would not, however, have the ambiance or camaraderie. Remember, people buy something only if they perceive a value.

- Psychological pricing. **Psychological pricing** theory takes into account how the customer reacts to certain pricing structures. Psychological pricing has a long history in retailing; however, only recently has it been incorporated into the pricing structure of the hospitality industry. One of the primary theories behind psychological pricing is the odd-cents price. This pricing method reduces the customers' resistance to buy because it gives the illusion of a discount. Instead of charging $1.50 for an item, charge $1.49, and the customer perceives this as a better price–value relationship. The reason is the perception that the bar is charging the exact amount necessary rather than rounding up to the nearest even amount. When using odd-cents pricing, the best ending digit to use is 9.

Another factor is the importance of the left-most digit and the distance between two prices. For example, the customer perceives a greater distance between 69 and 71 than between 67 and 69, even though the distance is the same (2 cents).

The length of the price or the number of digits in the price is another factor in psychological pricing. As in the left-most digit theory, the customer also perceives distance here. In other words, greater distance is perceived between $9.99 and $10.25 than between $9.55 and $9.99, even though there is a $0.26 difference between the first set of numbers and a $0.44 difference between the second set. This strategy is of particular importance in a highly competitive situation. For example, a promotion featuring $2.00 draws could be priced at $1.99 and have a much greater impact, or $3.00 well drinks during happy hour could be $2.99.

Psychological pricing is not for everyone. Certainly it is very important when a bar's customers are very price conscience. It would not be necessary to use it in a situation where a bar or lounge is doing a brisk business without it or where entertainment is involved. At the far end of the spectrum, a white-table-cloth restaurant would go to the opposite extreme and price its drink and wine list in even dollars to create a fine dining ambiance.

- The business, the market, and the competition. The final consideration in menu pricing is the bar itself and the market in which it is operating. It is imperative that pricing be in keeping with the demographics of the market and within the means of the target audience. Many of the things previously discussed come into play, namely pricing your menu so that your customer perceives a value for the price paid for the product, utilizing psychological pricing where applicable, and being competitive. The selling price should also, most importantly, give the operation the opportunity to make a profit.

CONCLUSION

All too often in the hospitality industry, business owners go up the street to see what their competition is charging for a drink and come back to their own bar and sell it for the same price. This is a disaster waiting to happen. No two bars are alike. Their fixed costs are different; their marketing strategies, their product mixes, their investments, in short, everything about them is different except for the fact that they both sell drinks. While it is important to know what your competition is up to and the fact that you need to be competitive, it is just plain dumb to copy selling prices.

Astute bar managers will analyze their income statement to see if they are producing an adequate profit as a return on their investment. They will use the cost of beverage sold as the fulcrum to overcome their expenses and achieve a profit. They will establish a product mix so that they know what gross profit can be expected from each category of drinks on their menu. They will create their selling prices based on this data. Then and only then will they be successful.

QUESTIONS

True/False

1. A noncontrollable cost can be classified as a fixed cost.
2. Due to the minimum wage law and in some cases union contracts, labor cost is classified as a noncontrollable cost.
3. To achieve a profit, sales must exceed costs.
4. Sales are the number of units sold time the selling price of those units.
5. To obtain a percentage you divide sales by cost.
6. Gross profit is sales minus beverage cost.

7. Product mix is the actual number of items sold at their various markups that make up the cost of beverage sold on the income statement.
8. The selling price of a drink is based on the cost of the liquor plus all of the other ingredients in the drink.

Multiple Choice

1. A controllable cost can also be known as a
   1) fixed cost.
   2) variable cost.
   A. (1) only
   B. (2) only
   C. Both (1) and (2)
   D. Neither (1) nor (2)
2. A semi-variable cost is
   1) a combination of a fixed cost and a variable cost.
   2) labor cost on an income statement.
   A. (1) only
   B. (2) only
   C. Both (1) and (2)
   D. Neither (1) nor (2)
3. If a bar had an opening inventory of $8000, purchases of $25,000 and a closing inventory of $6000, its cost of beverages sold would be
   A. $27,000.
   B. $39,000.
   C. $23,000.
   D. $11,000.
4. Assuming the bar in question 3 had sales of $100,000, its beverage cost percentage would be
   A. 27 percent.
   B. 37 percent.
   C. 23 percent.
   D. 35 percent.
5. To obtain a gross profit percentage,
   (1) divide gross profit dollars by sales dollars.
   (2) subtract cost of beverages sold percentage from sales percentage.
   A. (1) only
   B. (2) only
   C. Both (1) and (2)
   D. Neither (1) nor (2)
6. Assume that you sold about the same amount of J&B Scotch as you did Cutty Sark Scotch, but that their costs were different. Both being call drinks, you would figure your selling price based on

A. the cost of each individually, with a different selling price for each.
B. the cost of the more expensive of the two.
C. the average cost of both.
D. both B and C are acceptable methods.

7. A case of beer cost $15 for 24 bottles. You would like to achieve a 25 percent beverage cost on your bottled beer. What would you sell a bottle for?
   A. $1.60
   B. $4.00
   C. $1.56
   D. $2.50
8. The term *bundling* most nearly means
   A. grouping together items in the storeroom for inventory purposes that are close together in cost.
   B. grouping together items that are close in cost for the purpose of setting uniform selling prices.
   C. grouping together appetizers and certain well drinks for promotional purposes.
   D. dressing in warm clothing in the winter in North Dakota.
9. Psychological pricing would most likely be used
   A. at a sports stadium.
   B. for fine wine at a white-tablecloth restaurant.
   C. in an area where there are several neighborhood bars.
   D. at a popular nightclub with entertainment.
10. There are several methods that can be employed in setting selling prices. These could include
    1) charging what your competition charges.
    2) figuring what your overall beverage cost should be in order to cover all costs and profit and charging accordingly.
    A. (1) only
    B. (2) only
    C. Both (1) and (2)
    D. Neither (1) nor (2)

Essay

You are employed by the Dimmick Drinking Emporium, which is a chain that operates upscale bars across the United States. You have been selected to teach a class of management trainees. Tell how you would explain the following items:

1. The various classifications of cost and how they affect the bar's profitability.
2. The meaning of the term *gross profit*.
3. The term *product mix*, how it can change from bar to bar, and its importance in figuring the selling price of various categories of products.
4. How price–value relationship is an important consideration when determining selling prices for drinks.
5. How to effectively use psychological pricing in a highly competitive situation.

RESOURCES

Dopson, Lea R. and Hayes, David, *Food and Beverage Cost Control*, 5th ed . (New York, NY: John Wiley & Sons, 2010).

Drysdale, John A. and Galapeu, Jennifer, *Profitable Menu Planning*, 4th ed. (Upper Saddle River, NJ: Pearson Prentice Hall, 2008).

Keister, Douglas C., *Food and Beverage Control*, 2nd ed. (Upper Saddle River, NJ: Prentice Hall, 1990).

Pavesic, David V. and Magnant, Paul F., *Fundamental Principles of Restaurant Cost Control*, 2nd ed. (Upper Saddle River, NJ: Pearson Prentice Hall, 2005).

Plotkin, Robert, *Successful Beverage Management*, (Tucson, AZ: Bar Media, 2001).

12
Controlling to a Profit

Objectives

Upon completion of this chapter, the reader should be able to:

- Write a product specification for alcoholic and nonalcoholic beverages.
- Develop a par stock figure for each beverage item in inventory.
- Explain the importance of using purchase orders.
- Describe a control state and how it affects the purchase of alcoholic beverages.
- Employ the proper procedure for receiving goods.
- Demonstrate the two methods for issuing beverages from the storeroom.
- Establish a set of controls that ensure that all beverages served are suitably paid for.
- Generate a plan to ensure that cash received is deposited in the bank.

Key Terms

Bin card
Bottle exchange
Control state
Cost of beverage sold
Credit card
Debit card
Par stock
Perpetual inventory
Physical inventory
Product specification
Purchase order
Requisition
Standard

OVERVIEW

As learned in Chapter 11, sales play an integral part in making a profit. Equally important to profit is controlling costs. In order for a bar to be profitable, sales must exceed costs. One of the most important costs that needs to be controlled is the cost of beverages. Keep in mind that alcoholic beverages are for the most part very expensive. While they are sitting in the storeroom, they represent cash that you have invested in them. You do not get a return on your investment until that inventory is sold. Therefore, it is extremely important that the inventory is on the shelf for the least amount of time. The quicker it moves through the cycle of purchasing, receiving, storage, issuing, and sales, the quicker you will receive an investment return.

Alcoholic beverages are very prone to theft. Because of this, it is imperative that tight controls be exercised throughout the process from the time they are purchased to the time they are sold. In this chapter, we will study the control of alcoholic beverages from purchasing to receiving, storing, issuing, sales, and cash. This is an important chapter as it will outline the steps necessary to achieve a profit. Skip any one of these controls, and you could lose your job or your bar.

The primary control in purchasing is the product specification. It gives a detailed account of exactly what it is that you want to purchase. Specifications should always be in writing with copies of them going to the purveyor, the receiving clerk, the bar manager, and accounting. In addition to purchasing the correct product, it is necessary to purchase the correct amount. To facilitate this, the par stock system should be used. This system ensures that the dollars invested in inventory are maximized in that there is sufficient product on hand to conduct business without wasting money on excess inventory.

Another control is the purchase order. It is a written document showing what has been ordered and the price quoted for that item. Purchase orders are important as they leave a paper trail of what has been ordered, received, placed in storage, and approved for payment. One factor that makes purchasing easier is that many states control the wholesale distribution of alcoholic beverages. These are called control states and as such control the price that is paid for product.

After the product is purchased, it is delivered and received. The receiving clerk should check the order for accuracy and put it into storage as quickly as possible to avoid theft. The storage areas should be secure, well organized, clean, and temperature controlled. Inventory should be kept in the storeroom until needed at the bar. The inventory at the bar should be kept at a minimum with sufficient product for that day's business. In order to maintain tight controls, inventory leaving the storeroom should be issued either by a bottle exchange or a requisition.

Controlling sales is an important part of the process. It is imperative that everything that is produced by the bar is paid for. Thus, a set of controls is necessary for ensuring that the cash, credit, or debit cards reflect the sales. After these are collected, it is necessary to guarantee that they arrive at the bank.

In order to figure the cost of beverages sold, an accurate inventory must be taken. Once the beverage cost is known, it can then be measured against the company standard. This quickly tells management if their controls are working.

PURCHASING ALCOHOLIC BEVERAGES

Purchasing alcoholic beverages is a relatively easy process, certainly much simpler than procuring groceries, meats, and other goods for a restaurant. The reason for this is that beverages are purchased primarily by brand name, unlike food. When purchasing produce, for example, attributes such as growing area, size of the product, variety, and degree of ripeness among other virtues need to be written into the specification. On the other hand, if you were ordering Bud Lite, you would simply specify the brand rather than going into detail about the water source, type of hops, time of aging, and other factors that go into the brewing process.

Control States

The first challenge to be encountered when purchasing alcoholic beverages is who to purchase them from. Unlike food supplies, where there are several wholesalers from which to choose, alcoholic beverage distribution normally is very limited. This is due primarily to state regulation.

While a few states allow open competition, the majority severely limit distribution. Some states control it to the point of holding a monopoly over the wholesale (and retail) selling of beer, wine, and spirits. These are known as **control states**. In a control state, the state either operates the distribution system itself or it licenses a company to do it for them. Either way, alcoholic beverages are purchased from one distributor only. There is no competition, and the state sets the price. Some states control all three—beer, wine, and spirits—while others control only one or two.

Specifications

Prior to purchasing anything, a **product specification** should be determined for each item purchased. Specifications should always be in writing and a copy given to the purveyor so that they know exactly what you want. For some items purchased, specifications must be very detailed, while for others, a brand name will suffice.

Specifications for alcoholic beverages are a prime example of using a brand name for a specification. For example, a Coors Light differs from a Miller Lite. There are subtle differences in the ingredients used and the amount of those ingredients. The brewing process is different, as is the water. The result is that the two beers taste different. Rather than writing a lengthy specification outlining the ingredients, brewing process, and so forth, the prudent operator simply states the brand name.

In addition to the brand name, the specification should include the product name, intended use, grade (in this case brand name), product size, type of container, how the containers are to be packaged, product characteristics (if any), acceptable substitutions, and general instructions to the bidders (acceptable delivery times, when payments will be made, etc.). For example,

- Product name: Light beer
- Intended use: Bottled beer sales
- Grade: Coors Light beer
- Product size: 12 ounce
- Type of container: Bottles
- Container packaging: 24 bottles to the case
- Product characteristics: Deliver chilled
- Acceptable substitutions: None
- General instructions: Invoices paid net 30. Deliveries accepted after 2:00 P.M. on our dock.

Domestic beers are sold by the U.S. ounce while imported beer, lager, and ale are normally sold in metric measurements. Wine and spirits are all sold in metric. Some of the more common containers that are used in bars and cocktail lounges, and their sizes, are as follows:

- Beer. In the United States, the sizes for beers, lagers, and ales are quite common. Note, however, there are always exceptions, particularly with imports. Domestic brews served in bars typically come in 12 ounce containers, either bottles or cans. Bottles are the most popular; however, cans are used where ambiance is not of the utmost importance. Canadian sizes are the same as in the United States for cans, but bottles are 12 Imperial ounces, which is 11.5 U.S. ounces. Imports from Europe are typically 330 milliliters or 11.2 U.S. ounces. Again, there are many exceptions to these sizes with imports. For draft beer, the most popular size of kegs for bar use are half barrel (15.5 gallons) and quarter barrel (7.75 gallons).
- Wine. Metric measurements for wine sold in the United States began in 1979. The standard size wine bottle is 750 milliliters or 25.4 ounces. This is very close to what is referred to as a fifth, which used to be a common size when purchasing spirits. This size is most popular for restaurants and bars when selling wine. Other sizes available include 50, 10, 187 (often referred to as a split), 375 (half bottle), and 500 milliliters. Larger sizes for dispensing "jug" or "house" wines include 1, 1.5 (referred to as a magnum), and 3 liter containers. The terms *split*, *half bottle*, and *magnum* are a popular nomenclature when referring to Champagne.
- Spirits. The most common sizes are 0.750 liter, close to what used to be called a fifth, and 1 liter, which is slightly bigger and close to a quart.

What to Purchase

While the makeup of alcoholic beverages is covered in other chapters, the emphasis here is on which of these beverages to purchase for a particular bar. There are many factors that affect these decisions; first and foremost are the local and state laws, which determine if you can sell beer, wine, or spirits or all three. Other factors include the availability of product, the demographics of your trade area, the type of establishment, and the clientele.

Another factor to consider is that a bar, local laws notwithstanding, must be all inclusive. That is, when customers order a drink, they expect the bar to carry it. What spirits to carry, or what types of wine, is not a consideration. Which brands to carry is a consideration, but not what types. Being "all things to all people" and carrying a tight inventory are constantly at odds with each other. The savvy operator will keep careful track of sales to determine what is selling and what has fallen out of favor with their customers.

- Beer. In days gone by, stocking beer was quite simple. Carry a half a dozen bottled brands and one or two draft beers and you were in business. Then along came regional beers, microbreweries, and craft beers, not to mention the increased interest in imported ales and lagers, and all of a sudden purchasing beer became more complex. How extensive the beer menu, and consequently the inventory, should be depends on the type of bar and the customers' demands. A small neighborhood bar in a blue-collar area can probably get by on the aforementioned six or so bottled beers and one or two draft beers, while a sophisticated upscale bar catering to the affluent twenty-something crowd will need an extensive listing of beers, both bottled and draft. Speaking of bottled and draft, this is another consideration. Should the bar carry one or the other or both? There is no question that bottled beer is easier to inventory and control, but it does not have the taste of draft beer that some customers demand. Additionally, draft beer can generate a higher profit if, and that is a big if, it is handled properly. How many times have you seen a bartender pull a draft beer from an improperly calibrated tap and continuously keep pouring beer down the drain trying for a perfect head? So much for profit. What to carry, draft and/or bottled, will ultimately be decided by the customer.
- Wines. Essential to a good wine list is variety and price. The types of wine that can be offered are red, white, rose, sparkling, and dessert. All of these categories can be offered to the customer or only a few. Sparkling and dessert wines are often omitted from bar menus but are offered on restaurant wine lists. The number of types that should be carried and the number of labels in each category depend on the clientele, the menu, and the image that you are trying to project. A rule of thumb for the average restaurant is 35 percent white and 65 percent red. However, this would change depending on the menu being offered.
- Spirits. Spirits can be broken down into four categories: well (sometimes referred to house), call, premium, and super premium. Well is the least expensive of the spirits and is used often when mixing multiple-ingredient drinks or when the customer does not have a preference and/or does not want to spend a lot of money. Well drinks are often used in promotions such as happy hours when drinks are discounted. Call spirits are more expensive than well and are used when a customer asks for a specific brand. The selling price of call drinks is usually higher than for well. Premium spirits are expensive calls and are priced accordingly, as are super premiums, which are very expensive calls. Deciding what to stock depends on the clientele of your operation.

Amount to Purchase

Because of the high cost of alcoholic beverages and the high potential for theft, it is imperative that the inventory be tightly controlled. The larger the inventory is, the greater the propensity for theft. Excess inventory will also result in a lower cash flow. Every business wants its assets in cash rather than inventory. A tight inventory is an excellent control to thwart the possibility of theft as well as to keep business's assets in cash rather than inventory.

The method used to control inventory is called **par stock**. Each and every item in inventory has a usage factor assigned to it. This usage factor is based on two things: the normal consumption of that product, from the time it is received until the time it is reordered, plus a safety factor. Keep in mind that as products are promoted or the general public's taste changes that adjustments to par stock should be made to reflect those changes.

Product	Grey Goose Vodka
Size	750 ML
Par Stock	12 Bottles

FIGURE 12.1
Example of a bin card.

The par stock is posted in the storeroom by each item in inventory. This is referred to as a **bin card**. It lists the product name, its container size, and its par stock. When the comes time to order, management goes through the storeroom, looks at the bin card, notes the item's par stock, counts the inventory on hand, and subtracts the amount in inventory from the par stock figure. The result is the amount of that product to purchase. This is then placed on the order sheet.

For example, let's assume that liquor is ordered weekly. The normal usage of Grey Goose vodka is ten bottles a week. Management has determined that it wants a safety factor of two bottles. Thus the par stock of Grey Goose is twelve bottles. When it comes time to place the liquor order, management goes through the storeroom and records the order for each item on the order sheet. When it comes to the Grey Goose shelf, it notes that there are three bottles on hand. Three bottles from the par stock of twelve leaves nine bottles to order. Figure 12.1 gives an example of a bin card.

A bin card is not to be confused with a bin number. A bin number refers to a wine inventory control number. In operations that have an extensive wine list, each wine is assigned a bin number. When a customer orders a particular bottle of wine the sommelier, wine steward, or server looks on the master list, obtains the bin number, and goes to the corresponding bin and retrieves the wine. This system greatly expedites wine service as the server does not have to search up and down racks of wine looking for a particular bottle. Coincidently each bin number has a bin card listing the name of the wine, bottle size, and par stock for that particular wine.

In larger operations where the storerooms are managed by a storeroom steward, the **perpetual inventory** method is sometimes used to reorder. A perpetual inventory is maintained on paper. It lists the amount on hand for each item in the storeroom at the beginning of the period as well as the par stock for that item. When bottles are issued to the bar from the storeroom, they are subtracted from this amount, leaving a new amount on hand. When it comes time for the steward to order, the amount on hand is subtracted from par stock and becomes the amount to order. Thus, the steward does not have to go into the storerooms and coolers to physically see what is on the shelves and execute the order from his or her desk. Refer to Figure 12.2 to see how this works.

Par stock should be followed faithfully when ordering. There are, however, exceptions to the rule. For example, when Saint Patrick's Day rolls around, most bars can expect a large sales spike in imported ales, Irish whisky, and (tacky as it is) green beer. At this time, par stock should be ignored and purchases made on the expectation of sales of those items. After the event, revert back to using par stock for those items.

Purchase Orders

Large beverage outlets or multiple-unit operations, such as hotels, use **purchase orders** when ordering. A purchase order contains the following information:

- The purveyor's name, address, and phone number.
- The purchaser's name, address, and phone number.
- The date the order is made.

FIGURE 12.2
Perpetual inventory example.

ITEM: Grey Goose vodka
PAR STOCK: 12 bottles

DATE	ON HAND	ORDERED	ISSUED	BALANCE
MM/DD/YY	12		3	9
	9		6	3
	3	9		12

- An item description, the amount ordered the unit cost, and the extension.
- The total dollar amount of the order.
- Other pertinent information such as delivery date and time, how payment is to be made, or if substitutions will be accepted.

Figure 12.3 shows an example of a purchase order.

Once a purchase order has been filled out, a copy of it goes to the following people:

- The purveyor
- The receiving clerk
- The accounts payable department
- The person authorizing the purchase order

Purchase orders are important as they leave a paper trail of what has been ordered, received, placed in storage, and approved for payment. In smaller operations that do not use purchase orders, the order sheet will suffice. In any event, a written document should be on hand for every item that has been ordered, showing the amount ordered and the price quoted for that item. With so many items to keep track of in the average bar, it is probable that the person ordering will forget the amount ordered or the price quoted for each and every item. An unscrupulous purveyor could take advantage or a common error could be made. Either way you could end up paying too much for an item or receive too little or too much. Any of these scenarios would affect the profitability of the operation.

Overland Bar and Grill
1234 Beverly
Midway KS

	Purchase Order
	#0000
	P.O. number must appear on all invoices and packages

Date: _____

Vendor: _____
_____
_____

Ship To:

Send Invoices To:	Overland Bar and Grill Attn: Accounts Payable 1234 Beverly
Same	

Quantity	Unit	Catalog#	Description	Unit Price	Total

Total: _____

Authorized Signature   Date

FIGURE 12.3
Illustration of a purchase order.

RECEIVING PROCEDURES

As mentioned earlier, alcoholic beverages have a high propensity for theft. Therefore it is imperative that they be received accurately and put into a secure storeroom as quickly as possible. When the goods arrive on the dock, the receiving clerk checks them against the invoice and the purchase order. Note that these two documents should agree as to product ordered, container size, quantity, and price. The product received should be the same as stated on the invoice and purchase order. The receiving clerk also checks for any leakage, which would indicate that the container has been damaged. Should there be a discrepancy in the order or if there is damage, it should be noted on the invoice and initialed by the receiving clerk and the driver.

When the order is verified as being correct, or any discrepancies duly noted, a copy of the invoice is signed and given to the driver. The order is then put immediately into the liquor storage room, wine storage area, or beer cooler and locked. The receiving clerk then takes the purchase order, signs it as being received, and along with the invoice sends these documents to the accounting office.

STORAGE

There are primarily three storage areas for alcoholic beverages; a liquor storage room, a wine storage room, and a walk-in cooler for beer, ale, and lager. As previously mentioned, these areas should be locked, with a member of management being the only person who has access to a key. As theft is the primary reason for a beverage cost to go out of line, it is imperative that these rooms be secure.

The storage areas should be well organized with a place for everything and everything in its place. The liquor storage room should have like products together. For example, there should be a section for Scotch, and likewise sections for Irish whisky, bourbon, domestic whiskey, gin, vodka, and liqueurs. The same holds true for the wine storage area as well. Each category should have its own section. The beer cooler should be organized in a like manner with kegs and cases of individual containers stored on pallets and off of the floor to facilitate cleaning. Speaking of cleaning, the storage areas should be kept meticulously clean at all times.

There should be a bin card for every item showing the name, brand, container size, and par stock. When stock is received, it should be stored in its proper place. This will facilitate taking inventory and replacing supplies for the bar.

Another important consideration for storage of alcoholic beverages is temperature. Spirits and liqueurs should be stored in a temperate room at 65–70°F. Wine should be stored at 56–58°F. Note that a rule of thumb is that most red wines can be served at storage temperature while most white wines should be refrigerated prior to serving. Warm storage of beer should not exceed 70°F because high temperature can cause the flavor of beer to depreciate rapidly. The best cold storage range for beer is 36–38°F. It should be noted that all keg beer and some bottled or canned beer is not pasteurized, and these products need to be refrigerated.

ISSUING

Since the storage areas for alcoholic beverages are securely locked, items needed for the bar are issued. There are two methods of issuing: a bottle exchange, used in smaller operations, or a requisition, which is used in larger operations.

With a **bottle exchange**, an empty bottle is exchanged for a full one. During the shift, as the bartender empties a bottle, it is placed in a carton and a replacement is taken off of the bar shelf. At the end of the shift, the cartons of empties are given to a member of management who goes to the storeroom and replaces the empties with full bottles. The bartender then restocks the shelves in the bar with the full bottles and the empties are destroyed by management to avoid them being used again by an unscrupulous bartender. Bottle exchanges are used for spirits and house wines only. Bottled or canned beers and ales are replaced at the bar by the case using the par stock method.

Another method of issuing alcoholic beverages is by using a requisition. A **requisition** is an order sheet requesting merchandise from the storeroom to be released to the bar. Requisitions are used in larger operations with multiple units and are usually handled by a storeroom steward. A requisition looks much like a purchase order because in many respects is serves the same function. In effect, the bar is "purchasing" items from the storeroom. Figure 12.4 shows an example of a requisition form.

A requisition is filled out by the shift bartender and is approved and signed by the bar manager. It then goes to the storeroom steward who fills the order (issues the merchandise) and delivers it to the bar. The bartender signs the requisition as having received the merchandise and then restocks the bar. What has happened here is that the responsibility for the product has shifted from the storeroom steward to the bar. It is now the responsibility of the bartender to ensure that the product is secure, properly

FIGURE 12.4
Image of a requisition.

Location _____   Requested By _____

Date   /   /   Approved By _____

Requisition

No.	Description	Quantity	Unit Price	Total
1				
2				
3				
4				
5				
6				
7				
8				
9				
10				
11				
12				
13				
14				
15				
16				
17				
18				
19				
20			TOTAL	

dispensed, and paid for by the customer in order to achieve the bar cost expected by management. After the steward has issued the merchandise, the requisition is then priced, extended, and sent to the accounting office.

Because issuing merchandise from the storeroom is done by a storeroom steward and not management, a strong set of controls is necessary to ensure that the product does not go astray while it is in the storeroom. The formula for reconciling the storeroom inventory and issues is as follows:

> Opening inventory
> + Purchases
> − Closing inventory
> = Issues

In looking at the formula more closely,

> Opening inventory (the same as the closing inventory of the previous period)
> + Purchases (the total of all invoices going into the storeroom)
> − Closing inventory (a physical inventory is taken at the end of the period)
> = Issues (the requisitions are totaled and should equal this number)

Assume that the ending inventory of the previous period was $12,000, the invoices totaled $18,000, and the closing inventory came to $10,000, the formula would look like this:

> Opening inventory $12,000
> + Purchases $18,000
> − Closing inventory $10.000
> = Issues $20,000

The total of all requisitions issued to the bars should equal $20,000. If they do not, either sloppy bookkeeping has taken place or theft has occurred, both of which are bad. In most operations, inventory reconciliation is done on a weekly basis.

PHYSICAL INVENTORY

Taking a **physical inventory** is an important part of the control process. When taking inventory, all products are counted, priced, extended, and totaled.

Counting Product

An accurate count of all products is important because if everything is not counted or the count is inflated, inaccurate information will be given to management regarding the control system or the cost of beverages sold. When counting, all bar inventory, the liquor storeroom, wine storage, and the beer cooler should be included. In addition to all alcoholic beverages, ingredients such as maraschino cherries, limes, lemons, olives, and mixes should be included. Some operations include nonfood items such as napkins, straws, and stir sticks in the beverage inventory while others categorize these as supplies.

Taking inventory is a two-person process; one person counts and one person records. At least one person, if not both, should be a member of management. There are two reasons to have a two-person team. First, the process is quicker with two people, and second, it decreases the possibility of padding the inventory to obtain a favorable, but inaccurate, beverage cost.

When counting, start at one end of the back bar and work across it and then do the front bar. Counting the bar is difficult because most, if not all, of the bottles are only partially full, and it is necessary to estimate their contents. It is best to do this in tenths, which will make it easier to price the inventory (e.g., $3/10$ of a bottle, $8/10$ of a bottle). When counting the storerooms and cooler, start on one shelf, count the entire shelf, and then go on to the next shelf. While this is a time-consuming process, it is an important function of the inventory process.

Pricing

After the inventory is taken, it should be priced. The pricing for all of the items comes from the invoice. Occasionally, the units in storage will differ from the units on the invoice. When this happens, it will be necessary to convert the invoice units to the inventory units. For example, if the bar Scotch is House of Stuart and it is invoiced by the case but inventoried by the bottle, it will have to be converted from the case price to the bottle price. Assume there are twelve bottles to the case and a case costs $100.00. The bottle price would be:

$$\$100/12 = \$8.33$$

Likewise, if on the bar, 4/10 of a bottle was inventoried, the price for the partial bottle would be:

$$\$8.33 \times 0.4 = \$3.33$$

Extending

To extend the cost of the inventory, simply multiply the number of the units by the unit price to get the extension. For example, tanking the example above of the House of Stuart Scotch, assume we had 8 and $4/10$ bottles at a cost of $8.33 per bottle. The extension would look like this:

$$\$8.33 \times 8.4 = \$69.97$$

Totaling

The extension column is then totaled to give a total for that page. All of the pages are then totaled to obtain a total beverages inventory for the period. While an inventory can be taken for any period of time, it is normally done on a monthly basis. Refer to Figure 12.5 for an example of an inventory sheet.

Electronic Applications

As can be seen, obtaining an inventory figure takes a great deal of time if it is done manually. Since this is such an important number for getting an accurate beverage cost, it is necessary to take the time to get an exact figure. In larger operations, much of the tedious work is done electronically.

The most sophisticated systems have a scanner that is passed over the bar code on the container. The person taking the inventory then counts the product and inputs the amount on a portable keypad. Since the cost of the product was put into the system when it was received, the program takes the amount of the product and multiplies it by the cost, extends it, and keeps a running total. Thus when the team finishes counting the inventory, the closing inventory number is there. While there are less sophisticated programs available, they are not as quick. However, any system that can reduce the overall amount of time spent conducting manual inventories is a plus.

FIGURE 12.5
Example of an inventory sheet.

Overland Bar and Grill
1234 Beverly
Midway KS

Physical Inventory Report				
Date:		Taken by:		
Quantity	Description	Item#	Unit Price	Total
			Total	

COST OF BEVERAGE SOLD

We have already seen how an inventory is used for reconciling the issues from the storeroom. In addition to that procedure, inventory is also a component of figuring cost of goods sold or in this case **cost of beverage sold**. Some people think that beverage cost is the cost of beverages purchased during a period. This simply is not true. While purchases are a key component of beverage cost, they are not all of the equation. We do not start a period with an empty bar or storeroom, nor do we end with one. As we learned in Chapter 11, the cost of beverage sold looks like this:

   Opening inventory
+ Purchases
= Total available
− Closing inventory
= Cost of beverage sold

Taking inventory using a scanner which is passed over a bar code.
Anatoly Vartanov/Fotolia

Once the cost of beverage sold is known, it is then divided by sales for that period to get a cost of beverage sold percentage:

$ cost of beverage sold/$ sales = cost of beverage percentage

This is important because it gives management a meaningful number to compare. For example, if the dollar cost of beverage sold in August was $10,000 and in September was $11,000, could management say that September was a bad month because the beverage cost was $1,000 higher than August? No, because the sales are unknown. If sales were $50,000 in August and $55,000 in September, the beverage cost for both months would be 20 percent.

August: $10,000/$50,000 = 20 percent cost of beverage sold

September: $11,000/$55,000 = 20 percent cost of beverage sold

We also learned in Chapter 11 that there are adjustments to be made to cost of beverages sold. After the adjustments are made to the cost of beverage sold, the formula now looks like this:

      Opening inventory
+   Purchases
=   Total available
−   Closing inventory
=   Cost of beverage sold
+   Transfers from kitchen
−   Transfers to kitchen
−   Comps
=   Net cost of beverage sold

BEVERAGE COST STANDARD

By using a beverage cost percentage, management can compare one period against other periods and can also compare the cost against a **standard**. A standard is what a cost should be and is compared to what a cost actually is. Standards are established by management to ensure that the operation is on track to achieve a profit.

For example, if it is determined that a bar must achieve a 25 percent beverage cost to be profitable, management will set the standard beverage cost at 25 percent. If the bar produces a 27 percent beverage cost, it has not met standard and corrective action needs to be taken to bring it back into line. Most costs that can be controlled—food, labor, supplies, and beverage—have standards. Quite often a manager's bonus is tied to the operation meeting the standard costs.

PRODUCTION CONTROL

While the art of mixology and tending bar is covered in detail in Chapter 10, the discussion here is limited to briefly mentioning the controls used in bartending and their importance in controlling costs. There are two primary controls used in production, and they are the standardized recipe and portion control.

Standardized recipes are an important component of the cost control system in any bar. They control the quantity and quality of ingredients used to prepare a particular drink as well as the portion that is to be served. Simply having standardized recipes in an operation is not enough; it is imperative that everyone follow them. Any deviation from the standardized recipe results not only in poor quality but also in inaccurate costs being figured for that item and, consequently, an incorrect selling price.

Portion control is equally important. It is a well-known fact that may bartenders overpour to increase their tips. There are many devices used in tending bar to control portions, including but not limited to glassware, shot glasses, jiggers, controlled pourers, and automated dispensing systems.

This is an area that management needs to keep a constant vigilance over. When bartenders overpour for patrons seated at the bar, they will underpour on the servers' drinks to make everything come out even in the end. While this may increase their tips, it will result in some disgruntled customers who are not getting what they expected. Disgruntled customers result in lost sales. Regardless, by not following standardized recipes or not pouring the correct portion, profit is lost.

SALES CONTROL

After purchasing, receiving, storage, and issuing, the product has arrived at the bar and the controls continue. It is as this juncture where product control is most important, as this is the point where most loss occurs. The action of dispensing beer and wine or producing cocktails is quite involved and is covered in Chapter 10 on mixology and production. The focus here is on making sure that the proper amount of money is received for the product that is dispensed. There are four methods that are used in the industry; however, there are only three that should be used to make sure that this happens:

- Guest check. This system is used in smaller bars. Serially numbered checks are used. Servers are issued a set of checks at the start of their shift, and their serial numbers are recorded by management. The server is responsible for these checks. When the guests order their drinks, the server records the order on the check. The check is presented to the bartender, who fills the order and, using a grease pencil, places a line under the order. This prevents the server from using the order twice to receive a second round of drinks without recording it. Another method is for the bartender to take the check and put it into the cash register, enter the dollar amount of the drinks, with that amount being printed on the guest check, and return it to the server with the drinks. This is often referred to "franking" the check. Note that the cash register must have the capability of franking checks.

  When the guests are finished, they are presented with the check and pay by cash, credit, or debit card. At the end of the shift, the server pays management

A POS system in which the server inputs the order on the touch screen and it prints out at the bar.
Courtesy of Conroy's Public House

the total of all guest checks with cash, credit, or debit card receipts. If there are any checks missing, most operations will charge the server a penalty for the missing checks. (*Note*: The penalty amount cannot bring the server's wages below the state or federal minimum wage.)

- Server pays. With this system, the server is issued a bank at the start of the shift. The servers then pay the bartender for the drinks when they pick them up. At the end of the shift, the bank is returned to management. While this system is an excellent control system, it is somewhat cumbersome in that the bartender has to ring up every order and in some cases give change to the server. Also, its use is limited to those operations that have high cash sales. In bars where credit or debit cards are the preferred method of payment, its use would cause an extremely large bank being given to the server.

- POS system. The point of sale (POS) system is the most widely used system in the industry. While originally used in large operations only, its cost has come down so that today many smaller operations are using it. The reason it is the most widely used system is that it has a very strong set of controls. The server inputs the guest's order into the system. The order is printed out at the bar. The bartender fills the order, and the server delivers it to the guest. It is quick and efficient, and all orders are in the system. An extension of the POS system is the automated bar distribution system. It will not dispense product until it has been put into the POS system.

- Oral orders. This system is used in many small bars. It operates on blind trust. The server takes the guest's order and calls it out to the bartender, who fills it, and the server takes it to the guest. There is no paper trail. The server collects the money from the guest and either turns it in to the bartender or turns it in at the end of the shift. While this system is used frequently in small bars, it is not secure and should only be used where the bartender and the owner are one and the same person.

When choosing a system of cash controls, keep in mind that none of them are foolproof. Any person with a minimal degree of common sense can figure out a way to beat a system. The objective is to put as many deterrents as possible in their way to discourage theft. The oral order system has no deterrents. The bartender or the server can easily steal. When using the guest check, server pays, or POS systems, there has to be collusion between the server and the bartender. This is a strong deterrent, but not unbeatable. The POS in conjunction with the automated pour system is the strongest in terms of control.

Management should always be vigilant by making frequent trips behind the bar to ensure there is no money being left out and that all bottles are in their place. This is also an excellent opportunity to visit with customers and make them feel welcome. If the bartender and servers know that you are going to be in and out on a frequent basis, they will be less apt to steal.

The income statement should also be reviewed to see if the beverage cost is meeting the company's standard. This is the surest way to find out if there is anything amiss in the operation. If the beverage cost is higher than standard, everything from purchasing through service should be checked for any leakage in the system.

CASH CONTROL

One of the most crucial functions in the control system is sales control, be it cash, check, or credit or debit card. While all of these controls are important, cash is probably the most important as it is the most susceptible to theft. Before a discussion on cash controls can be started, management needs to decide how cash is to be handled. There are two methods that are predominately used in the beverage industry: (1) each server is given a bank and is responsible for handling his or her own cash, or (2) the server pays the bartender for drinks as they are prepared and the bartender is then responsible for all cash. In either case the procedure is as follows:

- The person responsible is issued a bank containing coin and bills.
- At the end of the shift, the sales for that person (server or bartender) are totaled by either obtaining a total from the POS system or the cash register, or by totaling the guest checks. The person then turns in that total plus the bank total that was issued to him or her at the start of the shift. The amount turned in can be made up of cash, checks (if accepted), and credit or debit card receipts.
- When using a cash register, a key is needed to total the register at the end of the shift. This is also known as the Z key and the process is called Z'ing the register. The Z key should only be used by a member of management. Some operations subtotal the register at the end of the shift, and this subtotal is subtracted from the previous subtotal to get the sales for that shift.

Figure 12.6 shows an example of a cash reconciliation sheet that is used at the end of a shift to ascertain that all income is accounted for.

FIGURE 12.6

Example of a cash reconciliation sheet.

```
Date:   / /        Shift: _____
Manager:      _____
Cashier:      _____
Audited By: _____


Register Reading                    $_____
Less Previous Register Reading  $_____
Sales                               $_____

Less Approved Overings          $_____
Net Sales                                        $_____

Cash                                $_____
Checks                              $_____
Credit                              $_____
Other                               $_____
Total Receipts                                   $_____

Less Authorized Paid Outs       $_____
Less Authorized Comps           $_____
Net Receipts                                     $_____

Over <Short>                                     $_____
```

CHECK CONTROL

First, the operation must decide if it is going to accept checks. With the amount of "bad paper" floating around it is probably a wise decision not to accept checks. Shakey's Pizza used to have a sign that read:

Shakey made a deal with the bank.

Shakey's won't cash checks and the bank won't make pizza.

However, it is sometimes necessary to cash checks to retain customers. This is particularly true of neighborhood bars. If checks are accepted, there should be a clear policy that outlines the procedure. Many a bar has wound up in legal trouble because it cashed some checks but not others, as the person did not look trustworthy. Accept checks for the amount of purchase only (including tip). The check should be written on a local bank. The check should look normal, that is, have a perforated edge, be numbered, and have the name address and phone number of the person or business writing the check. When cashing the check, have the person show a picture ID and make sure that the numerical amount agrees with the written amount, that the check is signed, and that the name of the bar is written on the payee line.

CREDIT AND DEBIT CARD CONTROL

From the point of view of the bar owner/manager, credit cards and debit cards are handled the same way. The primary difference is with the customer. When a **credit card** is used, the customers have a specified period of time before they have to pay the charge. They also have the option of paying the amount over a period of time. If they pay their charges in full on or before the due date, there is no finance charge. If they pay it off over a period of time, a finance charge is added to the amount that has been charged. A **debit card**, on the other hand, is much like writing a check. When a debit card is used, that amount is immediately deducted from the account.

There are two ways to handle credit and debit cards. One is manual, which is all but obsolete. When the customer charges, the card number and amount is phoned into a processing center and approved. The bar then manually writes in the amount of the transaction along with the approval number and runs it through an impression machine, which transposes the credit card number and expiration date. The customer signs the slip and the bar sends it to the bank with the regular cash deposit.

The second and most common method of handling credit and debit cards is to transmit them electronically. The customer, upon receipt of the check, gives his or her credit or debit card to the server. The server runs it through a terminal. An alternative means of handling this is that the customer is given a handheld device wherein the customer runs the card through the terminal. Some of the advantages of having the customers complete the transaction themselves are as follows:

- An unscrupulous server cannot copy the customer's credit card number and code number and use these numbers for online purchases.
- A server or bartender cannot add a tip or change the amount of the tip by adding a digit such as a $6.00 tip becoming a $16.00 tip.
- An employee cannot create a second bogus charge to the card and turn the receipt in with the cash at the end of the shift after taking that amount in cash out of the register or their bank. Everything would balance.

In either case, the magnetic strip on the card contains the card number, which is sent to the processing center with the amount charged. The customer's account is charged for that amount and the bar's bank account is credited with that amount. The customer then signs the charge slip. In some cases where the charge is minimal, say under $20, a signature is not required.

In both cases the charge slip is very similar to cash. It is also the only evidence the bar has that the transaction occurred should a discrepancy arise with the credit card company.

Many people have a false sense of security with credit and debit cards. Consider that during the transmission, the credit card information can be "hacked" with the customer's personal information being compromised by individuals who then sell this information to a third party.

CONCLUSION

In this chapter, we learned that alcoholic beverages are very prone to theft. The author recalls several bar consulting jobs where controls were installed and several of the staff quit. In most cases, it is assumed that since they could no longer augment their income, they went elsewhere where it was easier to ply their trade. If you are a single proprietor tending your own bar, you do not need controls. As soon as you hire another bartender and some servers, you need controls. Keep in mind that people who steal sooner or later get caught. The purpose of controls is to make it sooner rather than later. The longer theft goes on, the more money you lose. While it is a fact that most employees are honest, a few will steal if given the opportunity and a few will attempt to subvert the system. It is for these few that controls are necessary.

Alcoholic beverages are controlled from the purchasing process to receiving, storing, issuing, production, sales, and finally cash control. The controls in purchasing involve the product specification and the purchase order. When receiving goods, they should be checked against the invoice and the purchase order and be put away in a locked storage room. Goods should be dispensed from the secure store room by management. Production of alcoholic beverages should be tightly controlled through the use of standardized recipes and portion control devices. Sales and cash should be closely monitored.

A story has been told of a bar manager who hired a new bartender. I'll pay you $100 a shift, the manager told the bartender. I'll take $100 a shift, the bartender told the manager. Sure enough, he did.

Case Study

You have just received your degree from one of the better hospitality management programs in the country. After weighing several offers, you have decided to accept a proposal from a dinner theater to become their beverage manager. They have offered you a good salary, with a very generous bonus if you meet a standard beverage and labor cost.

The operation is located in a large midwestern city and seats around 1,000 patrons. The plays are mostly comedies and musicals and normally feature a well-known star. The guests have reserved seating at tables that are arranged so that all guests are facing the stage. The dinner is served buffet style prior to the play. The majority of the patrons order cocktails, wine, or beer prior to dinner and during intermission. There is also a small bar located off of the lobby that serves cocktails as the guests arrive.

While the dinner theater is open six nights a week, the hours are great in that you normally report to work at 4:00 P.M. to supervise the set up and since not drinks are served after intermission, you are usually out of there by 10:00 P.M. Once a week you have to go in early to order supplies, make out schedules, attend a staff meeting, and perform other administrative duties.

As you settle into your job, you start to notice several things that bother you. The general manager has told you to order all of the liquor from one distributor that happens to be owned by his brother-in-law. The chef helps herself to wine for cooking purposes, bottles of wine or spirits are sent to the star's dressing room, and management "comps" drinks. None of this is accounted for. Drinks are ordered verbally from three service bars with no records being made. The bartender in the lobby bar free pours all of his drinks.

Because of these and other problems, you are not making the standard beverage cost and therefore not receiving any bonus. Explain how you would proceed to bring costs into line so that you can get your bonus.

QUESTIONS

1. Explain what a control state is and how it affects the purchase of alcoholic beverages.

2. What is the difference between a purchase specification and a purchase order, and how does each of them play a part in the control of alcoholic beverages?

3. For each of the following beverages, give the unit of measurement that it is produced and sold in:
   Domestic wine
   Bourbon
   Imported wine
   Domestic beer
   Gin
   Vodka
   Imported ale

4. Assume the par stock of Heinekens is six cases, on average a case is used every day, the order you are preparing will be delivered in two days, and there are three cases on hand. How many cases do you order?

5. Differentiate between a perpetual inventory and a physical inventory. Which is more accurate? Why?

Which could be used when purchasing stock? Which is used in figuring cost of beverage sold?

6. You are the general manager of a very hip nightclub on the Strip in Las Vegas. You have just hired a new receiving clerk. Explain her duties to her.

7. What are the two methods of issuing alcoholic beverages from the storeroom? Give an application for each.

8. Give and explain the formula for a storeroom check and balance.

9. What is the step-by-step procedure for figuring the ending inventory for a beverage outlet?

10. After cost of beverage sold is figured, what adjustments are made to arrive at the net cost of beverage sold?

11. Define the term *standard* and give an example of how it helps management control their beverage cost.

12. Explain the four methods of cash control used in beverage management. Which one(s) are best and which ones(s) are unacceptable? Why?

RESOURCES

Dopson, Lea R. and Hayes, David, *Food and Beverage Cost Control*, 5th ed. (New York, NY: John Wiley & Sons, 2010).

Katsigris, Costas and Thomas, Chris, *The Bar & Beverage Book*, 4th ed. (Hoboken, NJ: John Wiley & Sons, 2007).

Keister, Douglas C., *Food and Beverage Control*, 2nd ed. (Upper Saddle River, NJ: Prentice Hall, 1990).

Kotschevar, Lendal H. and Tanke, Mary L., *Managing Bar and Beverage Operations* (East Lansing, MI: Educational Institute of the American Hotel and Motel Association, 1996).

Pavesic, David V. and Magnant, Paul F., *Fundamental Principles of Restaurant Cost Control*, 2nd ed. (Upper Saddle River, New Jersey, Pearson Prentice Hall, 2005).

Plotkin, Robert, *Successful Beverage Management*, 1st ed. (Tucson AZ, Bar Media, 2001).

13
Marketing

Objectives

Upon completion of this chapter, the reader should be able to:

- Design a marketing plan for a beverage outlet.
- Compare the importance of demographics as it relates to the existing and potential customer.
- Apply feasibility studies, demographic surveys, psychographic studies, and personal knowledge to the development of a marketing plan.
- Conduct a SWOT analysis to determine the strengths, weaknesses, opportunities, and threats of an existing beverage operation.
- Describe how place, product, price, and promotion fit into the marketing strategy of a business.
- Implement a pricing strategy that will increase sales and customer satisfaction.
- Compare the advantages and disadvantages of happy hour promotions.
- Demonstrate how to carry out a tasting or pairing promotion.
- Explain the methods of promotion to communicate the marketing message to potential customers.
- Plan a public relations campaign using personal contacts and publicity.
- Analyze and measure the return on investment from the results of a marketing program.

OVERVIEW

As we develop our discussion of marketing, it is helpful to discuss two of the key terms and definitions used. First, what is meant by the term "marketing"? Perhaps the most basic definition is that **marketing** is the creation of a want or desire and the provision of a product or service that satisfies that want or desire. Contrast this definition with one for **sales**, which can be defined as the actual transaction of exchanging money or an asset for the means of fulfillment. For example, you are watching television, and during the commercial break you see an ad for a new menu offering at Cousin Billie's Bar and Grill. The commercial tells you that it is available for a limited time only. You do not want to miss this new menu item, so you go to try it. The ad has succeeded in creating a need and provided you with a means of fulfilling it. When you arrive at Cousin Billie's, you are given their regular menu that highlights the special offering. There is even a table-tent that promotes it further. These all serve to remind you of the "need" you came to the restaurant to fulfill. When you order the item, the marketing cycle is complete, and the sales cycle begins.

Marketing starts with the study of the beverage outlet's location and ascertaining who the potential customer is. This is known as demographics. To comprehend an operation's demographics, surveys and psychographic studies are used along with management's own personal knowledge of the area.

In addition to referring to the demographics of the area, it is a good idea to take an internal inventory to investigate the strengths and weaknesses of the operation as well as looking at opportunities and threats to the business. This is known as a SWOT analysis.

Four key marketing aspects are place, product, price, and promotion. These are known as the four Ps of marketing. Customers come to the bar; the bar does not go to customers. The important marketing concept with place is that the bar must attract customers to go to it. Product refers to what the bar sells and what it is known for. The product must fit the demographic makeup of the bar's trade area. Price is not only the amount charged for beverages; it also takes into account discounts such as those given during happy hour or for a specific promotional campaign. Advertising, also called promotion, is used to encourage customers to come into the bar. Promotion is also conducting various events such as wine tastings or pairings.

There are some other Ps in marketing: public relations, publicity, and personal contact. Public relations involve establishing an image for the business, what it stands for, and how it interrelates with the community. Publicity is free advertising such as the bartender appearing on a local television show demonstrating how to make a martini. Publicity for the most part is good for the bar, but it can also be negative, such as a fight outside the bar being shown on the local news. Personal contact is the bar owner or manager being involved in community clubs and organizations and networking with people who could be potential customers of the business.

After examining the demographics, doing a SWOT analysis, and exploring the vehicles available to promote the business, it is time to create a plan. The plan should include the specific objectives that management wants to achieve. These objectives should be measurable. A budget should be established and analyzed to see if the objectives can be achieved given the resources available. After the marketing campaign, the results should be determined by measuring the results against the projections and performing a return on investment (ROI) analysis.

Throughout the entire process the employees should be consulted and kept appraised of the process as it evolves. After all, the success of any marketing campaign is dependent on the employees buying into it. If they are not on board, it will not be successful.

MARKET SEGMENTATION

The study of location and the potential customer is known as **demographics**. More specifically, it is the statistical data of an area and its population's characteristics, including, but not limited to, the average age, income, education, ethnicity, rental housing versus owned, and number of cars per household. In order to use demographics properly in marketing, two factors must be evaluated: (1) the demographic study itself—in other words, identifying the customer in the market and (2) the matching of these customers, along with their needs and preferences, to the proper beverage offerings and, in the case of a restaurant, the menu. First, let's look at the demographic study itself. How does it develop? There are four sources for this information:

- Feasibility studies. A **feasibility study** is a creative, objective, and rational process whereby marketing and financial data are collected and analyzed. It is an in-depth study that attempts to predict with reasonable accuracy whether a potential business will succeed or fail. Feasibility studies are quite large, sometimes running several hundred pages in length. They are very complete documents that explore every variable that would indicate whether a business has the potential to make a profit.
- Demographic surveys. For those beverage outlets and restaurants that do not feel a complete feasibility study is needed, **demographic surveys** are available from a number of companies for a reasonable fee. These firms have the demographics for the entire United States computerized. Many of them even make this information available on the Internet. To be helpful in planning a marketing strategy, demographic studies must be focused on the particular location, such as a specific zip code or a street intersection. Fortunately, these studies

Matador/Fotolia

can be broken down to any size quadrant for any area that the customer desires. Demographic studies list the general population by age group, median age, ethnic origins, household type, marital status, occupation, education, housing, income, number of vehicles, and other related data. Specialized data can also be obtained that detail consumer restaurant and bar expenditures for the area and can further refine this statistic by giving a breakdown by category such as quick service, coffee shop, fine dining, and so on.

- Psychographic studies. In addition to demographic studies, **psychographic studies** can also be helpful to the marketing undertaking. This data is sometimes referred to as a VALS study as it concentrates on information about the values, attitudes, and lifestyle preferences of the population being studied. For example, a psychographic study might reveal information about how frequently the people in a community dine out, how much they spend on average, and what their habits are with regard to recreational, educational, and cultural activities. These studies can also reveal information about how daring or traditional a group of people is. This information can be of notable assistance when designing a marketing strategy. It can also be very useful in planning not only a bar concept but the actual bar menu for the operation as well. Just as in the case of demographic profiles, the Internet can be an excellent source of preliminary psychographic information.

- Personal knowledge. Finally, do not discount your own knowledge, even a feeling, for an area when developing a marketing plan. After all, you know your customers: their product preferences, their price point tolerance, and their penchant for service. If used properly, a personal feel for the market is an important tool because demographic studies look at an area with cold, hard facts. Knowledge of situations behind these facts is very important. For example, if the demographic study of an area indicates that the average income is in the upper middle range and that a large share of the market owns their home, this indicates at the outset that your customer is willing to spend money. However, if the majority of people in the target area have their homes heavily mortgaged, their disposable income is lower and their propensity to spend is less. They may be more driven to two-for-one happy hour promotions than to purchasing premium beverages.

On the other hand, even though you know your customers, there are many others in your market area who are not frequenting your establishment. By studying the demographics of your market area, you will most likely uncover potential customers. By concentrating your marketing efforts towards these people, you will develop new customers and therefore increase sales and profit.

SWOT ANALYSIS

After studying the external market area and determining the customer's wants and needs, it is time to turn the focus inward and study the internal environment. In order for a marketing strategy to be successful, the external forces must be combined with internal information to develop a successful program. This is best accomplished by conducting a **SWOT analysis**. This study helps management determine the operations strengths, weaknesses, opportunities, and threats (SWOT). The first two parts, strengths and weaknesses, are primarily internal; that is, what are the strong points of your bar and what are the weak points? The second two parts, opportunities and threats, are primarily external, although some could be internal as well. For example, if you identified holes in the parking lot pavement as a weakness of your operation, repaving it could turn the weakness into a strength as well as a marketing opportunity.

Taking into consideration the SWOT analysis along with the demographic study, a comprehensive marketing plan can now be developed.

It is extremely important when conducting a SWOT analysis that the person or persons doing the evaluation be completely neutral in their observations. For this reason it is best to have an outside consultant come in and perform the evaluation. If this is not economically feasible, it can be done internally. If it is done internally, it is best to use several people in order to keep partiality at a minimum.

Strengths

First off, what does the operation excel at? What does it do better than any other business in the market area? Look at all of the operational aspect of your bar: service; quality of drinks; extent of the wine list; selection of beers, lagers, and ales; price point; atmosphere; décor; cleanliness; location; and parking, among others. Is it the only operation of its type, such as brew pub, sports bar, or dance club? Look for any other characteristics that your business has that others do not. Are you the only one in the market, or do you do whatever it is you do better than anyone else in the market?

Weaknesses

In evaluating the strengths of your bar, if the answer to any of the operational aspects was no, then these are probably weaknesses. If the service is not outstanding, then it is a weakness. Weaknesses are not all bad because management can eliminate them and turn them into strengths. In the case of service, additional training may be necessary, or in severe cases maybe some personnel need to be replaced. If service is lacking due to high turnover, the reason needs to be found. Are the working conditions poor, tips low, management's attitude bad? The reason needs to be found and corrected.

Not every negative response to a strength is necessarily a weakness. If you are running a brew pub, customers do not expect you to have the most extensive wine list in the market area. However, if the beverage operation is part of a white-tablecloth restaurant, the wine list should be extensive. If not, then in this case it is a weakness.

When evaluating weaknesses, look outside the business. Are there any barriers that affect it? Lack of parking, train tracks blocking traffic, or construction can all be weaknesses. Some can be corrected; some cannot. The marketing plan should address those weaknesses that can be corrected and neutralize those that cannot.

Opportunities

Some of the weaknesses, particularly those in the operational analysis, can be turned into opportunities. As previously mentioned, upgrading and training the staff can improve service. When operational weaknesses have been corrected and improved, these should be marketed. Previous customers who were put off by bad service, poor quality drinks, a dirty operation, or whatever could be persuaded to return.

Additionally, external opportunities should be sought. This could be a change in the competitive landscape, a new office building in the market area, or neighborhood improvements, to name a few. These should be marketed as well. For example, if a competitor were to go out of business, find out the demographic makeup of its customers and market to their wants and needs.

Threats

Threats are normally external. It is very important to recognize threats that are on the horizon in order to attack them. It could be a new competitor coming into your market, or it could be road construction outside of your establishment. In this case, work with the city in advance to set up an alternate plan to get to your place of business.

Have them erect signage to direct customers to the alternate route. Make this a part of your marketing plan. Introduce a new "hard hat" drink, extend happy hour, and give away free hors d'oeuvres to offset the loss of business during the construction period.

Other forms of threats include but are not limited to a price war with a competitor, recession, bad publicity resulting from a fight in your parking lot, and ordinances passed by the city council or the state alcoholic beverage commission affecting your ability to do business; the list goes on and on. Threats must not be taken lightly or ignored because they will influence your sales. Rather, tackle them head on by putting a positive spin on whatever is that is threatening the business.

THE FOUR MARKETING Ps

The four Ps—place, product, price, and promotion—are key aspects of marketing. They serve as the framework of the marketing plan and ensure that the unique aspects of the operation are considered. Many times they are referred to as the marketing mix. In the case of beverage operations, the four Ps are used by management to categorize their marketing strategies.

Place

Place refers to the actual beverage outlet, its location, and its means of distribution. For bars, location is really the most important element, because they typically distribute their products and services only through their location. An exception to this would be an off-premise catering company that served alcoholic beverages as well. Be that as it may, this means that the customers must make a decision to go to the bar rather than having the bar come to them.

For this reason, other elements such as the demographics surrounding the operation and the local competition are very important to the operations success. For example, a blue-collar bar that sells primarily draft and bottled beer and well or house liquor would not do well in an upscale, high-income neighborhood. Conversely, a martini bar using premium liquor would not do well in a lower-income neighborhood location.

Place refers to the beverage outlet.
Dimitri Surkov/Fotolia

Product

Product is what is for sale along with the business's concept and theme. In the case of a bar, we have tangible products (beer, wine, and spirits) and intangible products (service, atmosphere). A successful marketing plan therefore focuses on the unique aspects of the operation, both tangible and intangible. Product can be presented in advertisements before a guest even sets foot in the operation or sees the menu. It is important to remember that although you are marketing a product, an expectation is formed in the potential customer's mind, and when the customer visits the bar, this expectation must be met.

Two methods of getting customers into your establishment and introducing them to your products, service, and atmosphere are through tastings and pairings.

- **Tastings.** Wine tastings are the most popular example of this method of marketing. However, beer tastings as well as single malt scotch tastings are trendy as well. Often an expert such as a vintner or distiller is brought in to conduct such tastings. This is an especially good promotion if the bar can legally sell beverages by the bottle or case. Customers, particularly if they taste something for the first time, will want to purchase more of the product to take home with them. Quite often, food is served that is compatible to the product being tasted. If the bar is in conjunction with a restaurant, this serves a twofold purpose as it shows off the culinary offerings of the operation and also helps maintain a reasonable alcohol level for the customer.

- **Pairings.** Very similar to tastings that serve food, but in pairings, the compatibility between the beverage and the food is emphasized. Frequently, these are cohosted, with the chef explaining the food and the beverage expert describing the beverage. These can be conducted using wine, beer, or spirits.

Tangible products of a bar: beer, wine, and spirits.
draghicich/Fotolia

Pairings are often cohosted with the chef and beverage experts.
CandyBox Images/Fotolia

Price

Price is the charge for the products and services provided by the bar. The price must be set at a level that the customer perceives as a good value as well as being competitive with other operations in the market area. At the same time, the selling price must allow the bar to achieve its profit goals. Sometimes an operation decides to offer one or more items at a reduced price, even below profitable levels, as a special promotion to entice more customers into the bar. A word of caution: Several states do not allow customers to be enticed to drink in any way, while some others do not allow pricing to be used to entice customers into a drinking establishment. Make sure you understand your state's laws before trying any of these enticements. If the law is not standing in the way, there are several ways to increase awareness of a beverage operation. Following are some examples:

Happy hour advertisement.
Brad Pict/Fotolia

- **Discounting.** A percentage is taken off the normal retail price of the item. Discounts can be 10 percent, 25 percent, or even 50 percent (half off) of the regular price. This can be an effective way to entice regular customers to trade up. Discounting can be an ongoing promotion or used on a one-time basis. For example, a regular who frequents your bar always drinks bar scotch on the rocks. By discounting one of the single malt scotches, she is persuaded to purchase it. She likes it and thereafter orders the single malt. By discounting the single malt on one night, a regular has been converted to purchasing it at the normal price on successive nights.
- Buy one, get one free (**BOGO**). With this promotion, the customer buys a particular drink or beer determined by management, and the second is free. A variation of this promotion, where food is sold, is one in which the customer selects any sandwich or entrée from the menu and gets the second (which has the same or lesser value) free. Because the discount is so steep on this promotion, it often comes with restrictions such as only being available on slow nights or during slow periods. Discounting and buy one get one free BOGO are often used during an operation's happy hour.

On the subject of happy hours, many operators do not like the idea for several reasons. One is the risk of a lawsuit or citation by the state for an overly intoxicated customer who was "enticed" into buying extra drinks because of the value offered. Another reason is that happy hours are usually held during what is one of the bar's highest demand periods, which is immediately after the customer gets off of work. There are very few industries that discount their product during a high-demand period. The reason many bars conduct happy hours is that everyone else does and they are afraid of discontinuing it as they will lose sales to their competitors. Some states have outlawed happy hours and discounting to reduce the number of DUIs and alcohol-related accidents. In doing so, they have inadvertently solved one of a bar manager's greatest problems and unknowingly increased the bar's profits.

- **Bundling.** This method is taking two or three items and bundling them together to create better value. Often a restaurant that has a Sunday brunch will offer free Champagne, Bloody Marys, or mimosas to its customers.
- **Coupons.** Many drinking establishments use coupons in conjunction with any one of the previously discussed promotions. The customer must present a coupon in order to participate. The use of coupons helps control the amount of promotional activity generated. There are two schools of thought on coupons: One is to use them sparingly, because you do not want your regular customers to wait

for a coupon to visit your bar. The other is to present coupons regularly. Resort areas such as Las Vegas and Reno use this method of promotion repeatedly, giving away free Bloody Marys or free draws to entice customers into the casinos to gamble. Few people pay regular price for these items.

- **Co-op marketing.** This is quite popular in the beverage business. Co-op marketing is where a beverage manufacturer or wholesaler works with a bar to promote its product. This becomes a win–win as the beverage company increases exposure to its product and the bar increases its sales. Beer companies use this promotional method quite often as do companies that distribute spirits.

Promotional pricing should be managed carefully to ensure that discounts do not have a negative impact on the bottom line of the operation.

Promotion

Promotion refers to all the methods used to communicate the marketing message to potential customer. If successful, promotional activities generate more patrons for the operation, resulting in higher revenues. Without question, the menu is one of the most important promotional tools and serves as the foundation of the entire marketing effort. The menu must be compatible with the demographics of the restaurant's customer. The same goes for promotion, in that the promotional media must cater to the demographics of the targeted guest. Sponsoring a sports talk show makes perfect sense for a sports bar but is hardly worth the money for a high-ticket white-tablecloth restaurant. Methods for promotion are limitless. Some are costly, whereas for others the cost is negligible. There are many opportunities that bar managers have to promote their operations. Some of the more popular options are as follows:

Television   Without a doubt, television is the most costly of all of the mass media promotional opportunities. First, the spot must be produced, which is costly because it usually involves actors or animation, sound, and visuals. Second, the airtime must be purchased. National network television advertising is usually limited to large chain operations that sell food in addition to alcoholic beverages.

Although television is very expensive, there are strategies that smaller operations can use, such as placing advertisements on cable television channels viewed by their target markets. Cable-channel advertising is much less expensive than broadcast-channel advertising. Sports bars can advertise on sports channels while upscale bars can advertise on the food channels. Spot ads run during local breaks of nationally syndicated shows on network television can also, at times, be less expensive. Of course, even small operations must be sure that the video used to produce the commercial is of good quality and has a professional air about it. The major advantage of television advertising is that, because of sound and visuals, viewers tend to retain the message longer. It also has the advantage of reaching a large number of potential customers quickly.

Radio   Radio is lower in cost than television, thus making it affordable to both large chains and smaller, independently operated bars because of lower production costs, as only sound is involved and there is a lower rate for airtime. By carefully selecting programs that appeal to the demographic makeup of their customer base, a bar can saturate the market with information about its operation: its theme, décor, ambiance, beverage and food menu, and promotional activities. Although retention is less than with television ads, the lower cost allows restaurants to repeat the ads more often. If the local radio station has a special program focused on food and entertainment, placing an ad during that program can be very effective, because the operation

Radio is an effective
promotional strategy.
Tsian/Fotolia

has direct access to people who are interested in food, drink, and dining out. Other promotional strategies can be used as well, such as hosting a broadcast from the bar and giving away gift certificates through the program (assuming they are allowed by local law).

Newspaper Newspaper advertising is another low-cost marketing format. While circulation has been dropping recently, it can still be a viable option. Again, two costs are involved. First, the layout must be produced professionally, and second, the advertising space must be purchased. Newspaper advertising is very flexible in that it can be changed quickly. It has immediacy about it. It is news; it is what is happening now. The fact that a newspaper reaches a large number of people is both an advantage and disadvantage. Reaching the masses has the potential to bring in a number of new customers; however, many of the readers are not in the demographic realm of the bar, and therefore the coverage is wasted. The fact that a newspaper is normally read quickly and sometimes only skimmed by its reader means that the advertisement must be eye catching and state its message quickly and succinctly.

Newspapers are a low-cost
marketing format.
jfv/Fotolia

Magazines Magazines, although an effective marketing tool for many businesses, are probably not as useful for the beverage industry because they have a relatively high cost in comparison to newspaper advertising and there is a much longer production time required. Thus, they have little immediacy and cannot be used for a short-term promotional activity. As opposed to newspapers, which are read quickly and then recycled, magazines are often read several times over a given period. Because of this, magazine advertising should be used for a more long-term approach and espouse a restaurant's theme, atmosphere, ambiance, décor, or service as opposed to a short-term promotional activity. An advantage of magazine advertising is that you can target specific demographic audiences as well as reach several people per issue, because more than one person typically reads them. They also have excellent reproductive qualities as opposed to newspapers and can therefore be used to show pictures of plate presentations or interior or exterior shots of the restaurant. Many bars and clubs use local magazines to promote their business.

Outdoor Advertising   Outdoor advertising refers primarily to billboards as opposed to a bar's exterior signage on a building. As it is relatively expensive, its use is normally restricted to large chains. There are several costs associated with outdoor signs. One is the design of the sign, the second is the production costs, and the third is the rental fee of the billboard itself. If properly located, it can reach a large number of potential customers; however, not all of them will be demographically linked with the operations customer base. Because the majority of viewers pass it by relatively quickly, the message must be limited, succinct, and eye catching to have any lasting effect on the reader.

Direct Mail   Direct mail, like almost all forms of advertising, has several costs involved with it, including design and production costs as well as delivery costs, either by door-to-door distribution or via postage. Direct mail can be easily targeted to the desired demographic base using zip codes. Because of this, it can have a direct and personalized message. Although reaching many potential customers at a relatively low cost, many people perceive direct mail as "junk mail" and do not bother to read it.

The Internet   The Internet can be a very cost effective tool for promotion. Social media has become a very important part of the marketing process. It includes forms of electronic communication such as websites for social networking and microblogging through which users create online communities to share information, ideas, personal messages, and other content, such as videos.

The Internet can be an effective promotional tool if used properly.
bloomua/Fotolia

Website A website for a bar can be established for a minimal cost. For example, the entire menu can be presented as well as photographs, awards, special offerings, customer testimonials, and staff profiles. The key here is that the website should look and function as professionally as possible. A poorly designed website can give a poor impression of the operation. You may want to view other professional websites before designing one for your business.

While you may opt to do it yourself, keep in mind that there are numerous companies available to assist you with creating and maintaining a professional website for a fee. Many of them provide a one-stop-shopping experience, including purchasing a domain name and building the actual website, as well as various additional services for the website creation and maintenance process. You can use all of their services or a few depending on your level of involvement and expertise.

You may want to investigate and utilize a third-party vendor which will do all of the work for you. A professionally developed website has the capability of allowing customers to take a virtual video tour of the establishment, allowing them to see the business first-hand, as if they were actually on site. Consideration should also be given to creating links on other related websites. Use caution when adding your bar's website link to other related websites. Ensure the proper audience is included, and the website you are adding your link to is appropriate to your business.

In addition to a website, there are other Internet options. Social media resources such as Facebook, Twitter, LivingSocial, and Groupon have become commonplace in the marketing arena.

Facebook Facebook, a social networking website, reaches over 400 million people. With Facebook, you can create a "page" for your business, which can include logistical information, current promotions, special announcements, and other marketing tactics in an attempt to entice potential customers to visit your establishment. Facebook also has a marketing section of their site titled "Facebook offers," which brings people to your business with an offer they can claim and share with their friends. An example of an offer could be a buy one get one free drink offer or a meal at a discounted price. You may also influence your audience by creating unique posts and updates on your page, whether it is to visit your establishment, purchase a discounted offer, or update your audience on the latest and greatest drink selections for your business. Options for posting a message include text, web links, pictures, and videos.

Twitter Twitter, another social media resource for promoting your business, allows your customer to "follow" people or businesses which they find interesting. You can create "Tweets"—short messages of 140 characters or less, which can include a website link or a link to a specific picture or video. Although Twitter does not post videos directly on the site itself as part of the tweet, you can create a link to another site, such as your website, and post it in your tweet.

When creating your Twitter account, you have the option of adding a personalized profile within your account. This is important as your profile assists in the branding of your business. Within your profile, you can create a background, post a small message describing your business, as well as add a picture to represent your business. The profile also lists the amount of tweets you have created thus far, the amount of people or businesses you are following, and the number of people or businesses that are following you.

LivingSocial LivingSocial is a website that lists daily deals specific to your city. For a fee, LivingSocial can publicize your business by offering discounted deals with the expectation of drawing customers to your business.

The website contains a features section, which includes "Feature Deals," "Popular Deals," and "Most Shared," as well as categories for family deals, food and drink, and health and beauty, to name a few. Consumers can create an account, select their home city or nearby vicinity, and receive offers via email for deals in their particular area or peruse the website to find deals. The consumer can then buy the deal by providing his or her payment information

It is very important to remember when creating a deal for your bar that you must be very descriptive with the deal when creating the contract with LivingSocial. Ensure you include the exact details on any and all exclusions which need to be specifically listed in the deal details itself. Examples include deal quantity limitations (i.e., one coupon per person) and expiration date. Otherwise, this may lead to negative experiences for new customers when visiting your establishment, which may cause you to lose a potential repeat customer. Also make sure you are not violating state or local liquor laws in enticing customers to your establishment.

Groupon Groupon, similar to LivingSocial, is also a deals website. Groupon offers include overall discounts from a total cost perspective. For example, a deal may consist of "$25 for $50," meaning you pay $25 for $50 worth of services depending on the specific details of the deal. As with LivingSocial, it is extremely important to ensure all exclusions and details are listed in the "fine print" section and that you can legally do this in your state or locale.

Social Media Marketing Tool	Website Address	Site Details	Capabilities	Limitations	Marketing Links
Facebook	http://www.facebook.com	Facebook provides tools which enable a business to market themselves via a unique Facebook page, ad creation, and status updates to include promotions, giveaways, and other marketing tactics.	• Text • Pictures (automatically displayed) • Video (automatically displayed) • Website link	• None	https://www.facebook.com/marketing
Twitter	http://www.twitter.com	Twitter provides a communications mechanism for quick updates in the form of limited text and web-links.	• Text • Website link • Video link • Picture link	• Limited amount of 140 characters allowed • Pictures need to be manually opened, are not automatically displayed	https://business.twitter.com/
LivingSocial	http://www.livingsocial.com	Deals website where businesses can offer discounted deals to potential customers for services at their establishment.	• Text • Pictures • Website link • Map and location of business • Fine Print section	• None	https://getfeatured.livingsocial.com/getfeatured/us-escapes/
Groupon	http://www.groupon.com	Deals website where businesses can offer discounted deals to potential customers for services at their establishment. Offers overall discount on total bill verses specific Item(s).	• Text • Pictures • Website link • Fine Print section	• None	https://www.grouponworks.com/

Social media reference chart.

THE "OTHER Ps"; PUBLIC RELATIONS, PUBLICITY, AND PERSONAL CONTACT

Public relations can be an effective tool to market a bar. It involves creating and promoting a public image for the operation. This public image is not promoted through advertising but rather through participation in community events and activities. Some specific examples include participating in food drives; local contests, such as a chili cook-off, sponsoring a little league or youth soccer team, and neighborhood beatification efforts such as Adopt-a-Street. These efforts can build public goodwill by helping your guests to see the bar as good neighbor who cares about and contributes to the community. It also does not hurt that your bar's name is constantly in the forefront during these events, thus reinforcing brand name recognition on the part of the public.

Closely related to public relations is **publicity**, or free advertising. Very often, this free advertising takes the form of press coverage. Bars can help create their own publicity through press releases sent to media outlets. Press releases should announce such newsworthy events as an award given to the bar or a staff member, a new menu, upcoming entertainment, or promotions.

Another strategy is to become an expert. Media are always looking for people to quote. For example, the local media may choose to quote your bartender regarding a hot new drink that has hit the market, and he or she could give a demonstration on how to make it. Wine tasting or pairings could be discussed either in print media or on the air. Responsible drinking is always a good subject to discuss, and who better to do it than a local bartender or manager? The key is to get yourself known with the local media persons, so that when a news feature comes up, they think of you as the contact.

Publicity can be either controlled or uncontrolled. An example of controlled publicity is the aforementioned expert. In situations where you as the expert are concerned, you control the content. Uncontrolled publicity happens when you have no control over the situation. Often this can cast a negative light on an operation, for example if a local paper publishes a negative restaurant review or if there are negative stories about

Personal contact is important when dealing with customers.
Tyler Olson/Shutterstock

the bar's clientele getting into an altercation. All too often sports personalities or local celebrities are constantly followed by the paparazzi that are looking for news flashes, and they will blow an incident out of proportion as well as damage the reputation of your establishment.

Personal contact is yet another way to generate business with minimal, if any, cost. Personal contact can be internal or external. Internally, it is interfacing with your customers, getting to know them and their wants. For example, when Joe walks into the bar, he is greeted by name, asked if he wants the usual, and is engaged in conversation on topics that interest him, such as sports, family, or job. Joe likes this personal treatment. As a matter of fact, he likes it so much he tells his friends about it and they start coming into the bar as well. This is also known as word-of-mouth promotion and is perhaps the most effective method of marketing there is. It is direct, personal, and comes from someone the recipient respects. Keep in mind, however, that it can work the other way. Joe walks into the bar, is largely ignored, and while he is waiting to be served notices that the place is fairly dirty. It is when the cockroach walks across the bar that Joe gets up and leaves. He tells his friends, who tell their friends, and before you know it, the bar is closed.

External personal contact is when the owner or manager gets out in the community and makes new acquaintances. It could be as simple as belonging to a church, synagogue, or mosque or joining the chamber of commerce, a civic club, fraternal organization, country club, or professional organization. Better yet is serving on the board or being an officer of one of these organizations. It shows involvement on the owner's part as well as the business's in the affairs and welfare of the community. Additionally, it serves as a great vehicle to network.

CREATING THE PLAN

Before embracing any of the methods described in this chapter, it is important that management identify the specific objectives that they hope to achieve as well as carefully researching their **target markets**, the competition, and their operation's internal resources. Often, management may embrace marketing efforts to increase sales, but it is important to quantify what level of increase they hope to achieve and how it will be measured. For example, are they looking to increase the number of guests who visit the bar, or are they looking to increase how much the average customer spends after coming to the bar?

Research the Market

Management should specifically define what outcome they are working toward and track results of the marketing efforts carefully. It is important to research the target market that the operation is hoping to reach in order to design marketing approaches that will appeal to them directly. As discussed earlier in the chapter, psychographic studies can be quite helpful in this regard, because they provide insight on the media utilized by a particular group as well as their recreational habits. For example, if you were trying to reach college students with your marketing efforts, an advertisement on a talk radio station would be a poor choice. Conversely, if you are operating a sports bar, running ads during the local team's broadcasts or hosting a sports talk radio show would be ideal.

Establish a Budget

Ultimately, the operation's internal resources determine how broad or narrow the marketing plan's reach is. When ample dollars are available, expensive media buys such as television advertising and full-color print ads may be possible. However, most of the time resources are limited, especially for smaller operations. This presents management with the challenge of determining how to get the most impact for their investment. The key here is getting a return on your investment (ROI). No matter how much you spend on marketing, be it a large amount or a small amount, there should be a return, either in the number of customers coming into your establishment or the amount of money they spend when they get there or both. In other words, the campaign should pay for itself in real dollars, plus some.

Plan the Promotion

What do you want to do: Increase customer count? Increase sales? Make the public aware of your operation? Promote a product? Attack the competition? Some of these? All of these? As all of these are admirable goals, keep in mind that your potential customer is bombarded daily with hundreds of advertisements. A generic promotion trying to do too much will not be as successful as concentrating on one theme. By driving home one point, a successful campaign will have residual effects. For example, a bar and grill owner specializing in Tex-Mex teamed with a tequila manufacturer to promote margaritas. The goal of the campaign for the bar and grill owner was to bring new customers into the establishment. The goal of the tequila company was to expose its brand name to the consumer. The marketing plan concentrated on premium margaritas served in a take-home souvenir glass available at that operation only. The promotion was featured on the

establishment's website. Radio and newspaper advertising were used. Additionally, the owner appeared on a local television show and demonstrated how to make a perfect margarita. The campaign was successful and bought in new customers. Even though the campaign focused on one idea, which was to bring in new customers, there was a residual effect in that once the new customers got there they ordered food as well, thus increasing the average check. This obviously affected the competition. By concentrating on one idea, the campaign accomplished its goals plus more.

Notice also that more than one type of promotion was used in the campaign. Radio and newspaper were a cost to the operation. Publicity in the form of the television appearance did not cost the operation and more than likely had as great or greater impact than the paid media. Additionally, by using the website to promote the event, the word got out at a very nominal, almost free, cost.

The Competition

Who is the competition, and what are they up to? **Competition**, in a broad sense of the word, is any business that sells alcoholic beverages. Thus, a liquor store or supermarket that sells beer and wine could be considered competition for a bar. In a stricter sense of the word, competition includes any bar with a comparable theme and ambiance that sells a similar product at a price equivalent to your operation.

Competition can also be categorized as indirect competition (in the case of the liquor store) or direct competition (in the case of other bars). Of course, some types of direct competition are more direct than others. If potential customers want to go out for a night of dancing and a few drinks, they are going to go to a bar that has a dance floor and a band or DJ. In this case, although there may be many bars in the area to choose from, the fact that they want to dance means that the most direct competition comes only from bars that promote dancing. Conversely, a few friends that want to go out for a few drinks and conversation after work will not be as fussy about the venue, and all bars in the area would be considered direct competition.

Many people and companies are afraid of competition, but competition is healthy. It promotes a good price–value relationship, excellent service, and a quality product. In a competitive market, businesses are forced to excel in order to succeed. Care must be exercised when planning a business because a market will support only a given number of similar operations. When the maximum numbers of competing businesses are operating in a market, the situation is known as market saturation. Market saturation, however, is not a healthy situation because the number of available customers can be spread only so thin. Rather than copy the competition, attack it with a different theme, décor, and ambiance, thus turning a problem into an opportunity. For example, an area that has an overabundance of sports bars would probably welcome a brew pub that features excellent on-premise quality and unusual brews. Another strategy is to increase the quality of service and atmosphere. It is not enough to be as good as the competition; you must offer something different and do it better.

When planning a **marketing strategy**, examine what the competition is doing, either for embracing a similar approach or to take an entirely different path. Take for example the quick service restaurants that assault each other with price points with a dollar value menu. Each one tries to offer more items than the other for a dollar. After they go toe to toe on price, one of them will offer a new item. Pretty soon they are all offering new items. Then they attack each other. Then they go back to dollar menu items and the cycle repeats. Conversely, some quick service operations take an entirely different approach by offering quality, service, and unique menu items and lure customers into their operations by offering something different.

The important thing is to look at how others take on their competition and learn from them. Then look at your own competition. What are their strong points and what are their weak points? Where are they vulnerable? What can you do to outmaneuver them? Given this knowledge, you can then plan your strategy.

Employees

Keep your key employees involved throughout the planning process. After all, they are the ones who have the first line contact with the customer. They know the guests' wants and needs as well as their likes and dislikes. If they are a part of the planning process, they will have already bought into the plan when it is executed. When the plan is fully developed and ready for launching, bring the rest of the crew into the picture. Everyone should be on board, the front of the house as well as the back of the house.

Explain to them exactly what the promotion consists of, why you are doing it, and the results expected. Tell them how they can help make it successful. Possibly throw in some incentives for them. For example, the owner of Lawrensen's Vivacious Libations notices that other bars in the area have an increase in sales on Fridays, while his sales are the same as any other day. He discusses this with his staff. The bartender suggests a pep rally for the local professional football team on Fridays. One of the servers suggests that they all wear team jerseys. Another wants to decorate the bar with team logos and colors. Lawrensen calls the radio station, and they agree to have a sports talk show do a remote from the bar on those days if he buys some ads on the station. He agrees to that and also takes an ad out in the local newspaper. The webmaster puts the event on the bar's web page and sends a broadcast email to all of the patrons. The sales increase 60 percent on Fridays during the football season.

Get the staff involved with the promotion.
aletia2011/Fotolia

MEASURING RESULTS

In order to evaluate the impact of marketing effort, a method for tracking results should be established. Results can be measured in various ways. Perhaps the easiest method is guest counts and check average, because most operations track this information on a regular basis. Also, managers can collect information through comment cards that ask how a guest heard about the restaurant. If coupons are used, they can be collected and tracked by source. All these methods help managers determine the return on investment (ROI) of a particular marketing effort. In other words, managers should carefully consider how much return (e.g., additional guests, increased check average) they see after investing and multiply that by the amount of money in each aspect of the marketing campaign.

For example, Jerome's Jazz Joint has a trio that plays every Friday and Saturday evening. On an average, the lounge brings in $7000 for those two nights. Jerome would like to increase that by 15 percent, or an additional $1050. He takes out an ad in the weekly *Jacksonville Jazz Journal* for a month at a cost of $2000. He figures the ad should increase his sales during that month plus have a residual effect the following two weeks. The results show an increase by week as follows:

1st week	$100
2nd week	$450
3rd week	$500
4th week	$550
5th week	$450
6th week	$300

To figure ROI, take the amount returned, divide by the amount invested, and subtract 1:

$$\$ \text{ returned}/\$ \text{ invested} - 1 = \text{ROI}$$

Jerome had an increase for six weeks of $2350 and invested $2000. His ROI was

$$\$2350/\$2000 - 1 = 0.175, \text{ or } 17.5 \text{ percent}$$

The ROI should be compared to an investment rate such as a money market account or certificate of deposit. In this case Jerome did better by investing in the advertisement than he would have if he did not advertise and left the money invested. An operation that spends thousands of dollars on marketing efforts that result in little or no change in guest count or check average would be considered a poor ROI and therefore a poor investment.

Finally, one should consider the fact that it is easier to get someone to continue a behavior than it is to get someone to change a behavior. In other words, it is easier and less expensive to keep an existing customer than it is to create a new customer. For this reason, many operations direct much of their marketing efforts toward their established clientele and addressing their needs. Simple gestures that costs nothing, like calling customers by their name or remembering what they drink, are examples of how rewarding repeat guests can become part of the restaurant marketing plan.

MENUS

One of the key components of the overall marketing plan is the operation's menu. After an advertisement gets the potential customer into the bar, product in the form of food and drink is marketed via the menu. Keep in mind, however, that many of the bar's customers are creatures of habit and know exactly what they want before they even enter the building. The menu is for those who are undecided. While some bartenders and servers do an excellent job of selling, do not depend on it, especially when the bar is very busy. Consider the menu your silent salesperson, because it is through the menu that an unsure guest determines what to order. This is one of the major reasons why the bar's menu content and its layout should be planned carefully. It is not a haphazard list of items offered for sale; rather it is a carefully crafted marketing device, which is geared to enticing the customer to purchase those items that are high profit and serve to enhance the bar's reputation.

All menus, regardless of type, are broken down into various categories. The type of menu and consequently the number of categories used is determined by the needs of that particular bar. The categories, which are groups of food or drink, are listed on the menu as headings, and under these headings are the items themselves. The traditional categories for restaurant menus are appetizers, soups, salads, cold entrées, hot entrées, sandwiches, vegetables, side dishes, starches, desserts, cheeses, fruits, and beverages. In a high-ticket, white-tablecloth, fine-dining restaurant, most of these categories are used, whereas in other operations, such as theme, ethnic, or family-style restaurants, only a selected few are used on the menu.

The categories for a bar are draft beer, bottled beer, spirits, cocktails, wine by the glass, and wine by the bottle. Again, not every bar will have all of these categories.

Once the categories have been decided along with the food or drink items that are to be sold within those categories, it is time to write the bar menu. Writing the menu can be and is a challenging task. The categories become the headings on the menu, and the food or drinks are listed beneath them. Unless the items are self-explanatory, **descriptive terminology** should be used. The language and vocabulary used when writing the menu must do one major thing: sell the product to the customer in an honest and forthright manner. A secondary thing it must do is to explain the item to the customer, especially if it is one in which the customer is unfamiliar. For example, if you have developed a specialty drink for a promotion, list the ingredients and how it is prepared, for instance blended, shaken, or stirred. Accurate descriptive terminology will result in menu descriptions which in turn will result in a satisfied customer receiving the product expected.

The next step is to design the layout. This should be done in a logical and scientific manner. The categories should be in larger print, while the items listed beneath the category heading should be in smaller print. Keep in mind that because of a lower lighting level in most bars, the print size should never be smaller than 12 points (a point being a printer's measure of type size). When placing all of this on the menu itself, another factor must be considered. When the customers open the menu, the spot that their eyes hit first is known as the **prime space**. Studies have shown that the customer is more likely to order what is seen first. Thus, the prime space on the menu becomes an extremely important merchandising area. Many people are unaware of this fact, because few menus use it to its best advantage. The prime space is determined by the type of menu. On a two-page menu, it is located in the middle of the right-hand page. On a three-page or a single menu, it is in the center of the upper third of the menu. Figure 13.1 shows the location of prime space on menus.

Because this is prime space, it stands to reason that management should place the item that they most want to sell in this spot. Quite naturally, this item should be popular and bring the bar a higher gross profit than normal.

There are three types of menus used in beverage outlets. They are the food menu, the bar menu, and the wine list. Bars that do not sell food obviously will not have a food menu, and bars that have a limited selection of wine will not have a wine menu. Some bars will combine all three into one, and some will have separate menus for each group.

FIGURE 13.1
Prime space illustration.

Prime Space on a One-Page Menu

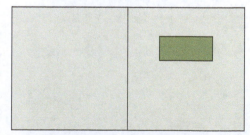

Prime Space on a Two-Page Menu

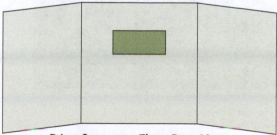

Prime Space on a Three-Page Menu

Food Menus

Is the operation a bar that sells food or a restaurant that sells drinks? There is a major distinction between the two when it comes to designing the beverage outlet's food menu. A bar that sells food is at an advantage over a bar that does not sell food because it keeps the customers in the bar longer as they do not have to leave to get something to eat. It also contributes to the bottom line with add-on sales.

If the operation is a bar that sells food, care must be taken so that the menu does not overpower the kitchen. Most bar kitchens have limited production and storage facilities, and the menu must take this fact into consideration. A minimal bar kitchen should have a deep fryer, a grill or griddle, a refrigerated salad and sandwich makeup unit, a dish machine, adequate refrigeration and storage, and a hand sink. Again, this is minimal. With this equipment, a bar menu can offer the following categories: appetizers, hot and cold sandwiches, salads, soups, and a limited number of entrées.

Portion sizes for appetizers for an individual serving should be small, with larger portions available for groups. Many bar menus have one size, super large, which curtails sales to customers who are alone. While some people go to a bar to eat, the majority of customers simply want something to nibble on while they are enjoying a cocktail, beer, or wine. A bar menu should contain primarily popular items with maybe one or two house specialties. These house specialties are what help draw customers to your establishment. Look at what happened to that little neighborhood bar in Buffalo, New York, that decided to put chicken wings on its menu long before anyone knew what they were.

If the operation is a restaurant that sells drinks, a decision needs to be made as to whether the regular restaurant menu will be used in the bar or a separate bar food menu will be developed. A typical restaurant menu will have many categories. The number of categories used will depend on such factors as style, décor, type of service, price range, and area demographics.

Should a separate menu be used in the bar, the same concepts pertaining to a bar food menu should be followed, that is, a limited selection and smaller portions While the bar food menu can contain many of the restaurants regular listings, the smaller portions can be served and merchandised as tapas, small plates, or appetizer portions. While fewer categories are used on a bar menu, some interesting categories can be added that are not on a normal restaurant menu such as fruit and cheese. These, paired with some wine selections, can make for some very attractive offerings.

Bar Drink Menus

Keep in mind that not every bar has to be all things to all people. By carefully studying the previously mentioned demographics for your area, you can come up with menu that will satisfy the majority of your clientele. Listing drinks on your menu that do not sell well will slow down service as well as create an excess inventory, which will slow down cash flow. The next time you visit a bar, watch the bartender waste time hunting for the ingredients for a rarely called for drink. Look on the back shelf and see how many premium brands are sitting up there collecting dust, when an offering of only a few premiums would satisfy 99 percent of the customers. The categories for a bar menu are as follows:

- Wines. Red, white, rose, sparkling, dessert. *Note*: If a limited number of wines are offered, they should appear on the bar menu. If a larger number are offered, a separate wine list should be developed.
- Beers. Domestic, imported, lagers, ales, bottled, draught.

The draft beer menu listed on a chalkboard.

Photo Courtesy of Conroy's Public House

- Spirits. Bar, call, premium, by brand separated by price, bourbon, domestic whiskey, Scotch whisky, Irish whisky, gin, tequila, rum, vodka.
- Standard mixed drinks. Highballs, rocks, mists.
- Specialty drinks. Martinis, margaritas, blended drinks.
- Alcohol-free drinks. Juices, carbonated beverages, flavored teas (hot and iced), virgin drinks.

Wine List

Equally important as the bar drink menu is the **wine list**, particularly if the operation has a fine dining component. As previously mentioned, if the operation offers a minimal selection of wines by the glass, they can be listed on the regular bar menu. However, if a wider assortment of wines is offered both by the bottle and the glass, a separate wine list should be presented. Essential to a good wine list is variety and price. How much variety and at what price will be determined by the demographics of the establishment and also on the type of operation and the menu served. For example, a German restaurant in a middle-class neighborhood with a moderately priced menu would have a number of moderately priced German wines on wine list. However, a few American or even a few French or other imported wines would be appropriate to give the guest a plethora of choices.

Another decision that must be made is which and how many of the wine selections should be made available by the glass or carafe. Obviously all of them would be available by the bottle. The number available by the glass should be determined by the popularity of the wine as well as its price. Once a bottle is opened, it should be consumed in a relatively short period of time. For example, a rare wine carrying a high selling price would not be purchased as often as a more moderately priced wine and therefore would not be offered by the glass. Carafe sales are most often limited to moderate or lower priced wines and are used in moderately priced restaurants and bars.

Like the bar menu, the wine list should be broken down into categories. The categories for wine are red, white, rose, sparkling, and dessert. All of these categories can be offered to the customer or only a few. Sparkling and dessert wines are often omitted. A subcategory would be the country or region of origin. Another way to arrange the wine list is to reverse the above with the country or region becoming the category and the type of wine the subcategory.

How many wines in each category, again, depends on the clientele, the menu, and the image that you are trying to project. A rule of thumb for the average restaurant is 35 percent white and 65 percent red. However, this could change depending on the menu being offered, with steak houses offering more reds and seafood restaurant offering more whites. A minimal list would be twenty selections total, but most wine lists offer more than that. Keep in mind that the greater the selection, the greater the investment in inventory. Wines that sit in storage lower the cash flow of the operation.

Once the wines have been selected and how to categorize them decided, it is time to write the menu. As previously discussed, descriptive terminology is important. With wine it is probably more important to describe the product than it is to sell the product. Many wine lists do not do this, and an important component is missed in helping the customer, particularly those that are neophytes, make an informed decision. All Burgundies are not the same, and one or two sentences describing each one will help the customers make a wise selection that they will enjoy.

While the menu goes a long way to explain the various nuances of the wine to the customer, nothing replaces the personal knowledge of the server. If the operation does not have a sommelier to address this function, it is up to management to train each server. A good way to do this is to have employee wine tastings. This should

Wine Menu.
© food pictures studio - Fotolia.com

Sample text

Sample text Your text here
text Here sample text text sample
Your text here Sample text
Here Your text Sample
Text sample here

include all servers as well as some of the culinary staff. Have your distributor bring in someone knowledgeable about wines and taste several of them. By doing this the server will be able to explain the wine to the customers, telling them about the distinctive attributes of each wine. Additionally, the culinary staff will be able to create dishes that are compatible with particular wines.

CONCLUSION

Large corporations operating multi-unit beverage outlets for the most part get their marketing strategy right. It is the small business operations that have problems in this area. With no plan or measurable objectives, they go about marketing their bar in a haphazard manner. If a coupon salesperson comes by, they will purchase space in the coupon book. If business is down, they take out an ad in the local paper. If an unforeseen event happens that threatens their bar, without a plan, they will go out of business.

Marketing is an important subject for the owner or manager because, if properly done, it maximizes sales by getting patrons into the bar and keeps those patrons. Marketing starts with demographics, the study of location and determining who the potential customer is. Feasibility studies, demographics surveys, and psychographic studies are used along with managements own knowledge of the area. In addition to studying demographics, a SWOT analysis should be taken. This is an internal inventory of the business which investigates its strengths and weaknesses and looks at opportunities and threats.

Four key marketing aspects are place, product, price, and promotion. These are known as the four Ps of marketing. Place concerns itself with getting customer to the establishment, in this case the bar. What are the best means to get potential customers to try it out? The product the bar serves must fit the demographic makeup of its trade area. Well, spirits sell best in a blue-collar bar, while premium spirits sell best in a high-income area. Price is the amount charged for beverages as well as discounts given such as a happy hour. Advertising, also called promotion, is used to encourage customers to come into the bar. Promotion is also conducting various events such as wine tastings or pairings.

There are some other Ps in marketing: public relations, publicity, and personal contact. Public relations involve establishing an image for the business, what it stands for, and how it interrelates with the community. Sponsoring a little league team or underwriting a charity event demonstrates that the bar is involved with its neighborhood. Publicity is free advertising such as being quoted in the newspaper. Publicity for the most part is good for the bar, but it can also be negative. Personal contact is the bar owner or manager being involved in community clubs and organizations and networking with people who could be potential customers of the business.

After all of this, a plan should be written. It should include the specific objectives that management wants to achieve. These objectives should be measurable. A budget should be established and analyzed to see if the objectives can be achieved given the resources available. After the marketing campaign, the results should be determined by measuring the results against the projections and performing an ROI analysis.

Throughout the entire process the employees should be consulted and kept appraised of the process as it evolves. After all, the success of any marketing campaign is dependent on the employees buying into it. If they are not on board, it will not be successful.

Case Study

You have been approached by the president of your university or college to work on a campus project. The board of trustees has decided to open a club for the faculty and alumni of the institution. It will be housed on campus in one of the original buildings that has a great view of the campus commons green. The club will have meeting rooms, a library, a large reading room with a large stone fireplace, a dining room, and a lounge. The décor will be wood-paneled walls with comfortable furniture and a relaxing atmosphere.

You have been asked to come up with menus for the lounge. Write a brief summary of the demographics of the clientele of this club and three menus: a food menu for the lounge, a bar menu, and a wine list. Assume that the club will be on the campus where you are presently going to school.

QUESTIONS

True/False

1. Demographics are the study of a bar's location and its potential customers.
2. A feasibility study is often referred to as VALS (values, attitudes, and lifestyle)
3. Regarding the four Ps of marketing, price concerns itself solely with what the customer is charged.
4. Even though it is very unscientific, personal knowledge of an area is considered a part of market segmentation.
5. Tastings and pairings, while different, are also very similar in their makeup.
6. When planning a marketing campaign, it is important that management identify the specific objectives that they hope to achieve.
7. Due to the complex nature of planning a marketing campaign, it is wise to keep the employees out of the planning stage.
8. There is little correlation between a marketing plan and the operations menus.
9. Menu categories and headings are essentially the same thing.
10. Most well-run bars have a wine list separate from the drink list.

Multiple Choice

1. When evaluating demographics, consideration should be given to
   1) identifying the customer in the market.
   2) matching of the customers, along with their needs and preferences, to the proper beverage offerings.
   A. (1) only
   B. (2) only
   C. Neither (1) nor (2)
   D. Both (1) and (2)

2. A SWOT analysis concerns
   A. internal analysis only.
   B. external concerns that influence internal factors.
   C. external concerns only.
   D. situations, weaknesses, outside influences, and threats.

3. The four Ps of marketing are
   A. place, product, price, and promotion.
   B. place, production, publicity, and price.
   C. product, public relations, publicity, and price.
   D. product, price, publicity, and promotion.
4. Happy hour promotions
   1) often have a discount or BOGO associated with them.
   2) are legal in all fifty states.
   A. (1) only
   B. (2) only
   C. Both (1) and (2)
   D. Neither (1) nor (2)
5. Any discussions regarding a marketing campaign should *not* involve
   A. suppliers.
   B. employees.
   C. landlord.
   D. none of the above should be involved in the discussion.
6. When calculating a return on investment (ROI) for a marketing campaign, which of the following is used?
   A. Customer count.
   B. Average check.
   C. $ returned/$ invested – 1.
   D. All of the above are used.
7. Which one of the following is a true statement regarding menu categories?
   A. They are virtually the same for most bars.
   B. They are determined by the needs of that particular bar.

C. They are the same thing as menu listings.
D. They are regulated in most, but not all, states.
8. Descriptive terminology
   1) is used to sell a menu listing.
   2) is used to explain a product.
   A. (1) only
   B. (2) only
   C. Both (1) and (2)
   D. Neither (1) nor (2)
9. Which of the following is *not* true regarding prime space?
   A. It is located on the middle of the left-hand page on a two-page menu.
   B. It is the space that should feature a high-profit, popular drink.
   C. It is located on the upper middle page of a three-page menu.
   D. It is the spot on a menu that a customer's eye hits first.
10. Regarding the wine menu and keeping in mind that there are exceptions,
    A. a minimum of forty wines should be offered.
    B. a minimum of thirty wines should be offered.
    C. wines offered on a typical menu should be about 65 percent white and 35 percent red.
    D. wines offered on a typical menu should be about 35 percent white and 65 percent red.

Essay

1. Define *demographics* in your own words and give an example of the four sources for demographic information.
2. Rationalize how a demographic study should be used with a SWOT analysis to help formulate a marketing plan.

3. Discuss the various media outlets, including the advantages and disadvantages of each, the costs associated with each, and which one(s) would be most advantageous to a bar.
4. Differentiate between publicity and public relations.
5. Name and define all of the categories that could be found on a bar menu.

RESOURCES

Davis, Bernard and Stone, Sally, *Food and Beverage Management*, 5th ed. (Oxford, UK: Lineacre House, 2008).

Drysdale, John A. and Galapeu, Jennifer, *Profitable Menu Planning*, 4th ed. (Upper Saddle River, NJ: Pearson Prentice Hall, 2008).

Katsigris, Costas and Thomas, Chris, *The Bar & Beverage Book*, 4th ed. (Hoboken, NJ: John Wiley & Sons, 2007).

Kotschevar, Lendal H. and Tanke, Mary L., *Managing Bar and Beverage Operations* (East Lansing, MI: Educational Institute of the American Hotel and Motel Association, 1996).

14

The Entrepreneur in You

OVERVIEW

This chapter delves into the intricacies of opening your own business. Some of what you have already learned is contained in this chapter. Even if you have no intention of opening your own bar or restaurant, this chapter is important to you as it will serve to tie together all you have learned about the business of managing a business.

At the heart of any successful new business is the business plan. It takes a lot of work and research to complete one, but it pays dividends in that it forces the potential business owners to think through things that they might not have otherwise thought of. It points out potential pitfalls so that they can be resolved before the business opens. The hospitality industry is one of the most difficult industries in which to succeed. For those that do succeed, the rewards are great. A sound business plan will get you off on the right foot to success.

CHOOSING A LOCATION

As we learned in Chapter 2, the study of location and the potential customer is known as **demographics**. More specifically, according to *Webster's New Collegiate Dictionary*, demographics is "the statistical study of populations with reference to size, density, distribution, and vital statistics and the ability (of the market) to expand or decline." In order to use demographics properly in choosing a location for a proposed bar, two factors must be taken into account. One is the demographic study itself, in other words, who exactly are the customers in the proposed market, and the second factor is the matching of these customers, along with their needs and preferences, to the proper theme and ambiance of the bar.

For example, if the demographic study indicated a blue-collar, working-class, middle-income neighborhood, with families, you could opt to open a sports bar with a good selection of beer and feature basic mixed drinks. Another option would be to open a family-oriented restaurant with reasonably priced comfort food that served drinks. Conversely, if the demographic study showed a young twenty-something population, upper-middle-income bracket, with single persons and married couples without children, you could opt for a wine bar with tapas. Another option would be a hip nightclub with a martini bar and live entertainment.

Objectives

Upon completion of this chapter, the reader should be able to:

- Design, write, and execute a business plan for a beverage outlet.
- Describe how location is important to the success of a business.
- Write a mission statement along with determining a company's goals and objectives.
- Execute a plan for determining what food and drink to offer the customer.
- Determine a staffing chart indicating what positions need to be filled, how many positions are needed, and the expertise each person should bring to the business.
- Research and develop a pro forma income statement and cash flow analysis.
- Analyze and figure a break-even point.
- Understand how the legal environment relates to the opening of a bar as well as its day-to-day operation.

Key Terms

Break-even analysis
Business plan
Company goals and objectives
Competition
Demographic survey
Demographics
Feasibility study

Market niche

Market saturation

Mission statement

Pro forma statement

As we learned in Chapter 13, the sources of information for determining the demographic makeup of the market area could come from the following sites:

- **Feasibility study**. A complete analysis of the proposed location which would determine if the planned business would have a reasonable chance of success.
- **Demographic survey**. A study, normally purchased from a company that has statistical information about specific areas that include the area's general population by age group, median age, ethnic origins, household type, marital status, occupation, education, housing, income, number of vehicles, and other related data. Specialized data can also be obtained that detail consumer restaurant and beverage expenditures for the area and can further refine this statistic by giving a breakdown by category such as bar, restaurant/bar, nightclub, or fine dining. A demographic survey is not as complete as a feasibility study in that it does not predict the possibility of success or failure.
- **Psychographic study**. This data is sometimes referred to as VALS because it contains information about the values, attitudes, and lifestyle preferences of the population being studied. It tells if the lifestyle of the residents in the proposed location meets the market objectives of the bar, restaurant, or nightclub.
- **Personal knowledge**. A personal feel for the market is an important tool if used properly. Demographic studies look at an area with cold, hard facts. Knowledge of situations behind these facts is quite important. A person should not open a business based on personal knowledge alone but rather in conjunction with the previous aforementioned data.

We also discussed competition, which can be a good or bad thing. It is good if it draws people into the area. Several similar bars in an area will attract people who like to bar hop. It is bad if the market has reached, or gone beyond, **market saturation** resulting in the customer pool being spread too thin.

THE BUSINESS PLAN

Anybody going into business should have a plan, and it should be in writing. The importance of creating a **business plan** lies in the procedure of conducting research and thinking about your proposed business in a systematic way. This planning helps you to think your proposals through comprehensively. As you go through the process, it will be necessary to study and research facts if you are not sure of them. It will also be necessary for you to look at your ideas critically. The time spent on the business plan will pay dividends in the long run as it will avoid costly mistakes down the road.

As you research, keep careful notes on your sources of information, where did you read it or who you talked to. Most of your time spent on the business plan will be expended in research. As it develops, you will be rethinking the plan and making changes based on what you have learned. This is good. It is better to change now when the plan is on paper than later when change could be very costly. It usually will take several weeks of full-time work to complete a good plan.

No two business plans are alike, but most of them follow a certain format and contain the following information:

- Table of contents
- Executive summary
- General company description
- Products and services
- Marketing plan
- Operational plan
- Management and organization

- Personal financial statement
- Startup expenses and capitalization
- Financial plan
- Appendices

Table of Contents

This is basically self-explanatory as you will divide the report into the chapters cited above. You will want to put the page number of the start of each chapter in the table of contents so the readers can quickly go to the source of information that they are interested in.

Executive Summary

While this section appears at the start of the report, it should be written last. It contains an abstract of everything that is in the report. It should be no more than two pages. The purpose of an executive summary is to give the reader an overview of the project. Who is the customer? What are the demographics of the area? What will the bar look like? What is the organizational structure? What is the expertise of the management team? What does the future hold for the business and the beverage industry as a whole? How much capital will the project need and how will it be repaid?

Assume that you are going to make a presentation on your project to the president of a bank and you have five minutes. Everything you would tell that president in five minutes should be in the executive summary. Write it in a concise, professional manner, and above all be enthusiastic about your project.

General Company Description

Here you will give a general description of the business. Let's assume that you are planning on opening a nightclub for young singles and couples. The club will have live entertainment on weekends and during the week will serve as a gathering place where people can converse. It will feature upscale, cutting-edge drinks prepared by mixologists as well as a menu featuring locally grown food. A brief statement about the market area could go here, although that would be covered in more detail in the marketing section. You could state that the club would be located in an area of apartments and condos inhabited by young professionals near a major teaching hospital.

Next would come a description of the beverage industry as a whole. State that it is a growth industry and back it up with statistics. These can be obtained from statistical studies conducted by the National Restaurant Association or the American Hotel and Lodging Association as well as a plethora of other associations. Explain how you will take advantage of these opportunities.

At the core of any successful business is a **mission statement**. This is a brief declaration of your reason for being and what your guiding principles will be. It should be brief and concise, containing one or two sentences and no more than thirty words. It will give the reader of your business plan a general overview of what you are all about. For example, your mission statement could be, "To be the leading provider of food and drink to the young people of Centerville, served in an environmentally responsible and sustainable atmosphere."

In addition to a mission statement, **company goals and objectives** are needed. A goal is an end. An objective is an assessment of how well you are doing to meet the end. For example, a goal could be to have a successful nightclub that is a leader in the market. An objective of that goal would be meeting an annual sales budget, or it could be meeting a monthly customer count. A business could have several goals and the objectives to meet those goals.

How a company carries out its mission statement, goals, and objectives depends a great deal upon the leadership of that company. Assuming that you are going to be the leader of the business, you will want a brief description of your background and your expertise. For example, you could say that you graduated from one of the top hospitality management programs in the country and spent the last ten years as the general manager of a successful bar and restaurant for a leading national chain. You should then go on to say how this background will help the company succeed, how you have honed your leadership skills and are now ready to lead your own company. Do not go into detail about who you are bringing on board to help you in this endeavor, as that will be detailed later in the plan in the organizational chapter.

Finally, what will be the legal form of ownership? Will it be a sole proprietor, partnership, corporation, or limited liability corporation (LLC)? There are advantages and disadvantages as well as legal and tax implications for each of these forms. The advice and council of an attorney and a certified public accountant should be sought when making this decision. Which form you have chosen and why should be included in the business plan.

Products and Services

Since you are opening a bar/restaurant/nightclub, your product is obviously going to be food and drink along with service. Include a copy of your proposed menu. Also include an example of your proposed drink menu. Figures 14.1 and 14.2 illustrate a proposed menu.

If you are stressing a sustainable environment, in the narrative of your business plan, stress that locally grown produce along with locally raised meats are going to be featured. They will be from farmers who emphasize chemical- and hormone-free farming techniques. Also mention that while you will offer a typical bar offering of beer, wine, and spirits, the emphasis will be on cutting-edge, original, hand-crafted drinks made by an experienced mixologist. You will also feature regional beers from a local brewery and wine from local vineyards. Emphasize that the service staff will be well trained to give exceptional service. Tie it all together by pointing out that the young generation of today is concerned about the environment and the source of food and drink that they consume. Also state that your menu and operating beliefs share these same philosophies and that these ideas will put you head and shoulders above the competition.

In this section you should state your pricing strategy. While locally grown products often cost more, your unique treatment of them will allow you to sell your product at a slightly higher price than your competition. This along with your unique décor and ambiance will also allow you to charge more than the competition.

This chapter should include an artist's sketch or photographs of the proposed décor of the operation. It should give the reader a feel for the ambiance and theme you with to project. Figure 14.3 gives an example. A drawing of the floor plan showing the number of seats, the bar area, and the sound stage would also be fitting. Do not include a great deal of minutiae here as this would be more appropriate in the appendices.

Marketing Plan

Chapter 13 goes into quite a bit of detail how the marketing plan should be put together. The following is a review.

Location   Much of what was previously discussed regarding location will be included in the marketing plan. Make the plan as specific as possible; give statistics, numbers, and sources. Again, do not bog the reader down with minutiae. Just state the relevant facts. Put the finer points backing up your assessment of the location in the appendices. If there are any negatives regarding your project, do not ignore them but list them and give your plan for overcoming them. The marketing plan will be the basis, later on, of the sales projection.

The Slippery Noodle

Starters

Grilled Gulf Prawns
Curly endive with Dijon vinaigrette

Goat Cheese and Caramelized Onion Tart

Sweet Potato Gnocchi
Ham hock and chanterelles

Smoked Salmon
Crème fraiche, toasted baguette

Dungeness Crab Fritters
Bosc pear relish

Chicken Liver and Foie Gras Mousse
Red onion confit

Soups & Salads

Maryland Clam and Corn Chowder

French Onion Soup Gratinee

Soup du Jour

Salad Nicoise
Seared tuna

Roasted Beet Salad
Baby spinach, hazelnuts, vinaigrette

Mixed baby greens
Maytag Blue Cheese, candied pecans, bosc pears

Entrees

Grilled Durac Farms Pork Chop
Potatoes gratin, wilted spinach

Seared Diver Scallops
Root vegetable hash, baby asparagus

Slow Braised Short Ribs of Beef
Potato pancake, Vichy carrots

Sautéed Calf's Liver
Bacon, caramelized onions, root vegetable hash, baby asparagus

Seared Atlantic Salmon
Buttered new potatoes, wilted spinach

Lobster Macaroni and Cheese
Minted peas and pearl onions

Vincent Ranch Rib Eye Steak
Root vegetable hash, baby asparagus

Roasted Free Range Farm Chicken
Potatoes gratin, minted peas and pearl onions

Locally Raised Vegetable Omelet
Fresh herbs, potato pancake

Sandwiches

Ham and Chicken Club
With apple wood bacon, gruyere cheese, lettuce and tomato, French fries

Vincent Ranch Hamburger
With your choice of cheese, lettuce, tomato, red onion, French Fries

Shrimp Salad Sandwich
On toasted twelve grain bread, fresh fruit salad

FIGURE 14.1 Proposed menu.

The Slippery Noodle

Domestic Beers
Budweiser
Coors Light
Michelob
Miller Light

Imports
Amstel Light
Corona
Heinekin
New Castle

Scotch
Chivas Regal
Cutty Sark
Dewar's
J & B
Johnnie Walker
Glenfiddich
Glenlivit
Oban

Irish
Bushmill
Jameson
Tryconnell

Bourbon
Ancient Age
Early Times
Jim Beam
Makers Mark

Whiskey
Canadian Club
Crown Royal
Seagrams VO
Jack Daniels
George Dickel
Jim Beam Rye

Rum
Bacardi
Captain Morgan
Myers

Gin
Beefeater
Booth's London Dry
Gordon's
Tanqueray London Dry
Seagram's Extra Dry

Vodka
Smirnoff
Absolut
Finlandia
Grey Goose

Tequila
Sauza 100
Jose Cuervo

CLASSIC MARTINI
Beefeaters Gin and a splash
of vermouth

MOJITO
Bacardi Limon, mint leaves,
fresh lime juice, sugar and
club soda

BLOODY MARY
Grey Goose vodka,
tomato juice, dash of
Worcestershire sauce, and a
dash of Tabasco

MAI TAI
Bacardi rum, orange
curagao, orgeat syrup and
limes.

MARGARITAVILLE
Jose Cuervo Clasico Silver
tequila, Cointreau' and lime
juice

**LONG ISLAND ICED
TEA**
Beefeater gin, Skyr vodka,
Bacardi rum, Jose Cuervo
tequila and Cointreau, mixed
with citrus and a splash of
Coca-Cola.

TOM COLLINS
Old Tom gin, freshly
squeezed lemon juice,
simple syrup, and a splash of
soda water

BLACK RUSSIAN
Smirnoff vodka and Kahlua

Wines by the Glass
White
White Blend, Conundrum
White Zinfandel, Barefoot
Moscato, Castello Del Poggio
Pinot Gris, Four Graces
Pinot Grigio, Ecco Domani
Sauvignon Blanc, Oyster Bay
Sauvignon Blanc, Long
        Meadow Ranch
Chardonnay, Santa Carolina
Chardonnay, Sonoma Cutrer,
Chardonnay, Barefoot
Chardonnay, Bogle
Chardonnay, La Crema
Chardonnay, Frank Family
        Vineyards

Red
Pinot Noir, Kings Ridge
Pinot Noir, Mirassou
Pinot Noir, Pedroncelli
Pinot Noir, Kendall-Jackson
Zinfandel, Artezin
Zinfandel, Twisted
Merlot, Santa Carolina
Merlot, Murphy Goode
Merlot, Burgess Cellars
Merlot, Kendall-Jackson, VR
Cabernet Sauvignon
        Allomi Vineyard
Cabernet Sauvignon,
        Barefoot
Cabernet Sauvignon,
        Hess Select
Malbec, Santa Julia
Shiraz, Peter Lehmann
        Weighbridge

Sparkling
Barefoot Brut, California
Champagne Brut, Piper
        Heidsieck,
Blanc de Blancs,
        Schramsberg

Ports
Dow's 20 Year Tawny
Graham's Six Grapes
Sandeman Port

Cognacs & Brandies
Hardy, X.O.
Remy Martin, V.S.O.P.

FIGURE 14.2 Proposed bar menu.

FIGURE 14.3
A picture of the proposed décor. Fotolia Images.

Competition   We also talked about **competition** in Chapter 13. Recall that we talked about competition: direct (anyone selling food and drink in your price range with a like ambiance) and indirect (anyone selling food and/or drink). You should list your direct competitors and how you stack up against them. A chart as exhibited in Figure 14.4 would be a good way to illustrate this. After the competition chart is filled out you should have a good idea about your niche in the marketplace. A **market niche** is your unique position in the marketplace.

The Plan   How will you get the word out to customers? Remember the four P's: promotion, publicity, public relations, and personal contact. Promotion includes advertising. In the business plan tell what types of advertising you will use, its projected cost, and benefits expected from it. Explain what promotions you will run. Publicity could include one of your mixologists appearing on a noon-time show demonstrating how to make a perfect martini. Joining the Chamber of Commerce will give you personal

Factor	Your business	Strength	Weakness	Competitor A	Competitor B	Importance to Customer
Products						
Price						
Quality						
Selection						
Service						
Reliability						
Stability						
Expertise						
Company Reputation						
Location						
Appearance						

FIGURE 14.4
A competitive analysis worksheet. Courtesy of SCORE.

contact with the business leaders in the community. Getting the word out is crucial to the success of the business.

In addition to the four P's, include in this section of the business plan examples of your graphic images. For example, your logo design, sketches of your signage, menu design, letterhead, business cards, and brochures should all be included.

Promotional Budget   The promotional budget will be broken down into two parts: the startup budget and the operational budget. The startup budget will include such items as the design element and signage. The operational budget will include the ongoing promotional expense. Include such items as printing costs, media costs, and signage maintenance. The industry average for promotional expense is 2 percent of sales.

Proposed Location   Earlier in the chapter we talked about location. At this point you should have a location picked out. You should also have a backup plan in case things do not work out. Any number of things can happen, for example the inability to get a liquor license for that location or the landlord renting to another tenant. In this section of the plan, describe how the location will affect your customer. The physical needs of the location will be covered in the operational plan section. Cover such things as convenience to your potential customer, available parking, and whether the area is consistent with your image. Also discuss the competition. In the case of a nightclub, many people like to bar hop. If you are clustered with several other bars and clubs, this will increase your potential as opposed to being located alone at a remote site

Operational Plan

This section of the business plan concerns itself with location as it relates to the physical properties of the establishment, the staffing of the business, quality control, suppliers, inventory, credit policies, and controlling your accounts payable.

Location   Location as it relates to the customer was discussed in the previous section. This section discusses location as it relates to the physical properties that are necessary to run a food and beverage outlet. First and foremost is the amount of space needed to make the venture profitable. Approximately one third of the space will be back of the house for the kitchen and storage and two thirds of the space will be front of the house for the bar, dining area, sound stage, dance floor, waiting area, and rest rooms. The front of the house must contain enough square footage to accommodate the number of seats to make the operation profitable. This will be discussed in further detail in the "Financial Plan" section.

The type of building you have selected should be discussed here. Is it freestanding, part of a shopping center, or located in a strip mall? Fortunately, a bar can go into almost any type of building. A number of successful ventures have been opened in old warehouses. For example, the world-famous Copa Cabana Club in New York City is located in just such a setting.

Another consideration to address is the zoning. First and foremost, the location must be zoned for a retail business, and furthermore you must be able to get a liquor license for that location. Most cities and counties have a limitation as to how many licenses are available, as well as restrictions regarding their location relative to nearby places of worship and schools. There are a number of other permits and licenses to obtain; these will be discussed in detail later in the chapter.

As we learned in Chapter 6 on equipment, the available power sources are an important component of location. If you are using gas equipment in the kitchen, does the location have gas service available? While any location that has electricity has 120 volt service, not every location has 220 or 440 volt service available. Some of your electrical equipment will operate at these voltages. Is this service available?

Next the type of building should be discussed. Will it be owned by the business or leased? If you already own the building, this is okay. It is generally not recommended to build if you are starting a new business due to the high cost of construction. This will greatly add to the startup costs and could be a deal breaker when obtaining capital. If you opt to build, then the construction strategies should be included in this section. The building's cost will be included in the section on startup costs. If the property is to be leased, negotiate a remodeling allowance into the lease. In this way the landlord pays for the costs to change the building to accommodate your business, thus freeing up capital for other startup costs. You will probably pay a higher rent, but this will spread the cost out over the length of the lease. Also negotiate a period of free rent while you are getting the property ready to open, as this will also reduce your startup costs.

Whether you build or lease, a drawing of the layout should be included in this section. It should be to scale and preferably professionally drawn by an architect. It should show the location of the entrance, waiting area, restrooms, dining area, bar dance floor or stage, kitchen, and storage areas. Also include the architect's sketches of the décor if available.

This section should also address access to the location. For example, we have chosen to open a nightclub catering to young people in the area. For those that will drive, is the parking adequate? Is it in close walking distance to apartments and condos? Is public transportation such as buses, streetcars, and taxis available?

Finally, discuss the businesses operating hours. Since we are opening a nightclub, the hours will be late and dependent on local laws governing the serving of alcohol. If the feasibility study warrants it, will we open for lunch? Opening for lunch will require an additional staff and management due to the time spread. These issues should be decided here.

Personnel   The number of employees that will be needed should be determined. It is wise to start out with more employees than the projections would indicate, as some of those that are hired will not work out and some will quit. A mock schedule should be made based on the sales projection. From this schedule you can determine how many professionals you need to hire as well as how many skilled and unskilled workers will needed.

Once the number of employees is projected, the rate of pay for each position should be decided. This will be predicated on the minimum wage laws as well as the prevailing wage scale in the area. Conventional wisdom says that you should meet or exceed what your competitor is paying in order to attract the best employees. In addition to the wage scale, the fringe benefits should be decided. Will you offer paid holidays, vacation days, personal days, sick days, health insurance, life insurance, disability insurance, some of these, or all of these? Include also your contribution to FICA and Medicare. Include in this section how you will recruit employees—job fairs, newspaper, online services, word of mouth, or by other means. A written job description for each position should be prepared, including the employees' duties and who they report to. Include in this section how they will be trained and who will train them.

Finally, if any positions are going to be contracted out, they should be listed here. Such services could include security, cleaning, and payroll. Note that these are services that are traditionally provided in house. They do not include professional services such as accounting or legal. Those will be addressed in a subsequent section.

Production   How your product is to be made should be included in this section. You should incorporate the fact that you will have standardized recipes for all food items and bar drinks. Standardized portion sizes should also be mentioned here as well as how they will be monitored. The standardized food and drink recipes as well as the standardized portions should not be given here, just mentioned. If you feel a need to present them to your investors, they should be placed in the appendices.

Mention the fact that the product will be delivered to the customer by way of table service (as opposed to self-service) by a well-trained and uniformed service staff.

As we are running a higher check average than the normal bar, the servers will have fewer seats assigned to them in order to increase level of service.

Cover in this section also new product development. Explain that the culinary staff will constantly be exploring new ideas and innovations to keep your club on the leading edge. Also convey the fact that the bar staff will be mixologists rather than bartenders and will be constantly innovating new cocktails.

Inventory   In this section, go into some detail about the kind of inventory you will carry. Stress that some of it is perishable and some of it is nonperishable. Tell how the perishable inventory is to be rotated to minimize or eliminate spoilage. Explain to your investors that the food service industry is a manufacturing plant as well as a retail outlet. You bring raw product in, produce a finished product out of it, and sell it to the customer all under one roof.

Cover what the value of your startup inventory will be and what the average value of the inventory will be once you get opened and established. Tell what your inventory turnover rate will be and how this will compare to the national average for the hospitality industry of one to two times. For some reason investors, particularly banks, put a great deal of weight on this number.

What will be your controls over your inventory? Tell how the storage areas, particularly the liquor storage, will be secured. Convey that the monthly food and liquor cost percentage will be an indicator of how well the control system is working.

Suppliers   Identify who your key suppliers will be and what goods they will be supplying you. You will probably want one full-line supplier for your groceries and supplies. In addition, since we are stressing locally grown herbicide- and hormone-free meats and produce, a list of local farmers and ranchers should be developed. A "plan B" should also be developed identifying sources when local products are not available. These could be environmentally friendly farms and ranches located in other parts of the country.

A similar list should also be developed for beverages. Again you will probably, depending on state and local laws, be purchasing from a full-line distributor. Local wineries and microbreweries that you will be purchasing from should also be included.

Include with each supplier their credit policies and their delivery schedules.

Credit Policies   It is customary in the hospitality industry to extend credit to customers via established credit card companies. You should establish which companies you will do business with. Customers normally will limit their credit cards to one or two companies, so you should accept several of the more predominate firms. Carefully research the charges that the credit card companies will make to you for the service of accepting their cards.

Many bars have historically let their customers, particularly the good ones, run a tab and pay it off periodically. This is not a good idea. As most customers have at least one credit card, let the credit card company take the risk of payment.

A policy regarding personal checks, traveler's checks, and money orders should also be established and included in this section.

Accounts Payable   Managing your cash flow is an important task. Paying an invoice too soon can deplete your cash; however, paying late can cost you valuable discounts and damage your credit. Also, take advantage of prompt payment discounts. Prompt payment to your venders goes a long way when you are negotiating prices with them. If they have to "carry" you, they will charge you a higher price for goods to offset their credit costs.

Management and Organization

In this section of the business plan, you will tell the potential investor about the management team, develop an organizational chart, and identify your professional and advisory support.

The Management Team   Assuming that you will be the general manager of the operation, you should give a brief biography of yourself. Include such things as your experience in food and beverage management, your organizational and analytical skills, as well as your entrepreneurial spirit. Also include your resume. Since the whole organization revolves around you, a succession plan should be included in the possibility that you become incapacitated and are unable to run the business.

At this stage of the project, your management staff, namely your assistant general manager, bar manager, service manager, and executive chef, should be identified. Include their resumes as well, along with a brief bio of the unique skills they bring to the enterprise.

Organization   Since you already know your hours of operation, the number of seats, and the level of service that you wish to provide, now is the time to determine how many and what type of employees it will take to operate. For example, if you determine that each server will handle 20 seats and you have 300 seats, you will need 15 servers per shift. What skill sets do they need, and how much is it going to cost per hour to get a person with these skill sets? This should be done for each position in the operation. Once this task is completed, you can determine a projected payroll, which we will use in figuring the labor cost in the pro forma section.

In order for the operation to function smoothly, an organizational chart should be developed and placed in this section. First, determine how the duties will be divided among your management team. Second, determine which groups of employees will report to which members of management. Figure 14.5 gives the proposed organizational chart. One of the most common complaints of employees in startup businesses is that there are "too many bosses who give different directions." This confusion leads to high turnover, and management is constantly training new employees while the business is struggling to get on its feet.

Everyone in the organization needs to know what is expected of him or her. For this reason, job descriptions should be developed. Include the job descriptions of your management team in this section, and put the staff job descriptions in the appendices.

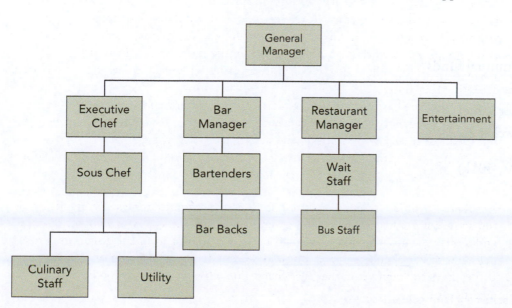

FIGURE 14.5
Proposed organizational chart.

Professional and Advisory Support   If the proposed organization is a corporation, it will need a board of directors. The number of directors should be included in the article of incorporation. You should have a sufficient number to properly advise you on the policies and direction of the company but not too many as to make the board unwieldy. It would be wise to have an accountant and an attorney on the board as well as some of your investors or a banker. A person familiar with the hospitality business, but not a competitor, should be included as well. The names, addresses, and professional affiliations of the board members should be included in the business plan.

If the proposed organization is a sole proprietorship, a partnership, or a closed LLC, it would be a good idea to establish an advisory committee made up of individuals similar to the makeup of a board of directors.

In addition to a board of directors or advisory board, you will have other professionals whom you can rely on for advice. These would include your banker, accountant, attorney, insurance agent, consultants, and mentors.

Personal Financial Statement

A copy of your personal financial statement should be shown here. If there are other investors in the project, include their financial statements as well. Refer to Figure 14.6 for an example of a personal financial statement form. While your home, IRA or retirement accounts, and college saving funds are included in your personal financial statement, they

Personal Financial Statement

Personal Financial Statement of:
Enter your name here
As of mm/dd/yyyy

Assets	Amount in Dollars
Cash - checking accounts	$ -
Cash - savings accounts	-
Certificates of deposit	-
Securities - stocks / bonds / mutual funds	-
Notes & contracts receivable	-
Life insurance (cash surrender value)	-
Personal property (autos, jewelry, etc.)	-
Retirement Funds (e.g., IRAs, 401k)	-
Real estate (market value)	-
Other assets (specify)	-
Other assets (specify)	-
Total Assets	$ -

FIGURE 14.6
An example of a personal financial statement form. Courtesy of SCORE.

Liabilities	Amount in Dollars	
Current Debt (Credit cards, Accounts)	$	-
Notes payable (describe below)		-
Taxes payable		-
Real estate mortgages (describe)		-
Other liabilities (specify)		-
Other liabilities (specify)		-
Total Liabilities	$	-
Net Worth	$	-

Signature: Date:

Personal Finance Statement of:

Enter your name here

As of mm/dd/yyyy

Details

1. ASSETS - Details

Notes and Contracts held

From Whom Owing	Balance Owing	Original Amount	Original Date	Monthly Payment	Maturity Date	History / Purpose
	$ -	$ -		$ -		

Securities: stocks | bonds | mutual funds

Name of Security	Number of Shares	Cost	Market Value	Date of Acquisition
		$ -	$ -	

FIGURE 14.6   *(Continued)*

Stock in Privately Held Companies

Company Name	No. of shares	$ Invested	Est. Market Value
		$ -	$ -

Real Estate

Description / Location	Market Value	Amount Owing	Original Cost	Purchase Date
	$ -	$ -	$ -	

2. LIABILITIES - Details

Credit Card & Charge Card Debt

Name of Card / Creditor	Amount Due
	$ -

Notes Payable (excluding monthly bills)

Name of Creditor	Amount Owing	Original Amount	Monthly Payment	Interest Rate	Secured by (Leine)
	$ -	$ -	$ -		

Mortgage / Real Estate Loans Payable

Name of Creditor	Amount Owing	Original Amount	Monthly Payment	Interest Rate	Secured by (Leine)
	$ -	$ -	$ -		

FIGURE 14.6 *(Continued)*

should not be included as collateral for the business. Should the business fail you do not want to lose these assets. Make sure you consult an attorney before signing any loan agreements. Herman Cain, the former president of Godfathers Pizza, referring to going into business for yourself, once said "you will lose everything before the bank loses a dime"

Startup Expense and Capitalization

Before the business gets up and running, there will be startup expenses. How much depends on circumstances. On one end of the spectrum, let's say you have vacant land on which you will build a building; equip it; and add décor, landscaping, parking, signage, and so forth. You would expect a significant investment. On the other hand, if you were to lease a building that previously housed a bar and restaurant, then your investment would be considerably smaller. You would avoid such expenses as a hood and exhaust system, restrooms, and an HVAC system designed for restaurants.

This is a crucial part of your business plan. One of the pitfalls that most new enterprises fall into is not accurately estimating the startup costs. They either overlook some expenses or underestimate them. For example, in taking over an existing restaurant, the owner decided to add some gas ranges and ovens. The gas line coming into the restaurant was not large enough. To put the larger gas line in, a trough had to be jackhammered through the parking lot. Ca Ching! The Health Department requires another hand sink in the kitchen. Ca Ching! A neighborhood group has organized a protest of your bar opening in their vicinity. Ca Ching! Too many Ca Chings and you are out of money before the doors are even opened. Each overlooked expense cuts into your working capital.

The best of research will not cover every unanticipated expense. Therefore you should have a line on your start up expense statement titled contingency expense. This will be to cover anything that may have been overlooked. A rule of thumb for contingencies is 20 percent of the total of your startup expenses.

In this section explain how you arrived at your estimated startup expenses. Give your source of information. Also include bank loans and loans from others, if applicable. If the proposed business will be a partnership or corporation, list how much will be invested by each person and what their percentage of ownership will be. Figure 14.7 gives an example of a startup and capitalization statement,

Financial Plan

Now we come to the centerpiece of the business plan: the financial plan. This is made up of a pro forma income statement and a cash flow projection. A **pro forma statement** shows what you believe will occur financially in your business in the future. In addition to the pro forma statements, you will need a break-even analysis.

FIGURE 14.7
An example of a startup and capitalization statement.
Courtesy of SCORE.

Startup Expenses

Enter your company name here

Sources of Capital
Owners' Investment (name and percent ownership)

Your name and percent ownership	$	-
Other investor		-
Other investor		-
Other investor		-
Total Investment	$	-

FIGURE 14.7   (*Continued*)

Bank Loans

Bank 1	$	-
Bank 2		-
Bank 3		-
Bank 4		-
Total Bank Loans	**$**	**-**

Other Loans

Source 1	$	-
Source 2		-
Total Other Loans	**$**	**-**

Startup Expenses

Buildings/Real Estate

Purchase	$	-
Construction		-
Remodeling		-
Other		-
Total Buildings/Real Estate	**$**	**-**

Leasehold Improvements

Item 1	$	-
Item 2		-
Item 3		-
Item 4		-
Total Leasehold Improvements	**$**	**-**

Capital Equipment List

Furniture	$	-
Equipment		-
Fixtures		-
Machinery		-
Other		-
Total Capital Equipment	**$**	**-**

Location and Admin Expenses

Rental	$	-
Utility deposits		-
Legal and accounting fees		-
Prepaid insurance		-
Pre-opening salaries		-
Other		-
Total Location and Admin Expenses	**$**	**-**

FIGURE 14.7 (Continued)

Opening Inventory

Category 1 $ -
Category 2   -
Category 3   -
Category 4   -
Category 5   -
Total Inventory $ -

Advertising and Promotional Expenses

Advertising $ -
Signage   -
Printing   -
Travel/entertainment   -
Other/additional categories   -
Total Advertising/Promotional Expenses $ -

Other Expenses

Other expense 1 $ -
Other expense 2   -
Total Other Expenses $ -
Reserve for Contingencies $ -
Working Capital $ -

Summary Statement

Sources of Capital

Owners' and other investments $ -
Bank loans   -
Other loans   -
Total Source of Funds $ -

Startup Expenses

Buildings/real estate $ -
Leasehold improvements   -
Capital equipment   -
Location/administration expenses   -
Opening inventory   -
Advertising/promotional expenses   -
Other expenses   -
Contingency fund   -
Working capital   -
Total Startup Expenses $ -

FIGURE 14.7   *(Continued)*

<u>**Security and Collateral for Loan Proposal**</u>

Collateral for Loans		Value	Description
Real estate	$	-	
Other collateral		-	
Other collateral		-	
Other collateral		-	

Owners
Your name here
Other owner
Other owner

Loan Guarantors (other than owners)
Loan guarantor 1
Loan guarantor 2
Loan guarantor 3

Pro Forma Income Statement   The pro forma income statement shows your projected sales, expenses, and hopefully a projected profit. It is much like a budget except in the case of a budget you have historical data on the business, on which the budget is built. In the case of a pro forma, you have no historical data, so there is more guesswork involved. Some expenses you will have a good grasp on such as rent (assuming you have picked a location) or insurance. Other numbers will be more elusive, such as sales. Whatever the number, be as realistic as possible. When in doubt, err on the side of caution. Do as much research as possible. Consult with industry experts and employ industry figures put out by the National Restaurant Association and other trade organizations. A step-by-step illustration to put together a pro forma income statement follows. Refer to Figure 14.8 as you go through it.

Assumptions: 160 seat restaurant, 70 seat club (lounge) including 20 seats at the bar. Restaurant open 11 A.M.–10 P.M. seven days a week, club open 11 A.M.–1 A.M., seven days. Average check per person for the restaurant: lunch $10, dinner $25; bar lunch $5, bar happy hour and evening $20 (bar figures are for drinks only and do not include food served at the bar, which would be included in food sales).

Food Sales This, along with bar sales, is the most important number on the pro forma income statement because all of the variable costs will be predicated on sales. Unfortunately, it is also the most difficult number to predict. However, we do have some clues. We know how many seats there are. What we need to do is predict how many customers will occupy those seats. Trade associations will give figures by region for operations similar to yours. Use these to get a rough idea of what to expect. Use your SWOT analysis to further define this number. For example, an association study indicates that a restaurant in your region with the same average check will turn a seat one and a half times during a lunch period. By consulting your SWOT analysis, you conclude that the area in which you are located is not very conducive to business traffic. You therefore estimate that you will do only a half turn for lunch. The same procedure is used for dinner business.

Once the number or turns is figured, it is multiplied by the number of seats to get the number of customers per meal period. This number is then multiplied by the estimated average check to get the dollar sales for the meal period. The sales for the meal period are then multiplied by the number of days the business is open in the

	Jan	Feb	Mar	Apr	May	June	Jul	Aug	Sep	Oct	Nov	Dec	Total
Food Sales	$175,000	$150,000	$215,000	$228,000	$235,600	$228,000	$240,000	$235,600	$237,500	$250,000	$225,000	$295,000	$2,714,700
Beverage Sales	$ 95,000	$ 91,000	$140,000	$164,500	$189,000	$189,000	$204,500	$200,000	$175,500	$219,000	$195,000	$220,000	$2,082,500
Total Sales	$270,000	$241,000	$355,000	$392,500	$424,600	$417,000	$444,500	$435,600	$413,000	$469,000	$420,000	$515,000	$4,797,200
Cost of goods sold													
Food Cost	$ 70,000	$ 60,000	$ 86,000	$ 91,200	$ 94,240	$ 91,200	$ 96,000	$ 94,240	$ 95,000	$100,000	$ 90,000	$118,000	$1,085,880
Beverage Cost	$ 23,750	$ 22,750	$ 35,000	$ 41,125	$ 47,250	$ 47,250	$ 51,125	$ 50,000	$ 43,875	$ 54,750	$ 48,750	$ 55,000	$ 520,625
Total C/GS	$ 93,750	$ 82,750	$121,000	$132,325	$141,490	$138,450	$147,125	$144,240	$138,875	$154,750	$138,750	$173,000	$1,606,505
Gross Profit	$176,250	$158,250	$234,000	$260,175	$283,110	$278,550	$297,375	$291,360	$274,125	$314,250	$281,250	$342,000	$3,190,695
Expenses													
Payroll													
Salaries	$ 38,333	$ 38,333	$ 38,333	$ 38,333	$ 38,333	$ 38,333	$ 38,333	$ 38,333	$ 38,333	$ 38,333	$ 38,333	$ 38,333	$ 459,996
Wages	$ 54,000	$ 48,200	$ 71,000	$ 78,500	$ 84,920	$ 83,400	$ 88,900	$ 87,120	$ 82,600	$ 93,800	$ 84,000	$103,000	$ 959,440
Payroll taxes	$ 7,063	$ 6,620	$ 8,364	$ 8,938	$ 9,429	$ 9,313	$ 9,733	$ 9,597	$ 9,251	$ 10,108	$ 9,358	$ 10,812	$ 108,587
Total Payroll	$ 92,333	$ 86,533	$109,333	$116,833	$123,253	$121,733	$127,233	$125,453	$120,933	$132,133	$122,333	$141,333	$1,419,436
Employee benefits	$ 10,000	$ 10,000	$ 10,000	$ 10,000	$ 10,000	$ 10,000	$ 10,000	$ 10,000	$ 10,000	$ 10,000	$ 10,000	$ 10,000	$ 120,000
Rent	$ 28,000	$ 28,000	$ 28,000	$ 28,000	$ 28,000	$ 28,000	$ 28,000	$ 28,000	$ 28,000	$ 28,000	$ 28,000	$ 28,000	$ 336,000
Utilities	$ 8,000	$ 8,000	$ 8,000	$ 8,000	$ 8,000	$ 8,000	$ 8,000	$ 8,000	$ 8,000	$ 8,000	$ 8,000	$ 8,000	$ 96,000
Telecommunications	$ 1,000	$ 1,000	$ 1,000	$ 1,000	$ 1,000	$ 1,000	$ 1,000	$ 1,000	$ 1,000	$ 1,000	$ 1,000	$ 1,000	$ 12,000
Supplies	$ 5,400	$ 4,820	$ 7,100	$ 7,850	$ 8,492	$ 8,340	$ 8,890	$ 8,712	$ 8,260	$ 9,380	$ 8,400	$ 10,300	$ 95,944
Advertising	$ 8,000	$ 8,000	$ 8,000	$ 8,000	$ 8,000	$ 8,000	$ 8,000	$ 8,000	$ 8,000	$ 8,000	$ 8,000	$ 8,000	$ 96,000
Music & Entertainment	$ 25,500	$ 25,500	$ 25,500	$ 25,500	$ 25,500	$ 25,500	$ 25,500	$ 25,500	$ 25,500	$ 25,500	$ 25,500	$ 25,500	$ 306,000
Legal & accounting	$ 2,000	$ 2,000	$ 2,000	$ 2,000	$ 2,000	$ 2,000	$ 2,000	$ 2,000	$ 2,000	$ 2,000	$ 2,000	$ 2,000	$ 24,000
Insurance	$ 4,500	$ 4,500	$ 4,500	$ 4,500	$ 4,500	$ 4,500	$ 4,500	$ 4,500	$ 4,500	$ 4,500	$ 4,500	$ 4,500	$ 54,000
Repairs & Maintenance	$ 2,500	$ 2,500	$ 2,500	$ 2,500	$ 2,500	$ 2,500	$ 2,500	$ 2,500	$ 2,500	$ 2,500	$ 2,500	$ 2,500	$ 30,000
Miscellaneous	$ 4,000	$ 4,000	$ 4,000	$ 4,000	$ 4,000	$ 4,000	$ 4,000	$ 4,000	$ 4,000	$ 4,000	$ 4,000	$ 4,000	$ 48,000
Depreciation	$ 5,500	$ 5,500	$ 5,500	$ 5,500	$ 5,500	$ 5,500	$ 5,500	$ 5,500	$ 5,500	$ 5,500	$ 5,500	$ 5,500	$ 66,000
Total Expenses	$196,733	$190,353	$215,433	$223,683	$230,745	$229,073	$235,123	$233,165	$228,193	$240,513	$229,733	$250,633	$2,703,380
Pre tax profit (loss)	-$ 20,483	-$ 32,103	$ 18,567	$ 36,492	$ 52,365	$ 49,477	$ 62,252	$ 58,195	$ 45,932	$ 73,737	$ 51,517	$ 91,367	$ 487,315

FIGURE 14.8 The pro forma income statement for the proposed club.

month. The same formula is used for dinner, and the two are added together. Thus our formula looks like this:

Number of turns $\times$ number of seats = customers per meal period

Customers per meal period $\times$ average check = sales per meal period

Sales per meal period $\times$ days open per month = sales per meal period per month

Lunch sales per month + dinner sale per month = food sales per month.

For example, along with the assumptions given above, let's assume that the restaurant will turn a seat 0.5 times during lunch and 1.5 turns during dinner. Our formula now looks like this:

Lunch number of turns $\times$ number of seats = customers per meal period
$$0.5 \times 160 = 80$$

Customers per meal period $\times$ average check = sales per meal period
$$80 \times \$10 = \$800$$

Sales per meal period $\times$ days open per month = sales per meal period per month
$$\$800 \times 30 = \$24,000 \text{ lunch sales per month}$$

Dinner number of turns $\times$ number of seats = customers per meal period
$$1.5 \times 160 = 240$$

Customers per meal period $\times$ average check = sales per meal period
$$240 \times \$25 = \$6,000$$

Sales per meal period $\times$ days open per month = sales per meal period per month
$$\$6,000 \times 30 = \$180,000$$

Lunch sales per month + dinner sale per month = food sales per month
$$\$ 24,000 + 180,000 = \$204,400$$

This gives you a rough idea of what to expect in terms of food sales. Refer to Figure 14.8 to see how the sales were allocated for this example. Keep in mind that this is an average. Sales on Monday will probably be lower than sales on Saturday. Sales will also vary month to month depending on your location. For example, a restaurant and club operation in Fargo, North Dakota, will probably have poor sales in January and February while the same operation in Miami Beach, Florida, will have high sales during those months. When putting together your sales projections make sure that you look at all of the variables that could affect your sales. As stated previously this is a very important number. Take the time to get it as near to reality as you can.

Beverage Sales The beverage sales are figured in the same manner as food sales. That is, you know the number of seats in the operation. Estimate the number of turns for a period and multiply it by the number of seats. Multiply this by the average check to get the sales for that period. Multiply that number by the days in the month to gets sales for that period for the month. Add the monthly sales for the time periods to get total beverage sales for the month. For example, we estimated a 0.5 turn for the bar for lunch with a $5.00 average check, a 2.5 turnover for happy hour with a $20 average check, and a 2.0 turnover for the rest of the evening also with a $20 average check:

Bar number of turns $\times$ number of seats = customers per lunch period
$$0.5 \times 70 = 35$$

Customers per meal period $\times$ average check = sales per meal period
$$35 \times \$ 5 = \$175$$

Sales per meal period × days open per month = sales per meal period per month
$ 175 × 30 = $5250 lunch sales per month

Bar number of turns × number of seats = customers per happy hour period
2.5 × 70 = 175

Customers per meal period × average check = sales per meal period
175 × $ 20 = $3500

Sales per meal period × days open per month = sales per meal period per month
$ 3500 × 30 = $105,000 happy hour sales per month

Bar number of turns × number of seats = customers per evening period
2.0 × 70 = 140

Customers per meal period × average check = sales per meal period
140 × $ 20 = $2800

Sales per meal period × days open per month = sales per meal period per month
$ 2800 × 30 = $84,000 evening period sales per month

Lunch bar sales + happy hour sales + evening sales = monthly beverage sales
$5,250 + $105,000 + $84,000 = $194,250

Again, this is an average and should be allocated by month based on your projected sales cycle. Refer to Figure 14.8 to see how the beverage sales were allocated for this operation.

Cost of Goods Sold This is a variable cost; that is, it goes up or down as sales go up or down. After the menus, both bar and food, are planned, you should have a good idea of what your aggregate food or beverage cost (product mix) percentages should be. Take these percentages and multiply them by their respective sales. For example, assume that we have calculated our food cost of goods sold percentage to be 40 percent. In Figure 14.8 the food sales for January are $175,000. Multiply this by 40 percent or 0.40 to get a cost of food sold of $70,000.

It should be noted that cost of goods sold is figured by taking opening inventory plus purchases less closing inventory to get cost of goods sold. Since we do not know what those numbers will be, we will use our standard cost of goods sold percentage, in this case 40 percent for food, and multiply it by food sales.

Do the same for cost of beverage sold. Assume that our cost of beverage sold percentage is 25%. In Figure 14.8 the beverage sales for January are $95,000. Multiply $95,000 by 25 percent or 0.25 to get a cost on beverage sold of $23,750.

The cost of food sold is then added to the cost of beverages sold to get a total cost of goods sold. This is then divided by total sales to get a cost of goods sold (both food and beverage) percent. For example, January's cost of food sold was $70,000, and the cost of beverage sold was $23,750. Added together they equal $93,750. The sales for January were $270,000 (both food and beverage). Cost divided by sales equals a percentage:

$93,750/$270,000 = 34.7 percent

Gross Profit Gross profit is the amount of money made on cost of goods sold. To figure gross profit, subtract cost of goods sold from sales. For example our cost of goods sold in January for both food and beverage was $93,750, and our sales for food and beverage were $270,000. Subtracting $93,750 from $270,000 gives a gross profit in dollars of $176,250. To figure the gross profit percentage, divide $176,250 by $270,000 to get a gross profit percentage of 65.3 percent.

Payroll Payroll will be split into two parts: salaries, which are a fixed cost, and wages, which are a variable cost. Salaries are paid to management and do not change as sales volume changes. Wages paid to the hourly employees go up and down as sales go up and down, thus making them a variable cost.

As far as management is concerned, assume that we have a general manager, an assistant general manager, a dining room manager, a bar manager, a relief manager, a chef, and two sous chefs. Their combined salaries are $460,000 per year or $38,333 per month, or about 10 percent of total sales. Budgeting 30 percent of sales for payroll, this will leave 20 percent of sales for the variable cost employees. Because it is a variable cost, it will go up and down as sales go up and down each month. In addition to payroll, any business must pay 7.65 percent into FICA and Medicare as the employer's share of these taxes (7.65 percent is also take out of the employees' pay). Refer to Figure 14.8 to see how the payroll is allocated each month.

Prime Cost While this number is not a part of the pro forma income statement, it is an important check-and-balance number. Prime cost is the total of food, beverage, and payroll costs. The rule of thumb in the hospitality industry is that prime cost should not exceed 65 percent in order for an operation to be profitable. In our example, the prime cost is 63.1 percent, which is well within an acceptable range.

$$\text{Food cost} + \text{beverage cost} + \text{payroll} = \text{prime cost}/\text{total sales}$$
$$= \text{prime cost percentage}$$
$$\$1,085,880 + \$520,625 + \$1,419,436 = \$3,025,941/\$4,797,200$$
$$= 63.1 \text{ percent}$$

Employee Benefits This is a number that could vary greatly from operation to operation depending on the benefits given to employees. Benefits could include such things as paid holidays, vacation time, personal days, health insurance, life insurance, or retirement (401K). Some benefits could be given to salaried employees only, hourly employees only, or all employees. While employee benefits could go a long way in attracting outstanding personnel, care must be exercised as this could be a very expensive proposition depending on which benefit you choose to give. In our example we have determined that the benefits that we will give our employees will cost on average $10,000 per month. Note that many operations chose to include employee benefits as a part of payroll rather than listing it as a separate expense.

Rent This is one of the easier numbers to predict. At this stage in the process, you should have a location picked out, have negotiated with the landlord, and have a pretty good idea of what the rent will be. In our example, we have determined that the rent will be $28,000 per month.

Utilities This number can be provided to you by your utility companies. If you furnish them with a layout of your operation including the cubic feet, along with your equipment list, they can give you a reasonable estimate of what your utilities will be. In our example, Figure 14.8, we have spread the utility costs out evenly over the twelve-month period. In all likelihood this will not happen. It could go up or down in the winter or summer, depending on your location. Note that this cost will not go up or down with sales but rather up or down with the temperature. Thus it is not considered a variable cost but rather a fixed cost.

Telecommunications This includes land phone, cell phones, computer broadband hookups, and cable or satellite television hookups.

Supplies This includes all cleaning and janitorial supplies and office supplies. Some operations include supplies associated with food and beverage, such as to-go containers, aluminum foil, paper napkins, stir sticks, and so on. in this category, while others choose to include those items in cost of goods sold.

Advertising This number is obtained after consulting with various media outlets in the area and putting together an effective advertising campaign that targets our demographic audience. Since it is predetermined and relatively the same month after month, it is a fixed cost. Some operations base their advertising budget on sales, and in that case it would be a variable cost.

Music and Entertainment The lounge will provide entertainment on certain nights of the week. Decide how often it will occur and the average cost of a band or DJ in your area, and multiply the two to come up with this cost.

Legal and Accounting These two expenses are typically lumped together. Accounting is a rather easy number to predict, while legal is another matter. Restaurants and lounges usually do not have an accounting department unless they are a part of a chain. Rather they will have a bookkeeper or relegate the duties to an office aide. This person will record deposits, prepare payroll, and pay bills. They are part of the staff, and their expense will go under payroll. The accounting expense that goes on this line is for the fees paid to a certified public accountant (CPA). The professionals will take the numbers that the bookkeeper provides to them and prepare the financial statements as well as prepare the various tax forms. They will also advise you on such financial matters as depreciation, buying versus leasing, and so forth.

Legal expenses are harder to predict because you do not know how often you will need an attorney. Some businesses will hire an attorney on a retainer to review contracts, permits, and leases, which evens this expense out a bit. However, you do not know when, or how often, you could be sued by a customer or be a party to a lawsuit involving a dram shop law liability. While liability insurance will pay a large part of the expense of a lawsuit, you will still have some expenditures. Unfortunately, the bar business has more than its share of lawsuits, and this expense should be figured accordingly.

Insurance This line pertains to insurance that is relevant to the business. It would include such items as liability as well as contents of the building such as equipment, furniture and fixtures, and leasehold improvements. If the insurance involves employee perks such as health, life, or loss of income, it would go on the fringe benefit line. An exception to this could be life insurance on one or more of the partners of the business or the general manager, where the beneficiary is the business rather than an individual.

Repairs and Maintenance In the first year of business, repairs and maintenance expenses will depend largely on the type of equipment you purchased. If used equipment was bought, this expense will run higher than if you bought new. This is because new equipment rarely breaks down, and if it does, it is probably under a warranty. Also included in this category is maintenance such as hood and ductwork cleaning, as well as refrigeration maintenance contracts if applicable.

Miscellaneous This is the "catch all" line. If money is spent and does not fit under any other category, it goes under miscellaneous.

Depreciation This is money that is theoretically set aside for replacement of equipment, furniture, and fixtures that have worn out and need replacing or have outlived their useful life. There are several forms of depreciation, and each one has its advantages and disadvantages. Your accountant will advise you on the type that best fits your situation and will prepare your depreciation schedules.

Total Expenses This is the sum of all expenses including payroll, but not including food and beverage cost.

Pretax Profit (loss) Subtract total expenses from gross profit to obtain the pretax profit or loss line. This represent the amount of money left over after all expenses have been covered. If you will notice on the example (Figure 14.8), our operation lost money in January and February but made money on all of the successive months. This is because the sales were not high enough during those months to cover expenses, while in the succeeding months sales were greater than expenses, thus giving us a profit.

As you can see, a pro forma income statement is a very time-consuming process if done correctly. However, it is probably the most important thing you will do to ensure the success of your business. The pro forma should be accompanied by a narrative that explains the major assumptions that were made in the preparation of the document. By all means keep documentation on the source of your information and your research resources because you will need them in case revisions are necessary or if some material needs to be updated.

Pro Forma Cash Flow   At this point a lot of hard work, research, and calculations have gone into the business plan. However, none of it means anything if you run out of cash. The pro forma cash flow statement will point out just how much cash will be needed to open the business and to keep it running over the long term.

As you can see on Figure 14.9, in the first column titled Start Up, our investment in the business is $150,000 and we have secured a loan in the amount of $450,000. This represents the amount of cash we have to open the doors.

Before that happens, we will need to purchase kitchen equipment, bar equipment, furniture, and do some leasehold improvements such as plumbing and electrical, décor, and signage among other things. All of these go on the Capital Purchases line. Opening inventory, costs associated with hiring and training the staff, pre-opening advertisements, and any other costs associated with opening the business go on the Other Start Up Costs line. After these are paid for we will have $50,000 left over on opening day.

That $50,000 goes on the next column, January, under cash on hand. In January there are sales of $270,000. This number comes from the pro forma income statement (Figure 14.8). Therefore in January we have $320,000 in which to operate. Our expenses in January total $292,046. These numbers again come from the pro forma income statement in Figure 14.8. Note that depreciation is missing. This is because we do not write a check for depreciation. It does not affect our cash flow. In addition to the total expenses, the payment on our loan must be made. The loan payment is not included on the pro forma income statement; however, it represents a deduction of cash; therefore it goes on the pro forma cash flow statement. After all is said and done, we have a positive cash balance at the end of January of $23,954. This number again goes on the cash on hand line for February.

February's sales were $241,000, which when added to the cash on hand equals $264,954 cash available for February. Our expenses in February were $274,000 plus the loan payment of $4000 for a total of $278,223. However, we only had cash on hand of $264,954 leaving us short $13,269. In this case there are two alternatives: invest more money or borrow it. A third alternative would be to not pay some invoices; however, this is not a sound business practice. We have decided to borrow the money from the bank on a sixty-day short-term loan which will show up on March's cash column under loans. In May when we pay it back it will show up on the loan payment line, which will increase our normal monthly loan payment of $4000 to $19,000 (4000 normal payment + 15,000 short − term loan = 19,000).

In June, the owners decide that the business is financially stable and decide to take out $25,000 a month for the rest of the year. This is recorded on the Owners Withdrawal line.

Since opening, the sound system, which was purchased used, has not worked properly. In September, the owners decide to put in a totally new system at a cost of $40,000. This expense goes on the Capital Purchases line in September.

	Start up	Jan	Feb	Mar	Apr	May	Jun	Jul	Aug	Sep	Oct	Nov	Dec
Cash on hand	$ 0	$ 50,000	$ 23,954	-$ 13,269	$ 13,434	$ 42,488	$ 71,924	$ 88,588	$117,607	$ 42,705	$ 15,886	$ 56,015	$ 74,674
Sales		$270,000	$241,000	$355,000	$392,500	$424,600	$417,000	$444,500	$435,600	$413,000	$469,000	$420,000	$515,000
Investments	$150,000												
Loans	450,000			$ 15,000									
Cash available	600,000	$320,000	$264,954	$356,731	$405,934	$467,088	$488,924	$533,088	$553,207	$455,705	$484,886	$476,015	$589,674
Cash paid out													
Food Cost		$ 70,000	$ 60,000	$ 86,000	$ 91,200	$ 94,240	$ 91,200	$ 96,000	$ 94,240	$ 95,000	$100,000	$ 90,000	$118,000
Beverage Cost		$ 23,750	$ 22,750	$ 35,000	$ 41,125	$ 47,250	$ 47,250	$ 51,125	$ 50,000	$ 43,875	$ 54,750	$ 48,750	$ 55,000
Salaries		$ 38,333	$ 38,333	$ 38,333	$ 38,333	$ 38,333	$ 38,333	$ 38,333	$ 38,333	$ 38,333	$ 38,333	$ 38,333	$ 38,333
Wages		$ 54,000	$ 48,200	$ 71,000	$ 78,500	$ 84,920	$ 83,400	$ 88,900	$ 87,120	$ 82,600	$ 93,800	$ 84,000	$103,000
Payroll taxes		$ 7,063	$ 6,620	$ 8,364	$ 8,938	$ 9,429	$ 9,313	$ 9,733	$ 9,597	$ 9,251	$ 10,108	$ 9,358	$ 10,812
Employee benefits		$ 10,000	$ 10,000	$ 10,000	$ 10,000	$ 10,000	$ 10,000	$ 10,000	$ 10,000	$ 10,000	$ 10,000	$ 10,000	$ 10,000
Rent		$ 28,000	$ 28,000	$ 28,000	$ 28,000	$ 28,000	$ 28,000	$ 28,000	$ 28,000	$ 28,000	$ 28,000	$ 28,000	$ 28,000
Utilities		$ 8,000	$ 8,000	$ 8,000	$ 8,000	$ 8,000	$ 8,000	$ 8,000	$ 8,000	$ 8,000	$ 8,000	$ 8,000	$ 8,000
Telecommunications		$ 1,000	$ 1,000	$ 1,000	$ 1,000	$ 1,000	$ 1,000	$ 1,000	$ 1,000	$ 1,000	$ 1,000	$ 1,000	$ 1,000
Supplies		$ 5,400	$ 4,820	$ 7,100	$ 7,850	$ 8,492	$ 8,340	$ 8,890	$ 8,712	$ 8,260	$ 9,380	$ 8,400	$ 10,300
Advertising		$ 8,000	$ 8,000	$ 8,000	$ 8,000	$ 8,000	$ 8,000	$ 8,000	$ 8,000	$ 8,000	$ 8,000	$ 8,000	$ 8,000
Music & Entertainment		$ 25,500	$ 25,500	$ 25,500	$ 25,500	$ 25,500	$ 25,500	$ 25,500	$ 25,500	$ 25,500	$ 25,500	$ 25,500	$ 25,500
Legal & accounting		$ 2,000	$ 2,000	$ 2,000	$ 2,000	$ 2,000	$ 2,000	$ 2,000	$ 2,000	$ 2,000	$ 2,000	$ 2,000	$ 2,000
Insurance		$ 4,500	$ 4,500	$ 4,500	$ 4,500	$ 4,500	$ 4,500	$ 4,500	$ 4,500	$ 4,500	$ 4,500	$ 4,500	$ 4,500
Repairs & Maintenance		$ 2,500	$ 2,500	$ 2,500	$ 2,500	$ 2,500	$ 2,500	$ 2,500	$ 2,500	$ 2,500	$ 2,500	$ 2,500	$ 2,500
Miscellaneous		$ 4,000	$ 4,000	$ 4,000	$ 4,000	$ 4,000	$ 4,000	$ 4,000	$ 4,000	$ 4,000	$ 4,000	$ 4,000	$ 4,000
Sub total		$292,046	$274,223	$339,297	$359,446	$376,164	$371,336	$386,481	$381,502	$370,819	$399,871	$372,341	$428,945
Loan payment		$ 4,000	$ 4,000	$ 4,000	$ 4,000	$ 19,000	$ 4,000	$ 4,000	$ 4,000	$ 4,000	$ 4,000	$ 4,000	$ 4,000
Capital Purchases	450,000									$ 40,000			
Other Start up costs	100,000												
Owners withdrawal		$ 25,000	$ 25,000	$ 25,000	$ 25,000	$ 25,000	$ 25,000	$ 25,000	$ 25,000	$ 25,000	$ 25,000	$ 25,000	$ 25,000
Total cash paid out	550,000	$296,046	$278,223	$343,297	$363,446	$395,164	$400,336	$415,481	$410,502	$439,819	$428,871	$401,341	$457,945
Cash position	50,000	$ 23,954	-$ 13,269	$ 13,434	$ 42,488	$ 71,924	$ 88,588	$117,607	$ 42,705	$ 15,886	$ 56,015	$ 74,674	$131,729

FIGURE 14.9 The pro forma cash flow for the proposed club.

As you can see, with the exception of February, when the business was just getting started, the cash flow has been positive. It is not at all unusual, at the start of a new business, for it to run low on cash or even out of cash. Therefore it is very important to have a line of credit set up at a bank or investors who are willing to invest additional money to keep the business afloat until it can establish itself.

Break-even Analysis   A **break-even analysis** predicts the sales volume required to recover total costs. In other words, it is the sales level that is the dividing line between operating at a loss and operating at a profit. It is an important number to know because when it is broken down on a per day basis it gives management a goal. If it achieves more sales than the break-even point, it will achieve a profit for that day. It is also a number that the banks and investors are interested in. The formula for a break-even analysis is as follows:

Break-even point = fixed cost $/contribution margin percent

That is, the break-even point equals fixed costs expressed in dollars divided by the contribution margin expressed in percentage. The contribution margin percentage is figured by adding together all of the variable costs and subtracting them from sales. (Sales are represented as 100 percent). The contribution margin is figured as follows:

Contribution margin = 100 percent (sales) − total variable costs percentage

To illustrate, refer to Figure 14.8, the pro forma income statement. The first thing is to separate the variable costs from the fixed costs. To review, a variable cost is a cost that goes up or down as sales go up or down and does so in direct proportion. A fixed cost is one that remains the same regardless of sales. You will recall that we also have semi-variable costs. While these are not a part of the break-even formula, they will have to be accounted for. To do this, take the variable portion of a semi-variable cost and separate it from the fixed portion. For example, recall that payroll is made up of salaried personnel, which are fixed; that is, their salary does not change because of sales. Payroll is also made up of variable rate personnel who are paid by the hour, and the number of these employees that will be scheduled will go up or down as sales go up or down.

Figure 14.10 illustrates the breakdown of these expenses as well as the break-even point for January. The numbers were taken from the pro forma income statement (Figure 14.8). The variable costs include cost of goods sold (both food and beverage), wages (hourly personnel), FICA tax on hourly wages, the portion of benefits paid to the hourly personnel (58 percent of total payroll is hourly; therefore 58 percent of the $10,000 benefits is allocated to hourly personnel), and supplies. The total of variable cost is $163,081, which is divided by January's sales of $270,000 to get a variable cost percentage of 58 percent.

The rest of the expenses are fixed costs and are listed under that heading. An exception is depreciation, which is not listed because no dollars are spent on depreciation. Another exception is the loan payment, which is not an expense on the income statement but is dollars going out. The fixed costs are totaled and for January are $91,700.

The contribution margin is figured by subtracting the variable cost percentage from 100 percent (sales) to get 42 percent. The fixed costs of $91,700 are then divided by the contribution margin of 42 percent to get a break-even point of $218,333. This number is then divided by 31, the days the operation is open in January, to get a break-even point of $7043 per day.

It should be noted that we made certain assumptions in the foregoing illustration regarding fixed and variable costs. Most noteworthy are advertising and rent. For example, we categorized advertising as a fixed cost because the partners agreed to spend $8000 per month on advertising. If they had agreed to spend 2 percent of sales on advertising, then it would have been categorized as a variable cost as the amount spent would have increased or decreased as sales increased or decreased. The same can be said for rent. The lease we signed called for a rent of $28,000 per month. If we had agreed

January Sales		$270,000
Variable Costs		
Cost of goods sold	$ 93,750	
Wages	$ 54,000	
FICA Tax on Wages	$ 4,131	
Employee Benefits	$ 5,800	
Supplies	$ 5,400	
Total Variable Costs	$163,081	
Variable Cost %		58%
Fixed Costs		
Salaries	$ 38,333	
FICA tax on salaries	$ 2,932	
Employee benefits	$ 4,200	
Rent	$ 28,000	
Utilities	$ 8,000	
Telecommunications	$ 1,000	
Advertising	$ 8,000	
Music & Entertainment	$ 25,500	
Legal & accounting	$ 2,000	
Insurance	$ 4,500	
Repairs & Maintenance	$ 2,500	
Miscellaneous	$ 4,000	
Loan Payment	$ 4,000	
Total Fixed Costs	$ 91,700	
January Break-Even Point		$218,333
January Daily Break-Even Point		$ 7,043

FIGURE 14.10
Break-even point for January. Separation of costs and break-even point for January

with the landlord to pay 8 percent of sales, then rent would have been a variable cost. If we had agreed to pay $10,000 per month plus 4 percent of sales then it would have been a semi-variable cost with $10,000 being a fixed cost and 4 percent being a variable cost.

Legal Environment

Any business, regardless of its location, is regulated. Some jurisdictions regulate more than others, and some businesses are regulated more than others. The business of selling alcoholic beverages to others is arguably one of the most heavily regulated businesses in the United States today. To make matters worse there is no consistency among laws and regulations. They vary from state to state, county to county, city to city, and even in some cases from voting precinct to voting precinct.

Before You Start Before you start on the business plan, have a complete understanding of all the laws pertaining to the sale of alcoholic beverages in your community.

- Zoning. Most cities and many counties have zoning laws which restrict the type and size of a business that can operate at a given location. While you may be able to sell food at a site you deem desirable, you may not be able to sell alcohol. Practically all jurisdictions will outlaw the sale of alcoholic beverages near a church or school. What is considered near varies greatly from area to area. Sometimes it is measured door to door and sometimes property line to property line. The distances also vary.

- License availability. Most jurisdictions have restrictions on the number of liquor licenses that can be issued. This could be city or county wide, or it could be broken down into neighborhoods or voting precincts. For example, more licenses could be issued in a downtown or entertainment district than would be issued in a residential area. Whatever the distribution formula, it is absolute. Once all of the licenses are issued, there are no more. Should you desire to open in an area where there are no available licenses, the only way you can open is to buy out an existing business. This can be quite costly as the license is likely to cost more than the existing business is worth. Also, you are locked into that location as the license is normally issued to that address specifically.

- Opposition. The location that you selected is properly zoned and a liquor license is available, but the neighbors do not want a bar in their neighborhood. This is called the NIMBY syndrome (for Not In My Back Yard). If the opposition is well organized and vocal, it is very possible that a license will not be issued. Occasionally, law enforcement will oppose the issuing of a license, particularly if you are buying an existing license and the location has had problems in the past.

- Hours. The hours you are permitted to conduct business are governed locally. This could be important if your business plan calls for you to be open until 3:00 A.M. and the law says that that location can only stay open until 1:00 A.M.. It is common for cities to allow a later closing time in a downtown, entertainment district, or convention area and an earlier closing time in neighborhoods.

Building or Remodeling   There are a plethora of laws, regulatory agencies, permits, and regulations that must be adhered to if you are building or remodeling. It is important that you know all of them and adhere to them to the letter. Many a business has delayed its opening because at the last minute, a permit was not obtained or a regulation followed. In extreme cases a floor has to be jackhammered, a wall torn down, and plumbing or electrical moved because a building regulation was not followed. Some of the more common requirements follow, but check with your local jurisdiction regarding regulations. City or county offices as well as the chamber of commerce will help you get through the maze of requirements.

Most jurisdictions, whether building or remodeling, will require a building permit. In most cases a drawing prepared by a licensed architect must accompany the permit request. The drawing should detail the general construction, all electrical and plumbing requirements, the location of all kitchen and bar equipment, as well as restroom fixtures and layout. The application for a building permit, along with the plans, will normally go first to the codes department, who will ascertain that the construction meets all of the building, electrical, and plumbing requirements. From there, more often than not, it goes to the fire department's inspection unit to make sure that the hood, ventilation system, and fire suppressant system in the kitchen meet requirements. They also check for adequate exits and will normally place a maximum on the number of persons who can occupy that space at any one time.

The health department also checks the plans for such thing as adequate hand sinks in the kitchen and back bar, sufficient refrigeration, as well as scrubbable walls and flooring material. Note that all equipment must be NSF (National Sanitation Foundation) approved.

A relative newcomer to the building permit assemblage is the environmental control department. While not all jurisdictions have this department, many are adding it out of concern for air and water pollution. If you are remodeling they will look for hazardous materials, such as asbestos and lead-based paint, in the existing structure.

Should they exist, special precautions must be taken in their removal. (This could be one of the unforeseen expenses mentioned earlier in the chapter.) They will also look at the exhaust system plans to ascertain that there will be little or no air pollution. If the plumbing code people do not check for grease traps, the environmental people will.

In addition to local laws, there are federal laws that must be adhered to in remodeling or construction. Most notable are OSHA (Occupational Safety and Health Agency) and the ADA (Americans with Disabilities Act). While these are federal programs, in some cases they have turned over authority to the states to enforce the law. Many local jurisdictions have also embraced these regulations and made them a part of their own codes.

One last detail, which is arguably the most important, and that is obtaining the liquor license. The liquor control board will want to know all about you and your management team: are you a citizen of the United States, of good moral character, creditworthy, with no prior arrests or convictions, and so forth? Does the location meet the requirements of the law, that is, not being near a school or place of worship? Is a license available for that location? If the answers to these questions are favorable, you will more than likely get a license.

Operating   After opening, there will still be regulatory agencies scrutinizing your operation, most notably the heath department and the liquor control board. The health department, among other things, will randomly check for temperatures of food (both hot and cold), proper storage of goods, sanitary practices of employees, absence of insects and vermin, and overall cleanliness of the operation. They may also require that management (or in some cases all employees) undergo training and/or pass a safety and sanitation test.

The liquor control board will conduct random checks on the operation as well. It will look for such things as serving alcohol to minors or serving intoxicated guests. These visits may be made in conjunction with laws enforcement agencies. The board may require that employees who make, dispense, or serve alcoholic beverages have a permit to do so.

Appendices

The business plan is now complete except for the appendices. Not only will your idea for a successful business be judged, but the quality and appearance of the study will give the reader an impression of you as a person. Make sure that this impression is favorable. Go back over the study and edit it for spelling and sentence structure. Make sure it flows well. Have another person, preferably an English professor or a professional writer, go over it.

The last thing to do is put together an appendices. These will consist of items that go into detail or illustrate what you have presented in the body of the plan. They should include such items as the following:

- Menus, brochures, and advertising materials
- Industry studies
- Blueprints and plans
- Maps and photos of location
- Trade journal, research studies, or other articles
- Detailed list of equipment
- Copies of leases and contracts
- Market studies
- List of assets available as collateral for a loan
- Any other materials needed to support the assumptions in the plan

CONCLUSION

Running a hospitality enterprise involves many small details, and each one of them affects the overall performance of the operation. "Expect the unexpected" is the catchphrase on opening a new business. When you execute a well-conceived business plan, you confront many of these issues before you open. This will give you the time and resources you need to overcome the unforeseen issues that you did not see coming. As you can see, opening or managing a business is a lot of hard work. It does, however, have its rewards. The hospitality industry is one of providing good food, good drink, and a good time for our customers. It is quite satisfying to see friends and family gather together in your establishment to enjoy the camaraderie.

Good luck as you continue your studies in the field of the hospitality business.

QUESTIONS

True/False

1. A psychographic study is undertaken to ascertain the mental stability of a person who desires to go into the bar business.

2. Personal knowledge of an area is not a good device to use when studying a proposed location for a bar as it is not scientific and is subject to bias.

3. A mission statement is a brief declaration of a business's reason for being and what its guiding principles will be.

4. A company's goals are an assessment on how well it is doing to meet its objectives.

5. One of the pitfalls that most new enterprises fall into is not accurately estimating the startup costs.

6. An estimation of a proposed business's sales and expenses is known as a pro forma income statement.

7. In organizing a pro forma income statement, the preparer relies heavily on historical data.

8. A break-even analysis predicts the sales volume required to recover total costs.

9. Some federal programs such as the Occupational Safety and Health Administration and Americans with Disabilities Act have turned over enforcement of their regulations to state or local jurisdictions.

10. Once you have obtained your liquor license, you are through with the liquor control board until it is time to renew your license.

Multiple Choice

1. In choosing a location for a proposed bar, one must
   1) ascertain the demographics of the location's trade area.
   2) match the demographics of the area to the theme and price point of the proposed bar.
   A. (1) only
   B. (2) only
   C. Both (1) and (2)
   D. Neither (1) nor (2)

2. An executive summary of a business plan is a summary
   A. giving an overview of the proposed business.
   B. that is to be read solely by executives of a lending bank.
   C. written by an executive.
   D. describing the ability of those responsible for running the establishment.

3. If you are operating a bar, a liquor store opening in the neighborhood could be considered
   A. a direct competitor.
   B. an indirect competitor.
   C. invading your market niche.
   D. invading your customer base.

4. When planning a layout for a restaurant and bar, the ratio of the front of the house to the back of the house should be:
   A. ⅓, ⅔
   B. ⅔, ⅓
   C. ¼, ¾
   D. ¾, ¼

5. Gross profit is
   1) the amount of money made after the cost of goods sold is subtracted.
   2) figured by subtracting sales from the cost of goods sold.
   A. (1) only
   B. (2) only
   C. Both (1) and (2)
   D. Neither (1) nor (2)

6. The document that shows how much money will be needed to open a business and keep it running is known as a
   A. pro forma income statement.
   B. pro forma balance sheet.
   C. pro forma break-even analysis.
   D. pro forma cash flow statement.

7. If advertising for a bar is allocated at 2 percent of sales, it is a
   1) variable cost.
   2) fixed cost.
   A. (1) only
   B. (2) only
   C. Both (1) and (2)
   D. Neither (1) nor (2)

8. Assume that you have obtained a liquor license to open a bar; you may not be able to open if
   A. a neighborhood group opposes the bar.
   B. law enforcement objects.
   C. This not possible. Once you have the license you can open.
   D. Either A or B.

9. The liquor control board will randomly check your operation for
   1) serving alcohol to underage guests.
   2) exceeding the occupancy limit of your establishment.
   A. (1) only
   B. (2) only
   C. Both (1) and (2)
   D. Neither (1) nor (2)

10. Appendices go at the end of your proposal and consist of
   A. a summary of your business plan.
   B. items supplementing or backing up the business plan.
   C. an index showing the page numbers of the sections.
   D. an acknowledgement to those who have contributed to the business plan.

Essay

1. Choose a bar in your area. Assume that it does not have a mission statement and management has hired you to write one for it. In thirty words or less, write a mission statement for that bar.

2. What factors go into choosing a location for a bar? Include market as well as legal in your discussion.

3. Assume that you are opening a 300 seat restaurant and bar. Make a list of all of the positions that will be necessary to staff that operation and then develop an organizational chart. (Do not include the number of employees, just the positions.)

4. Assume a bar is open six days a week and has a happy hour from 4:00 P.M. to 7:00 P.M. with drinks being sold two for the price of one. It has 75 seats and expects two turns per night during this period with an average check of $5.50 per person. Calculate the weekly happy hour sales.

5. If a bar has sales of $125,000, variable costs of $65,000, fixed costs of $49,000, a profit of $11,000, and is open six days a week, what is its break-even point?

RESOURCES

http://www.feasibleproject.com/
http://managementhelp.org/strt_org/prep.htm

glossary

Additive Antioxidants, enzymes, and preservatives added to simplify the beer brewing process and prolong shelf life.

Adjunct Fermentable material used as a substitute for traditional grains to make beer lighter bodied or cheaper.

Administrative liability Applies to the issuing of licenses and/or permits to sell alcoholic beverages. These are normally issued to the business, and in some jurisdictions they are issued to the bartenders and servers as well. Establishments or servers not adhering to the law can be fined or have their license suspended. In rare cases, usually involving several violations, they could have their license revoked.

Age Discrimination in Employment Act (ADEA) A law passed by Congress in 1967 to protect individuals over the age of forty from discrimination based upon their age.

Air-cooled system (refrigeration) These are the most popular refrigeration systems and are therefore found in most commercial refrigerators and freezers. In this system, a fan blows the hot air off the condenser into the surrounding air in the room. It is critical that, for this system to operate most efficiently, the fins on the condenser be cleaned on a regular basis, preferably monthly.

Alcohol content For beer normally runs at around 5 percent, but can be as low as almost 0 percent (near beer) and as high as 15 percent and in a few cases even higher.

Ale A type of beer.

American proof system One of three types of systems used for the strength of alcoholic beverages. In the United States the proof is twice the alcohol content expressed as a percentage by volume. For example, 120 proof rum is 60 percent alcohol.

Ampere Commonly called an amp, it measures the amount of electricity. There is a limited amount of amps going into any building. You need to know this number to avoid purchasing more electrical equipment than the system will allow.

Amylase A digestive enzyme which facilitates conversion of starch into sugars.

Aperitif wine A wine served prior to a meal. Aperitif wines are normally fortified and some are flavored by herbs and spices.

Aperitifs A type of liqueur developed to stimulate the appetite, served prior to the start of a meal.

Arabica One of the two main types of coffee beans, the other being robusta. The arabica bean has less caffeine and is deemed superior in flavor.

Automated beverage control system A fully computerized beverage dispensing system that is designed to control beverage pour sizes.

Back bar The area behind the bar. It is usually 3 feet wide. This area is used for storage and often displays the call and premium brand spirits.

Bar back An assistant to the bartender. Quite often bar backs are actually bartenders in training. Their primary role is to take over some of the bartender's more mundane duties so that the bartender can concentrate solely on mixing drinks and keeping up with the volume.

Bar die What people normally refer to as "the bar" is technically called the bar die. It is almost always custom built to fit the room both in terms of size and aesthetics.

Barley A cereal grain that is malted for use in the grist that becomes the mash in the brewing of beer.

Barspoon A long-handled, stainless steel spoon approximately 10 inches long, often with a bead on the top. Barspoons are used to stir cocktails in either a mixing glass or cocktail glass.

Bartender A person who serves usually alcoholic beverages behind the bar in a licensed establishment. He or she is essentially responsible for the functional operation of the bar itself.

Beer stein A heavy glass, usually with a handle, used to serve beer. Also called a beer mug.

Beverage manager A person who is responsible for the entire operation of the bar

Beverage outlet A place where alcohol, namely, beer, wine, spirits, and/or liquor, is sold to be consumed on the premises.

Bid A process by which several companies quote prices for items that have been specified by the buyer.

Bid conditions When purchasing new bar equipment the first part of the bid process concerns itself with the bid conditions, sometimes referred to as conditions to bid or invitation to bid. This is an important document as it eliminates any confusion between the buyer and the seller. It also makes it a level playing field for all bidders.

Bid process Manufacturers do not generally sell equipment directly to the end user. The markup on equipment from the manufacturer to the dealer is quite high, leaving ample room for the dealer to negotiate price. For this reason the best and only way for the buyer to obtain the lowest price for equipment is to have several dealers bid on the equipment. In order for the bidding to be accurate, a specification for the equipment must be written. A specification lists all of the important data pertaining to the equipment so that each dealer is bidding on the exact same piece.

Bin card   The par stock posted in the storeroom by each item in inventory.

Binge drinking   Defined by the Centers for Disease Control as men drinking five or more alcoholic drinks within a short period of time or women drinking four or more drinks within a short period of time.

Black tea   One of the major varieties of tea. It is the most popular of all the varieties.

Blend   The process whereby two or more grape varieties are combined after separate fermentation. The opposite of a varietal.

Blended drink   A drink of several ingredients that is mixed using a blender or spindle mixer.

Blended rate of pay   A method of calculating overtime pay.

Blender stand   Normally located immediately adjacent to the workstation either to the left or right. Either way it should be handy for the bartender to fill the blender with ingredients from the speed rail and the mix bin and blend the drink without taking any steps. Some bars will use a malt mixer rather than a blender for blended drinks.

Blood alcohol content (BAC)   Defined as the weight of alcohol per unit volume of blood, normally measured in grams and expressed as a percentage.

BOGO   Buy One, Get One free. Expression for when an operation decides to offer one or more items at a reduced price, even below profitable levels, as a special promotion to entice more customers into the bar.

Boiling hops   One of the two types of hops used in the brewing process. They are taken from the female hop vine. They are put in during the first boil and give the beer its bitter flavor.

Bottle exchange   A control method where an empty bottle from the bar must be turned in to get a full bottle of the same product from the storeroom.

Bottled in Bond   To be labeled "Bottled in Bond" whiskey must come from one distiller, be distilled in one distillery, and be the product of one distillation season. It must be aged for a minimum of four years in a bonded

warehouse. It must be bottled at 100 proof with the label showing the distillery's DSP number.

Bottom line   Net income after tax.

Bouquet   A term referring to the complex aromas of wine.

Brandy snifter   A footed glass without a stem, with a rounded bowl, popularly used for whisk(e)y and brandy.

Break-even analysis   Predicts the sales volume required to recover total costs.

Breathalyzer test   A test using a device that detects and measures alcohol in expired air to determine the concentration of alcohol in a person's blood.

British thermal unit   Abbreviated BTU, this is the amount of heat needed to raise 1 pound of water 1 degree.

Brix   The sugar content of grapes is measured in Brix. Knowing the sugar content, the vintner can predict the alcohol content of the wine by using the formula of Brix $\times$ 0.55 = percent alcohol

Brown ale   Light to dark brown in color and unlike other beers has a tan head. It has a degree of popularity in Belgium, England, and the United States.

Brown goods   These are stored and aged in oak barrels. The aging of brown goods does two things: One, it gives the spirit color, and two, it develops its flavor and aroma. Two types of oak are generally used, French and American, with French oak being subtler, while American oak gives stronger aromas.

Budget   An estimate of costs, revenues, and resources over a specified period, reflecting a reading of future financial conditions and goals.

Built-in refrigeration system   Where the refrigeration system is part of the unit as opposed to being located at a remote area. These systems are the most popular as they are less costly.

Bundling   Taking two or more items from the menu and putting them together to create better value. Also can refer to the grouping together the selling prices of various drinks or beverages within a category.

Business plan   A formal statement of a set of business goals and the plan for reaching those goals.

Cage   The wire mechanism covering the cork on a bottle of champagne or sparkling wine.

Call stock   A higher-cost liquor that a customer will order by brand.

Carbonation   The sparkle caused by carbon dioxide, either created during fermentation or injected later.

Carbonation method   A method of carbonating wine by makers who want to produce a low-cost sparkling wine. Carbon dioxide is forced into the wine under pressure.

Cash bar   A bar where each guest pays for his or her own drinks as opposed to having the host pay for all drinks. When cash bars are utilized, the bartender usually is allowed to receive gratuities, and often a tip jar is placed on the bar.

Chaptalization   The process of adding sugar to fermenting grapes in order to increase alcohol if the grapes have not been picked at an optimal time.

Charmat method   A method used to make sparkling wine.

Château   French for "castle." An estate with its own vineyards.

Circular bar   Design layout of a bar that is most prevalent where the building has been designed in a circle to house a circular bar and the tables are arranged in a circular manner around the bar.

Civil liability   Allows a person who has been victimized to bring a lawsuit against another person or company. In the case of the bar business, a person could bring a lawsuit against a bar that served alcohol to a customer that resulted in that customer becoming intoxicated.

Classic Champagne   A sparkling white wine made from a blend of grapes, especially Chardonnay and Pinot, produced in Champagne, France.

Clear goods   Also known as white goods. All spirits when distilled are clear. As a general rule, white or clear goods are not aged and are stored in stainless steel or glass barrels prior to bottling. Examples of clear goods are vodka, gin, tequila, and some rums.

Closed question   An interview question that requires a short, sometimes one-word response.

Cocktail server   Responsible for taking drink orders and delivering those drinks to tables of customers in a dining establishment or other public place that serves alcohol.

Cocktail shaker   Also known as a hand shaker, mixing cup, or mix can. It is used for mixing cocktails by shaking rather than by stirring as in a mixing glass. It is made of stainless steel and has a strainer that fits over the top of the can for straining ice and fruit pulp and seeds before entering the serving glass. In cases where the ice is part of the drink, the strainer is not used or in some cases a mixing glass is placed over the cocktail shaker; the drink is shaken and then poured into the serving glass.

Cold storage   Normally a walk-in cooler used for storing bottled and keg beer. Wine can go here as well; however, bars that have a large wine selection will have a separate locked storage area.

Common negligence law   Is concerned with negligent behavior on the part of a person or persons. Negligent behavior, in this case, is defined as not doing what a reasonable person would do given a specific set of circumstances. With regard to alcohol, bartenders or cocktail servers are expected to monitor the behavior of their customers.

Company goals and objectives   A goal is an end. An objective is an assessment of how well you are doing to meet the end.

Compensatory award   Money awarded to the plaintiff for damages incurred.

Competition   The efforts of two or more parties acting independently to secure the business of a third party by offering the most favorable terms.

Compressor   The part of the refrigeration cycle where the refrigerant R-22, which is in a gaseous state, is compressed until it gets very hot.

Computer assisted drawing (CAD)   a software program used by architects to execute layouts and architectural drawings.

Conceptual layout   Deciding where each work center is going to go and how they will be joined together.

Condenser   Takes hot R-22 refrigerant gas and condenses it into a liquid form. Can also be referred to as the part of the still where the vapors condense and become distilled spirits.

Condiment tray   A tray holding garnishments for drinks.

Congeners   Substances that give a particular spirit its unique taste as well as its aroma. They are inherent in the ingredients that are used in the fermented liquid. As a rule, the more expensive a spirit, the fewer the congeners, as the distillation process will filter out a higher percentage of them. Another rule of thumb states that the darker the spirit, the greater the number of congeners. Therefore, whiskey, brandy, and red wine will have more congeners than will vodka, gin, and white wine.

Consolidated Omnibus Reconciliation Act of 1985 (COBRA)   An act that generally requires that group health plans sponsored by businesses with twenty or more employees offer employees and their families the opportunity for a temporary extension of health coverage in certain instances where coverage under the plan would otherwise end.

Control state A state in which the state either distributes alcoholic beverages itself or controls the number of distributors, often giving a distributorship a monopoly in a given area.

Controllable cost A cost that management can control. A variable cost.

Co-op marketing This is where a beverage manufacturer or wholesaler works with a bar to promote their product. The beverage company increases exposure to their product and the bar increases its sales.

Coordination The ability of the muscles to produce complex movements.

Cordial Cordials are synonymous with liqueurs, although in the United Kingdom and its Commonwealth countries a cordial refers to a nonalcoholic drink.

Corkscrew A tool for pulling corks from wine bottles.

Cost of beverage sold An accounting line item. It is figured by taking opening inventory plus purchases minus closing inventory, which equals cost of beverage sold. The actual cost of all ingredients and goods that were used to create beverage sales during the period.

Cover charge A cost paid by the guest to enter the site. The cover charge helps absorb the cost of the entertainment to management.

Credit card A payment card issued to users as a system of payment. It allows the cardholder to pay for goods and services based on the holder's promise to pay for them.

Criminal law An application of law that relates to the owner of a bar and the staff. Criminal liability gives the state the right to bring suit against a licensee, the owner of a bar, and/or their employees. These suits are different from civil suits in that they deal with the criminal aspect of irresponsible alcohol service. Many times, particularly in cases involving injury or death, a lawsuit could be brought in both civil and criminal courts and could result in both civil and criminal charges. While the cases are tried separately, the penalty in either case is not dependent on the other. Thus a party could be found innocent in the civil trial but guilty in the criminal trial or versa visa, or they could be found innocent in both or guilty in both.

Cru The highest ranking for a wine in France.

Cubic feet per minute Abbreviated CFM, this is used to measure air movement in heating and cooling the building. It is also used in the kitchen for air movement in the exhaust hood and makeup air systems.

Customer satisfaction The degree of satisfaction provided by the goods or services sold as measured by the number of repeat customers.

Cut sheet A method of selecting equipment by going through manufacturers' catalogs. Each piece of equipment is listed on a page which explains the equipment, its design, its capacity, how it is constructed, its dimensions, and any electrical, gas, or water data.

Cuvee The process of blending wine.

Debit card A plastic card that provides the cardholder electronic access to his or her account at a financial institution. Some cards have a stored value with which a payment is made, while most relay a message to the cardholder's bank to withdraw funds from a payee's designated bank account. The card, where accepted, can be used instead of cash when making purchases.

Decant A method to remove the sediment from wine that has been aging by pouring it into another vessel; also aerates the wine before drinking.

Decibel A unit measuring the loudness of sound.

Defendant A person being sued.

Demographic survey Determines and analyzes characteristics such as age, gender, income levels, and lifestyles and is used in planning a marketing strategy. Such a study is focused on the particular location where a bar wants to set up business. It lists the general population by age group, median age, ethnic origins, household type, marital status, occupation, education, housing, income, number of vehicles, and other related data. Specialized data can also be obtained that detail consumer restaurant and bar expenditures for the area and can further refine this statistic by giving a breakdown by category such as quick service, coffee shop, and fine dining.

Demographics Statistical characteristics of a population.

Department of Labor A Cabinet level department of the federal government of the United States responsible for occupational safety, wage and hour standards, unemployment insurance benefits, re-employment services, and some economic statistics.

Descriptive terminology The language and vocabulary used when writing a menu must do one major thing: sell the product to the customer in an honest and forthright manner. A secondary thing it must do is to explain the item to the customer.

Dessert wine A wine served at the end of a meal. These are almost always a sweet wine. While most are fortified, some are not. Those that are not fortified are made from overripened grapes which have an extremely high sugar content.

Digestif   A type of drink developed to aid in the digestion of the meal and served at the end.

Distillation   Water boils at 212°F. In the process of boiling, the water turns into a vapor. Alcohol boils at 176°F, and at that point, like water, it turns into a vapor. Because alcohol boils at a lower temperature than water, a fermented mixture can be heated to 176°F or higher (but lower than 212°F) and the alcohol in that mixture will vaporize, thus setting itself apart from the fermented liquid.

Distillery   A place where the distilling of hard liquor is done.

Distribution system   This starts with the manufacturer who designs and builds the equipment. They hire manufacturer representatives that represent their products to dealers. The dealers then sell, deliver, and in some cases install the equipment to the restaurants, bars, and lounges.

Dosage   A sweetened spirit added at the very end to Champagne and other traditionally made sparkling wines. It determines whether a wine is brut, extra dry, dry, or semisweet.

Dram shop law   A law that governs the liability of pubs, bars, liquor stores, or any other business that sells alcoholic beverages. Dram shop laws have been enacted by some state legislatures to place the responsibility of damages to a third party squarely on the shoulders of the retailer as well as the person who is responsible for the damages, that is, the person who has been drinking. Hence, dram shop laws are also known as third-party laws or third-party liability.

Driving while intoxicated (DWI)   Driving a vehicle with a blood alcohol count at or over 0.08, which is illegal.

Dry   A wine containing no more than 0.2 percent unfermented sugar.

Dry county   Counties within a state which does not allow the sale of alcoholic beverages.

Dry state   A state which does not allow the sale of alcoholic beverages.

Dry storage   Dry storage should be a locked storeroom. Liquor and room temperature wines would go directly into this room immediately after they are inspected and signed for.

Elevation drawing   An architectural drawing viewed as if you were standing in a room looking straight ahead at a wall, using length and height.

Employee evaluation   A procedure that employers use to review the performance of an employee.

Employee Retirement Income Security Act (ERISA)   A federal law that contains detailed requirements for businesses that offer their employees a welfare benefit plan or retirement plan.

Employee training   A function of management that ensures that all employees are aware of the standards and procedures of the business.

Employment application   Allows management to look over several applicants quickly and ascertain which ones have the qualifications and background necessary to become a longtime employee. It is a document that becomes a part of an employee's permanent record.

Employment eligibility verification   Form I-9 is used by an employer to verify an employee's identity and to establish that the worker is eligible to accept employment in the United States.

Equal Employment Opportunity Commission (EEOC)   A federal law enforcement agency that enforces laws against workplace discrimination. The EEOC investigates discrimination complaints based on an individual's race, color, national origin, religion, sex, age, disability, or genetic information as well as retaliation for reporting, participating in, or opposing a discriminatory practice.

Equal Pay Act   This act reads in part that no employer shall discriminate between employees on the basis of sex by paying wages to employees at a rate less than the rate at which it pays wages to employees of the opposite sex for equal work on jobs the performance of which requires equal skill, effort, and responsibility, and which are performed under similar working conditions.

Estate bottled   Wine bottled at the winery of origin.

Etched line   The line that is sometimes marked onto jiggers to show different measures.

Ethics   Distinguishing between right and wrong, determined by the standards that a society or group deems appropriate.

Evaporator   Takes the R-22 refrigerant which is in a liquid state and circulates it. As it circulates throughout the refrigerator or freezer, it picks up heat from the air in the box as well as from the product. As it picks up this heat, it heats up until it comes to the boiling point and turns to a gas. It returns to the compressor, where the process starts over and repeats itself.

Exit interview   A meeting between the business and a departing employee. The departing employee usually has voluntarily resigned rather than getting laid off or fired.

Factor method   A process by which the selling price of an item is determined that will cover all costs and profit.

Fair Labor Standards Act (FLSA)   An act was passed into law in 1938 primarily to level the playing field between management and labor. It also sought to end child labor, among other things. It has been amended several times since then, including the addition of the minimum wage provision. In additions to the minimum wage there are a few other provisions to the law regarding wages and hours worked that affect bars, clubs, and restaurants.

Family Medical Leave Act (FMLA)   Under FMLA, employers must allow employees to take the equivalent of twelve weeks of unpaid leave each year due to the birth or adoption of a child, to attend to a serious health condition of an immediate family member, or to attend to their own serious health condition.

Feasibility study   A creative, objective, and rational process whereby marketing and financial data are collected and analyzed. It is an in-depth study that attempts to predict with reasonable accuracy whether a potential business will succeed or fail.

Federal and State Unemployment Compensation Program   One of the provisions of the Social Security Act of 1935. One objective of the program is to provide an unemployed worker time to find a new job, which is the same or similar to the one lost, without undue financial burden.

Federal Unemployment Tax Act (FUTA)   The Federal Unemployment Compensation Program is financed through the Federal Unemployment Tax Act (FUTA). The tax is paid by businesses at the rate of 0.8% on the first $7,000 of annual pay to each employee. In addition, many states impose an additional tax on employers to cover administration costs.

Ferment   To convert sugars into ethyl alcohol and carbon dioxide through the action of yeast.

Fermentation   The conversion of sugars into alcohol.

FIFO (first in, first out)   An accounting method whereby goods are used in the order in which they are purchased.

Fining   Part of the clarification process whereby elements are added to the wine in order to capture solids prior to filtration.

Finishing hops   One of the two types of hops used in the brewing process. They are put in at the end of the boil and give the beer aroma.

Fixed cost   A cost that remains the same regardless of sales volume.

Flaming drink   An alcoholic drink where the glass and alcohol are both heated and the alcohol is then ignited with a lighter.

Floated drink   A very colorful drink where various alcohols are layered on top of each other.

Flor   A film that develops on some sherries as they go through the aging process. This slows the oxidization and gives the sherry flavor. The longer it is in contact with the film, the finer the sherry.

Foot candle   A measurement of light defined as the amount of light provided by a candle 1 foot from an object.

Footed ware   A glass with a base but without a stem.

Forecast   Projection of achievable sales revenue, based on historical sales data, analysis of market surveys, and trends.

Fortified wine   A wine that is much higher in alcohol content than natural wines, ranging anywhere from 14 to 24 percent.

French knife   A large knife used for cutting larger items such as watermelon or pineapple garnishes.

Fruit liquor   Any spirit distilled from a fermentation of fruit, for example brandy, which is distilled from fermented grape juice.

Fruit squeezer   A handheld device that squeezes a lemon or lime wedge to extract juice.

Garde manger kitchen   A cool, well-ventilated area where cold dishes are prepared and other foods are stored under refrigeration.

Garnish   An edible item added to a drink to enhance its appearance and its taste.

Gay-Lussac proof system   A system used to measure the alcoholic content of spirits, especially in Europe. Known as the Gay-Lussac method, it is the actual percentage of alcohol by volume in the spirit. This system is the one used by the European Union.

General bottler   If vintners do not bottle their own wine, they sell it to a general bottler. The bottler goes to the vineyard, samples the wine, and negotiates with the vintner. When a deal is struck, the wholesaler loads the casks of wine onto a truck and ships it to the bottling plant where it is bottled as is or blended and then bottled.

General manager   The person who oversees both the food and beverage sides of the business. In larger operations these duties are split with a restaurant manager overseeing the food production and restaurant service side of the business and a beverage manager overseeing the bar and its service. In independent operations, the manager(s) report to the owner or, in the case of a partnership, the owner's representative. Many of these types of operations are owned by regional and national chains, in which case the unit management reports to a district or regional manager.

Generic wine   A wine where a large blend of grape varieties is used.

Genever   The Dutch word for the juniper berry. It is also a style of gin, also known as Dutch or Holland gin.

Gin-head   A device in which as the alcohol vapors pass through on their way to the condenser, they pick up additional flavors.

Glass rail   This is located on top of the bar die directly above the ice bin. It is a 4 inch wide trough that is usually lined with a webbed rubber or plastic matting.

Glass rimmer   A plastic device that is used to rim a glass with either salt or sugar.

Goblet   A drinking vessel usually made from heavy glass, with a bowl shape sitting on a stem.

Grain liquors   Any spirit distilled from fermented grain mash; for example, whiskey can be distilled from corn or barley.

Green tea   A variety of tea that is lower in caffeine and high in antioxidants.

Grist   Ground barley sprouts, used in the production of Scotch.

Gross profit   The amount of money that is left over after food cost has been subtracted from sales.

Hops   An herb added to boiling wort or fermenting beer to impart a bitter aroma and flavor.

Hosted bar   A hosted bar is often referred to as an open bar. With this method, the host, rather than the guests, pays for the drinks.

House wine   A wine featured by a restaurant and often served in a carafe or by the glass.

Form I-9   *See* Employment Eligibility Verification.

Income statement   An accounting form that shows the monetary sales, expenses, and either the profit or loss for a business.

Ignition interlock law   A system that tests a driver's breath for alcohol. The driver blows into a small hand-held device that is attached to the vehicle's dashboard. The vehicle will not start if the BAC is above a preset level, usually 0.02 to 0.04. In addition to needing a test to start the engine, it also requests a test every few minutes while driving. This prevents another person from starting the car and then giving the wheel to an impaired driver. While this is cumbersome for the guilty party, it does have an advantage in that it allows such persons to operate a motor vehicle as opposed to having their driver's license revoked. With an ignition interlock system they can get to work and run errands without having society worrying about whether they are endangering the safety of others.

Immigration Reform and Control Act   An act making it illegal for employers to discriminate with respect to hiring, firing, or recruiting based on an individual's citizenship or immigration status.

Inhibition   An inhibition is a psychological or mental process that suppresses our actions, thoughts, and emotions. It is what keeps us from saying or doing things that we would find ethically or morally wrong while sober. However, when alcohol gets into the bloodstream and ultimately to the brain, this suppression is relaxed and we say and do things we would not say or do otherwise.

Intoxication   The condition of being drunk as the result of drinking alcoholic beverages and/or use of narcotics.

Jigger   A control device used in mixing cocktails.

Judgment   The ability to make sound decisions. Judgment is impaired when alcohol enters the system.

Kilowatt   1,000 watts. This is the number seen on an electric bill showing the electrical usage for a period.

Krausening   The addition of a small proportion of partly fermented wort to a brew during lagering. It stimulates secondary fermentation and imparts a crisp, spritzy character.

"L" shaped bar   A long straight line bar that has a right angle at one end with a short bar.

Labor cost   The cost of wages paid to workers during an accounting period.

Lager   A beer made by the bottom fermentation method.

Leadership style   The type or types of leadership that a person uses, usually selected from: autocratic, bureaucratic, participative, and laissez-faire.

Lease   Written or implied contract by which an owner (the lessor) of a specific asset (such as a parcel of land, a building, equipment, or machinery) grants a second party (the lessee) the right to its exclusive possession and use for a specific period and under specified conditions, in return for specified periodic rental or lease payments.

Lees   The sediment in the wine that settles to the bottom of the storage container during the aging process.

License suspension law   This law is in effect in most states. The license suspension law requires the officer who conducts the arrest to suspend the driver's license of the person who did not pass the sobriety test.

Liqueurs   A liqueur has its start as a distilled spirit. To this is added one or more of any one of a myriad of other ingredients.

Liquor   A synonym for a spirit.

Maceration   One method of making liqueurs, in which the ingredients are soaked in the base spirit until it has taken on the flavorings of the fruits and other additives.

Malt   The process by which barley is steeped in water, germinated, then kilned to convert insoluble starch to soluble substances and sugar. The foundation ingredient of beer.

Malted barley   The majority of beers produced use a malted barley. It is produced from the seeds of the barley plant.

Maltose   A water-soluble, fermentable sugar contained in malt.

Manufacturer   designs and builds equipment. Very few of them sell direct to a restaurant or lounge.

Manufacturer representatives   represent the manufacturer's products to a dealer, consultant, architect, or builder. They also work with large corporations and chains to induce them to purchase their manufacturer's brand. Most manufacturer reps will speak for several manufacturers.

Market niche   A small but profitable segment of a market suitable for focused attention by a marketer.

Market saturation   Point at which a market is no longer generating new demand for a firm's products, due to competition, decreased need, obsolescence, or some other factor.

Marketing   The creation of a want or desire and the provision of a product or service that satisfies that want or desire.

Marketing strategy   a plan devised to meet the wants and needs of potential customers.

Markup on cost   A method of price calculation. Take the beverage cost of the item and divide it by the desired beverage cost percentage; the result is the selling price to be charged for that item.

Mash   The process by which malt and grains are combined with hot water to create a mixture called mash. The mash liquid is then combined with yeast which causes fermentation and is subsequently distilled.

Mash tun   A vessel used to convert starches into sugar in the fermentation process.

Material flow   A component of the layout process that decides how materials are going to flow in the operation.

Meritage   Blended wines created originally in California, summed up as "American Bordeaux."

Metabolism   The method the body uses to process items ingested, such as food or alcohol.

Méthode Champenoise   A method of bottling and infusing bubbles into wine. Sugar is added to the wine when it is bottled to create a secondary fermentation. After the wine is recorked a wire cage is put over the cork to secure it, as it is under extreme pressure, and the cork and cage are covered with foil. The bottles are then returned to the caves, where they are aged from one to five years.

Minimum wage   The federal minimum wage for covered, nonexempt employees is $7.25 per hour effective July 24, 2009.

Mission statement   A brief declaration of a company's reason for being and its guiding principles.

Mix bin   A storage area for mixes usually located to the right or left of the ice bin in the bartender's work area. While they are separated from the ice bin itself, they should be kept iced down to prevent spoilage.

Mixing glass   A heavy glass for mixing cocktails such as martinis or manhattans.

Mixologist   An employee who specializes in the art of bartending and creating and developing new cocktails.

Mocktail   A nonalcoholic version of an alcohol-containing drink.

Moonshine   Illicitly distilled liquor.

Mug   A tumbler with a handle.

Must   The liquid resulting when grapes are crushed.

National Labor Relations Act   Congress enacted the National Labor Relations Act (NLRA) in 1935 to protect the rights of employees and employers, to encourage collective bargaining, and to curtail certain private sector labor and management practices which can harm the general welfare of workers, businesses, and the U.S. economy.

Natural wine   A wine made without additional alcohol or sugar.

Near beer   A beer with an alcohol content of near 0 percent.

Neat   An alcoholic drink with no ice or additives.

Noble rot   A mold that grows on the grapes, causing sweetness in a wine. The mold causes the moisture in the grapes to shrivel, which concentrates the sugars.

Nonalcoholic beverage   A beverage containing no alcohol.

Noncontrollable cost   A cost that management cannot control, usually fixed costs.

On the rocks   A drink served with ice.

Oolong tea   A medium-bodied brew that has the freshness of green tea and the aroma of black tea.

Open bar   A bar at a banquet or reception in which the host, rather than the guests pays for the drinks.

Open-ended question   A question requiring a response with a considerable degree of information.

Ordinary   A term used in the 17th century for an inn in the English colonies of America. It also refers to a type of bitter ale.

Overtime pay   Management that requires or permits an employee to work overtime is generally required to pay the employee premium pay for such overtime work. Employees covered by the Fair Labor Standards Act must receive overtime pay for over 40 hours worked in a workweek. The rate for overtime is at least one and one-half times the regular rate of pay.

Pale ale   A type of top-fermented beer.

Par stock   The method used to control inventory. Management determines an inventory level for each item, and purchases are made to bring the stock back up to that level.

Paring knife   A small knife that is used for cutting small items.

Pasteurization   Heating of beer to 140–174°F to stabilize it microbiologically. Flash pasteurization is applied very briefly, for 15–60 seconds, by heating the beer as it passes through a pipe. Alternatively, the bottled beer can be passed on a conveyor belt through a heated tunnel. This more gradual process takes at least 20 minutes and sometimes longer.

Patent still   Also called a continuous still, column still, or Coffey still after the Irishman Aeneas Coffey, who patented it in 1831.

Per se laws   *Per se* is a Latin phrase meaning "by itself." In regard to drunk driving it means that anyone operating a motor vehicle with a BAC at or over 0.08 is intoxicated in the eyes of the law, and no further proof is needed to convict the driver.

Percolation   A method of making liqueurs. The spirit is poured over the flavorings and pumped back up over the flavorings, and this is repeated several times.

Performance review   An interview between a manager and an employee wherein the employee's job performance is evaluated.

Perishable   A product with a relatively short life.

Perpetual inventory   System of inventory control in which the number of units of any inventory item (and the total value of inventory) on any day can be obtained from the stock records.

Personal contact   A way to generate business with a minimal cost. Personal contact can be internal or external. Internally, it is interfacing with your customers, getting to know them and their wants. External personal contact is when the owner or manager gets out in the community and makes new acquaintances.

Physical inventory   An important part of the control process. When taking inventory, all products are counted, priced, extended, and totaled.

Pilsner   A tall glass shaped like a funnel with a base.

Place   One of the four key Ps of marketing. Place concerns itself with getting customer to the establishment, in this case the bar.

Plaintiff   A person instituting a lawsuit.

Plan drawing   A drawing showing the entire area of the building that a business will occupy and where each piece of equipment will go.

Plant liquor   A distilled spirit made from the juice of plants. Examples are rum, distilled from sugar cane juice or a by-product of sugar cane, and tequila, made from the juice of the blue agave plant.

Postmix   Postmix is when the syrup and carbonated water are mixed when dispensed.

Pot still   A pot which is covered with a funnel device at the top. The vapors are captured at the top of the funnel and go into a pipe which carries them to the condenser, where they are condensed and become distilled spirits.

Pounds per square inch (PSI)   Used to measure water pressure and steam. Water pressure is what cleans glasses and dishes.

Pour station   A bartender's work center or work station.

Pourer   A plastic or metal control device that fits into the top of the bottle and has a channel through which the liquor is poured.

Premium stock   A liquor that costs more than call, normally single malt Scotch or Irish whiskey and high-end domestic whiskey.

Premix   Premix is where the syrup and carbonated water are mixed at a factory and filled into cartons.

Price One of the four marketing Ps of marketing. The amount charged for beverages and food, as well as discounts given such as a happy hour.

Price point The dollar point at which a customer regards the price of a commodity as too high and will therefore no longer purchase it.

Price–value relationship The connection that consumers make between price and quality. Products with a higher price are commonly perceived to be of better quality

Prime cost Labor expense and beverage cost added together. These two expenses are the largest operating costs that can be controlled by management.

Prime space The place on a menu that a customer sees first. Studies have shown that the customer is more likely to order what is seen first. Thus, the prime space on the menu becomes an extremely important merchandising area.

Pro forma statement What a company believes will occur financially in its business in the future.

Product One of the four marketing Ps. This refers to what the bar sells and what it is known for. The product must fit the demographic makeup of its trade area.

Product mix The actual number of items sold at their various markups, making up the cost of beverages sold on the income statement.

Product specification A written statement containing exactly what the purchaser wants from the vender. A primary control in purchasing.

Professional development A term referring to education outside of the normal work environment. For the most part it is conducted off premises.

Prohibition A period of nearly fourteen years of U.S. history, 1920–1933, in which the manufacture, sale, and transportation of liquor was made illegal. It led to the first and only time an Amendment to the U.S. Constitution was repealed.

Promotion One of the four marketing Ps. This refers to all the methods used to communicate the marketing message to potential customer.

Proof A measure of how much alcohol is contained in an alcoholic beverage. Proof is twice the amount of alcohol content, thus 80 proof equals 40 percent alcohol.

Psychographic study Analysis of consumer lifestyles to create a detailed customer profile.

Psychographics The use of demographics to study and measure attitudes, values, lifestyles, and opinions for marketing purposes.

Psychological pricing The theory that takes into account how a customer reacts to certain pricing structures.

Public relations This is an effective tool to market a bar. It involves creating and promoting a public image for the operation. This public image is not promoted through advertising but rather through participation in community events and activities.

Publicity Free advertising. This takes the form of press coverage. Restaurants can help create their own publicity through press releases sent to media outlets.

Punitive award An award given to punish the defendant.

Purchase order A written document showing what has been ordered and the price quoted for that item.

Racking The process of moving wine from barrel to barrel while leaving sediment behind.

Railway Labor Act of 1926 This act gave workers the right to join unions.

Reaction time The delay between an initiated stimulus and the corresponding response. In terms of alcohol consumption the reaction or response time gets progressively slower.

Rectangular bar A four sided bar which is enclosed on all sides.

Refrigerant The substance used to pull heat particles out the air and out of products. The refrigerant presently being used is R-22 and is being replaced by R-410A.

Remote refrigeration system With a remote refrigeration system the heat generated by the compression system will be away from the bar area, making it more comfortable for customers. When repairs are necessary, a remote system can be worked on without having the repair person working behind the bar and getting in everyone's way.

Requisition An order sheet requesting merchandise from the storeroom to be released to the bar.

Robusta One of the two major species of coffee, the robusta bean has a higher caffeine content than the Arabica bean and is more acidic.

Sales The actual transaction of exchanging money or an asset for the means of fulfillment.

Sales to minors Sales to any person under the age of 21 are illegal in all states.

Scale refers to the number of feet represented by one inch on a drawing. There are two scales used by architects when drawing bar layouts; ¼ inch and 1/8 inch scale. Thus a ¼ inch scale will represent 4 feet of actual space for every inch used on the drawing and a 1/8 inch scale will represent 8 feet for every inch on the drawing.

Semi-variable cost   An expense containing both fixed costs and variable costs.

Service area   The area where the cocktail servers pick up their drinks.

Service bar   A compact bar used only by the wait staff.

Severance pay   An amount of money that is given to employees when they are terminated. It is over and above the amount that they earned during their last pay period.

Sexual harassment   A form of sex discrimination that violates Title VII of the Civil Rights Act of 1964 and applies to employers with fifteen or more employees.

Shaken drink   A shaken drink is a multiple-ingredient drink. Ice is placed in the shaker with the ingredients. The bartender then places a lid on the shaker and proceeds to shake the drink until it is well chilled. The lid is removed, a strainer is placed over the top of the shaker, and the drink is poured into the serving glass.

Shot glass   A jigger made from glass.

Social host   This term does not apply directly to an alcoholic beverage business but rather to a person or persons who would host a private party or function.

Solera system   A method of blending whereby barrels are placed in a row and stacked four or five high. Each row contains product of a different age with the youngest on the top row and the oldest on the bottom row. When the bottom row is ready to be bottled, approximately one third of it is drawn off. The barrels in the bottom row are then filled up from the row above it and so on. The top row is then replenished with "young" product. As it progresses down, it picks up the flavor of the older product with the end result being a consistent product.

Sommelier   A wine steward, mostly employed in fine dining establishments.

Sparkling wine   A wine with bubbles.

Speakeasy   Any establishment selling alcoholic drinks illegally, especially in reference to the Prohibition period in America from 1920–33.

Specification   A document initiated by the buyer listing everything he/she wants in a product and given to the seller for bidding purposes.

Speed rail   Also called a speed rack or liquor well. It contains all of the well brands or house brands. These are used to mix drinks when the customer does not specify a particular brand. They normally, but not always, cost less than call brands and consequently sell for a lower price.

Spirits   Spirits are alcoholic beverages that are distilled from liquids that have already been fermented.

Standard   A standard is what a cost should be and is compared to what a cost actually is. Standards are established by management to ensure that the operation is on track to achieve a profit.

Standard beverage cost   The cost percentage that management has determined is necessary for the operation to make a profit.

Standardized recipe   A formula that should be followed each and every time a drink is made.

Stemware   A drinking glass that stands on a stem above a base.

Sterile filtration   A process in which beer goes through a series of filters to eliminate the bacteria that causes spoilage.

Still   A vessel in which a fermented mixture is heated to between 176°F and 190°F. At this point the alcohol in the mixture boils and the alcohol's vapor goes into a condenser, where it is cooled; as it cools it is condensed into a liquid state. See also *Pot still* and *Patent still*.

Still wine   A wine with no bubbles.

Stirred drink   A drink where one or more ingredients are added to a spirit or spirits and the drink is stirred as opposed to being shaken.

Stout   A generic category of beer in which the malt is roasted until it is very dark, almost black, giving stout a dark color.

Straight line bar   A bar best utilized in a building that is long and narrow.

Straight pour   A spirit poured straight into a shot or in a rocks glass.

Straight up   An alcoholic drink that is shaken or stirred with ice and then strained and served without ice in a stemmed glass.

Sweet wine   A wine that is sweet due to its residual sugar content.

SWOT analysis   A study helps management determine the operations strengths, weaknesses, opportunities, and threats (SWOT).

Tab   A means for customers to charge their drinks and pay for them periodically, usually on their payday, rather than paying for each individual drink. This practice is being replaced by the use of credit and debit cards. A tab also refers to a customer's bill while he or she is at the bar, which should be paid upon leaving the bar.

Table wine   These belong to the largest classification of wines and are so called because they are often served at the table with food every day. They can be further classified as to their color: red, white, and rose.

Taft–Hartley Act   A United States federal law enacted in 1935 that restricts the activities and power of labor unions.

Target market those persons within a given area that the business has deemed as potential customers.

Termination The ending of employment. There are two types, voluntary and involuntary.

Terroir The soil, moisture, temperature, weather conditions, fertilizer, and climate along with the skill of the farmer, which all determine the outcome and the quality of the grape harvest.

Thermometer Most commercial units contain exterior thermometers on their refrigerators and freezers. These work by use of a probe that is in the interior cabinet of the refrigerator or freezer. The probe relays the interior temperature to the exterior thermometer.

Thermostat Controls the temperature in the box. There are normally two temperatures on the thermostat, a low setting and a high setting. When the temperature in the box reaches the high setting, the refrigeration system is turned on, and it is turned off when it reaches the low point.

Tip credit provision If an employee's tips combined with the employer's direct wages of at least $2.13 an hour do not equal the federal minimum hourly wage, the employer must make up the difference.

Tip pooling The requirement that an employee must retain all tips does not preclude a valid tip pooling or sharing arrangement among employees who customarily and regularly receive tips, such as waiters, waitresses, bellhops, counter personnel (who serve customers), bussers, and service bartenders. Tipped employees may not be required to, although they can at their own discretion, share their tips with employees who have not customarily and regularly participated in tip pooling arrangements, such as dishwashers, cooks, chefs, and janitors. Only those tips that are in excess of tips used for the tip credit may be taken for a pool. Tipped employees cannot be required to contribute a greater percentage of their tips than is customary and reasonable.

Third-party law A law which places responsibility for the actions of a person on another person or business. In the case of the bar business, if a person becomes intoxicated in a bar and goes out and causes damage or injury, the bar could be held responsible for some or all of the damages.

Title VII of the Civil Rights Act of 1964 Prohibits employers from discriminating against employees on the basis of race, color, national origin, religion, or gender in all parts of the employment process from recruitment through termination. In order to comply with Title VII, an employer must make employment decisions on the basis of business necessity rather than based upon a particular individual's membership in a protected class.

Topping off As wine ages in the casks, some of it evaporates. Since the vintner want the casks full to prevent further oxidation, which could ruin the batch, more wine is added to keep the casks full.

Traffic flow Refers to how products and people travel through an operation. These should flow in a line with no cross traffic or backtracking.

Transfer method A method for bottling sparkling wine or champagne.

Triple Trinity The three characteristics that identify Marsala wine from Sicily: sweetness, color, and quality.

Tumbler A straight line glass with no foot, stem, or handle.

Tun A large vessel in which the mashing is done.

"U" shaped bar A rectangular shaped bar that is open at one end.

Use/lose law Several states beginning in the 1980s began passing use/lose laws as a penalty for minors purchasing, possessing, or consuming alcohol. As the name implies, if you use alcohol, you lose your drivers license. Not only does the law include alcohol, it includes other drugs as well.

Utility knife A knife for cutting small fruit such as limes, lemon, and oranges.

Variable cost A cost that rises and falls in the same proportion that sales do.

Varietal A wine made from just one grape type and named after that grape; the opposite of a blend.

Vehicle forfeiture law A law allowing the vehicle a drunk driver is driving to be impounded.

Vintage Champagne When only one year of a champagne is used exclusively and the harvest is of high quality.

Vintner The person or company that processes grapes into wine.

Virgin drink A beverage with no alcohol in it.

Vitis vinifera The common grape vine.

Volstead Act An act named after a congressman from Minnesota, which defined intoxicating liquor as anything containing more than one-half of 1 percent alcohol and gave the government the power to enforce the 18th Amendment to the Constitution prohibiting the manufacture, transportation, or sales of alcoholic beverages.

Volt Measures the force or push of electricity. Some equipment operates on 110, 115, or 120 volts; some operates on 208, 210, 220, 230, or 240 volts; and some operates on 440 or 480 volts. Each piece of electrical equipment is designed to operate on a specific voltage. You need to know the voltage coming into your building to specify the correct piece of equipment. Too much voltage will burn the equipment out; too little will not allow it to run at its full potential. Additionally, some equipment will not even run on the incorrect voltage. All buildings with electricity will have the 100 series of volts. They may or may not have the 200 or 400 series.

Wage garnishment   Occurs when an employer is required to withhold the earnings of an individual for the payment of a debt in accordance with a court order or other legal procedure.

Wait stands   house the supplies used by the servers such as napkins, glassware, flatware, condiments, and some beverages. It can also house the POS system.

Water-cooled systems (refrigeration)   A series of pipes containing water. The water picks up the heat particles given off by the condenser and becomes quite hot. In state-of-the-art facilities, this water is circulated into the hot water system. By doing this the water heater does not have to work as hard to get the water up to the desired temperature and therefore have uses less energy. In operations that do not do this, the hot water is simply wasted and emptied into a floor drain.

Watt   Is the amount and force of electricity, or amps times volts (amps × volts = watts).

Well stock   A drink made from the lowest cost liquor when a customer orders a drink without expressing preference.

White tea   A minimally processed tea that tastes like fresh leaves or grass.

Wine list   used in establishments that have a wider selection of wines. It should contain an assortment of wines offered both by the bottle or glass and have a variety of red, white and sparkling wines.

Wine steward   A waiter managing wine service in an upscale restaurant or hotel.

Work aisle   The area between the bar die and the back bar where the bartender works.

Work center   An area where one task or a group of similar tasks are completed by one employee.

Work section   An area where a group of similar functions takes place.

Wort   The solution of grain sugars strained from the mash tun.

Yeast   A microorganism of the fungus family. When it is added to the wort the fermentation process begins to take place.

Zero tolerance legislation   A law passed in 1998. The reasoning behind it was that since it was illegal for minors to drink in the first place, then any amount of alcohol in their systems was illegal. As a result of the financial incentives established in this legislation, all states and the District of Columbia have enacted very low legal BAC limits of 0.02 or less for drivers under the legal drinking age of 21.

Zester   An implement used to peel the outer skin of a lemon for drinks that call for a twist of lemon.

index